BIBLIOGRAPHIES OF WRITINGS BY AMERICAN AND BRITISH WOMEN TO 1900

VOLUME 2

POETRY BY WOMEN TO 1900

A BIBLIOGRAPHY OF AMERICAN AND BRITISH WRITERS

COMPILED BY GWENN DAVIS AND BEVERLY A. JOYCE

UNIVERSITY OF TORONTO PRESS
TORONTO AND BUFFALO

Published in North America 1991 by
University of Toronto Press
Toronto and Buffalo
Reprinted in paperback 2015
ISBN 978-0-8020-5966-6 (cloth)
ISBN 978-1-4426-3973-7 (paper)

First published 1991 by
Mansell Publishing Limited, *A Cassell imprint*
Villiers House, 41/47 Strand, London WC2N 5JE, England

Canadian Cataloguing in Publication Data
Davis, Gwenn
Poetry by women to 1900 : a bibliography of
American and British writers.

Includes index.
ISBN 978-0-8020-5966-6 (bound) ISBN 978-1-4426-3973-7 (pbk.)

1. American poetry—Women authors—Bibliography.
2. English poetry—Women authors—Bibliography.
I. Joyce, Beverly A. II. Title.

Z1229.W8D38 1991 016.821008'09287 C91-093475-4

CONTENTS

INTRODUCTION

Poetry by Women to 1900: A Bibliography of American and British Writers is the second volume in a series designed to make accessible literary works by well known and neglected writers in order to re-establish the range and variety of books published by women from 1475–1900. Other volumes in the series cover personal writing, drama, short fiction, long fiction, and juvenile literature. A dictionary of pseudonyms and alternative names will be the final volume. The series deals with printed books and offers a comprehensive listing of writers whose works appear in a variety of sources. Each bibliography presents the writers in alphabetical order. An appendix places them in order of publication date; an index to types of works and topics appropriate to the genre under consideration further defines the subject of each volume. The entries for the whole series were developed from a complete reading of *The National Union Catalog, Pre–1956 Imprints* (NUC) and the catalog of the British Museum (now the British Library), Department of Printed Books, *General Catalogue of Printed Books* (BL), supplemented by the data base of the Online Computer Library Center (OCLC), other standard bibliographies and biographical dictionaries, and inspection of many of the works. The individual volumes are intended to be useful on their own as guides to particular literary forms. Taken together as a series, they will permit their users to compare an individual author's work to others in a given genre and by consulting the other volumes to discover the full range of that writer's literary publications.

The focus of this volume, poetry, is self explanatory. Its relationship to the other parts of the series should, however, be made clear. *Poetry* includes a few works that are cited in other volumes, as for example, autobiographies that include poems or collections that combine poetry and short fiction or juvenile literature. This has been done so that each bibliography may be used independently. The relationship to *Drama by Women to 1900* is more complex. Plays in verse that were published as separate works such as Aphra Behn's *The Amorous Prince* will be cited only in *Drama*. Collections of poetry that include plays in verse, Sally Caulfield's *The Innocents, a sacred drama. Ocean; and The Earthquake at Aleppo; Poems*, for example, will appear in both volumes. The index to *Poetry* lists works that contain dramatic poems, while the index to *Drama* indicates plays in verse. This will eliminate extensive duplication, yet enable the reader to trace the extent of each form. Further information on the indexes may be found below in the section on the development and organization of this volume.

Women published in every field of letters. Though they are traditionally thought to have concentrated on the novel, on children's literature, and on matters of domestic economy, they produced many works beyond those covered in this series, including biographies, histories, volumes of essays and controversial pamphlets. Translations, unless they form part of a collection that includes original work in English, are excluded. Periodical publication, also beyond our scope, would no doubt add greatly to the roster of women writers. Our purpose is to show that they published a considerable number of printed books in the major literary genres, a point the more than 6,000 entries here can clearly demonstrate. Poets, except for the great names, Elizabeth Barrett Browning or Anne Bradstreet, or the popular figures such as Frances Ridley Havergal or Lucy Larcom whose work is now more often alluded to than read, have received little scholarly attention, and the general impression left by literary histories is that their number is small. The impressive record of women's participation in the literary marketplace that this bibliography reveals should open the way for fresh consideration of their achievements.

Poetry is the most ancient form of literary expression and arguably the most universally practised. Histories and anthologies include a few women poets: Sappho, Marie de France, some of the Medieval lyricists, Emily Dickinson, Christina Rossetti. Recent anthologies have added some names to the canon. Anne Finch, Charlotte (Turner) Smith, Eliza Jane Nicholson have long been unavailable in standard texts. In some ways women's poems are the most obscure of their literary contributions. The ratio of printed volumes to poems concealed in writing tables, circulated in manuscript, or published in small literary journals is doubtless as tiny for women as for men. Yet women's poems are even less known than their other works, in part, perhaps, because poetry generally attracts small audiences and few reviews. Plays were produced, if only for home entertainment; autobiographies are shared with friends or collected by mourners. Children's books and popular fiction are known to make money, a powerful incentive for release. More important, women's names quickly vanish from the rolls of notable poets, and each new generation finds it hard to discover those who wrote before them. The works listed here show that women wrote nearly every form of poem and that their numbers increased steadily from the sixteenth century on.

To judge from the standard anthologies of American and British literature, few women ever published their poems. There have been collections of poetry by women, but they confine themselves to a few prominent writers, and they tend to re-establish the same handful of poets. The major nineteenth century sources, Caroline May's *American Female Poets* (1848), Thomas Buchanan Read's *The Female Poets of America* (1869), and Rufus Griswold's *The Poets and Poetry of America* (1842), cover only a fraction of the writers whose works appear in this bibliography. They do mention some who published primarily in periodicals, but the same names recur: Bradstreet, Warren, Gilman, Hale. The sources are similarly incomplete for British writers. David Moir's lectures on *The Poetical Literature of the Last Half Century* (1851) do cover what he calls "The Female Constellation": Joanna Baillie, Felicia Hemans, Mrs Jameson, Letitia Landon, Caroline Bowles, Mary Howitt, Mary Mitford, Maria Jewesbury, Mrs Norton, and Elizabeth Barrett Browning, whom he faults for "a careless self-satisfaction." A. H. Miles's *Poets and Poetry of the Nineteenth Century* has an especially skimpy selection. Women writers not only go out of print rapidly, they become invisible. In the introduction to the new Oxford anthology of *Eighteenth Century Women Poets*, Roger Lonsdale documents the comments the more than 100 poets he includes occasioned and the indignation some male reviewers felt at the number of women who were writing. Nonetheless, in 1861, Jane Williams (Ysgafell), working on a critical biography of Felicia Hemans and looking for other poets with whom to compare her, could find reference to very few of these. Having judged the major sources, Ballard, Wharton, Duncombe, Read and others "bare, bald, and often inaccurate," she wrote her own history. Ysgafell's own work, *The Literary Women of England*, so thoroughly, lovingly researched and so full of fascinating anecdotes and insights into mid-nineteenth century tastes, has itself been ignored.

Recent anthologies have begun to make available poets whose work has long been inaccessible. From Sara Teasdale's *The Answering Voice: One Hundred Love Lyrics by Women* (1926) to *The Distaff Muse: An Anthology of Poetry Written by Women*, compiled by Clifford Bax and Meum Stewart in 1949 to the two pioneering collections of the seventies, *Salt and Bitter and Good* and *The World Split Open*, to the new Oxford anthology, one can trace the increasing interest in women writers and the increasing sophistication in scholarly treatment of them. Many neglected poets, Renaissance writers and Americans of the colonial period in particular, are being studied. Feminist theorists and critics have begun to look at what constitutes women's writing and to establish feminist poetics. This bibliography should help to provide the context for these studies. It clearly demonstrates a long tradition of women's poetry, a participation in all literary forms. There are epics here, long narratives presented in cantoes. There are ballads, sonnets, masques, satires and epistles. Women poets wrote in the popular forms of their own time, and their history parallels the history of male poets. Many eighteenth century women favored heroic couplets; the Romantic period popularized nature poems and ballads and saw an increase in the number of working class and rural women who published their verse. Victorians wrote often of bereavement. Women's themes were the preoccupations of the day. There are some indications of the particular concerns of women's lives. The largest single category of works in this volume is religious poetry, perhaps because from the time of the Countess of Pembroke it was permissible for women to express themselves on spiritual matters. The great causes for nineteenth century women, abolition and temperance, are well represented. Two special types of poems, domestic verse and poems on the language of flowers give some indication of women's responsibilities and pastimes. In general, though, these poets shared the concerns, the styles and sensibilities of their male counterparts. Indeed some may have originated poetic forms which were then adopted by the more famous men. Anna Seward, "the inventress of the epic elegy," knew most of the writers of her time and was admired not only by Hannah More and the ladies of Llangollen but by Robert Southey and Sir Walter Scott who edited her work. Women poets were fully involved in the ages in which they lived and many actively pursued a literary career.

While the majority of the writers in this bibliography, close to 60 percent, published only one volume of poetry, many, about 20 percent, also wrote in other genres. Sarah Elizabeth (Knowles) Bolton published fiction as well as poetry as did Jane Hornblower, Margaret Oliver (Woods) Lawrence and Felicia Skene, to cite only a few. Some, Sarah Lawrence or Julia Webster, for example, not only wrote fiction but drama and juvenile literature as well. About 20 percent published two or three volumes; 5 percent issued four or more. This group includes the famous, Elizabeth (Barrett) Browning, for instance, the prolific popular writer of gift books such as the Havergals, and some who wrote on local topics for their own small communities such as Elizabeth Davies' poems on the coming of the railway to Wales or Miss Child's memoirs of the Salisbury Exhibition. The remaining 15 percent are represented in volumes of collected works including memorial volumes brought out by family or admirers after their death. Mary Noel (Bleeker) Meigs issued her sister, Sophia Bleeker's poems in *Lays of a Lifetime* (1857); Sophia Woodrooffe's uncle edited three posthumous volumes of her narrative and dramatic verse. Some of the collections represent years of work some of which had previously been published in periodicals. Lady Camilla Gurdon's *Suffolk tales and other stories. Fairy legends. Poems. Miscellaneous articles.* is such a volume, as is Maria L. (Doud) Scott's *Autumn Leaves* which includes poems she had already published in newspapers under her pseudonym, "Ella Vale."

The works included here indicate that women's published books of poetry increased exponentially from the sixteenth century to the end of the nineteenth. Barely 2 percent were published before 1750; nearly 45 percent appeared in the last quarter of the nineteenth century. This may account for the rough parity between American and British writers here. While only eighteen American women published before 1800, compared to 210 British women, in the nineteenth century 1,687 British writers published their poems compared to 1,609 Americans. Differences in population probably mean that a smaller percentage of the women in the New World were issuing books of verse, but they were catching up quickly. A market for women writers had developed on both sides of the Atlantic by the second quarter of the nineteenth century when 15 percent of these works were published. The writers came from increasingly diverse backgrounds, and wrote on more disparate themes. The majority were, like their audience, middle class, though by the end of the nineteenth century both poets and readers more nearly paralleled the composition of their society.

During the Middle Ages and the Renaissance, poetry was an aristocratic occupation. Ladies of leisure and exceptional education are the first poets in this bibliography: Lady Diana Primrose, the Countess of Pembroke and her niece, Lady Mary Wroth, Lady Colville of Culross, the Duchess of Newcastle. Katherine Philips, one of the first middle class women to publish her poems, owes her recognition at least in part to her classical tastes, Royalist sympathies and tireless cultivation of literary friendships. Her near contemporary in Restoration England, Aphra Behn, began her professional career in poetry and in the theatre a full century after Marlowe and the Cambridge wits, the middle class upstarts of their time, began to eke out a livelihood in literature. By the eighteenth century, however, women from all strata of society began to publish. The authors in this volume represent a true cross section of American and British life.

The salons of the court of Henry VIII, of the Countess of Pembroke at Wilton, of aristocratic families at their country seats were, to the dismay of some, widely imitated in the eighteenth century. Lady Anne (Lindsay) Barnard, whose work was published in a family collection, *Lays of the Lindsays*, composed the ballad "Auld Robin Gray" to a traditional Scottish air in 1771. She confessed her authorship to Sir Walter Scott fifty years later, maintaining that now that the middle classes had taken up verse, noblewomen ought not to be pursuing it. Many middle class poets began by writing for a family literary circle. Eleanor Anne (Porden) Franklin, the daughter of an architect, first composed poems to place in the salt box her family kept for their literary efforts. One of her earliest contributions, *The Veils*, was published in 1815 when she was eighteen. The most determined hostess in Bath, Anna Riggs, Lady Miller, kept a Roman urn in her garden. Her guests were to place poems on set topics in it when they came to her morning breakfasts, and a contest was held for the best poem of the day. Several collections of the results of these competitions were published for the aid of the poor in the 1770s. Though she entertained Anna Seward, Thomas Whalley, and David Garrick, Lady Miller never won the social standing she hoped for. Poetry had become a universal art, not an exclusive pastime. Rather than serving as an entrée to the most exclusive circles, it became in the Romantic age associated with the most ordinary people.

Working class women began to write in the mid-eighteenth century; some titled women resumed publishing extensively in the nineteenth. Perhaps there was still a sense that poetry had become common, as a number of women, Margaret McKay or Margaret Russell Dow, for instance, called their work "Lays of Leisure Hours." A few of the most prolific gentlewomen disguised their identities. Mary Montgomerie (Lamb) Singleton, Baroness Currie, did use a pseudonym, Violet Fane, for her seven volumes of poetry. Elizabeth Susan Law who became Baroness Colchester used the pseudonym, An Amateur, in one work, but she published six volumes of her poems. Lady Emmeline Stuart-Wortley must be considered a professional writer. She not only published plays but occasional verse including *The Great Exhibition. Honour to labour, a lay of 1851*, narratives, travelogues and elegiac verse. All three were serious writers who published extensively and for a general rather than a coterie audience.

It is more difficult to determine the economic circumstances and social class of American authors; no titles clearly denote the gentry and aristocracy. There is evidence, though, of a similar diversity of background. There are women from influential families: Phebe Ann (Coffin) Hanaford, Laura (Winthrop) Johnston or Sara Wentworth (Apthorp) Morton; literary dynasties: Maria (White) Lowell; and publishing families: Sara Jane (Clarke) Lippincott, herself a great granddaughter of Jonathan Edwards. There are settlers who write of their experiences on the plains, Amanda Theodosia Jones wrote *Utah* in 1861 and *A prairie idyll* in 1892. The great humorist, Marietta Holley, grew up on her family farm and lived her whole life there. Lucy Larcom, daughter of a shipmaster, moved with her family to Lowell, Massachusetts, when he died and became the most famous writer that the Mill Workers writing movement produced. At least two women became publishers. Eliza Jane (Poitevent) Nicholson, who took her pseudonym, Pearl Rivers, from the region where she was raised, inherited the most influential newspaper in Louisiana, *The Daily Picayune*, from her first husband and went on to run it successfully. Though she is perhaps best known as a poet and writer for children, Alice (Bradley) Neal Haven, having inherited *Neal's Gazette*, became its editor as well as publisher.

There are few women of color here, yet some did publish their work. Margaret Jane Blake, born a slave, was freed before the Civil War; Ann Plato, a black woman from Connecticut, published her *Essays; including biographies and miscellaneous pieces, in prose and poetry* in 1841. The best known and most influential, Phillis Wheatley, was read on both sides of the Atlantic. Philanthea, Mary Deverell, was uncertain of her origin, thinking she came from "India's swarthy shore." Her tribute, published in 1781, shows that she did understand both Wheatley's talent and her enslavement: "Go on, sweet maid, of Providence once more/ Divinely sing, and charm another shore;/ No fetters thus thy genius shall controull,/ Nor iron laws restrain thy towering soul." Frances Ellen Watkins Harper became famous in the later nineteenth century as an advocate for abolition and temperance. Like Wheatley, she had an audience and influence beyond the restrictions of her sex, race, and class.

In both America and Britain, then, by the end of the nineteenth century women from all social orders and economic circumstances were publishing volumes of poetry. The same cultural conditions and literary movements that encouraged them also restricted them. The more middle and working class poets published, the less favorable critical commentary became, and the faster they disappeared from the canon. A few aristocratic ladies might be considered exemplars of their rank rather than their sex; a regiment of ordinary women could only produce popular poetry. Three parallel developments in the eighteenth and nineteenth centuries altered the climate for women poets: the increasing number of writers from all parts of society, the commercial success of many kinds of poetry, and the changing public conceptions of literature to which literary movements, especially Romanticism, responded.

The eighteenth century brought an enormous increase in the numbers of women who offered their poems for publication. The number of volumes published from 1700–1749 represents a 25 percent increase over all previous printed books and the number from 1750–1799 is nearly a 300 percent increase over that. While the majority of volumes of personal writings in the age are memorial collections published by the authors' admirers after their deaths, most of the poets, over 90 percent, saw their works through the press themselves. Roger Lonsdale traces the increasing activity of women poets in the age, the condescension they faced from male reviewers, and the class conflict that met their efforts. He concludes that "in the 1780s women virtually took over, as writers and readers, the territories most readily conceded to them, of popular fiction and fashionable poetry (p. xxxv)." The distinction between art and popular verse established in this age ultimately served to exclude women from the literary history. Placing them in the ranks of the fashionable, the ephemeral, while it made publishers more receptive to their efforts, caused them to be ignored by students of serious poetry. Their audience may have been primarily female, not because of the disdain of male critics, but because more women were reading magazines and books than ever before, and as with personal writings and fiction, women who bought books or subscribed to lending libraries were looking for a literature of their own. Readers sought out works by those who shared their experiences, their attitudes and values. The larger the audience, the easier and the more profitable it was to publish. The more daunting task was to make their way into anthologies and literary histories.

By the close of the eighteenth century, not only were the wives and daughters of prosperous business and professional men writing, working class women also published their verse. *Sketches of Obscure Poets*, 1833, mentions one woman, Christian (Ross) Milne, the daughter of a carpenter, who published a volume by subscription in 1805. She was not the first. Janet Little, "the Scotch Milkmaid" published in 1792; Ann More Candler, a Suffolk cottager, in 1803. Some were self taught. Susannah Watts' father died when she was a young child. She taught herself French and Italian and supported herself by translating Tasso and writing children's books and ballads. Janet Thompson Hamilton, daughter of a Scottish shoemaker, who was married at age thirteen, did not learn to write until she was fifty. She published three volumes of poems and essays in the 1860s, and her son edited a fourth collection which suggests that she was highly regarded beyond her family circle. Eliza Frances Robertson composed her *Consolatory Verses* (1808) while imprisoned for debt; Frances Britton wrote bitterly of her poverty and her arrest as a vagabond. Isabella Bourne's *Lays of Labour's Leisure Hours* includes poems and a novella that reflect her working class experience. Mary Collier, a washerwoman, presented a woman's view of working life in *The woman's labour; an epistle to Mr. Stephen Duck; in answer to his late poem called The thresher's labour* in 1739. While she was the first to record the complaint that women who work outside the home must work again within it, throughout the nineteenth century women proclaimed themselves as Eliza Dupe did in 1860, as "a member of the working class." The title page of Ellen Johnston's poems (1867) calls her a "factory girl"; Lizzie Smith's *Poems of a Dairy Maid* were issued in 1898. Interest in working class writers reached a peak in the 1820s and 1830s; it also enlarged the market for poetry from which women in a variety of circumstances benefited.

Whether the Romantic Movement established a fashion for the writings of working class writers or the spread of literacy led more of them to aspire to publication is hard to calculate. As Collier and Smith would indicate, working women began to write well before the publication of *The Lyrical Ballads* and continued to identify themselves with labor from then on. Their numbers were never great in any period, though their impact on critical constructions of the history of poetry has been profound. More central to the increase in middle class writers was the recognition, towards the end of the eighteenth century, that money could be made or raised by the publication of volumes of poetry. The prosperous donated their profits: Lady Miller's collections were sold for the poor of Bath, Elizabeth Knipe Cobbold's *Ode* for the veterans and orphans of Waterloo. Mary (Blatchford) Tighe assigned the proceeds of the second edition of her *Psyche, with Other Poems* to the Orphan Asylum at Wicklow. In gratitude, the wing these funds built was called the "Psyche Ward." Some "distressed gentlewomen," widowed, orphaned, the sole supports of their families, undertook to support themselves by selling their work by subscription. Others, less well connected, found patrons. Mary Maria Colling's *Fables and other pieces in verse* was published in 1831. Her employer took pains to establish on the title page her own standing in literary and charitable circles by adding "with some account of the author in letters to Robert Southey . . . by Mrs. Bray." Ann Yearsley had the patronage of Hannah More. Subscribers, of course, could find their names in the prefatory pages and patrons in the dedications. Both groups had an interest in the book's success.

American women also turned to verse to support themselves. Lydia Howard (Huntley) Sigourney's father was a gardener. His employer, Mrs Lathrop, was the first person to encourage her to study and to write. When her husband's hardware business failed, Mrs Sigourney returned to poetry. She came to dominate the American market as Mrs Hemans did the British as a poet, arbiter of taste and advisor on moral and domestic issues. Similary, when Anna Cora (Mowatt) Ritchie's husband lost his memory, she gave poetry readings to raise funds for the family. Contrary to the common assumption, true today but not for the nineteenth century, fiction was not the only literary pursuit of women in financial difficulties.

The early nineteenth century was both hospitable and hostile to women writers. Romanticism, as Christopher Clausen points out in his provocative study, *The Place of Poetry: Two Centuries of an Art in Crisis*, attempted to reassert the importance of poetry and to re-establish its efficacy for society. In the Romantic view, "Peasants, children, and savages—these were the kinds of people who could produce and appreciate poetry. That Romantic poetry idealized all three could hardly be an accident if the modern adult world offered such stony soil to the seeds of a poetic revival (pp. 15–16)." Women could easily be added to this list of the disenfranchised. They might then be seen—even think of themselves—as natural poets. Romantic theorists, while redefining the sources of poetry and granting a place to poets of humble origin, introduced a new form of exclusivity. It was no longer an aristocratic pursuit, it was the spontaneous outpouring of a sensitive soul. If late eighteenth century arbiters of taste whom the Romantics were answering, considered poetry, especially popular poetry, a feminine art, then women writers of the early nineteenth century might take as a virtue especially highly developed in their gender the intensity of feeling the Romantics considered the definitive characteristic of the artist.

Although they are not generally considered among its founders, women poets were very much a part of the Romantic Movement and echoed its themes into the middle of the century. Odes and reflective poems were published in the early decades of the nineteenth century, from Harriet Cope's *Suicide* (1815) to Louisa Poulter's *Imagination* (1820), to Miss Edgar's *Tranquility* (1824). Mary Anne Lloyd's "Sonnet to a star", Mary Kerr Hart's *Heath Blossoms: or, Poems Written in Obscurity and Seclusion* (1830?) and Catherine Ponsonby's *Lays of the Lakes, and Other Poems of Description and Reflection* (1850) clearly refer to more famous male Romantic poets. Some poetic forms, developed but hardly invented by the Romantics, were widely imitated; nature poems like those in Mary Mackey's *Scraps of Nature* (1810) do show their influence. Collections of ballads were published before this period and continued to be popular beyond it. They represent about 1½ percent of all titles before 1850, about 2½ percent until 1880 and then return to their earlier frequency. Percy's *Reliques*, celebrated in an ode by Jessie Stewart in 1804, gave the form new life, but mainly among the Scottish writers. Women also commented on the more glamorous figures of the movement, especially Lord Byron, the subject of a Poetical Address (Mrs Henry Rolls, 1816), an Admonitory Appeal (Mrs Isaac Henry Robert Mott, 1824), an Elegy (Catherine Napier, 1844) and several satires. As more women began to publish, they were eager to join the major issues of their time.

The Victorian corollary to the Romantic ideal of the sensitive artist and the natural wisdom of the—at least relatively—untutored, that manly men were pursuing science, classifying rocks and exploring the antipodes, was not entirely true of the nineteenth century. The cult of domesticity and the defensive reassertion of the values of the age put women back in the home, but gave poets an official role in instilling virtue. Some male laureates became patrons and sponsors of women writers, most notably John Greenleaf Whittier, Sir Walter Scott, and Robert Southey. The Brownings were as loved for their domesticity and her invalidism, the icons of the age. If women's writing was devalued by being linked to the "peasants, children and savages," it was also judged useful in promoting the roles and age hoped to impose on them. In Britain the burden of empire required its builders to codify the values they were imparting to their colonies, while in the United States the rawness of the western settlements gave those who had established their homes an appetite for culture. This made both nations place a certain value on their poets and gave some women a place. Unfortunately, it is a utilitarian place, one that carries a built in obsolescence that has helped many women poets into obscurity. As values and fashions changed, the women writers were forgotten.

Accustomed to serving as models of virtue, angels in the house, educators of the young, and gentle tamers of the outposts of civilization, women wrote poems that fulfilled these missions. Francis Mary Sutcliffe, influenced perhaps by Hannah More and the early Tractarians, published poems on the conversion of the poor and ungodly (*Long Tom, Otherwise, Thomas Long*, 1836) and offered advice on the conduct appropriate to each station in life (*Mount Pleasant and Pleasant Row*, 1838; *The Squire and his Man; or, The Way to Get Up in the World*, 1839). Mary Wright Sewell published fifteen volumes of "Homely Ballads for the Working Man's Fireside" from 1858 to 1870. Other women wrote narrative and dramatic poems that could entertain and instruct. Biblical narratives and stories of the heroes of Christianity were popular, such as Gertrude Grey's *Claudius and Eudocia: A Tale of the Early Martyrs* (1868) as were classical myths (Virginia Vaughn's *Orpheus and the Sirens: A Drama in Lyrics*, 1882) and Gothic legends (Sallie Bridges' *Marble Isle, Legends of the Round Table, and Other Poems*, 1864). There were some obviously commercial works, instructional verses such as Mary (Russell) Gardner's histories of England, America, and France in rhyme and volumes of poems suitable for presentation on various occasions such as Dora Read Goodale's *A Birthday Book of Birds* and *Heralds of Easter*. As they had with the Romantics, women adapted forms popularized by male writers to their own concerns. Lucy Larcom called her narrative of the mill workers, *An Idyll of Work* (1875); Amanda Theodosia Jones, poet of Western settlement, published her *A Prairie Idyll, and Other Poems* in 1892. There were works on the preoccupation of the day, bereavement (Lady Lindsay's *The Christmas of the Sorrowful*, 1898), on private occasions (Margaret Junkin Preston's *Epithalamium 1878. October 10th.*), on the great events, the Civil War, on the causes of abolition, temperance, and women's rights, and on other contemporary themes. In the second half of the nineteenth century women began to publish in great numbers. Close to 70 percent of all the works in this bibliography are from this period. Having been inspired by the Romantic emphasis on creativity and having found in the Victorian Age a place as exemplars in the domestic sphere and commentators on the public, they offered the results to a receptive, often a paying, audience.

The American and the British poets represented in this volume contradict some general assumptions about women writers. They did not hide behind male pseudonyms, they were not always obscure in their own lifetimes, and they did compete in the literary marketplace. At mid-century, as the concepts of Romanticism were absorbed, there was a stock taking of poetry; the collections of May, Read, Griswold and Miles fixed the cannon of earlier poets. For the latter half there are fewer comprehensive anthologies. As a result, some of the notions of women's writing—that ladies did not publish or took care to do so anonymously, that poets were poor and wrote only for art's sake—seem to be based more on the earlier part of the nineteenth century than the later. The entries in this bibliography expand and alter those ideas considerably.

Only a small number of these poets, 8 percent, took care to conceal their identities, and of that fraction, a third signed some of their works with their initials. If one discounts this group, then only 5 percent of these women chose a pseudonym, and this does not change significantly over time. Renaissance and eighteenth century writers were no more likely to adopt a false identity than Victorians. In fact, women were more likely to reserve their pseudonyms for fiction as did Ellen Gilbert (Maples) Cook ("Ray Merton") or Elizabeth (Okes) Smith ("Ernest Helfenstern"). Perhaps because the Brontes first published under the names Acton, Currer and Ellis Bell and because Marian Evans has remained better known as George Eliot, the notion of the woman writer choosing a male name in order to gain credibility persists. Only twenty-one of these published poets did so. If out of diffidence or under family pressure they chose a disguise, it was more likely to be Jane Austen's simple designation, A Lady. Close to a quarter of the women in this volume who used pseudonyms follow this form which suggests that they were not concerned that their gender would prevent them from publishing. When they did alter their own names, it was often through an anagram that would do little to conceal their accomplishments from their friends. Eiggam Strebor (Maggie Roberts), Jay Peabee (Julia P. Burge), and Ekalenna (Anne Lake) are three of the most transparent.

Those who used pseudonyms clearly did so for some literary purpose or fashion. Restoration and eighteenth century women chose classical or pastoral names. Katherine Philips was Orinda (others added the adjective Matchless); Mary Deverell, Philanthea; Elizabeth Teft, Orinthia; and Elizabeth Thomas, Corinna. Some were assigned titles. Anna Seward was referred to as The Swan of Litchfield, Julia Mildred Harriss as The Minstrel Maiden of Mobile. Satire called for appropriate personae. Miss Barker chose "One of the small fry of the lakes" for her address to Lord Byron, while Mary Cowden Clarke took on the most frequently parodied American poet as Henry Wandsworth Shortfellow. Nature poetry inspired such choices as Eva Evergreen (Mrs E. H. Hough), Waif Woodland (Mrs C. P. Blair), and Ruth Rustic (Cornelia J. Orme). Most writers, even those who made artful use of pseudonyms for some of their works, also published under their own names.

Women poets' desire for recognition may be traced in a number of ways. Through occasional verse and addresses to royalty, literary and public figures they linked themselves to the major issues, events and people of their times. Some wrote on the Chicago fire, the Johnstown flood of 1889 or the shipwreck of the Birkenhead; others commemorated, as did Rebecca Reavis the St

Louis Exhibition of 1884 or Mary Brown the Manchester Royal Jubilee Exhibition of 1887. Some events in the lives of the famous called for sympathetic and loyal odes: the assassination of Abraham Lincoln, the death of Princess Charlotte, Queen Victoria's Jubilee or nearly any event in the life of the Prince of Wales. May Baird Finch composed campaign songs for the Democratic Party. Women wished to participate in events local and national.

Some of the poets here were famous for other pursuits, Mary Baker Eddy for her religious leadership, Sarah Stickney Ellis for her moral and social pronouncements. Some wrote works that made them immediately famous, though their names are no longer associated with their work. Sarah Fuller (Flower) Adams, for example, composed the hymn, "Nearer My God to Thee." Others were well known as poets in their own time. Isa (Craig) Knox, who published five volumes, including a collection of dramatic poems and *Songs of Consolation*, was also recognized for *The Burns Festival, Prize Poem Recited at the Crystal Palace, January 25, 1859*. Sarah A. (Ulrich) Kelley, the Bard of Shanty Hill, was nominated in the 1880s as "National Poetess of the United States." Others were celebrated, even notorious, in the nineteenth century, but have been overlooked since. Laetitia Elizabeth Landon, the "Byronic" woman Romantic, published over a dozen volumes and was a member of the first poetic circles of her time. Bulwer Lytton gave her away when she married George Maclean in June 1838, but it is the mystery of her death—she was found four months after the wedding dead with an empty vial of prussic acid by her side—that has continued to occasion comment. These women sought and sometimes gained fame in their own time, but like earlier poets, they have since disappeared from literary history. Not all, of course, were great writers, some were strictly commercial or local writers, but women who were important voices in their own time have been obscured.

In their day the writers listed here found major presses for their writing. Close to half (47 percent) of all these volumes were issued by the standard houses: Little, Macmillan, Longmans, Lippincott, etc. The authors who publish with them are by no means simply the famous and popular poets. Cecilia and Florence Havergal, whose sumptuous gift books were generally published by Nister, Randolph, Dutton and other established names, were also issued by much smaller houses. Some writers now obscure published with major houses: Caroline (Crane) Marsh, for example, with Scribner and Sampson Low, and Catherine M. Marsh with James Nisbet. While some of these presses did do vanity publishing, they generally make it clear when they print a book at the author's request. Publishing arrangements were more fluid then. Some best selling writers, Washington Irving and James Fennimore Cooper among them, financed their own works because they earned more by underwriting their works and giving the publisher a percentage. In the 1820s, Susan H. Gardner, a widow, published two extensive volumes of verse, *The Basket of Fragments* and *The Village Rambler*, in order to support herself and her children. Only 8 percent of these works are designated as privately printed, but the number may in fact be greater, as a third of them (30 percent) were issued by small concerns, by newspapers and job presses. Some of those, especially the presses in more remote locations such as Nashville, Denver, Pasadena, may only indicate that a writer had a local reputation and that the area was beginning to develop a readership. Caroline Lee (Whiting) Hentz wrote poems to be read before philosophical societies in Alabama and Massachusetts and was evidently commissioned to write a dramatic poem for "The Georgia Citizen." In fact these represent only a small number of the total volumes, and they do reveal the writers' interest in placing their works in a format more permanent than a magazine would afford. No information was available for 13 percent of the works in this volume. A tiny fraction (2 percent) were printed by church publishing houses or other organizations such as the Society for the Prevention of Cruelty to Animals, and these of course are written for specific purposes and audiences. One cannot tell how many works from small presses were not preserved and can no longer be considered.

There is no doubt that most of the works were published in the major cities. This is perhaps not surprising for Great Britain where 73 percent of the works were issued in London, 4 percent in Edinburgh and 3 percent in Dublin. The remainder came from provincial cities: Birmingham, Sheffield, Newcastle on Tyne, etc. There is less diversity in the United States, however, than one might expect. New York and Boston, which became the major publishing center after the railroad gave it access to western markets, account for about 28 percent each of the publications. Philadelphia, the dominant center before 1820, issued 7 percent, Chicago 4 percent. Other locations in New England account for 12 percent and California and the Deep South for 4 percent each. Two small firms, Moulton in Buffalo, New York and Clarke in Cincinnati, Ohio were the most important provincial presses. American women sought, as the British poets did, the centers of culture and publishing activity. They hoped for recognition and the widest possible audience. They were aware that other women were their audience. Quite a number published domestic verse: Emily Foote Baldwin's *Flora: and Other Poems, Grave and Humorous, For the Domestic Circle* (1879), Isabella Caulton's *The Domestic Hearth* (1843) and *Poems for Home* (1851) or Margaret Elizabeth Sangster's *Poems of the Household* (1882). Many wrote on children, on love, friendship and the affections. They created a sentimental cult of the language of flowers that could be used to express the highest themes (Rebecca Hey's *The Moral of Flowers*, 1833 or Katherine Keene's *Voiceless Teachers*, 1885), serve as the decoration for birthday gift books or even give practical advice (Pauline Garcia's *Flirtation Made Easy; or, The Art Revealed. Together with Poetry of Love and Flowers*, 1882). They shared their experiences of the western settlements: Wyoming (Lizzie Gordon), Colorado (Virginia McClurg), and Indiana (Alice Greenwood's *Husks and Nubbins*, 1899) and did not neglect to cover the difficulties of establishing a home in them. They chose heroines of the Bible, Eliza Cushing's *Esther, a Sacred Drama: With Judith, a Poem* (1840) is one of nine works on Esther. They wrote on goddesses, (*Astraea* by Mrs E. P. Thorndyke), famous women (Mrs Sigourney's *Pocahontas*), and the first woman poet, Sappho, the subject of seven volumes.

Most important, they spoke throughout the nineteenth century, from Agnes Semple's *Miscellanies, Designed Chiefly for the Benefit of Female Readers* (1810) to Catharine Scott's *Idylls of Womanhood* (1892) of women's roles. Some poems such as Jessee Butler's *Home: Femme Heroic* (1875) glorified the angel in the house; others provided a humorous perspective, as Jane Campbell's *The Nineteenth Century Woman* (1890), a satire on the expansion or lack thereof of women's roles. Others looked back to the tradition of the "female advocates" of the eighteenth century, Chudleigh and Scott. Frances Rowley made her advocacy clear in *Poems for the Times: Devoted to Woman's Rights, Temperance, etc.* (1871). Josephine Pollard's *Co-education* (1883), divided into four sections: Helpmate, Slave, Toy, and Equal anticipates twentieth century feminist critiques. Women poets may not always have been aware of their predecessors, but they were aware of the issues that concerned women in their day and conscious that they were writing for them.

The more than 6,000 volumes of poetry in this bibliography indicate that women were far more prolific, particularly in the second half of the nineteenth century, than has been supposed. Some trends are clear. Although poetry, unlike fiction or juvenile literature, was first a pursuit of upper class women, it was practised in the eighteenth and especially in the nineteenth century by women of all backgrounds. Although the label of popular poet was used to relegate most women to swift oblivion, there is a much larger and more persistent tradition of women writing than has been supposed. These poets responded to the same issues and themes that male poets did, yet they were also conscious that they were writing as women for women. Though aristocrats might not need money and Romantics ought, at least theoretically to disdain it, many women wrote poetry for a living. Commercial success is no more incompatible with art for women than for men, and they surely hoped for both, for bread and roses.

SCOPE AND ARRANGEMENT

The entries for this series of bibliographies were first developed by a complete reading of NUC and BL because they represent the most complete collections of works in English by American and British authors, and they offer the further advantage of guiding the reader to locations where the works may be seen. OCLC and other standard bibliographical and biographical sources were used to establish the most complete list possible. We have consulted other general sources, a selected list of which is supplied, to help in identifying and characterizing the works and to provide biographical background for the authors. In some cases the older sources, written before the canons of literature were established, have been most helpful because they treat authors who have since been forgotten. In other cases, more recent scholarship has offered information not available in the earlier reference works. We also consulted more specialized sources on poetry, a selected bibliography of which is included below. Each volume of this series has a similar list of the most useful general and specialized sources. Finally, we inspected about half the works included here in order to be sure they fit the parameters of this volume, and we examined others that were excluded.

In reading the catalogs to develop the materials for this series we established only a few guidelines for exclusion. We chose to end our collection with the nineteenth century, as more work has been done and more resources are available for twentieth century writers. Of course, some works by earlier writers were not published until the twentieth century and some women who began writing in the nineteenth century continued to publish into the next, but the volume of information was so large, that we chose to confine ourselves to works that were available to readers before 1900. We looked for original literary works, not scholarly or practical ones such as Elstob's Anglo-Saxon grammars or Mrs Beeton's cookbooks. Manuscripts, materials in translation, and periodical publications are not covered unless they were later collected in a book. We also excluded single sheets and broadsides, though we include volumes of very few pages so long as they might reasonably be considered a printed book. Having collected this information for all the genres in the series this way, we separated it into the constituent volumes in several ways, using reference works such as the ones listed in our bibliographies, library classifications, publishers' descriptions and advertisements, biographies and literary criticism. We also read a large number of the works themselves. NUC, BL and OCLC doubtless do not hold every book ever printed and tired eyes have undoubtedly missed some works, but we hope we have provided as full a listing within the guidelines as possible. This is not intended to be an analytic or descriptive bibliography. The scope of the entire series is too great to permit full annotation of each entry. Instead brief notes intended to clarify the character of the work if that is not made evident by its full title and subtitle are provided.

The entries in *Poetry* supply for each author the following information: her name, following the way it is listed in NUC; her husband's name; nationality; birth and death dates where known or century; alternative forms of her legal name under which she published or was known; and pseudonyms under which she published poetry. Birth names are placed in parentheses. Where a birth name is known and the husband's name is not, the title, Mrs, is omitted. Where the birth name is not clear, we do supply the title Mrs. In cases where the woman is identified only by initials which may be either hers or her husband's, we also include the title, Mrs. We list all known forms of a woman's legal name(s) as alternative names. For example, Katherine Sherwood (Bonner) McDowell who published under both her birth and her married names is listed as:

> MC DOWELL, Katherine Sherwood (Bonner) [Am. 1849–1883] ALT: Bonner, Katherine Sherwood; Bonner, Sherwood PSEUD: Atom, An

She is cross-referenced under both Bonner, Katherine Sherwood and Bonner, Sherwood. We consider the second name an alternative rather than a pseudonym because it is a part of her legal name. Similarly, initials are considered alternative forms of a woman's name. McDowell does also use a pseudonym, An Atom, for one of her works. Pseudonyms used in other literary genres are not listed in this volume. So, for example, Anna Cummings Johnson, who published essays and poems under the pseudonym, Minnie Myrtle, the travel literature as A Lady is identified as:

JOHNSON, Anna Cummings, Miss [Am. 1818–1892] PSEUD: Myrtle, Minnie

In *Personal Writings* she is identified and cross-indexed as: Lady, A, pseud. In the *Dictionary of Pseudonyms and Alternative Names* she will be listed under her real name and cross-references from both pseudonyms will be supplied. We follow NUC form for names, and include alternative spellings found in other sources, for example, Elizabeth, Lady Tyrwhitt is listed as: ALT: Tirwit, Elizabeth, Lady. Editors and compilers are also cross-referenced to their subjects.

As our main focus is on the women writers themselves, memorial volumes are listed under the subject's name as the primary entry even though they may appear under the editor's or compiler's name in NUC and BL. So, though Sarah (Hall) Boardman Judson's work is sometimes listed under the pseudonym, Fanny Forester, of the sister-in-law who collected it, Emily E. (Chubbuck) Judson, it is listed here under her name. Cross-references are provided from Forester, Fanny, pseud., comp. and from Judson, Emily E. (Chubbuck), comp. In the case of multiple authorship, works are listed under the name of the woman who appears first on the title page of the book and cross-references are given from all known forms of the names of the co-author(s).

For each work we list the title, the name of pseudonym under which it was written where this differs from the author entry, co-authors, place, publishers, date of first publication, page numbers, and catalog(s) in which it was found. Information from multiple sources is merged to form the most complete entry possible. We give only the first edition of a work. When new editions add a substantial number of new poems or include revisions, those editions are covered in the annotation to the first edition. Works that have been completely revised and really constitute a new work are given separate entries.

We try whenever we can to present the information in its fullest possible form. Any omissions within the entries indicate that the information was not available. We print, in most cases, the full title, as this often gives the character and flavor of the work. We do omit information not relevant to the primary work, as, for example, notices of other works by the same author or lists of appendices. We list compilers and editors, but not illustrators. Cross-references are also supplied from all known forms of the legal name for all co-authors, editors, and compilers. Wherever possible we give full names rather than initials in both entries and cross-references. We do use a few standard abbreviations (L for London, NY for New York, and U.S. for United States) within the entries. We also supply standard abbreviations of U.S. states as part of the place of publication, except for cities (Philadelphia or Chicago, for example) whose location is well known.

APPENDIX

The appendix is a chronological listing and sets the writers into their appropriate general time frame. The list is divided by century to 1700, by half century for the eighteenth and by quarter century for the nineteenth century. Because a number of works were published some time after the woman's death, we place names in parentheses to indicate posthumous publication. The names of these authors are also listed in the time period in which they lived, marked with an asterisk. We use date of death in assigning a writer to a given period. Exact dates of publication and precise dates of birth and death where known may be found in the main entries.

SUBJECT INDEX

The subject index to this volume is intended as a general guide to traditional forms of poetry as well as to particular themes which occupied women writers. Every work is not represented in the index as many of them are too heterogeneous to describe. Poets experiment in many forms and individual collections may include a great variety. A miscellany may contain lyrics on different topics, a single sonnet, a few occasional or memorial verses, and a narrative. Unless there are clearly designated groupings of poems, "songs and sonnets", for example, such works cannot usefully be indexed. We have not attempted to classify collections we have not seen unless one of the index terms is included in the title of the work.

This index covers traditional poetic forms: sonnets, odes, ballads, etc. and certain themes popular in the eighteenth and nineteenth centuries: legends, Biblical themes, nature poetry, etc. It includes particular topics that were important to women writers: domestic life, children, and flowers. Some key words have been used where they seem to indicate a particular theme or mood and occur in a significant number of works: Affection, Death, Echoes, Evening, Sunshine, Thoughts. A few special categories have been set up to distinguish within broader categories. Biblical Themes refers to poems that deal with characters or events in the Bible; Scripture Verses covers poems based on or published with passages from the Bible. Epic refers to any poem written in Books or Cantos. Poems indexed as Elegies were so designated by the author. Memorial Poems refers to other verses written on a particular person's death, while Bereavement covers poetry that focuses on the themes of grief and consolation. Poems listed in one of these categories are not then listed in the others. Lays, Legends, and Ballads may all be forms of narrative, but if they are so classified, they are not then listed under Narrative Verse. The subjects of poetic addresses and tributes are listed under one of three categories: Literary Figures, Public Figures, and Royalty. Poems on Places includes travel verses, descriptions of buildings, landscapes, regions, etc. Instructional Verse refers to a small group of poems which seek to provide geography lessons to or give mnemonic devices for the monarchs of England or Presidents of the United States. Charities covers works written for the benefit of a particular cause. Abolition and Temperance cover poems about two of women's historical concerns. While the index cannot begin to cover the diverse works in the bibliography, we hope it will give a general sense of the most popular poetic forms and themes.

Some of these index terms will be found in other volumes in the series. Abolition, Country Life, Juvenile Authors, Memorial Volumes, for example, are indexed for each genre. We have not tried to indicate any other literary activities of these authors, as they will be covered in the appropriate volume. We hope that this volume will stand on its own as a resource for the study of poetry by women. Taken together with the others in the series, it will enable users to trace an individual woman's career, to compare the frequency of memorial volumes or works on rural life, and to gain an overview of the publications of women before 1900.

ACKNOWLEDGEMENTS

Finally, we would like to thank some people whose help has been invaluable: Kristy Wallisch and Alison Circle for research assistance, and Wayne Joyce for research and moral support. Martha Burris for her skill in setting up the earliest files. Jan Valouch who has entered this material, edited it, and found many solutions to seemingly insoluable problems. George Economou for his unfailing support of the project. We thank especially The National Endowment for the Humanities for their generous research grant.

The librarians and staff of the Library of Congress and the British Library have given valuable help. Two collections of materials have been among our greatest resources, the Harris Collection of American Poetry at Brown University and the Stainforth Collection in the British Library. We would also like to thank for their special assistance the librarians of: Boston Public Library, Brown University, Buffalo and Erie County Public Library, Case Western Reserve University Library, Cornell University, Duke University, The Houghton and Harvard College Libraries of Harvard University, Huntington Library, Newberry Library, New York Public Library, Princeton University Library, Rutgers University Library, University of British Columbia Library, University of Kansas Libraries, University of Texas Libraries, University of Virginia Library and Yale University Library.

Gwenn Davis
Norman, Oklahoma
1990

SELECTED SOURCES

GENERAL

ADAMS, Oscar. *A Dictionary of American Authors*. 6th ed. Boston: Houghton Mifflin, 1904. Repr. Detroit, MI: Gale, 1969.

ADAMS, William Henry Davenport. *Celebrated English Women of the Victorian Era*. London: F. V. White, 1884.

ADBURGHAM, Alison. *Women in Print: Writing Women and Women's Magazines from the Restoration to the Accession of Victoria*. London: Allen and Unwin, 1972.

ADELMAN, Joseph. *Famous Women*. New York: Ellis Lonow Co., 1926

ALDERMAN, Edwin Anderson, ed. *Library of Southern Literature*. New Orleans, LA & Atlanta, GA: Martin & Hoyt Co., 1908–13.

ALEXANDER, William. *The History of Women From the Earliest Antiquity; Giving Some Account of Almost Every Interesting Particular Concerning That Sex, Among All Nations Ancient and Modern*. 2 vols. London: W. Strahan & T. Cadell, 1779.

ALLIBONE, S. Austin. *A Critical Dictionary of English Literature and British Authors*. 3 vols. Philadelphia: J. B. Lippincott, 1899.

ALTICK, Richard D. *The English Common Reader: A Social History of the Mass Reading Public, 1800–1900*. Chicago: U of Chicago P, 1957.

American Authors 1600–1900. Ed. Stanley J. Kunitz and Howard Haycraft. New York: H. W. Wilson, 1938.

American Women Writers: A Critical Reference Guide from Colonial Times to the Present. Ed. Lina Mainiero. 4 vols. New York: Frederick Ungar, 1979.

American Women Writers: Bibliographical Essays. Ed. by Maurice Duke, Jackson R. Bryer, and M. Thomas Inge. Westport, CT: Greenwood Press, 1983.

American Writers Before 1800: A Biographical and Critical Dictionary. Ed. James A. Levernier and Douglas R. Wilmas. Westport, CT: Greenwood Press, 1983.

AMORY, Thomas. *Memoirs of Several Ladies of Great Britain*. 2 vols. London: Pr. for John Noon, 1775.

Annals of English Literature, 1475–1950: The Principal Publications of Each Year Together with an Alphabetical Index of Authors with their Works. 2nd ed. Ed. Robert W. Chapman and W. K. Davin. Oxford: Clarendon, 1961, repr. 1969.

BAIN, Robert and Flora, Joseph M., eds. *Fifty Southern Writers Before 1900: A Bio-bibliographical Source Book*. New York: Greenwood Press, c1987.

BAKER, Ray Palmer. *History of English-Canadian Literature to the Confederation. Its Relation to the Literature of Great Britain and the United States*. New York: Russell & Russell, 1920 [repr. 1968].

BALD, Marjory A. *Women Writers of the Nineteenth Century*. Cambridge: Cambridge UP, 1928.

BALLARD, George. *Memoirs of British Ladies, Who Have Been Celebrated for Their Writings or Skill in the Learned Languages, Arts and Sciences*. London: Pr. for J. Evans, 1775. Repr.; ed. Ruth Perry. Detroit, MI: Wayne State UP, 1985.

BASKERVILL, William Malone. *Southern Writers: Biographical and Critical Studies*. 2 vols. Nashville, TN: Pub. House M.E. Church, South, 1902–3.

BETHAM, Mary Matilda. *A Biographical Dictionary of the Celebrated Women of Every Age and Country*. London: B. Crosby & Co., 1804.

The Biographical Cyclopaedia of American Women. Comp. Mabel Ward Cameron and Erma Conckling Lee. New York: Halvord Pub. Co., 1924.

Biographium Femineum. The Female Worthies: or Memoirs of the Most Illustrious Ladies of All Ages and Nations. 2 vols. London: S. Crowder, 1766.

BLACK, Helen C. *Notable Women Authors of the Day*. Glasgow: David Bryce & Son, 1893.

Black American Writers, Past and Present: A Biographical and Bibliographical Dictionary. Ed. Theresa Gunnels Rush, Carol Fairbanks Myers, and Esther Spring Arata. 2 vols. Metuchen, NJ: Scarecrow, 1975.

Black American Writers, 1773–1949: A Bibliography and Union List. Comp. Geraldine O. Matthews, et al. Boston: Hall, 1975.

BLANCK, Jacob Nathaniel. *Bibliography of American Literature*. New Haven: Yale University Press, 1955.

BOASE, Frederic. *Modern English Biography, Containing . . . Many Concise Memoirs of Persons Who*

Have Died Since . . . the Year 1850 . . . With An Index of the Most Interesting Matter. 6 vols. Truro: Netherton & Worth, 1892–1921.

BRADFORD, Gamaliel. *Portraits of American Women*. Boston & New York: Houghton Mifflin, 1916.

British Authors Before 1800; A Biographical Dictionary. Ed. Stanley J. Kunitz and Howard Haycraft. New York: Wilson, 1952.

British Authors of the Nineteenth Century. Ed. Stanley J. Kunitz and Howard Haycraft. New York: Wilson, 1936.

British Museum. Department of Printed Books. General Catalogue of Printed Books. Photolithographic edition to 1955. London: Trustees, 1959–66.

The Cambridge History of American Literature. Ed. by William Peterfield Trent, John Erskine, Stuart P. Sherman & Carl Van Doren. NY: The McMillan Co., 1944.

The Cambridge History of English Literature. Ed. A. W. Ward and A. R. Waller. New York & London: G. P. Putnam's Sons, 1907–17.

CAMERON, M. W. *The Biographical Encyclopedia of Women*. New York: Halvord, 1924.

CASEY, Elizabeth. *Illustrious Irishwomen*. 2 vols. London: Tinsley Bros., 1887.

CHAMBERS, Robert. *A Biographical Dictionary of Eminent Scotsmen*. New Ed. Rev. by Thomas Tomson. 3 vols. London: Blackie & Son, 1870.

CHARVAT, William. *Literary Publishing in America, 1790–1850*. Philadelphia: U of Pennsylvania P, 1959.

CHARVAT, William. *The Profession of Authorship in America, 1800–1870*. Columbus: Ohio State UP, 1968.

CLARKE, Mary Cowden. *World-Noted Women*. New York: D. Appleton, 1857.

COSTELLO, Louisa Stuart. *Memoirs of Eminent Englishwomen*. 4 vols. London: R. Bentley, 1844.

CRONE, John S. *A Concise Dictionary of Irish Biography*. Dublin: The Talbot Press, 1928.

DABYDEEN, David, ed. *The Black Presence in English Literature*. Manchester: Manchester UP, 1985.

Dictionary of American Biography. Ed. Allen Johnson, et al. 11 vols. New York: Scribner, 1946–58.

Dictionary of National Biography. Ed. Sir Leslie Stephen and Sir Sidney Lee. 22 vols. London: Oxford UP, 1921–22.

Dictionary of Welsh Biography Down to 1940. Under the Auspices of the Honourable Society of Cymmrodorion. London: 1959.

DUYCKINCK, Evert Augustus and George Long. *Cyclopedia of American Literature*. 2 vols. New York: C. Scribner, 1835.

Eighteenth-Century Short-Title Catalogue. London: British Museum; Baton Rouge, LA: Lousiana State U, [In prep.]

ELLIOTT, Emory, ed. *American Colonial Writers, 1606–1734*. Detroit, MI: Gale, 1984.

The Europa Biographical Dictionary of British Women. Ed. Anne Crawford, Tony Hayter, Ann Hughes, Frank Prochaska, Pauline Stafford, Elizabeth Vallance. Detroit, MI: Gale Research Co., 1983.

EVANS, Charles. *American Bibliography: A Chronological Dictionary of All Books, Pamphlets and Periodical Publications Printed in the United States of America from the Genesis of Printing in 1639 down to and including the year 1820, with Bibliographical and Biographical Notes*. 14 vols. Chicago: Blakely, for Evans, 1903–34; Worcester, MA: Am. Antiquarian Soc., 1955–59.

FAUST, Langdon Lynne, ed. *American Women Writers: A Critical Reference Guide from Colonial Times to the Present*. Abr. ed. New York: Ungar, 1988.

The General Biographical Dictionary . . . Ed. Alexander Chalmers. 32 vols. London: Pr. for J. Nichols, 1812–17.

HALE, Sarah Josepha Buell. *Woman's Record; or, Sketches of All Distinguished Women, From "The Beginning" Till A.D. 1850*. New York: Harper & Bros., 1853.

HANAFORD, Phebe A. *Daughters of America, or Women of the Century*. August, ME: True & Co., 1883.

Handbook of American-Jewish Literature: an Analytical Guide to Topics, Themes, and Sources. Ed. Lewis Fried, et al. Westport, CT: Greenwood P, 1988.

HARRIS, Trudier, ed. and foreword; Davis, Thadious M., ed. *Afro-American Writers Before the Harlem Renaissance*. Detroit, MI: Gale, 1986.

HASKELKORN, Anne, M. and Betty S. Travitsky, eds. *The Renaissance Englishwoman in Print: Counterbalancing the Canon*. Amherst: U. of Massachusetts P., 1990.

HAYS, Mary, *Female Biography; or, Memoirs of Illustrious and Celebrated Women of All Ages and Countries*. 3 vols. London: R. Phillips, 1803.

INGE, M. Thomas, ed. *Handbook of American Popular Literature*. Westport, CT: Greenwood, 1988.

The International Dictionary of Women's Biography. Comp. and ed. Jennifer S. Uglow. New York: Continuum Pub. Co., 1982.

JAMES, Edward T., et al. *Notable American Women: A Biographical Dictionary*. 3 vols. Cambridge, MA: Belknap Press of Harvard UP, 1971.

KANNER, Barbara, ed. *The Women of England From Anglo-Saxon Times to the Present: Interpretive Bibliographical Essays*. Hamden, CT: Shoe String, 1979.

KLAUS, Gustav. *The Literature of Labour: Two-Hundred Years of Working Class Writing*. New York: St. Martin's, 1985.

LEE, Anna Maria. *Memoirs of Eminent Female Writers*. Philadelphia: T. Desilver & Towar & Hogan, 1827.

MADISON, Charles A. *Book Publishing in America*. New York: McGraw-Hill, 1966.

MATTHEWS, Geraldine O., and the African-American Materials Project Staff School of Library Science, North Carolina Central University, comp. *Black American Writers, 1773–1949: A Bibliography and Union List*. Boston: Hall, 1975.

MILLER, Elizabeth W. *The Negro in America: A Bibliography Compiled By Elizabeth W. Miller for the American Academy of Arts and Sciences*. Cambridge, MA: Harvard UP, 1966.

MOERS, Ellen, *Literary Women: The Great Writers*. Garden City, NY: Doubleday & Co., Inc., 1976.

MOORE, Virginia. *Distinguished Women Writers*, New York: E. P. Dutton & Co., 1934.

NADEL, Ira Bruce. *Jewish Writers of North America*. Detroit, MI: Gale, 1981.

NATHAN, Rhoda B, ed. *Nineteenth-Century Women Writers of the English-Speaking World*. New York: Greenwood, 1986.

National Union Catalog. Pre-1956 Imprints. London: Mansell, 1968–1981.

New Cambridge Bibliography of English Literature. Ed. George Watson. 4 vols and index. Cambridge: Cambridge UP, 1969–76.

Notable American Women, 1607–1950; A Biographical Dictionary. Ed. Edward T. James et al. Cambridge, MA: Belknap P of Harvard UP, 1971.

OCLC (Online Computer Library Center). Dublin, OH: 1967–

The Oxford History of English Literature. Ed. F. P. Wilson and Bonamy Dobree. Oxford: Oxford UP, 1944.

POLLARD, Alfred W., and Gilbert R. Redgrave. *A Short-Title Catalogue of Books Printed in England, Scotland, and Ireland and of English Books Printed Abroad 1475–1640*. London: Bibliographical Soc., 1926. [Reprint 1969. 2d ed. Oxford UP, 1985]

PRIOR, Mary, ed. and pref.; Thirsk, Joan, foreword. *Women in English Society, 1500–1800*. London: Methuen, 1985.

RIVERS, Isabel, ed. *Books and Their Readers in Eighteenth-Century England*. Leicester: Leicester UP, 1982.

ROORBACH, Orville Augustus. *Bibliotheca Americana . . . 1820–61*. 4 vols. New York: Roorbach, 1852–61.

The Schomburg Library of Nineteenth-Century Black Women Writers. Henry Louis Gates, Jr., gen. ed. 30 vols. New York: Oxford UP, 1988– .

SHEVELOW, Kathryn. *Women and Print Culture: Constructing Femininity in the Early Periodicals*. New York: Routledge, 1989.

SHIRLEY, J. *The Illustrious History of Women*. London: J. Harris, 1686, 1702.

SHOCKLEY, Ann Allen. *Afro-American Women Writers, 1746–1933: An Anthology and Critical Guide*. Boston & London: G. K. Hall & Twayne, 1988.

SHOEMAKER, Richard H. *A Checklist of American Imprints for 1820–1829*. 10 vols. Metuchen, NJ: Scarecrow, 1964–71.

TEBBEL, John. *A History of Book Publishing in the United States*. 4 vols. NY: R. R. Bowker, 1972.

TODD, Janet. *British Women Writers: A Critical Reference Guide*. New York: Continuum, 1989.

TODD, Janet, ed. *A Dictionary of British and American Women Writers 1600–1800*. Totowa, NJ: Rowman & Allanheld, 1985.

WAGES, Jack D. *Seventy-four Writers of the Colonial South*. Boston: G. K. Hall & Co., 1979.

WILLARD, Frances E. and Mary A. Livermore *A Woman of the Century: 1400 Biographies of Leading American Women*. Buffalo: C. W. Moulton, 1893. Repr. Detroit, MI: Gale, 1967.

WILLIAMS, Franklin B., Jr. *The Index of Dedications and Commendatory Verses in English*. London: Bibliographical Society, 1962.

WILSON, Katharina M., ed. *Women Writers of the Renaissance and Reformation*. Athens, GA: U of Georgia P, 1987.

WING, Donald, ed. *Short-Title Catalogue of Books Printed in England, Ireland, Wales, and British America and of English Books Printed in Other Countries 1641–1700*. 2d ed. New York: Modern Language Association of America, 1989.

WRIGHT, Thomas *Womankind in Western Europe*. London: Groombridge & Sons, 1869.

POETRY SOURCES

ABDY, Georgiana B. *A Victorian Potpourri of Verses, Known, Unknown, and Forgotten. Collected and Edited by G. B. Abdy*. London: Lane, 1930.

BARBER, Mary. *Poems By Eminent Ladies*. Ed. George Colman and Bonnell Thornton. 2 Vols. Dublin: Sarah Cotter, 1757.

BARNSTONE, Aliki and Willis Barnstone, eds. *A Book of Women Poets from Antiquity to Now*. New York: Schocken, 1978.

BAX, Clifford and Meum Stewart. *The Distaff Muse: An Anthology of Poetry Written by Women*. London: Hollis & Carter, 1949.

BELL, Robert, E.; G. B. Tennyson; Marilyn J. Sharrow, John W. McConnell; Peter Allan Dale. *Minor British Poets 1789–1918: Part Two: The Early Victorian Period 1840–1869; Part Three: The Later Victorian Period 1870–1899*. Davis: Univ. of California, 1985, 1986.

BERDAN, John Milton. *Early Tudor Poetry, 1485–1547*. Repr. Hamden, CT: Shoe String, 1961.

BETHUNE, George Washington, ed. *The British Female Poets; With Biographical and Critical Notices*. Philadelphia: Lindsay & Blakiston, 1848.

Black Sister. Poetry by Black American Women, 1746–1980. Ed. Erlene Stetson. Bloomington, IN: Indiana UP, 1981.

BRATTON, Jacqueline S. *The Victorian Popular Ballad*. London: Macmillan, 1975.

BOGAN, Meg, ed. *The Women Troubadours*. New York: Paddington, 1976.

BUYZE, Jean. *The Tenth Muse: Women Poets Before 1806: A Rediscovery of Women Poets Lost to History*. Berkeley, CA: Shameless Hussy, 1980.

CHAPMAN, Dorothy H. *Index to Black Poetry*. Boston: Hall, 1976.

CLAUSEN, Christopher. *The Place of Poetry: Two Centuries of an Art in Crisis*. Lexington, KY: U of Kentucky P, 1981.

COGGESHALL, W. T. *The Poets and Poetry of the West*. New York: Arno, 1975.

COPPEE, Henry. *A Gallery of Distinguished English and American Female Poets*. Philadelphia: E. H. Butler & Co., 1860.

DAY, Cyrus Lawrence, and Eleanore Boswell Murrie. *English Songbooks, 1651–1702: a Bibliography with a First-Line Index of Songs*. London: The Bibliographical Society, 1936.

DUGAW, Dianne. *Warrior Women and Popular Balladry, 1650–1850*. Cambridge: Cambridge UP, 1989.

DYCE, Alexander. *Specimens of British Poetesses*. London: T. Rodd, 1827.

FAIRCHILD, Hoxie Neal. *Religious Trends in English Poetry*. 6 vols. New York: Columbia UP, 1939–68.

FOXON, D. F. *English Verse 1701–1750: A Catalogue of Separately Printed Poems with Notes on Contemporary Collected Editions*. 2 vols. London & New York: Cambridge UP, 1975.

GILBERT, Sandra M., and Susan Gubar, eds. *Shakespeare's Sisters: Feminist Essays on Women Poets*. Bloomington IN: Indiana UP, 1979.

GRISWOLD, Rufus Willmot. *The Female Poets of America*. Philadelphia: Carey & Hart, 1849.

GRISWOLD, Rufus Willmot. *The Poets and Poetry of America*. Philadelphia: Carey & Hart, 1842.

HESSELGRAVE, Ruth Avaline. *Lady Miller and the Batheaston Literary Circle*. New Haven, CT: Yale UP, 1927.

HICKOK, Kathleen. *Representations of Women: Nineteenth-Century British Women's Poetry*. Westport, CT: Greenwood, 1984.

HOMANS, Margaret. *Women Writers and Poetic Identity: Dorothy Wordsworth, Emily Brontè, and Emily Dickinson*. Princeton, NJ: Princeton UP, 1980.

JANTZ, Harold S. *The First Century of New England Verse*. New York: Russell & Russell, 1962.

JULIAN, J. *A Dictionary of Hymnology*. New York: Dover Publications, 1957.

KAPLAN, Cora, ed. *Salt and Bitter and Good: Three Centuries of English and American Women Poets*. New York & London: Paddington, 1975.

KOLB, Elene Margot. *A Tapestry of Voices: the Medieval Woman's Song*. Bloomington, IN: Indiana UP, 1979. 1980.

LONSDALE, Roger. *Eighteenth Century Women Poets: An Oxford Anthology*. Oxford: Oxford UP, 1989.

MAY, Caroline. *American Female Poets*. Philadelphia: Lindsay & Blakiston, 1848.

MAYO, Sara Carter (Edgarton). *The Poetry of Woman*. Boston: A. Tompkins & B. B. Mussey, 1841.

MILES, Alfred Henry. *Poets and Poetry of the Nineteenth Century*. 12 vols. London: Routledge; New York: Dutton, 1905–07.

MOIR, David Macbeth. *Sketches of the Poetical Literature of the Past Half-Century, in Six Lectures, etc.* Edinburgh & London: n.p., 1851.

NYE, Russel B. *The Unembarrassed Muse*. New York: Dial P, 1970.

ONDERDONK, James Lawrence. *History of American Verse, 1610–1897*. Chicago: A. C. McClurg, 1901.

OSTRIKER, Alicia Susan. *Stealing the Language: The Emergence of Women's Poetry in America*. Boston: Beacon Press, 1986.

READ, Thomas Buchanan. *The Female Poets of America*. New York: Garret Press, 1969. Repr. Detroit, MI: Gale, 1978.

ROBERTSON, Eric S. *English Poetesses*. London: Cassell & Co., 1883.

ROGERS, Charles. *The Modern Scottish Minstral: or, the Songs of Scotland of the Past Half Century*. 6 vols. Edinburgh: A. & C. Black, 1855–57.

ROWTON, Frederic, Williamson, Marilyn L., ed. *The*

Female Poets of Great Britain. A Facsim. of the 1853 ed. with a Crit. Introd. and Bibliog. Appendices. Detroit, MI: Wayne State UP, 1981.

SAINTSBURY, George, ed. *Minor Poets of the Caroline Period*. 3 vols. Oxford: Clarendon P. 1905–21.

SELDEN, Raman. *English Verse Satire, 1590–1765*. London: Allen & Unwin, 1978.

SHERMAN, Joan Rita. *Invisible Poets: Afro-Americans of the Nineteenth Century*. Urbana, IL: U of Illinois P, 1974.

Sketches of Obscure Poets. With Specimens of Their Writings. London: Cochrane & McCrone, 1833.

TEASDALE, Sara, comp. *The Answering Voice: One Hundred Love Lyrics by Women*. New York: MacMillan, 1926.

WAGNER, Jean. *Black Poets of the United States: From Paul Laurence Dunbar to Langston Hughes*. Trans. Kenneth Douglas. Urbana, IL: U of Illinois P, 1973. c1962.

WALKER, Cheryl. *The Nightingale's Burden: Women Poets and American Culture Before 1900*. Bloomington, IN: Indiana UP, c1982.

WATTS, Emily Stipes. *The Poetry of American Women from 1632–1945*. Austin, TX & London: U of Texas P, 1977.

WEGELIN, Oscar. *Early American Poetry: A compilation of the Titles and Broadsides by Writers Born or Residing in North America, North of the Mexican Border*. 2d ed. rev. & enl. New York: P. Smith, 1930.

WHITE, Peter, ed. and pref.; Meserole, Harrison T., Advisory ed. *Puritan Poets and Poetics: Seventeenth-Century American Poetry in Theory and Practice*. University Park, PA: Pennsylvania State UP, 1985.

WILLIAMS, Jane. *The Literary Women of England*. London: Saunders & Otley, 1861.

Women Poets in Pre-Revolutionary America, 1650–1755. Ed. Pattie Cowell. Troy, NY: Whitson Pub. Co., 1981.

The World Split Open, Four Centuries of Women Poets in England and America, 1552–1950. Ed. Louise Bernikow. New York: Vintage, 1974.

SELECTED ABBREVIATIONS

BL	British Museum, Department of Printed Books. *General Catalogue of Printed Books*.
DLC	The Library of Congress.
NUC	*National Union Catalog, Pre–1956 Imprints*.
OCLC	Online Computer Library Center.
RPB	Brown University Library.
TXU	University of Texas Library.

THE BIBLIOGRAPHY

*, pseud., co-author see OWEN, Frances Mary (Synge)

A. see ALLENBY, Mrs.

A. see SHORE, Arabella

A., F.E. see ASHLEY, Florence Emily

1. A., M., Mrs. [19c]
The remembrance.
Paris: Pr. E. Briere, 1845. 221p. NUC

A., M. see ARTHINGTON, Maria

ABBOT, Elizabeth Susan (Law), Baroness see COLCHESTER, Elizabeth Susan (Law) Abbot, Baroness Colchester

ABBOTT, Mrs. L. Smith see ABBOTT, Mary Persons (Briggs)

2. ABBOTT, M., Mrs. W. Abbott [Br. 19c]
The garden, and other poems. By Mrs. W. Abbott.
L: Robert Hardwicke, 1855. 88p. NUC BL

3. ABBOTT, Mary Persons (Briggs), Mrs. L. Smith Abbott [Am. 1823-1849]
Poetical and prose writings of Mrs. Mary P. Abbott.
Painesville, OH: Scofield's Book & Job Office, 1851. 91p. NUC OCLC
[Misc. poems, addresses, essays & 1 short story]

ABBOTT, Mrs. W. see ABBOTT, M.

4. ABDY, Maria Smith, Mrs. [Br. d. 1867]
Poetry.
8 Ser. L: J. Robins & co., 1838-62. 98p. NUC BL OCLC

5. -----Poetry. By Mrs. Abdy.
L: Pr. J. Robins & sons, for priv. circ., 1834. 78p. NUC BL OCLC
[With this is bound her: Poetry. Second Series 1838. Most of these were first published in periodicals]

6. ACKROYD, Laura G. [Br. 19/20c]
Homer's wine, and other poems.
L: Roxburghe Press, 1896. 196p. NUC BL

ACOTES, Rosemary A. see COTES, Rosemary A.

7. ACTON, Eliza [Br. 1799-1859]
Poems.
Ipswich: R. Deck, 1826. 140p. NUC BL OCLC

8. -----The voice of the north.
L: R. & J.E. Taylor, 1842. 7p. BL

9. ACTON, Harriet [Br. 19c]
Poems. By Harriet and Rose Acton.
L: Pr. for the authors by J. Rogerson, 1846. 150p. NUC BL OCLC

ACTON, Rose, co-author see ACTON, Harriet

10. ADAMS, Ann Olivia, Mrs. [Am. 19c]
PSEUD: Astarte
Lines on a Japanese fan, presented to Mrs. Richard W. Schieffelin. By Astarte.
NY: D.N. Carvalho, 1879? 4p. NUC
[Inside title: The Japanese flutist.]

11. -----Poems by Astarte.
NY: W.H. Kelley & bros., 1865. 83p. NUC OCLC

ADAMS, Bertha Leith see LAFFAN, Bertha Jane (Grundy)

12. ADAMS, Catherine A. Van Buren [Am. 19c]
Music: an apotheosis: and other poems.
NY: Eckler, pr., 1870. 66p. NUC OCLC

13. ADAMS, Mrs. Clayton [Br. 19c]
The church universal.
L: E.W. Allen, 1886. 8p. BL

14. -----Out in the sunshine.
L: G. Stoneman, 1892. 39p. BL

15. ADAMS, Edith C. [Br. 19c]
Idyls of love and life.
L: K. Paul, Trench, Trubner, & co., 1893. 148p. NUC BL

16. ADAMS, Jane [Br. 18c]
Miscellany poems.
Glasgow: Pr. James Duncan, 1734. 189p. NUC BL OCLC

17. ADAMS, L. B., Miss [Am. 19c] ALT: L.
The plays and poems of L. In three parts.
NY: Delisser & Procter, 1859. 100p. NUC OCLC
[Part 1. Eva, a tragic poem. Part 2. A tragic poem in 3 acts. Part 3. Ballads, etc. NUC lists only under pseud. L.]

18. -----Sybelle, and other poems. By L.

NY: Carleton, 1862. 192p. NUC OCLC

ADAMS, M.J.M. see ADAMS, Mary Jane (Mathews)

19. ADAMS, Mary Jane (Mathews) [Am. 1840-1902] ALT: Adams, M. J. M. PSEUD: Barnes, Mary Mathews
The choir visible.
Chicago: Way & Williams, 1897. 185p. NUC OCLC

20. -----Commencement ode. By M.J.M. Adams.
Madison, WI: Tracy, Gibbs & co., pr., 1894. 15p. NUC OCLC

21. -----Epithalamium. By Mary Mathews Barnes.
NY & L: G.P. Putnam's sons, 1889. 31p. NUC

22. -----The message of the dead. A poem written for Memorial Day, 1895, at Madison, Wisconsin.
Madison, WI: Priv. pr., 1895? 15p. NUC

23. ADAMS, Nellie E. [Am. b. 1864]
Blossoms. A book of poems.
Exeter, NH: E.A. Kaharl, 1885. 22p. NUC OCLC

24. ADAMS, Sarah Fuller (Flower)
Nearer my God to thee.
Boston: Lee and Shepard, 1876. 16 l. NUC BL
[The hymn first appeared in a collection: Bethany, NY: Fourth Ward Mission, 1860.]

25. -----Vivia Perpetua.
L: Charles Fox, 1841. 200p. NUC BL OCLC
[Dramatic poem; 5 acts. On early Christians martyrs, Saints Perpetua & Felicitas]

26. ADAMS, Vesta [Am. 19c]
Ivy leaves.
Cincinnati, OH: Standard pub. co., 1887. 51p. NUC

ADELINE, pseud., comp. see SERGEANT, Emily Frances Adeline

ADELINE, pseud. see SERGEANT, Jane (Hall)

ADIDNAC, pseud. see WHITAKER, Lily C.

AEMILIA JULIA, pseud. see BLACK, Emily Julia

AFTON, EFFIE, pseud. see HARPER, Frances Ellen (Watkins)

AFTON, EFFIE, pseud. see MONMOUTH, Sarah Elizabeth (Harper)

AGATHA, pseud. see LAWRENCE, Bessie

AGNEW, E.C. see AGNEW, Eleanor C.

27. AGNEW, Eleanor C. [Br. 19c] ALT: Agnew, E. C.; Agnew, Emily C.
The convent prize book. A selection of verses on the festivals of the church, feasts of the Blessed Virgin, festivals of the principal saints, and miscellaneous poems.
L: R. Washbourne, 1868. 132p. BL

AGNEW, Emily C. see AGNEW, Eleanor C.

28. AGNEW, Emily C.
Saint Mary and her times; a poem, in fourteen cantos.
L: n.p., 1851. BL

29. AGUILAR, Grace [Br. 1816-1847]
The spirit of Judaism. Ed. Isaac Leeser.
Philadelphia: C. Sherman & co., pr., 1842. 255p. NUC BL OCLC
[Includes her poetry]

30. AIKIN, Lucy [Br. 1781-1864]
Epistles on women, exemplifying their character and condition in various ages and nations. With miscellaneous poems.
L: J. Johnson & co., 142p.; Boston: W. Wells & T.B. Wait & co., 1810. 154p. NUC BL OCLC

AIKIN, Anna Letitia see BARBAULD, Anna Letitia (Aikin)

AIKIN, Lucy, comp. see BARBAULD, Anna Letitia (Aikin)

AILENROC, pseud. see STRYKOR, Cornelia

31. AITKEN, Cora Kennedy [Br. 19c]
Legends and memories of Scotland.
L: Hodder & Stoughton, 1874. 155p. NUC BL OCLC
[Travel literature in verse]

32. -----Sonnets, songs, and stories.
L: Hodder & Stoughton, 1875. 240p. NUC BL

33. AKERMAN, Lucy Evelina [Am. 1816-1874]
Nothing but leaves. A poem.

Philadelphia: D. Ashmead, 1868. 7 l. NUC OCLC
[Later pub. as: Nothing but leaves and other poems. Providence, RI: 1875. Not expanded]

AKERS, Elizabeth Ann (Chase) <u>see</u> ALLEN, Elizabeth Ann (Chase) Akers

34. AKERSTROM, Ullie R. [Am. 19/20c]
ALT: Ullie
Poems by Ullie.
Chicago: The author, 1884. 85p. NUC OCLC

35. -----"Toot yer horn" and other poems, by Ullie.
New Britain, CT: The authoress, 1886. 94p. NUC OCLC

36. ALCOCK, Mary Cumberland [Br. d. 1798]
The air-balloon: or, Flying mortal. A poem.
L: E. Macklew, 1784. 7p. BL

37. -----Poems, &c., &c. Ed. Joanna Hughes.
L: C. Dilly, 1799. 183p. NUC BL OCLC

38. ALDRICH, Anne Reeve [Am. 1866-1892]
Nadine and other poems.
NY: Pr. for priv. circ., 1893. 96p. NUC OCLC
[Includes sonnets addressed to her by others]

39. -----The rose of flame and other poems of love.
NY & L: G.P. Putnam's sons, 1889. 92p. NUC

40. -----The rose of flame and other poems of love.
2d ed. NY: American News co.; C.T. Dillingham, 1889. 108p. NUC BL OCLC
[With added poems considered too intense, so omitted from first edition. Third edition pub. same year.]

41. -----Songs about life, love and death.
NY: C. Scribner's sons, 1892. 133p. NUC OCLC

42. ALDRICH, Julia Carter [Am. b. 1834] PSEUD: Peters, Petresia
Hazel bloom. By Petresia Peters.
Buffalo, NY: C.W. Moulton, 1899. 213p. NUC OCLC

43. ALEXANDER, Adelaide Windsor [Am. 19c]
Four poems.
Providence, RI: n.p., 1860-90. 4 pt. NUC

44. ALEXANDER, Cecil Frances (Humphreys), Mrs. William Alexander [Br. 1818-1895] ALT: A., C. F.; H., C. F.; Humphreys, Cecil Frances
Legend of the golden prayers and other poems.
L: Bell & Daldy, 1859. 228p. NUC BL OCLC

45. -----Moral songs.
L: n.p., 1849. 64p. NUC BL OCLC

46. -----Poems on subjects in the Old Testament. By C.F.A.
L: J. Masters, 1854. 2v. NUC BL

47. -----Poems. By C.F.A. Ed. William Alexander.
L & NY: Macmillan & co., 1896. 463p. NUC BL OCLC
[Religious poetry]

48. -----Verses for holy seasons. By C.F.H. Ed. Walter Farquhar Hook.
L: F. & J. Rivington, 1846. 232p. NUC BL OCLC
[Christian poetry for the church year]

49. -----Verses written on the accession of Her Majesty the Queen.
n.p.: n.p., 1837. 15p. NUC OCLC

ALEXANDER, Mrs. William <u>see</u> ALEXANDER, Cecil Frances (Humphreys)

ALEXANDER, William, ed. <u>see</u> ALEXANDER, Cecil Frances (Humphreys)

50. ALICE GEORGINA, pseud. [Br. 19c]
Wild rosebuds. By Alice Georgina, aged nine years old.
L: David Bogue, 1853. 46p. BL

51. -----Wild spring flowers. By Alice Georgina, aged eight years.
Darmstadt: G.G. Lange, 1852. 24p. BL

52. ALICE MARGARET [Br. 19c]
Lines on the loss of Her Majesty's steamer "Birkenhead." By the orphan of a naval officer. Contributed to the bazaar in aid of Queen Adelaide Naval Fund.
Liverpool: n.p., 1852. BL

53. ALLARDYCE, Anne Dundas (Blair) [Br. 1777-1857] PSEUD: Lady, A
The goodwife at home; in metre, illustrating the dialect of the

north-west district of Aberdeenshire. By a lady.
Aberdeen: Brown, 1867. 19p. NUC BL

ALLEGRO, pseud. see ELDRED, O.P., Mrs.

54. ALLEN, Almira L., Mrs. [Am. 19c]
Hymns of joy, and songs of faith.
Boston: J.H. Earle, 1896. 75p. NUC

55. ALLEN, Brasseya Johnson [Am. 19c]
Pastorals, elegies, odes, epistles, and other poems.
Abingdon, MD: Pr. Daniel P. Ruff, 1806. 163p. NUC BL OCLC

56. ALLEN, Charlotte, Mrs. [Am. 19c]
Poems.
Boston: Saxton & Peirce, 1841. 143p. NUC BL OCLC

ALLEN, Mrs. E.M. see ALLEN, Elizabeth Ann (Chase) Akers

57. ALLEN, Eleanor [Am. 19c]
The siege of Agrigentum, a poem.
Boston: C.C. Little & J. Brown, 1841. 79p. NUC BL OCLC

58. ALLEN, Elizabeth, Miss [Am. 19c]
The silent harp; or, Fugitive poems.
Burlington, VT: Edward Smith, 1832. 119p. NUC BL OCLC
[Sketch of Green Mountain life]

59. ALLEN, Elizabeth Ann (Chase) Akers, Mrs. E.M. Allen [Am. 1832-1911] ALT: Akers, Elizabeth Ann (Chase); Chase, Elizabeth Ann PSEUD: Percy, Florence
Forest buds from the woods of Maine. By Florence Percy.
Portland, ME: F. Blake; Boston: Brown, Bazin & co., 1856. 207p. NUC OCLC
[88 poems, sonnets & lyric]

60. -----The high-top sweeting, and other poems.
NY: C. Scribner's sons, 1891. 142p. NUC OCLC

61. -----Poems.
Boston: Ticknor & Fields, 1866. 251p. NUC BL OCLC

62. -----Poems.
Boston: Ticknor & Fields, 1867. 251p. BL

63. -----Rock me to sleep, Mother.
L: Sampson, Low & co., 1883. 37p.
Boston: Estes & Lauriat, 1883. 20 l. NUC BL OCLC

64. -----The silver bridge and other poems.
Boston & NY: Houghton, Mifflin & co., 1886. 124p. NUC BL

65. -----The triangular society. Leaves from the life of a Portland family.
Portland, ME: Hoyt, Fogg & Donham, 1886. 381p. NUC OCLC
[Novel about a family literary society. Incl. 56 poems]

66. -----Two saints. A tribute to the memory of Henry Bergh, founder of the first American Society for the Prevention of Cruelty to Animals.
Portland, ME: B. Thurston & co., 1888. 12p. NUC

67. ALLEN, Esther Charlotte Anne [Br. 19c]
Echoes of heart whispers.
Manchester: John Heywood, 1866. 192p. BL OCLC

ALLEN, MRS. FAIRCHILD, pseud. see MCINTYRE, Anne E., Mrs.

68. ALLEN, Gertrude Frances [Br. 19c]
Sketches and poems.
L: Army & Navy coop. soc., 1893. 152p. BL
[Sketches are narrative poems; the others chiefly religious]

69. ALLEN, Hannah Bowen
A poetical geognosy.
Boston: C.C. Little & J. Brown, 1841. 34p. NUC OCLC
[On the geologic & geographic wonders of the Creation]

70. ALLEN, Lavilla E. [Am. 19c]
Aunt Betsy's pumpkin pie, and other poems.
Hillsdale, MI: Wright & Green, 1878. 28p. NUC OCLC

71. ALLEN, Lucy [Am. 18c]
Hymns.
Windsor, VT: Repr. A. Spooner, 1795. NUC

72. ALLENBY, Mrs. [Br. 19c] ALT: A.
The starling of the spire; or, A bird's-eye view of the church as it was. By A.
Louth: J. & T. Jackson, 1866. 39p. NUC BL

73. ALLERDICE, Elizabeth Winslow [Am. b. 1829]

"From high to higher." Over the hill to the White House and our President.
NY: Denison & co., 1881. 26p. NUC OCLC
[Also pub. as: Over the hill to the White House. Tribute to the mother of Pres. Garfield.]

74. ALLERTON, Ellen Palmer, Mrs. [Am. 1835-1893]
Annabel, and other poems.
NY: J.B. Alden, 1885. 153p. NUC OCLC
[Cover title: Poems of the prairies]

75. -----Walls of corn, and other poems.
St. Louis, MO & NY: A. Gast & co., 1884. 29p. NUC BL OCLC

76. -----Walls of corn and other poems. Collected and published with a memorial sketch by Eva Ryan.
2d ed. Hiawatha, KS: Harrington pr. co., 1894. 254p. NUC BL OCLC

77. ALLEYNE, Sarah Frances [Br. 1836-1884]
Verses.
L: Priv. pr., 1885. 74p. NUC

ALLIN, Abby see CURTISS, Abby Allin

78. ALLINGHAM, Helen Maria [Br. 19c]
A closet companion for the daughter of Zion: being original poems on the person, work, sufferings and triumphs of ... Jesus Christ.
2 pt. L: Houlston & Stoneman, 1850,51. BL

79. -----A poem for the times; being a word of encouragement and advice for Zion.
L: Houlston & Stoneman; J. Paul, 1855? 8p. BL

80. ALLNUT, Mrs. Alfred [Br. 19c]
The day-star prophet.
L: Hurst & Blackett, 1865. 103p. NUC BL

81. ALLOM, Elizabeth Anne [Br. 19c]
Death scenes, and other poems.
Hackney: Caleb Turner; L: Simpkin & Marshall, 1844. 48p. BL

82. ALLYN, Eunice Gibbs [Am. 19c]
Thanksgiving hymn of the Republic.
Platteville, WI: Youmans, 1898. 3p. NUC

83. ALMA-TADEMA, Laurence, Miss [Br. d. 1940] ALT: Tadema, Laurence Alma
Realms of unknown kings.
L: G. Richards, 1897. 78p. NUC BL OCLC

84. ALMY, Annie Whittier [Am. 19c]
Early poems.
Boston: The author, 1866. 56p. NUC

85. ALT, Florence May [Am. b. 1869]
A child of song. Verses by Florence May Alt.
Rochester, NY: Rodell bros., pr., 1890. 114p. NUC

AMATEUR, AN, pseud. see COLCHESTER, Elizabeth Susan (Law) Abbot, Baroness Colchester

AMBLER, Theresa J., ed. see JORDAN, Cornelia Jane (Matthews)

AMELIA see WELBY, Amelia Ball (Coppuck)

AMELIA OF WESTERN N.Y., pseud. see KEELER, Amelia

AMERICAN GENTLEMAN, AN, co-author see BLENNERHASSETT, Margaret Agnew

86. AMES, Jane, Mrs. [Am. 19c]
Compositions, original and selected.
Boston: Pr. E. Lincoln, 1805-08. 2v. NUC OCLC
[Poems & essays, mostly religious]

AMES, Mary Clemmer, ed. see CARY, Alice

87. AMES, Mary E. (Clemmer) [Am. 1839-1884] ALT: Clemmer, Mary E.; Hudson, Mary E. (Clemmer) Ames
Poems of life and nature. By Mary Clemmer.
Boston: James R. Osgood & co., 1883. 278p. NUC BL OCLC

AMICA RELIGIONIS, pseud. see DODGE, H.M., Mrs.

88. ANAGNOS, Julia Romana (Howe) [Am. 1844-1886]
Stray chords.
Boston: Cupples, Upham & co., 1883. 146p. NUC OCLC

89. ANDERSON, Jane W. [Am. 19c]
Verses by Jane W. Anderson of Portland.
Boston: n.p., 1896. 57p. NUC OCLC

ANDERSON, John, co-author see ANDERSON, Mary Christina

90. ANDERSON, Martha J. [Am. 19c]
Social gathering dialogue, between six sisters.
Albany, NY: Weed, Parsons & co., 1873. 18p. OCLC

91. -----Social life and vegetarianism.
Mount Lebanon, NY: n.p., 1893. 27p. NUC OCLC
[Essays, poems, and recipes by a Shaker sister]

92. ANDERSON, Mary Christina [Br. 19c]
In memory of John Anderson and Mary Christina Anderson.
L: n.p., 1863. BL
[Collection of short poems by both]

93. ANDREW, Mrs. [Br. 19c]
Original poems on various and interesting subjects.
Paisley: Caldwell & son, 1852. 36p. BL

94. ANDREWS, Hannah [Br. 19c]
Miscellaneous pieces in verse.
L: T. Jones, 1805. 93p. BL

95. ANDREWS, Mary J. [Br. 19c]
The quiet hour.
Brighton: C. Wilmott, 1850. 68p. BL

96. ANGEL, Rosa Evangeline [Am. d. 1895]
This side and that, poems.
Cincinnati, OH: R. Clarke & co., 1889. 160p. NUC OCLC

97. ANGIER, Annie Lanman, Mrs. [Am. 19c]
Poems.
Boston: A. Williams & co., 1883. 245p. NUC OCLC

ANN OF SWANSEA, pseud. <u>see</u> HATTON, Ann Julia (Kemble)

98. ANNA MARIA [Br. 18c]
The poems of Anna Maria.
Calcutta: Thomson & Ferris, 1793. 68p. NUC BL OCLC

ANNA MATILDA, pseud. <u>see</u> COWLEY, Hannah (Parkhouse)

ANNIE <u>see</u> GARRETT, Annie

ANODOS <u>see</u> COLERIDGE, Mary Elizabeth (Anodos)

99. ANSELL, Martha [Br. 19c]
In commemoration of the birth, the christening, and the marriage of H.R.H. the Prince of Wales.
L: A.M. Pigott, 1863. 7p. BL

ANTONIA, pseud. <u>see</u> IVORY, Bertha May

100. APPLETON, Elizabeth [Br. 19c]
The spring bud; or, Rural scenery in verse.
L: J. Harris, 1818. 31p. BL

101. ARABEL [Br. 19c]
Letters from a young lady in Scarbro', to her cousin in London.
Beverley: Kemp & son, 1871. 39p. BL

102. ARBUTHNOT, Constance Angelena (Milman), Lady [Br. 19c]
Wishes kind and true.
L: Ernest Nister, 1898. BL

103. ARCHBOLD, Ann [Am. 19c]
A book for the married and single, the grave and the gay, and especially designed for steamboat passengers.
East Plainfield, OH: N.A. Baker, pr., 1850. 192p. NUC BL OCLC
[13 poems on Indian Territory & its missions. A few essays]

104. ARCHER, M. A., Mrs. [Am. 19c]
Echoes. Vol. I.
Hartford, CT: Case, Lockwood & co., 1867. 204p. NUC OCLC
[No other vols. pub. Chiefly elegies for children]

105. ARCHER, Ruby [Am. 19c]
Little poems.
Brooklyn, NY: Braunworth, Munn & Barber, c1900. 296p. NUC OCLC

106. -----Notes and poems in Europe.
Kansas City, MO: n.p., 1896. 101 l. NUC
[Travel journal with poems]

107. ARCHIBALD, Elizabeth L. (Goodhue) [Am. 1839-1877]
Memorials of Mrs. Elizabeth L. Archibald, with occasional verses of her writing.
Hartford, CT: Case, Lockwood & Brainard co., 1878. 89p. NUC

AREY, Mrs. H.E.G. <u>see</u> AREY, Harriet Ellen (Grannis)

108. AREY, Harriet Ellen (Grannis) [Am. b. 1819]
Household songs and other poems. By Mrs. H. E. G. Arey.

NY: J.C. Derby; Boston: Phillips Sampson & co., 1855. 254p. NUC BL OCLC

109. -----"Myself."
Rochester, NY: J. Vick, 1890. 24p. NUC

110. ARGALL, Annie E. [Br. 19c]
The inspiration of song, and other poems.
Truro: Netherton & Worth, 1894. 155p. BL OCLC

111. ARGENT, Alice E. [Br. 19c]
Poems.
Chelmsford: E. Durrant & co., 1890. 124p. BL OCLC

112. ARMOUR, Margaret [Br. 19/20c]
ALT: Macdougal, Margaret Armour
The shadow of love, and other poems.
L: Duckworth & co., 1898. 124p. BL

113. -----Songs of love and death, etc.
L: J.M. Dent & co., 1896. 136p. NUC BL OCLC

114. -----Thames sonnets and semblances.
L: Elkin Mathews, 1897. 57p. BL OCLC
[Poems by Armour; Pictures by W.B. Macdougall]

115. ARMSTRONG, Clara J. [Am. 19c]
La Porte in June.
Chicago: R.R. Donnelly & sons, 1899. 44p. NUC OCLC
[15 poems; title poem is in praise of La Porte, IN]

116. ARMSTRONG, Florence C. [Br. 19c]
The King in his beauty, and other hymns.
L: A. Richardson; W. Wells Gardner, 1875. 29p. NUC BL

ARNOLD, Charlotte, co-author <u>see</u> ARNOLD, Henrietta

117. ARNOLD, Eunice C. Sprague [Am. 19c]
Maple leaves and myrtle wreaths. Being a collection of short poems and essays, many of which were written in youth. Including "Scraps from a school-girl's portfolio," and "Incidents of the war".
Charlotte, MI: J. Saunders & co., 1872. 124p. NUC OCLC

118. ARNOLD, Harriot Stone (Frizell) [Am. b. 1826]
Birthday gift: consisting of original poems, and original and selected prose.
Dedham, MA: Pr. H.A. Mann, 1853. 128p. NUC OCLC
[50 original poems. Essays from periodicals.]

119. ARNOLD, Henrietta [Br. 19c]
Village lyrics. By Henrietta and Charlotte Arnold.
L: Provost & co., 1878. 101p. BL

120. ARTHINGTON, Maria [Br. d. 1863]
ALT: A., M.
Queries for women Friends, affectionately addressed to members of the Society.
L: Charles Gilpin, 1847. 24p. NUC BL

121. -----Thoughts in verse concerning Mary Wright who lived to the age of 103.
Leeds: n.p., 1859. NUC

122. -----To Mary Wright, on completing her 100th year.
Leeds: n.p., 1855. NUC

123. ARTHUR, Clara May (Stevens) [Am. 1844-1884]
The cherry-blooms of Yeddo, and other poems.
Boston: D. Lothrop & co., 1882. 140p. NUC BL OCLC

124. ARTHUR, Grace [Br. 18c] PSEUD: Lady, A
The temple of health, a poetic vision. Occasioned by the universal joy expressed on His Majesty's most happy recovery. By a lady.
L: Pr. for author by W. Chalklen, 1789. 12p. NUC
[Attributed to her]

125. ASHBY, Anna E., Mrs. Edmund Ashby [Br. 19c]
Elidure.
Southampton: Priv. pr., 1880? 56p. BL

ASHBY, Caroline W., co-author <u>see</u> HAVERGAL, Frances Ridley

126. ASHBY, Caroline W. [Br. 19/20c]
Talitha cumi, and other verses.
L: Houghton & co., 1878. 28p. BL

ASHBY, Mrs. Edmund <u>see</u> ASHBY, Anna E.

127. ASHE, Cecilia [Br. 19c]
Lays for harp and voice: songs devotional and patriotic.
L: J. Ogden & co., 1875. 108p. BL

ASHLEY, Annie Louise see GREENSTREET, Annie Louise (Ashley)

128. ASHLEY, Florence Emily [Br. 19c]
ALT: A., F. E.
Darmayne, and other poems.
L: Pr. for the author by Cassell, Petler & Galpin, 1872. 162p. NUC BL OCLC

ASHLEY, Mary see TOWNSEND, Mary Ashley (Van Voorhis)

129. ASHTON, Kate, Miss [Am. 19c]
Allspice, gathered from the sunny side of the world to be sprinkled over the shady side.
Boston: Rand, Avery, 1873. 24p. NUC OCLC
[Riddles and verse]

130. ASTLEY, Gertrude Emma, Mrs. [Br. d. 1862]
Poems by Gertrude Emma Astley.
L: n.p., 1863. 23p. NUC OCLC

ASTARTE, pseud. see ADAMS, Ann Olivia, Mrs.

131. ASTON, Marie [Br. 19c]
Linked lyrics.
Congleton: Robert Head, 1887. 52p. BL OCLC

132. ATHERTON, Maria [Br. 19c]
Centzontli, and other poems.
L: Hodder & Stoughton, 1872. 190p. BL

133. ATKINSON, Jane [Br. 19c] PSEUD: Wren, Jenny
Facts and fancies, in prose and verse. By Jenny Wren.
Keighley: A. Shackelton; L: Hall, Smart & Allen, 1864. BL
[8 poems; 15 short stories]

134. ATKINSON, Mary Ellen [Am. 19c]
The architect of Cologne, and other poems.
Boston: D. Lothrop & co.; Dover, NH: G.T. Day & co., 1873. 101p. NUC BL OCLC

135. -----Ivy leaves.
Philadelphia: J.B. Lippincott & co., 1870. 112p. NUC OCLC

136. -----On the mountain, and other poems.
Philadelphia: Henry Longstreth, 1870. 32p. NUC OCLC

ATOM, AN, pseud. see MCDOWELL, Katherine Sherwood (Bonner)

137. ATTENBOROUGH, Florence Gertrude [Br. 19/20c] PSEUD: Chrystabel
Cameos, and other poems. By Florence G. Attenborough ("Chrystabel").
L: W. Reeves, 1898. 168p. BL OCLC

138. ATTERIDGE, Mary Ellen [Br. 19c]
Immaculata.
L: T. Richardson & son, 1871. 94p. BL

139. ATWATER, Emma M. [Am. 19c]
Poems ... lovingly dedicated to her many friends.
New Haven, CT: n.p., 18--? 23p. NUC

140. AUBIN, Penelope, Mrs. [Br. 1679-1731]
The extasy. A Pindarick ode to ... the Queen.
L: Pr. for the author, 1708. 16p. BL

141. -----The Stuarts: a Pindarique ode.
L: John Morphew, 1707. 12p. BL

142. -----The welcome: a poem to His Grace the Duke of Marlborough.
L: John Morphew, 1708. NUC

AUNT ALICE, pseud. see GRAVES, Adelia Cleopatra (Spencer)

AUNT MATTIE, pseud. see LAMB, Martha Joanna Reade (Nash)

AUNT MAY, pseud. see LATHBURY, Mary Artemisia

AURA, pseud. see IRVINE, Mary Catherine

AURINGER, O.C., co-author see SMITH, Jeanie Oliver (Davidson)

AUSTIN, Alfred, comp. see BLAGDEN, Isa Jane

AUSTIN, Mrs. Harrington see AUSTIN, Maria (Carter)

143. AUSTIN, Maria (Carter), Mrs. Harrington Austin [Am. 19c]
A bundle of poems.
Buffalo, NY: Charles Wells Moulton, c1894. 47p. NUC OCLC

144. AUSTIN, Mary Evelyn [Am. 19c]
Poems selected from the writings of Mary Evelyn Austin. Arranged in loving remembrance for her friends.
Buffalo, NY: Peter Paul & bro., 1885? 36p. NUC OCLC

AUSTRAL, pseud. see WILSON, Annie, Lady

145. AVERY, R. J., Mrs. [Am. 19c]
Wood notes wild.
Nashville, TN: Cameron & Fall, 1843. 204p. NUC OCLC

146. AVERY-STUTTLE, Lilla Dale, Mrs. [Am. 19/20c]
Poems of the Christ life, arranged in a series of recitations for use in Sabbath school entertainments.
Lansing, MI: Beacon pub. co., 1893. 48p. NUC
[Poems arranged chronologically, to be used with suitable music, not for children only.]

147. -----Satan's first lie; or, Man in death.
Battle Creek, MI: The author, 1893. 36p. NUC

148. AYARS, M. Morton, Mrs. [Am. 19c]
Mythology in rhyme.
Philadelphia: Pr. for author, 1895. 63p. NUC

149. AYRE, Elizabeth Georgiana [Br. 19c]
Wild flowers: or the produce of uncultivated genius.
L: Simpkin, Marshall & co., 1842. 202p. BL

B., A. see BEATTIE, Anne

B., A. see BEHN, Aphra (Amis)

B., A.C. see BUSSING, Alice Cary

150. B., E.M.
The snow storm, and other poems. Ed. Carrie F. Young.
San Francisco: Pr. E. Bosqui & co., 1877. 16p. NUC
[Title poem by E.M.B., a "Young Miss in her teens."]

B., I.M. see BRAIKENRIDGE, Isabella M.

B., K.G., comp. see BAKER, Ella Maria

B., M.E. see BENNETT, Mary E.

B., M.E. see BLAKE, Mary Elizabeth (McGrath)

B., N.K. see BRADFORD, Nellie Knight, Mrs.

151. B****, R. [Br. 19c] PSEUD: Lady, A
Lines written by a lady on hearing of the execution of Peter Blanchard; Drink and its consequences, with an affectionate appeal to Christians, parents, and all well-wishers.
L: Charles Akrill, pr.; Louth: Mawer, 1875. 9p. BL

152. B---N, Mrs. [Br. 19c]
A collection of miscellaneous poems.
Edinburgh: n.p., 1819. BL

153. BACHMAN, Sophie E. [Am. 19c]
Posers unaware. A series of booklets, with sketches from life, for children of all ages.
Providence, RI: c1889. 57p. NUC

154. BACKUS, Elizabeth Welch [Am. 19c]
Three friends' fancies. With Jannet Carruthers and Ella A. Germain Carruthers.
Philadelphia: J.B. Lippincott & co., 1880. 136p. NUC OCLC

BACON, Charles W., co-author see NICHOLS, Alice S.

155. BACON, Eliza Ann (Munroe) [Am. 19c] PSEUD: Lady, A
The fruit of the spirit; or, The Christian graces. By a lady.
Boston: A. Tompkins, 1842. 151p. NUC OCLC
[Primarily prose. The graces incl. temperance, gentleness, etc. Brief poems interspersed.]

156. BACON, Fanny Elizabeth [Am. 1832-1881]
A reminiscence of Fanny Elizabeth Bacon. Ed. William Johnson Bacon.
Utica, NY: n.p., 1881? 84p. NUC OCLC
[Includes poems]

BACON, M.A. see BACON, Mary Ann

157. BACON, Mary Ann [Br. 19c] ALT: Bacon, M. A.
Flowers and their kindred thoughts.
L: Longman & co., 1848. 34p. NUC OCLC

158. -----Fruits from the garden and field.
L: Longman & co., 1850. 32p. BL OCLC

159. -----Winged thoughts.
L: Longman & co., 1851. 24p. NUC BL OCLC

160. BAHN, Rachel [Am. 19c]
Poems.
York, PA: H.C. Adams & co., 1869. 200p. NUC OCLC

[In PA Dutch dialect]

161. BAILEY, Alice Ward [Am. b. 1857]
Flower fancies.
Boston: L. Prang & co., c1889. 24 l.
NUC OCLC

162. -----Outside of things: a sky book.
NY: E.P. Dutton & co., 1899. 30 l.
NUC BL OCLC

163. BAILEY, Elizabeth Rainier [Br. 19c]
Lady Jane Grey, and other poems.
L: Longman, Brown, Green & Longmans, 1854. 2v. NUC BL OCLC

164. BAILEY, Flora Hazelton [Am. 19c]
Belle Zoe. A Canadian ballad.
Des Moines, IA: Conway & Shaw, 1898. 30p. NUC OCLC

165. BAILEY, Mary Walker [Br. 19c]
ALT: Walker, Mary
The months and other poems.
2d ed. L: C.J.G. & F. Rivington, 1833. 48p. NUC BL

166. -----Musae sacrae.
Ballingdon; L: n.p., 1835? 163p. BL
[Hymns & sacred poetry]

167. -----Palmyra.
2d ed. L: C.J.G. & F. Rivington, 1833. 22p. NUC

168. BAILEY, Sarah Loring [Am. 19c]
Poems.
Chicago: Dial Press, 1897. 24p. NUC OCLC

169. BAILEY, Urania Locke (Stoughton) [Am. 1820-1882]
Star-flowers.
NY: G.P. Putnam's sons, 1882. 152p.
NUC OCLC

BAILLIE, Alexander, ed. see BAILLIE, Marianne

170. BAILLIE, E. C. C., Mrs. [Br. 19c]
Snatches of sacred song.
L: Wertheim & Macintosh, 1854. 70p.
NUC BL

171. BAILLIE, Joanna [Br. 1762-1851]
Ahalya Baee: a poem.
L: Pr. for priv. circ. by Spottiswoode and Shaw, 1849. 39p. NUC BL OCLC
[About India]

172. -----The complete poetical works of Joanna Baillie.
1st Am. ed. Philadelphia: Carey & Lea, 1832. 574p. NUC BL OCLC

173. -----The dramatic and poetical works of Joanna Baillie.
L: Longman, Brown, Green & Longmans, 1851. 847p. NUC BL OCLC
[Incl.: Plays on the Passion, Miscellaneous Plays, Miscellaneous Poetry]

174. -----Fugitive verses.
L: Edward Moxon, 1840. 408p. NUC BL OCLC

175. -----Metrical legends of exalted characters.
L: Longman, Hurst, Rees, Orme and Brown, 1821. 373p. NUC BL OCLC

176. BAILLIE, Marianne, Mrs. [Br. 1795?-1831]
Guy of Warwick: a legende. And other poems.
Kingsbury: A. Baillie, priv. pr., 1817. 74p. BL

177. -----Trifles in verse. Ed. Alexander Baillie.
L: Pr. for priv. circ., 1825. 48p.
NUC BL OCLC

178. BAILY, Florence [Am. 19c]
Gleanings from the fields of life, an old year reverie.
Philadelphia: Porter & Coates, c1882. 15 l. NUC OCLC

179. BAINES, Wilhelmina [Br. 19c]
Lays from legends, and other poems.
L: W.H. Allen, 1885. 143p. NUC BL OCLC

180. BAKER, E. A., Mrs. [Br. 19c]
The fruits of the spirit, and other poems.
L: R. Groombridge & sons, 1847. 51p. BL

181. BAKER, Ella [Br. 19c]
Kingscote essays and poems. Ed. Thomas Baker.
L: Kegan Paul & co., 1888. 187p. NUC BL

182. BAKER, Ella Maria [Am. 1848-1884]
Clover-leaves. A collection of poems. Comp. K.G.B.
Boston: D. Lothrop & co., c1885. 234p. NUC BL OCLC
[Early poems; nature, religious, in memoriam, misc.]

183. BAKER, Florence Hooper (Tilghman) [Am. 19c]
Love thoughts of the war, composed by Florence Hooper Tilghman Baker, during the war between America and Spain. In the year 1898.
NY: G.W. Bowers, 1899. 24 l. NUC

184. BAKER, Georgiana M. A. [Br. 19c]
Pen-rambles: poems.
L: Longmans & co., 1869. 96p. BL

185. BAKER, Mrs. Isadore [Am. 19/20c]
In memoriam.
Iowa City, IA: n.p., 1896. 23p. NUC

186. -----Sonnets and other verse.
Iowa City, IA: n.p., 1896. 33p. NUC OCLC

187. BAKER, Louise Southard [Am. 1846-1896]
By the sea.
Nantucket, MA: L.S. Baker, c1893. 59p. NUC OCLC

188. -----By the sea. Nantucket in summer and winters.
Providence, RI: Snow & Farnham, pr., c1890. 18 l. NUC OCLC

189. BAKER, Sarah Schoonmaker (Tuthill) [Am. 1824-1906]
A legacy of love. A compilation of prose and poetry.
Richmond, VA: Pr. at the Hummingbird Office, 1869. 126p. NUC BL OCLC
[Essays & about 40 poems, some original, some memorized in childhood]

BAKER, Thomas, ed. see BAKER, Ella

190. BALCOMB, Amelia [Br. 19c]
Rambles in the realms of thought.
L: Whitbread, 1855. 70p. BL
[History and description of Brighton with moral observations in verse.]

191. BALDWIN, A. E. Corey, Mrs. [Am. 19c]
James Abraham Garfield, died at seven. Elegia horologium. The spectral clock. Pastoral-memorial leaves.
Newark, NJ: n.p., 1882. 8 l. NUC

BAKEWELL, Thomas, co-author see CAMPBELL, Nancy W.

192. BALDWIN, Emily Foote [Am. 19c]
Flora: and other poems, grave and humorous, for the domestic circle.
Hartford, CT: Brown & Gross, 1879. 480p. NUC OCLC

193. BALDWIN, Nancy [Am. 19c]
Leaves of affection.
Detroit, MI: E.B. Smith & co., 1878. 248p. NUC

194. BALDY, Lizzie F. [Am. 19c]
The California pioneer, and other poems.
San Francisco: Bacon & co., pr., 1879. 159p. NUC OCLC

195. BALFOUR, Clara Lucas (Liddell) [Br. 1828-1878]
The garland of water flowers, a collection of poems and tales. Ed. Rev. Jabez Burns.
L: Temperance depot, 1841. 192p. NUC OCLC

196. BALFOUR, Mary [Br. 19c]
Hope, a poetical essay; with various other poems.
Belfast: Smyth & Lyons, 1810. 192p. BL

197. BALL, Alice M. [Am. 19c]
Buttercups and clover.
Buffalo, NY: Office of Triumphs of Faith; Baker, Jones & co., pr. 1885. 86p. NUC OCLC
[Ballads]

198. -----Cheerful hours at home.
Pittsfield, MA: Chickering & Axtell, 1873. 64p. NUC OCLC
[7 prose sketches and 27 poems]

BALL, C.A., Mrs. see BALL, Caroline A. (Rutledge)

199. BALL, Caroline A. (Rutledge) [Am. b. 1825] ALT: Ball, C. A., Mrs.
The jacket of grey, and other fugitive poems. By Mrs. C.A. Ball.
Charleston, SC: Joseph Walker, stationer & pr., 1866. 29p. NUC OCLC
[13 poems in memory of son killed in Civil War]

200. BALLANTYNE, Jane B. [Br. 19c]
Aesop's fables in verse.
Edinburgh: A. Elliot, 1877. 167p. TXU

201. -----Peace in search of a home; an allegory.
Edinburgh: Ballantyne, Hanson, 1878. 38p. NUC OCLC

202. -----Poetical fragments.
Edinburgh?: n.p., 1870? 128p. BL OCLC

203. -----A summer trip to the Highlands: poems.
Edinburgh: Ballantyne press, 1880 31p. TXU

204. BALLANTYNE, Mrs. John [Br. 19c]
PSEUD: Lady, A
Birds, British and foreign. By a lady.
L: n.p., 1843. 96p. BL

205. -----The Kelso souvenir; or, Selections from her scrap-book. Entirely original. By a lady.
L: Pr. T. Barclay; Edinburgh: Blackwood, 1832. 99p. NUC BL
[Epigrams, narrative & lyric verse]

206. BALLARD, Julia Perkins (Pratt) [Am. 1828-1894]
The scarlet oak, and other poems. With Annie Lenthal Smith.
NY: G.P. Putnam's sons, 1878. 116p. NUC

207. BALMANNO, Mary, Mrs. Robert Balmanno [Am. 19c]
Pen and pencil.
NY: D. Appleton & co., 185-? 299p. NUC BL OCLC
[About half verse; essays on British royalty; personal reminiscences of famous people. Incl. engravings.]

208. -----Poems.
L: n.p., 1830. 19p. NUC BL

BALMANNO, Mrs. Robert <u>see</u> BALMANNO, Mary

209. BALMER, Catherine Gordon [Am. 19c]
The nonsense rhyme of my birthday ball.
n.p.: n.p., 1898. NUC

210. BANGS, Ella Matthews [Am. 19c]
The bells of memory.
Portland, ME: L.H. Nelson co., 18--? 4p. NUC

211. BANKS, Ellen [Am. 19c]
Songs in the house of my pilgrimage.
Boston: Henry Wark, c1885. 104p. NUC OCLC

BANKS, George Linnaeus, co-author <u>see</u> BANKS, Isabella (Varley) Linnaeus

BANKS, Mrs. George Linnaeus <u>see</u> BANKS, Isabella (Varley) Linnaeus

212. BANKS, Isabella (Varley) Linnaeus, Mrs. George Linnaeus Banks [Br. 1821-1897] ALT: Varley, Isabella
Daisies in the grass: a collection of songs and poems. With George Linnaeus Banks.
L: R. Hardwicke, 1865. 208p. NUC BL OCLC
[All original poems, slightly more than half by him. Misc. lyrics, no music incl.]

213. -----Ivy leaves: a collection of poems.
L: Simpkin, 1844. 196p. NUC BL OCLC

214. -----Ripples and breakers, a volume of verse.
L: C. Kegan Paul, 1878. 198p. NUC BL OCLC

215. BANNERMAN, Anne [Br. d. 1829]
Poems.
Edinburgh: Mundell & son, 1800. 110p. NUC BL OCLC

216. -----Tales of superstition and chivalry.
L: Pr. for Vernor & Hood by J. Swan, 1802. 144p. NUC BL OCLC
[On ghosts]

217. BANNERMAN, Frances [Br. 19c]
Milestones: a collection of verses.
L: G. Richards, 1899. 197p. NUC BL

218. BANTA, Melissa Elizabeth (Riddle) [Am. 1834-1907]
Songs of home.
Menasha, WI: Phenix press, 1895. 136p. NUC OCLC

219. BARBAULD, Anna Letitia (Aikin) [Br. 1743-1825] ALT: Aikin, Anna Letitia
Eighteen hundred and eleven; a poem.
L: J. Johnson, 1812. 25p. Boston: Bradford & Read; Philadelphia: Anthony Finley, 1812. 40p. NUC BL OCLC

220. -----Epistle to William Wilberforce, esq. on the rejection of the bill for abolishing the slave trade.
L: J. Johnson, 1791. 14p. NUC BL OCLC

221. -----Memoir, letters, and a selection from the poetry and prose writings of Anna Letitia Barbauld. Comp. Grace A. Ellis.
Boston: J.R. Osgood & co., 1874. 2v. BL OCLC
[Vol. 1: a biography; Vol. 2: pp. 1-172 poems; prose, essays & fables; Legacy for young ladies: essays & fiction with educational purpose.]

222. -----Poems.
L: Joseph Johnson, 1773. 138p. NUC BL OCLC

223. -----The works of Anna Letitia Barbauld. Memoir by Lucy Aikin.
L: Longman, Hurst, Rees, Orme, Brown & Green, 1825. 2v. NUC BL OCLC
[Vol. 1: poems; Vol. 2: correspondence & misc. prose, incl. tales]

224. BARBER, Mary [Br. 1690?-1757]
Poems on several occasions.
L: C. Rivington, 1734. 283p. NUC BL OCLC

225. BARBOUR, Margaret Fraser [Frayer NUC] [Br. 19c]
The soul-gatherer.
L: n.p., 1864. 228p. NUC BL
[Religious poems and prose]

226. BARCLAY, Kate [Am. 19c]
Minnie May; with other rhymes and stories.
Boston: John P. Jewett & co., 1854. 32p. NUC OCLC
[Anti-slavery poetry]

BARD OF SHANTY HILL, THE, pseud. <u>see</u> KELLEY, Sarah A. (Ulrich)

227. BARKER, Miss [Br. 19c] PSEUD: One of the small fry of the lakes
Lines addressed to a noble lord by one of the small fry of the lakes.
L: W. Pople, 1815. 23p. NUC BL
[Satire on Byron and his admirers]

228. BARKER, Alice J., Mrs. [Am. 19c] PSEUD: Melbourne, Grace
Poems, by Grace Melbourne.
Cleveland, OH: n.p., 1888. 220p. NUC OCLC

229. BARKER, Eliza H. [Am. 19c]
Marguarite, Baroness Leichenstein, and other poems.
Philadelphia: J.B. Lippincott & co., 1870. 103p. NUC

230. BARKER, H. Anne [Br. 19c]
Crown jewels, scattered for youth.
L: Charles Bean, 1854. 120p. BL

231. BARKER, Jane [Br. c1675-1743]
Poetical recreations; consisting of original poems, songs, odes, etc. with several new translations. In two parts. Part I. Occasionally written by Mrs. Jane Barker. Part II. By several gentlemen of the universities and others.
L: Benjamin Crayle, 1688. 287p. NUC BL OCLC

232. BARKER, Jemima [Br. 19c]
Poems, on miscellaneous subjects.
L: Lypton Relfe, 1822. 145p. BL

233. BARLAND, Katharine [Br. 19c]
Poems.
L: David Bogue, 1845. 208p. BL

234. -----Songs of consolation.
Edinburgh: James Hogg, 1851. 59p. BL

235. BARLOW, Jane [Br. 1860-1917]
Bog-Land studies.
L: T. Fisher Unwin, 1891. 104p. NUC BL OCLC
[Narrative of Irish working people in brogue.]

236. -----The end of Elfintown.
L: Macmillan & co., 1894. 77p. NUC BL OCLC
[An adult fable]

237. BARNARD, Anne (Lindsay), Lady [Br. 1750-1825] ALT: Lindsay, Lady Anne
Auld Robin Gray; a ballad. Ed. Sir Walter Scott.
Edinburgh: J. Ballantyne, 1825. 16p. NUC BL OCLC

238. -----Lays of the Lindsays; being poems by the ladies of the House of Balcarras.
Edinburgh: Pr. James Ballantyne & co., 1824. 123p. NUC BL

239. BARNARD, Charlotte Alington [Br. 1830-1869] PSEUD: Claribel
Fireside thoughts, ballads, etc. etc.
L: J. Nisbet & co., 1865. 150p. NUC BL

240. -----Thoughts, verses and songs. By Claribel.
L: J. Nisbet & co., 1877. 314p. BL

241. -----Verses and songs.
L: J. Nisbet & co., 1870? 55p. BL

242. BARNARD, Elizabeth [Am. 18c]
Heart offerings.
Chatfield, MN: Pub. for the authoress, 1873. 158p. NUC

243. BARNARD, Frances Catherine [Br. 19c]
The doleful death and flowery funeral of Fancy.
L: Harvey & Darton, 1837. 42p. NUC BL

244. BARNES, Charlotte Mary Sanford, Mrs. E.S. Conner Barnes [Am. 1819?-1863]

The night of the coronation: written on reading the account of the coronation of Victoria I.
NY: n.p.; L: D. Cahn, 1838. 8p. NUC BL

245. -----Plays, prose and poetry.
Philadelphia: E.H. Butler & co., 1848. 489p. NUC BL
[Fugitive pieces, incl. 3 poems]

BARNES, Mrs. E.S. Conner see BARNES, Charlotte Mary Sanford

246. BARNES, Esther [Br. 18c]
The disengaged fair.
Bristol: S. Bonner, 1796. 32p. BL

247. BARNES, Mrs. George [Am. 19c]
A poem, Columbus.
Howell, MI: n.p., c1892. 11 l. NUC

BARNES, Howard C., comp. see BARNES, Sarah L.

BARNES, Mrs. J.B. see BARNES, Nellie L. Davis

248. BARNES, M. L. Francis, Mrs. [Am. 19c]
Story of Job: some of its lessons, and other poems.
Hartford, CT: Press of the Case, Lockwood & Brainard co., 1893. 126p. NUC OCLC

BARNES, MARY MATHEWS, pseud. see ADAMS, Mary Jane (Mathews)

249. BARNES, Nellie L. Davis, Mrs. J.B. Barnes [Am. 19c]
Flowers of remembrance.
Louisville, KY?: n.p., 1893? 85 l. NUC OCLC

250. -----In harbor.
Louisville, KY: Flexner bros., c1892. 13 l. NUC

251. BARNES, Sarah L. [Am. 1843-1882]
Poems .... Arr. her brother, Howard C. Barnes.
Cambridge, MA: J. Wilson & son, c1883. 39 l. NUC OCLC

252. BARNETT, Henrietta Octavia (Rowland) [1851-1936]
Miscellaneous poems.
Reading: Pr. Crosby, 1872. 106p. NUC OCLC

BARON-WILSON, Mrs. Cornwell see WILSON, Margaret (Harries) Baron-

253. BARR, Catherine [Br. 19c]
Verses by Catherine Barr, a poor blind woman, better known in the church militant as "Kitty.".
L: Rixon & Arnold, 1859. 23p. BL

254. BARRAND, Elizabeth [Br. 19c]
PSEUD: Lady, A
The willows of Amwell. By a lady.
Hertford: G. & S.E. Simson, 1853. BL

255. BARRELL, P., Miss [Br. 19c]
The test of virtue, and other poems.
L: C. Chapple, 1811. 154p. NUC BL

256. BARRETT, Angelica Bishop [Am. 19c]
The linden-tree cottage, and the accepted sacrifice.
NY: Hurd & Houghton, 1868. 58p. NUC OCLC

BARRETT, Elizabeth see BROWNING, Elizabeth (Barrett)

257. BARRETT, Roxanna Mae (Stephens) [Am. 19c] ALT: Barrett, Roxie M.
Evening meditations. A book of poems. By Roxie M. Barrett.
Gainesville, GA: Baptist Sun pub. co., c1888. 95p. NUC

BARRETT, Roxie M. see BARRETT, Roxanna Mae (Stephens)

258. BARROWS, Elizabeth A. (Cate) [Am. b. 1823?] ALT: Barrows, Ellen A.
Friendship and wayside gleanings.
Boston: J.H. Earle, 1887. 110p. NUC OCLC
[Ellen A. Barrows on t.p. 56 poems]

259. BARTER, Laura Anne [Br. 19/20c]
ALT: Snow, Laura Anne (Barter)
Led on.
L: J.E. Hawkins, 1891. BL

BARROWS, Ellen A. see BARROWS, Elizabeth A. (Cate)

260. BARTHOLOMEW, Anne Charlotte Turnbull [Br. 19c] ALT: Turnbull, Anne Charlotte; Turnbull, Mrs Walter
The song of Azrael, the angel of death. Recollections of a village school, and other poems.
L: J.W. Southgate, 1840. 100p. BL

261. BARTHOLOMEW, Julia Mersilvia [Br. 19c]
The young poet's offering.
Winchester: D.E. Gilmour, 1838? 194p. BL

262. BARTON, Anna [Am. 19c]
For friendship's sake.
Kalamazoo, MI: H.H. Everard & co., pr., 1882. 133p. NUC OCLC

263. BARTON, Ardelia Maria (Cotton) [Am. b. 1843]
An offering.
San Francisco: The Murdock press, 1898. 236p. NUC OCLC

264. BASKIN, Mary [Br. 19c]
Wild violets; a collection of poems and sketches.
L: F.E. Longley, 1873. 125p. NUC BL OCLC

265. BASS, Cora C. [Am. 19/20c]
PSEUD: Vane, Harley
Poems. By Cora C. Bass (Harley Vane).
Lowell, MA: Lawler & co., pr., 1899. 75p. NUC OCLC

266. BASS, Matilda, Mrs. [Br. 19c]
Silent ministry; poems.
L: Hamilton, Adams & co., 1880. 94p. BL

267. BASSETT, Matilda, Mrs. [Br. 19c]
Bible gleanings.
Woolwich: Boddy & son, 1849. 106p. BL

268. -----Bible gleanings.
L: Partridge & Oakey, 1851. 115p. BL
[Different work from 1849 vol.]

269. BATCHELOR, Harriet [Br. 19c]
Original poetry. (Faith, hope, and charity, etc.)
L: Ashfield, 1866. 4p. BL

270. -----Original poetry. (God is love, etc.)
L: Ashfield, 1865. 4p. BL

271. -----Original poetry. (A welcome to Christmas, etc.)
L: Ashfield, 1866. 4p. BL

272. -----Original poetry. (Wisdom is justified of her children.)
L: G. Nutton, 1862. BL

273. -----Poetry by Miss Harriet Batchelor. The voice of prayer on behalf of missionaries in heathen lands.
L: H. Weede, 1864. 4p. BL

274. BATEMAN, L. M. Beal, Mrs. [Am. 19c] PSEUD: Glenn, Grace
A book of rhymes to suit the times.
Chicago: N. Chapin & sons, c1886. 18p. NUC

275. -----The prohibition speaker, a collection of readings, recitations, dialogues, tableaux and songs. By Grace Glenn.
Cincinnati, OH: Fillmore bros., 1889. 80p. NUC
[65p. of temperance poetry, 4 dialogues & pantomimes, 1 tableau, 10 songs with music]

276. BATEMAN, May Geraldine Frances [Br. 19/20c]
Sonnets and songs.
L: Elkin Mathews, 1895. 53p. NUC BL

277. BATEMAN, Susanna Begin [Br. 17c]
I matter not how I appear to man, a witness in my soul there lives that can bear record to the Father, etc.
L: n.p., 1656. 8p. NUC BL
[BL: Religious tract, begins with poem quoted as title.]

278. BATES, Alice Pease [Am. 19c]
Memory bells.
Buffalo, NY: C.W. Moulton, 1894. 48p. NUC OCLC

279. BATES, Clara Doty [Am. 1838-1895]
From heart's content.
Chicago: Morrill, Higgins, & co., c1892. 128p. NUC OCLC

280. BATES, Theodora [Am. 19c]
Poems.
n.p.: n.p., 1894. 17p. NUC

281. BATH, Elizabeth [Br. 19c]
Poems on various occasions.
Bristol: J. Desmond, 1806. 187p. NUC BL

282. BATHAM, Lucy [Br. 19c]
A wreath of wild flowers: poems.
L: J. Nisbet & co., 1869, 315p. BL

283. BATLEY, E., Mrs. [Br. 19c]
Beamings of the future.
L: H.K. Lewis, 1873. 53p. BL

BATTERSBY, Anne Jane Elizabeth (Jessop) see JESSOP, Anne Jane Elizabeth

284. BATTERSBY, C. Maud [Br. 19c]
Twilight and dawn: hymns, fragments and poems.
L: S.W. Partridge, 1899. 96p. BL

285. BATTERSBY, Hannah S. [Br. 19c]
Home lyrics. A book of poems.
2nd ed. L: Ward, Lock & Tyler, 1876. 184p. NUC BL OCLC

286. -----Home lyrics. A book of poems. Vol. II.
Toronto, Canada: Hunter, Rose & co., 1887. 143p. NUC

BAUGHAN, B.E. see BAUGHAN, Blanche Edith

287. BAUGHAN, Blanche Edith [Br. 1870-1958] ALT: Baughan, B. E.
Verses. By B.E. Baughan.
L & Westminster: A. Constable & co., 1898. 144p. NUC BL OCLC
[Alt. title: Poems. Selections]

288. BAXTER, Lydia [Am. 1809-1874]
Gems by the wayside; or, Religious and domestic poems.
NY: Sheldon, Lamport, & Blakeman, 1855. 283p. NUC OCLC

289. BAYFIELD, E. G., Mrs. [Br. 19c]
Fugitive poems.
L: Lindsell; Warde & Betham, 1805. 192p. NUC BL OCLC

BAYLEY, F.W.N., ed. see SIGOURNEY, Lydia Howard (Huntley)

BAYLY, E.B., comp. see SEWELL, Mary (Wright)

290. BAYNE, Emily [Br. 19c]
Sighs of hope.
L: B.M. Pickering, 1870. 69p. BL

291. BEACH, Emily J. [Am. 19c]
Misunderstood.
Boston: The author, 1876. 421p. NUC OCLC

292. BEADLE, Jane E. [Am. 19c]
The play of gold, a versified story of moral interest.
Milwaukee, WI: Riverside prntg. co., 1887. 82p. NUC

293. BEALE, Anne [Br. 19c]
Poems.
L: Longman, Brown, Green, & Longmans, 1842. 227p. NUC BL

294. BEALE, Mary [Br. 19c]
St. John. A poem.
L: Digby & Long, 1892. 35p. BL

295. BEARCROFT, Susannah [Br. 19c]
Eva of Chepstow; A new year's tale, in verse.
L: W. Edwards, 1841. 88p. NUC BL

296. BEARDSLEY, Jane Margaret Matthews [Am. 1824-1851]
The unforgotten and other poems.
New Haven, CT: Pr. Tuttle, Morehouse & Taylor, 1891. 90p. NUC OCLC

297. BEATTIE, Anne [Br. 19c] ALT: B., A.
Songs in the desert. By A.B.
L: The author, 1845. 142p. BL

298. BEATTIE, Elise [Am. 19c]
Echoes.
Atlanta, GA: n.p., 1883. 84p. NUC OCLC
[Twenty-two poems and "Poppies," ten prose pieces, incl. a short story, "Mud Pies."]

299. BEAUCHAMP, Ellen [Am. 19c]
Sweet messengers.
NY: Hard & Parsons, c1888. 6 l. NUC OCLC

300. -----Voices of nature.
Boston: L. Prang, c1890. 6 l. NUC OCLC

301. BEAVAN, Mary [Am. 19c]
The water brook, and other verses.
NY: A.D.F. Randolph & co., 1895. 61p. NUC OCLC

302. BECK, Leonora [Am. b. 1862]
Star heights, and other stories, pastels, and poems.
Atlanta, GA: The Foote & Davies co., 1895. 240p. NUC OCLC
[5 poems, 10 short stories, several prose sketches, studies of Browning, etc.]

303. BEDNALL, Jeannie [Br. 19c]
Sea spray; and other poems.
L: Elliot Stock, 1894. 82p. BL OCLC

BEERS, Ethel Lynn see BEERS, Ethelinda Elliot

304. BEERS, Ethelinda Elliot [Am. 1827-1879] ALT: Beers, Ethel Lynn
All quiet along the Potomac, and other poems. By Ethel Lynn Beers.
Philadelphia: Porter & Coates, 1879. 352p. NUC OCLC

305. BEGG, Mary Miller [Br. 19c]
My mother's marriage ring, and other poems.
Glasgow: D. Bryce & sons, 1893. 172p. NUC BL

306. BEHENNA, Kathleen [Br. 19c]
The history of a soul.
L: Digby, Long & co., 1896. 104p. BL

BEHN, A. see BEHN, Aphra (Amis)

307. BEHN, Aphra (Amis) [Br. 1640-1689] ALT: B., A.; Behn, A.
A congratulatory poem to her most Sacred Majesty [Mary Beatrice of Modena, Queen Consort of James II] on the universal hopes of all loyal persons for a Prince of Wales.
L: Will Canning, 1688. 7p. NUC BL

308. -----A congratulatory poem to the King's most Sacred Majesty, on the happy birth of the Prince of Wales.
L: W. Canning, 1688. 2p. NUC BL

309. -----"The Gods are not more blessed than he," in Chorus Poetarum; or, Poems on several occasions by the Duke of Buckingham and other eminent poets. Ed. Charles Gildon.
L: B. Bragg, 1694. 176p. BL

310. -----The land of love. A poem.
L: H. Meere, pr., 1717. 1v. NUC

311. -----Lycidus: or the Lover in fashion. Being an account from Lycidus to Lysander of his voyage from the Island of Love. From the French. By the same author of the Isle of love. Together with a miscellany of new poems. By several hands.
2 pt. L: J. Knight & F. Saunders, 1688. NUC BL
[Many of the poems by A. Behn, & the dedication signed by her]

312. -----Miscellany, being a collection of poems by several hands. Together with Reflections on morality, or Senecca unmasqued.
L: J. Hindmarsh, 1685. 301-382p. NUC BL
[The dedicatory epistle signed: A. Behn]

313. -----A pindaric poem to the Reverand Doctor Burnet, on the honour he did me of enquiring after me and my muse. By Mrs. A. Behn.
L: R. Bentley, sold by Richard Baldwin, 1689. 8p. NUC BL

314. -----A pindarick on the death of our late sovereign: with an ancient prophecy on his present Majesty.
L: J. Playford, for Henry Playford, 1685. 5p. NUC BL

315. -----Pindarick poem on the happy coronation of His ... Majesty James II and his illustrious Consort Queen Mary.
L: J. Playford, for Henry Playford, 1685. 20p. NUC BL

316. -----A poem humbly dedicated to the great patern of piety and virtue Catherine Queen Dowager, on the death of her dear Lord ... King Charles II.
L: J. Playford for Henry Playford, 1685. 6p. BL

317. -----A poem to Sir Roger L'Estrange on his third part of the history of the times; relating to the death of Sir Edmund Bury-Godfrey.
L: Randall Taylor, 1688. 7p. NUC BL

318. -----Poems upon several occasions: with a Voyage to the island of love.
2 pt. L: R. Tonson & J. Tonson, 1684. NUC BL

319. -----To the most illustrious Prince Christopher Duke Albemarle, on his voyage to his government of Jamaica. A pindarick. By Mrs. A. Behn.
L: John Newton, 1687. 9p. NUC BL

320. BEL, Sarah F. [Am. 19c]
Ornaments of rhyme.
Middletown, CT: n.p., 1891. 54p. NUC OCLC

BELASCO, Mme. Isaac Dolaro <u>see</u> DOLARO, Selina

BELCHER, J., comp. <u>see</u> SIGOURNEY, Lydia Howard (Huntley)

321. BELL, A., Mrs. [Br. 19c]
The lays of a lady: or, Poetical tales and poems.
L: T.H. Rice, 1840. 203p. BL

322. BELL, A. S., Mrs. [Br. 19c]
Fanny, or true benevolence: to which are added, miscellaneous poems.
Whitby: R. Rogers, 1821. 168p. NUC BL

BELL, ACTON, pseud., co-author <u>see</u> BRONTE, Charlotte

323. BELL, Clara L. [Am. 19c]
Poems.
Boston: Farrington pr. co., 1894. 27p. NUC

BELL, CURRER, pseud. <u>see</u> BRONT, Charlotte

BELL, ELLIS, pseud., co-author <u>see</u> BRONTE, Charlotte

324. BELL, Emma M., Mrs. [Am. 19c]
Poems.
Philadelphia: J.B. Lippincott & co., 1872. 197p. NUC OCLC

325. BELL, Frances Augusta [Br. 1809-1825]
A memoir of Miss Frances Augusta Bell ... with specimens of her compositions, in prose and verse. Ed. Rev. Johnson Grant.
L: Hatchard & son, 1827. 175p. NUC BL
[15 year-old girl. Incl. religious essays, letters & 5 brief poems.]

326. BELL, Helen [Am. 19c]
Man's catastrophe, and other poems.
Middlebury, VT: Pr. at the Register Office, 1869. 43p. NUC OCLC

327. BELL, Laura [Am. 19c]
In verse proportion.
Philadelphia: J.B. Lippincott co., 1893. 45p. NUC OCLC

BELL, LURA, pseud. see WILLIAMSON, Julia May

BELL, M. Bettie see BELL, Mary Elizabeth (Stone)

328. BELL, Margaret Thomson (Beveridge) [Br. 1833-1890]
Poems and other pieces. Ed. D. Beveridge.
L: Leadenhall Press, 1894. 191p. NUC BL
[Mainly poetry. Includes three prose narratives]

329. BELL, Maria [Br. 19c]
Songs of two homes.
Edinburgh & L: Oliphant, Anderson & Ferrier, 1899. 139p. BL

330. BELL, Martha Ann (Penney) [Am. 1817-1881]
Poems of Mrs. Martha A. Bell.
Louisville, KY: Educational Courant, c1893. 135p. NUC OCLC

331. BELL, Mary Elizabeth (Stone) [Am. b. 1848] ALT: Bell, M. Bettie
Christmas, a poem. By M. Bettie Bell.
Chicago: The author, c1895. 8p. NUC

332. BELL, Orelia Key [Am. b. 1864]
Poems of Orelia Key Bell.
Philadelphia: The Rodgers co., c1895. 218p. NUC OCLC

333. BELLER, Lizzie I., Mrs. [Am. 19c]
The star of light.
Perth, KS: n.p., 1898. 78p. NUC OCLC
[Religious poetry & prose; 4 long poems, 1 story, dedicated to the Masonic Fraternity]

334. BELLOC, Bessie Rayner (Parkes) [Br. 19/20c] ALT: Parkes, Bessie Rayner
Ballads and songs.
L: Bell & Daldy, 1863. 216p. NUC BL OCLC

335. -----Gabriel.
L: J. Chapman, 1856. 110p. NUC BL
[Poem on Percy Bysshe Shelley]

336. -----Poems. By Bessie Rayner Parkes.
L: J. Chapman, 1852. 94p. NUC BL OCLC

337. -----Summer sketches and other poems.
L: John Chapman, 1854. BL
[Poems and letters on travel; lyrics & commemorative verse]

338. BELT, Miss [Br. 19c]
The sons of the martyrs, and other poems.
L: Pr. the Jewish youths at the Institution, 27 Red Lion Square, 1847. 135p. BL

BELSON, Mary see ELLIOTT, Mary (Belson)

BENEDICT, HESTER A., pseud. see DICKINSON, Hester A.

339. BENEDICT, Sarah Ward [Am. 19c]
A strike at King Alcohol.
Jamesville, IL: Jamesville Signal Steam pr., 1887. 48p. NUC
[Poems and one story on temperance]

340. BENGER, Elizabeth Ogilvie [Br. 1778-1827]
The female geniad; a poem.
L: T. Kookham; J. Carpenter; C. & G. Kearsley, 1791. 55p. NUC BL

341. -----A poem, occasioned by the abolition of the slave trade in 1806. In poems on the abolition of the slave trade, written by James Montgomery, James Grahame and E. Benger. Comp. R. Bowyer.
L: Pr. J. Bensley, 1809. 141p. NUC BL OCLC

342. BENN, Mary [Br. 19c]
Lays of the Hebrews, and other poems.
L: Joseph Masters, 1854. 69p. BL

343. -----The solitary; or, A lay from the west; with other poems, in English and Latin.
Dublin: James McGlashan; L: Joseph Masters, 1853. 156p. BL

344. BENN, Rose [Br. 19c]
The two great powers, alcohol versus love! Which is the greater? By E.L.W.C.T.U.
L: Nat. Temperance pub. depot, 1890. 12p. BL

345. BENNET, Georgiana [Br. 19c]
Ianthe and other poems.
2d ed. L: Longman, Orme, Brown, Green & Longmans, 1841. 144p. BL OCLC

346. -----A lay and songs of home.
L: Longman, 1843. 142p. BL

347. -----The new year's eve, and other poems.
L: Longman, 1865. 168p. BL

348. The poetess, and other poems.
L: Longman, 1844. 140p. BL

349. -----The studio, and other poems.
L: Darton & Clark, 1846. 145p. OCLC

350. BENNETT, Anna R. (Gladstone) [Br. 19c]
Iphigenia in Tauris. From the German of Goethe. With original poems.
Liverpool: Priv. pr., 1851. 200p. BL
[Also trans. from Italian. Original poems, pp. 109f.: Nature, Hymns, Philosophical]

351. BENNETT, Edith M. [Br. 19c]
The path of life. A poem.
L: Digby & Long, 1892. 84p. BL

352. BENNETT, Emily Thatcher B. [Am. 19/20c]
Song of the rivers and other poems.
NY: Dexter & co.; Cincinnati, OH: R.W. Carroll & co., 1865. 262p. NUC BL OCLC

353. BENNETT, Lucy Ann [Br. 1850-1927]
Afterward. A poem.
L: Castell bros., 1890. BL

354. -----Alleluia songs.
L: S.W. Partridge & co., 1882. BL

355. -----"Daybreak." Easter poems.
L: Castell bros., 1888. BL

356. -----Evermore, and other poems.
L: Castell bros., 1891. BL

357. -----Evermore. Poem.
L: Castell bros., 1890. BL

358. -----Every day.
7 pt. L: Castell bros., 1890. BL
[Religious poems]

359. -----Far and near.
L: Castell bros., 1888. BL
[Christmas verses]

360. -----Garnered grain. With Horatius Bonar.
L: Castell, 1889. BL

361. -----"Gleanings." Scripture texts for Easter with verses.
L: Castell bros., 1887. BL

362. -----Good night.
L: Castell bros., 1890. BL

363. -----"Harpstrings." A poem.
L: Castell bros., 1887. BL

364. -----"He ever liveth." Easter poems.
L: Castell bros., 1888. BL

365. -----Heavenward. A poem.
L: Castell bros., 1886. BL

366. -----I never expected such happiness. The last days of a young cyclist.
L: Marshall bros., 1896. 28p. BL

367. -----Lifted loads.
L: Marshall bros., 1895. 107p. BL

368. -----Little Phoebe. A dream of Christmas.
L: Castell bros., 1888. BL

369. -----"My redeemer liveth." An Easter memorial.
L: Castell bros., 1888. BL

370. -----Near and far.
L: Castell bros., 1889. BL

371. -----Neath sun and star.
L: Castell bros., 1890. BL

372. -----On the wing. Scripture texts for each day, with verses.
L: Castell bros.; NY: E. & J.B. Young, 1887. 35p. NUC BL OCLC

373. -----Open secrets. A poem.
L: Castell bros., 1887. BL

374. -----"Otherwhere." A poem.
L: Castell, 1888. NUC BL

375. -----"Our Father who art in heaven."
L: Castell, 1888. BL

376. -----"Risen with Christ."
L: Castell, 1889. BL

377. -----Some better thing, and other poems.
L: Castell bros., 1890. BL

378. -----Songs for Christmastide.
L: Castell, 1887. BL

379. -----Songs for silent hours.
L: W. Mack, 1878. 112p. BL

380. -----"This same Jesus." A poem.
L: Castell, 1888. BL

381. -----Verses for Christmas and the New Year.
L: Castell, 1885. BL

382. -----White hyacinths, and other poems.
L: Marshall bros., 1898. 164p. BL

383. BENNETT, Mary Anne [Br. 19c]
Poems.
L: Griffith Farran & co., 1894. 96p. BL

384. BENNETT, Mary E. [Am. 19c] ALT: B., M. E. PSEUD: Campbell, Mary; Mel, Mary
Poems and tales, by Mary Campbell, Mary Mel, etc., noms de plume of M.E.B.
NY: T.W. Strong, 1851. 160p. NUC BL
[7 short stories, 63 poems]

385. BENNETT, Nancy P. K. [Am. 19c]
From a mother's only legacy to her three orphan children.
Portland, ME: n.p., c1889. 5 l. NUC
[Short poems, 1 to each child: Lillie Irene, Neddie, & the baby.]

386. BENNISON, Deborah Matilda (Lunt) [Am. 1789-1852]
Poems, original and selected.
Boston: Pr. for the author, 1847. 144p. NUC BL OCLC
[Mostly original]

387. BENSON, Eliza [Br. 19c]
Lays of memory, sacred and social. By a mother and son.
L: Hurst & Blackett, 1856. 304p. BL
[Pt. 1 by mother, pt. 2 by son, Richard Meux Benson]

BENSON, Richard Meux, co-author see BENSON, Eliza

388. BENT, Naomi [Br. 19c]
Games for tables.
L: J. Williams, 1899. 20p. BL

389. BENTLEY, Elizabeth [Br. 1767-1839]
Genuine poetical compositions, on various subjects.
Norwich: Pr. Crouse & Steverson for the authoress, 1791. 69p. NUC BL OCLC

390. -----Miscellaneous poems; being the genuine compositions of Elizabeth Bentley, of Norwich.
Norwich: Matchett, 1835. NUC

391. -----Ode on the glorious victory over the French and Spanish fleets, on the 21st of October, 1805, and the death of Lord Nelson.
Norwich: Stevenson & Matchett, 1805? 4p. BL

392. -----Poems; being the genuine compositions of Elizabeth Bentley, of Norwich.
Norwich: The author, 1821. 168p. NUC

393. BERRY, Lizzie [Br. 19c]
Heart echoes; original miscellaneous and devotional poems.
Otley: W. Walker & sons, 1886. 320p. BL

394. -----Poems.
Rugby: J.W. Kenning, 1879. 2v. NUC

395. BERRY, Sarah [Br. 19c]
Thoughts in prose and verse on the grace and love of God.
Ramsgate: Burgess & Hunt, 1837. 70p. BL
[Spiritual autobiography; religious poems, pp. 38-70]

396. BERTONI, Ada, Mrs. [Am. 19c]
Charms.
Bloomington, IL: n.p., 1899. 76p. NUC OCLC
[11 poems & 8 prose pieces, several on spiritualism]

397. BESEMERES, Jane [Br. 19c]
Vanished faces, and other poems.
L: J. Nisbet & co., 1884. 110p. BL

398. BETHAM, Mary Matilda [Br. 1776-1852]
Elegies and other small poems.
Ipswich: Jermyn & Forster; pr. W. Burrell, sold by Longman, 1797. 128p. NUC BL OCLC

399. -----The lay of Marie: a poem.
L: Rowland Hunter, 1816. 276p. NUC BL OCLC
[With "Extracts from a dissertation on the life and writings of Marie, an Anglo-Norman poetess of the thirteenth century]

400. -----Poems.
L: J. Hatchard, 1808. 116p. NUC BL OCLC

401. -----Vignettes: in verse.
L: Rowland Hunter, 1818. 80p. BL

402. BETHELL, E. M., Mrs. [Br. 19c]
Poems.
Chippenham: Pr. for priv. circ. by J. & G. Noyes, 1854. 138p. NUC

BETHUNE, Divie, comp. <u>see</u> GRAHAM, Isabella Marshall

403. BEVAN, Emma Frances A., Mrs. [Br. 19c] ALT: Bevan, Frances A.
Service of song in the house of the Lord.
L: Hatchards, 1884. 118p. BL

404. -----Songs of praise for Christian pilgrims.
L: Hamilton, 1832. 152p. NUC BL

BEVAN, Frances A. <u>see</u> BEVAN, Emma Frances A., Mrs.

BEVERIDGE, D., ed. <u>see</u> BELL, Margaret Thomson (Beveridge)

405. BEVERLEY, Charlotte [Br. 18c]
Poems on miscellaneous subjects.
Hull: E. Foster, 1792. 247p. NUC BL OCLC

406. BEVERLEY, Elizabeth, Mrs. R. Beverley [Br. 19c]
The actress' ways and means to industriously raise the wind! Containing the moral and entertaining poetical effusions of Mrs. R. Beverley.
L: The author, 1818? 31p. NUC BL

407. -----The bee; containing letters from Mrs. Elizabeth Beverley in town, to her friend, Poll Curious, in the country.
L: Pr. for authoress, 1827. 34p. NUC

408. -----The book of variety; containing laughable anecdotes, entertaining poetry, and various other pieces of interest and amusement.
L: The authoress, 1823. 23p. NUC BL
[Jests, satiric verses & essays extolling elocution.]

409. -----Entertaining moral poems on various subjects, expressly designed for the use of the rising generation.
2d ed. L: the authoress, 1826. NUC BL

410. -----A new dish of all sorts.
L: The authoress, 1824. 23p. NUC BL

411. -----A poetical olio.
L: the author, 1819. 24p. NUC BL

412. -----Useful subjects in prose and verse.
4th ed. L: the authoress, 1828. 24p. NUC BL
[Opinions on training servants, educating poor children, etc. in prose and misc. verse]

BEVERLEY, Mrs. R. <u>see</u> BEVERLEY, Elizabeth

413. BEVINGTON, Louisa Sarah [Br. b. 1845] ALT: Guggenberger, Louisa Sarah (Bevington) PSEUD: Leigh, Arbor
Key-notes. By L.S. Bevington.
L: C.K. Paul & co., 1879. 137p. NUC BL

414. -----Liberty lyrics. By L.S. Bevington.
L: J. Tochatti, 1895. 16p. NUC

415. -----Poems, lyrics and sonnets. By L.S. Bevington.
L: E. Stock, 1882. 158p. NUC BL

416. BEVIS, Sophia Cortoulde (Hazlett) [Am. b. 1846]
Poems.
Cincinnati, OH: H.H. Bevis, 1890. 99p. NUC

417. BEWSHER, Amelia [Br. 19c]
Early musings. A collection of sacred and other poems.
L: Hope & co., 1854. 95p. BL

418. BIANCHI, Martha Gilbert (Dickinson) [Am. 1866-1943] ALT: Dickinson, Martha Gilbert
Within the hedge.
NY: Doubleday & McClure co., 1899. 127p. NUC OCLC

419. BIANCIARDI, Elizabeth Dickinson (Rice) [Am. 1833-1885] ALT: R., E. D.; Rice, Elizabeth Dickinson
A quiet life, and other poems. By E.D.R.
New & enl. ed. NY: Anson D. F. Randolph & co., c1879. 73p. NUC OCLC

420. BICKFORD, Lelia B. [Am. 1852-1873] PSEUD: May, Morna
Songs of May morning.
Albany, NY: Joel Munsell, 1874. 81p. NUC OCLC

421. BICKNELL, Emeline Larkin [Am. 1825-1916]
Violets, and other poems.
NY: Eaton & Mains press, 1897. 170p. OCLC

BIGELOW, Andrew Frank, ed. see BIGELOW, Marion Albina (Purmont)

422. BIGELOW, Marion Albina (Purmont) [Am. 19c]
The northern harp: containing songs from the St. Lawrence, and forest melodies. Ed. Andrew Frank Bigelow.
Auburn, NY: Derby & Miller, 1852. 400p. NUC OCLC BL

423. -----Songs from the St. Lawrence: or, Occasional poems. Ed. Andrew Frank Bigelow.
NY: Lane & Scott, 1851. 176p. NUC OCLC
[130 poems from 300 prev. pr. in periodicals.]

424. BIGELOW, Mary Ann Hubbard (Townsend) [Am. d. 1870]
The kings and queens of England, with other poems.
Boston: Pub. for author by S.K. Whipple & co., 1853. 142p. NUC OCLC

425. BIGG, Louisa [Br. 19c] PSEUD: Brand, Louis
Oenone. A poem.
Luton: O'Doherty, 1875. 27p. BL

426. -----Pansies and asphodel.
L: Chapman & Hall, 1878. 163p. BL OCLC

427. -----Urban grandier, and other poems. By Louis Brand.
L: Chapman & Hall, 1872. 81p. NUC BL

428. BILLER, Sarah Kilham [Br. 19c]
Halkam, the scenes of my childhood: and other poems.
L: Foster & Hextall, 1839. 64p. BL

429. BINGHAM, Ashton, Mrs. [Br. 19c]
The autumn leaf poems.
Edinburgh: Colston & co., 1891. 104p. BL

430. BINGHAM, Frances Lydia [Br. 19c]
Hubert, or the orphans of St. Madelaine; a legend of the persecuted Vaudois.
L: Simpkin, 1845. 75p. NUC BL

431. -----Short poems, religious and sentimental. By the late Miss F.L. Bingham. Ed. her father, Richard Bingham.
2d ed. L: Simpkin, Marshall & co.; Bolton-le-Moors: Henry Bradbury, Jr., 1848. 59p. BL

BINGHAM, G.C., co-author see COTTON, Mrs. F. Percy

BINGHAM, Graham Clifton, co-author see COTTON, Mrs. F. Percy

BINGHAM, Graham Clifton, co-author see REED, Alice

432. BINGHAM, Jane M. [Br. 19c]
"Amy of the peak;" or, The triumph of principle.
2d ed. Chesterfield: C. Gallimore, 1847. 35p. NUC OCLC

433. -----Joys and sorrows; where to find and how to exchange them: comprising Agnes; or, a word for women ... and other poems.
L: C. Gilpin, 1847? 136p. BL

BINGHAM, Richard, ed. see BINGHAM, Frances Lydia

BIRCH, C.M. see SALWAY, Charlotte Maria (Birch)

434. BIRCH, Eliza [Br. 19c]
Poems on various subjects; to which is added a selection of hymns.
Manchester: C. Wheeler & son, 1800. 69p. BL

BIRCH, Thomas, comp. see COCKBURN, Catherine (Trotter)

BIRDSALL, Fannie, co-author see NELSON, Flora Birdsall

435. BIRKETT, M., Miss [Br. 18c]
A poem on the African slave-trade; addressed to her own sex by M. Birkett.
2 pt. Dublin: J. Jones, 1792. 25p. NUC BL

436. BISHOP, Harriet E. [Am. 1817-1883] ALT: Macconkey, Harriet E. (Bishop)
Minnesota; then and now.
St. Paul, MN: D.D. Merrill, Randall & co., 1869. 100p. NUC OCLC
[Descriptive & historical verse]

437. BISHOP, Kate [Br. 19c]
A life's requiem, and other poems.
L: Marlborough & co., 1890. 199p. BL

438. BISHOP, Maria J. [Am. 19c]
Bells of Saint Matthew.
n.p.: n.p., n.d. NUC

439. -----The hospital offering.
n.p.: n.p., n.d. 9p. NUC

440. -----Hours with the lonely.
Boston: B.B. Russell, 1872. 64p. OCLC
[Misc. poetry, brief prose essays, & a fictional sketch of Queen Elizabeth I]

441. -----"Marah;" or, The sweets of trial.
Boston: B.B. Russell & co., 1873. 64p. NUC OCLC
[16 short poems and misc. prose: 1 moral short story, essays on consolation, resignation, etc.]

442. -----Sunset clouds.
Boston: B.B. Russell, 1873. 64p. OCLC
[Misc. poetry & prose: parables, stories & brief sermons]

443. BISHOP, Mary [Br. 19c]
Poetic tales and miscellanies.
2d ed. Liverpool: William Robinson; Liverpool: Pr. J. Smith; L: James Ibery, 1812. 151p. NUC BL OCLC

BISSICKS, Lolo Julia, ed. see TUPPER, Margaret Elenora

444. BLACK, Anita Ciprico [Am. 19c]
Sketches in prose and verse.
San Francisco: H.S. Crocker co., 1897. 50p. NUC OCLC
[Misc. poems & 4 short stories]

445. BLACK, Emily Julia [Br. 19c]
PSEUD: Aemilia Julia
Byron: Salathiel, or the martyrs; and other poems. By Aemilia Julia.
L: G. Routledge & co., 1855. 143p. BL

446. -----Leon de Beaumanoir; or, The twin-born. By Aemilia Julia.
L: Chapman & Hall, 1865. 215p. BL

447. BLACKETT, Mary Dawes [Br. 18c]
Suicide; a poem.
L: Pr. W. Justins, 1789. 14p. NUC BL OCLC

BLACKLOCK, Thomas, co-author see SCOT, Elizabeth (Rutherford)

448. BLACKWELL, Anna [Br. 19c]
Poems.
L: J. Chapman, 1853. 248p. NUC BL OCLC

449. -----A vision.
L: G. Redway, 1898. 14p. BL

450. BLACKWELL, Elizabeth, Mrs. Thomas Blackwell [Am. d. 1897]
Poems by Mrs. Thomas Blackwell.
Toledo, OH: The Toledo Evening Bee, pr., 1884. 50p. NUC OCLC

BLACKWELL, Mrs. Thomas see BLACKWELL, Elizabeth

BLACKWOOD, Helen Selina (Sheridan), Baroness Dufferin and Clandeboye see DUFFERIN and CLANDEBOYE, Helen Selina (Sheridan) Blackwood, Baroness

BLACKWOOD, Mrs. Price see DUFFERIN and CLANDEBOYE, Helen Selina (Sheridan) Blackwood, Baroness

451. BLAGDEN, Isa Jane [Br. 1816-1873]
Poems. With a memoir by Alfred Austin.
Edinburgh & L: W. Blackwood, 1873. 166p. NUC BL OCLC

452. BLAIR, C. P., Mrs. [Am. 19c]
PSEUD: Woodland, Waif
Poems.
Buffalo, NY: n.p., 1884. 139p. OCLC NUC
[Cover title: The silver cup and other poems.]

453. -----Poems of Mrs. C.P. Blair (Waif Woodland).
Binghamton, NY: Binghamton Republican, 1884. 139p. NUC OCLC

454. BLAIR, Ophelia E. [Am. 19c]
PSEUD: Dean, Adam
Poems of humanity by Adam Dean.
Little Rock, AR: The Press pr. co., 1892. 136p. NUC OCLC

BLAKE, Emilia Aylmer see GOWING, Emilia Aylmer (Blake)

455. BLAKE, Emma M. [Am. 19c]
Reliquiae.
Charleston, NC: Priv. pr. for D. Blake, 1854. 140p. NUC BL OCLC

456. BLAKE, Louisa [Am. 19c]
Supper flies, and other pieces; a Christmas booklet of original verse.
Wellington: Edward Russell & co., 1895. NUC

457. BLAKE, Louisa Dumaresque [Am. 19c]
Poems.
Boston: Carter Hendee & co., 1832. 138p. NUC

458. BLAKE, Margaret Jane [Am. 1811-1880]
Memoirs of Margaret Jane Blake of Baltimore, Md., and selections in prose and verse, by Sarah R. Levering.
Philadelphia: Press of Innes & son, 1897. 48p. NUC
[Blake was a slave in Baltimore, freed before the Civil War]

459. BLAKE, Mary Elizabeth (McGrath) [Am. 1840-1907] ALT: B., M. E.
An epic of travel; gotten up without regard to cost, sense, or meter; in eight cantos, dedicated to the third Raymond California party of 1822, by M.E.B.
Boston: n.p., 1884. 12p. NUC OCLC

460. -----The merry months all. Poems by M.E.B.
Boston: D. Lothrop & co., 1885. 24p. NUC

461. -----Poems, by Mary E. Blake (M.E.B.).
Boston: Houghton, Mifflin & co., 1882. 208p. NUC OCLC

462. -----Verses along the way, by Mary Elizabeth Blake.
Boston & NY: Houghton, Mifflin & co., 1890. 151p. NUC BL OCLC

463. -----Youth in twelve centuries. Poems by M.E.B.
Boston: D. Lothrop & co., 1886. 78p. NUC OCLC

464. BLAKE, Nancy [Am. 19c]
Nancy Blake, letters to a western cousin.
NY: Sinclair Tousey; John Bradburn, 1864. 36p. NUC BL OCLC

465. BLAMIRE, Susanna [Br. 1747-1794] PSEUD: Muse of Cumberland, The
The poetical works of Miss Susanna Blamire. Comp. Henry Lonsdale.
Edinburgh: J. Menzies, 1842. 262p. NUC BL OCLC

466. -----Songs and poems by Miss Blamire; together with songs by her friend Miss [Catherine] Gilpin. Ed. Sidney Gilpin.
L: Geo. Routledge, 1866. 184p. OCLC

467. BLANCHARD, Anne [Br. 19c]
Midnight reflections, and other poems.
L: J. Arliss, 1822. 111p. NUC BL

BLANCHARD, Laman, comp. <u>see</u> LANDON, Letitia Elizabeth

BLANCHARD, Mary Ellen <u>see</u> BLANCHARD, May Ellen

468. BLANCHARD, May Ellen [Am. b. 1851] ALT: Blanchard, Mary Ellen
A story of Psyche, and other poems.
Boston: A.C. Getchell, 1885. 257p. NUC OCLC

469. BLAND, Edith (Nesbit), Mrs. Hubert Bland [Br. 1858-1924] ALT: Nesbit, Edith
Autumn songs. Sel. & arr. by E. Nesbit and Robert Ellice Mack.
L: Griffith Farran & co., n.d. 30p. TXU
[2 orig. poems each by E. Nesbit & Caris Brooke; selections from Keats, Swinburne, etc.]

470. -----Babes in the wood.
L: E. Nister, 1896. 14p. OCLC

471. -----The better part and other poems, by E. Nesbit.
L: H.J. Drane & co., 1888? 16p. NUC

472. -----Corals, sea songs. By E. Nesbit.
NY: E.P. Dutton & co., n.d. 6p. TXU

473. -----Easter-tide. Poems by E. Nesbit & Caris Brooke.
NY: E.P. Dutton & co., 1888. 24p. NUC

474. -----Fading light. Verses by E. Nesbit.
L & NY: W. Hagelberg, 18--? 16p. NUC OCLC

475. -----Lays and legends by E. Nesbit.
1st ser. L: Longmans, Green, 1886. 197p. 2d ser. L & NY: Longmans, Green, 1892. 160p. NUC BL OCLC
[Narrative & lyric poems.]

476. -----Leaves of life by E. Nesbit.
L & NY: Longmans, Green, 1888. 185p. NUC BL OCLC

477. -----The lily and the cross.
L: Griffith, Farran & co., 1887. BL

478. -----A pomander of verse by E. Nesbit.

L: John Lane, 1895. 88p. NUC OCLC

479. -----Rose leaves.
L: Ernest Nister, 1895. BL

480. -----Songs of love and empire by E. Nesbit.
Westminster: Archibald Constable & co., 1898. 168p. NUC BL OCLC

481. -----Songs of two seasons.
L: R. Tuck & sons, 1890. BL

482. -----Sweet lavender.
L: Ernest Nister, 1892. BL

483. -----Winter snow, selected, written and arranged by E. Nesbit.
NY: E.P. Dutton, 18--? 28p. NUC
[4 poems signed E. Nesbit; others by Tennyson, Shelley, Herrick, etc.]

484. -----Winter songs and sketches. By E. Nesbit and Caris Brooke. Arr. E. Nesbit & Robert Ellice Mack.
NY: E.P. Dutton & co., 18--? 24p. NUC OCLC
[4 poems signed E. Nesbit; others by Tennyson, Shelley, Herrick, etc.]

BLAND, Mrs. Hubert <u>see</u> BLAND, Edith (Nesbit)

485. BLANKENSHIP, Mattie A., Mrs. [Am. 19c]
A statistical and descriptive poem of Texas.
Dallas, TX: J.M. Colville, 1892. 23p. NUC OCLC

486. BLEASE, Elizabeth Bower [Br. 19c]
Poems, on various subjects.
L: the author, 1817. 108p. BL

487. BLEECKER, Ann Eliza (Schuyler) [Am. 1752-1783] ALT: Bleecker, Eliza
The posthumous works in verse and prose. To which is added a collection of essays, prose and poetical by Margaretta V. Faugeres.
NY: Pr., T. & J. Swords, 1793. 375p. NUC BL OCLC
[36 poems, 2 stories, & letters on Revolutionary War experiences. Incl. 4 prose essays and 33 poems by Faugeres.]

BLEECKER, Eliza <u>see</u> BLEECKER, Ann Eliza (Schuyler)

488. BLEECKER, Sophia [Am. 19c]
PSEUD: Katy-did; Katy-didn't
Lays of a lifetime. The record of one departed. By Mary Noel (Bleecker) Macdonald Meigs.
NY: Dana & co.; L: S. Low & son & co., 1857. 157p. NUC
[Sophia's poems under pseuds., "Katy-did" and "Katy-didn't", are included.]

489. BLENNERHASSETT, Margaret Agnew [Am. 1788?-1842] PSEUD: Lady, A
The widow of the rock, and other poems, by a lady.
Montreal: E.V. Sparhawk, pr., 1824. 192p. NUC
[Misc. poetry. Incl.: 1 dialogue, 1 poem in Negro dialect. Also includes some poems by an American gentleman]

490. BLEVINS, Louisa [Br. 19c]
Poems green and grey.
Romsey: C.L. Lordan, 1869. 79p. BL

491. -----Poetic musings in shade and sunshine.
2d ed. Romsey: C.L. Lordan, 1864. 72p. OCLC

492. BLIND, Mathilde [Br. 1841-1896]
PSEUD: Lake, Claude
The ascent of man.
L: Chatto & Windus, 1889. 200p. NUC BL OCLC
[Incl. The ascent of man, Poems of the open air, and Love in exile.]

493. -----Birds of passage; songs of the Orient and Occident.
L: Chatto & Windus, 1895. 147p. NUC BL OCLC

494. -----Dramas in miniature.
L: Chatto & Windus, 1891. 113p. NUC BL OCLC

495. -----The heather on fire: a tale of the Highland Clearances.
L: Walter Scott, 1886. 117p. NUC BL OCLC

496. -----Poems. By Claude Lake.
L: A.W. Bennett, 1867. 94p. NUC OCLC

497. -----The prophecy of Saint Oran, and other poems.
L: Newman & co., 1881. 135p. NUC BL OCLC

498. -----Songs and sonnets.
L: Chatto & Windus, 1893. 119p. NUC BL OCLC

499. BLODGETT, Lydia, Mrs. [Am. 19c]
Temperance and other poems.

Berlin, NH: Pub. by the authoress, The Independent pr., 1888. 43p. NUC

500. BLOEDE, Gertrude [Am. 1845-1905]
PSEUD: Sterne, Stuart
Angelo, a poem. By Stuart Sterne.
Boston & NY: Houghton, Mifflin, c1877. 104p. NUC OCLC

501. -----Beyond the shadow, and other poems. By Stuart Sterne.
Boston & NY: Houghton, Mifflin & co., 1888. 146p. NUC BL OCLC

502. -----Georgio, and other poems. By Stuart Sterne.
Boston: Houghton, Mifflin, 1881. 195p. NUC BL OCLC

503. -----Piero da Castiglione. By Stuart Sterne.
Boston & NY: Houghton, Mifflin & co., 1890. 121p. NUC BL OCLC

504. -----Poems by Stuart Sterne.
NY: F.B. Patterson, 1874. 244p. NUC OCLC

505. BLOOMFIELD-MOORE, Clara Sophia (Jessup) [Am. 1824-1899]
Character and descriptive songster.
NY: n.p., 1877. NUC

506. -----Gondaline's lesson. The warden's tale. Stories for children and other poems; by Mrs. Bloomfield Moore.
L: C.K. Paul & co., 1881. 226p. NUC OCLC
[Incl. some poems for children, but predominately adult: In memoriam, Voices of the past, The seasons, Sonnets, etc.]

507. -----Miscellaneous poems: Stories for children, The warden's tale, and Three eras in life.
Philadelphia: Pr. for priv. circ., 1875. 288p. NUC OCLC
[Misc. poetry]

508. -----Poems. A chapter from the modern pilgrim's progress. Slander and gossip.
Philadelphia: Pr. for priv. circ., 1882. 105p. NUC

509. -----The warden's tale; San Moritz; the Magdalene, and other poems.
L: Remington, 1883. 131p. OCLC

510. BLOUNT, Annie R. [Am. 19c]
Poems.
Augusta, GA: H.D. Norrell, 1860. 276p. NUC OCLC

511. BLOUNT, Lady Charlotte [Br. 19c]
The old palace, a retrospect, with other poems.
L: Chapman & Hall, 1876. 175p. BL OCLC

512. BLYTON, Emma [Br. 19c]
The pleasures of freedom. A poem.
L: Saunders, Otley & co., 1860. 53p. NUC BL OCLC

513. -----Poetical tributes to the memories of British bards, and other poems.
L: A.W. Bennett, 1858. NUC BL

514. BOATE, Mrs. Wellington [Br. 19c]
Carlo Marillo: and other poems, including national lyrics; or, Recollections of Ireland.
L: Judd, 1857. 163p. NUC

515. BODDINGTON, Mary [Br. 19c]
Poems.
L: Longmans & co., 1839. 412p. NUC BL

516. BOGART, Elizabeth [Am. b. 1806]
Driftings from the stream of life; a collection of fugitive poems.
NY: Hurd & Houghton; Boston: E.P. Dutton, 1866. 307p. NUC BL OCLC

517. BOIES, Lura Anna [Am. 1835-1859]
Rural rhymes, by Lura Ann Boies.
Saratoga Springs, NY?: Steam presses of G.M. Davison, 1859. 189p. NUC OCLC

BOLTON, Charles Knowles, co-author
<u>see</u> BOLTON, Sarah Elizabeth (Knowles)

518. BOLTON, Sarah Elizabeth (Knowles) [Am. 1841-1916] ALT: Knowles, Sarah Elizabeth
From heart and nature. With Charles Knowles Bolton.
NY: T.Y. Crowell & co., 1887. NUC OCLC
[61 pp. poems by her, 82 pp. by him]

519. -----The inevitable, and other poems.
NY & Boston: T.Y. Crowell & co., 1895. 100p. NUC BL

520. -----Orlean Lamar, and other poems.
NY: D. Appleton, 1864. 167p. NUC BL OCLC

521. BOLTON, Sarah Tittle (Barrett) [Am. 1814-1893]

The life and poems of Sarah T. Bolton.
Indianapolis, IN: F.L. Horton & co., 1880. 555p. NUC

522. -----Paddle your own canoe and other poems. Ed. John Clark Ridpath. With an introduction by Gen. Lew Wallace and a poem by James Whitcomb Riley.
Indianapolis, IN & Kansas City, MO: Bowen-Merrill co., 1897. 161p. NUC OCLC

523. -----Poems.
NY: Carleton, 1865. 300p. NUC

524. -----Songs of a lifetime. Intro. by General Lew Wallace and a poem by James Whitcomb Riley. Ed. John Clark Ridpath.
Indianapolis, IN: Bowen-Merrill co., 1892. 161p. NUC OCLC

BONAR, Horatius, co-author see BENNETT, Lucy Ann

525. BOND, Alessie [Br. 19c]
The Cairns of Iona, and other poems.
Dublin: George Herbert, 1873. 92p. NUC BL

526. -----Leaves.
Dublin: George Herbert, 1873. 101p. BL

527. -----The triumph of faith: and other poems.
Dublin: G. Herbert, 1870. 110p. NUC

528. BOND, Mrs. Henry [Br. 19c]
Miscellaneous poems.
L: Whittaker & co., 1838. 184p. BL

529. -----Sacred poems.
L: Whittaker & co., 1838? 159p. NUC BL
BOND, LEDA, pseud. see FELDSMITH, Mattie Doherty, Mrs.

530. BONHOTE, Elizabeth, Mrs. [Br. 1744-1818] PSEUD: Lady, A
Feeling, or Sketches from life; a desultory poem. With other pieces. By a lady.
Edinburgh: Manners & Miller; A. Constable & co.; L: Longman, Hurst, Rees, & Orme, 1810. 162p. NUC BL
[Feeling, pp. 1-120; also incl. narrative poems: The Maniac, The Misanthrope, Ode to Death]

BONNER, Katherine Sherwood see MCDOWELL, Katherine Sherwood (Bonner)

BONNER, Sherwood see MCDOWELL, Katherine Sherwood (Bonner)

531. BOOKER, Ellen [Br. 19c]
Meditations in poetry and prose.
L: Aylott & son, 1861. 92p. BL OCLC
[Religious poems & 15 brief prose pieces.]

532. BOONE, Susanna (Waring) [Br. 18/19c] ALT: Waring, Susanna
The minstrelsy of the woods; or, Sketches and songs connected with the natural history of some of the most interesting British and foreign birds.
L: Harvey & Darton, 1832. 227p. NUC BL

533. -----The wild garland: or, prose and verse illustrative of English wild flowers and forest trees.
L: n.p., 1837. BL

534. BOOT, Charlotte [Br. 19c]
The pirate; and other poems.
L: J.F. Hope, 1859. 79p. BL

535. BOOTH, Emma Scarr [Am. b. 1835]
The family of three, Iasuina, and other poems.
Buffalo, NY: C.W. Moulton, 1893. 398p. NUC OCLC
[Incl. poems of childhood, patriotism, the seasons, the affections, devotional poems, etc.]

BOOTH, Eva Selina Gore- see GORE-BOOTH, Eva Selina

536. BOOTH, Mary H. C., Mrs. [Am. 1831-1865] ALT: Chamberlain, Mary Booth PSEUD: Carlton, Carrie
Wayside blossoms among flowers from German gardens. By Mary H.C. Booth.
Milwaukee, WI: S.C. West, 1864. 190p. NUC BL
[70p. of orig. poems; 120p. trans. from German]

537. -----Wayside flowers. By Carrie Carlton.
Milwaukee, WI: Strickland & co., 1862. 163p. NUC BL OCLC

538. BORRON, Elizabeth Willesford (Mills) [Br. 19c] ALT: Mills, Elizabeth Willesford
Sybil's leaves: poems and sketches.
L: Longman, Rees, Orme & co. & G.B. Whittaker, 1826. 260p. NUC BL
[Chiefly poetry; four short prose pieces: 2 stories, 2 character sketches]

539. BORTHWICK, Jane Laurie [Br. 1813-1897]
Thoughtful hours.
L & Edinburgh: T. Nelson, 1863. 120p. NUC BL OCLC
[Enlargement of Thoughts for thoughtful hours]

540. -----Thoughts for thoughtful hours.
L: n.p., 1859. 36p. BL
[1st ed. 1857.]

541. BOSTWICK, Helen Louisa (Barron) [Am. 1826-1907]
Four-o'-clocks. Poems.
Philadelphia: E. Claxton & co., 1880. 111p. NUC OCLC

542. BOSWORTH, Elizabeth Asbyn [Am. 19c]
Poems.
Chicago: The author, 1893. 41p. NUC OCLC

543. BOTSFORD, Margaret, Mrs. [Am. 19c] PSEUD: Lady of Philadelphia, A
Viola; heiress of St. Valverde. An original poem, in five cantos. To which is annexed patriotic songs, sonnets, etc. By a lady of Philadelphia.
Louisville, KY: Pr. S. Penn, jr., 1820. 96p. NUC BL OCLC
[2d ed. Philadelphia: R. Desilver, T. Town, pr., 1829. 198p. NUC BL OCLC]

544. BOTTA, Anne Charlotte (Lynch) [Br. 1815-1891] ALT: Lynch, Anne Charlotte
Memoirs of Anne C.L. Botta, written by her friends. With selections from her correspondence and from her writings in prose and poetry. Ed. Vincenzo Botta.
NY: J.S. Tait & sons, 1894. 459p. NUC BL OCLC
[22 short poems; selections from her journal & letters]

545. -----Poems. By Anne C. Lynch.
NY: G.P. Putnam, 1849. 189p. NUC BL OCLC
[New ed. enl. NY: G.P. Putnam, 1852. 203p. NUC OCLC]

546. -----Rhode Island book. 1841. Selections in prose and verse from the writings of Rhode Island citizens, including several original pieces. By Anne C. Lynch.
Providence, RI: H. Fuller; Boston: Week, Jordan & co., 1841. 352p. NUC OCLC
[2 poems by Lynch.]

BOTTA, Vincenzo, ed. see BOTTA, Anne Charlotte (Lynch)

547. BOULGER, Margaret C. [Am. 19c]
The fiat of faith, or ambition's dream.
Minneapolis, MN: Harmon & Moe, pr., 1887. 298p. NUC OCLC
[Civil War narrative poem, 24 p., and misc. lyrics]

548. BOURKE, Hannah Maria [Br. 19c]
O'Donoghue, Prince of Killarney; a poem: in seven cantos.
Dublin: W. Curry, 1830. 284p. NUC OCLC
[Epic poem about historical figure]

549. BOURNE, Isabella [Br. 19c] ALT: Bovine, Isabella
Lays of labour's leisure hours.
L: Judd & Glass, 1858. 224p. BL
[67 poems and a 56p. novelette. Working class author]

550. BOURNE, Jane [Br. 19c]
A companion to the Noah's ark, being conversations between a mother and her children, on the animals contained in the ark, interspersed with pieces of poetry and remarks on heathen mythology, particularly that of the Egyptians.
Swaffham: F. Skill, 1833. 165p. NUC

551. -----Northern reminiscences.
Whitehaven: J. Robinson, 1832. 145p. BL
[Tour of northern England where she grew up. Poetry and prose]

552. BOURNE, Mary Anne [Br. 19c]
The evergreen: a miscellaneous collection of original poetry.
L: Whittaker & co., 1839. 252p. BL OCLC
[Nature & occasional poetry; some written "at a very early age"]

553. BOUTELLE, Ann L. [Am. 1819-1835]
Biographical sketch of Ann L. Boutelle.
Boston: Benjamin H. Greene, 1836. 35p. NUC
[Incl. brief excerpts from her poetry]

BOVINE, Isabella see BOURNE, Isabella

554. BOWDEN, Hannah Marsh [Br. 1823-1859]

Poetical remains of Hannah Bowden, of Croydon, formerly Hannah Marsh ... Ed. her sister, Priscilla Marsh.
L: A.W. Bennett, 1860. 230p. NUC BL OCLC
[Religious poetry, member of Society of Friends]

555. BOWDLER, Henrietta Maria [Br. 1754-1830]
Creation, and other poems: to which are added, The Bowers of happiness, a vision, and an essay on sacred poetry.
L: Cadell & Davies; Hatchard, 1818. 155p. BL
[Creation pp. 11-46; occasional poems. Bowers, a prose allegory, pp. 95-123]
BOWDLER, Henrietta Maria, ed. <u>see</u> SMITH, Elizabeth

556. BOWEN, Harriet M. (Gardiner) [Am. 1832-1852] ALT: Brown, Harriet M. (Gardiner)
A brief memoir of Harriet, with some of her essays in prose and verse. By her mother, Mrs. William Gardiner [Marilla (Dunton) Gardiner].
Oberlin, OH?: J.M. Fitch, 1855. 129p. NUC OCLC
[OCLC lists Bowen as Brown]

557. BOWEN, Melesina [Br. 19c]
Kenilworth Castle, and other poems.
L & Wellington: F. Houlston & son, 1818. 111p. NUC BL

558. -----Ystradffin, a descriptive poem.
L: Longman, Orme, Brown, Green & Longmans; Llandovery: W. Rees, 1839. 189p. NUC BL OCLC
[Narrative poem recounting Welsh history & legends]

BOWEN-GRAVES, Frances E., co-author <u>see</u> OWEN, Frances Mary (Synge)

559. BOWES, Emily [Br. 19c] ALT: B., E.
Hymns and sacred poems. By E.B. 2d ser. Bath: A.E. Binns; L: Hamilton, Adams & co., 1834. 110p. NUC BL

BOWLES, Caroline Anne <u>see</u> SOUTHEY, Caroline Anne (Bowles)

560. BOWLES, Emily [Br. 19/20c]
The three kings, and other poems.
L: Burns & Oates, 1874. 135p. BL

561. BOWLES, Mrs. George Cranley [Br. 19c]
Life's dissolving views.
L: Trubner & co., 1865. 108p. NUC BL
[One essay and 75p. of poems, chiefly religious]

562. BOWMAN, Anne [Br. 19c]
The Norman invasion, and the Day of Rinrory. Poems.
L: Richardson bros., 1857. 78p. BL OCLC

563. -----Rhymes from the shadows.
Guelph, Ontario: n.p., 18--? 15p. NUC

564. BOWMAN, Henrietta [Br. 1838-1872] ALT: Bowman, Hetty
Songs amid the shadows. By Hetty Bowman.
L: Simpkin, Marshall & co., 1871. 72p. NUC BL OCLC

565. -----Speaking yet: or, Remains in prose and verse of the late Hetty Bowman. Ed. M.M. Gordon.
L: Book society; Bristol: W. Mack, 1874. 157p. BL
[88p. of poetry; 69p. essays on religious topics]

BOWMAN, Hetty <u>see</u> BOWMAN, Henrietta

BOWYER, R., comp. <u>see</u> BENGER, Elizabeth Ogilvie

566. BOYD, Elizabeth [Br. 18c] PSEUD: Louisa
Admiral Haddock: or, the progress of Spain. A poem.
L: J. Applebee, sold by Elizabeth Boyd, 1740? 14p. NUC BL

567. -----Altamira's ghost; or, Justice triumphant. A new ballad.
L: Charles Corbett, pr., 1744. 8p. BL OCLC

568. -----Don Sancho: or, the student's whim, a ballad opera of two acts, with Minerva's triumph, a masque.
L: C. Corbet, the booksellers of L & Westminster, 1739. 20p. NUC BL

569. -----Glory to the highest, a Thanksgiving poem, on the late victory at Dettingen. To which is subjoin'd a sacred hymn on the same occasion.
L: The author, 1739. 8p. BL

570. -----The happy North-Briton. A poem. On the marriage of His Grace the Duke of Hamilton and Brandon with Miss Spencer.
L: The author, 1737. 4p. NUC

571. -----The humourous miscellany; or, Riddles for the beaux.
L: J. Slow, 1733. 32p. NUC BL

572. -----Truth, a poem. Address'd to the Right Honourable William Lord Harrington.
L: The author, 1740. 8p. BL

573. -----Variety: a poem, in two cantos ... To which is annex'd an answer to an Ovid's epistle. By Louisa.
Westminster: T. Warner & B. Creake, 1727. 92p. OCLC

574. -----Verses most humbly inscrib'd to His Majesty King George IId on his birthday.
L: n.p., 1730. 6p. NUC BL

575. BOYD, Nellie [Am. 19c] PSEUD: Idler, An
Vagabond rhymes, by an idler.
Boston: J.G. Cupples co., 1892. 110p. NUC

576. BOYDEN, Emily Maria (Blakeslee) [Am. b. 1828]
Intermittent thoughts, by Mrs. Emily M. Blakeslee Boyden.
Chicago: Union pub. co., 1897. 127p. NUC OCLC

577. BOYDEN, Helen F. [Am. 19c]
Echoes of peace.
NY: G.L. Shearer, c1889. 83p. NUC OCLC

578. BOYES, Mrs. [Br. 19c]
Widow Gray: a ballad for humble homes.
L: Emily Faithfull, 1864. 16p. BL

579. BOYLAN, Grace Duffie [Am. 1861?-1935]
If Tam O'Shanter'd had a wheel, and other poems and sketches.
NY: E.R. Herrick & co.; Chicago: Palmer & co., 1898. 112p. NUC OCLC
[Light-hearted poems and stories, not juvenile. 2d ed., expanded, NY: E.R. Herrick, 1898. 222p. NUC OCLC]

580. -----The old house, and other poems and sketches.
Chicago: Palmer & co.; NY: E.R. Herrick & co., 1897. 112p. NUC OCLC
[Incl. in a larger collection, If Tam O'Shanter'd ....]

BOYLE, Emily Charlotte (DeBurgh-Canning), Countess of Cork and Orrery see CORK AND ORRERY, Emily Charlotte (DeBurgh-Canning) Boyle, Countess of

581. BOYLE, Esmeralda [Am. b. 1840]
Songs of the land and sea.
NY: E.J. Hale & son, 1875. 76p. NUC OCLC

582. -----The story of Felice.
L: Trubner & co., 1873. 55p. BL OCLC
[Civil war narrative]

583. -----Thistle-down.
Philadelphia: J.B. Lippincott & co., 1871. 150p. NUC OCLC

584. BOYLE, Lady Henrietta [Br. 18c]
A poem sacred to the memory of the Lady Harriot Boyle.
Dublin: Halhed Garland, 1747. 24p. BL

585. BOYLE, Margaret [Am. 19c]
Johnstown flood.
Steubenville, OH: Press of W.W. MacKay, 1889. 4p. NUC

586. BOYLE, Mary Louisa [Br. 1810-1890]
The bridal of Melcha; a dramatic sketch.
L: Henry Colburn, 1844. 133p. NUC BL
[Not written for performance. 4 acts, based on an Irish legend.]

587. -----My portrait gallery, and other poems.
L: Priv. pr., 1849. 50p. BL

588. BOYLE, Sarah Roberts [Am. 19c]
ALT: Roberts, Sarah
The voice of the grass. By Sarah Roberts.
Boston: L. Prang & co., 1887. 102p. NUC OCLC

589. BOYLE, Virginia Frazer [Am. 1863-1938]
The other side, an historic poem.
Cambridge, MA: Pr. at the Riverside press, 1893. 64p. NUC OCLC
[Civil War poem, Southern side]

590. BOYNTON, Julia P. [Am. 19c]
Lines and interlines.
NY & L: G.P. Putnam's sons, 1887. 103p. NUC BL OCLC

591. BRACKENBURY, Catherine Ada [Br. 19c]
A legacy of verse. Ed. Sir Henry Brackenbury.
L: G. Routledge & sons, 1893. 192p. BL

BRACKENBURY, Sir Henry, ed. see BRACKENBURY, Catherine Ada

592. BRADBURN, Eliza Weaver [Br. 19c]
The endless story in rhyme.
L: the author, 1843. 36p. BL

593. BRADBURY, Mary R. [Am. 19c]
Cochituate Park, and other poems.
Cambridge, MA: Riverside press, 1882. 71p. NUC

BRADDON, Mary Elizabeth see MAXWELL, Mary Elizabeth (Braddon)

594. BRADFIELD, Mary Bertha [Br. 19c]
Songs of faith and hope and love.
L: C.H. Kelly, 1898. 112p. BL

BRADFORD, Annie Chambers see KETCHUM, Annie (Chambers) Bradford

595. BRADFORD, Nellie Knight, Mrs. [Am. 19c] ALT: B., N. K.
Elberon; or, The ride for life. By N.K.B.
Washington, D.C.: R.H. Darby, pr., 1881. 11p. NUC
[About Pres. Garfield]

596. -----Songs of real children.
Springfield, MA: C.W. Bryan & co., 1877. 40p. NUC BL

597. BRADLEE, Lucy Hall [Am. 19c]
Christus Victor.
Boston: William Spencer, 1865. 28p. NUC OCLC

598. -----Max Overmann.
Boston: W.V. Spencer, 1866. 64p. NUC OCLC

599. -----Three crowns.
Boston: Spencer, 1866. 134p. NUC

BRADLEY, Gertrude M., co-author see MARK, Amy

600. BRADLEY, Kate A. [Am. 19c]
Songs in the night.
Buffalo, NY: C.W. Moulton, 1894. 46p. NUC OCLC

601. BRADLEY, Katherine Harris [Br. 1843-1914] PSEUD: Field, Michael [With Edith Emma Cooper, Br. 1862-1913]; Leigh, Arran
Long ago. By Michael Field.
L: G. Bell, 1889. 132p. NUC BL OCLC
[Poems based on Sappho]

602. -----The new minnesinger and other poems. By Arran Leigh.
L: Longmans, Green & co., 1875. 174p. BL OCLC

603. -----Noontide branches. A small sylvan drama interspersed with songs and invocations. By Michael Field.
Oxford: Pr. H. Daniel, 1899. 44p. NUC BL OCLC
[1-act drama in verse]

604. -----Sight and song. By Michael Field.
L: E. Mathews & J. Lane, 1892. 125p. NUC BL OCLC

605. -----Underneath the bough; a book of verses. By Michael Field.
L & NY: G. Bell; Chiswick press, 1893. 135p. NUC OCLC

606. BRADLEY, Mary Emily (Neely) [Am. 1835-1898]
Hidden sweetness.
NY & Boston: Roberts bros., 1886. 64p. NUC OCLC

BRADLEY, Thomas Bibb, co-author see PLEASANTS, Julia

BRADNACK, Isaac R., co-author see BRADNACK, Mary Anne

607. BRADNACK, Mary Anne [Br. 19c]
Lays of the valley. With Isaac R. Bradnack.
L: J. Mason, 1843. 108p. BL

608. BRADSTREET, Anna [Br. 19c]
The six legends of King Golden Star.
L: Smith, Elder & co., 1858. 216p. BL

609. BRADSTREET, Anne (Dudley) [Am. 1612-1672]
Several poems ... .
Boston: Pr. J. Foster, 1678. 255p. NUC BL
[1st Am. ed. of The tenth muse. 2d ed. of her poems]

610. -----The tenth muse lately sprung up in America. Or severall poems, compiled with great variety of wit and learning, full of delight ... By a gentlewoman in those parts (Anne Bradstreet).
L: Stephen Bowtell, 1650. 207p. 255p. NUC BL
[First ed. of her poems]

611. -----The works of Anne Bradstreet in prose and verse. Ed. John Harvard Ellis.
Charlestown, MA: A.E. Cutter, 1867. 434p. NUC BL OCLC
[The 'Poems' are printed from 2d ed., pub. in Boston, 1678. Incl. prose, misc. & relig. poetry]

612. BRADT, Edith Virginia [Am. 19/20c]
For the quiet hour.
Philadelphia: H. Altemus, 1897. 32p. NUC OCLC

613. BRAGG, Jane [Br. 19c]
Extracts on various subjects, religious and secular. Selected and original.
L: Darton & Hodge, 1862. 112p. BL
[Includes original religious poetry]

614. -----Lays of early years.
L: n.p., 1839. 94p. BL

615. BRAIKENRIDGE, Isabella M. [Br. 19c] ALT: B., I. M.
The lady's bay, and other poems. By I.M.B.
L: Thomas Bosworth, 1853. 71p. BL

616. BRAINARD, Mary [Am. 19c]
Esther Gray and other poems.
Rockford, IL: Gazette steam book & job pr. house, 1871. 160p. OCLC NUC

617. -----Heart offerings: a book of poems.
Rockford, IL: Golden Censer co., 1881. 288p. NUC OCLC

618. -----Memorial pictures of war and peace.
Rockford, IL: Gazette steam pr. house, 1873. 208p. NUC OCLC
[Narrative poems, incl. one on Civil War, and religious lyrics]

619. BRAITHWAITE, Adeline [Br. 19c]
Scripture spoil in sacred song.
L: J. Nisbet, 1886. 119p. BL

620. BRAMHALL, Mae St. John [19c]
Japanese jingles: being a few little verses.
Tokyo: T. Hasegawa, 1891. 66 l. NUC BL OCLC
[Prev. pr. in the "Japan Gazette." Also pub. as: Niponese rhymes and Japanese jingles. L: S. Low, Marston & co., 1892? 61p. NUC]

621. BRAMSTON, Mary [Br. 19c]
The little treasure book of hymns and poems.
L: Wells Gardner & co., 1891. 63p. BL

BRAND, Barbarina Ogle Wilmot, Baroness Dacre <u>see</u> WILMOT, Barbarina, Baroness Dacre

622. BRAND, Hannah [Br. d. 1821]
Plays and poems.
L: F. & C. Rivington; Norwich: Beatniffe & Payne, 1798. 424p. NUC BL OCLC
[6 poems, incl. The tale of The Monk of LaTrappe.]

BRAND, LOUIS, pseud. <u>see</u> BIGG, Louisa

623. BRANHAM, Adelia Pope- [Am. 19/20c]
Grandma tales and others.
Greenfield, IN: n.p., 1899. 42p. NUC OCLC
[15 poems, some depicting life in Grandma's day, a few in dialect]

BRAY, Mrs., comp. <u>see</u> COLLING, Mary Maria

624. BREESE, Carrie A. [Am. 19c]
Many days, and other poems.
Dover, NJ: "The Iron Era," 1886. 53p. NUC OCLC

625. BREMONT, Anna (Dunphy), Comtesse de [Br. 19/20c]
Love poems.
Capetown: Argus pr. co., 1889. 80p.

626. -----Sonnets and love poems.
NY: Press of J.J. Little & co., 1892. 121p. NUC BL OCLC

BRERETON, Charlotte, co-author <u>see</u> BRERETON, Jane

627. BRERETON, Jane [Br. 1685-1740] PSEUD: Melissa
Poems on several occasions, with letters to her friends and an account of her life.
L: Edward Cave, 1744. 303p. NUC BL
[Incl. 2 poems by her daughter, Charlotte Brereton (Br. b. c1720), under the pseud. "Carolina."]

628. BRETT, Helena [Br. 19c]
Emmanuel.
L: J.T. Hayes, 1875. 32p. BL

629. BRETTELL, Mrs. [Br. 19c]
Meriden; or, Memoirs of Matilda.
L: R. Edwards, 1819. 134p. NUC

630. -----Susan Ashfield and other poems.
L: Richard Edwards, 1820. 101p. NUC BL

631. BREWSTER, Clara Evelyn S. [Am. 19c]
Wayside blossoms.
Montrose, PA: C.E.S. Brewster, 1899. 31p. NUC

BREWSTER, Margaret Maria <u>see</u> GORDON, Margaret Maria (Brewster)

632. BREWSTER, Martha Wadsworth [Am. 1710-c1759]
Poems on divers subjects.
New London, CT: Pr. & sold by John Green; Boston: Sold by Edes & Gill, 1757. 35p. NUC OCLC

633. BRIDGES, Sallie [Am. 19c]
Marble isle, legends of the round table, and other poems.
Philadelphia: J.B. Lippincott, 1864. 272p. NUC OCLC

BRIGGS, Caroline Atherton <u>see</u> MASON, Caroline Atherton (Briggs)

634. BRIGGS, Edith [Br. 19c]
"Little feet".
L: Simpkin & Marshall, 1893. 12p. BL

BRIGHTWELL, Cecelia Lucy, ed. <u>see</u> OPIE, Amelia (Alderson)

635. BRINE, E., Mrs. [Br. 19c]
Allington, and other poems.
L: Simpkin, Marshall & co.; Swansea: C.F. Edwards, 1884. 255p. BL

636. BRINE, Mary Dow (Northam) [Am. 19/20c]
From gold to grey. Being poems and pictures of life and nature. NY: Cassell & co., 1886. 192p. NUC BL OCLC

637. -----Grandma's attic treasures; a story of old-time memories.
NY: E.P. Dutton & co., 1882. 94p. NUC BL OCLC

638. -----Grandma's memories.
NY: E.P. Dutton & co., 1888. 47p. DLC

639. -----The home concert.
NY: Cassell & co., 1885. 10 l. NUC

640. -----Madge, the violet girl, and other poems.
NY: G.W. Harlan, 1881. 114p. NUC OCLC

641. -----Memories of home. Poems and pictures of life and nature.
NY: Cassell pub. co., 1890. 80p. DLC

642. -----A mother's song.
NY: Cassell & co., 1886. 42p. NUC OCLC

643. -----My boy and I; or, on the road to slumberland.
Cambridge, MA: J. Wilson and son, 1881. 60 l. NUC OCLC

644. -----Somebody's mother. A poem.
L: E. Nister; NY: E. P. Dutton & co., 1891. 12p. NUC BL

645. -----The story of Aunt Patience.
NY: E.P. Dutton & co., 1893. 110p. NUC OCLC

646. -----Sunny hours.
NY: Am. Tract soc., 1899. 46p. NUC

647. -----"Sunshine" and other poems and pictures of life and nature.
Boston & Chicago: United Society of Christian Endeavor, 1899. 62p. NUC
[All misc. poems]

648. -----Thoughts and fancies; poems and pictures of life and nature.
NY: Cassell pub. co., 1891. 80p. NUC OCLC

649. -----Uncle Amos and his Christmas gifts.
NY: T.E.D. Darling, 1887. 28p. NUC

650. -----A wish for Christmas and the New Year.
NY: n.p., 1886. NUC

651. BRINTON, Bulah, Mrs. [Am. 19c]
Behold the woman. Parable sequel to Man is love.
Milwaukee, WI: Pub. for the author by Bay New Herald pub. co., 1886. 171p. NUC BL
[Religious allegory in poetry and prose, 20 cantos; also misc. poetry and prose]

652. BRISTOL, Augusta Cooper [Am. 1835-1910]
Poems.
Boston: Adams & co., 1868. 190p. NUC BL OCLC

653. -----The web of life.
Buffalo, NY: C.W. Moulton, 1895. 71p. NUC OCLC

654. BRISTOW, Amelia [Br. 19c]
The maniac, a tale; or, A view of Bethlehem Hospital; and The merits of women, a poem from the French, with poetical pieces ... original and translated.
L: J. Hatchard, 1810. 145p. NUC BL OCLC
[Chiefly original lyric & occasional verse. Three beast fables trans. from Dorat.]

655. -----The scrapbook: containing a variety of prose and verse. Chiefly original.

L: R.B. Seeley, 1833. 115p. NUC
[8 religious poems; essays on Jewish beliefs]

BRITISH MATRON, A, pseud. see JONES, Hannah Watts-

656. BRITTINGHAM, Florence Virginia (Shearer) [Am. 1856-1891]
Verse and story.
Buffalo, NY: C.W. Moulton, 1892. 220p. NUC OCLC
[Poems and short stories]

657. BRITTLE, Emilly [Br. 18c]
The Indiaguide; or, Journal of a voyage to the East Indies in the year MDCCLXXX in a poetical epistle.
Calcutta: Pr. George Gordon, 1785. 79p. NUC BL OCLC
[Includes other poems]

658. BRITTON, Frances [Br. 19c]
Short and true sketches on the conflicts of life and other subjects.
L: the author, 1828. 16p. BL
[Poetry about poverty & England]

659. BROADUS, Annie Maud [Am. 1867-1897]
Poems.
NY: n.p., 1897-1900. 152p. NUC OCLC

660. BRODIE, Elizabeth Rowton [19c]
Miscellaneous poems.
Hereford: Hereford Times, 1880? 46p. NUC BL OCLC

661. BROMFIELD, Elizabeth [Br. 19c]
Recollections of Brittany, in prose and verse.
L: James Blackwood, 1863. 201p. BL
[5 poems; essays on Roman Catholicism]

BRONTË, Anne, co-author see BRONTË, Charlotte

662. BRONTË, Charlotte [Br. 1816-1855] PSEUD: Bell, Currer
Poems by Currer, Ellis [Emily Jane Brontë (1818-1848)], and Acton [Anne Brontë (1820-1849)] Bell.
L: Smith, Elder & co., 1846. NUC BL

BRONTË, Emily Jane, co-author see BRONTË, Charlotte

BROOKE, Caris, co-author see BLAND, Edith (Nesbit)

663. BROOKE, Elizabeth Tilghman, Mrs. [Am. 19c]
The days of sixty-three.
Philadelphia: the benefit of the Sanitary Commission by C. Sherman son & co., 1864. 54p. NUC BL OCLC
[Poem on U.S. Civil War]

BROOKE, Frances Moore see BROOKE, Frances More

664. BROOKE, Frances More [Moore NUC], Mrs. John Brooke [Br. 1724?-1789]
Virginia, a tragedy, with odes, pastorals, and translations.
L: The Author, 1756. 159p. NUC BL
[5-act verse tragedy, based on story of Appius & Virginia. Two pastorals, dialogues, p. 131-38; 10 odes; trans. of Guarine's poems.]

665. BROOKS, Constantina E. [Am. 19c]
Ballads and translations.
NY & L: D. Appleton & co., 1866. 144p. NUC BL OCLC
[22 original ballads & 10 trans. from Anacreon, Alcestis, and Norwegian folk legends.]

666. BROOKS, Louise Winsor [Am. 1835-1892]
A year's sonnets.
Boston: n.p., c1855. 18p. NUC
BROOKE, Mrs. John see BROOKE, Frances More

BROOKS, James Gordon, co-author see BROOKS, Mary Elizabeth (Aiken)

BROOKS, Mrs. James Gordon see BROOKS, Mary Elizabeth (Aiken)

667. BROOKS, Maria A. (Gowen) [Am. 1795-1845] PSEUD: Lover of the Fine Arts, A
Judith, Esther, and other poems. By a lover of the fine arts.
Boston: Cummings & Hilliard, 1820. 112p. NUC OCLC

668. -----Zophiel, a poem. By Mrs. Brooks.
Boston: Richardson & Lord, 1825. 70p. NUC BL OCLC

669. BROOKS, Maria Sears, Mrs. [Am. d. 1893]
A vision of the mistletoe.
Buffalo, NY: Press of Moulton, Wenborne & co., 1888. 13 l. NUC

670. BROOKS, Mary Elizabeth (Aiken), Mrs. James Gordon Brooks [Am. 19c]
PSEUD: Norma
The rivals of Este. By James Gordon Brooks and Mary E. Brooks.

NY: J. & J. Harper, 1829. 260p. NUC BL OCLC

671. BROOKS, Sarah Warner, Mrs. [Am. d. 1906]
Blanche; or, The legend of the angel tower.
NY: Budd & Carleton, 1861. 43p. NUC OCLC

672. -----Even-songs, and other poems.
Boston: Little, Brown, & co., 1868. 100p. NUC OCLC

673. -----The legend of St. Christopher, and other poems.
Providence, RI: G.H. Whitney, 1859. 172p. NUC OCLC

674. BROTHERSON, Frances Bennett (McReynolds) [Am. 19c]
Poems.
Peoria, IL: Press of Franks & sons, 1880. 518p. NUC OCLC

675. BROTHERTON, Alice Williams [Am. 1848-1930]
Beyond the veil.
Chicago: Charles H. Kerr & co., 1886. 14p. NUC OCLC

676. -----The sailing of King Olaf, and other poems.
Chicago: C.H. Kerr & co., 1887. 145p. NUC BL

677. BROTHERTON, Mary Isabella Irwin [Br. 19c]
Poems.
2d ed. Brussels: J.H. Briard, 1855. 118p. BL

678. -----Rosemary for remembrance.
L: J. Lane, 1895. 75p. NUC BL

679. BROWN, Alice [Am. 1857-1948]
The road to Castaly.
Boston: Copeland & Day, 1896. 70p. NUC OCLC

680. -----The rose of hope.
Cambridge: J. Wilson & son, pr., 1896. 15p. NUC OCLC

681. BROWN, Annie Johnson- [Br. 19c]
Myths of the dawn. Poems by A. Johnson-Brown and other members of the Daisy Guild.
L: Kegan Paul, Trench & co., 1885. 123p. BL
[Primarily by Brown: "Myths of the Dawn," misc. poems & translations. Also incl. poems by: Elsie Higgins, Bertha Synge, Alice Greenwood, Mrs. James Owen, Mrs. Van Glenn]

682. -----Rejected of men, and other poems.
L: Sampson Low & co., 1890. 87p. BL

683. BROWN, Carrie L. [Am. 19c]
Poems by a girl of fifteen.
Boston: C.M. Brown, 1867. 112p. NUC OCLC

684. BROWN, Elizabeth [Am. fl. 1815]
Lines on the unfortunate persons who were drowned in the Delaware, March 19, 1815.
Philadelphia: n.p., 1815. 8p. NUC

685. BROWN, Elizabeth [Br. 19c]
Original poems.
New ed. Northampton: The author, 1842. 24p. BL

686. BROWN, Ellen Anne Boyer- [Br. 19c]
The true story of the sisters of Reculver.
L: E. Boyer-Brown, 1897. 12p. BL

687. BROWN, Emma Elizabeth [Am. b. 1847] PSEUD: E., B.E.
Huldah; a daughter of the revolution, and other poems of American patriotism. By Emma E. Brown.
Boston: Lothrop pub. co., 1897. 77p. NUC OCLC

688. -----A hundred years ago, by B.E.E.
Boston: D. Lothrop & co., 1876. 42p. NUC OCLC
[Romantic poetic narrative of Revolutionary War]

BROWN, Harriet M. (Gardiner) <u>see</u> BOWEN, Harriet M. (Gardiner)

689. BROWN, Helen E., Mrs. [Am. 19c]
Easter lilies.
Richfield Springs, NY: n.p., n.d. 1p. NUC

690. -----Songs by the way.
NY: H.H.B. Angell, 1888. 72p. NUC OCLC
[Religious poetry]

691. BROWN, Lelah Harrison [Am. 19/20c]
A book of poems. The golden rod.
St. Louis, MO: n.p., c1892. 70p. NUC OCLC

692. -----The golden leaf, poems.

2d ed. St. Louis, MO: Klug & Sterling, c1899. 33p. NUC

693. BROWN, Margaret [Br. 19c]
Lays of affection.
Edinburgh: Waugh & Innes, 1819. 224p. BL

694. BROWN, Mary [Br. 19c]
Lines on the trip promoted by the members of the Littleborough and Smallbridge Reform Clubs ... 1888, to Chester and Hawarden, the residence of the right Hon. W.E. Gladstone, M.P.
Littleborough: Wm. Brown, 1888. BL

695. -----A pleasant remembrance of my visit to the Manchester Royal Jubilee Exhibition of 1887 in 52 verses.
Littleborough: Wm. Brown, 1888. 11p. BL

696. BROWN, Mary Chadwick (Barrett) [Am. 1827-1887]
Poems and charades.
NY: Press of J.J. Little & co., 1888. 215p. NUC OCLC
[Charades are poetic puzzles, not for acting]

697. BROWN, Mary Eugenia [Br. 19c]
ALT: Mary Eugenia
Crumbs from the table of the muses.
L: Elliot Stock, 1873. 205p. BL

698. -----The months in floral costume. The floral meeting, etc. By Mary Eugenia.
L: n.p., 1850? BL

699. BROWN, Minnie Frances [Am. 19/20c]
The harvest rune, a thanks-giving entertainment; original verse and prose.
Chicago: A. Flanagan, 1899. 61p. NUC OCLC
[Pub. in special issue of "The teacher's helper."]

700. BROWN, Nellie Larue, Mrs. [Am. 19c]
Brother Aleck.
Louisville, KY: n.p., 1896. 15p. NUC OCLC

BROWN, Sara Hall, ed. <u>see</u> WHITTEN, Mary Delano

BROWNE, Charlotte Elizabeth <u>see</u> TONNA, Charlotte Elizabeth (Browne) Phelan

BROWNE, Felicia Dorothea <u>see</u> HEMANS, Felicia Dorothea (Browne)

701. BROWNE, Frances [Br. 19c]
Lyrics and miscellaneous poems.
Edinburgh: Sutherland & Knox, 1848. 144p. BL

702. -----Pictures and songs of home.
L: T. Nelson & sons, 1856. BL

703. -----The star of Atteghei; the vision of Schwartz; and other poems.
L: Edward Moxon, 1844. 261p. BL

704. BROWNE, Frances Elizabeth [Am. 1816-1879]
Poems.
Cambridge, MA: Metcalf & co., 1846. 155p. NUC BL OCLC

705. -----Ruth: a sacred drama, and original lyrical poems.
NY: Wynkoop & Hollenbeck, 1871. 121p. NUC
[Prose drama for performance. Misc. lyric poems]

BROWNE, Isaac Hawkins, ed. <u>see</u> LEAPOR, Mary, Mrs.

706. BROWNE, Isabella [Br. 19c]
Poems.
Bath: S. Hayward, 1854. 32p. NUC

BROWNE, Jane Euphemia <u>see</u> SAXBY, Jane Euphemia (Browne)

707. BROWNE, Lucy Lovina [Am. 19c]
Prophetic visions of national events and spirit communications.
Oakland, CA: The author, 1882. 158p. NUC OCLC
[Includes poems]

708. BROWNE, Martha Griffith [Am. d. 1906] ALT: Griffith, Mattie
Poems, by Mattie Griffith; now first collected.
NY & L: D. Appleton & co., 1853. 167p. NUC OCLC

BROWNE, Mary Ann <u>see</u> GRAY, Mary Ann (Browne)

BROWNE, Sara Hall, ed. <u>see</u> WHITTEN, Mary Delano

709. BROWNELL, Anna Gertrude (Hall) [Am. b. 1863] ALT: Brownell, Gertrude Hall; Hall, Gertrude
Age of fairy gold. By Gertrude Hall.
Boston: Little, Brown & co.; L: Gay & Bird, 1899. 79p. NUC BL OCLC

[66 misc. poems]

710. -----Allegretto.
Boston: Roberts bros., 1894. 111p. NUC OCLC

711. -----Verses.
NY: J.W. Lovell & co.; L: D. Heinemann, 1890. 125p. NUC BL OCLC

BROWNELL, Gertrude (Hall) see BROWNELL, Anna Gertrude (Hall)

712. BROWNING, Elizabeth (Barrett), Mrs. Robert Browning [Br. 1806-1861]
ALT: Barrett, Elizabeth
Aurora Leigh.
L: Chapman & Hall, 1856. 403p. BL

713. -----The Battle of Marathon. A poem.
L: W. Lindsell, 1820. 72p. NUC BL OCLC

714. -----Casa Guidi windows. A poem.
1st ed. L: Chapman & Hall, 1851. 140p. NUC BL OCLC

715. -----Elizabeth Barrett Browning's poetical works.
NY: Crowell, 1856. 520p. 12th ed. L: Smith, Elder, & co., 1866. NUC OCLC

716. -----An essay on mind, with other poems.
L: James Duncan, 1826. 152p. NUC BL OCLC

717. -----Last poems. Ed. Robert Browning.
L: Chapman and Hall, 1862. 142p. NUC BL OCLC

718. -----Poems before Congress.
L: Chapman and Hall, 1860. 65p. NUC BL OCLC

719. -----Poems by E. Barrett Browning.
L: E. Moxon, 1844. 2v. NUC BL OCLC
[Another ed. pub. as: A drama of exile: and other poems. NY: H.G. Langley, 1845. 2v. NUC BL OCLC]

720. -----Poems by E. Browning.
New ed. L: Chapman and Hall, 1850. 2v. NUC BL OCLC

721. -----Prometheus bound (translated) and miscellaneous poems, by the translator.
L: A.J. Valpy, 1833. 163p. NUC OCLC

722. -----The runaway slave at Pilgrim's Point.
L: Edward Moxon, 1849. 26p. NUC OCLC
[First printed in The Liberty bell. By friends of freedom. Boston: American Anti-slavery soc., 1848.]

723. -----The Seraphim and other poems.
1st ed. L: Saunders & Otley, 1838. 360p. NUC BL OCLC

724. -----Two poems. With Robert Browning.
L: Chapman & Hall, 1854. 15p. NUC OCLC
[Contents: "A plea for the ragged schools of London," by E.B. Browning. "The twins 'Give' and 'it shall be given unto you.'" By Robert Browning]

725. BRUCE, Charlotte Ann Brownsword [Br. 19c]
Poems. Ed. Andrew Leslie.
Calcutta: Baptist Mission press, 1846. 111p. BL

BROWNING, Mrs. Robert see BROWNING, Elizabeth (Barrett)

BROWNING, Robert, co-author see BROWNING, Elizabeth (Barrett)

726. BRUCE, Mrs. Henry [Br. 19c]
Scripture sonnets.
L & Cambridge: Macmillan & co., 1863. 86p. BL OCLC

727. BRUCE, Jane [Br. 19c]
Poems on various subjects ... printed for private distribution by ... William Downing Bruce ... and Robert Cathcart Dalrymple Bruce.
Edinburgh: T.G. Stevenson, 1857. 11p. BL

728. -----Sacred poems. Ed. her son, William Downing Bruce.
L: R. Groombridge, 1846. 47p. BL OCLC

BRUCE, Rev. William, comp. see BURMAN, Ellen Elizabeth

BRUCE, William Downing, ed. see BRUCE, Jane

729. BRYAN, Hannah M. [Am. 19c]
Dreams and aspirations, a collection of poems.
Saguache, CO: Crescent press, 1896. 83p. NUC OCLC

730. BRYAN, J. M., Mrs. [Am. 19c]

"Nellie." A summer rhyme.
NY: G.P. Putnam's sons, 1882. 55p.
NUC OCLC

731. BRYAN, Mary, Mrs. [Br. 19c]
Sonnets and metrical tales. By Mrs. Bryan.
Bristol: Pr. & sold at City pr. off., 1815. 141p. NUC BL

732. BRYAN, Mary (Edwards) [Am. 1846?-1913]
Poems and stories in verse.
Atlanta, GA: C.P. Byrd, 1895. 119p. NUC OCLC
[Mostly narrative poems. No prose]

733. BRYAN, Mary M.
Poems.
n.p.: n.p., 18--. 10p. NUC OCLC
[Religious poetry]

734. BRYANT, Mary [Am. 19c]
Fantasma and other poems.
Kansas City, MO: Ramsey, Millet & Hudson, 1879. 318p. NUC OCLC

735. BRYTON, Anne [Br. 18c]
Richmond, a pastoral.
L: Printed for the author, 1766? 1780? 16p. NUC BL
[Dated 1780? BL, but refers only to first four children of George III, so presumably written before 1767.]

736. BUCKINGHAM, Emma May [Am. 19c]
Pearl. A centennial poem.
NY: S.R. Wells & co., 1877. 82p. NUC OCLC

737. -----The silver chalice, and other poems.
NY: S.R. Wells & co., 1878. 80p. NUC OCLC

738. BUCKLEY, Sarah Ann, Mrs. [Am. 19c]
The whisperings of angels, and spirit breathings; adapted to man's use on earth.
Worcester, MA: Chas. Hamilton, pr., 1854. 400p. NUC
[Hymns given by spirits of John Wesley and others to uneducated woman.]

BUDDINGTON, Zadel Barnes see GUSTAFSON, Zadel (Barnes) Buddington

739. BUDGE, Jane [Br. 19c]
Poems.
L: S. Harris & co., 1877. 144p. NUC BL OCLC

740. BUDGETT, Mary Elizabeth [Br. 19c]
Lays and legends of many lands.
L: Cradock & co., 1848. 74p. BL

741. -----The priest. A poem.
L: William Walker, 1852. 38p. BL

742. BUDINE, Angeline Jenette [Am. 19c]
A prophetic poem, which is rapidly being fulfilled. Written August 11, 1880, by the Indian doctress, Angeline Jenette Budine.
Elkland?, PA: Budine & Kimball, 1890. 7p. NUC

743. BULL, Lucy Catlin [Am. 19c] ALT: Robinson, Lucy Catlin (Bull)
A child's poems from October to October, 1870-1871. By Lucy Catlin Bull.
Hartford, CT: Case, Lockwood & Brainard, 1872. 171p.
[10 yr.-old author. 64 lyrics, 1 narrative poem, & 3 verse dramas, 5 acts each]

BULL, Lucy Catlin see ROBINSON, Lucy Catlin (Bull)

744. BULLENS, A. N., Mrs. [Am. 19c]
Beyond the clouds.
Troy, NY: H.B. Nims & co., 1885. 28p. NUC

745. -----Buds and blossoms. Original and selected.
NY: Hard & Parsons, 1885. 24p. NUC
[From the Gem series: Emerald Sprays, Echoings, & Buds & Blossoms. 4 poems by Bullens]

746. -----Chains of golden thought, original and selected.
NY: Hard & Parsons, 1885. 28p. NUC
[7 of 36 entries are Bullens' work. Incl. aphorisms & quotes from others.]

747. -----Christmas in song: a Christmas poem.
Troy, NY: Nims & Knight, 1886. 19 l. NUC OCLC

748. -----Easter cheer; or, Melodies for Easter-tide.
NY: Hard & Parsons, 1885. 28p. NUC

749. -----Emerald sprays. Original and selected.
NY: Hard & Parsons, 1885. 24p. NUC

750. -----Fair thoughts and happy havens. Original and selected.

Troy, NY: H.B. Nims & co., 1885. 26p. NUC

751. -----Gems by the wayside. Original and selected.
NY: Hard & Parsons, 1884. 14 l. NUC

752. -----Gleams of memory. Original and selected.
NY: Hard & Parsons, 1885. 38p. NUC OCLC
[On flowers]

753. -----Heralds of the morn. Original and selected.
NY: Hard & Parsons, 1885. 38p. NUC

754. -----Rays of remembrance, or words of golden cheer.
NY: Hard & Parsons, 1885. 27p. NUC

755. -----Silver and gold. Original and selected.
NY: Hard & Parsons, 1885. 40p. NUC

BULLOCK, C., ed. see HAVERGAL, Frances Ridley

756. BULLOCK, Cynthia [Am. b. 1821]
A bunch of pansies.
NY: Pr. J.A. Gray, 1852. 143p. NUC OCLC
[Mainly poetry; seven brief prose pieces]

757. -----A cluster of roses. Ed. G.P. Quackenbos.
NY: the author by Styles & Cash, 1877. 228p. NUC OCLC
[Approx. half poetry and half prose, fiction and reminiscences]

758. -----Washington, and other poems.
NY: The author, 1847. 108p. NUC OCLC
[About George Washington]

759. BULMER, Agnes Collinson [Br. 1775-1836]
Memoir of Mrs. Agnes Bulmer ... to which is subjoined, Mrs. Bulmer's last poem, Man the offspring of Divine Benevolence. By her sister, Anne Ross Collinson.
L: J.G. & F. Rivington, 1837. NUC BL

760. -----Messiah's kingdom. A poem. In twelve books.
NY: B. Waugh & T. Mason, 1833. 364p. NUC BL

761. BULWER, Elizabeth Barbara (Lytton) [Br. 19c] ALT: L., Eliz. B. B.
The Abbey de la Trappe: a poem.
L: n.p., 1826. 67p. NUC BL OCLC

BULWER, Rosina Doyle (Wheeler), Baroness Lytton see LYTTON, Rosina Anne Doyle (Wheeler) Bulwer-Lytton, Baroness

762. BUMSTEAD, Mary E. [Br. 19c]
Heart breathings.
3d ed. Southport: T. Greener, 1888. 64p. BL

763. BURBANK, Mary M. [Am. 19c]
A choral wreath.
NY: Adriance, Sherman & co., 1854. 155p. NUC

BURDER, George, ed. see BURDER, Sophia Maria

764. BURDER, Sophia Maria [Br. 19c]
Poetical effort. Ed. George Burder.
L: Westley & Davis, 1826. 67p. BL

765. BURGE, Julia P. [Am. 19c] PSEUD: Peabee, Jay
Life at Greene Farm.
n.p.: n.p., 1870. 12p. NUC
[On Greene Farm, historic home visited by Ben Franklin, Tom Paine, etc.]

766. -----Old Grime's wife; a ballad.
Providence, RI: Sidney S. Rider, 1885. 8 f. NUC OCLC

767. -----Work, watch, and pray.
NY: T.B. Ventres, Sunday School bookseller, 31p.
[2 hymns, 1 short story & 2 essays]

768. BURGESS, Adelaide Maria, Mrs. [Am. 19c]
From the cradle to the grave. By Mrs. A.M. Burgess.
Brooklyn, NY: 1880. 61 l. NUC OCLC

769. -----A poem on the garden of Eden.
Brooklyn, NY: n.p., 1889. NUC

770. -----The talisman.
Brooklyn, NY: n.p., 1887. 16p. NUC

771. BURGESS, Elisa [Am. b. 1801?]
Life thoughts and memorials of Mrs. Elisa Burgess.
Brooklyn, NY: Press of Rogers & Sherwood, 1878. 91p. NUC OCLC
[Includes poems]

772. BURGESS, Elizabeth [Br. 19c]
Life and history of Betty Bolaine, late of Canterbury, a well known

character for parsimony and vice ... interspersed with original poetry by Elizabeth Burgess.
Canterbury: H. Ward, 1832. 40p. NUC BL

773. BURLEIGH, Clare Hoyt [Am. 19c]
A four-leaved clover, and wayside rhymes.
Boston: G.H. Ellis, pr., 1884. 57p. NUC OCLC

774. BURMAN, Ellen Elizabeth [Br. 1837-1861]
Poetical remains of Ellen Elizabeth Burman, with a brief memoir by the Rev. William Bruce.
L: Seeley, Jackson & Halliday; Bristol: I.E. Chillcott, 1862. 114p. NUC BL

775. BURNELL, Harriet P. [Am. 19c]
Poems.
Oberlin, OH: 1841. 21p. NUC

BURNS, Rev. Jabez, ed. see BALFOUR, Clara Lucas (Liddell)

BURNS, Robert, co-author see SCOT, Elizabeth (Rutherford)

776. BURNSIDE, Helen [Br. 19c]
Poems. Ed. R.J. Burnside.
L: Hatchard & co., 1864. 117p. BL

777. BURNSIDE, Helen Marion
Bright leaves and ruddy berries.
L, Paris, NY: Raphael Tuck & Sons, 18-? 10p. NUC OCLC

778. -----Drift weed. Verses and lyrics.
L: Hutchinson & co., 1897. 274p. NUC BL OCLC

779. -----A happy greeting.
L: Ernest Nister; NY: E.P. Dutton & co., 1898. BL

780. -----The three angels.
L: R. Tuck & sons, 1890. BL

BURNSIDE, R.J., ed. see BURNSIDE, Helen

781. BURR, Sylvia E. [Am. 19c]
A stone: or, The highest church after the apostolic order.
Southford, CT: Seymour Print., 1871. 78p. NUC OCLC
[Inspirational essay, poems interspersed]

782. BURRELL, Sophia (Raymond), Lady [Br. 1750?-1802]
Poems.
L: Pr. J. Cooper; Leigh & Sotheby, 1793. 2v. NUC BL OCLC

783. -----Telemachus.
L: Sold by Leigh & Sotheby, 1794. 78p. NUC BL OCLC
[A poem based on the work of Fenelon]

784. -----The Thymbriad, from Xenophon's Cyropoedia.
L: Sold by Leigh & Sotheby, 1794. 154p. NUC BL OCLC

BURR LINGTON, D.L.L., pseud. see NARAMORE, Gay Humbolt

785. BURT, Eveline F. [Am. 19c]
Autumn leaves: poems.
Mt. Gilead, OH: Sentinel pr. house, c1890. 44p. NUC OCLC

786. BURTON, Margaret, Mrs. [Br. 19c]
Poetical effusions, on subjects religious, moral and rural.
L: Pr. for author by Paris & Cowell; sold by Messrs. Butterworth & son, 1816. 149p. NUC BL

BURTON, Phillipina see HILL, Phillipina (Burton)

787. BUSH, BELLE, pseud. [Am. 19c]
The clock of gold.
NY: Frank L. Hamilton, 1870? 12p. NUC

788. -----October.
Shirley, MA: n.p., n.d. 11 stanzas. NUC

789. -----Voices of the morning.
Philadelphia: J.B. Lippincott & co., 1865. 270p. NUC BL OCLC

790. BUSH, Clara [Am. b. 1853]
Poems ... with a memoir.
Jackson, TN: Cisco & Hawkins, 1883. 275p. NUC OCLC

791. BUSH, Olivia Ward [Am. b. 1869]
Original poems.
Providence, RI: O. Bush, Press of Louis A. Basinet, 1899. 19p. NUC OCLC

792. BUSHBY, Anne S. [Br. 19c]
Poems.
L: R. Bentley & son, 1876. 399p. BL

793. BUSSING, Alice Cary [Am. 19c]
ALT: B., A. C.
Some verse, by A.C.B.
NY: The De Vinne press, 1897. 63p. NUC OCLC

794. BUTCHER, Edith Louisa (Floyer) [Br. 19/20c] ALT: Floyer, Edith Louisa
Poems.
L: Griffith & Farran, 1877. 128p. BL

BUTE, Marchioness of, ed. see HASTINGS, Lady Flora Elizabeth Rawdon-

795. BUTLER, Ann [Br. 19c]
Fragments in verse; chiefly on religious subjects.
Oxford: Bartlett & Minton, 1826. 155p. NUC BL OCLC

796. BUTLER, Anne [Br. 19c]
A selection of sacred poems. Ed. G. Smith.
L: Benrose & sons, 1878. 67p. BL

797. BUTLER, Ellen Hamlin [Am. b. 1860]
In rhyme and measure; poems.
Cambridge, MA: J. Wilson & sons, 1892. 94p. NUC OCLC

798. BUTLER, Harriette [Br. 19c]
Lays of the heart.
Manchester: J. Gleave, 1833. 104p. BL

799. BUTLER, Jessee H. [Am. 19c]
Home: femme heroic, and miscellaneous poems.
Boston: Colby & Rich, 1875. 236p. NUC BL OCLC

800. BUTLER, Marie Radcliffe [Am. 1839-1884]
Poetry and prose of Marie Radcliffe Butler. Ed. Thomas D. Butler.
Cincinnati, OH: Standard pub. co., 1884. 361p. NUC OCLC
[Misc. poems, religious essays, novelette]

801. BUTT, Geraldine [Br. 19c]
My picture and other poems.
L: Houlston & sons; Wellington, Salop.: R. Hobson, 1874. 48p. BL

BUTLER, Mrs. Pierce see KEMBLE, Frances Anne

BUTLER, Thomas D., ed. see BUTLER, Marie Radcliffe

802. BUTTON, Susan S. [Am. 19c]
Poems.
Litchfield, OH: Pub. for authoress; NY: Pr. John A. Gray, 1858. 336p. NUC OCLC

803. BUTTS, Mary F. [Am. 19c]
A fence of trust.
Boston & Chicago: United Soc. of Christian Endeavor, 1898. 45p. NUC OCLC

BYRNE, Charlotte Dacre see DACRE, Charlotte

BYRON, George Gordon Noel, Baron Byron, co-author see HEMANS, Felicia Dorothea (Browne)

BYRON, George Gordon Noel, Baron Byron, co-author see LAMB, Lady Caroline (Ponsonby)

804. BYRON, May Clarissa (Gillington) [Br. d. 1936] ALT: Gillington, May Clarissa
Poems. With A.E. Gillington.
L: Elliot Stock, 1892. 99p. BL

805. -----Twelve original Christmas carols.
L: R. Cocks & co., 1893. 8p. BL

C., pseud. see STEELE, Anna Caroline (Wood)

C., A. see CROSS, Ada Cambridge

C., A.R. see COUSIN, Anne Ross (Cundell)

C., E.S. see COLCHESTER, Elizabeth Susan (Law) Abbot, Baroness Colchester

C., F., ed. see NASH, Caroline

C., F.D. see CARTWRIGHT, Frances Dorothy

C., I. see CLARK, Isabella Golding

C., I.G. see CLARK, Isabella Golding

C., M., pseud. see MARTIN, Catherine Edith Macaulay (Mackay)

C., M.A. see CURSHAM, Mary Anne

C., M.F. see CROW, Martha Foote

C., M.T. see CANBY, Margaret T.

C., S. see CARSON, Sallie

C---, Ellen see CULLEY, Ellen

806. CABELL, Julia (Mayo) [Am. b. 1860]

An odd volume of facts and fiction, in prose and verse.
2d ed. Richmond, VA: Nash & Woodhouse, 1852. 276p. OCLC
[Incl. letters, 35 poems, 3 short stories, & travel journals]

807. CAILLARD, Emma Marie [Br. b. 1852]
Charlotte Corday and other poems.
L: Kegan Paul & co., 1884. 98p. BL OCLC

808. -----The lost life and other poems.
L: Eyre & Spottiswoode, 1889. 189p. BL OCLC

809. -----A poem of life.
L: London Literary Society, 1884. 120p. BL OCLC

810. CAIRD, Eliza [Br. 19c]
Christian songs and elegies. Ed. John Caird.
Perth: Pub. for priv. circ., 1846. 49p. BL

CAIRD, John, ed. see CAIRD, Eliza

811. CAIRNS, Christiana Victoria [Br. 19c]
Fugitive poems.
L: Jones & Causton, 1860. 248p. BL

812. CAKE, Lu B. [Am. 19/20c]
Decoration day.
Clarinda, IA: n.p., 1878. 8p. NUC

813. -----The devil's tea-table, and other poems.
NY: L.B. Cake, 1898. 195p. NUC OCLC

814. CAKE, Susan McDonough [Am. 1816-1896]
Aunt Susan's own story of her life. With additional incidents, her favorite hymns and quaint sayings. Comp. William U. Cake.
Philadelphia: J.J. Hood, c1897. 70p. NUC OCLC
[Includes poetry]

815. CALDWELL, Maggie [Am. 19c]
Bird notes from the mountains. Poems.
Lebanon, VA: E.K. Harding, 1888. 76p. NUC

CAKE, William U., comp. see CAKE, Susan McDonough

CALIFORNIAN, A, pseud. see SMITH, Minna Caroline

816. CALLANAN, Helena
Verses old and new.
Cork: Pr. at the Eagle Works, 1899. 108p. NUC BL

817. CALLICOTTE, Alma Francis (Brown) [Am. b. 1863]
Seeds of truth.
New Windsor, CO: n.p., 1896. 63p. NUC OCLC
[Incl. sketches of author's life]

818. CALVERT, Elizabeth Henderson (McRobie) [Am. 19/20c]
The boat-man God and other poems.
Seattle, WA: The Calvert co., c1898. 69p. NUC OCLC

819. CALVERT, Elizabeth Henderson (McRobie)
Sealth, the city by the inland sea.
n.p.: n.p., c1897. 22p. NUC BL
[Poems and prose sketches. Sealth is the Indian name for Seattle.]

820. CAMP, Frances Griswold [Am. 19c]
ALT: C., F. G.
Echoes. By F.G.C.
Columbus, OH: A.H. Smythe, 1885. 92p. NUC

CAMBRIDGE, Ada see CROSS, Ada Cambridge

821. CAMPBELL, Ann Raymond [Br. 19c]
A wreath of poesy; or, Effusions of the heart.
L: the author, 1828. 88p. BL OCLC

822. CAMPBELL, Arabella Georgina [Br. 19c]
Cranmer: a poem.
L: Hamilton, Adams & co.; Reading: T. Buchanan, 1855. 67p. BL

823. CAMPBELL, Dorothea Primrose [Br. d. 1863]
Poems.
Inverness: Pr. & pub. for authoress by J. Young, 1811. 198p. NUC BL OCLC

824. -----Poems.
L: Pr. for authoress and pub. by Baldwin, Cradock, & Joy, 1816. 226p. NUC BL

825. CAMPBELL, Elizabeth Anne [Br. 19c]
Life triumphant. A poem.
L: William Macintosh, 1863. 273p. BL

826. CAMPBELL, Elizabeth [Br. 19c]
Poems.
Arbroath: the author, 1862. 26p. BL

827. CAMPBELL, Mrs. Graham [Br. 19c]
One hundred voices from nature: or, Apples of gold in a net-work of silver.
Cheltenham: For the authoress, 1861. 131p. BL
[Poems on animals, flowers, and natural phenomena]

828. CAMPBELL, Jane [Am. 19c]
Mother Goose's protest.
Philadelphia: Sherrerd bros., 1888. 15p. NUC OCLC
[Humorous poem on educational value of Mother Goose rhymes.]

829. -----The nineteenth century woman.
Philadelphia: W.J. Campbell, 1890. 18p. NUC OCLC
[Humorous poem on expanded opportunities for women.]

830. -----Origin of the fan.
Philadelphia: Campbell, 1891. NUC OCLC

831. CAMPBELL, Jean (Morison) [Br. 19/20c] ALT: Morison, Jean
Aeolus. A romance in lyrics.
Edinburgh & L: W. Blackwood & sons, 1892. 108p. NUC BL

832. -----Ane booke of ballades.
Edinburgh: Bell & Bradfute, 1882. 54p. NUC BL

833. -----Doorside ditties.
L: W. Blackwood & sons, 1893. NUC BL

834. -----Gordon: an our-day idyll.
L: Kegan Paul, Trench & co., 1889. 126p. NUC BL

835. -----Pontius Pilate, a drama. And other poems.
L: Daldy Ibister & co., 1878. NUC BL

836. -----The purpose of the ages.
NY, L & Edinburgh: Macmillan & co., 1887. 384p. NUC BL OCLC

837. -----Rifts in the reek.
Edinburgh: W. Blackwood & son, 1898. 323p. NUC BL

838. -----Sabbath songs and sonnets, and By-way ballads.
Edinburgh: W. Blackwood & son, 1899. BL

839. -----Saint Isadora; and other poems.
Edinburgh: Bell & Bradfute, 1885. NUC BL

840. -----Snatches of song.
L: Longmans & co., 1873. 145p. NUC OCLC

841. -----There as here: hints and glimpses of the unseen.
Edinburgh & L: Blackwood & sons, 1891. 99p. BL

842. CAMPBELL, Juliet H. (Lewis) [Am. b. 1823]
Legend of the infancy of our Savior. A Christmas carol.
Philadelphia: J.B. Lippincott & co., 1862. 36p. NUC

CAMPBELL, MARY, pseud. see BENNETT, Mary E.

843. CAMPBELL, Mary Jane [Am. b. 1865]
Strangers: a little book of poems.
Farmington: Press of the News, 1896. 28p. NUC OCLC

844. CAMPBELL, Nancy W. [Am. d. 1862]
Poetry and prose. With Thomas Bakewell.
Pittsburgh, PA: Pr. Bakewell & Marthens, 1872. 100p. NUC

845. CANBY, Margaret T. [Am. 19c]
ALT: C., M. T.
Flowers from the battle-field, and other poems by M.T.C.
Philadelphia: H.B. Ashmead, pr., 1864. 36p. NUC OCLC
[U.S. Civil War poetry]

846. CANDLER, Ann More [Br. 1740-1814]
Poetical attempts, by Ann Candler, a Suffolk cottager; with a short narrative of her life.
Ipswich & L: Pr. & sold by J. Raw; also sold by T. Hurst, 1803. 68p. NUC BL

847. CANNON, M. Maria [Br. 19c]
Maria and St. Flos, a poem, in a series of letters: to which is added, A search after happiness.
L: W.C. Wright; J. Hatchard & son, 1825. 64p. BL

848. CANTRELL, Mrs. John Blackwall [Br. 19c]
Melodies from the mountains, with other poetical pieces.
L: Wertheim & co., 1861. 92p. BL

849. CAPADOSE, Emily Anne Ximenes [Br. 19c]
Jamaica and her children. A poem.

L: John Nicols, 1840. 16p. BL

850. CAPP, Mary Elizabeth [Br. 19c]
The African princess, and other poems.
Yarmouth: J. Keymer; L: Longman, Hurst, Rees, Orme & Browne, 1813. 188p. NUC BL OCLC

CAPPE, Catherine (Harrison), ed. <u>see</u> RICHARDSON, Charlotte

851. CAPPER, Louisa [Br. 19c]
A poetical history of England.
L: Pr. Nichols, son, & Bentley for the author, 1810, 1815. 154p. BL OCLC

CARDALE, Mrs. <u>see</u> COWPER, Frances Maria (Madan)

852. CAREY, Elizabeth Sheridan [Br. 19c]
Ivy leaves; or offerings in verse.
L: n.p., 1837. 206p. BL

CAREY, H.M. <u>see</u> CAREY, Harriet Mary, Mrs.

853. CAREY, Harriet Mary, Mrs. [Br. 19c] ALT: Carey, H. M.
Echoes from the harp of Normandy. Ed. G.S. Trebutien.
Caen: A. Hariel, 1857. 32p. BL NUC

854. -----For ever! By H.M. Carey. To which is added an imitation in French verse by A. le Flaguais. Ed. G.S. Trebutien.
Caen: V. Pagny, 1857. 12p. BL

855. -----Matilda of Normandy. A poetical tribute to the Imperial Academy of Caen.
L: Saunders & Otley, 1859. 93p. BL

CARLTON, CARRIE, pseud. <u>see</u> BOOTH, Mary H.C., Mrs.

CARLYLE, Jane Welsh, co-author <u>see</u> SMITH, Mary

CARLYLE, Thomas, co-author <u>see</u> SMITH, Mary

856. CARMICHAEL, Rebekah [Br. 18c]
ALT: Hay, Rebekah Carmichael
Poems.
Edinburgh: Pr. for author, sold by Peter Hill, 1790. 92p. NUC BL OCLC

857. CARMICHAEL, Sarah E. [Am. 19c]
Poems.
San Francisco: Towne & Bacon, 1866. 72p. NUC BL OCLC

858. CARNES, Hannah, Mrs. [Br. 19c]
ALT: Garwood, Hannah Carnes PSEUD: Female, A
The beauties of Halstead ... and other original poems by a female.
Chelmsford: n.p., 1861. 24p. BL

859. -----The beauties of Walden: a poem.
Saffron Walden: H. Hart, 1842. 27p. BL
[Descriptive verse]

860. -----The life of Hannah Carnes. Compiled from her own papers.
Weymouth: B. Benson, 1833. 60p. BL
[Incl. "Albion weeping for the loss of her children."]

861. -----Truthful pathetic poetry.
Chelmsford: J. Shawcraft, 1855. 21p. BL

862. -----The widow's cottage, and other pathetic poems.
Gloucester: William Verrinder, 1829. 36p. BL

863. CARNEY, Julia Abigail (Fletcher), Mrs. T. J. Carney [Am. b. 1823]
The poetry of the seasons.
Boston: A. Tompkins & B.B. Mussey, 1842, c1841. 136p. NUC OCLC
[Verses with prose commentary]

CARNEY, Mrs. T.J. <u>see</u> CARNEY, Julia Abigail (Fletcher)

CAROLINA, pseud., co-author <u>see</u> BRERETON, Jane

CAROLINA PETTY PASTY, pseud. <u>see</u> COBBOLD, Elizabeth Knipe

864. CARPENTER, Alice Dimmick [Am. 19c]
Poems, original and translated.
Chicago: Cowles & Dunkley, 1882. 76p. NUC

CARR, Gabrielle, co-author <u>see</u> CARR, Helen

865. CARR, Helen [Br. 19c]
Ephemera. By Helen and Gabrielle Carr.
L: E. Moxon & co., 1865. 330p. BL

866. CARR, Laura Garland [Am. b. 1835]
Memories and fancies.
Boston: The Writer pub. co., 1891. 144p. NUC OCLC

867. CARRINGTON, E., Mrs. [Br. 19c]
A metrical outline of historical events from the beginning of the Christian era to the Norman conquest.
L: Simpkin, Marshall & co., 1836. 110p. BL

868. CARROLL, Octavia Dorell [Br. 19c]
On that glorious day, May 24th, 1899.
n.p.: n.p., 1899. BL

CARROLL, Susanna <u>see</u> CENTLIVRE, Susanna Freeman Carroll

CARRUTHERS, Ella A., co-author <u>see</u> BACKUS, Elizabeth Welch

CARRUTHERS, Jannet, co-author <u>see</u> BACKUS, Elizabeth Welch

869. CARSHORE, Mary [Br. 19c]
Songs of the East.
Calcutta: D'Rozario & co., 1855. 143p. BL

870. CARSON, Sallie [Am. b. 1847] ALT: C., S.
Wayside flowers. A collection of short poems. By S.C.
Philadelphia: J.B. Lippincott & co., 1881. 163p. NUC OCLC

871. CARTER, Agnes Louisa [Am. 19c]
The white nun, and other poems.
NY: G.P. Putnam's sons, 1883. 88p. NUC OCLC

872. CARTER, Agnes P. [Br. 19c] ALT: C., A. P.
Songs in the wilderness.
L: D. Walker; W.G. Bartlett, 1845. 105p. BL

873. -----Sunshine and shadow. Poems.
L: S.W. Partridge, 1861. 172p. NUC BL

874. CARTER, Elizabeth [Br. 1717-1806] PSEUD: Charissa; Eliza
Poems.
L: n.p., 1789. BL

875. -----Poems on several occasions.
L: John Rivington, 1762. 104p. NUC BL

876. -----Poems upon particular occasions.
L: n.p., 1738. 24p. NUC BL

877. CARTER, Mary Ann [Br. 19c]
The deluge, The general resurrection and other poems.
L: Hamilton, 1838. 136p. NUC BL

878. CARTWRIGHT, Frances Dorothy [Br. 1780-1863] ALT: C., F. D.
Poems, chiefly devotional. By F.D.C.
L: G. Woodfall, 1835. 55p. NUC BL

879. CARY, Alice [Am. 1820-1871]
Ballads, lyrics, and hymns.
NY: Hurd & Houghton, 1866. 333p. NUC OCLC

880. -----Early and late poems of Alice and Phoebe Cary.
NY & Boston: Houghton, Mifflin & Co., 1887. 321p. NUC BL OCLC

881. -----The last poems of Alice and Phoebe Cary. Ed. Mary Clemmer Ames.
NY: Hurd & Houghton; Cambridge, MA: Riverside press, 1873. 306p. NUC OCLC

882. -----A lover's diary.
Boston: Ticknor & Fields, 1868. 240p. NUC BL

883. -----Lyra, and other poems.
NY: Redfield, 1852. 172p. NUC BL OCLC

884. -----Pictures of country life.
NY: Derby & Jackson; Cincinnati, 1859. 359p. Cincinnati, OH: H.W. Derby, 1859. 425p. NUC OCLC

885. -----Poems. With Phoebe Cary.
Philadelphia: Moss & bro., 1850. 264p. NUC

886. -----Poems.
Boston: 1855. 399p. NUC BL
[Authorship hers alone. Misc. poetry incl. a narrative poem on the Aztecs, pp. 327-399]

887. -----Poetical works. With Phoebe Cary. Ed. Mary Clemmer Ames.
NY: Hurd & Houghton, 1876. 435p. NUC BL OCLC

888. CARY, Mary E. [Am. 19c]
Sunshine and shadows, poems.
NY: George F. Nesbitt, pr., 1875. 80p. NUC OCLC

CARY, Phoebe, co-author <u>see</u> CARY, Alice

889. CARY, Phoebe [Am. 1824-1871]
Poems.
NY: Hurst, n.d. 205p. NUC

890. -----Poems and parodies.
Boston: Ticknor, Reed, & Fields, 1854. 200p. NUC BL OCLC

891. -----Poems of faith, hope, and love.

NY: Hurd & Houghton, 1868. 249p. NUC BL OCLC

892. CASE, Venelia R. [Am. 19c]
Grange poems.
Bloomfield, CT: n.p., 1892. 92p. NUC OCLC

893. CASSAN, Sarah (Mears), Mrs. Stephen Cassan [Br. 19c]
Poems.
L: Pr. G. Sidney, 1806. 96p. NUC BL

CASSAN, Mrs. Stephen see CASSAN, Sarah (Mears)

894. CASTLEN, Eppie Bowdre [Am. 19c]
PSEUD: Chiquita
Autumn dreams. By Chiquita.
NY: D. Appleton, 1870. 108p. NUC BL OCLC

CAULFEILD, Mrs. Edwin Toby see CAULFEILD, Frances Sally

895. CAULFEILD, Frances Sally, Mrs. Edwin Toby Caulfeild [Br. 19c]
The deluge. A poem. By Mrs. Edwin T. Caulfeild.
L: Baldwin & Cradock, 1837. 170p. BL

896. -----The innocents; a sacred drama. Ocean; and the earthquake at Aleppo; poems.
Bath: S. Simms, 1824. 63p. NUC BL

897. CAULFEILD, Sophia Frances Anne [Br. 1824-1911]
Avenele, and other poems.
L: Longmans & co., 1870. 220p. NUC BL OCLC

898. -----Desmond and other poems.
L: Longmans & co., 1870. 243p. NUC BL

899. CAULKINS, Frances Mainwaring [Am. 1795-1869]
Bride Brook. A legend of New London.
New London, CT: Colfax & Holt, 1852. 11p. NUC BL

900. -----The children of the Bible: as examples and as warnings.
NY: American Tract Soc., 1842. 52p. NUC
[Poems about Ishmael, Moses, Josiah, etc. as children]

901. -----Colporteur songs written for the American Messenger.
New London, CT: n.p., 1847. 12p. BL

902. -----Eve and her daughters of holy writ; or, Women of the Bible.
NY: Am. Tract Soc., 1861. 144p. NUC
[Poems on: Dorcas, Leah, Rachael, Rebecca, etc.]

903. CAULTON, Isabella [Br. 19c]
The domestic hearth, and other poems.
Manchester: Bradshaw & Blacklock, 1843. 181p. BL OCLC

904. -----Poems for home.
Leamington Spa: Richard Russell, 1851. 96p. BL OCLC

CAVE, Harriet see MORTON, Harriet (Cave)

CAVE, Jane see WINSCOM, Jane Cave
CAVENDISH, Georgiana (Spencer), Duchess of Devonshire see DEVONSHIRE, Georgiana (Spencer) Cavendish, Duchess of

CAVENDISH, Margaret (Lucas), Duchess of Newcastle see NEWCASTLE, Margaret (Lucas) Cavendish, Duchess of

CAZIRE, pseud. see SHELLY, Elizabeth

CECIL, LADY FRANCES H., pseud. see SAYERS, Frances H.

905. CELESIA, Dorothea (Mallet) [Br. 1738-1790]
Indolence; a poem.
L: T. Becket, 1772. 23p. NUC BL OCLC

906. CENTLIVRE, Susanna Freeman Carroll [Br. 1667-1723] ALT: Carroll, Susanna
Abelard to Heloise. A poem. In answer to that wrote by Mr. Pope. In: 1755. By Mrs. C____ER. In: The lover's cabinet: a collection of poems.
2 pt. Dublin: L. Flin, 1855. 84, 22p. BL

907. -----The masquerade. A poem.
L: B. Lintott, 1713. 7p. NUC

908. -----A poem. Humbly presented to George, His Most Sacred Majesty, King of Great Britain, France and Ireland. Upon his accession to the throne.
L: T. Woodward, 1715. 8p. BL

909. CHADWICK, Mrs. [Br. 19c]
Rural and other poems.
Ludlow: Procter & Jones; L: Longmans & co., 1828. 178p. NUC BL OCLC

910. CHADWICK, Ellen R. [Am. 19c]
Poems ... published by her mother.
South Boston: R.J. Gilkie, pr., 1876. 107p. NUC OCLC

911. CHAFA, Sara Genevra [Am. 19c]
Napoleon Bonaparte, and other poems.
Cambridge, MA: Riverside press, 1872.
211p. NUC BL OCLC

912. CHALENOR, Mary, Mrs. [Br. 19c]
The poetical remains of Mary Chalenor.
L: Longmans & co., 1843. 78p. NUC BL

913. -----Walter Gray; a ballad: and other poems.
L: Longman, Brown, Green & Longmans, 1841. 72p. BL OCLC

914. -----Walter Gray; a ballad: and other poems.
2d ed. L: Longman, 1843. 162p. BL
[Expanded edition]

915. CHALMERS, Margaret [Br. 19c]
Poems.
Newcastle: S. Hodgson, 1813. 160p. BL

CHAMBERLAIN, Mary Booth see BOOTH, Mary H.C., Mrs.

CHAMBERLIN, Mrs. Alden see CHAMBERLIN, Mary Jane (Wilson)

916. CHAMBERLIN, Mary Jane (Wilson), Mrs. Alden Chamberlin [Am. b. 1832]
Life thoughts; book of poems on religion, love, temperance.
Charlevoix, MI: The author, 1893.
319p. NUC

CHAMBERS, Anna see TEMPLE, Anna (Chambers) Grenville-Temple, Countess

917. CHAMBERS, Augusta [Am. 19c]
My book.
Buffalo, NY: The author, 1880. 141p.
NUC OCLC
[Poems, chiefly lyric; one narrative poem, "Caleb Plummer"]

918. CHAMBERS, Edith C. [Br. 19c]
Fragments.
Sheffield: Loxley bros., 1867. 56p.
BL

CHAMBERS-KETCHUM, Mrs. see KETCHUM, Annie (Chambers) Bradford

919. CHAMPION DE CRESPIGNY, Mary (Clark), Lady [Br. d. 1812] ALT: De Crespigny, Mary (Clark) Champion
A monody to the memory of the Right Honourable the Lord Collingwood.
L: Cadell & Davis, 1810. 23p. NUC BL OCLC

920. CHANDLER, Elizabeth Margaret [Am. 1807-1834]
Poetical works of Elizabeth M. Chandler. With a memoir of her life by Benjamin Lundy.
Philadelphia: Lemuel Howell, 1836.
180p. NUC BL OCLC

CHANDLER, Ellen Louise see MOULTON, Ellen Louise (Chandler)

921. CHANDLER, Julia Knapp [Am. 19c]
Broken hearted; an o'er true tale of the fever.
New Orleans, LA: T.H. Thomason, pr., 1878. 18p. NUC OCLC
[New Orleans fever epidemic.]

922. CHANDLER, Mary [Br. 1687-1745]
A description of Bath: a poem. In a letter to a friend.
L: J. Robert, J. Jackson, J. Gray, J. Leake, & S. Lobb, booksellers, c1733.
18p. NUC BL

923. -----The description of Bath: a poem. In a letter to a friend. To which are added, several poems by the same author.
3d ed. L & Bath: James Locke, 1736.
77p. NUC BL OCLC

924. -----A description of Bath: a poem. In a letter to a friend. To which is added, a true tale, by the same author.
6th ed. L & Bath: James Leake, 1744.
85p. BL

925. CHANT, Laura Ormiston (Dibbin) [Am. 1848-1923]
Four sonnets written for the benefit of Wellesley students.
Boston: Damrell & Upham, 1888. NUC

926. -----Ode to the parliament of religions. Farewell ode to the United States. Columbian year 1893.
Boston: n.p., 1893? NUC

927. -----Verona, and other poems.
L: David Stott, 1887. 157p. NUC BL

928. CHANTRELL, Mary Ann [Br. 18c]
Poems on various subjects.
L: the author, 1798. 109p. BL OCLC

929. CHAPLIN, M. A., Mrs. [Br. 19/20c]
Chimes for the times.
L: William Wileman; E. Wilmshurst, 1891. 126p. BL

930. -----Sunlit spray from the billows of life.
L: G. Stoneman, 1898. 109p. BL

931. CHAPMAN, Elizabeth Rachel [Br. 1850-1897]
A little child's wreath.
NY: Dodd, Mead & co.; L: Elkin Mathews & John Lane, 1894. 41p. NUC BL OCLC
[Sonnet sequence in memory of her son, Roger, who died age seven.]

932. -----The new purgatory, and other poems.
L: T. Fisher Unwin, 1887. 158p. NUC BL

933. CHAPMAN, Maria Weston [Am. 1806-1885]
Songs of the free, and hymns of Christian freedom.
Boston: I. Knapp, 1836. 227p. NUC OCLC
[Abolitionist poems]

934. CHAPONE, Hester (Mulso) [Br. 1727-1801]
Miscellanies, in prose and verse.
L: E. & C. Dilly, 1775. 178p. NUC BL OCLC
[Poems and plays. Incl. 3 essays & 1 short story: Fidelia.]

935. -----Posthumous works ... [incl.] some fugitive pieces, never before published.
Edinburgh: A. Constable & co.; L: J. Murray, 1807. 2v. NUC BL OCLC

936. CHAPPEL, Sarah [Br. 18c]
Divine poems.
n.p.: n.p., 1750. 8p. BL

CHARISSA, pseud. see CARTER, Elizabeth

937. CHARKE, Charlotte (Cibber) [Br. d. 1760]
The art of management; or, Tragedy expell'd.
L: W. Rayner 1735. 47p. BL N
[Farce; apparently written when she was fired as an actress from Drury Lane. Followed by 2 1/2 pp. of airs, short poems.]

938. CHARLES, Beatrice Ethel [Br. 19c]
Songs in the night.
L: Simpkin, Marshall & co., 1894. 104p. BL

939. CHARLES, Elizabeth (Rundle) [Br. 1828-1896]
Collected poems.
L: Soc. for Prom. Christ. Knowl., 1894. 340p. OCLC

940. -----Songs old and new.
L & NY: T. Nelson & sons, 1887. 340p. NUC BL

941. -----The three wakings and other poems.
L: James Nisbet & co., 1859. 194p. NUC BL OCLC
[Pub. anon.]

942. -----The women of the gospels.
NY: M.W. Dodd, 1867. 275p. BL OCLC
[Expanded version of The three wakings]

943. CHARLES, Emily Thornton [Am. b. 1845] PSEUD: Hawthorne, Emily
Hawthorne blossoms. By Emily Thornton Charles (Emily Hawthorne).
Philadelphia: J.B. Lippincott & co., 1876. 165p. NUC OCLC

944. -----Lyrical poems, songs, pastorals, roundelays, war poems, madrigals. By Emily Thornton Charles (Emily Hawthorne).
Philadelphia: J.B. Lippincott & co., 1886. 266p. NUC OCLC

CHARLOTTE ELIZABETH see TONNA, Charlotte Elizabeth (Browne) Phelan

CHARLTON, pseud. see PENDLETON, Charlotte

CHARNOCK, J.H., ed. see CHARNOCK, Mary Anna E.

945. CHARNOCK, Mary Anna E. [Br. 19c]
Legendary rhymes, and other poems. Ed. J.H. Charnock.
L: Longman & co., 1843. 238p. BL OCLC

CHASE, Elizabeth Ann see ALLEN, Elizabeth Ann

CHASE, Lydia M., comp. see MILLER, Mary Morgan

946. CHASE, Mary M. [Am. 1822-1852]
Mary M. Chase and her writings. Ed. Henry Fowler.
Boston: Ticknor & Fields, 1855. 336p. NUC BL OCLC
[Songs, flower poems, misc. poems.]

CHATELAIN, The Chevalier de, ed. see CHATELAIN, Clara de (de Pontigny)

947. CHATELAIN, Clara de (de Pontigny) [Br. 1807-1876]
Photographs of familiar faces by a female photographer ... . Ed. The Chevalier de Chatelain.

L: B.M. Pickering, 1878. 275p. BL
[Character sketches; The months: a photographic calendar for 1858, in verse, pp. 200-251.]

CHATTERTON, Georgiana, Lady see CHATTERTON, Henrietta Georgiana Marcia Lascelles (Iremonger), Lady

948. CHATTERTON, Henrietta Georgiana Marcia Lascelles (Iremonger), Lady [Br. 1806-1876]
Lady May, a pastoral.
L: T. Richardson & sons, 1869. 109p. BL OCLC

949. -----Lenore, a tale: and other poems.
L & Cambridge: Macmillan & co., 1864. 324p. NUC BL OCLC

CHEEVER, Elizabeth Hopkin Wetmore see CHEEVER, Elizabeth Hoppin Wetmore

950. CHEEVER, Elizabeth Hoppin [Hopkin BL] Wetmore, Mrs. George Barrell Cheever [Am. 1814-1886]
Memorabilia of George Barrell Cheever, D.D. late pastor of the Church of the Puritans ... and of his wife Elizabeth Wetmore Cheever.
NY: J. Wiley & sons; Fleming H. Revell, 1890. NUC BL OCLC
[Incl. her poems and letters]

CHEEVER, Mrs. George Barrell see CHEEVER, Elizabeth Hoppin Wetmore

CHENEY, Ednah Dow Littlehale, ed. see SEWALL, Harriet Winslow

951. CHESSON, Nora Hopper [Br. 1871-1906] ALT: Hopper, Nora
Ballads in prose.
Boston: Roberts bros.; L: John Lane, 1894. 186p. NUC BL OCLC
[9 poems; 10 stories & legends of Ireland]

952. -----Mildred and her mills, and other poems.
L: R. Tuck & sons, ltd., 189-? 64p. NUC BL OCLC

953. -----Under quicken boughs.
L: J. Lane; NY: G. Richmond & co., 1896. 151p. NUC BL OCLC

CHESTER, NORLEY, pseud. see UNDERDOWN, Emily

954. CHETWYND, Mary Anne [Br. 19c]
PSEUD: Daughter of a clergyman, The
Choice selections, and original effusions; or, Pen and ink well employed. By the daughter of a clergyman.
Brighton: n.p., 1828. BL

955. -----A poetical history of England.
Stafford: R. & W. Wright, 1849. 61p. BL

956. -----A short poetical compendium of the history of Russia.
Stafford: R. & W. Wright, 1854. 51p. BL

957. CHEVES, Elizabeth Washington (Foote) [Am. 19c]
Sketches in prose and verse.
Baltimore, MD: Pr. at Publication Rooms, 1849. 264p. NUC BL OCLC
[Based on her homes in Virginia & Louisiana]

958. CHILD, Anne Page [Am. 19c] ALT: Page, Ann
The banner of freedom: a collection of patriotic songs, original and selected.
Providence, RI: S.M. Millard & co., 1841. 24p. NUC OCLC
[Without music]

959. CHILD, F., Miss [Br. 19c]
"A little while after she was at it again." The Royal Agricultural Assemblage, Salisbury. July, 1857.
2d ed. Salisbury: F.A. Blake, 1857. BL

960. -----The Salisbury exhibition. A poem.
2d ed. Salisbury: F.A. Blake, 1852. 24p. BL

961. -----The Salisbury jubilee for the peace of 1856. A poem.
Salisbury: F.A. Blake, 1856. 20p. BL

962. -----The spinster at home, in the close of Salisbury. No fable. Together with tales and ballads.
Salisbury: W.B. Brodie, 1844. 395p. BL
[Incl. poem in 7 cantos on Salisbury & environs]

963. CHILD, Lydia Maria (Francis) [Am. 1802-1880] ALT: Francis, Lydia Maria
Autumnal leaves: Tales and sketches in prose and rhyme.
NY & Boston: C.S. Francis & co., 1857. 365p. NUC BL OCLC
[Short stories, essays & misc. poetry]

964. -----The [western BL] coronal; a collection of pieces written at various times.
Glasgow: n.p.; NY: B. Carter, 1831. 287p. NUC BL
[Short stories interspersed with poems]

965. CHILDE-PEMBERTON, Harriet Louisa [Br. 19/20c] ALT: Pemberton, Harriet Louisa Childe-
Dead letters, and other narrative and dramatic pieces.
L: Ward, Lock & co., 1896. 125p. BL
[9 poems; 4 dramatic pieces]

966. -----Original readings and recitations. "Prince," a story of the American war, and other ... poems.
L: Ward & co., 1883. 79p. BL
[Narrative poems based on well known stories written and/or adapted for recitation. Incl. Geese: a dialogue.]

967. CHILTERN, Faith [Br. 19c]
Watching for the dead, and poems.
L: Provost & co., 1877. 91p. BL

CHIQUITA, pseud. <u>see</u> CASTLEN, Eppie Bowdre

968. CHITWOOD, Mary Louisa [Am. 1832-1856]
Poems ... selected and prefaced by George D. Prentice.
Cincinnati, OH: Pr. Moore, Wilstach, Keys & co., 1857. 288p. NUC OCLC

969. CHOATE, Clara Elizabeth [Am. 19c]
Songs of truth.
2d ed. Boston: Lee & Shepard, 1894. 42 l. NUC OCLC
CHRYSTABEL, pseud. <u>see</u> ATTENBOROUGH, Florence Gertrude

CHRISTABEL, pseud. <u>see</u> DOWNING, Mary

970. CHRISTIAN, Ann [Br. 18c]
Cambridge. A poem.
L: W. Reeve, 1756. 10p. BL

971. CHUBBUCK, Lavinia [Am. 19c]
My two sisters: a sketch from memory. By Emily E. (Chubbuck) Judson.
Boston: Ticknor, Reed & Fields, 1854. 112p. NUC BL OCLC
[Incl. poetry by Lavinia]

972. CHUDLEIGH, Mary (Lee), Lady [Br. 1656-1710] PSEUD: Eugenia; Quality, A lady of
Essays upon several subjects, in prose and verse.
L: R. Bonwicke, et al, 1710. 240p. NUC BL OCLC

973. -----The female preacher. By a lady of quality.
L: H. Hills, 1699? 24p. NUC

974. -----The ladies' defence; or, the Bride-woman's counsellor answered in a poem. Written by a lady.
L: John Deeve, 1699, 1701. 23p. NUC BL
[Published 1700 as: The female advocate; and in 1707 as: The female preacher.]

975. -----Poems on several occasions; together with The song of the three children paraphras'd.
L: Bernard Lintott, 1703. 125, 73p. NUC BL OCLC

976. CHURCHILL, Amelia Laman [Am. 19c]
Masonic poems.
2d ed. La Porte, IN: Pub. by author, Millikan & Cullaton, pr., 1865. 63p. NUC

977. CHURCHILL, Rosie [Br. 19c]
Poems and song words.
L: Simpkin, Marshall & co., 1889. 48p. BL

978. CLAIBORNE, Martha J. (Haden) [Am. 19c] PSEUD: Clark, Martha J.
Hawthorne leaves by Martha J. Clark.
Baltimore, MD: Cushing & co., 1894. 200p. NUC OCLC

979. CLAPP, Eliza Thayer [Am. 1811-1888]
Essays, letters, and poems.
Boston: Priv. pr., 1888. 200p. NUC
[Transcendentalist, later Unitarian religious writer; poems pp. 214-273]

980. CLAPP, Mabelle P. [Am. 19c]
Sunshine 'mid shadows.
Boston: George H. Ellis, 1898. 108p. NUC OCLC

981. CLAPP, Susan Francis (Preston) [Am. 1817-1859]
Quiet hours.
Salem: H. Whipple & son, 1859. 131p. NUC OCLC
[Religious poetry]

CLARA AUGUSTA <u>see</u> JONES, Clara Augusta

CLARIBEL, pseud. see BARNARD, Charlotte Alington

982. CLARK, Annie E. [Am. 19c]
Poems.
Philadelphia: J.B. Lippincott & co., 1866. 146p. NUC BL OCLC

983. CLARK, Annie Maria (Lawrence) [Am. b. 1835] ALT: Lawrence, Annie Maria
Verses and versions.
Lancaster, MA: Pr. for author by W.J. Coulter, c1898. 36 l. NUC OCLC
[26 misc. poems]

984. CLARK, Annie R. [Am. 19c]
Light amid the shadows; poems by Annie Clarke.
Chicago, NY & Toronto: Fleming H. Revell co., 1898. 143p. NUC OCLC

985. CLARK, Elizabeth Dwight [Am. 1837?-1906]
My ship; or, One day by the sea.
Portland, ME: Frank B. Clark, 1888. 16 l. NUC OCLC

986. CLARK, Emily [Br. 18/19c]
Poems: consisting chiefly of ballads.
L: F.C. & J. Rivington, 1810. 144p. BL

987. CLARK, Esther Lewis [Br. 1719?-1794]
Poems moral and entertaining.
Bath: Pr. and sold by S. Hazard; G.G.J. & J. Robinson, 1789. 336p. NUC OCLC

988. CLARK, Isabella Golding [Br. 19c] ALT: C., I.; C., I. G.
The legend of the chapel of St. Thomas of Acon, commonly called Mercers' Chapel. By I.C. [I.G.C. BL].
L: Church press co., 1865. 408p. NUC BL OCLC

989. CLARK, Jeannette R. [Am. 19c] ALT: Nettie
Nettie's poems, and a farce: Old fogy and young America.
Cincinnati, OH: 1880. 78, 24p. NUC OCLC
[44 misc. poems & 2-act play designed for home theatricals.]

990. CLARK, Julia [Am. 19c]
Driftwood. With Medora Clark.
Milwaukee, WI: Magann, Keege, & Aldrich, 1878. 172p. NUC OCLC

991. CLARK, Kate McCosh, Mrs. [Br. 19c]
Persephone, and other poems.
L: Sampson, Low, Marston & co., 1894. 192p. NUC BL OCLC

CLARK, MARTHA J., pseud. see CLAIBORNE, Martha J. (Haden)

CLARK, Medora, co-author see CLARK, Julia

992. CLARKE, Amy (Key), Mrs. Henry Clarke [Br. 19/20c] ALT: Key, Amy
Caerdyn and other poems.
L: n.p., 1873. BL

993. CLARKE, Ann [Br. 19c]
Poems, moral and entertaining.
Northampton: the author, 1824. 48p. BL

994. -----The saviour's triumph and Satan's downfall, a tragical poem.
L: n.p., 1824. 48p. BL

995. -----The world an inn; or, The soul's search after divine knowledge. An allegory.
L: the author, 1835? 106p. BL

996. -----The world an inn; or, Hephzibah's splendid wedding. An allegory.
Bath: the author, 1830? 254p. BL
[Part II of The world an inn]

997. CLARKE, Anne, Miss [Br. 19c] PSEUD: Lover of her country, A; Philanthropos
Small literary patchwork; or, A collection of miscellaneous pieces, in prose, and verse, written on various occasions, chiefly on moral and interesting subjects. By Anne Clarke, a lover of her country.
2d ed. L: the author by Nichols, son, & Bentley, 1814. 118p. BL
[On half t.p.: A country woman. On t.p.: A village muse--she claims no higher fame. Incl. letters to newspaper editors, signed Philanthropos; poems: satire, patriotic, elegies, lyrics.]

CLARKE, ELIZA, pseud. see COBBOLD, Elizabeth Knipe

CLARKE, Mrs. Henry see CLARKE, Amy (Key)

998. CLARKE, Katherine [Br. 19c]
Dew drops.
Cheltenham: Priv. pr. by William Clee, 1876. 27 l. NUC
[Religious and nature poetry]

999. CLARKE, Katherine A. [19c] ALT: Clarke, Katie A.
Gleanings from my portfolio. Original poems, by Katie A. Clarke.
Toronto: Pr. for priv. circ., 1894. 75p. NUC

1000. -----Lyrical echoes, by Katherine A. Clarke.
Toronto: W. Briggs, 1899. 157p. BL NUC

CLARKE, Katie A. see CLARKE, Katherine A.

1001. CLARKE, Mary Bassett [Am. b. 1831] PSEUD: Fairfield, Ida
Autumn leaves, by Mary Bassett Clarke (Ida Fairfield).
Buffalo, NY: C.W. Moulton, 1895. 238p. NUC OCLC

1002. -----Legend of Watch Hill.
n.p.: n.p., 189-? 15p. OCLC

1003. CLARKE, Mary Bayard Devereux [Am. 1827-1886] PSEUD: Tenella
The battle of Manassas, by Mrs. Clark, wife of Col. Clark, 14th Regiment, North Carolina.
n.p.: n.p., 1861? 1p. NUC
[Civil War poetry]

1004. -----Beauregard at Manassas.
n.p.: n.p., 1861? 1p. NUC
[Civil War poetry]

1005. -----Clytie and Zenobia; or, The lily and the palm, a poem.
NY: E.P. Dutton & co., 1871. 65p. NUC OCLC

1006. -----Mosses from a rolling stone; or, Idle moments of a busy woman. By Tenella.
Raleigh, NC: W.B. Smith & co., 1866. 168p. NUC BL OCLC

1007. -----Wood-notes; or, Carolina carols: a collection of North Carolina poetry. Compiled by Tenella.
Raleigh, NC: Warren L. Pomeroy, 1854. 2v. NUC OCLC
[30pp. of original poems by Tenella. Incl. others by North Carolina women: Mrs. S.C. Chunn, Mrs. E.A. Dare, Mrs. Joseph Gales, Miss M.A. Hoye, Laura Linton, Ellen Lloyd, Luola, Mrs. George C. Mendenhall, Miss Ann Pope, Sarah B. Winston.]

CLARKE, Mary Cowden see CLARKE, Mary Victoria (Novello) Cowden-

1008. CLARKE, Mary Victoria (Novello) Cowden- [Br. 1809-1898] ALT: Clarke, Mary Cowden PSEUD: Shortfellow, Henry Wandsworth
Honey from the weed. Verses.
L: C. Kegan Paul & co., 1881. 350p. NUC BL OCLC

1009. -----An idyl of London streets, by Mary Cowden Clarke.
Rome: Italian-American school press, 1875. 19p. NUC

1010. -----Memorial sonnets.
L: Pr. Novello, Ewer, 1888. 112p. NUC

1011. -----A score of sonnets to one object.
L: Kegan Paul, Trench, 1884. 28p. NUC OCLC

1012. -----The song of drop o'wather. By Harry Wandsworth Shortfellow.
L & NY: G. Routledge, 1856. 120p. NUC OCLC
[Parody of Longfellow's Hiawatha]

1013. -----Verse-waifs: forming an appendix to Honey from the weed.
L: K. Paul, Trench, 1883. 79p. NUC OCLC

CLARKE, Sara Jane see LIPPINCOTT, Sara J. (Clarke)

1014. CLARKE, Sara Jane, Lippincott [Am. 1823-1904] PSEUD: Greenwood, Grace
Poems. By Grace Greenwood.
Boston: Ticknor, Reed, & Fields, 1851. 190p. NUC BL

CLARKSON, L., comp. see WHITELOCK, Louise Clarkson

CLARKSON, Lida see WHITELOCK, Louise Clarkson

1015. CLAY, Geraldine, Mrs. John Randolph Clay [Br. 19c]
A "ray" from the "land of the sun!" Peru! By Geraldine, Mrs. J. Randolph Clay.
L: n.p., 1870? 19p. BL

CLAY, Mrs. John Randolph see CLAY, Geraldine

1016. CLEAVELAND, Elizabeth Hannah (Jocelyn) [Br. 1824-1911]
The dark river.
NY: A.D.F. Randolph, Clark & Maynard, 1863. 16p. NUC

1017. -----Easter flowers.

n.p.: n.p., n.d. 7p. NUC

1018. -----No sect in heaven.
NY: Broughton, Jr., 1860. 16p. NUC OCLC

CLEMANS, Mrs. F.M. see CLEMANS, Sarah Isabella

CLEMANS, Rev. F.M., comp. see CLEMANS, Sarah Isabella

1019. CLEMANS, Sarah Isabella, Mrs. F.M. Clemans [Am. 19c]
Flowers from the pathway of a consecrated life ... . Comp. her husband, Rev. F.M. Clemans.
Columbus, OH: William G. Hubbard, 1836 [1886 OCLC]. 296p. NUC

CLEMENCE, F., ed. see NASH, Caroline

1020. CLEMENT, Ada [Br. 19c]
Original writings. Ser. 1.
Kensington: J.W. Wakeham & son, 1886. 20p. BL
[Inspirational essays and poems]

CLEMMER, Mary E. see AMES, Mary E. (Clemmer)

1021. CLEPHANE, Anna Jane Douglas Maclean [Br. 19c]
The journey of life ... verses.
n.p.: n.p., 1847. BL

1022. -----Plays and poems.
Northampton: Priv. pr. Stanton & son, 1864. 40p. BL OCLC
[Pub. as memorial. Incl. 3 tragedies. Poems pp. 285-383, chiefly ballads and occasional verse.]

CLERGYMAN'S WIFE, A, pseud. see SMITH, Bithiah, Mrs.

1023. CLERKE, Ellen Mary [Br. 1840-1906]
The flying Dutchman and other poems.
L: Satchell & co., 1881. 107p. BL

CLEVELAND, FLORENCE, pseud. see TWEDDELL, Elizabeth (Cole)

1024. CLEVELAND, Lucy [Am. 19c]
Lotus-life, and other poems.
L & NY: G.P. Putnam's sons, 1893. 111p. NUC OCLC
[Incl. poems on Egypt]

1025. -----The scarlet-veined, and other poems.
NY: A.D.F. Randolph co., 1897. 135p. NUC OCLC

1026. CLEVELAND, Mary A., Mrs. [Am. 19c]
Poems written ... during her blindness.
Winsted, CT: n.p., 1872. 30p. NUC OCLC

1027. CLIVE, Caroline Archer (Wigley) [Br. 1801-1873] PSEUD: V.
I watched the heavens: a poem, by V.
L: n.p., 1842. BL

1028. -----IX poems by V.
L: Saunders & Otley, 1840. NUC BL

1029. -----The Morlas; a poem by V.
L: Hope, 1853. 59p. BL OCLC

1030. -----Poems by V.
L: n.p., 1872. 62p. L: Longmans, Green & co., 1890. 207p. BL

1031. -----Poems. Including a new edition of IX poems by V., with former and recent additions.
L: Saunders & Otley, 1856. 229p. NUC OCLC

1032. -----The queen's ball, a poem. By V.
L: Saunders, 1847. 15p. BL OCLC

1033. -----Saint Oldooman: a myth of the nineteenth century.
L: Simpkins, Marshall & co., 1845. 22p. BL
[22p. satire on lives of the English saints]

1034. -----The valley of the Rea. By V.
L: n.p., 1851. 15p. BL

1035. CLOUD, Virginia Woodward [Am. 1861-1938]
Down Durley Lane, and other ballads.
NY: The Century co., 1898. 99p. NUC BL OCLC

1036. CLYMER, Ella Maria (Dietz) [Br. b. 1856] ALT: Dietz, Ella
The triumph of life. Mystical poem. By Ella Dietz.
L: E.W. Allen, 1885. 345p. NUC

1037. -----The triumph of love. A mystical poem in song, sonnets, and verse. By Ella Dietz.
L: E.W. Allen, 1877. 175p. NUC OCLC

1038. -----The triumph of time. Mystical poem. By Ella Dietz.
L: E.W. Allen, 1884. 227p. NUC

COATES, Ellen see FREEMAN, Ellen Coates

1039. COATES, Florence Earle [Am. 1850-1927]
Memorial ode, written by request of the city of Philadelphia ... .
Cambridge, MA: Pr. at Riverside Press, 1898. 5 l. NUC

1040. -----Poems.
Boston: Houghton, 1895. 136p. NUC

1041. -----Poems.
Boston & NY: Houghton, Mifflin & co., 1898. 136p. NUC OCLC

1042. COATS, J. B., Mrs. [Am. 19c]
Poems and fragments in prose.
Cincinnati, OH: Walden & Stowe, pr. for the author, c1880. 200p. NUC OCLC
[Poems on Lake Seneca & Watkins Glen, NY; Prose recollections; fictional letter from the Queen of Sheba.]

1043. COBBETT, Maria, Mrs. [Br. b. c1800]
Poems.
L: Pr. for priv. circ., 1880. 88p. NUC BL

1044. COBBIN, Mary Eliza [Br. 19c]
Simple poems: sacred and miscellaneous.
L: S.W. Partridge, 1867. 104p. BL

1045. COBBOLD, Dorothy [Br. 19c]
Domestic rhymes.
L: Rivingtons, 1856. 65p. BL

1046. COBBOLD, Elizabeth Knipe [Br. 1767-1824] ALT: Knipe, Eliza; Clarke, Eliza PSEUD: Carolina Petty Pasty; Clarke, Eliza
Cliff Valentines.
Ipswich: J. Raw, 1813. 26p. or 1814. 32p. BL

1047. -----Ode on the victory of Waterloo.
Ipswich: The Author; Pr. J. Raw; Sold by Messrs. Longman, Hurst, Rees, Orme and Brown, 1815. 18p. NUC BL OCLC
[Sold to benefit the Waterloo Subscription]

1048. -----Poems.
Ipswich: J. Raw, 1825. 383p. NUC BL OCLC
[Incl. memoir of author by Laetitia Jermyn]

1049. -----Poems on various subjects. By Eliza Knipe.
Manchester: C. Wheeler, 1783. 112p. NUC BL

1050. -----Six narrative poems. By Eliza Knipe.
L: Pr. & sold by C. Dilly, 1787. 74p. NUC BL OCLC

1051. COBBY, Eleanor F. [Br. 19c]
The auto-biography of war, being a brief account of its private pedigree and public transactions.
Bognor: Henry Lovett, 1884. 16p. BL

COCHERON, Augusta (Joyce) see COCHERON, [Crocheron OCLC], Augusta (Joyce)

1052. COCHERON, [Crocheron OCLC], Augusta (Joyce) [Am. 19c]
Wild flowers of Deseret. A collection of efforts in verse.
Salt Lake City, UT: Pr. at the Juvenile Instructor off., 1881. 240p. NUC OCLC

1053. COCHRANE, Mrs. Alexander [Br. 19c] PSEUD: Lady, A
Flights of fancy, consisting of a variety of poetical pieces, satirical, humourous, pathetic, etc. By a lady.
Arbroath: P. Wilson, 1844. 83p. BL

1054. COCKBURN, Catherine (Trotter) [Br. 1679-1749] ALT: Trotter, Catherine
The works of Mrs. Catherine Cockburn, theological, moral, dramatic, and poetical. Several of them now first printed. By Thomas Birch.
L: J. & P. Knapton, 1751. 2v. NUC BL OCLC

1055. COCKE, Zitella [Am. b. 1848?]
A Doric reed.
Boston: Copeland & Day, 1895. 91p. NUC OCLC

1056. -----Easter lilies, an original poem.
NY: The Art Lithographic pub. co., 189-? 8p. NUC OCLC

1057. COCKLE, Mary, Mrs. [Br. 19c]
Elegy on the death of his late Majesty George the Third.
Newcastle upon Tyne: S. Hodgson, 1820. 20p. NUC BL

1058. -----Elegy to the memory of her royal highness the Princess Charlotte of Wales.
Newcastle upon Tyne: S. Hodgson, 1817. 7p. NUC BL

1059. -----The fishes grand gala.
L: C. Chapple, 1808. 16p. NUC BL

1060. -----Lines addressed to Lady Byron.
Newcastle: S. Hodgson, 1817. 6p. NUC BL

1061. -----Lines on the lamented death of Sir John Moore. By E.C.
L: D.N. Sharp, 1810. 11p. BL

1062. -----Lines to a boy pursuing a butterfly.
Newcastle: T. & J. Hodgson, 1826. 4p. NUC BL

1063. -----Reply to "fare thee well".
L: Kirby, 1816. 12p. NUC

1064. -----Simple minstrelsy.
L: C. Chapple, 1812. 237p. NUC BL

1065. COCKLE, Rita Francis Moss-, Mrs. [Br. 19c] ALT: Mosscockle, Rita Frances, Mrs.
Fantasies.
L: K. Paul, Trench & co., 1886. 78p. NUC BL OCLC

1066. -----The golden quest and other poems. By Mrs. Moss-Cockle.
L: K. Paul, Trench, Trubner & co., ltd., 1890. 72p. NUC BL OCLC

1067. COCKS, S., Mrs. [Br. 19c]
Original hymns for the family and the closet.
L: Hamilton Adams & co., 1831. 201p. NUC BL
[With an appendix of 11 hymns by the author's mother]

1068. COGHILL, Annie Louisa (Walker), Mrs. Harry Coghill [Br. 1836-1907] ALT: Walker, Annie Louisa
Oak and maple: English and Canadian verses.
L: Kegan Paul, Trench, Trubner, 1890. 114p. BL OCLC

COGHILL, Mrs. Harry <u>see</u> COGHILL, Annie Louisa (Walker)

1069. COLBORNE-VEEL, Mary [Br. d. 1923] ALT: Veel, Mary Colbourne-
The fairest of the angels, and other verse.
L: H. Cox, 1894. 157p. NUC BL

1070. COLBURN, Maria Southwick [Am. 19c]
Golden gems. Miscellaneous poems.
Oakland, CA: Pacific Press pub. co., 1891. 33p. NUC OCLC

1071. COLCHESTER, Elizabeth Susan (Law) Abbot, Baroness [Br. 1799-1883] ALT: Abbot, Elizabeth Susan (Law), Baroness Colchester; C., E. S.; Law, Elizabeth Susan; L., E. S. PSEUD: Amateur, An
Giustina: a Spanish tale of real life. A poem in three cantos. By E.S.L.
L: Ibotson & Palmer, prs., 1833. 63p. NUC BL OCLC

1072. -----Home reminiscences and other poems ... . By E.S.C.
L: Pr. Spottiswoode & co., 1861. 144p. NUC BL OCLC

1073. -----The Lady "Arabella Stuart." A poem. By E.S.L.
L: Pr. E. Barclay, 183-? 126p. NUC OCLC

1074. -----Miscellaneous poems. By E.S.L.
L: Ibotson & Palmer, 1832. 104p. NUC BL OCLC

1075. -----Views in London. By an amateur.
L: Chiswick press, pr. C. Whittingham, 1833. 66p. NUC BL OCLC

1076. COLCHESTER, Lady Elizabeth Sophia (Law) [Br. 19c] ALT: L., E. S.
Miscellaneous poems dedicated to Joseph Jekyll, esq., by E.S.L.
L: Ibotson & Palmer, priv. pr., 1832. 104p. NUC BL OCLC

1077. COLCORD, Millie [Am. 1859-1878]
For thy name's sake, and other poems.
Portland, ME: Hoyt, Fogg & Donham, 1878. 100p. NUC OCLC

1078. COLDWELL, Mary [Br. 19c]
A congratulatory poem, addressed to Her Majesty Queen Victoria and His Royal Highness Prince Albert, on their marriage.
L: Hatchard & son, 1840. 16p. BL

1079. COLE, Jessie Adella [Am. 19c]
Poems.
Denver, CO: F.W. Wood & co., pr., 1885. 291p. NUC

1080. COLERIDGE, Mary Elizabeth (Anodos) [Br. 1861-1907] ALT: Anodos
Fancy's following. By Anodos.
Oxford: Daniel, 1896. 58p. NUC BL OCLC

1081. -----Fancy's guerdon. By Anodos.

2d ed. L: E. Mathews, 1897. 30p. NUC BL OCLC

COLES, Ada, co-author see COLES, Clara (Leake)

1082. COLES, Clara (Leake) [Am. 19c]
Clara's poems.
Philadelphia: J.B. Lippinncott & co., 1861. 304p. NUC OCLC
[Poems by author's daughter, Ada Coles, pp. 283-296]

1083. COLLET, Fanny [Br. 19c]
Building of the Leviathan 1856-57-58. A poem.
L: Deeks, 1859. 18p. BL

1084. COLLIER, Martha [Br. 19c]
Lines to Mademoiselle Lind.
Manchester: the author, 1849. 15p. BL

COLLIER, Mary (Peach) see COLLIER, Mary (Leach)

1085. COLLIER, Mary [Br. 18c]
Poems, on several occasions.
Winchester: Pr. M. Ayres for the author, 1762. 68p. NUC BL
[New ed. Petersfield: n.p., 1765. 68p. Incl. some remarks on her life]

1086. COLLIER, Mary [Br. 18c]
The woman's labour; an epistle to Mr. Stephen Duck; in answer to his late poem called The thresher's labour.
L: the author & sold by J. Roberts, 1739. 32p. NUC
[Author was a washerwoman]

1087. COLLIER, Mary (Leach) [Peach OCLC] [Br. 19c]
Poetic effusions.
2d ed. Derby: Jewitt, 1835. 94p. NUC OCLC

1088. COLLING, Elizabeth [Br. 19c]
PSEUD: Ita; Mawr, Eta
Far and near; or, Translations and originals. By Ita [NUC].
L: T. Nelson & sons, 1864. 270p. NUC BL OCLC
[Part III original odes, occasional verse. Also pub. as: Far and near; or, Stories of a Christmas tree.]

1089. -----The old, old woman of Elton. A true ballad of modern times. North of England Tractates No. 6.
L: John Russell Smith; Stokesley: Twiddell & sons, 1868-90. 7p. BL

1090. -----The story of Count Ulaski: Aurelia: or, The gifted: and other poems.
L: n.p., 1870. BL

1091. -----A tour of times gone by. By Eta Mawr.
Darlington: Peter Rhodes, 1871. 72p. NUC BL OCLC

1092. COLLING, Mary Maria [Br. b. 1805]
Fables and other pieces in verse ... with some account of the author in letters to Robert Southey ... by Mrs. Bray.
L: Longman, Rees, Orme, Brown & Green, 1831. 178p. NUC BL OCLC
[Colling was Mrs. Bray's servant; poems pp. 89-178]

COLLINGRIDE, Henrietta Isabella, comp. see DRING, Mrs.

1093. COLLINGS, Linda B.M. [Br. 19c]
A rhyming record of English history and other poems.
L: Dibgy, Long & co., 1892. 51p. BL

1094. COLLINS, Miss [Br. 19c]
Poems.
L: Pr. M. Bird, sold by T. Hookham, 1816. 64p. NUC

1095. COLLINS, Emma (Gowdy), Mrs. William Leslie Collins [Am. 19c]
Sea waifs, and other poems.
Louisville, KY: J.P. Morton & co., 1888. 186p. NUC OCLC

1096. COLLINS, Laura G. (Case) [Am. 1826-1912]
Immortelles and asphodels; poems.
Cincinnati, OH: The Robert Clarke co., 1898. 106p. NUC OCLC

COLLINS, Mrs. William Leslie see COLLINS, Emma (Gowdy)

COLLINSON, Anne Ross, comp. see BULMER, Agnes Collinson

COLMORE, G., pseud. see WEAVER, Baille Gertrude (Renton) Dunn

COLQUHOUN, Frances Sara Fuller Maitland see MAITLAND, Frances Sara Fuller

1097. COLTHURST, E., Miss [Br. 19c]
Futurity.
Cork: O. Savage, 1837. 202p. NUC BL OCLC
[Narrative poems & 2 short stories]

1098. -----Futurity continued.
Cork: Osborne Savage & son, 1838. 100p. BL

1099. -----Home.
Cork: n.p., 1836. 140p. BL

1100. -----Life, a poem.
Cork: n.p., 1835. 79p. BL

1101. -----Love and loyalty. A poem.
L: W. Pickering, 1851. 46p. BL OCLC

1102. -----Loyalty, a poem.
L: n.p., 50p. BL
[With additional poems]

1103. -----The storm; a poem, in five cantos: and other poems.
Liverpool: Arthur Newlins; L: J. Hatchard & son, 1840. 164p. NUC BL OCLC

1104. COLVILLE, Elizabeth (Melvill), Lady Colville of Culross [Br. 17c] ALT: Culross, Elizabeth (Melvill) Colville, Lady; M.M.; Melvill, Elizabeth
Ane Godlie dreame compylit in Scottish meter by M.M. (Mistress Melville) gentlewoman in Culross, at the request of her freindes.
Edinburgh: Pr. Robert Charteris, 1606, 1610. NUC BL OCLC
[Also pub. as: A Godlie dreame, compiled by Elizabeth Melvill, Ladye Culross younger, at the request of a friend. Edinburgh: Andrew Hart, 1620]

1105. COLVIN, Laura M. [Am. 19c]
Belles and beaux, with other poems.
Rochester, NY: Charles Mann, c1882. 271p. NUC OCLC

1106. COMBERMERE, Mary Woolley Stapleton (Gibbings) Cotton, Viscountess [Br. d. 1889] ALT: Cotton, Mary Woolley Stapleton (Gibbings), Viscountess Combermere
A friar's scourge. Nonsense verses.
L: Pr. A. Schulze, 1876. 170p. NUC BL OCLC

1107. COMMELIN, Anna Olcott, Mrs. [Am. 19c]
Of such is the kingdom, and other poems.
NY: Fowler & Wells, 1894. 110p. NUC OCLC

1108. -----Poems.
NY: A.D.F. Randolph & co., 1888. 60p. NUC OCLC

COMPTON, Margaret (Clephane), Marchioness of Northampton <u>see</u> NORTHAMPTON, Margaret (Clephane) Compton, Marchioness of

COMPTON, Spencer Joshua Alwyne, Marquis of Northampton, ed. <u>see</u> NORTHAMPTON, Margaret (Clephane) Compton, Marchioness of

1109. CONDON, Lizzie G. [Br. b. 1857]
Killeeny of Lough Corrib, and miscellaneous poems.
Dublin: McGlashan & Gill, 1872. 207p. NUC BL

1110. CONE, Helen Gray [Am. 1859-1934]
Baby sweethearts.
NY: Frederick A. Stokes co., 1890. 13 l. NUC

1111. -----Bonnie little people ... new verses.
NY: F.A. Stokes co.; L: Dean & son, 1890. NUC BL OCLC

1112. -----The ivy leaf; a book of college and alumnae poems.
NY: The Knickerbocker Press, 1899. 34p. NUC OCLC
[Hunter College, NY]

1113. -----Oberon and Puck, verses grave and gay.
NY: Cassell & co., 1885. 140p. NUC BL OCLC

1114. -----The ride to the lady, and other poems.
Boston & NY: Houghton, Mifflin & co., 1891. 95p. NUC BL OCLC
[Misc., narratives & sonnets]

1115. CONGDON, Caroline M. [Am. 19c]
The guardian angel; and other poems.
Auburn, NY: W.J. Moses, 1856. 250p. OCLC

1116. CONKEY, M., Mrs. [Am. 19c]
Cottage musings; or, Select pieces in prose and verse.
NY: Press of H.R. Piercy, 1835. 184p. NUC OCLC

1117. CONKLIN, Jane Elizabeth (Dexter) [Am. b. 1831]
Poems.
NY: Press of J.J. Little & co., 1884. 148p. NUC OCLC

1118. CONNERS, Maria Wheeler, Mrs. [Am. 19c]
A wreath of maple leaves; or, A collection of household poems.
Seattle, WA: William H. Hughes co., pr., 1888. 95p. NUC OCLC

CONSTANTIA, pseud. see MURRAY, Judith (Sargent)

1119. CONVERSE, Harriet Maxwell [Am. 1836-1903]
The Ho-de'-no-sau-nee, the Confederacy of the Iroquois.
L & NY: G.P. Putnam's sons, 1884. 13p. NUC OCLC

1120. -----Sheaves, a collection of poems.
NY: G.P. Putnam's sons, 1882. 160p. NUC OCLC

1121. CONWAY, Katherine Eleanor [Am. 1853-1927]
A dream of lilies.
Boston: J.G. Cupples co., c1893. 64 l. NUC OCLC

1122. -----Love's quest and other poems.
Boston: Flynn & Mahony, c1895. 51p. OCLC

1123. -----On the sunrise slope.
NY: The Catholic pub. society, 1881. 153p. NUC
[Author's first book of poetry, much of it religious]

1124. CONYNGHAM, Elizabeth (Emmet) Lenox-, Mrs. George Lenox-Conyngham [Br. 19c]
The dream, and other poems. By Mrs. George Lenox-Conyngham.
L: E. Moxon, 1833. 166p. BL NUC OCLC

1125. -----Eiler and Helvig; a Danish legend.
L: Chapman & Hall, 1863. 37p. NUC BL

1126. -----Hella and other poems.
L: E. Churton, 1836. 241p. NUC OCLC BL

1127. -----Horae poeticae; lyrical and other poems.
L: Longman, Brown, Green, Longmans & Roberts, 1859. 426p. NUC BL OCLC

CONYNGHAM, Mrs. George Lenox- see CONYNGHAM, Elizabeth (Emmet) Lenox-

1128. COOK, Ann G. [Am. d. 1826]
... some poetical pieces.
KY: n.p., c1854. 91p. NUC

1129. COOK, Clara F. [Am. 19c]
Leaves from life.
Owosso, MI: The Times pr. co., 1885. 44p. NUC OCLC

1130. COOK, Eliza [Br. 19c]
Lays of a wild harp; a collection of metrical pieces.
L: John Bennett; E. Spettigue, 1835. NUC BL

1131. -----Melaia, and other poems.
L: R.J. Wood, 1838. 202p. NUC BL
[Expanded with poems from Lays of a wild harp. L: Charles Tilt, 1840. 286p. NUC BL]

1132. -----New echoes and other poems.
L: Routledge, Warne & Routledge, 1864. 254p. NUC BL

1133. -----The old arm-chair.
Boston: D. Lothrop & co., 1856. 26p. NUC

1134. -----The old farm gate.
L & NY: R. Tuck & son, 188-? 15p. NUC OCLC

1135. -----Poems. With her miscellaneous pieces.
Philadelphia: Uriah Hunt & son; NY: Leavitt & Allen, 1845. 288p. NUC BL OCLC

1136. -----Poems: second series.
L: Simpkin, Marshall, 1845. 275p. OCLC

1137. -----The poetical works of Eliza Cook.
Philadelphia: Sorin & Ball, 1848. 392p. L: F. Warne & co.; NY: Scribner, Welford & co., 1870. 624p. NUC BL OCLC

COOK, Mrs. James C. see COOK, Mary Louise (Redd)

1138. COOK, Mary Louise (Redd), Mrs. James C. Cook [Am. 19c]
A legend of lover's leap and poems. By Mrs. James C. Cook.
Columbus, GA: Thos. Gilbert, pr., 1892. 23p. NUC OCLC

COOKE, Belle Walker see COOKE, Susan Isabella (Walker)

1139. COOKE, Elizabeth Harriet [Br. 19c]
The widow's mite.
L: R.J. Michell & sons, 1874. 71p. BL

1140. COOKE, Helen M., Mrs. [Am. 19c]
PSEUD: Linwood, Lottie
Gold-thread, and other poems. By Helen M. Cooke (Lottie Linwood).

NY: E.B. Treat, 1874. 195p. NUC OCLC

1141. -----Pine needles. By Helen M. Cooke (Lottie Linwood).
NY: E.B. Treat, 1886. 64p. NUC OCLC

1142. COOKE, Mrs. M. A. [19c]
The exhibition Bible stall. A poem.
Guernsey: William Maillard, 1862. 15p. BL

1143. -----A legend of La Haye du Puits. A Guernsey home.
6 pt. L: Provost & co., 1882. BL

1144. -----Marie de Saint Roman: suggested by an incident of the sixteenth century.
L: Sold by Frederick Le Lievre, 1865. 22p. BL

1145. -----Marion; or, The two crowns.
Guernsey: William Maillard, 1859. 15p. BL

1146. COOKE, Rose Terry [Am. 1837-1892] ALT: Terry, Rose
Poems.
Boston: Ticknor & Fields, 1861 [1860 OCLC]. 231p. NUC BL OCLC

1147. -----Poems.
NY: W.S. Gottsberger, 1888. 412p. NUC BL OCLC

1148. COOKE, Susan Isabella (Walker) [Am. 1834-1919] ALT: Cooke, Belle Walker
Tears and victory, and other poems. By Belle W. Cooke.
Salem, OR: E.M. Waite, pr., 1871. 253p. NUC OCLC

1149. COOKSON, Mary Ann [Br. 19c]
Poems on various subjects, never before published.
Leith: William Heriot, 1829. 86p. BL

1150. COOLBRITH, Ina Donna [Am. 1842-1928]
A collection of wild flowers of California pressed and arranged by Miss E.C. Alexander. With appropriate sonnets specially written by Miss Ina D. Coolbrith and Grace Hibbard.
4th ed. NY: Dodge book & stationery co., 1898. San Francisco: The popular bookstore, 1894. 5 l. NUC BL OCLC

1151. -----A perfect day and other poems.
San Francisco: J.H. Carmany & co., pr., 1881. 173p. NUC OCLC

1152. -----The singer of the sea.
San Francisco: The Century Club of California, 1894. 8 l. NUC OCLC

1153. -----Songs from the Golden Gate.
Boston & NY: Houghton, Mifflin & co., 1895. 159p. NUC OCLC

1154. COOLEY, Hattie A.
Ripples of song.
Cleveland, OH: William W. Williams, 1883. 112p. NUC OCLC
[Sixty-four poems in four parts: Sketches; Memorials songs; Three sunsets; & other poems]

1155. COOLIDGE, Katherine Scollay (Parkman) [Am. 1858-1900]
Voices.
Boston: Little, Brown & co., 1899. 118p. NUC OCLC

COOLIDGE, SUSAN, pseud. <u>see</u> WOOLSEY, Sarah Chauncey

1156. COOMBE, Sarah Matilda [Br. 19c]
Auristine; a tale of fancy.
Portsea: Williams & son, 1829. 45p. BL

1157. COOPER, Mrs. [Br. 18c]
An address to the people of Wapping and its envirions.
L: the author, 1770? 23p. BL

1158. COOPER, Cecilia [Br. 19c]
The battle of Tewkesbury. A poem written on a view of the entrenchments near the town.
Tewkesbury: Pr. E. Reddell, for the author, 1820. 46p. NUC BL OCLC

COOPER, Edith Emma, co-author <u>see</u> BRADLEY, Katherine Harris

1159. COOPER, Edith Emma [Br. 1862-1913] PSEUD: Field, Michael [With Bradley, Katherine Harris, Br. 1848-1914]; Leigh, Isla
Bellerophon. Pub. as: Isla Leigh. With Arran Leigh [Katherine Harris Bradley].
L: C. Kegan Paul, 1881. 180p. NUC BL

1160. -----Long ago. By Michael Field.
L: G. Bell, 1889. 132p. NUC BL OCLC
[Extension of Sappho's fragments into lyrics]

1161. -----Noontide branches, a small sylvan drama interspersed with songs and invocations, by Michael Field.

Oxford: Pr. Henry Daniel, 1899. 44p. NUC BL OCLC
[A woodland idyll, suited to reading. No acts or scenes.]

1162. -----Sight and song, by Michael Field.
L: Elkin Mathews & John Lane, 1892. 125p. NUC BL OCLC
[Poems written after viewing particular works of art. Painter & museum identified]

1163. -----Sight and sound. By Michael Field.
L: E. Matthews, 1892. 125p. NUC OCLC

1164. -----Under [Underneath NUC] the bough. By Michael Field.
L & NY: G. Bell & sons, 1893. 135p. NUC BL OCLC

1165. COOPER, Emma Louise (Adams) [Am. 19c]
Maidenhair.
n.p.: n.p., 1884? 10p. NUC

1166. COOPER, Maria Susannah [Br. 18c]
Jane Shore to her friend. A poetical epistle.
L: T. Becket, sold by J. Fiske, 1776. 16p. NUC BL OCLC

1167. COOPER, Mary Grace
Orletta; or courtly ways and cottage conclusions.
L: William Macintosh, 1866. 47p. BL

1168. COOPER, Mary Grace
Thamuta the spirit of death and other poems.
L: R. Fenn, 1837. 144p. BL

1169. COPCUTT, Ann Elizabeth [Am. 19c]
Poems.
NY: T.J. Crowen, 1862. 94p. NUC

1170. COPE, Harriet [Br. 19c]
An address to the late Lord Byron translated from the French of Mons. La Martine; with original poems, respectfully inscribed to the Bishop of Durham, by Miss H. Cope.
L: Pr. W. Glindon, 1825. 30p. OCLC

1171. -----The brazen serpent, a sacred poem.
L: W. Morgan, 1827. BL

1172. -----A monody to the memory of Thomas, Lord Erskine.
L: the author & pub. by F.C. & J. Rivington, 1824. BL

1173. -----Suicide, a poem in four parts.
L: F.C. & J. Rivington, 1815. 198p. NUC BL

1174. -----The triumphs of religion, a sacred poem in four parts.
L: Pr. A.J. Valpy, 1811. 121p. NUC BL

1175. -----Waterloo: a poem in two parts, inscribed to ... the Duke of Wellington.
L: Pr. R.G. Gunnell, 1822. 162p. NUC BL

CORDER, Annie, co-author see LAYARD, Nina Frances

1176. CORF, Eliza [Br. 19c]
Moral and religious essays, poems, anecdotes, and extracts from my diary.
L: Simpkin Marshall & co., 1852. 2v. BL OCLC

CORINNA, pseud. see THOMAS, Elizabeth

1177. CORK and ORRERY, Emily Charlotte (DeBurgh-Canning) Boyle, Countess of [Br. b. 1828] ALT: Boyle, Emily Charlotte (DeBurgh-Canning), Countess of Cork and Orrery
Memories and thoughts.
L: G. Bell & sons, 1886. 140p. BL

1178. CORLETT, Theresa, Mrs. [Am. 19c]
Birthday ode to her most gracious Majesty, Queen Victoria of England.
San Francisco: A.L. Bancroft & co., 1877. 7p. NUC OCLC

CORNABY, Hannah Hollingsworth see CORNABY, Hannah Last

1179. CORNABY, Hannah Last [Br. b. 1822] ALT: Cornaby, Hannah Hollingsworth
Autobiography and poems.
Salt Lake City, UT: Pr. J.C. Graham & co., 1881. 158p. NUC OCLC

1180. CORNELIUS, Mrs. Edward G. [Am. 19c]
Crumbs.
Indianapolis, IN: W.B. Burford, pr., 1898. 38p. NUC
[Religious poetry]

1181. CORNISH, Miss [Br. 19c]
Echoes of our childhood.
L: n.p., 1865. 108p. BL

1182. CORNWALL, Clarice [Br. 19c]

Sweet innocence. Songs and sketches of childhood.
L: Hodder & Stoughton, 1890. BL

1183. CORNWALL, Sarah Jerusha [Am. b. 1837]
Roses and myrtles.
NY: D. Appleton & co., 1881. 203p. NUC OCLC

1184. CORNWALLIS, Caroline Francis [Br. 1786-1858]
Selections from the letters of Caroline Frances Cornwallis. Also some unpublished poems.
L: Trubner & co., 1864. 482p. NUC BL OCLC

1185. CORPIER, Lulu Belle [Am. d. 1898]
Dreams and realities.
Nashville, TN: Publishing house of the M.E. Church, South, Barbee & Smith agents, 1897. 110p. NUC OCLC

1186. CORRIE, Theodora [Br. 19c]
Siberian echoes.
Edinburgh: T. & A. Constable, 1896. 104p. NUC
[3 narrative poems, 5 stories]

1187. CORSTORPHAN, Wilhelmina Henrietta [Br. 19c]
Poems, &c.
St. Andrews: J. Cook; M. Fletcher; W. Henderson, 1852. 141p. BL

1188. CORTISSOZ, Ellen Mackay (Hutchinson) [Am. 19c] ALT: Hutchinson, Ellen Mackay
Songs and lyrics. By Ellen Mackay Hutchinson.
Boston: J.R. Osgood & co., 1881. 98p. NUC

1189. CORWIN, Jane H. [Am. 19c]
The harp of home; or, The medley.
Cincinnati, OH: Moore, Wilstach, Keys & co., 1858. 382p. NUC OCLC
[Poetry & prose: advice, short stories & poems.]

1190. CORY, Constance E. [Br. 19c]
Seeds and blossoms.
Bath: S.W. Simms, 1897. 115p. BL

1191. CORY, Elizabeth [Br. 19c]
Lilies of the valley.
L: Whittaker & co.; Wisbech: William Watts, 1841. 60p. BL

1192. COSTELLO, Louisa Stuart [Br. 1799-1870]
The lay of the stork.
L: William & Frederick G. Cash, 1856. 131p. NUC BL

1193. -----The maid of the Cyprus Isle and other poems.
L: Sherwood, Neely & Jones, 1815. BL

1194. -----Redwald; a tale of Mona; and other poems.
Brentford: P. Norbury, 1819. 70p. NUC BL

1195. -----Songs of a stranger.
L: Pub. for the author by Taylor & Hessey, 1825. 158p. NUC BL OCLC

1196. COSTLEY, Rosa Fairfax, Mrs. [Am. 19c]
Fantasma, and other poems.
Kansas City, MO: Ramsey, Millett & Hudson, 1879. 318p. NUC OCLC

1197. COTES [Acotes OCLC], Rosemary A. [Br. 19c]
Dante's garden, with legends of the flowers.
L: Methuen & co., 1898. 110p. NUC BL OCLC

1198. COTTON, Mrs. F. Percy [Br. 19c]
PSEUD: Walton, Ellis; Walton, Mrs. Ellis
The dear homeland. Two poems by G[raham] C[lifton] Bingham and E. Walton.
L: Ernest Nister; E.P. Dutton, 1894. NUC BL

1199. -----Lyrics. By Ellis Walton.
L: Elliot Stock, 1895. 60p. BL OCLC

1200. -----Playmates. By Ellis Walton.
NY: Art Lithographic pub. co.; L: Artistic Lithographic co., 1899? 2p. OCLC
[Poems for children]

1201. -----Seven love-songs and other lyrics.
L: Elliot Stock, 1894. 60p. BL

COTTON, Mary Woolley Stapleton (Gibbings), Viscountess Combermere <u>see</u> COMBERMERE, Mary Woolley Stapleton (Gibbings) Cotton, Viscountess

COULTHARD, Clara <u>see</u> TANNER, Clara (Coulthard)

1202. COUREY, Hattie M. [Am. 19c]
Gems from the poems of Hattie M. Courey.

Albany, NY: c1890.

1203. COURSEN, Charlotte H. [Am. 19c]
From daybreak to twilight. With Edith R. Crosby.
NY: G.P. Putnam's sons, 1882. 51p. NUC OCLC

1204. COURTNEY, Margaret [Am. 19c]
The poetical works.
Pittsburgh, PA: John L. Arthurs, 1850. 300p. NUC

1205. COUSIN, Anne Ross (Cundell) [Br. 1824-1906] ALT: C., A. R.
Immanuel's land and other pieces by A.R.C.
L: J. Nisbet & co., 1876. 267p. NUC BL OCLC

1206. COVENTRY, Mary [Br. 19c] PSEUD: Moi-Meme
Poems of the past. By Moi-Meme
Dublin: M.H. Gill & son, 1890. 332p. BL

1207. COWDERY, Charlotte [Br. 19c]
Island leaflets. Poems.
2d ed. L: Longmans, Green & co., 1871. 160p. BL

1208. -----Poems.
L: Dovey & Sheerman, 1870. 104p. BL

1209. COWELL, Christiana B. (Coffin), Mrs. D.B. Cowell [Am. 1821-1862]
Life and writings of Mrs. Christiana B. Cowell, consort of Rev. D.B. Cowell, who died in Lebanon, Maine, Oct. 8, 1862, aged 41 years.
Biddeford, ME: J.E. Butler & co., 1872. 296p. NUC
[Incl. poetry and a hymn]

COWELL, Mrs. D.B. <u>see</u> COWELL, Christiana B. (Coffin)

1210. COWELL, Elizabeth Susan [Br. 19c] PSEUD: Suffolk Villager, A
Historical reveries. By a Suffolk villager.
L & Salisbury: n.p., 1839. 117p. BL
[OCLC lists under Sarah Wilkinson, of Sudbury.]

1211. COWELL, Elizabeth Susan [Br. 19c]
Leaves of memory.
L: Seeley & co., 1892. 89p. BL
[Incl. poetry]

1212. COWEN, Helene E. A. (Gingold) [Br. 19/20c] ALT: Gingold, Helene E. A.
A cycle of verse.
3d ed. L: Remington & co., 1889. 160p. BL

1213. COWLEY, Hannah (Parkhouse) [Br. 1743-1809] ALT: Merry, Mrs. Robert PSEUD: Anna Matilda
The British album.
Boston: Pr. & for Belknap & Hall, 1793. Dublin: Pr. Bernard Dernin, 1790. 1st Am. ed. Boston: Belknap & Hall, 1793. 290p. NUC TXU
[OCLC & NUC: Contains poems of Della Crusca (pseud. of Robert Merry), Anna Matilda, and others. Originally pub. as: The poetry of the world. 2v.]

1214. -----Edwina. A poem.
L: Wm. F.S.A. Hutchinson, 1794. BL

1215. -----The poetry of Anna Matilda.
L: J. Bell, 1788. 139p. NUC BL OCLC

1216. -----The Scottish village; or, Pitcairne Green. A poem.
L: G.G.J. & J. Robinson, 1786. 23p. NUC BL OCLC

1217. -----The siege of Acre. An epic poem in six books.
L: Pr. at Oriental press by Wilson for J. Debrett, 1801. 127p. BL NUC

1218. -----Works; drama and poems.
L: Wilkie & Robinson, 1810. 1813. 3v. NUC BL OCLC
[1 v. misc. poetry]

1219. COWPER, Frances Maria (Madan) [Br. 1726-1797] ALT: Cowper, Maria Frances Cecilia PSEUD: Lady, A
Original poems on various occasions. By a lady. Revised by William Cowper.
L: J. Deighton, J. Mathews & R. Faulder, 1792. 115p. NUC BL OCLC
[Also attrib. to Mrs. Cardale]

COWPER, Maria Frances Cecilia <u>see</u> COWPER, Frances Maria (Madan)

COWPER, William, co-author <u>see</u> COWPER, Frances Maria (Madan)

1220. COX, Lydia Noyes [Am. 1814-1844]
Recollections and gathered fragments ... . Ed. Mrs. Phoebe Palmer.
NY: Piercy & Reed, 1845. 231p. NUC

1221. COX, May M. [Br. 19c]
Poems.
L: George Bell & sons, 1889 72p. BL

1222. COXE, Eliza C. [Am. 19c]
Memorial poems of the late Mrs. Eliza C. Coxe. Comp. her husband.
Utica, NY: n.p., 1868. 7p. NUC

1223. CRAIG, Catharine Pringle [Br. 19c]
Mary the mother of Jesus. A poem.
L: Hodder & Stoughton, 1872. 169p. BL

1224. -----Zella, and other poems.
L: Hodder & Stoughton, 1877. 200p. BL

CRAIG, Isa see KNOX, Isa (Craig)

CRAIGMYLE, Bessie see CRAIGMYLE, Elizabeth

1225. CRAIGMYLE, Elizabeth [Br. 19c]
ALT: Craigmyle, Bessie
Poems and translations.
Aberdeen: J. & J.P. Edmond & Spark, 1886. 134.p. NUC BL OCLC

1226. CRAIK, Dinah Maria (Mulock) [Br. 1826/36-1887] ALT: Mulock, Dinah Maria
Poems.
L: Hurst & Blackett, 1859. 324p. NUC BL OCLC

1227. -----Poems of thirty years, new and old.
L: Macmillan, 1880. 411p. NUC OCLC
[NUC title: Thirty years, being poems new and old. Pub. 1880 & 1881]

1228. -----Songs of our youth.
L: Daldy, Isbister & co.; NY: Harper, 1875. 93p. OCLC

1229. CRAIK, Ellen S. [Br. 19c]
Poems.
L: James Nisbet & co., 1877. 61p. BL

1230. CRANCH, Jane Bowring [Br. 19c]
Poems.
L: Provost & co., 1877. 40p. BL

1231. -----True greatness.
L: W. & T.G. Cash, 1855. 48p. BL

1232. CRAWFORD, Alice Arnold [Am. 1850-1874]
A few thoughts for a few friends.
Chicago: Jansen, McClurg & co., 1875. 162p. NUC BL OCLC
[Chiefly verse]

1233. CRAWFORD, M. J. E., Mrs. [Am. 19c]
Songs of early and later years.
Philadelphia: Pub. for the author by Claxton, Remsen & Haffelfinger, c1871. 180p. NUC OCLC

1234. CRAWFORD, Margaret [Br. 19c]
Rustic lays; or, The braes of Gala Water.
Edinburgh: Pr. Mould & Tod, 1855. 84p. NUC BL OCLC

CRAWLEY, Eliza see MURDEN, Eliza (Crawley)

CRESWELL, Julia (Pleasants) see PLEASANTS, Julia

1235. CRESWICK, Margaret [Br. 19c]
Spiritual songs, etc.
L: Creswick & co., 1861. BL

1236. CREWDSON, Jane (Fox), Mrs. T.D. Crewdson [Br. 1808-1863]
Lays of the Reformation and other lyrics, scriptural and miscellaneous.
L: Hatchard & co., 1860. 284p. NUC BL OCLC

1237. -----"A little while" and other poems.
Manchester: William Brenner & co., 1864. 108p. NUC BL OCLC

1238. -----The singer of Eisenach and Luther at Worms.
Manchester: Tubbs & Brook; L: Simpkin, Marshall & co., 1870. 51p. BL

CREWDSON, Mrs. T.D. see CREWDSON, Jane (Fox)

1239. CREWE, Annabel [Br. 19c]
Ichabod. The Hebrew's lamentacion.
L: William Poole, 1879. 32p. BL

1240. -----A medley. Poems.
L: William Hunt & co., 1878. 116p. BL

1241. CRISFIELD, Charlotte Lennox [Am. 19c]
A wayside flower, and other poems.
Baltimore, MD: Pr. Kelly, Piet & co., 1875. 91p. NUC OCLC

1242. CRIST, Maley Bainbridge [Am. 19c]
Patchwork; the poems and prose sketches of Maley Bainbridge Crist.
Atlanta, GA: Martin & Hoyt co., 1898. 238p. NUC OCLC
[12 short stories, 30 misc. poems]

CROCHERON, Augusta (Joyce) see COCHERON, Augusta (Joyce)

1243. CROGGON, Lucy (Emra) [Br. 19c]
ALT: Emra, Lucy PSEUD: Lover of Nature, A

Attempts at sketching.
L: n.p. 1846. BL

1244. -----Heavenly themes. A selection of original poetry.
L: n.p. 1832. NUC BL

1245. -----Onward and upward.
Sittingbourne: n.p., 1853. BL

1246. -----Scenes in the life and death of a missionary and other original poems.
L: n.p., 1832. BL

1247. -----A selection of original hymns.
Dublin: n.p., 1850. NUC BL

1248. -----Things new and old; or, Recollections by a district visitor in prose and verse. Pub. as: Lucy Emra.
L: Hamilton, Adams & co., 1839. BL
[9 poems, recollections in prose]

1249. -----Things seen and known: or, a book of remembrance.
L: Hamilton, Adams & co., 1844. BL
[Poetry & prose: meditations & sketches]

1250. -----Thoughts by the way side.
Canterbury: Henry Ward, 1836. 111p. BL

1251. -----Transcripts from my tablets. By a lover of nature.
Dublin: n.p., 1849. NUC BL

1252. CROKER, Margaret Sarah [Br. 19c]
Monody on His late Royal Highness the Duke of Kent.
L: Francis Westley, 1820. 14p. BL

1253. -----A monody on the lamented death of her Royal Highness the Princess Charlotte Augusta of Wales and of Saxe Cobourg.
Saalfield: J. Bush; Edmund Lloyd, 1817. 24p. BL

1254. -----Nugae canorae.
L: J. Souter, 1818. 94p. NUC BL OCLC

1255. -----A tribute to the memory of Sir Samuel Romilly.
L: J. Souter, 1818. 14p. BL

1256. CROLY, Jane Cunningham [Br. 1829-1901] ALT: Cunningham, Jane
Mystagogue.
Dublin: George Drought, 1851. 8p. BL

1257. CROMMELIN, Maria Henrietta de la Cherois [Br. 19/20c] ALT: Crommelin, May
Poets in the garden. By May Crommelin.
L: T. Fisher Unwin, 1886. 256p. BL NUC OCLC

1258. CROPPER, Hon. Mrs. [Br. 19c] PSEUD: Rednaxela
The hermit of the Pyrenees and other miscellaneous poems. By Rednaxela.
L: n.p., 1858. BL

CROMMELIN, May <u>see</u> CROMMELIN, Maria Henrietta de la Cherois

CROSBY, Edith R., co-author <u>see</u> COURSEN, Charlotte H.

1259. CROSBY, Frances Jane [Am. 1820-1915] ALT: Van Alstyne, Frances Jane (Crosby)
Bells at evening and other verses.
NY & Chicago: The Bigelow & Main co., 1897. 192p. NUC BL

1260. -----The blind girl and other poems.
NY: Wiley & Putnam, 1851. [1844 NUC] 159p. BL

1261. -----Monterey and other poems.
NY: R. Craighead, 1851. 203p. NUC BL OCLC

1262. -----The names of the books of the Bible in verse.
NY & Chicago: Biglow & Main, 1880. 4p. NUC

1263. -----A wreath of Columbia's flowers.
NY: H. Dayton, 1858. 138p. NUC OCLC

1264. CROSLAND, Camilla Dufour (Toulmin), Mrs. Newton Crosland [Br. 1812-1895] ALT: Toulmin, Camilla Dufour
The diamond wedding: a Doric story and other poems. By Mrs. Newton Crosland.
L: Houlston & sons, 1871. 293p. NUC BL

1265. -----Lays and legends, illustrative of English life. By Camilla Toulmin.
L: Jeremiah Howe, 1845. 194p. NUC OCLC
[A novel with poems interspersed.]

1266. -----Light in the valley. By Mrs. Newton Crosland.

L & NY: G. Routledge, 1857. 228p. TXU

1267. -----Poems.
L: n.p., 1846. BL

CROSLAND, Mrs. Newton see CROSLAND, Camilla Dufour (Toulmin)

1268. CROSS, Ada Cambridge [Br. 1844-1926] ALT: C., A.; Cambridge, Ada
Hymns on the Holy Communion.
NY: Randolph; L: Houlston & Wright, 1866. 127p. NUC BL OCLC

1269. -----Hymns on the Litany. By A.C.
Oxford & L: J.H. & J. Parker, 1865. 73p. BL

1270. -----The manor house and other poems.
L: Daldy, Isbister & co., 1875. 283p. BL

1271. -----Unspoken thoughts.
L: K. Paul, Trench, 1887. 142p. NUC BL OCLC

1272. CROSS, Constance [Br. 19c]
The children of holy baptism.
L: n.p., 1877. BL

1273. -----The coming of the Christ-child; or, The path of light.
L: n.p., 1877. BL

1274. CROSS, Elizabeth D. [Br. 19c]
An old story, and other poems.
L: Longmans, Green & co., 1868. 155p. NUC BL OCLC

CROSS, Marian (Evans) see EVANS, Marian

1275. CROSS, Mary [Br. 19c]
Poems.
Edinburgh & L: Oliphant, Anderson & Ferrier, 1895. 64p. BL

1276. CROSS, Sophia [Br. 19c]
Mental flowers; original pieces on various subjects.
L: the Booksellers, 1843. 128p. BL

1277. CROW, Martha Foote [Am. 1854-1924] ALT: C., M. F.
The ministry of a child; a book of verses, by Martha Foote Crow.
Chicago: Wind-Tryst press, 1899. 94p. NUC OCLC

1278. -----The thought and the song.
Boston: Damrell & Upton, 1887. 6 l. NUC

1279. CROWELL, R. H., Mrs. [Am. 19c]
Fruit of affliction.
Wilkes Barre, PA: Pr. W.H. Seacord, 1878. 56p. NUC

1280. CROWELL, Rose Harvey [Am. 19c]
Crushed rose leaves. Poems.
Baltimore, OH: J.W. Smith & co., pr., 1881. 124p. OCLC

1281. CROWTHER, Mrs. [Br. 19c]
Moral tales and poetic essays.
Huddersfield: Brook & Lancashire, 1802. 122p. BL

1282. CRUGER, Eliza [Am. 19c]
Regina, and other poems.
NY: G.W. Carleton, 1868. 378p. BL

1283. CRUGER, Julie Grinnell (Storrow), Mrs. Van Rensselaer Cruger [Am. d. 1920] PSEUD: Gordon, Julien
The moujik. By Julien Gordon.
n.p.: n.p., 1891. 4p. NUC

1284. -----Poems. By Julien Gordon.
L: n.p., 1895. NUC

CRUGER, Mrs. Van Rensselaer see CRUGER, Julie Grinnell (Storrow)

1285. CRUTE, Sallie Spotswood, Mrs. [Am. 19c]
Buds from memory's wreath.
Philadelphia: Claxton, Remsen & Haffelfinger, 1873. 180p. NUC OCLC [Pt. 1, misc. poems; Pt. 2, "Scattered leaves," personal recollections in prose.]

1286. CULL, Mary [Br. 19c]
An acknowledgment to his Royal Highness the Prince Albert by Mary Cull, for patronizing her lines on the death of his grace, Arthur, Duke of Wellington.
n.p.: n.p., 1853. 4p. BL

1287. -----Lines descriptive of the lying in state and funeral procession of his grace Arthur, Duke of Wellington, etc.
n.p.: n.p., 1852. 4p. BL

1288. -----Lines on the wreck of the Birkenhead near the Cape of Good Hope on the 26th of February, 1852.
n.p.: n.p., 1852. 4p. BL

1289. -----Poems, etc.
L: Sangster & Fletcher, 1854. 270p. BL

1290. CULLEY, Ellen [Br. 19c] ALT: C---, Ellen

Poems. By Ellen C---.
L: Charles Westerton, 1855. 70p. BL

CULROSS, Elizabeth (Melvill) Colville, Lady see COLVILLE, Elizabeth (Melvill), Lady Colville of Culross

1291. CULSHA, Mary [Br. 19c]
A pilgrim's Ebenezer.
L: Wertheim & Macintosh, 1853. 34p. BL

1292. -----The prayer of Jehoshaphat.
L: Seeleys, 1852. 4p. BL

CUMBERLAND, PRINCESS OF, pseud. see SERRES, Olivia (Wilmot)

1293. CUMMINGS, Annie M. [Am. 19c]
Mother and son.
Cliftondale, NY: n.p., 1888. 5 l. NUC
[Poem on the Virgin Mary]

1294. CUMMINS, Hester V. [Am. b. 1862]
A bundle of twigs.
Vinton, IA: The Telegrapher's pub. co., 1893. 306p. NUC OCLC

1295. CUMMINS, Margaret [Am. 19c]
Leaves from my portfolio, original and selected, together with a religious narrative.
St. Louis, MO: William E. Foote, pr., 1860. 181p. NUC OCLC
[Stories, recollections, & 35 brief poems]

CUNNINGHAM, Jane see CROLY, Jane Cunningham

CURLING, M.A., see CURLING, Mary Anne

1296. CURLING, Mary Anne [Br. 19c]
ALT: Curling, M. A.
Poetical pieces.
Dover: W. Batcheller, 1831. 52p. NUC BL
[2d ed. with some additions. L: Whitaker, Treacher & Arnot, 1831. 54p. BL]

1297. CURRIE, Helen [Am. 19c]
Poems.
Philadelphia: Pr. Thomas H. Palmer, 1818. 150p. NUC OCLC

1298. CURRIE, Mary Montgomerie (Lamb) Singleton, Baroness [Br. 1843-1905]
PSEUD: Fané, Violet
Autumn songs, by Violet Fane.
L: Chapman & Hall, 1889. 85p. NUC BL OCLC

1299. -----Betwixt two seas: poems and ballads written at Constantinople and Therapia. By Violet Fane.
L: J.C. Nimmo, 1899. 105p. NUC BL OCLC

1300. -----Collected verses. By Violet Fane.
L: Smith, Elder, 1880. 101p. NUC OCLC

1301. -----Denzil Place; a story in verse. By Violet Fane.
L: Chapman & Hall, 1875. 256p. NUC BL OCLC
[Pub. as: Constance's fate. 1876.]

1302. -----From dawn to noon: poems by Violet Fane.
L: Longmans, Green, & co., 1872. 140p. NUC BL OCLC

1303. -----Poems. By Violet Fane.
L: J.C. Nimmo, 1842 [1892 BL]. 2v. NUC OCLC

1304. -----The queen of the fairies (a village story), and other poems. By Violet Fane.
L: Chapman & Hall, 1876. 152p. NUC BL OCLC

1305. -----Under cross and crescent: poems. By Violet Fane.
L: John C. Nimmo, 1896. 129p. NUC BL OCLC

1306. CURRIER, Mary Mehetabel [Am. b. 1869] PSEUD: Darrow, Persis E.
Among the granite hills.
Cambridge: Pr. at Riverside press, 1894. 136p. NUC OCLC

1307. -----Fructus arboris vitae. By Persis E. Darrow.
Wentworth, NH: n.p., 1890. 8p. NUC

1308. CURSHAM, Mary Anne [Br. 19c]
ALT: C., M. A.
Emanuel Swedenborg, and other poems. By M.A.C.
L: F. Pitman, 1832? 80p. NUC

1309. -----Martin Luther. A poem.
L: Longman, Hurst, Rees, Orme, Brown & Green, 1825. 82p. NUC BL OCLC

1310. -----Poems, sacred, dramatic and lyric.
L: Hamilton, Adams & co; Nottingham: S. Bennett, 1833. 285p. NUC BL

1311. CURTIES, Marianne [Br. 19c]
Classical pastime, in a set of poetical enigmas on the planets and zodiacal signs.

Reading: Pr. Snare & Man, 1813. 103p. NUC BL OCLC

1312. CURTIS, Ann [Br. 18c]
Poems on miscellaneous subjects.
L: Millan & Rae, 1783. 56p. NUC

1313. CURTIS, Austice
One question.
NY & Chicago: Brentanos, 1889. 122p. NUC
[Dramatic poem, 2 acts, blank verse]

1314. CURTIS, Harriet J., Mrs. [Am. 19c] PSEUD: Ray, Hettie J.
Angel whisperings: for the searcher after truth. By Hettie J. Ray.
Chicago: Religio-Philosophical pub. house, 1889. 272p. NUC OCLC

1315. CURTISS, Abby Allin [Am. 19c]
ALT: Allin, Abby
Home ballads: a book for New Englanders. By Abby Allin.
Boston & Cambridge, MA: J. Munroe & co., 1851. 238p. NUC BL OCLC
[Chiefly poetry]

1316. CURZON, Sarah Anne [Br. 1833-1898]
Laura Secord, the heroine of 1812: a drama. And other poems.
Toronto: C. Blackett Robinson, 1887. 215p. NUC BL OCLC
[Misc. poems & 2 plays]

1317. CUSHING, Eliza Lanesford (Foster) [Am. b. 1794]
Esther, a sacred drama: with Judith, a poem.
Boston: Joseph Dowe, 1840. 118p. NUC BL
[Esther, 3-act verse drama, pp. 1-103; Judith, narrative religious poem, pp. 107-118]

CUSTANCE, Olive see DOUGLAS, Olive Eleanor (Custance), Lady

1318. CUTTS, Mrs. [Br. 18c]
Almeria: or, Parental advice: a didactic poem. Addressed to the daughters of Great Britain and Ireland by a friend of the sex.
L: E. & J. Rodwell, 1775. 47p. NUC BL OCLC

1319. CUTTS, Mary [Am. 1801-1882]
PSEUD: Idamore
The autobiography of a clock and other poems. By Mary Cutts.
Boston: W. Crosby & H.P. Nichols; NY: C.S. Francis & co., 1852. 247p. NUC BL OCLC

1320. -----Grondalla; a romance in verse. By Idamore.
NY: Sheldon & co.; Boston: Gould & Lincoln, 1866. 310p. NUC OCLC

1321. CZARNECKI, Louisa Agnes, Mrs. [Br. 19c]
General Bem, and other poems.
2d ed. Edinburgh: A. Fullarton & co., 1853. NUC BL

1322. -----The hero of Italy and other poems.
Edinburgh: Paton & Ritchie, 1861. 122p. NUC BL

D., pseud. see GILLETE, Lucia Fidelia (Woolley)

D., pseud., co-author see GILLETTE, Florence Lilian

1323. D., A.G., Mrs. [Am. 19c]
Writings of Mrs. A.G.D. with a sketch of her character.
Newburyport, MA: Charles Norris & co., 1810. 72p. NUC

D., A.J.G. see DUFF, Anna Julia Grant (Webster)

D., A.T. see DRANE, Augusta Theodosia

D., C.A. see DE WINDT, Caroline Amelia (Smith)

D., E., Mrs. see DORNFORD, Eleanor, Mrs.

D., M.B.M. see DUNCAN, Mary Balfour Manson

D., T.F., ed. see DEMAREST, Mary Augusta (Lee)

D****, S**** see DOWSON, Susanna

1324. DABBS, Miriam Adair [Am.]
Sonnets from India.
n.p.: Delta branch of the Nat. League of American pen women, n.d. 20p. NUC

1325. DABNEY, Julia Parker [Am. b. 1850]
Songs of destiny and others.
NY: E.P. Dutton & co., 1898. 180p. NUC OCLC

1326. DACRE, Charlotte [Br. 1782-1842] ALT: Byrne, Charlotte (Dacre)
PSEUD: Rose Matilda

George the Fourth. A poem ... to which are added lyrics, designed for various melodies.
L: n.p., 1822. 64p. BL

1327. -----Hours of solitude. A collection of original poems.
L: Pr. D.N. Shury for Hughes, 1805. 2v. NUC BL OCLC

1328. DALE, Althea, Mrs. Shallett Dale [19c]
"Adeline" and other poems, by Mrs. Shallett Dale.
n.p.: n.p., 188-? 87p. NUC

1329. DALE, Azania [Am. 19c]
Country verses.
Washington, D.C.: Philip & Solomons, 1865. 87p. NUC

1330. DALE, Carrie [Am. 19c]
Our order. A poem: dedicated to the Knights of Honor and Knights and Ladies of Honor throughout the United States.
St. Louis, MO: n.p., 1880. 3p. NUC

DALE, Mrs. Shallett <u>see</u> DALE, Althea

1331. DALL, Caroline Wells Healey [Am. 1822-1912]
Sordello: a history and a poem. By Caroline H. Dall.
Boston: Roberts bros., 1886. 36p. NUC OCLC

DALLOR, F., Mrs. <u>see</u> DALLOR, Frances, Mrs.

1332. DALLOR, Frances, Mrs. [Br. 19c]
ALT: Dallor, F., Mrs.
The duel, an original poem. By Mrs. F. Dallor.
L: n.p., 1832. 17p. BL

1333. DALTON, Edith Leverett [Am. 19c]
More rhymes.
Boston: Damrell & Upham, 1899. 45p. NUC OCLC

1334. -----Rhymes.
Boston: Damrell & Upham, 1897. 45p. NUC OCLC

DALY, Alethia, co-author <u>see</u> DALY, Mary Anne

DALY, Harriet, co-author <u>see</u> DALY, Mary Anne

DALY, Henriette, co-author <u>see</u> DALY, Mary Anne

DALY, Jane, co-author <u>see</u> DALY, Mary Anne

1335. DALY, Mary Anne [Br. 19c]
A retrospect: being memorials of some who have long since departed this life.
Dublin: George Herbert, 1882. 175p. NUC
[Includes letters & poems, also poems by her mother, Henriette Daly, and sisters, Alethia, Harriet & Jane]

1336. DALY, Myrtilla H.N. [Am. 19c]
From shadow into everlasting light, or Easter thoughts.
NY: Hard & Parsons, 1886. 16p. NUC

1337. DAMAN, Miss [Br. 19c]
The program.
Oxford: Priv. pr. by Browne, 1841. 90p. NUC BL
[Misc. poems]

1338. DAMAN, Julia [Br. 19c]
Church bells: or, Thoughts in verse for holy times. By the author of "Thoughts in verse for the hardworking and suffering;" "Second series of thoughts in verse;" "Household verses;" etc.
L: William Macintosh, n.d. 55p. NUC
[The other works not found]

1339. DAME, B.F., Mrs. [Am. 19c]
Poem written for the occasion. In Manchester, N.H., ceremonies at the dedication of the monument erected ... to the men who periled their lives to save the Union... .
Manchester, NH: n.p., 1880. pp. 90-93. NUC
[Civil War poetry]

1340. DAMON, Fannie A. [Am. 19/20c]
Heart treasures.
Buffalo, NY: C.W. Moulton, 1894. 64p. NUC OCLC

1341. DANA, Eliza A. (Fuller) [Am. 19c]
The broken fold: poems of memory and consolation.
NY: Priv. pr. by A.D.F. Randolph, 1868. 124p. NUC BL

1342. -----Gathered leaves.
Cambridge, MA: Priv. pr. by H.O. Houghton, 1864. 160p. NUC OCLC
[Misc. poetry]

DANA, Mary S.B. <u>see</u> SHINDLER, Mary Stanley Bunce (Palmer) Dana

1343. DANDRIDGE, Caroline Danske (Bedinger) [Am. 1858-1914] ALT: Dandridge, Danske Bedinger
Joy, and other poems.
NY & L: G.P. Putnam's sons, 1888. 110p. NUC BL OCLC

1344. -----Rose brake; poems.
NY: G.P. Putnam's sons, 1890. 110p. NUC BL OCLC

DANDRIDGE, Danske Bedinger see DANDRIDGE, Caroline Danske (Bedinger)

DANIEL, Marion Delana see MCCONNELL, Marion Delana (Daniel)

1345. DANIEL, Martha A., Miss [Am. 19c]
The dew of Hermon.
Newburyport: n.p., 1856. 112p. NUC OCLC
[2d ed. Lewiston, ME: J.A. Smith, pr., 1858. 128p. NUC OCLC Rev. ed. with additions.]

1346. -----Golden moments and fragments of the year.
Bath, ME: Pr. for the author, 1864. 82p. NUC OCLC
[Revision & reissue of earlier works]

DANIEL, Samuel, co-author see PEMBROKE, Mary (Sidney) Herbert, Countess of

1347. DANIELL, Irene Stiles Munsell [Am. 19c]
Pastime poems.
Milwaukee, WI: King-Fowle McGee co., pr., 1896. 66p. NUC OCLC

1348. DANIELS, Adeline L.F. [Am. 19c]
Verses.
Uxbridge, MA: Compendium steam print, 1898. 66p. NUC OCLC

1349. DANIELS, Cora Linn (Morrison) [Am. b. 1852]
Poem.
Milwaukee, WI: Pabst Brewing co., 1895? 24p. NUC
[Cover title: In Colorado]

1350. -----The windharp.
Wrentham, MA: n.p., n.d. 142p. NUC

1351. DANIELS, Eunice K. (True) [Am. 1806-1841]
Poems: with a memoir of her life.
NY: Pr. John F. Trow [True BL], 1843. 184p. NUC BL OCLC
[Preface signed. B.K.T., ie., Benjamin K. True]

1352. DANNELLY, Elizabeth Otis (Marshall) [Am. 1838-1896] PSEUD: Lady of Georgia, A
Cactus; or, Thorns and blossoms: a collection of satirical and miscellaneous, embracing religious, temperance and memorial poems.
NY: Atlantic pub. & engr. co., 1879. 378p. NUC OCLC

1353. -----Destruction of the city of Columbia, South Carolina. A poem by a lady of Georgia. A true statement of facts.
Charleston, SC: J. Walker, 1866. 24p. NUC OCLC
[Later pub. as: The burning of Columbia. Civil War]

1354. -----Wayside flowers: religious and miscellaneous poems.
Chicago: American Publishers' Assn., 1892. 142p. NUC OCLC

1355. D'ANVERS, Alicia, Mrs. [Br. 17c]
Academia: or, The humours of the University of Oxford. In burlesque verse.
L: Pr. & sold by Randal Taylor, 1691. 67p. NUC BL OCLC

1356. -----The Oxford-act: a poem.
L: Pr. for Randal Taylor, 1693. 22p. NUC BL

1357. -----A poem upon His Sacred Majesty ... .
L: Pr. for Randal Taylor; pr. for Tho. Bever, 1691. 8p. NUC

1358. DARBY, Eleanor [Br. 19c]
Lays of love and heroism, legends, lyrics and other poems.
L: Hope & co., 1855. 244p. BL

1359. -----Legends of many lands; sonnets, songs and other poems.
L: William Freeman, 1870. 232p. BL

1360. -----Ruggiero Vivaldi, and other lays of Italy; with Ninfea, a fairy legend and a few lyrics.
L: Trubner & co., 1865. 208p. BL OCLC

1361. -----The sweet south; or, A month at Algiers. With a few short lyrics.
L: Hope, 1854. 126p. NUC BL

1362. DARK, Mariann [Br. 19c]
Sonnets and other poems.
L: Pr. for the author by S. Curtis, 1818. 120p. NUC BL

1363. DARLING, Elizabeth [Br. 19c]
Spare moments; a little book of poems.
Kingston: British Whig steam presses, 18--? 25p. NUC

1364. DARLING, Isabella Fleming [Br. 1861-1903]
Poems and songs.
Glasgow: H. Nisbet & co., 1889. 240p. NUC BL OCLC

1365. -----Whispering hope.
Edinburgh & Glasgow: John Menzies, 1893. 240p. NUC BL

1366. DARLING, Patricia Rolland [Br. 19c]
Poetical pieces.
Edinburgh: Pr. for the author's family by Oliver & Boyd, 1817. 84p. NUC BL

DARROW, PERSIS E., pseud. <u>see</u> CURRIER, Mary Mehetabel

1367. DARTON, Alice Weldon (Wasserbach) [Am. 19/20c]
Hexandria.
Washington, D.C.: Pathfinder pub. co., 1894. 85p. NUC OCLC
[Short stories and poems]

1368. DARWALL, Elizabeth [Br. 18/19c]
Poems on several occasions. With Mary (Whateley) Darwell.
L: n.p., 1794. NUC BL

1369. -----The storm, with other poems.
L: J. Ridgway, 1810. 159p. NUC BL

DARWALL, Mary (Whateley), co-author <u>see</u> DARWALL, Elizabeth

1370. DARWALL, Mary (Whateley) [Br. d. 1794] ALT: Whateley, Mary
Original poems on several occasions. By Miss Whateley.
L: Pr. for R. & J. Dodsley, 1764. 117p. NUC BL OCLC
[Also attr. to Elizabeth Darwall]

1371. -----Poems ... . By M. Whateley.
L: n.p., 1763. NUC

1372. DASH, Mary [Br. 19c]
Sacred and moral pieces.
Brighton: n.p., 1827. 102p. BL

1373. DAUGHTER OF KENTUCKY, A., pseud. [Am. 19c]
Sunlight upon the landscape, and other poems. By a daughter of Kentucky.
Cincinnati, OH: Moore, Anderson, Wilstach & Keys, 1853. 48p. NUC OCLC
[Protest against bill forbidding any Negro to settle or reside in KY.]

DAVENPORT, R.A., co-author <u>see</u> LEHARDY, Esther

1374. DAVID, Edith M. [Br. 19c]
Poems.
Oxford: Pr. for priv. circ. by Upstone & Due, 1872. 200p. NUC OCLC
[Written between ages of 11 & 17]

1375. DAVIDSON, Lucretia Maria [Am. 1808-1825]
Amir Khan, and other poems: the remains of Lucretia Maria Davidson. Ed. Samuel Finley Breese Morse.
NY: G. & C. & H. Carvill, 1829. 174p. NUC BL OCLC
[First collected edition]

1376. -----Poetical remains of the late Lucretia Maria Davidson, collected and arranged by her mother, Margaret (Miller) Davidson.
Philadelphia: Lea & Blanchard, 1841. 312p. NUC BL OCLC

1377. DAVIDSON, Margaret [Br. 18c]
The extraordinary life and Christian experience of Margaret Davidson, as dictated by herself. To which are added some of her letters and hymns. By the Rev. Edward Smyth.
Dublin: Pr. for the ed., 1782. 164p. BL

DAVIDSON, Margaret (Miller), comp. <u>see</u> DAVIDSON, Lucretia Maria

1378. DAVIDSON, Margaret Miller, Mrs. [Am. 1787-1844]
Selections from the writings of Mrs. Margaret M. Davidson, the mother of Lucretia Maria and Margaret M. Davidson.
Philadelphia: Lea & Blanchard, 1843. 272p. NUC BL OCLC
[Incl. misc. historical poems; 70p. novella about the War of 1812.]

1379. DAVIDSON, Margaret Miller [Am. 1823-1838]
Biography and poetical remains of the late Margaret Miller Davidson. Ed. Washington Irving.
Philadelphia: Lea & Blanchard, 1841. 359p. NUC BL OCLC

[Younger sister of author Lucretia Davidson. Remains are one unfinished tale and 84 poems.]

1380. DAVIE, Elizabeth [Br. 19c]
Wayside verses; or, Pilgrim melodies.
L: Adams & King, 1859. 91p. BL

1381. DAVIES, Elizabeth [Br. 19c]
A description of the Vale of Neath.
2d ed. Neath: Whittington, 1849. BL

1382. -----A full description of the proceedings at Swansea on the opening of the South Wales Railway, on Tuesday, June 18th, 1850.
Neath: Mary Whittington, 1850. BL

1383. -----Lines on the departure of an ancient ... Welsh family from Dyffryn House near Neath, it is to be hoped for a short period.
Neath: Whittington, 1850? BL

1384. -----Lines on the Gnoll Castle.
2d ed. Neath: Mary Whittington, 1849. BL

1385. -----Lines on the Neath and Red Jacket Junction Canal.
Swansea: F. Fagg, 1824. 4p. BL

1386. -----Lines on the passing of the South Wales Railway Bill in the House of Lords.
2d ed. Neath: Mary Whittington, 1849? BL

1387. -----Lines on the text selected for the funeral sermon of Mrs. Tennant, of Cadoxton Lodge ... .
Neath: Mary Whittington, 1850. BL

1388. -----Lines to Master Thomas Everet Tennant ... who is going to leave his native land to serve his Queen and country in India.
Neath: Mary Whittington, 1850. BL

1389. -----Lines to the memory of Mrs. Tennant ... who departed this life on the 22nd of June, 1850 ... .
Neath: Mary Whittington, 1850. BL

1390. -----On the ruins of the vale of Neath Monastery.
Neath: Mary Whittington, 1851. BL

1391. -----Reflections on the grave of a young officer who destroyed himself in a fit of despair at Neath.
Neath: Mary Whittington, 1850. BL

1392. -----To the memory of Mr. Peter Price: formerly, iron master of Neath Abbey.
Swansea: H. Griffith, pr., 1821? 4p.
BL OCLC

1393. -----To the memory of Robert P. Leyson, esq., surgeon and mayor of ... Neath, died on the 2nd of August, 1849 ... .
Neath: May Whittington, 1849. 4p. BL

1394. -----Verses to the Ivorites for their great love of the Welsh language.
Neath: Mary Whittington, 1850. BL

DAVIS, Clarkson, co-author see DAVIS, Hannah E. (Brown)

DAVIS, Mrs. Clarkson see DAVIS, Hannah E. (Brown)

1395. DAVIS, Cora M. A. Bemis, Mrs. [Am. 1841-1885]
Immortelles. Ed. F.M. Davis.
NY & L: G.P. Putnam's sons, 1887. 178p. NUC OCLC
[Misc. poems, many of nature, reflecting her life in Colorado.]

1396. DAVIS, Gertrude Cree [Am. 19c]
This and that in homespun rhyme.
Macon, NC: n.p., n.d. 31p. NUC

DAVIS, Emerson, comp. see GILBERT, Elizabeth, Mrs.

DAVIS, F.M., ed. see DAVIS, Cora M.A. Bemis, Mrs.

1397. DAVIS, Hannah E. (Brown), Mrs. Clarkson Davis [Am. 1841-1898]
Poems, papers and addresses of Clarkson and Hannah E. Davis.
Richmond, VA: Nicholson prt. & mfg. co., 1898. 178p. NUC OCLC
[Memorial volume; Her poems pp. 19-40]

1398. DAVIS, Isabel [Am. 19c]
"Her picture for heaven" and other poems.
Mt. Hermon, CA: n.p., n.d. 29p. NUC

1399. DAVIS, Jane Maria [Am. 19c]
The white chief's urn: containing poems and other contributions; with a brief memoir of Lieutenant Sam Smith R.M., the celebrated chief of the Cherokee Indians in Florida.
L: R. Spencer, 1850. 200p. NUC BL
[Memoir of her father, 2 essays, and 116 p. of poems]

1400. DAVIS, Katharine Bement [Am. 1860-1935]
From my window. Poems.
n.p.: n.p., n.d. NUC

DAVIS, M.E.M. see DAVIS, Mary Evelyn (Moore)

1401. DAVIS, Martha Ann, Mrs. [Am. 19c]
Poems of Laura; an original American work.
Petersburg, VA: Whitworth & Yancey, pr., 1818. 106p. NUC OCLC
[Misc. poems]

1402. DAVIS, Mary Ann [Br. 19c]
The wild flower wreath. A collection of miscellaneous poems. With reflections, etc. in poetic prose.
Birmingham: Pr. J. Moore, 1835. 150p. NUC BL

1403. DAVIS, Mary Anne [Br. 19c]
Fables in verse: from Aesop, La Fontaine, and others.
L: Pr. for J. Harris, 1813. 190p. NUC BL

1404. DAVIS, Mary Elizabeth (Moragne) [Am. 1815?-1903]
Lays from the sunny lands.
Buffalo, NY: Moulton, Wenborne & co., 1888. 160p. NUC OCLC

1405. DAVIS, Mary Evelyn (Moore) [Am. 1852-1909] ALT: Davis, M.E. M.; Moore, Mollie E.
Glenorie, and other poems.
Montpelier, VT: Argus & Patriot steam book & job pr. works, 1877. 349p. NUC OCLC

1406. -----Minding the gap, and other poems. By Mollie E. Moore.
Houston, TX: Cushing & Cave, 1876. [1867 TXU]. 240p. NUC BL OCLC
[Poems on New Orleans]

1407. -----Ode to Texas, written for the occasion of the ladies' bazaar for the benefit of the San Jacinto battle ground, by Mollie E. Moore Davis.
n.p.: n.p., n.d. 8p. NUC

1408. -----Poems. By Mollie E. Moore.
Houston, TX: E.H. Cushing, c1867. 275p. NUC BL OCLC

1409. DAVIS, Rebecca Ingersol [Am. b. 1828]
Gleanings from Merrimac Valley.
Portland, ME: Hoyt, Fogg & Donham, 1881. 128p. NUC BL OCLC
[Sketches of New England people & places, misc. poetry]

1410. DAVIS, S. W., Mrs. [Am. 19c]
Wayside gleanings. Poems.
Washington, N.J.: T.S. Dedrick, Jr., c1889. 200p. NUC OCLC

1411. DAVIS, Sadie O. (Prince), Mrs. [19c]
Poems.
Toronto: W. Briggs, 1890. 179p. NUC

DAVISON, Francis, ed. see PEMBROKE, Mary (Sidney) Herbert, Countess of

1412. DAWE, Frances [Br. 19c]
The silver cord. A book of poems.
L: Elliot Stock, 1888. 144p. BL OCLC

1413. DAWES, Sarah Elizabeth, Mrs. [Am. b. 1832]
Light from the star of Bethlehem. A poem.
Boston: J.S. Locke & co., 1871. 69p. NUC OCLC

DAWSON, C. Amy see SCOTT, Catharine Amy (Dawson)

DAWSON, Ethel, co-author see WOOD, Helen J.

1414. DAWSON, Jane Flower [Br. 1760-1825]
The life and writings of Mrs. Dawson, of Lancaster.
Kirkby Lonsdale: Arthur Foster, 1828. 187p. NUC BL

1415. DAWSON, M. A., Miss [Br. 19c]
A poem occasioned by the partial burning of York Cathedral.
L: Hatchard & son, 1829. 24p. NUC BL

1416. DAWSON, Marjorie [Am. 19c]
"Rhymes and jingles, jingles and rhymes, very good things for Christmas times.".
NY: Wright, c1899. 31p. NUC

DAWSON-SCOTT, C.A. see SCOTT, Catharine Amy (Dawson)

1417. DAY, Beth [Am. 19c]
Anemonies and clover, poems.
Belvidere, IL: Whitney pub. co., n.d. 192p. NUC

DAY, ELIZA, pseud. see DAY, Esther (Milnes)

1418. DAY, Elizabeth H.
Thoughts occasioned by the death of Maria: who departed this life, August 8, 1788. Also on a beloved friend: likewise on visiting Eusebia's tomb. By E. Day.
L: n.p., 1789. 16p. BL

1419. DAY, Esther (Milnes) [Br. d. 1792] PSEUD: Day, Eliza; Eliza
A poem on the proclamation of peace which took place the twentieth of the sixth month, one thousand, eight hundred and fourteen; the fifty-fourth year of the reign of King George the Third.
Tottenham: n.p., 1814. 8p. BL

1420. -----Poems and fugitive pieces, by Eliza.
L: Pr. W. Bulmer, 1796. 172p. NUC

1421. -----Poems on various subjects with several pieces on the death of relatives and friends, written during the last fifty-seven years of the author's life.
Liverpool: J.M. Creery, 1798. 258p.
Tottenham: Pr. for the author, 1814. 158p. NUC BL

1422. -----Select miscellaneous productions of Mrs. Day and Thomas Day, esq., in verse and prose. Ed. [and some poems by] Thomas Lowndes.
L: Cadell & Davies; T. Jones, 1805. 204p. NUC BL OCLC
[Most of her work written between ages 11-16. Incl. misc. poetry, letters, & school essays. "A conversation piece between Camillus and Emilia, upon fame" also incl.]

1423. -----Serious reflections on the death of Johannes, who was shot by his friend, July 12, 1789. Likewise on the triumphant death of Josephus, aged eighteen years. By Eliza.
L: Pr. for the author by Mr. Trays, 1789. 31p. NUC BL

1424. DAY, Holly [Am. 19c]
Notes of the phull, phamous, and phantastical phantasmagorium: compiled from despatches received by Holly Day and Ju. B. Lee, proprietors of the terrible, tremendous and terrestrial telegraph terminus. In six cantos (no heels).
Boston: Day & Lee, 1872. NUC
[No indication of pseud. in NUC]

1425. DAY, Julia [Br. 19c]
Poems.
L: William Pickering, 1847. 168p. BL

1426. -----Poems.
2d Series: L: William Pickering; Romsey: C.L. Lordan, 1849. 108p. BL

1427. DAY, Maie Dove, Mrs. [Am. 19c]
The blended flags.
Danville, VA: Dance bros. co., 1898. 46p. NUC OCLC
[Poems relating to the U.S. war of 1898]

DAY, Thomas, esq., co-author see DAY, Esther (Milnes)

DEAN, ADAM, pseud. see BLAIR, Ophelia E.

1428. DEAN, C.A., Mrs. [Am. 19c]
Inspirational poems.
Portland, OR: The author, 1898. 102p. NUC OCLC

1429. DEANE, Eleanor Sherburne (Reed) [Am. 19c]
As travellers in foreign climes. In: Annual reunion of the Emery family ... .
Taunton, MA: n.p., 1888. 18p. NUC

1430. -----History of Joseph.
Boston: Mass. Sabbath school soc., 1852. 54p. NUC

1431. DEBENHAM, Anna M. [Br. 19c]
The hero's child, and other poems.
L: Hughes, 1852. 152p. BL

1432. DE BLAQUIRE, Hon. Anna Maria (Wormald), Baroness [Br. d. 1894]
Pilgrims: a poem.
L: Priv. pr. by Swift & co., 1869. 103p. NUC BL

1433. -----Poems.
n.p.: Crawley, 1882. 26p. OCLC

1434. DEBNEY, Ellen Elizabeth [Aus. 19c] PSEUD: Ellie
Poems, by Ellie.
Adelaide: Andrews, Thomas & Clark, 1873. 209p. NUC

1435. DE BURGH, Emma Maria (Hunt) [Br. d. 1851]
The voice of many waters. A selection from the compositions, in prose and verse ... . Ed. her sister, Miss Caroline Hunt.
L: J.F. Shaw, 1858. 90p. NUC BL
[A travel journal of Niagara Falls, and occasional poetry from her diary]

1436. DE BURGH, Marianne [Br. 19c]
Chimes.
L: Smith, Elder & co., 1858. 112p.
NUC BL OCLC

1437. DE CRESPIGNY, Caroline [Br. 19c]
My souvenir: or poems with translations.
L: Longmans, Brown, Green & Longmans; Heidelberg: Hoffmeister, 1844. 296p.
NUC BL

1438. DE CRESPIGNY, H.C., Mrs. [Br. 19c]
Remembrances of friendship.
Cheltenham: n.p., 1830. BL

DE CRESPIGNY, Mary (Clark) Champion see CHAMPION DE CRESPIGNY, Mary (Clark)

1439. DE FLEURY, Maria [Br. 18c]
British liberty established and Gallic liberty restored; or, The triumph of freedom.
L: The author, 1790. 38p. NUC BL
[1789 on title page; epic poem tracing Britain's history]

1440. -----Divine poems and essays on various subjects.
L: The author, pr. T. Wilkins, 1791. 244p. NUC BL OCLC

1441. -----Hymns for believer's baptism.
L: Pr. W. Justins, 1786. 54p. NUC BL
[23 p. of original lyrics; the rest collected]

1442. -----An ode occasioned by the death of Mrs. Elizabeth Dowland.
L: Pr. & sold at the Chapel in Rose-Lane & at Mr. Miller's, 1783. 7p. NUC BL

1443. -----Poems occasioned by the confinement and acquittal of ... Lord George Gordon, etc.
L: The author, pr. by R. Denham, 1781. 24p. NUC BL OCLC

1444. -----Unrighteous abuse detected and chastised; or, A vindication of innocence and integrity, being an answer to a virulent poem entitled, The Protestant Association ... .
2d ed. L: The author, 1781. 23p. NUC BL

DE FLORI, C., pseud. see LEE, Floride (Clemson)

DE FONBLANQUÉ, Ethel Maud see HARTER, Ethel Maud (De Fonblanqué)

1445. DE GEER, M. E., Mrs. [19c]
Addresses, debates and poems.
Toronto: W. Briggs, 189-? 64p. NUC
[Poems; prose writings on: temperance, women's rights, the Bible]

1446. -----Marion Lee; or, One woman's trials and triumphs.
Chicago: Pr. Chicago Legal News co., 1874. 216p. NUC OCLC
[Incl. "temperance poems"]

1447. DE GRUCHY, Augusta Chambers [Br. 19c]
Under the hawthorn, and other verse.
L: E. Mathews & John Lane, 1893. 83p.
NUC BL OCLC

1448. DE HUMBOLDT, Charlotte [Br. 19c]
Corinth, a tragedy; and other poems.
L: Ellerton, 1821. 111p. BL OCLC
[5 act dramatic poem, others are chiefly occasional.]

1449. -----Corinth, a tragedy; and other poems.
L: Longman, Orme, Brown, Green & Longmans, 1838. 188p. BL OCLC
[Expanded ed.; more poems, also mainly occasional]

1450. DE KANTZOW, Theodosia [Br. 19c]
Poems, original and translated.
L: Priv. pr. at the Chiswick press, 1896. 23p. NUC BL

1451. DE KRAFFT, Mary [Am. 19c]
PSEUD: Lady, A
Poems, chiefly amatory, by a lady.
Washington, D.C.: Pr. for pub., M'Kay & De Krafft, pr., 1809. 112p. NUC

DE LA GARDE, Charles, co-author see GUPPY, Sarah

1452. DELAND, Margaret Wade (Campbell) [Am. 1857-1945]
The old garden and other verses.
Boston & NY: Houghton, Mifflin & co., 1886. 97p. NUC BL OCLC

1453. DE LAUNAY, Pauline [Am. 19c]
Pen pictures and other gleanings.
Columbia, GA: T. Gilbert, 1898. 162p.
NUC
[Verse & prose]

1454. DE LESDERNIER, Emily Pierpoint, Mrs. [Am. 19c]

Voices of life. By Mrs. Emily P. Lesdernier.
NY: Cornish, Lamport & co., 1853. 38p. NUC BL OCLC

1455. -----Voices of life. By Mrs. Emily P. Lesdernier.
Paris: E. Briere, 1862. 104p. NUC BL
[Poems and "Heloise," drama in four acts]

DELLA CRUSCA, pseud., co-author see COWLEY, Hannah (Parkhouse)

1456. DEMAREST, Mary Augusta (Lee), Mrs. Theodore Frelinghuysen Demarest [Am. 1838-1888]
My ain countree, and other verses.
NY: A.D.F. Randolph & co., 1882. 146p. NUC OCLC

1457. -----Verse and prose writings of Mary Lee Demarest. Ed. her husband, T.F.D. [Theodore Frelinghuysen Demarest].
Passaic, NJ: Passaic Daily News Office, 1888. 408p. NUC OCLC
[Supplement. Greenfield, MA: T. Morey, 1888. 131p. OCLC. Cover title: Gathered writings. Incl. poems, a novella, short stories, character sketches & parables.]

1458. -----Veteran Tom and the surgeon.
Philadelphia: Presbyterian board of publication, 1880. 8p. NUC

DEMAREST, Mrs. Theodore Frelinghuysen see DEMAREST, Mary Augusta (Lee)

DEMAREST, Theodore Frelinghuysen, ed. see DEMAREST, Mary Augusta (Lee)

1459. DENISON-KEENEY, Dora [Am. 19c]
Heartsease; poems.
Springfield, MA: Homestead job print, 1885. 190p. NUC OCLC

1460. DENNING, Elizabeth [Am. d. 1820]
Poems of Elizabeth Denning.
NY: A. Paul, pr., 1826. 123p. NUC BL OCLC

1461. DENNIS, Amanda Elizabeth [Am. 19c]
Asphodels and pansies.
Philadelphia: J.B. Lippincott co., 1888. 337p. NUC OCLC

1462. DENNIS, Ellen A., Mrs. [Am. 19c]
Poems.
Auburn, ME: Merrill & Webber, 1893. 128p. NUC OCLC

1463. DENSLOW, Olie C., Mrs. [Am. 19c]
Songs of progress and other poems.
South Bend, IN: C.L. Murray & sons, 1882. 42p. NUC

1464. DENT, Amelia Jane [Br. 19c]
Ceylon. A descriptive poem, with notes.
L: Kegan Paul & co., 1886. 32p. BL

1465. DENTON, Elizabeth M. Foote [Am. 19c]
Life. A poem.
Wellesley, MA: n.p., c1899. 7p. NUC OCLC

DENVER, Jane Campbell, co-author see DENVER, Mary Caroline

1466. DENVER, Mary Caroline [Am. 1821-1860]
Poems. By Mary Caroline and Jane Campbell Denver [1821-1847].
NY: Pr. for their brother, J.W. Denver, by Lange, Little & co., 1875. 347p. NUC OCLC

1467. DE PATON, Isabella [Br. 19c]
Iscah; or, Jephtha's vow. A poem in six cantos.
L: Binns & Goodwin, 1866. 174p. NUC

1468. DERBY, Caroline Rosina [Am. 19c]
The ruler's daughter and other poems.
Salem, MA: Press of the Salem Gazette, 1877. 192p. NUC

1469. DERENZY, Margaret Graves [Br. d. 1829] PSEUD: Widowed wife, A
The flowers of the forest.
Wellington, Salop: Houlston & son, 1828. 142p. BL

1470. -----The juvenile wreath.
L: n.p., 1828. 86p. BL

1471. -----Poems appropriate for a sick or melancholy hour.
L: n.p., 1824. 203p. BL

1472. -----A whisper to a newly-married pair from a widowed wife.
5th ed. Philadelphia: E.L. Carey & A. Hart, 1833. BL
[Appendix pp. 91-103. Contains poems on desertion & on the death of loved ones.]

DE STAËL, Mme. see LANDON, Letitia Elizabeth

1473. DE VERE, Cecelia [Am. 19c]
Monopoly!
Mount Lebanon, NY: Lebanon press, 1890? 2p. NUC

1474. DE VERE, Mary Ainge [Am. 19/20c]
Love songs and other poems.
NY: Fifth Ave. pub. co., 1870. 101p. NUC

1475. DEVERELL, Mary, Mrs. [Br. b. 1737?] PSEUD: Philanthea
Mary, Queen of Scots; an historical tragedy, or, dramatic poem.
L: Pr. & sold by author, 1792. 116p. NUC BL
[Blank verse, 5 acts]

1476. -----Miscellanies in prose and verse, mostly written in the epistolary style: chiefly upon moral subjects and particularly calculated for the improvement of younger minds.
L: Pr. for author by J. Rivington, 1781. 2v. NUC BL OCLC
[Essays & poems by Philanthea and members of her literary circle, esp. Thomas Swift]

1477. -----Theodora and Didymus or the exemplification of pure love and vital religion. An heroic poem, in three cantos.
L: The author, 1784. 80p. NUC BL
[2d ed. contains an appendix, consisting of a Pindaric ode, for the Queen's birthday, 1786; and poetical epistles. 2 pt. L: the author, 1786. BL]

1478. DEVEREUX, Rachel, Mrs. [Am. 19c]
Poetical pieces written on several occasions of unfortunate and unhappy facts.
NY: Pr. Lazarus Beach for authoress, 1803. 29p. NUC

DEVEY, Louisa, comp. see LYTTON, Rosina Anne Doyle (Wheeler) Bulwer-Lytton, Baroness

1479. DEVONSHIRE, Georgiana (Spencer) Cavendish, Duchess of [Br. 1757-1806] ALT: Cavendish, Georgiana (Spencer), Duchess of Devonshire
The passage of the mountain of Saint Gothard.
Gameau & co., 1803. 41p. NUC BL OCLC
[1st pub. 1802 with French trans. Travel journal in verse.]

1480. DE WINDT, Caroline Amelia (Smith) [Am. 19c] ALT: D., C. A.
Melzinga: a souvenir, by C.A.D.
NY: n.p., 1845. 175p. NUC OCLC
[Collection incl. her journal & misc. poems, plus favorite poems by others]

1481. DE WITT, Susan (Linn) [Am. 1778-1824]
The pleasures of religion; a poem.
NY: Wiley & Halstead, 1820. 72p. NUC OCLC

1482. DE WOLF, Abigail [Am. 1804-1888]
A glance at the nations, with other poems.
Boston: Russell, Odiorne, & Metcalf, 1835. 60p. NUC OCLC

1483. -----Heart poems.
Providence, RI: Sayles, Miller & Simons, pr., 1855. 105p. NUC OCLC

1484. DEY, Agnes Christall [Br. 19c]
Songs and poems.
Paisley: J. & R. Parlane, 1896. 123p. BL

1485. DICKINS, Clara Swain [Br. 19/20c]
Margaret and Margarites.
L: Sampson, Low, Marston & co., 1896. 112p. BL

1486. -----Sonnets sacred and secular.
L: Simpkin, Marshall & co.; Manchester: J.E. Cornish, 1886. 202p. BL

1487. DICKINSON, Eleanor Blakey [Br. 19c]
The Mamluk. A poem.
L: Effingham Wilson, 1850. 224p. BL

1488. -----The pleasure of piety, with other poems.
L: Sherwood, Jones & co., 1824. 84p. NUC BL

1489. DICKINSON, Ellen E. [Am. 19c]
The Christmas wreath; original and selected Christmas poems, arranged by E.E.D.
NY: White, Stokes & Allen, 1883. 12 l. NUC
[2 of the 13 poems are Dickinson's]

1490. -----His glorious cross, an Easter poem.
Munich & NY: Obpacher bros., 188-? 16p. NUC OCLC

1491. -----Wayside flowers; original and contributed poems, arranged by E.E.D.

NY: White & Stokes, 1882. 51 l. NUC

1492. DICKINSON, Emily [Am. 1830-1886]
Poems. Series 1-3.
Boston: Roberts bros., 1891-96. 3v. NUC BL OCLC
[1st & 2d series Ed. Mabel Loomis Todd & T.W. Higginson; 3d series Ed. Mabel Loomis Todd.]

1493. DICKINSON, Hester A. [Am. 19c]
PSEUD: Benedict, Hester A.
Fagots. By Hester A. Benedict.
Buffalo, NY: Charles Wells Moulton, 1895. 102p. NUC OCLC

1494. -----Vesta. By Hester A. Benedict.
Philadelphia: Claxton, Remsen & Haffelfinger, 1872. 170p. NUC BL

DICKINSON, Martha Gilbert see BIANCHI, Martha Gilbert (Dickinson)

1495. DICKINSON, Mary Lowe [Am. 1839-1914]
Easter greeting.
NY: H.H.B. Angell, 1885. 13p. NUC OCLC

1496. -----Edelweiss: an Alpine rhyme.
NY: n.p., 1876. 102p. NUC OCLC

1497. -----Home from the war; a rhyme of Thanksgiving.
n.p.: n.p., 1898. 10p. NUC OCLC

1498. -----If we had but a day.
n.p.: n.p., 187-? 3 l. NUC OCLC

1499. -----The living Christ: Easter thoughts for the King's daughters.
NY & Chicago: F.H. Revell co., 1891. 31p. NUC

1500. DICKSON, Emma Dodimeade [Br. 19c]
A posy of stray wildings.
2d ed. L: Robert Theobald; Edinburgh: Johnstone & Hunter, 1853. 151p. BL

DIETZ, Ella see CLYMER, Ella Maria (Dietz)

1501. DIEUDONNÉ, Florence Lucinda (Carpenter), Mrs. F. J. Dieudonné [Am. b. 1850]
Prehistoric romanza.
Minneapolis, MN: The Falls pr. co., 1882. 24p. NUC

DIEUDONNÉ, Mrs. F.J. see DIEUDONNÉ, Florence Lucinda (Carpenter)

1502. DIGNOWITY, Mattie Bell, Mrs. [Am. 19c]
The historic and picturesque San Antonio River.
San Antonio, TX: n.p., 1895. 37p. NUC
[Photographs accompanied by lyric poetry about the region]

1503. DIMMICK, Irene Sophie (du Pont) [Am. 1845-1877]
Verses.
NY: Pr. for priv. dist. by A.D.F. Randolph, 1880. 111p. NUC
[35 of the 64 poems dated 1860. Written chiefly between ages of 10 & 12]

1504. DIMOND, Elizabeth, Mrs. [Am. 19c]
A Christmas offering.
Providence, RI: Pr. Knowles & Vose, 1847. 18p. NUC

1505. DINNIES, Anna Peyre (Shackleford) [Am. 1805-1886]
The floral year ... .
Boston: B.B. Mussey, 1847. 256p. NUC OCLC
[Poems on flowers, arr. in 12 bouquets for the year.]

1506. DIXON, Charlotte Eliza [Br. 19c]
"Bread cast upon the waters.".
L: n.p., 1830. BL

1507. -----The Mount of Olives, or The resurrection and ascension; a poem: in continuation of Calvary.
L: n.p., 1824. BL

1508. DIXON, Constance E. [Br. 19c]
The chimney piece of Bruges and other poems.
L: Eliot Stock, 1886. 131p. NUC BL OCLC

1509. DIXON, Jane [Br. 19c]
Sacred lyrics and other poems.
Cambridge: T. Stevenson, 1843. 35p. BL

1510. DIXON, Lucy [Br. 19c]
Flowers from Gethsemane, hymns.
L: n.p., 1850. BL

1511. DIXON, Margaret [Am. 19c]
Chronicles of Christopher Columbus in twelve cantos.
NY: G.P. Putnam's sons, 1893. 310p. NUC BL OCLC

1512. DIXON, Sarah, Mrs. [Br. 18c]
Poems on several occasions.

Canterbury: Pr. J. Abree, 1740. 203p. NUC BL OCLC
[Pub. anon.]

1513. DIXON, Sophie [Br. 19c]
Castalian hours. Poems.
L: Longman, Hurst, Rees, Orme, Brown & Green, 1829. 212p. NUC OCLC

1514. DOBELL, Elizabeth Mary (Fordham), Mrs. Horace Benge Dobell [Br. 19c]
Ethelstone, Eveline, and other poems.
L: Pr. J. Wertheimir & co., 1852. 51p. NUC OCLC
[Pub. with subtitle: Legends of the castle and tales of the village. L: Kegan Paul & co., 1881. 303p. BL
Incl. legends, occasional pieces, songs & poems written between ages 10-16]

1515. -----In the watches of the night. Poems.
L: Remington & co., 1884. 18v. BL

DOBELL, Mrs. Horace Benge <u>see</u> DOBELL, Elizabeth Mary (Fordham)

1516. DODD, Mary Ann Hanmer, Miss
Poems.
Hartford, CT: Case, Tiffany & Burnham, 1844. 184p. NUC OCLC

1517. DODGE, Ellen Ada Phelps, Mrs. [Am. 19c]
Poems and letters.
NY: Pr. for the family, 1894. 127p. NUC OCLC

1518. DODGE, H.M., Mrs. [Am. 19c]
PSEUD: Amica Religionis
Hesebrigge; or, The death of Lady Wallace; with other poems. By Amica Religionis.
Utica, NY: Hastings & Tracy, 1827. 158p. NUC OCLC

1519. DODGE, Maria J., Mrs. [Am. 19c]
Echoes from Cape Ann. A book of poems, recitations, and memorial tokens.
Boston: Cupples & Hurd, 1889. 261p. NUC OCLC
[All in verse]

1520. DODGE, Mary Abigail [Am. 1833-1896] PSEUD: Hamilton, Gail
English kings in a nutshell. By Gail Hamilton.
NY & Chicago: Amer. Bk. co., 1893. 81p. NUC
[1st pub. 1885]

1521. DODGE, Mary Barker (Carter) [Am. 19c]
Arcadian club: ode for the reception to Peter Cooper.
Brooklyn, NY: n.p., 1874. 4p. NUC OCLC

1522. -----Belfrey voices.
Brooklyn, NY: E.J. de Selding, 1869. 38 l. NUC OCLC

1523. -----The gray masque, and other poems.
Boston: D. Lothrop & co., 1885. 285p. NUC BL OCLC

1524. DODSWORTH, Anna Barrell [Br. 19c]
Fugitive pieces.
Canterbury: Pr. Simmons & Kirkby, 1802. 107p. NUC BL OCLC

1525. DOLARO, Selina [Am. 1849-1889]
ALT: Belasco, Mme. Isaac Dolaro
"Mes amours." poems ... written to me ... and my answers to some of them.
Chicago & NY: Belford Clarke & co., 1888. 71p. NUC OCLC

1526. DONNE, Alicia [Br. 19c]
Peeps into bird life.
Chester: Phillipson & Golder, 1896. 112p. NUC BL

1527. DONNELLY, Eleanor Cecilia [Am. 1838-1917]
The children of the golden sheaf and other poems.
Philadelphia: n.p., 1884. 64p. NUC OCLC

1528. -----Christian carols of love and life.
Philadelphia: H.L. Kilner & co., 1898. 55p. NUC BL OCLC

1529. -----The conversion of Saint Augustine and other sacred poems.
Philadelphia: Press of D.J. Gallagher, 1887. 69p. NUC OCLC

1530. -----Crowned with stars.
Notre Dame, IN: Notre Dame Univ., 1881. 131p. OCLC

1531. -----Domus Dei: a collection of religious and memorial poems, by Eleanor C. Donnelly.
Philadelphia: P.F. Cunningham & son, 1875. 106p. NUC OCLC

1532. -----Hymns of the sacred heart adapted to original and selected melodies.

Philadelphia: n.p., 1893. 2v. NUC

1533. -----Legend of the best beloved, and other poems in honor of the sacred heart of Jesus.
NY: P. O'Shea, c1880. 108p. NUC OCLC

1534. -----Out of sweet solitude.
Philadelphia: J.B. Lippincott & co., 1873. 105p. NUC OCLC

1535. -----Poems.
Philadelphia: H.L. Kilner & co., 1892. 108p. NUC BL OCLC
[Civil War poems, sacred legends, & misc. poetry]

1536. -----Prince Ragnal, and other holiday verses.
Philadelphia: H.L. Kilner & co., 1898. 40p. NUC BL OCLC
[Christmas poetry]

1537. -----The rhyme of the Friar Stephen: a legend.
Philadelphia: H.L. Kilner & co., 1898. 46p. NUC BL OCLC

1538. -----A Tuscan Magdalen, and other legends and poems.
Philadelphia: H.L. Kilner & co., 1896. 205p. NUC BL OCLC

1539. DORNFORD, Eleanor, Mrs. [Br. 18c] ALT: D., E., Mrs.
Some memoirs of the life and death of Mrs. E.D.
L: Andrews & sons, 1790. 101p. BL
[Includes journal & poems]

1540. DORR, Julia Caroline (Ripley) [Am. 1825-1913] PSEUD: Thomas, Caroline
Afternoon songs.
NY: C. Scribner's sons, 1885. 184p. NUC BL OCLC

1541. -----A Christmas ballad: the legend of the Baboushka.
NY: A.D.F. Randolph & Co., 188-? 13 f. NUC

1542. -----Daybreak: an Easter poem.
NY: A.D.F. Randolph & Co., 1882. 14 l. NUC BL OCLC

1543. -----The fallow field.
Boston: Lee & Shepard, 1893. 28p. NUC OCLC

1544. -----Friar Anselmo and other poems.
NY: C. Scribner's sons, 1875. 178p. NUC BL OCLC

1545. -----Midnight chimes.
Boston: L. Prang & co., 1889. 14p. OCLC
[Christmas poetry]

1546. -----Periwinkle.
Boston: Lee & Shepard, 1894. 39p. NUC OCLC

1547. -----Poems.
Philadelphia: J.B. Lippincott & co., 1872. 192p. NUC BL OCLC

1548. -----Poems.
NY: Scribner's sons, 1892. 471p. NUC OCLC
[Incl. later poems.]

1549. -----Santa Claus souvenir.
Rutland, VT: Tuttle & co., c1882. 12p. NUC

1550. -----Vermont: a centennial poem.
Maplewood, MA: Pr. Perry & Austin, 1877. 12p. Boston: Milliken, 1877. NUC OCLC

1551. DORR, Louise S. [Am. 19c]
Fountain spray and miscellaneous poems.
Raleigh, N.C.: E.M. Uzzell, 1885. 100p. NUC OCLC

1552. DORSET, Catherine Ann (Turner) [Br. 1750-1817] PSEUD: Lady, A
The lion's masquerade. Written by a lady.
L: John Harris, 1807. 16p. NUC BL OCLC
[A sequel to The peacock at home.]

1553. -----The lioness's rout.
L: B. Tabart, 1808. 32p. NUC BL OCLC

1554. -----The peacock "at home." By a lady.
L: John Harris, 1807. 16p. NUC BL OCLC
[A sequel to The butterfly's ball, an original poem by Mr. Roscoe.]

1555. -----The peacock at home and other poems.
L: John Murray, 1809. 126p. BL TXU
[Author says title poem written for youngest listeners; but others are for adults.]

1556. DORSEY, Anna Hanson (McKenney) [Am. 1815-1896]
Flowers of love and memory.
Baltimore, MD: J. Murphy; Philadelphia: J. Fullerton, 1849. 137p. NUC OCLC

[Verse & prose]

1557. -----"They're coming, Grandad!" A tale of east Tennessee.
Washington, D.C.: n.p., 1865. 10p. NUC OCLC
[Civil War poetry]

1558. DOTEN, Elizabeth [Am. b. 1829]
ALT: Doten, Lizzie
The inner mystery. An inspirational poem. By Lizzie Doten.
Boston: Adams & co., 1868. 34p. NUC BL OCLC

1559. -----Poems from the inner life. By Lizzie Doten.
Boston: W. White & co., 1864. 171p. NUC BL OCLC

1560. -----Poems of progress. By Lizzie Doten.
Boston: W. White & co.; NY: The Am. News co., 1871. 252p. NUC BL OCLC

DOTEN, Lizzie <u>see</u> DOTEN, Elizabeth

1561. DOUDNEY, Sarah [Br. 1843-1926]
Christmas angels.
L: Castell bros., 1890. BL

1562. -----Drifting leaves.
L: Marcus Ward & co., 1892. 32p. BL

1563. -----Easter morning: verses.
L, Belfast, NY: Marcus Ward & co. ltd., 189-? 16p. OCLC

1564. -----My message.
L: Castell bros., 1892. BL

1565. -----Psalms of life.
L: n.p., 1871. BL

1566. -----Violets for faithfulness.
L & NY: M. Ward & co., 1893. 24p. NUC BL OCLC

1567. -----Voices in the starlight.
L: Marcus Ward & co., 1892. BL

1568. DOUGLAS, Miss [Br. 19c]
Prize poem. The auld Brig O'Slittrick's last address to the magistrates, town council and inhabitants of Hawick.
Hawick: n.p., 1851. 20p. BL

1569. DOUGLAS, Alice May [Am. b. 1865]
Phlox.
Bath, ME: Times press, 1888. 22p. NUC

1570. DOUGLAS, BESSIE, pseud. [Br. 19c]
Excelsior: an ethical poetasm.
Dublin: n.p., 1857. BL

1571. DOUGLAS, Lucretia J. [Am. b. 1830]
Grace for every trial, containing sketches of the author's life and family and her wonderful religious experience, with original poems and letters ... .
Dublin, GA: K.N. Walker, 1893. 258p. NUC OCLC

1572. DOUGLAS, Margaret [Am. 19c]
Poems.
Philadelphia: Times pr. house, c1892. 116p. NUC OCLC

DOUGLAS, Mrs. Alfred <u>see</u> DOUGLAS, Olive Eleanor (Custance), Lady

1573. DOUGLAS, Olive Eleanor (Custance), Lady [Br. 1874-1944] ALT: Douglas, Mrs Alfred; Custance, Olive
Opals. By Olive Custance.
L & NY: John Lane, 1897. 74p. NUC BL OCLC

1574. DOUGLAS, Sarah [Am. 19c] PSEUD: Philomath
A bird's-eye-view of the progress of science, religion and philosophy.
Providence, RI: The Rhode Island News co., 1883. 18p. NUC OCLC

1575. -----Expository paraphrase of the Song of Solomon. By Philomath.
Providence, RI: J.A. & R.A. Reid, pr., 1884. 30p. NUC OCLC
[Dialogue in verse]

1576. DOUGLAS, Sarah Parker [Br. 19c]
Poems and songs.
4th ed. Ayr: H. Henry, 1880? 216p. BL OCLC

1577. DOUGLASS, Anna S., Mrs. [Am. 19c]
Otsego Lake.
Berlin? NY: n.p., 1893. 10 l. NUC

1578. DOW, Margaret Russell [Br. 19c]
Lays for leisure hours.
Edinburgh: A. Elliot, 1881. 230p. BL

1579. -----Songs of nature and other poems.
Edinburgh: Edinburgh press, 1898. 228p. BL

1580. DOWD, Alice Mary [Am. b. 1855]
Vacation verses.
Buffalo, NY: C.W. Moulton, 1891. 49p. NUC OCLC

[Incl. several trans. from German]

1581. DOWDEN, Elizabeth Dickinson (West) [Br. 19c] ALT: W., E.D.; West, Elizabeth
Verses. E.D.W.
2 pt. Dublin: Ponsonby, 1876. 47p.
BL OCLC

DOWD, J. Luella see SMITH, Jane Luella (Dowd)

1582. DOWLING, Hannah Teresa [Am. 1845-1897]
Poems. Ed. William H. Dowling.
Boston: Washington press, 1898. 134p.
NUC OCLC

1583. DOWLING, Penelope [Br. 19c]
Wild flowers gathered by a wandering pilgrim.
L: n.p., 1862. BL

DOWLING, William H., ed. see DOWLING, Hannah Teresa

1584. DOWN, Eliza [Br. 19c]
Athelney: and other poems.
L: G. Bell & sons, 1884. 132p. NUC BL OCLC

1585. -----Kenwith Castle, and other poems.
L: S. Tinsley, 1878. 150p. NUC BL OCLC

1586. -----Messeria and other poems.
L: Jarrold & sons, 1875? 167p. BL

1587. DOWNING, Harriet [Br. 19c]
The bride of Sicily, a dramatic poem.
L: Hurst, Chance & co., 1830. 167p.
NUC BL
[Incl. stage directions]

1588. -----The child of the tempest and other poems.
L: J. Harwood, 1821. 74p. NUC BL OCLC

1589. -----Mary; or, Female friendship: a poem.
L: J. Harper & co., 1816. 182p. NUC BL

1590. -----Satan in love: a dramatic poem.
L: n.p., 1840. NUC BL

1591. DOWNING, Mary [Br. 19c] PSEUD: Christabel
Scraps from the mountains and other poems. By "Christabel".
Dublin: William Curry, jr., 1840.
278p. BL OCLC

1592. DOWNING, Mary Alphonsus, Sister [Br. 1828-1869]
Voices from the heart. Sacred poems.
Dublin: M.H. Gill & son, 1860. 302p.
NUC OCLC

1593. DOWNING, Sophie E. C., Mrs. [Am. d. 1873]
Songs in the valley of Achor.
NY: A.D.F. Randolph & co., 1874. 88p.
NUC OCLC

1594. DOWNS, Annie Sawyer [Am. 19c]
Poem: Historic Andover 1646-1896.
Andover, MA: The Andover press, 1896.
56p. NUC OCLC

DOWRICH, Anne see DOWRICHE, Anne

1595. DOWRICHE, Anne [Br. 16c] ALT: Dowrich, Anne
Commendatory verse in: The jaylors conversion ... . By Hugh Dowriche.
L: J. Windet, 1596. NUC BL

1596. -----The French historie. That is: a lamentable discourse of three bloodie broiles that have happened in France for the Gospell of Jesus Christ.
L: Thomas Orwin for Thomas Man;
Exeter: W. Russell, 1589. 37p. NUC BL

DOWRICHE, Hugh, co-author, see DOWRICHE, Anne

1597. DOWSON, Susanna [Br. 19c] ALT: D****, S****
Poems, domestic and miscellaneous. By S**** D****.
Norwich: Charles Muskett, 1844. 144p.
BL
[Sappho, dramatic poem in 10 scenes. Night before: metrical romance, 107 p. Several lyric poems.]

1598. DRANE, Augusta Theodosia [Br. 1823-1894] ALT: D., A.T.; Drane, Mother Frances Raphael
Songs in the night and other poems.
L: Burns & Oates, 1876. 211p. NUC BL OCLC

1599. DRANFIELD, Betsy [Br. 19c]
Poems.
Chesterfield: R.J. Smithson, 1872.
75p. BL

1600. DREYFUS, Lilian Gertrude (Shuman) [Am. 19/20c]
From me to you.
Boston: Lee & Shepard, 1898. 92p. NUC OCLC

1601. DRING, Mrs. [Am. 18c]
Poems, sacred & miscellaneous.
Newark, NJ: W. Tomlinson & son, 1858. 249p. NUC
[Inscribed Henrietta Isabella Collingride. Poems composed by her great grandmother, Mrs. Dring]

1602. DRINKER, Anna [Anne OCLC] [Am. b. 1827] ALT: Drinkwater, Anna PSEUD: May, Edith
Poems. By Edith May. Ed. N.P. Willis.
Philadelphia: E.H. Butler & co., 1852. 218p. NUC BL OCLC
[Expanded ed. pub. 1855]

DRINKER, Anne see DRINKER, Anna

DRINKWATER, Anna see DRINKER, Anna

1603. DRUMMOND, Mrs. [Br. 18c]
The female speaker; or, The priests in the wrong, a poem.
L: n.p., 1735. BL

1604. DRUMMOND, Hon. Adelaide [Br. 19c]
"Baby."
L: Day & son, 1862. BL

1605. DRURY, Anna Harriet [Br. 19c]
Annesley, and other poems.
L: W. Pickering, 1847. 74p. NUC BL OCLC

1606. -----The first of May. A new version of a celebrated modern ballad.
L: n.p., 1851. 16p. NUC BL

1607. DRURY, Susie [Can. 19c]
Maple leaves.
London, ONT: Daily Free press steam book & job pr. estab., 1871. 200p. NUC

1608. DU BOIS, Lady Dorothea (Annesley) [Br. 1728-1774] PSEUD: Lady of Quality, A
Poems on several occasions. By a lady of quality.
Dublin: Pr. for the author, 1764. 159p. NUC BL OCLC

1609. DUCKWORTH, Eleanor [Br. 19c]
Poems and sketches. With Milly Wentworth.
Edinburgh: W. Winter, 1856. 104p. Cincinnati, OH: Wentworth co., 1857. 104p. NUC BL OCLC
[Duckworth's poems first appeared in the Edinburgh Waverly Journal. Wentworth was from New Orleans. Sketches are brief essays.]

1610. DUCLAUX, Agnes Mary Frances (Robinson), formerly Mme. James Darmester [Br. 1856/7-1944] ALT: Robinson, A. Mary F.
A handful of honeysuckle. By A. Mary F. Robinson.
L: C.K. Paul & co., 1878. 88p. NUC BL OCLC

1611. -----An Italian garden; a book of songs.
Boston: Roberts bros.; L: T.F. Unwin, 1886. 102p. NUC BL OCLC
[Misc. poetry]

1612. -----The new Arcadia and other poems. By A. Mary F. Robinson.
Boston: Roberts bros.; L: Ellis & White, 1884. 175p. NUC BL OCLC

1613. -----Retrospect and other poems.
L: T. Fisher Unwin; Boston: Roberts bros., 1893. 88p. NUC BL OCLC
[The Cameo Series]

1614. -----Songs, ballads and a garden play. By A. Mary F. Robinson.
L: 1883. 142p. L: T.F. Unwin, 1888. NUC BL OCLC

1615. DUDLEY, Marion Vienna (Churchill), Mrs. J.L. Dudley [Am. 19c]
Granada. A poem of the Moors in Spain. By Mrs. J.L Dudley.
Jacksonville, FL: n.p., 1899? 16p. NUC

1616. -----Poems.
Milwaukee, WI: Thomas S. Gray, 1885. 53p. NUC OCLC

DUDLEY, Mrs. J.L. see DUDLEY, Marion Vienna (Churchill)

DUER, Alice Maud, co-author see DUER, Caroline King

1617. DUER, Caroline King [Br. b. 1865]
Poems. With Alice Maud Duer [Miller; Br. 1874-1942].
NY: G.H. Richmond & co., 1896. 62p. NUC BL OCLC

1618. DUFF, Anna Julia Grant (Webster) [Br. 19c] ALT: D., A. J. G.
Verses. By A.J.G.D.
Edinburgh: Edinburgh UP, 1882. 47p. BL OCLC

1619. DUFF, Anne Jane Wharton [Br. 19c]

Poems.
Edinburgh: Pr. for priv. circ., W. Blackwood & sons, 1859. 64p. NUC

1620. DUFF, Henrietta Anne [Br. 1842-1879]
Fragments of verse.
L: M. Ward, 1880. 175p. BL OCLC

DUFFERIN and AVA, The Marquess of, ed. see DUFFERIN and CLANDEBOYE, Helen Selina (Sheridan) Blackwood, Baroness

1621. DUFFERIN and CLANDEBOYE, Helen Selina (Sheridan) Blackwood, Baroness [Br. 1807-1867] ALT: Blackwood, Helen Selina (Sheridan), Baroness Dufferin and Clandeboye; Blackwood, Mrs. Price; Gifford, Helen Selina (Sheridan) Blackwood Hay, Countess of; Hay, Helen Selina (Sheridan) Blackwood, Countess of Gifford
Helen's tower, Clandeboye. [By Alfred Lord Tennyson] Published with: To my dear son on his 21st birthday. [A poem by Baroness Dufferin].
n.p.: Pr. for priv. circ., 1861? 5p. NUC BL

1622. -----[Lament of] the Irish emigrant: a ballad.
n.p.: n.p., 1840. BL OCLC

1623. -----Songs, poems and verses. By Helen, Lady Dufferin ... . Ed. with a memoir, and some account of the Sheridan family, by her son, the Marquess of Dufferin and Ava.
2d ed. L: John Murray, 1894. 429p. NUC BL OCLC

DUFFUS HARDY, Lady see HARDY, Mary Anne (McDowell) Duffus, Lady

1624. DUFFY, Annie V. [Am. 19c]
Glenalban; and other poems.
NY: E.J. Hale & son, 1878. 155p. NUC OCLC

1625. DUGAN, Annie A. (Stevens), Mrs. George E. Dugan [Am. b. 1844] PSEUD: Myrtle, May
Myrtle leaves, a miscellaneous collection of poems, by May Myrtle, (Mrs. George E. Dugan).
Sedalia, MO: Democrat co., 1885. 200p. NUC

DUGAN, Mrs. George E. see DUGAN, Annie A. (Stevens)

DUNCAN, Mary (Grey) Lundie, comp. see DUNCAN, Mary (Lundie)

1626. DUNCAN, Mary (Lundie), Mrs. W.W. Duncan [Br. 1814-1839] ALT: Lundie, Mary
Memoir of Mrs. W.W. Duncan, being recollections of a daughter. By her mother, Mrs. J.C. Lundie [Mary (Grey) Lundie Duncan].
Edinburgh: W. Oliphant, 1841. 308p. NUC BL OCLC
[Numerous editions; includes letters, diary & poems]

1627. DUNCAN, Mary Balfour Manson [Br. 1835-1865] ALT: D., M.B.M.
Bible hours: being leaves from the note book of ... M.B.M.D.
Edinburgh: n.p.; L: James Nisbet & co., 1866. BL
[Includes poems]

1628. -----"Under the shadow" being additional leaves from the note book of ... M.B.M.D.
Edinburgh: n.p., 1867. BL
[Includes poems]

DUNCAN, Mrs. W.W. see DUNCAN, Mary (Lundie)

1629. DUNIWAY, Abigail Jane (Scott) [Am. 1834-1915]
David and Anna Matson.
NY: S.R. Wells & co., 1876. 194p. NUC OCLC
[Narrative poem & misc. lyrics]

1630. -----My musings; or, A few fancies in verse.
Portland, OR: Walling, 1875. 32p. NUC

1631. DUNLAP, Alice F. [Am. 19c]
A bullet from the battle-field of Mission Ridge.
Chattenooga, TN: n.p., c1895. 6 l. NUC
[Civil War poem]

1632. DUNLAP, Jane [Am. 18c]
Poems, upon several sermons, preached by the rev'd and renowned, George Whitefield, while in Boston.
Boston: n.p., 1771. 22p. NUC

1633. DUNLOP, Alison Hay [Br. 19c]
Anent old Edinburgh and some of the worthies who walked its streets, with other papers. Ed. her brother [John Charles Dunlop].
Edinburgh: R. & H. Somerville, 1890. 191p. NUC OCLC
[Historical descriptions, short fiction & poetry. Incl. biog. of author]

1634. DUNLOP, Frances Elizabeth [Br. 19c]
Edmond of Rydale Vale; or, The widowed bride, a poem in six cantos.
York: Bolland, 1822. 251p. NUC BL OCLC

DUNLOP, John Charles, ed. see DUNLOP, Alison Hay

1635. DUNN, C. A., Mrs. [Can. 19c]
Fugitive pieces, the production of leisure hours!
Woodstock, Ontario: Pr. for the author, 1867. 94p. NUC

1636. DUNN, Sarah Jane [Br. b. 1852]
Poems. Ed. Henry Shaw.
L: Chiswick press, Whittingham & Wilkins, 1870. 31p. NUC BL OCLC

1637. DUNN, Winifrid [Am. 19c]
Wild Alvin and other poems.
Allentown, PA: Harlacher, 1872. 96p. NUC OCLC

1638. DUNNETT, Jane [Br. 19c]
Poems on various subjects.
Edinburgh: Pr. J. Moir, 1818. 152p. NUC BL

1639. DUNNING, Frances A.B. [Am. 19c]
Gathered leaves. Poems.
Chicago: Palmer, Augir & co., 1877. 197p. NUC OCLC

1640. DUNSTERVILLE, Ann [Br. 19c]
Poems on several occasions.
Exeter: n.p., 1807. BL

1641. DUPE, Eliza [Br. 19c]
Happiness, or the secret spring of bliss and antidote of death. By Eliza Dupe, a member of the working class.
Oxford: W. Baxter, 1860. 107p. NUC BL
[Tract, incl. orig. poems]

1642. DU PUY, Elisabeth [Am. 1868-1932]
The dragon yoke; sonnets and songs.
NY: John B. Alden, 1890. 46p. NUC OCLC

1643. -----The queen's quire: being a book of songs, sonnets and ballads.
St. Louis, MO: Woodward & Tiernan pr. co., 1892. 44p. NUC OCLC

1644. DURANT, Heloise [19c]
Pine needles: or sonnets and songs.
NY & L: G.P. Putnam's sons, 1884. 160p. NUC OCLC

1645. DUTTON, Anne, Mrs. [Br. 1692-1765]
A discourse concerning the New-Birth.
L: n.p., 1740. NUC BL
[Incl.: A poem on Salvation in Christ by free grace and a poem on the safety and duty of a believer]

1646. -----A poem on the special work of the spirit in the hearts of the elect.
4th ed. L: n.p., 1818. BL

DUTTON, Henry Melzar, co-author see GRAVES, Mary Eliot (Dutton)

1647. DUVALL, Linda M. [Am. 19c]
Song waifs.
Delaware, OH: O.F.T. Evans, 1888. 33p. NUC

1648. DYKE, Ann [Br. 18c]
The female muse; a poem on the coronation of Her Sacred Majesty Queen Ann.
L: Pr. & sold by J. Nutt, 1702. 7p. NUC

1649. DYSON, Julia A. (Parker) [Am. 1818-1852]
Life and thought: or, Cherished memorials of the late Julia A. Parker Dyson. Ed. Miss E. Latimer.
Boston: Whittemore, Niles & Hall, 314p. NUC OCLC
[Includes poems and essays]

E., A.L.O., pseud. see TUCKER, Charlotte Marie

E., B.E., pseud. see BROWN, Emma Elizabeth

E., C. see EYTON, Elizabeth Charlotte

E., E.L. see POUCHER, Emma E.

E., E.S. see ELLIOTT, Emily Elizabeth Steele

E., M. see EVANS, Margaret Freeman

1650. EARLE, Miss [Br. 19c]
Corinth and other poems.
L: Pr. Ellerton & Henderson, 1821. 111p. NUC BL

1651. EASTER, Marguerite Elizabeth (Miller) [Am. 1839-1894]
Clytie and other poems.
Boston: A.J. Philpott & co., c1891. 163p. NUC OCLC

1652. EASTMAN, Elaine (Goodale) [Am. 1863-1953] ALT: Goodale, Elaine
All round the year verses from Sky farm. By E. Goodale and Dora Read Goodale.
NY: G.P. Putnam's sons, 1881. 202p. NUC OCLC

1653. -----Apple-blossoms: poems of two children. By Elaine Goodale and Dora Read Goodale.
NY: G.P. Putnam's sons, 1878. 253p. NUC BL OCLC

1654. -----The coming of the birds.
Boston: S.E. Cassino & co., 1883. 6 l.; Estes & Lauriat, 18--? 7 l. NUC OCLC

1655. -----In Berkshire with the wild flowers. With Dora Reed Goodale.
L: n.p., 1871. NY: G.P. Putnam's sons, 1879-80. 92p. NUC OCLC

1656. EASTMAN, Mary Henderson [Am. 1818-1890] ALT: Henderson, Mary
Easter angels.
Washington, D.C.: Globe pr. & pub. house, 1879. 8 numb. l. NUC
[Poem about death of child, followed by death of her father.]

1657. EATON, Imogene Cammett [Am. 19c]
Poems.
Fall River, MA: Press of Fiske & Monroe, c1881. 80p. NUC OCLC

1658. EATON, Marcia Jane, Mrs. [Am. 19c]
Poems.
Baltimore, MD: Steam press, 1876. 62p. NUC OCLC

1659. EBERLE, Eliza, Mrs. [Am. 19c]
Bunyan's pilgrim in verse. Stage first.
NY: S.T. Callahan, pr., 1853. NUC

1660. -----The Pilgrim's Progress, in verse.
Berlin, NY: J.J. Eberle, 1854. 322p. NUC OCLC

1661. -----The way to the cross, set forth in rhyming verses, founded upon the allegorical representation of Bunyan.
Philadelphia: J.J. Eberle, 1868. NUC

1662. ECKLEY, Sophia May [Br. 19c]
Minor chords.
L: Bell & Daldy, 1869. 277p. NUC BL OCLC

1663. -----Poems.
L: Longman, Green, Longman, Roberts & Green, 1863. 207p. NUC BL OCLC

1664. EDDINGTON, Emma Nevius [Am. 19c]
The daisy, and other poems.
Detroit, MI: J.F. Eby & co., pr., 1887. 31p. NUC

1665. EDDY, Mary Morse (Baker) Glover Patterson [Am. 1821-1910]
Poetical works.
Boston: Trustees under the will of Mary Baker G. Eddy, c1893-1897. 49, 79p. NUC BL

1666. EDELSTEN, Jane [Br. 19c]
Sunset thoughts.
L: n.p., 1895. BL

1667. EDGAR, Miss [Br. 19c]
Tranquility. A poem. To which are added other original poems and translations from the Italian and Spanish.
2d ed. L: n.p., 1824. BL

EDGARTON, Sarah Carter, comp. <u>see</u> SCOTT, Julia H. (Kinney)

1668. EDGWORTH, Temple, Miss [Br. 19c]
Metrical tales and romances in verse.
L: T. Tregg, 1809. 136p. BL OCLC

1669. -----The mysterious shriek, or Alexander and Livinia: a metrical tale. From the Greek.
L: n.p., 1809. BL

1670. EDIS, Mary [Br. 19c]
The friendly harp.
L: n.p., 1852. BL

EDITH <u>see</u> STEVENSON, Edith

1671. EDMOND, Amanda M. (Corey) [Am. 1824-1862]
The broken vow and other poems.
Boston: Gould, Kendall & Lincoln, 1845. 324p. NUC BL OCLC

1672. -----Religious and other poems.
Ed. James Edmond.
Boston: Gould & Lincoln, 1872. 263p. NUC BL OCLC

EDMOND, James, ed. <u>see</u> EDMOND, Amanda M. (Corey)

1673. EDMONDS, Elizabeth Mayhew (Waller) [Br. 19c]
Hesperas: rhythm and rhyme.

L: Kegan Paul & co., 1883. 166p. NUC BL

1674. EDRIDGE, Rebecca [Br. 19c]
The lapse of time, a poem for the new year.
Uxbridge: n.p., 1803. NUC BL

1675. EDSON, Helen R. [Am. 19c]
My soul, thou has much goods.
Philadelphia: Presbyterian Board of Publication, 1885. 64p. NUC

1676. EDWARDS, Mrs. [Br. 19c]
A few hymns, copied ... from the diary of the late Mrs. Edwards to be sung at the Baptist Chapel ... the 7th of February, 1836.
Lyme: n.p., 1836. BL

1677. EDWARDS, Miss [Br. 18c]
Miscellanies in prose and verse.
Edinburgh: Pr. for the author & sold by C. Elliot, 1776. 181p. NUC BL

1678. EDWARDS, Amelia Ann Blanford [Br. 1831-1892]
Ballads.
NY: Carleton, 1862. 127p. NUC BL OCLC

1679. -----Home thoughts and home scenes. In original poems. By A.B. Edwards et al.
Boston: J.E. Tilton & co., 1865. NUC

1680. EDWARDS, Anna Maria [Br. 18c]
The enchantress, or The happy island. A favorite musical entertainment; performed at the Opera House, Capel Street.
2 pt. Dublin: n.p., 1787. BL
[Also incl. songs, odes.]

1681. -----Poems on various subjects: pastoral, elegiac, etc. By the author of The enchantress (incl.).
2 pt. Dublin: Pr. for the author by H. Colbert, 1787. 144p. NUC BL OCLC
[Variant ed.; Enchantress also pub. sep.]

EDWARDS, EVELYN, pseud. see JACKSON, Lucy Evelyn

1682. EDWARDS, Matilda Barbara Betham- [Br. 1836-1919]
The lay of Marie: a poem.
L: Rowland Hunter, 1816. 244p. NUC OCLC

1683. -----Poems.
L: K. Paul, Trench, 1884. 155p. NUC BL

1684. EDWARDS, Matilda Caroline (Smiley) [Am. 19c]
The church and the world.
Oxford: Parker, 1883. 32p. L: J. Kensit, 1889. 10p. Yarmouth, ME: Scriptural pub. co., betw. 1872-95. 4p. BL OCLC

1685. -----Poems by Matilda.
Richmond, VA: Pr. Colin, Baptist & Nowlen, 1851. 311p. NUC OCLC

1686. EDWARDS, Viola Parks [Am. 19/20c]
After twenty years; or, Henry and Lamart, and other poems.
Bedford, IN: n.p., 1897. 145p. NUC OCLC

1687. EGERTON, Sarah (Fyge) [Br. 18c]
ALT: F., S., Mrs.
A collection of poems on several occasions. By Mrs. S.F.
L: Pr. & sold by the Booksellers of London & Westminster, 1706. 10p., 117p., 15p. NUC BL OCLC

EKALENNA, pseud. see LAKE, Anne

1688. ELDRED, Ellen E. [Am. 19c]
Reminiscences of a lecture tour.
Laurens, NY: n.p., 1885? 74p. NUC
[Comments in rhyme about a temperance tour]

1689. ELDRED, O.P., Mrs. [Am. 19c]
PSEUD: Allegro
Poems without a muse. By Allegro.
Cincinnati, OH: The Editor pub. co., 1899. 119p. NUC OCLC

1690. ELEMJAY, Louise [Am. 19c]
Censoria lictoria of facts and folks.
3d ed. rev. & enl. NY: John F. Trow, 1852. 208p. NUC
[Prose & poetry. Reviews call it a "grotesque mosaic of wit, sentiment, satire, and epigram, perfectly unique in style."]

1691. -----Censoria lictoria; or, Squibs and etceteras. From the notes and minutes of Miss Betsey Trotwood's official tour, under the Frank Pierce dynasty.
2d ed. NY: J.F. Trow, pr., 1857. 142p. NUC
[Incl. poetry, satires on politics, customs & foibles of the time.]

1692. -----Letters and miscellanies in prose, rhyme, and blank-verse.
Cincinnati, OH: Moore, Anderson, Wilstech & Keys, 1852. 278p. NUC OCLC
[Combines satiric essays, poetry, gossip]

ELIOT, GEORGE, pseud. see EVANS, Marian

ELIZA, pseud. see CARTER, Elizabeth

ELIZA, pseud. see DAY, Esther (Milnes)

1693. ELIZA, pseud. [Br. 18c]
Adversity; or, The tears of Britannia. A poem, by a lady.
L: James Kirby, etc., 1789. 36p. NUC BL OCLC
[A satire on John Wolcott]

1694. ELIZA, pseud. [Am. 19c]
The old elm and the fountain on Boston Common.
Boston: R.F. Foster, 1853. 12p. NUC

1695. ELIZA, pseud. [Am. 19c]
Poems.
n.p.: n.p., 1821. 123p. NUC

ELIZA see GORRINGTON, Elizabeth Sarah

1696. ELIZABETH [Br. 19c]
Poetry and prose. By Elizabeth. Including some original correspondence with distinguished literary characters.
Doncaster: C. & J. White, 1821. 137p. BL OCLC
[Occasional verse, hymns, prayers & meditations in prose. Letters anon. except for one from Anna Seward; many allude to women writers.]

1697. ELKINS, L.M., Mrs. [Am. 19c]
"Chaff".
Milwaukee, WI: The author, 1879. 87p. NUC

1698. ELLA, pseud. [Am. 19c]
Valentines. By Ella. Poems.
NY: T.J. Crowen, 1849. 27p. NUC

1699. ELLARD, Virginia G. [Am. 19/20c]
Grandma's Christmas day.
Cincinnati, OH: Robert Clarke, 1880. 97p. NUC OCLC

1700. ELLEN, pseud. [Am. 19c]
The minstrel lyre, a collection of metricals.
Philadelphia: Atkinson & Alexander, pr., 1827. 162p. NUC OCLC

ELLEN AMELIA, co-author see GARRETT, Annie

ELLER, pseud. see ELLERMAN, Anne Elizabeth

1701. ELLER, Mrs. Thorald [Br. 19c]
Verses.
L: n.p., 1897. 112p.

1702. ELLERMAN, Anne Elizabeth [Br. 19c] PSEUD: Eller
Ingatherings. By Eller.
L: Andrews & co., 1897. 184p. BL
[The liberator, pp. 1-50; poems, many on nature, short stories & prose allegories.]

1703. ELLET, Elizabeth Fries (Lummis), Mrs. William Henry Ellet [Am. 1818-1877]
Poems, translated and original.
Philadelphia: Key & Biddle, 1835. 229p. NUC BL OCLC
[Incl. 5-act tragedy: Teresa Contarini. Most poetry is original]

1704. ELLET, Emily [Br. 19c]
Emily Ellet's journal; or, helps [steps OCLC] towards a better life.
L: Religious Tract Society, 1874. NY: American Finale Guardian Society, c1873. 301p. BL OCLC
[Poetry & religious prose]

ELLET, Mrs. William Henry see ELLET, Elizabeth Fries (Lummis)

ELLIE, pseud. see DEBNEY, Ellen Elizabeth

1705. ELLIOT, Miss [Br. 19c]
Fancy's wreath: being a collection of original fables and allegorical tales in prose and verse.
L: Pr. T. Bensley, 1812. 159p. BL OCLC
[Lyric poems, dramatic poem, prose essay, fables, tales & juvenile literature.]

1706. ELLIOT, Anne [Br. 19c]
The heart's-ease.
Armagh: n.p., 1837. BL

1707. -----Serious thoughts in prose and poetry.
L: L. & G. Seeley; Exeter: W. Roberts, 1841. BL
[Religious poems, scripture texts; prose meditations]

1708. ELLIOT, Lady Charlotte [Br. 19c]
Mary Magdalene and other poems. Rev. & ed. The Earl of Southesk.
Edinburgh: Clark, 1880. 80p. BL OCLC

1709. -----Medusa, and other poems.
L: C. Kegan Paul & co., 1878. 153p. BL OCLC

1710. ELLIOTT, Charlotte [Br. 1789-1871] PSEUD: Lady, A
All I need; or, The Christian's confidence.
L: Religious Tract Society, 1874. BL

1711. -----Beautiful snow.
L: Ernest Nister, 1890. BL

1712. -----Hours of sorrow cheered and comforted. In verse.
2d ed. L: Seeley, 1840. 178p. NUC BL

1713. -----Leaves from the unpublished journals, letters and poems of Charlotte Elliott.
L: Religious Tract Society, 1874. 256p. NUC BL OCLC

1714. -----Morning and evening hymns for a week.
Brighton: n.p., 1836. BL

1716. -----Poetical leaflets. 16 nos.
L: Religious Tract Society, 1873. BL

1715. -----The pilgrim's wants.
L: Religious Tract Society, 1891. BL

1717. -----Thoughts in verse, on sacred subjects; with some miscellaneous poems written in early years and now published.
L: Hunt, 1869. 242p. NUC BL
[2d ed., expanded, 1871]

1718. ELLIOTT, Emily Elizabeth Steele [Br. 1836-1897] ALT: E., E. S.
Chimes of consecration and their echoes.
L: Seeley, Jackson & Halliday, 1875. 167p. NUC BL OCLC

1719. -----Glad voices. Verses by E.S.E. from chimes of consecration.
L: J.E. Hawkins, 1888. BL

1720. -----You may pick the daisies. In verse.
L: J.E. Hawkins, 1890. BL

1721. ELLIOTT, Julia Ann Marshall [Br. d. 1841]
Poems.
L: James Ridgway, 1832. 228p. NUC OCLC
[Part 2 has title: Poems on sacred subjects]

1722. ELLIOTT, Lydia Landon [Am. 19c]
The skeleton's message (and other poems).
Terre Haute, IN: The Inland pub. co., 1896. 131p. NUC OCLC

1723. ELLIOTT, Mary (Belson) [Br. 1794?-1870] ALT: Belson, Mary
The contrast; or, How to be happy.
L: W. Darton & Clarke, 1840? 36p. NUC BL

1724. -----Flowers of instruction: or, Familiar subjects in verse.
L: William Darton, 1820. 62p. BL

1725. -----Gems in the mine; or, Traits and habits of childhood, in verse.
L: William Darton, 1824. 104p. Salem, MA: J.R. Buffum; Lancaster, MA: James B. Buffam, 1828. 104p. NUC BL OCLC
[Poetry on children]

1726. -----Grateful tributes; or, Recollections of infancy. In verse.
NY: Samuel Wood & sons, 1818-1830. 46p. L: W. Darton, 1811. 32p. NUC BL OCLC

1727. -----The rainy day; or, The pleasures of employment.
L: William Darton, 182-? 36p. NUC

1728. -----The mice and their picnic. By a looking-glass maker.
L: Pr. W. & T. Darton, 1810. 30p. NUC BL

ELLIS, Grace A., comp. <u>see</u> BARBAULD, Anna Letitia (Aikin)

ELLIS, John Harvard, ed. <u>see</u> BRADSTREET, Anne (Dudley)

ELLIS, Lou Spencer <u>see</u> ELLIS, Louise Alverda (Spencer)

1729. ELLIS, Louise Alverda (Spencer) [Am. b. 1860] ALT: Ellis, Lou Spencer
Sunbeams and reflections. By Lou Spencer Ellis.
Chicago: Charles H. Kerr & co., 1898. 47p. NUC OCLC

1730. ELLIS, Sarah (Stickney) [Br. 1810/12-1872] ALT: Stickney, Sarah
Irish girl: and other poems. By Sarah Ellis.
NY: James Langley; Philadelphia: T. Cowperthwaite & co., 1844. 263p. NUC OCLC

1731. -----The island queen: a poem.
L: n.p., 1846. BL

1732. -----Janet: one of many. A story in verse.
L: E. Faithfull, 1862. 98p. BL OCLC

1733. -----The poetry of life.
Philadelphia: Carey, Lea & Blanchard; L: Saunders & Otley, 1835. 2v. NUC BL OCLC

1734. -----The sons of the soil; a poem.
2d ed. L: Fisher, son & co., 1840. 298p. NUC BL OCLC

1735. -----William & Mary; or, The fatal blow.
L: S.W. Partridge, 1865. 30p. NUC BL
[Temperance poetry]

1736. ELLISON, A., Mrs.
Original poems.
3d ed. Manchester: J. Heywood, 1875? 108p. BL

ELMORE, Ann Morrison see ELMORE, Lucie Ann (Morrison)

1737. ELMORE, Blanche [Can. 19c]
Poems. 5 series.
Toronto: C.M. Ellis & co.; Douglas bros. & Roberts, 1894-1899. 22 or 23p. NUC

1738. ELMORE, Lucie Ann (Morrison) [Am. 19c] ALT: Elmore, Ann Morrison
A beautiful city, set down by the sea. By Mrs. A. Elmore.
Newark, NJ: A. Pierson & co., 1880. 3p. NUC

1739. -----A mother's story.
Newark, NJ: A. Pierson & co., pr.; pub. by Women's Christian Temperance Union, 1879. 20p. NUC

1740. ELY, Clarissa Eunice [Am. 19c]
Mementos of past days and years.
Philadelphia: H.A. McKinney & co., 1874. 100p. NUC OCLC
[Occasional verse & memorials of her family]

1741. EMBURY, Emma Catherine (Manley) [Am. 1806-1863] ALT: Manley, Emma Catherine PSEUD: Ianthe
American wild flowers in their native haunts.
NY: D. Appleton & co.; Philadelphia: G.S. Appleton, 1845. 256p. OCLC
[Added t.p.: Nature's gems; or, American wild flowers. Verse & prose: botanical notes, misc. poetry, short stories]

1742. -----Guido: a tale; sketches from history, and other poems. By Ianthe.
NY: G. & C. Carvill, 1828. 200p. NUC BL OCLC
[Narrative & historical poems]

1743. -----Love's token flowers.
NY: J.C. Riker, c1845. 128p. NUC OCLC

1744. -----Poems of Emma C. Embury.
NY: Hurd & Houghton, 1869. 368p. NUC

1745. EMERSON, Adaline Elizabeth (Talcott) [Am. 1837-1915]
Love-bound, and other poems.
Cambridge, MA: UP, 1894. 193p. NUC OCLC

1746. EMERSON, Ellen Russell [Am. 1837-1907]
Poems.
Portland, ME: Bailey & Noyes, 1865. 160p. NUC OCLC

1747. EMERSON, Nannette Snow [Am. 1840-1884] PSEUD: Enesee
A Thanksgiving story, embodying the ballad of "Betsey and I are out," and other poems.
NY: G.W. Carleton & co., 1873. 200p. NUC OCLC
[Pub. 1877 as: Why wife and I quarreled; and 1883 as: Uncle Liab and other farm ballads]

1748. EMMA, Sister [Br. 19c]
Lanterns unto our feet and lights unto our path.
L: Masters & co., 1891. 48p. BL

1749. EMMONS, Mary Olive [Am. 19c]
Moods and whims.
Boston: Alfred Mudge & son, pr., 1892. 99p. NUC OCLC

EMRA, Lucy see CROGGON, Lucy Emra

ENESEE, pseud. see EMERSON, Nannette Snow

ENGALL, Thulia Susannah (Henderson) see HENDERSON, Thulia Susannah

ENGLAND, Olive S., Mrs. see ENRIGHT, Olive S. England, Mrs.

1750. ENGLE, Addie Clarissa (Strong) [Am. b. 1845]
Retrospect.
Indianapolis, IN: n.p., 1892. 10 l. NUC

1751. -----The vocal star.
Indianapolis, IN: W.D. Engle & bro., 1890. 16p. NUC

ENGLISHWOMAN, AN, pseud. see SARGANT, Jane Alice

1752. ENRIGHT, Olive S. England, Mrs. [Am. 19c] ALT: England, Olive S., Mrs.
Ceres, a harvest home festival, and other poems, essays, etc. By Mrs. Olive S. England.
Salem, OR: E.M. Waite pr. co., 1893. 99p. NUC OCLC

1753. ENSIGN, Martha Baldwin [Am. 19c]
The betrothal, a poem.
NY: The author, 1890. 68p. NUC OCLC

EPHELIA, pseud. see PHILIPS, Joan

EPHZIBA, pseud. see HOWELL, Annie, Mrs.

1754. ERICSON, Augusta C. [Am. 19c]
A collection of rhymes.
Earlville, IL: Press of the Ledger, 1893. 92p. NUC
[Mainly relating to local events]

1755. ERSKINE, Emma (Payne) [Am. 1854-1924] ALT: Erskine, Mrs. Payne
Iona, a lay of ancient Greece.
Boston: Cupples & Hurd, 1888. 186p. NUC

ERSKINE, Esme Steuart, Hon. Mrs. see NORTON, Eliza Bland (Smith) Erskine, Hon. Mrs.

ERSKINE, Mrs. Payne see ERSKINE, Emma Payne

ESDAILE, CLIFTON, pseud. see WALKER, Marie Woodruff

1756. ESLING, Catherine Harbeson (Waterman) [Am. b. 1812] ALT: Waterman, Catherine Harbeson
The broken bracelet and other poems. By Mrs. C.H.W. Esling. Ed. J.F.
Philadelphia: Lindsay & Blakiston, 1850. 288p. NUC BL OCLC

1757. -----Flora's lexicon: an interpretation of the language and sentiment of flowers: with an outline of botany and a poetical introduction. By Catherine H. Waterman.
Philadelphia: Hooker & Claxton, 1839. 252p. NUC BL OCLC

ESPENER, Isabella see ESPENSER, Isabella

1758. ESPENSER, [Espener OCLC], Isabella [Br. 19c]
Sentimental poetry, acrostics, etc.
Hull: Hutchinson, 1826. 47p. BL OCLC

ESTELLE, pseud. see HARRIS, Emily Marion

1759. ETA, pseud. [Br. 19c]
Echoes: translations from the French poets, with some original verse.
Oxford: T. Shrimpton & son, 1875. 78p. NUC

1760. -----Poems.
L: Cassell & co., n.d. 79p. NUC

EUGENIA, pseud. see CHUDLEIGH, Mary (Lee), Lady

EULALIE see SHANNON, Mary Eulalie (Fee)

EVA, pseud. see O'DOHERTY, Mary Anne (Kelly)

1761. EVANS, Ann [Am. 19c]
Africa, a poem. [Anon.].
Andover, MA: Pr. Flagg & Gould, 1826. 20p. NUC OCLC
[On slave trade]

1762. EVANS, Anne [Br. 1820-1870]
Anne Evans. Poems and music.
L: C. Kegan, Paul & co., 1880. 159p. NUC BL OCLC
[109p. poetry]

1763. EVANS, Elizabeth Hewlings (Stockton) [Am. 1817-1856]
Poems. By Mrs. E.H. Evans.
Philadelphia: Lippincott, Grambo & co., 1851. 251p. NUC OCLC

EVANS, M.A.B. see EVANS, Mary Anna (Buck)

1764. EVANS, Margaret Freeman [Br. d. 1893] ALT: E., M.
Dies Dominica; being hymns and metrical meditations for each Sunday in the natural year. With Isabel Southall.
L: E. Stock, 1897. 112p. NUC BL

1765. -----Songs of Siluria; to which is added Fluvius lacrymarum, by M.E. & I.S. [Isabel Southall].
L: E. Stock, 1890. 128p. NUC BL

1766. EVANS, Marian [Br. 1819-1880] ALT: Cross, Marian Evans; Evans, Mary Ann; Lewes, Marian PSEUD: Eliot, George
Agatha.
L: Trubner & co., 1869. 16p. NUC BL OCLC

1767. -----Complete poems; scenes of clerical life. By George Eliot.
Boston: Dana Estes & co., 18--? 442, 492p. TXU
[Incl. 4 short stories]

1768. -----How Lisa loved the king.
Boston: Fields, Osgood & co., 1869. 48p. NUC BL OCLC
[Later pub. in The legend of Jubal]

1769. -----The legend of Jubal: and other poems.
Berlin: A. Cohn, 1874. 242p. Author's ed. Boston: J.R. Osgood & co., 1874. 233p. Edinburgh & L: W. Blackwood & sons, 1874. 242p. NUC BL OCLC
[Original printer's proof copy, 1869.]

1770. -----The Spanish gypsy. A poem.
L & Edinburgh: W. Blackwood, 1868. 358p. Boston: Ticknor & Fields, 1868. 287p. NUC BL OCLC

EVANS, Mary Ann see EVANS, Marian

1771. EVANS, Mary Anna (Buck) [Am. 1857-1934]
In various moods. By M.A.B. Evans.
NY & L: G.P. Putnam's sons; Knickerbocker press, 1893. 90p. NUC OCLC

1772. -----Nymphs, Nixies and Naiads: Legends of the Rhine. By M.A.B. Evans.
NY & L: G.P. Putnam's sons, 1895. 111p. TXU

1773. EVELYN, Mary [Br. 1665-1685]
Mundus mulieribus; or, The ladies dressing-room unlock'd, and her toilette spread. In burlesque. Together with the fop-dictionary compiled for the use of the fair sex.
L: R. Bentley, 1690. 22p. NUC OCLC

EVERED POOLE, Mrs. see POOLE, Eva L. (Travers) Evered

EVERGREEN, EVA, pseud. see HOUGH, E.H., Mrs.

1774. EWER, Mary H. [Am. 19c]
Crazy Nell, a ballad; and other poems.
NY: Press of Bedell & bros., 1879. 32p. NUC

1775. -----Wild flowers.
NY: Edgar S. Werner, 1896. 113p. NUC OCLC
[3 sections, poems written in babyhood, girlhood, womanhood]

1776. EWING, Harriet [Br. 19c]
Dunrie: a poem.
Bath: Cruttwell, 1819. 202p. BL OCLC

1777. EWING, Martha [Am. 19c]
The language and poetry of flowers.
Rochester, NY: Union & adv. co's. pr., 1875. 119p. NUC

1778. EYTINGE, Pearl [Am. 19c]
Poems.
NY: A.S. Seer's pr., 1888. 18p. NUC

EYTON, Charlotte see EYTON, Elizabeth Charlotte

1779. EYTON, Elizabeth Charlotte [Br. 19c] ALT: E., C.; Eyton, Charlotte
Hymns of praise and prayer. By C.E.
Wellington, Salop: The author, 1868. 19p. BL

F. see OWEN, Frances Mary (Synge)

F., A. see FIELDS, Annie (Adams)

F., A. see FRANCIS, Ann

F., B. see FINCH, B., Mrs.

F., E. see FISHER, E., Miss

F., E. see FLETCHER, Eliza Dawson

F., E.S. see FRANCIS, Eliza S.

F., H.J. see FRY, Henrietta Joan

F., H.M. see FRERE, Helen M.

F., J., ed. see ESLING, Catherine Harbeson (Waterman)

F., M.F. see FRY, Matilda (Penrose) [F. BL]

F., S., Mrs. see EGERTON, Sarah Fyge

F., T.M., ed. see FALLOW, Mrs.

1780. FABBRI, Cora Randall [Am. 1871-1892]
Lyrics.
NY: Harper & bros., 1892. 162p. NUC OCLC

FABER, Rev. G.S., ed. see WOODROOFFE, Sophia

1781. FACKRELL, Mary S., Mrs. [Am. 19c]
Poems. With additional prose.
NY: Poole & Maclauchlan, pr., 1872. 164p. NUC OCLC
[Prose: short essays & fictional sketches]

1782. FAGAN, Fanny [Am. d. 1878]
In memoriam. A selection from the poems of Fanny Fagan.
Philadelphia: Pub. for priv. dist., 1878. 224p. NUC OCLC

1783. FAGE, Mary [Br. 17c]
Fame's roule: or, The names of our dread sovereigns Lord King Charles, his royall Queen Mary, and his most hopefull posterity: together with, the names of the dukes, marquesses, earles ... of ... England, Scotland and Ireland: anagrammatiz'd and expressed by acrosticke lines on their names.
L: Pr. by Richard Oulton, 1637. NUC BL OCLC

1784. FAIRBANKS, A. Loetta [Am. 19c]
A dream of heaven; or, Which way to heaven.
Lynn, MA: Pub. by the author, 1897. 163p. NUC OCLC
[Poem comparing religions of the world]

1785. FAIRBANKS, Cassie [Can. 19c]
The lone house: a poem, partly founded fact.
Halifax: n.p., 1859. 15p. NUC
[Relates to the murder of Rebecca Langley on August 24, 1854]

1786. FAIRBROTHER, Mary Ann [Br. 19c]
Poems: chiefly moral and pastoral.
L: Vernon, Hood & Sharpe, 1808. 112p. NUC BL

FAIRFIELD, IDA, pseud. see CLARKE, Mary Bassett

1787. FAIRWEATHER, Mary, Mrs. [Br. 19c]
Hymns and religious poems of a practical nature.
Agra: n.p., 1833. BL

FALCONAR, H., co-author see FALCONAR, Maria

FALCONAR, Harriet, co-author see FALCONAR, Maria

FALCONAR, M. see FALCONAR, Maria

1788. FALCONAR, Maria [Br. 18c]
Poems by Maria and Harriet Falconar.
L: J. Johnson & Messrs. Egertons, 1788. 124p. NUC BL OCLC

1789. -----Poems on slavery: by M[aria] Falconar ... and H[arriet] Falconar.
L: Egertons, 1788. 25p. NUC BL
[Pub. when Maria was 17 and Harriet 14]

1790. -----Poetic laurels ... for characters of distinguished merit, interspersed with poems, moral and entertaining.
L: n.p., 1791. BL

FALES, FANNY, pseud. see SWIFT, Frances Elizabeth (Chase)

1791. FALKNER, Rhoda Ann (Paige)
Wild notes from the backwoods, by R.A.P.
Cobourg: Pr. at Cobourg Star, 1850. 62p. NUC

1792. FALLON, Susan Ann [Br. 19c]
The May wreath.
L: Burns & Lambert, n.d. 35p. BL
[Prayers in verse to the Virgin]

1793. FALLOW, Mrs. [Br. 19c]
Poetical remains of a clergyman's wife. Ed. T.M. F[allow].
L: C. & J. Rivington, 1833. 124p. NUC BL

FALLOW, T.M., ed. see FALLOW, Mrs.

FANE, VIOLET, pseud. see CURRIE, Mary Mongtomerie (Lamb) Singleton, Baroness

1794. FANSHAWE, Catherine Maria [Br. 1765-1834]
The literary remains of Catherine Maria Fanshawe.
L: Basil Montagu Pickering, 1876. 79p.
[16 poems: odes, satires]

1795. -----Memorials of Miss Catherine Maria Fanshaw. Ed. William Harness.
Westminster, L: Priv. pr. by Vasher & sons, 1865. 56p. NUC BL OCLC

1796. FANSHAWE, Catherine Maria
Provision for a family.
L: Roake & Varty, 1830? 2p. NUC

1797. -----Speech of the member for Odium.

L: Roake & Varty, 1833. 3p. NUC BL
[A satire on William Cobbett]

1798. FANSHAWE, Lenora [Am. 19c]
A few buds ... .
n.p.: Allen, Lane & Scott, pr., 1887?
37p. NUC
[Written at 12-13 yrs.]

1799. FARLEY, Helen Hall (Moyer) [Am. 19c] PSEUD: Gilmore, Ernest
Unswerving. By Ernest Gilmore.
NY: T.Y. Crowell & co., 1877. 267p.
NUC OCLC
[A novel, 240p.; incl. 11 poems, pp. 243-67.]

1800. FARMER, P., Mrs. [Am. 19c]
The captives, and other poems.
Laporte, IN: Pr. Millikan & Holmes, 1856. 236p. NUC OCLC

FARNINGHAM, MARIANNE, pseud. see HEARN, Mary Anne

1801. FARQUHAR, Barbara H. [Br. 19c]
Poems.
L: Pitman, 1863. 208p. NUC BL OCLC

1802. FARQUHAR, Mary [Am. 19c]
A collection of verses.
Providence, RI: Snow & Farnham, pr., 1897. 39p. NUC OCLC

1803. FARRELL, Sarah, Mrs. [Br. 18c]
Charlotte; or, A sequel to the sorrows of Werther ... and other poems.
Bath: Campbell & Gainsborough, 1792. 80p. NUC BL

1804. FARRER, Georgiana [Br. 19c]
Miscellaneous poems.
L: Partridge & co., 1883. 356p. BL

1805. FARRIS, Edna Carrick [19c]
Mother's poems.
n.p.: n.p., n.d. 23p. NUC

1806. FARROW, Bertha S. [Am. 19c]
College rhymes.
Indianapolis, IN: The Bowen-Merrill co., 1893. 83p. NUC OCLC

FAUGERES, Margaretta V., co-author see BLEECKER, Ann Eliza (Schuyler)

1807. FAWCETT, Mary Huestis [Am. b. 1843]
Poems.
Cincinnati, OH: Robert Clarke & co., pr., 1880. 169p. NUC OCLC

1808. FAWKES, Miss [Br. 19c]
The Washburn and other poems.
L: Hatchards, 1879. 42p. BL

1809. FAY, Anna Maria [Am. 1828-1921]
Idylls and poems.
NY: G.P. Putnam's sons, 1879. 103p.
NUC OCLC

FAY, GERDA, pseud. see GEMMER, Caroline M., Mrs.

1810. FAY, Julia Douglas [Am. 19c]
Poems.
Albany, NY: J. Munsell [Mansell OCLC], 1878. 92p. NUC OCLC

FEARING, Blanche see FEARING, Lilian Blanche

1811. FEARING, Lilian Blanche [Am. 1863-1901] ALT: Fearing, Blanche
In the city by the lake; in two books: The shadow, and The slave girl. By Blanche Fearing.
2d ed. Chicago: Searle & Gorton, 1892. 192p. NUC OCLC

1812. -----The sleeping world, and other poems.
Chicago: A.C. McClurg & co., 1887. 116p. NUC

FEARN, J., comp. see FREMONT, Anne A.

1813. FELDSMITH, Mattie Doherty, Mrs. [Am. 19c] PSEUD: Bond, Leda
Dew drops. Poems by Leda Bond.
Milwaukee, WI: Press of the Evening Wisconsin co., 1896. 184p. NUC OCLC

FELKIN, Hon. Mrs. Alfred Laurence see FELKIN, Ellen Thorneycroft (Fowler)

1814. FELKIN, Ellen Thorneycroft (Fowler), Hon. Mrs. Alfred Laurence Felkin [Br. 1860-1929] ALT: Fowler, Ellen Thorneycroft
Verses grave and gay. By Ellen Thorneycroft Fowler.
L: Cassell, 1891. 148p. NUC BL OCLC

1815. -----Verses, wise or otherwise. By Hon. Ellen Thorneycroft Fowler.
L & Paris: Cassell, 1895. 139p. NUC BL OCLC

1816. FELKIN, Mrs. John [Br. 19c]
Original miscellaneous poems.
L: n.p., 1853. BL

FELL, Miss see FELL, Elizabeth

1817. FELL, Elizabeth [Br. d. 1780]
ALT: Fell, Miss

Fables, odes and miscellaneous poems.
L: J. Robson, 1771. 166p. OCLC

1818. -----A poem on the times.
Newcastle: Pr. T. Saint, sold by W. Charnley, 1774. 17p. NUC OCLC

1819. -----Poems.
L: J. Robson, 1777. 93p. BL OCLC

1820. FELLOWS, Mrs. Frank P. [Br. 19c]
Poems.
L: Smith, Elder, 1857. 83p. NUC BL OCLC

FEMALE, A, pseud. see CARNES, Hannah, Mrs.

FENNO, J., Miss see FENNO, Jenny, Miss

1821. FENNO, Jenny, Miss [Am. 18c]
ALT: Fenno, J., Miss
Original compositions, in prose and verse. On subjects moral and religious.
Boston: Pr. Joseph Bunstead, 1791. 125p. NUC BL

1822. FENTIMAN, Catherine [Br. 19c]
Scraps.
L: Bedford & Robins, 1824. 70p. BL

FERGUSON, Amos, co-author see FERGUSON, Mrs. Amos J.

1823. FERGUSON, Mrs. Amos J. [Am. 19c]
Bible poem ... by Amos Ferguson. Also, poems on the pioneer and his daughter; or, The lady of the forest; Elric and Earl, an allegory; and The lost boy. By Mrs. A.J. Ferguson. With Amos J. Ferguson.
Jamestown, NY: Journal pr. est., 1883. 280p. NUC OCLC

1824. FERRE, Ella [Am. b. 1856]
PSEUD: Gage, Hannah B.
The land by the sunset sea and other poems. By Hannah B. Gage.
San Francisco: P.I. Figel, 1884. 90p. NUC OCLC

1825. FERRIS, Mary Lanman (Douw), Mrs. Morris Patterson Ferris [Am. 1855-1932]
A legend of New Year's eve.
NY: n.p., 1896. 7 l. NUC

1826. -----The schepen's dream. A tale of Nieuw Amsterdam. A poem.
NY: Fort Orange Press, 1889. 7 l. NUC OCLC
[Pub. anon.]

FERRIS, Mrs. Morris Patterson see FERRIS, Mary Lanman (Douw)

1827. FESSENDEN, Laura Canfield Spencer (Dayton) [Am. d. 1924]
Beth.
NY: Brentano's literary emporium, 1878. 16p. NUC

1828. -----Essie. A romance in rhyme.
Boston: Lee & Shepard, 1895. 93p. NY: J.C. Graff, pr., 1878. 32p. NUC BL

1829. FEWKES, Charlotte Louisa [Br. 19c]
The royal album of great names. A jubilee offering to ... Queen Victoria.
L: Eyre & Spottiswoode, 1889. 45p. BL

1830. FFOULKES, L. Florence Wynne [19c]
Short poems in sunlight and shade.
L: Field & Tueretal; NY: Scribner & Welford, 1887. 117p. NUC BL OCLC

1831. FFRENCH, Evelyn [19c]
Verses from the bland.
Melbourne: Melville, Mullen & Slade, 1899. 31p. NUC

1832. FIELD, Caroline Leslie (Whitney) [Am. 1853-1902]
The unseen king, and other verses.
Boston & NY: Houghton Mifflin & co., 1887. 73p. NUC OCLC

1833. FIELD, Henriette (Deluzy-Desportes), Mrs. Henry Martyn Field [Am. d. 1875]
Home sketches in France, and other papers. Ed. Henry Martyn Field.
NY: G.P. Putnam's sons, 1875. 256p. NUC BL

FIELD, Henry Martyn, ed. see FIELD, Henriette (Deluzy-Desportes)

FIELD, Mrs. Henry Martyn see FIELD, Henriette (Deluzy-Desportes)

FIELD, MICHAEL, pseud. see BRADLEY, Katherine Harris

FIELD, MICHAEL, pseud. see COOPER, Edith Emma

1834. FIELDS, Annie (Adams), Mrs. James T. Fields [Am. 1834-1915] ALT: F., A.
The children of Lebanon.

Boston: n.p., 1872. 24p. NUC OCLC
[On the Shakers]

1835. -----Ode.
Cambridge, MA: Pr. Welch, Bigelow, & co., 1863? 11p. NUC

1836. -----The singing shepherd and other poems.
Boston & NY: Houghton Mifflin & co., 1895. 155p. NUC OCLC

1837. -----Under the olive.
Boston & NY: Houghton, Mifflin & co., 1880. 317p. NUC OCLC

FIELDS, Mrs. James T. see FIELDS, Annie (Adams)

FILLMORE, Charles Wesley, ed. see FILLMORE, Susan French

1838. FILLMORE, Mary Hawthorne, Mrs. [Am. 19c]
What the daisies told me.
Cushing, ME: n.p., 1888. 14p. NUC

1839. FILLMORE, Susan French [Am. b. 1795]
Our inalienable inheritance.
Providence, RI: n.p., 1882. 6p. NUC OCLC
[Written for the 6th anniversary of the Page Family Assn.]

1840. -----Poetic effusions. Ed. her son, Charles Wesley Fillmore.
Providence, RI: n.p., 1887. 35p. NUC OCLC

FINCH, Anne (Kingsmill), Countess of Winchilsea see WINCHILSEA, Anne (Kingsmill), Countess of

1841. FINCH, B., Mrs. [Br. 19c] ALT: F., B.
Sonnets and other poems: to which are added tales in prose. By B.F.
L: Blacks, 1805. 126p. BL OCLC

1842. FINCH, Constance [Br. 19c]
The vision of a beginner; and other poems.
L: Digby, Long, 1892. 88p. BL OCLC

1843. FINCH, Mary Baird [Am. 19c]
Silver party song book.
Pueblo, CO: n.p., 1896. 11p. NUC
[1896 Democratic campaign songs, without music.]

1844. -----Under the glory sheaves, and other poems.
Pueblo, CO: Mail publishing co., 1896. 11p. NUC

FINOLA, pseud. see VARIAN, Elizabeth Willoughby (Tracy)

1845. FIRE-FLY, FANNY, pseud. [Am. 19c]
The ducks and the frogs; a tale of the bogs.
Boston: J.H. Francis; W.D. Ticknor, 1849. 30p. NUC OCLC

1846. FISH, Angelina, Mrs. [Am. 19c]
Voices and echoes of the past.
Brooklyn, NY: n.p., 1885. 170p. NUC OCLC

1847. FISHER, E., Miss [Br. 19c] ALT: F., E.
Sketches and souvenirs; or, Records of other days. By E.F.
L: Simpkin, Marshall; Bath: Pocock Library, 1839. 239p. BL
[Biographical sketches, meditations, poems & stories]

1848. FISHER, Fanny E. [Br. 19c]
Ainsworth's heir, and other poems.
L: A.W. Bennett, 1866. 476p. NUC BL OCLC
[Incl. Lonely hours]

1849. -----Lonely hours: poems.
Dublin: n.p., 1864. BL

1850. -----Poems.
L: T. Fisher Unwin, 1889. 554p. BL

1851. -----Poems and notes descriptive of Killarney.
L: T. Fisher Unwin, 1890. 68p. NUC BL OCLC

1852. FISHER, Hannah [Aus. 19c]
Original poems.
Ballaret: F.W. Pinkerton, 1889. 320p. NUC OCLC

1853. FISHER, Lala Richardson [Br. 1872-1929]
A twilight teaching and other poems.
L: T. Fisher Unwin, 1898. 175p. BL

1854. FISHER, Laura Hope [Am. 19c]
Figures and flowers for serious souls.
Buffalo, NY: Moulton, Wenborne & co., 1888. 160p. NUC OCLC
[Misc. poetry, much of it homespun]

1855. FISHER, Mary J. (Acer) [Am. 19c]
Songs in the night.
Rochester, NY: Post Express pr. co., 1893. 35p. NUC OCLC

FISHER, Sarah C., ed. see WELLINGTON, Caroline Louisa (Fisher)

1856. FISHER, Susan [Br. 19c]
A legend of the Puritans, or, the influence of poetry and religion on the female character: with other poems.
L: Simpkin & Marshall, 1837. 92p. NUC BL

1857. FITCH, A. Mabel (Blackman) [Am. 19c]
Madaline: a poem.
Chicago: Henry A. Sumner & co., 1881. 165p. NUC OCLC

1858. FITCH, Anna Mariska, Mrs. [Am. 19c]
The loves of Paul Fenly.
NY & L: G.P. Putnam's sons, 1893. 119p. NUC BL OCLC
[Poem in 13 cantos.]

1859. FITZ-SIMON, Ellen [Br. 19c]
Darrynane in eighteen hundred and thirty-two, and other poems.
Dublin: W.P. Kelly, 1863. 250p. NUC BL

1860. FITZGERALD, M. Pauline [Am. 19c]
My thoughts: a book of poems.
Weldon, NC: Harrell's pr. house, 1896. 34p. NUC

1861. FITZGERALD, Marcella Agnes [Am. b. 1845]
Poems.
NY: Pub. for author by Catholic Pub. Soc., 1886. 504p. NUC OCLC

1862. FITZGERALD, Sarah A., Mrs. [Am. 19c]
Poems and fugitive pieces.
New Haven, CT: n.p., 1837-38. 10p. NUC

1863. FLEMING, Kate [Am. 19c]
Bi-centennial poems.
Wrentham, MA: n.p., 1873. 9p. NUC OCLC

1864. FLETCHER, Eliza Dawson [Br. 1770-1858] ALT: F., E.
Elidure and Edward. Two historical dramatic sketches. By E.F.
L: Pr. Thomas Davison, 1825. 125p. NUC BL OCLC
[5 acts each]

FLETCHER, Rev. Joseph, co-author see FLETCHER, Mary

1865. FLETCHER, Lisa A. [Am. 19c]
Beside still waters.
NY: A.D.F. Randolph co., 1899. 162p. NUC OCLC

FLETCHER, Lucy see MASSEY, Lucy (Fletcher)

1866. FLETCHER, Maria Jane Jewsbury [Br. 1800-1833]
Lays of leisure hours.
L: J. Hatchard & son, 1829. 189p. NUC BL OCLC

1867. FLETCHER, Mary [Br. 19c]
Poems. By the Rev. J[oseph] Fletcher ... and M[ary] Fletcher.
L: John Snow, 1846. 84p. BL OCLC

1868. FLINDERS, Anne [Br. 19c]
Naboth, the Jezreelite, and other poems.
Bath: n.p., 1844. BL

FLORENCE, pseud. see OSGOOD, Frances Sargent (Locke)

1869. FLORENZ [Br. 19c]
Stella, and other poems.
Edinburgh & L: n.p., 1867. BL

1870. FLOWERS, Sarah L. [Am. 19c]
Silver lined; a poem.
Rahway, NJ: W.L. Mershon & co., 1878. 112p. NUC OCLC

FLOYER, Edith Louisa see BUTCHER, Edith Louisa (Floyer)

FOGG, Mrs. F.B. see FOGG, Mary Middleton (Rutledge)

1871. FOGG, Mary Middleton (Rutledge), Mrs. F.B. Fogg [Am. 1800-1872]
Poems. By Mrs. F.B. Fogg.
Nashville, TN: n.p., 1850? 54p. NUC

1872. FOLLEN, Eliza Lee (Cabot) [Am. 1787-1860]
Poems.
Boston: W. Crosby & co., 1839. 192p. NUC BL OCLC

1873. FOLLETT, Mary A., Mrs. [Am. 19c] PSEUD: Hearthstone, Hetty
Golden heads. By Hetty Hearthstone.
Ware, MA: Press of C.W. Eddy, 1894. 18p. NUC

FOLSOM, Florence (Bluxome) see FOLSOM, Florens (Bluxome)

1874. FOLSOM, Florens [Florence OCLC] (Bluxome) [Am. b. 1874]

Love-lyrics.
Boston: The Idea pub. co., 1899. 64p. NUC OCLC

1875. FOOT, Alicia Julia [Br. 19c]
Thoughts in verse.
L: priv. pr., 1856. BL

1876. FOOT, Rose [Br. 19c]
Rose's offering.
L: Grattan; Cheshunt: T. Buck, 1856. NUC BL

1877. FOOTE, Ella Woodward [Am. 19c]
Poems.
Oakland, CA: G.A. Kelley, 1898. 40 l. NUC OCLC

1878. FOOTE, Louisa Young [Am. 1827?-1919]
In the Adirondacks.
Chicago: The Wind-tryst press, 1897. 2 l. NUC

1879. -----The old homestead.
Chicago: The Wind-tryst press, 1899. 20p. NUC

1880. FOOTT, Mary Hannay [Br. 1846-1918]
Morna Lee, and other poems.
2d ed. L: Gordon & Gotch, 1890. 72p. NUC BL OCLC

1881. FORBES, Lavinia C. M. [Br. 19c]
The Harringtons; and Select poetry.
Glasgow: Pickering & Inglis, 1894. 171p. BL

FORBES-LEITH, Mrs. James John see FORBES-LEITH, Williamina Helen (Stewart)

1882. FORBES-LEITH, Williamina Helen (Stewart), Mrs. James John Forbes-Leith [Br. d. 1866]
Whitehaugh: a poem.
Boulogne-sur-mer: Priv. pr. by H. Delahodde, 1848. 10p. NUC OCLC
[Addressed to her eldest son, after the death of his father]

1883. FORD, Anna M. [Am. 19c]
Garlands of thought.
Philadelphia: William Flint, 1885. 83p. NUC OCLC

1884. FORD, Anna P., Mrs. [Am. 19c]
Daisy's offering, and other poems.
Binghamton, NY: G.L. Harding, 1879. 41p. NUC OCLC

1885. FORD, Anna Perkins [Am. 19c]
Vesper voices; miscellaneous poems.
Asbury Park, NJ: M., W. & C. Pennypacker, 1899. 111p. NUC OCLC

FORD, Anne see THICKNESSE, Anne (Ford)

1886. FORD, Mrs. Augustine [Am. 19c]
Una.
Cincinnati, OH: n.p., 1863. 1v. NUC

1887. FORD, Emily Ellsworth (Fowler)
My recreations. Verses.
NY: Hurd & Houghton, 1872. 255p. NUC OCLC

1888. -----Poems. Comp. W.C. Ford.
Brooklyn, NY: Priv. pr., 1879. 19p. NUC OCLC

1889. FORD, Jane H. C. [Br. 19c]
Mara: a girl's story, and other poems.
Edinburgh: Pr. for priv. circ., 1879. 187p. BL

1890. FORD, Laura M. [Am. 19c]
Heart throbs.
Philadelphia: The Hathaway Press, 1895. 90p. NUC OCLC

1891. FORD, Mary Anne (McMullen) [Am. 1841-1876] PSEUD: Una
Poems. By Una.
Cincinnati, OH: S.G. Cobb, pr., 1863. 216p. NUC OCLC

1892. -----Snatches of song. By Mary A. McMullen (Una).
St. Louis, MO: P. Fox, 1874. 203p. NUC OCLC

FORD, W.C., comp. see FORD, Emily Ellsworth (Fowler)

1893. FORDE, Gertrude [Br. 19c]
Stray thoughts in verse.
Cheltenham: J.J. Banks, 1895. 128p. BL

1894. FORDHAM, Mary Weston [Am. 19c]
Magnolia leaves; poems.
Charleston, SC; Tuskegee, AL: Walker, Evans & Cogswell co., c1897. 104p. NUC OCLC

1895. FORDYCE, Henrietta, Mrs. James Fordyce [Br. 19c]
Memoir of the late Mrs. Henrietta Fordyce, relict of James Fordyce, D.D.; containing original letters, anecdotes, and pieces of poetry.
L: n.p., 1823. NUC BL

FORDYCE, Mrs. James see FORDYCE, Henrietta

FORESTER, FANNY, pseud. see JUDSON, Emily C. (Chubbuck)

FORESTER, FANNY, pseud., comp. see JUDSON, Sarah (Hall) Boardman

1896. FORMAN, Emily Shaw [Am. 19c]
A garland of love.
Boston: L. Prang & co., c1882. 1v. NUC OCLC
[Flowers in poetry]

1897. -----The life of Columbus in pictures, by Victor A. Searles. Historical poem, by Emily Shaw Forman.
Boston: L. Prang & co., 1892. NUC OCLC

1898. -----Sonnets. The sabbatia. With Jones Very.
U.S.?: n.p., 18--? 2p. NUC OCLC

1899. -----Wild-flower sonnets.
Boston: Joseph Knight co., 1895. 35 l. NUC

FORMAN, Harry Buxton, ed. see SHELLEY, Mary Wollstonecraft (Godwin)

1900. FORREST, Alice [Br. 19c]
Sunlight for the soul. Hymns for Christian readers.
L: n.p., 1873. BL

FORREST, MARY, pseud. see FREEMAN, Julia Deane, Mrs.

FORRESTER, Arthur M., co-author see FORRESTER, Ellen, Mrs.

1901. FORRESTER, Ellen, Mrs. [Br. 19c]
Songs of the rising nation: and other poems. With Arthur M. Forrester.
L: n.p., 1869. BL

1902. FORSAYTH, Frances Jane [Br. 19c]
Arno's waters, and other poems.
L: n.p., 1865. BL

1903. -----The student's twilight; or, Tales in verse.
L: n.p., 1878. BL

1904. -----The Maria-Steig, and other poems.
L: n.p., 1873. BL

FORTNUM, Sophia (King), co-author see KING, Charlotte

1905. FORTNUM, Sophia King [Br. 18/19c] ALT: King, Sophia
The fatal secret, or Unknown warrior; a romance of the twelfth century with legendary poems.
L: n.p., 1801. 1v. BL

1906. -----Poems; legendary, pathetic, and descriptive.
L: Pr. S. Burchett, 1804. 75p. NUC BL OCLC

1907. -----Trifles of Helicon. By C[harlotte] and S[ophia] K[ing].
L: n.p., 1798.

1908. FOSTER, Eleanor [Br. 19c]
With the tide, and other poems.
L: Gay & Bird, 1896. 95p. NUC

FOSTER, Hanna A. see FOSTER, Hannah A.

1909. FOSTER, Hannah A. [Am. 19c]
ALT: Foster, Hanna A.
Hilda. A poem.
Philadelphia: J.B. Lippincott & co., 1879. 101p. NUC OCLC

1910. -----Zululu, the maid of Anahuac. In verse.
NY: G.P. Putnam's sons, 1892. 119p. NUC OCLC

1911. FOSTER, Hannah (Webster), Mrs. John Foster [Br. 1759-1840]
Spirit-footprints.
n.p.: n.p., 1884.

1912. FOSTER, Harriet Townsend, Mrs. [Am. 19c]
The "wind-flower;" or, A legend of the Ozarks. By Mrs. Harriet Townsend Foster.
Chicago: R.R. Donnelley & sons, 1888. NUC

1913. FOSTER, Harriet W. [Am. 19c]
Reflections.
NY & Boston: Thomas Y. Crowell & co., c1895. 43p. NUC OCLC
[Verse & prose mixture, some epigrams, advice & sermonettes.]

FOSTER, Mrs. John see FOSTER, Hannah (Webster)

FOTHERBY, Henry Isaac, ed. see FOTHERBY, Marie J.E., Mrs.

FOTHERBY, Mrs. Henry Isaac see FOTHERBY, Marie J.E., Mrs.

1914. FOTHERBY, Marie J. E., Mrs. Henry Isaac Fotherby [Br. 19c]

Poems by the late M.J.E. Fotherby. Ed. her husband, Henry Isaac Fotherby.
L: Arthur Hall, Virtue & co., 1862. 186p. NUC BL

1915. FOUTY, Constance Bennett [Am. 19c]
Sea bride.
Whatcom, WA: Press of I.C. Parker, 1889? 144p. NUC

1916. FOWLE, Mary Louise Whelpley [Am. 1825-1898]
Where is heaven? and other poems.
San Francisco: Bancroft co., 1890. 48p. NUC OCLC

FOWLER, Ellen Thorneycroft see FELKIN, Ellen Thorneycroft (Fowler)

FOWLER, Henry, ed. see CHASE, Mary M.

1917. FOWLER, Lydia Folger [Br. 1823-1879]
Heart-melodies. Poems.
L & Manchester: Heywood, 1870. 175p. BL OCLC

1918. FOWLES, Mary A. [Am. 19c]
A sequence of songs.
Columbia, SC: W.J. Duffie; Atlanta, GA: Phillips & Crew, 1882. 42p. NUC

1919. FOX, Elizabeth [Br. 19c]
Wild blossoms and stray leaves gathered in sunshine and shade from the hedgerows of life.
L: Whittaker & co.; Westminster: W.H. Tayler, 1855. 160p. NUC BL

1920. FOX, Emma [Br. 19c]
"A village scene."
Brighton: n.p., 1870. BL

1921. FOX, Sarah Hustler [Br. 19c]
PSEUD: Sphinx
Catch who can ... original double acrostics. By Sphinx.
L: n.p., 1869. BL

1922. -----A metrical version of the book of Job.
Pt. 1 L: C. Gilpin, 1852. 57p. BL

FOXTON, E., pseud. see PALFREY, Sara Hammond

1923. FOXWORTH, Sophia Graves, Mrs. [Am. 19c]
The old mansion, and other poems.
Buffalo, NY: The Peter Paul book co., 1896. 100p. NUC OCLC

1924. FRAME, Elizabeth [Am. 1820-1913] PSEUD: Nova Scotian, A
Descriptive sketches of Nova Scotia, in prose and verse, by a Nova Scotian.
Halifax: A. & W. Mackinlay, 1864. 242p. BL

1925. FRAMPTON, Louisa Charlotte [Br. 19/20c]
A dream. Dedicated to "England's great hero, Arthur, Duke of Wellington."
Torquay?: n.p., 1845. BL

1926. FRANCIS, Miss [Br. 19c]
Santa Maura; Marion; and other poems.
L: n.p., 1821. BL

1927. FRANCIS, Ann [Br. 18c] ALT: F., A. PSEUD: Lady, A
Miscellaneous poems. By a lady.
Norwich: n.p., 1790. BL

1928. FRANCIS, Anne Gittins [Br. 1738-1800]
Charlotte to Werter. A poetical epistle.
L: T. Becket, 1789. 24p. NUC

1929. -----The obsequies of Demetrius Poliorcetes: a poem.
L: J. Dodsley, 1785. 20p. NUC OCLC

1930. FRANCIS, Eliza S. [Br. 19c]
ALT: F., E. S.
The rival roses; or, War of York and Lancaster. A metrical tale. By E.S.F.
L: Pr. for author, 1812. 2v. NUC BL OCLC

1931. -----Sir Wilibert de Waverley: or, The bridal eve. A poem.
L: n.p., 1815. BL

FRANCIS, Lydia Maria see CHILD, Lydia Maria (Francis)

1932. FRANCIS, Sophia L. [Br. 19c]
An elegy on Colonel R. Montgomery, written on the fatal spot, where the ... duel (with J. Macnamara) transpired.
L: n.p., 1803? BL

1933. FRANK, Mary [Br. 19c]
Glances in Palestine, and other poems.
L: n.p., 1860. 90p. BL

1934. -----Miscellaneous poems and paraphrases of select passages of the Hebrew scriptures.

L: n.p., 1833. BL

1935. -----Verses sacred and descriptive.
L: n.p., 1850. BL

1936. FRANKLAND, Sarah [Br. 19c]
Leaves of poesy, original and selected.
L: Harvey & Darton; Liverpool: Thomas Hodgson, 1838. 274p. NUC BL

1937. FRANKLIN, Cecile M. [Am. 19c]
The surgeon's reverie.
St. Louis, MO: Becktold & co., 1895. 19p. NUC OCLC

1938. FRANKLIN, Eleanor Anne (Porden) [Br. 1797?-1825] ALT: Porden, Eleanor Anne
The Arctic expeditions; a poem by Miss Porden.
L: J. Murray, 1818. 30p. NUC BL

1939. -----Coeur de lion; or, The third crusade; a poem in sixteen books.
L: G. & W.B. Whittaker, 1822. 2v. NUC BL OCLC

1940. -----Ode addressed to the Rt. Hon. Lord Viscount Belgrave on his marriage with ... Lady E.N.I. Gower.
L: Pr. Cox & Baylis, 1819. 16p. NUC BL OCLC

1941. -----The veils; or, The triumph of constancy. A poem, in six books.
L: J. Murray, 1815. 290p. NUC BL OCLC

1942. FRANTZ, Virginia, Mrs. [Am. 19c]
In a greenwood; or, Life mysteries, and other poems.
Asbury Park, NJ: Presbyterian pub. co., 1885. 512p. NUC OCLC

1943. FRASER, Janet Douglas [Br. 19c]
Poems on religious subjects.
Dumfries: Pr. J.Watson; Thornhill: D. Doig, 184-? 120p. NUC BL OCLC

1944. FRASER, Susan [Br. 19c] PSEUD: Officer's wife, An
Camilla de Florian, and other poems, by an officer's wife.
L: Pr. for author & sold by J. Dick, 1809. 159p. NUC BL

1945. FREEMAN, Eleanor [Am. 19c]
The rose's fate; a poem.
Cincinnati, OH: Standard pub. co., 1885. 16p. NUC

1946. FREEMAN, Ellen Coates [Br. 1818-1851] ALT: Coates, Ellen
Memorials of the mind and heart of Ellen Freeman.
L: Waterlow & sons, 1853. 273p. NUC BL
[Journal, letters, 5 poems & essays]

1947. FREEMAN, Julia Deane, Mrs. [Am. 19c] PSEUD: Forrest, Mary
Poems by Mary Forrest (Julia Deane Freeman).
n.p.: Priv. pr., n.d. 91p. NUC

1948. FREEMAN, Mary Eleanor (Wilkins) [Am. 1852-1930] ALT: Wilkins, Mary Eleanor
Decorative plaques. Designs by George F. Berner. Poems by Mary E. Wilkins.
Boston: D. Lothrop & co., 1883. 32p. NUC OCLC

1949. FREMONT, Anne A. [Br. 19c]
Poems and miscellaneous pieces. Collected, rev., and arr. J. Fearn.
L: n.p., 1872. BL

1950. FRENCH, Anna L. [Am. 19c]
Voices of welcome. A centennial poem for 1876.
Philadelphia: n.p., 1876. 10p. NUC OCLC

1951. FRENCH, Elizabeth Wilmshurst [Br. 19c]
Pebbles and shells.
L: R. Hardwicke, 1858. 80p. NUC BL

1952. FRENCH, Florence Virginia R. [Am. 19c]
Poems.
n.p.: n.p., 189? 20 l. NUC OCLC

FRENCH, L. Virginia (Smith <u>see</u> FRENCH, Lucy Virginia (Smith)

FRENCH, L. Virginia (Smith), co-author <u>see</u> MERIWETHER, Lide (Smith)

1953. FRENCH, Lucy Virginia (Smith) [Am. 1825-1881] ALT: French, L. Virginia (Smith)
One or two? By two sisters. With Lide (Smith) Meriwether.
St. Louis, MO: Meriwether bros., 1883. 228p. NUC

1954. -----Wind whispers.
Nashville, TN: The author, 1856. 272p. NUC OCLC

1955. FRENCH, Myriam Bedell, Mrs. [Am. 19c] PSEUD: Marvin, Jennie

Stray leaves and fragments, by Myriam Bedell French.
NY: M.J. Roth, pr., c1890. 45p. NUC OCLC
[A few previously pub. as Jennie Marvin]

1956. FRERE, Helen M. [Br. 19c] ALT: F., H. M.
Divots. By H.M.F.
n.p.: n.p., 1898. 19p. BL
[Poems on golf]

FRERE, M. see FRERE, Margaret

1957. FRERE, Margaret [Br. 19c] ALT: Frere, M.
England; a valediction. By M. Frere.
Cambridge: Metcalfe & co., ltd., 1890. 11p. NUC

1958. FRIEND, Sarah E. [Am. 19c]
A mother's bequest: poems, essays, extracts from the diary and religious experience.
Keyser, WV: Mountain Echo Water Power pr. house, 1894. 199p. NUC OCLC

FRIEND TO YOUTH, A, pseud. see HOARE, Sarah

1959. FRINK, Almira Louisa Corey [Am. 19c] PSEUD: Wild-bird
Beautiful Mollie, the Republican's song of the tariff.
Denver, CO: n.p., 1895. 8p. NUC

1960. -----Biddy's nest. By Wild-bird.
Denver, CO: n.p., 1891. 3p. NUC

1961. -----The cradle song of the Nile. By Wild-bird.
Denver, CO: n.p., c1891. 3p. NUC

1962. -----"He is risen." The coming glory. By Wild-bird.
Denver, CO: n.p., 1892. 6p. NUC

1963. -----Orion.
Denver, CO: n.p., 1891. 3p.

1964. FRINK, Mrs. Darius [Am. 19c]
Original ... thoughts suggested upon realizing that, as time passes on, I miss more and more, my brother, Nathaniel P. Coleman: who died March 28, 1876.
Newington, NH: n.p., 1878. 2p. NUC OCLC

1965. FRONDE, Mrs. [Br. 19c]
Poems and tales in verse.
L: Griffith, Farran & co., 1889. 131p. BL

FRY, Caroline see WILSON, Caroline (Fry)

FRY, Mrs. Francis Fry see FRY, Matilda (Penrose)

1966. FRY, Henrietta Joan [Br. 1800-1860] ALT: F., H. J.
Portraits in miniature; or, Tableaux du coeur.
L: C. Gilpin, 1848. 204p. NUC BL

1967. -----The wells of scripture, illustrated in verse, by ... H.J.F.
L: Charles Gilpin, 1842. 44p. BL

1968. FRY, Mary A. A., Mrs. [Am. 19c]
Tennesse centennial poem.
Chattanooga, TN: The author, 1896. 174p. NUC OCLC

1969. FRY, Mary C. [Am. 19c]
Poems.
Muscatine, IA: Neidig & Conaway, pr., 1893. 36p. NUC OCLC

FRY, Matilda F. see FRY, Matilda (Penrose)

1970. FRY, Matilda (Penrose) [F. BL], Mrs. Francis Fry [Br. 1808?-1888] ALT: F., M. F.
Historic memories and other poems.
L: Pr. Barclay & Fry, 1890. 257p. NUC BL OCLC

1971. -----Paul of Tarsus. A poem. By M.F.F.
Bristol: n.p., 1862. 16p. NUC BL

1972. FULLER, Angeline A. [Am. b. 1841] ALT: Fuller, Angie
The flying hours; the deaf girl's soliloquy; and Words of cheer.
Detroit, MI: n.p., 1883. 4p. NUC
[Fuller was deaf-mute]

1973. -----The venture.
Detroit, MI: J.N. Williams, 1883. 232p. NUC OCLC

FULLER, Angie see FULLER, Angeline A.

FULLER, Arthur B., ed. see OSSOLI, Sarah Margaret (Fuller), Marchesa d'

FULLER, Margaret see OSSOLI, Sarah Margaret (Fuller), Marchesa d'

FULLER, Metta Victoria, co-author see VICTOR, Frances Auretta (Fuller) Barritt

FULLER, VIOLET, pseud. see FULLERTON, Eleanor

1974. FULLERTON, Eleanor [Br. 19c]
ALT: Fullerton, Elizabeth Anderson
PSEUD: Fuller, Violet
Original poetry, by Violet Fuller.
L: n.p., 1870. 64p. NUC

FULLERTON, Elizabeth Anderson see FULLERTON, Eleanor

1975. FULLERTON, Lady Georgiana Charlotte (Leveson Gower) [Br. 1812-1885]
The gold-digger and other verses.
L: n.p.; Baltimore, MD: Kelly, Piet & co., 1872. NUC BL

1976. -----The old highlander, the ruins of Statta Florida and other verses.
L: Priv. pr., 1849. BL

1977. FURLONG, Mrs. [Br. 19c]
The spectre poverty: or, The realities of life, displayed under an allegory.
Edinburgh: n.p., 1834. BL

1978. FURLONG, Alice [Br. 19/20c]
Roses and rue.
L: Elkin Mathews, 1899. 63p. NUC BL OCLC

1979. FURLONG, N., Mrs. [Am. 19c]
Cozena, a tale of Italy, and other poems.
San Francisco: Pr. B.F. Sterett, 1880. 256p. NUC OCLC

G., A.E. see GUILD, Anne Eliza (Gore)

G., A.R. see GAZZAM, Anna Reading

G., C.H. see GILMAN, Caroline (Howard)

G., D. see GRUBB, Dorothea

G., E., Miss see GARLAND, Emma, Miss

G., E. see GRANT, Eleanor

G., F. see GREENSTED, Frances

G., H.A. see GLAZEBROOK, Harriet A.

G., J.C. see GRIMANI, Julia C.

G., J.T., comp. see GRANT, Emily Fredrica

G., Jeanie see LINCOLN, Jeanie Thomas (Gould)

G., L.F., ed. see WELLS, Ella Maria Wilson

1980. G., M. [Br. 19c] PSEUD: Lady, A
The Battle of the Ingogo. By a lady.
Southampton: Gutch & Cox, 1882. BL
[Signed M.G.]

G., Mrs. M.A. see GASCOIGNE, Caroline Leigh (Smith)

G., M.E. see GRANGER, Mary Ethel

G__, H. see GOODALL, Harriot Annabella

1981. GAGE, Frances Dana (Barker) [Am. 1808-1884]
Poems. By Mrs. Frances Dana Gage.
Philadelphia: J.B. Lippincott & co., 1867. 252p. NUC BL OCLC

GAGE, HANNAH B., pseud. see FERRE, Ella

1982. GALLAGHER, Caroline Harris [Am. 19c]
My crucifix and other verses.
Baltimore, MD: Gallery & McCann, 1896. 31p. NUC OCLC

1983. GALLOWAY, Lillie, Mrs. [Br. 19c]
Souvenir of the unveiling of the Holroyd memorial in Clayton Churchyard, May 25th, 1833.
Bradford: Pr. for priv. circ., 1893. 80p. BL

1984. -----Twilight musings. A volume of poems.
Bradford: Thornton & Pearson, 1893. 88p. BL

1985. GALWAY, Vere (Gosling) Monckton-Arundell, Viscountess [Br. 19c] ALT: Monckton-Arundell, Vere, Viscountess
The creed of love, and other poems. By Vere Viscountess Galway.
L: Priv. pr. by Messrs. Hatchard, 1895. 71p. NUC

1986. GAMMAGE, Anne [Br. 19c]
Spring flowers. A volume of poems.
Liverpool: n.p., 1843. BL

1987. GANGLOFF, N. S. S., Mrs. [Am. 19c]
Random lyrics.
Oberlin, OH: News office, 1865. 16p. NUC OCLC

1988. GANNETT, Abbie M., Mrs. [Am. 1845-1895]

The old farm home; a shadow of a poem.
Boston: D. Lothrop co., 1887. 83p. NUC OCLC

1989. GANNON, Anna [Am. 19c]
The song of Stradella, and other songs.
Philadelphia & L: J.B. Lippincott co., 1898. 85p. NUC OCLC

1990. GARCIA, Pauline Viardot [Am. 1821-1910?] ALT: Viardot-Garcia, Michelle Ferdinande Pauline
Flirtation made easy; or, The art revealed. Together with poetry of love and flowers.
NY: New York Popular pub. co., 1882. 60p. NUC

GARDINER, Marilla (Dunton), comp. see BOWEN, Harriet M. (Gardiner)

1991. GARDINER, Mary L. [Am. 19c]
A collection from the prose and poetical writings of M.L. Gardiner.
NY: J. Winchester, 1843. 359p. NUC OCLC
[Incl. short stories, brief essays & misc. poetry]

1992. GARDINER, Susan H., Mrs. [Am. 19c]
The basket of fragments; the employment of leisure hours.
Philadelphia: The author, Siegfried & Carter, pr., 1829. 165p. NUC OCLC
[Written by a widow to support herself and children. Many memorial poems, many on nature.]

1993. -----The village rambler; or, A collection of pathetic and rural poetry by S.H. Gardiner of Darby.
Philadelphia: The author, 1820. 231p. NUC

GARDINER, Mrs. William, comp. see BOWEN, Harriet M. (Gardiner)

1994. GARDNER, Anna [Am. b. 1816]
The golden rod, and other poems.
Nantucket, MA: Inquirer & Mirror press, 1892? 22p. NUC OCLC

1995. -----Harvest gleanings. In prose and verse.
NY: Fowler & Wells, 1881. 200p. NUC OCLC
[Abolitionist's misc. & occasional poetry. Prose is recollections of anti-slavery activities]

1996. GARDNER, Celia Emmeline [Am. b. 1844]
Broken dreams.
NY: Carleton & co., 1873. 252p. NUC BL OCLC

1997. -----Compensation. A study of experience.
NY: G.W. Carleton & co., 1880. 326p. NUC OCLC

1998. -----Stolen waters.
NY: G.W. Carleton & co.; L: S. Low, son & co., 1871. 326p. NUC OCLC

1999. -----A twisted skein, or, Out of the tempest.
NY: C.W. Carleton & co., 1881. 251p. OCLC

GARDNER, Mrs. Charles H. see GARDNER, Mary (Russell)

2000. GARDNER, E. P., Miss [Br. 19c]
Reflections in verse.
L: n.p., 1841. BL

2001. GARDNER, Mary (Russell), Mrs. Charles H. Gardner [Am. 19c]
American history in rhyme. By Mrs. Charles H. Gardner.
NY: The author, 1887. 48p. NUC OCLC

2002. -----English history in rhyme.
New Haven, CT: Stafford pr. co., 1884. 38p. NUC OCLC

2003. -----History of France in rhyme.
NY: The author, 1886. 90p. NUC OCLC

2004. GARDYNE, Hon. Amelia Anne Greenhill [Br. 19/20c]
Earl Beardie: a ballad of Finavon.
Edinburgh: W. Brown, 1899. 40p. BL

2005. -----Hakon the Good, and other verses.
Edinburgh: W. Brown, 1890. 95p. BL OCLC

2006. GARLAND, Alison L. [Br. 19/20c]
Eternity.
Birmingham: C. Caswell, 1887. 10p. BL

2007. GARLAND, Emma, Miss [Br. 19c]
ALT: G., E., Miss
Ovid's epistles in English verse; with some original poems ... by Miss E.G.
L: Rivington, 1842. 324p. BL OCLC

GARNETT, Catherine Grace see GODWIN, Catherine Grace (Garnett)

GARNETT, Richard, ed. see SHELLEY, Elizabeth

2008. GARNIER, Emily [Br. d. 1835]
A father's tribute to the memory of an amiable child. Ed. Thomas Henry Garnier.
Oxford: Pr. J.L. Wheeler, 1835. 86p. NUC
[Misc. poems composed before she died at 14]

GARNIER, Thomas Henry, ed. see GARNIER, Emily

2009. GARRARD, Eliza [Br. 18c]
Miscellanies, in verse and prose.
Bath: Pr. by William Meyler for the author, 1799. 235p. BL
[Essays, fiction & poetry]

2010. GARRETT, Annie [Br. 19c] ALT: Annie
The seven churches, and other poems. By Annie and Ellen Amelia [Garrett].
Winchester: H. Wooldridge; L: B. Wertheim, 1847. 210p. BL

GARRETT, Ellen Amelia, co-author see GARRETT, Annie

2011. GARRISON, Emma [Am. 19c]
A collection of brief poems, on various subjects.
Baltimore, MD: Pr. Sherwood & co., 1855. 250p. NUC

2012. GARTON, Anne [Br. 19c]
Poems of girlhood.
L: n.p., 1843. BL

GARWOOD, Hannah Carnes see CARNES, Hannah, Mrs.

2013. GARY, Anstiss Curtiss [Am. b. 1860]
A year's singing and other poems.
Chicago: Brentano's, 1895. 260p. NUC OCLC

2014. GASCOIGNE, Caroline Leigh (Smith), Mrs. M.A. Gascoigne [Br. b. 1813] ALT: Gascoyne, Caroline Leigh (Smith)
Belgravia: a poem.
L: Charles Westerton, 1851. 79p. NUC BL OCLC

2015. -----England's heroes.
L: n.p., 1855. BL

2016. -----The ladies' hand-book.
L: Priv. pr., 1846. 11 l. BL OCLC

2017. -----Recollections and tales of the Crystal Palace.
L: W. Shoberl, 1852. 150p. BL OCLC
[Her impressions of the exposition, in verse.]

GASCOIGNE, Mrs. M.A. see GASCOIGNE, Caroline Leigh (Smith)

GASCOYNE, Caroline Leigh (Smith) see GASCOIGNE, Caroline Leigh (Smith)

2018. GATES, Ellen Maria (Huntington) [Am. 1835-1920]
On Christmas day.
NY & L: G.P. Putnam's sons, 1898. 1p. NUC BL OCLC
[Love poem for Christmas]

2019. -----The treasures of Kurium and other poems.
NY & L: G.P. Putnam's sons, 1895. 128p. NUC BL OCLC

2020. -----Your mission.
NY: G.P. Putnam's sons, 1882. 8 l. NUC OCLC

2021. GATES, Jennie Elisabeth [Am. 19c]
Heart echoes.
Rutland, VT: The author, c1898. 75p. NUC OCLC

2022. GAY, E. Jane [Am. 1830-1919] PSEUD: Trumbull, Truman
The new Yankee Doodle; being an account of the little difficulty in the family of Uncle Sam. By Truman Trumbull.
NY: W.O. Bourne, 1868. 341p. NUC OCLC
[Civil war]

2023. GAY, Mary Ann Harris [Am. b. 1827] PSEUD: Georgia lady, A
The pastor's story, and other pieces; or, Prose and poetry.
6th ed. Nashville, TN: Pub. for the author, 1860. 266p. NUC OCLC
[Misc. poetry; prose is short stories & essays, moral & religious]

2024. -----Prose and poetry, by a Georgia lady.
Nashville, TN: Pub. for author, 1858. 199p. RPB
[First publication; material later included in The pastor's story.]

2025. GAYE, Selina [Br. 19c]
The maiden of the iceberg. A tale in verse.
L: Saunders and Otley & co., 1867. 100p. NUC BL OCLC

2026. GAYLORD, Mary Louisa [Am. 19c]
Heart echoes.

NY: The DeVinne press, 1895. 202p. NUC OCLC

2027. GAZZAM, Anna Reading [Am. 19c] ALT: G., A. R.
Gleams and echoes. By A.R.G.
Philadelphia: J.B. Lippincott co., 1893. 24 l. NUC OCLC

2028. -----Night etchings. By A.R.G.
Philadelphia: J.B. Lippincott co., 1893. 115p. NUC OCLC

2029. GEARY, Elizabeth [Br. 19c]
Juvenile effusions: moral and religious.
L: n.p., 1822. BL

2030. GELDART, Hannah Ransome, Mrs. Thomas Geldart [Br. 1820?-1861]
Thoughts for home in prose and verse.
Norwich: Josiah Fletcher; L: A. Hall, Virtue & co., 1850. BL
[Domestic poems; prose meditations; many on bereavement]

GELDART, Mrs. Thomas see GELDART, Hannah Ransome

2031. GEMMER, Caroline M., Mrs. [Br. 19c] PSEUD: Fay, Gerda
Fidelis, and other poems.
Westminster: A. Constable, 1897. 99p. NUC BL OCLC

2032. -----Lyrics and idylls. By Gerda Fay.
L: n.p., 1861. BL

2033. GENEVIEVE, pseud. [Am. 19c]
The wild rose.
NY: H.M. Onderdonk & co., 1846. 128p. NUC

2034. GENTLEWOMAN, A., pseud. [Br. 18c]
Advice to Sappho [i.e. Lady Mary Wortley Montagu]. Occasioned by her verses on the imitator of the first satire of the second book of Horace.
L: Pr. for the authoress, 1733. 8p. BL OCLC

GEORGIA LADY, A, pseud. see GAY, Mary Ann Harris

2035. GERALD, Florence M. [Am. 19c]
Adenheim, and other poems.
St. Louis, MO: G.I. Jones & co., 1880. 231p. NUC OCLC

GERTRUDE, pseud. see SIMPSON, Jane Cross (Bell)

2036. GERVIS, Marianne [Br. 19c]
Original Cornish ballads: chiefly founded on stories humorously told by Mr. Tregallas, in his popular lectures on "peculiarities"; to which are appended some drafts of kindred character from the portfolio of the editress [M. Gervis]: the whole prefixed by an introductory essay on the peculiar characteristics of the Cornish peasantry; from the gifted pen of Mrs. Miles, formerly Miss S[ibella] E[lizabeth] Hatfield.
L: Simpkin, Marshall & co., 1846. 60p. BL OCLC

2037. GIBBONS, Anne (Trelawny) [Br. 19c] ALT: Trelawny, Anne
An Easter offering. By Anne Trelawny.
Tavistock: W. Brendon; L: Edwards & Hughes, 1845. 44p. BL
[Religious poems, incl. 2 trans. from Borghi & Novalis]

2038. -----The tale of Trecarrell; or, Legend of Launceston Church, and other poems, etc.
Launceston: T.W. Maddox; L: Simpkin, Marshall & co., 1849. 48p. BL

2039. GIBBONS, Sarah Ann [Br. 19c]
Verses. Presented to Her most gracious Majesty the Queen, at the close of the Jubilee Year.
Wolverhampton: W. Gibbons, 1887. 27p. BL

2040. GIBBS, Ann, Mrs. [Br. 19c]
A selection, in prose and verse, with some original pieces by Mrs. A.G. of Lamberhurst, Kent.
Cranbrook: S. Waters, 1803. 123p. NUC BL
[Incl. original elegies, misc. verse and "The Invitation," poem on the most worthwhile authors and prose defense of literature.]

2041. GIBBS, Anna Skelton [Br. 19c]
Voice of the heart; a wife's love-offering.
L: Pr. for family by Whittingham & Wilkins, 1860. 52p. NUC OCLC
[Poems written to her husband on family occasions]

2042. GIBBS, Sarah Mather, Mrs. [Am. 19c]
The World's Fair poem.
Chicago: n.p., 1892. 3 l. NUC

GIBSON, Charlotte see GUBBINS, Charlotte Gibson

2043. GIELOW, Martha Sawyer [Am. 1854?-1933]
Mammy's reminiscences, and other sketches.
NY: A.S. Barnes & co., 1898. 100p. NUC OCLC
[Negro folklore. Incl. Blow li'l breezes, blow. A plantation lullaby. Words & music.]

2044. GIFFORD, Elizabeth [Br. 19c]
Poems.
L: Eden Fisher & co., 1897. 100p. BL

GIFFORD, Helen Selina (Sheridan) Blackwood Hay, Countess of see DUFFERIN and CLANDEBOYE, Helen Selina (Sheridan) Blackwood, Baroness

2045. GILBERT, Ann Taylor
Original anniversary hymns, adapted to the public services of Sunday schools.
L: B.J. Holdsworth, 1827. 76p. OCLC
[Without music]

2046. GILBERT, Elizabeth, Mrs. [Am. 1821-1846]
Memoir of Mrs. Elizabeth Gilbert. By Emerson Davis.
Westfield, MA: n.p., 1849. 115p. NUC
[Incl. her poems]

2047. GILBERT, Fannie Caldwell, Mrs. [Am. 19c]
Poems.
Philadelphia: I. Rindge, 1885. 262p. NUC OCLC

2048. GILBERT, Harriette Eliza (Phelps) [Am. 19c]
Promiscuous pieces. Addition to: The triumphs of divine grace, a poem in two parts. By Samuel Merrick Phelps.
NY: Pr. Craighead & Allen, 1835. 132p. NUC OCLC

2049. GILBERT, M. Jane [Br. 19c]
Lays of piety and affection.
L: F. Pitman; Birmingham: John Tonks, 1852. 144p. BL

2050. GILBERT, Rosa (Mulholland), Lady [Br. 1841-1921] ALT: Mulholland, Rosa
Vagrant verses.
L: Kegan Paul, Trench co., 1886. 155p. NUC BL OCLC

2051. GILBERT, Sophia Victoria [19c]
Wayside echoes. Poems.
Toronto: Pr. for author by W. Briggs, 1894. 179p. NUC

2052. GILCHRIST, Annie Somers [Am. 19c]
A souvenir of the Tennessee centennial; poems.
Nashville, TN: Gospel Advocate pr. co., 1897. 132p. NUC OCLC

2053. GILCHRIST, Catherine, Mrs. [Br. 19c]
Poems, moral and religious.
Manchester: n.p., 1839. BL

2054. GILDEA, Rachel C. [Br. 19c]
The morning, noonday and evening of life.
L: Charing Cross pub. co., 1877. 102p. BL
[Scripture verses and hymns]

GILDEN, Charles, ed. see BEHN, Aphra (Amis)

2055. GILDING, Elizabeth [Br. 19c]
The breathings of genius; being a collection of poems, to which are added essays, moral and philosophical.
L: W. Faden, 1776. 152p. NUC BL

GILES, Daphne S. see JENKINS, Daphne Smith (Giles)

2056. GILES, Daphne S. [Am. 19c]
The balm of Gilead.
NY: R. Craighead, 1852. 114p. NUC
[9 poems interspersed with devotional pieces, some in the form of letters to friends.]

GILES, Ella A. see RUDDY, Ella Augusta (Giles)

2057. GILES, Susan R. H., Mrs. [Am. 19c]
Memories and hopes.
Boston: The Fourth Baptist Church, 1887? 12p. NUC OCLC
[Poem on history of the church]

2058. GILL, Delia Mary [Br. 19c]
Poems.
Liverpool: J. Brakell, 1875. 88p. NUC

2059. GILLEN, Alma [Br. 19c]
The passion of passions.
L: n.p., 1896. 125p. BL

2060. -----Passionate passions.
L: Osgood & co.; Rahway, NJ: Pub. for author by Mershon co., 1895. 87p. NUC BL

2061. GILLETT, Ellen Elizabeth [Br. 19c]

A Christmas tale, and other poems.
Ed. her sons.
L: E. Stock, 1894. 58p. NUC BL

2062. GILLETTE, Florence Lilian [Am. 19c] PSEUD: M.
Floating leaves by M. & D. [Lucia Fidelia (Woolley) Gillette].
Tecumseh, MI: Herald Steam pr. house, 1881. 50p. NUC
[Chiefly prose. Short stories with a few poems.]

GILLETTE, Lucia Fidelia (Woolley), co-author see GILLETTE, Florence Lilian

2063. GILLETTE, Lucia Fidelia (Woolley) [Am. b. 1827] PSEUD: D.
Editorials and other waifs.
NY: F. Wells co., 1889. NUC
[Aphorisms]

2064. -----Pebbles from the shore.
New Sharon, IA: H.J. Vail, 1879. 168p. NUC
[Poems]

2065. GILLIGAN, Anna M. [Am. 19c]
Smiles and tears.
Boston: Press of Cashman Keating & co., 1889. 123p. NUC OCLC

GILLINGTON, A.E., co-author see BYRON, May Clarissa (Gillington)

GILLINGTON, May Clarissa see BYRON, May Clarissa (Gillington)

2066. GILMAN, Caroline (Howard), Mrs. Samuel Gilman [Am. 1794-1888] ALT: G., C. H.
The poetry of travelling in the United States: with additional sketches by a few friends, and a week among autographs by Samuel Gilman.
NY: S. Colman, 1838. 430p. NUC BL OCLC

2067. -----The rose-bud wreath.
Charleston, SC: S. Babcock, 1841. 152p. NUC OCLC

2068. -----Stories and poems by mother and daughter, Caroline Gilman and Caroline Howard Jervey.
Boston: Lee & Shepard, 1872. 293p. NUC OCLC

2069. -----Tales and ballads.
NY: n.p., 1834. 190p. Boston & Cambridge: J. Munroe & co., 1839. 190p. NUC BL OCLC

2070. -----Verses of a life-time.
Boston & Cambridge: J. Munroe & co., 1849. 263p. NUC BL OCLC

2071. GILMAN, Charlotte (Perkins) Stetson [Am. 1860-1935] ALT: Stetson, Charlotte Perkins
A clarion call to redeem the race!
Mt. Lebanon, NY: The Shaker press, 1890? NUC

2072. -----In this our world, poems and sonnets.
Oakland, CA: McCombs & Vaughan, 1893. 120p. L: F. Unwin, 1895. 132p. NUC BL OCLC

GILMAN, S., ed. see LEE, Mary Elizabeth

GILMAN, Mrs. Samuel see GILMAN, Caroline (Howard)

GILMORE, ERNEST, pseud. see FARLEY, Helen Hall (Moyer)

2073. GILMORE, Minnie L. [Am. 19c]
Pipes from prairie-land, and other places.
NY: Cassell & co., 1886. 150p. NUC OCLC

2074. -----Songs from the wings.
NY & L: F.T. Neely, 1897. 217p. NUC OCLC

GILPIN, Catherine, co-author see BLAMIRE, Susanna

GILPIN, Miss, co-author see BLAMIRE, Susanna

GILPIN, Sidney, co-author see BLAMIRE, Susanna

2075. GILSTRAP, Elizabeth Haigh, Lady [Br. 19c]
The harp of Colne.
L: Pr. for the author by Cassell & co., 1886. 230p. NUC BL OCLC
[Rev. ed. Ilkeston: n.p., 1894. 160p.]

2076. GIMSON, Harriet, Mrs. [Br. 19c]
Heart breathings. Arr. W. Willey.
L: n.p., 1872. BL

GINGOLD, Helene E.A. see COWEN, Helene E.A. (Gingold)

2077. GLADDING, E. N., Mrs. [Am. 19c]
Leaves from an invalid's journal, and poems.
Providence, RI: George H. Whitney, 1858. 235p. NUC OCLC

[Incl. journal, two short stories, and poems]

2078. GLAZEBROOK, Harriet A. [Br. 19c] ALT: G., H. A.
The Brooklet reciter for temperance societies.
L: National Temperance pub. depot, 1883. 176p. BL
[Temperance ballads.]

2079. -----Readings and recitations, chiefly upon temperance, written and selected by H.A.G.
L: Kempster's Home Library, 1874. BL

2080. -----Readings in rhyme, from the drama of drink.
L: J. Kempster & co., 1876. 144p. NUC
[New ed. L: Marshall bros., 1892. 223p. BL]

2081. GLEASON, Adele Amelia [Am. b. 1850]
Songs and verses for Christmas.
Boston: Cupples & Hurd, 1888. 90p. NUC OCLC

2082. GLEASON, M. Amarett [Am. 19c]
A leaflet from Elliot City Hospital.
Keene, NH: n.p., 1898. 14p. NUC OCLC

GLENN, GRACE, pseud. <u>see</u> BATEMAN, L.M. Beal, Mrs.

GLENN, Jessie <u>see</u> SCHENCK, Jessie (Glenn)

GLENN, Mrs. Van, co-author <u>see</u> BROWN, Annie Johnson-

GLENWOOD, IDA, pseud. <u>see</u> GORTON, Cynthia M.R., Mrs.

2083. GODDARD, Julia Bachope [Br. d. 1896]
The golden journey and other verses.
L: Longmans, Green, 1875. 192p. BL OCLC

2084. -----Psychologus: the story of a soul.
L: J. Masters & co., 1887. 77p. NUC BL
[Allegory]

2085. GODWIN, Catherine Grace (Garnett) [Br. 1798-1845] ALT: Garnett, Catherine Grace
The night before the bridal, a Spanish tale. Sappho, a dramatic sketch, and other poems.
L: Longman, Hurst, Rees, Orme, Brown & Green, 1824. 220p. NUC BL

2086. -----The poetical works of ... C.G.G., ed. with a sketch of her life, by A. Cleveland Wigan.
L: Chapman & Hall, 1854. 576p. NUC BL OCLC
[Incl. rev. versions of Sappho, and other early works. Lyric, dramatic & narr. poems.]

2087. -----The reproving angel: a vision.
L: n.p., 1835. 27p. NUC BL

2088. -----The wanderer's legacy; a collection of poems on various subjects.
L: S. Maunder, 1829. 277p. NUC BL
[Narrative & lyric]

2089. GODWIN, Elizabeth Ayton [Br. 19/20c]
Songs amidst daily life.
L: n.p., 1878. BL

2090. -----Songs for the weary: the school of sorrow and other poems.
L: n.p., 1873. BL

GOLDEN ROD, pseud. <u>see</u> LOOMIS, Submit (Chesebrough)

2091. GOLDIE, Emma Mary [Br. 19c]
Poems.
L: n.p., 1835. BL

2092. GOMERSALL, A., Mrs. [Br. 18/19c]
Creation; a poem.
Newport, Isle of Wight: n.p., 1824. BL

2093. GOOCH, Elizabeth Sarah (Villa-Real) [Br. b. 1754?]
Monody to the memory of His Grace the Duke of Bedford.
L: Pr. for the author, sold by William Miller, 1802. 12p. NUC

2094. -----Poems on various subjects.
L: n.p., 1793. BL

2095. GOOCH, Rebecca [Br. 19c]
Original poems, on various subjects.
2d ed. L: Sold by Longman, Rees, Orme, Brown & Green, 1828. 144p. NUC BL

GOODALE, Dora Read, co-author <u>see</u> EASTMAN, Elaine (Goodale)

2096. GOODALE, Dora Read [Am. b. 1866]
A birthday book of birds, new birthday verses.

NY: F.A. Stokes & bro., 1888. 16p. NUC

2097. -----Heralds of Easter, a new poem of Eastertide.
NY: White, Stokes & Allen, 1887. 16p. NUC OCLC

GOODALE, Elaine see EASTMAN, Elaine (Goodale)

2098. GOODALL, Harriot Anabella [Br. 19c] ALT: G__, H. PSEUD: Rector's Wife, The
The emigrants; a tale of truth. By the rector's wife.
Eton: Priv. pr., 1835. BL

2099. GOODENOUGH, Caroline Louisa (Leonard) [Am. b. 1856]
Natal lilies, and other poems.
Pietermaritzburg, Natal: P. Davis & sons, pr., 1897. 160p. NUC OCLC

2100. GOODLUCK, Maria [Br. 19c]
Blossom and fruit.
L: Darton & co., 1861. 71p. BL

GOODMAN, Mrs. Haskell C. see SHEPARD, Dolly Ellen (Ring)

GOODRICH, George, comp. see GOODRICH, Abigail (Spencer)

GOODRICH, Mrs. George see GOODRICH, Abigail (Spencer)

2101. GOODWIN, Caroline Georgiana [Br. 19c]
Amatum, and other poems.
L: n.p., 1862. BL

2102. GOODWIN, Marcia Melissa Bassett [Am. 19c]
Autumn leaves.
St. Louis, MO: Christian pub. co., 1880. 176p. NUC OCLC

2103. GORDON, D.H., Mrs. [Br. 19c] PSEUD: Violet
Poems by Violet.
Dunfermline: "Press" office, 1890. 146p. BL

2104. GORDON, Elizabeth [Am. b. 1823] ALT: Gordon, Lizzie
Among the flowers: a poem. By Lizzie Gordon. To which is added a selection of Wyoming poetry, by native writers of Luzerne County.
Wilkes-Barre, PA: The Leader co., 1879. 43p. NUC

2105. -----The world's future; or, The feast of the flowers.
Wilkes-Barre, PA: Union-loader steam pr. house, 1881. 37p. NUC

2106. GORDON, Helen [Br. 19c]
Eastern gleams: metrical essays and poems on the gospel history.
L: Longmans & co., 1866. 170p. BL

GORDON, JULIEN, pseud. see CRUGER, Julie Grinnell (Storrow)

GORDON, Lizzie see GORDON, Elizabeth

2107. GORDON, Margaret Maria (Brewster) [Br. b. 1823] ALT: Brewster, Margaret Maria
The covenant; or, The conflict of the church. With other poems, chiefly connected with the ecclesiastical history of Scotland.
Edinburgh: Johnstone, 1842. 160p. NUC BL

2108. -----Man and the animals, and other poems.
Edinburgh: F. Sinclair, 1840. 36p. NUC BL

2109. GORDON, Mary Antoinetta, Marchioness of Huntly [Br. 19c]
Thoughts in verse upon flowers of the field, illustrated by Mary Antoinetta, Marchioness of Huntly.
L: n.p., 1866. BL

2110. GORDON, Mary E. [Am. 19c]
Easter, the dawn. A story of the resurrection in verse.
Wooster, OH: n.p., 1892. 30p. NUC

2111. -----Songs of faith and love.
n.p.: n.p., n.d. 48p. NUC

GORDON, May E., ed. see SARTORIS, Adelaide Kemble

2112. GORDON, Rose [Br. 19c]
Childe Archie's pilgrimage.
L: G. Pulman, 1873. 65p. BL OCLC
[Parody of Lord Byron's "Childe Harold"]

2113. -----M.P.'s.
L: Edwards, 1876. 31p. BL OCLC
[Satire]

2114. -----The past and present. An historical humorous poem.
V. 1. L: J. Ivison, 1879. BL

2115. GORDON, Selma
Poems.
19p. NUC
[Lacks imprint]

GORE, C.G.F. see GORE, Catherine Grace Frances (Moody)

2116. GORE, Catherine Grace Frances (Moody), Mrs. Charles Gore [Br. 1799-1861] ALT: Gore, C.G.F.
The bond, a dramatic poem in the form of a play. By Mrs. Charles Gore.
L: John Murray, 1824. 100p. NUC BL OCLC
[3 acts]

GORE, Mrs. Charles see GORE, Catherine Grace Frances (Moody)

2117. GORE-BOOTH, Eva Selina [Br. 1870-1926] ALT: Booth, Eva Selina Gore-
Poems.
L & NY: Longmans Green, 1898. 128p. NUC BL OCLC

2118. GORRINGTON, Elizabeth Sarah [Br. 19c] ALT: Eliza
Spiritual recreations in the chamber of affliction; or, Pious meditations in verse. By Eliza.
L: F. Westley, 1821. 209p. BL OCLC

2119. GORTON, Cynthia M.R., Mrs. [Am. 19c] PSEUD: Glenwood, Ida
The wife's appeal. A poem. By Ida Glenwood.
Fenton, MI: W.H.H. Smith & son, 1873? 32p. NUC OCLC
[Gorton was known as "The blind bard of Michigan"]

2120. GORTON, M.J., Mrs. [Am. 19c]
The drama of the cycle and other poems.
Boston: Joseph George Cupples, 1891. 117p. NUC OCLC
[Dramatic poem meant for reading, not acting]

2121. GOSS, Almira J. [Am. 19c]
Ruins of the Maine Wesleyan Seminary, a poem. Dedicated to a friend.
Augusta, ME: n.p., 1847. 16p. NUC

GOTHERSON, Dorothea Scott see HOGBEN, Dorothea (Scott) Gotherson

2122. GOTT, Ada Augusta [Am. 19c]
Built upon a rock.
Baltimore, MD: D.H. Carroll, 1887. 84p. NUC

2123. GOULD, Abbie Walker [Am. 19/20c]
Flowers of thought.
Moline, IL: The author, 1896. 192p. NUC OCLC

2124. GOULD, Alta Isadore [Am. 19c]
The veteran's bride, and other poems.
2d ed. Grand Rapids, MI: P.D. Farrell & co., 1894. 253p. NUC OCLC
[Civil War poetry]

2125. GOULD, Elizabeth Porter [Am. 1848-1906]
Stray pebbles from the shores of thought.
Boston: Press of T.O. Metcalf & co., 1892. 220p. NUC OCLC
[Misc. poetry]

2126. GOULD, Hannah Flagg, Mrs. [Am. 1789-1865] PSEUD: Lady, A
The blind boy.
2d ed. Boston: O. Ditson, c1842. 7p. NUC

2127. -----The diosma, a perennial.
Boston: Phillips, Sampson & co., c1850. 287p. NUC BL OCLC
[Misc. poems, about half original & half by others.]

2128. -----Epitaphs.
Newburyport, MA: Newburyport, c1875. 7p. NUC OCLC

2129. -----Esther: a scripture narrative. By a lady. Together with an original poem by Miss H.F. Gould.
NY: D. Appleton & co., 1835. 77p. NUC BL OCLC

2130. -----Gathered leaves: or miscellaneous papers.
Boston: W.J. Reynolds, c1845. 304p. NUC OCLC
[Incl. 3 poems, several short stories, & misc. prose]

2131. -----The mother's dream, and other poems.
Boston: Crosby, Nichols & co., 1853. 240p. NUC

2132. -----New poems.
Boston: W.J. Reynolds & co., 1850. 287p. NUC BL OCLC

2133. -----Poems.
Boston: Hilliard, Gray, Little & Wilkins, 1832. 174p. NUC OCLC
[Issued in 1836 with additions as Vol. 1 of a 2-vol. ed. Vol. 3 appeared in 1841.]

2134. -----Poems.
Boston: Hilliard, Gray & co., 1839-41. 3v. NUC OCLC
[V. 1 first issued 1832, v. 2 1835, v. 3 1841.]

2135. GOULD, Sarah, Mrs. [Am. 19c]
Asphodels.
NY: Proof-sheets, 1856. 236p. NUC OCLC
[Rev. ed. pub. in 1860 as: Poems]

2136. GOULD, Tracy [Am. 19c]
The bride of the broken vow. A poem in four parts.
Troy, NY: William H. Young & Blake, 1874. 90p. NUC OCLC
[Poem on an unfaithful wife]

2137. GOULSTONE, S., Mrs. [Br. 19c]
Esther; or, The feast of Purim. A poem.
Liverpool: n.p., 1872. BL

2138. GOULTER, Eliza Eleanor [Br. 19c]
Souvenirs and reveries.
Bath: n.p., 1866. BL

2139. GOVION BROGLIO SOLARI, Catherine Hyde, Marquise de [Br. 1755/56-1844] ALT: Solari, Catherine Hyde
Wellington. Poemetto. Del Marchese A. Solari. And Wellington proved to be the greatest warrior of ancient and modern times by C.H. Solari.
L: n.p., 1820. BL

2140. GOWER, Jean Milne [Am. 19/20c]
A few verses written from 1883 to 1891.
Denver, CO: n.p., 1891. NUC

GOWING, Mrs. Aylmer <u>see</u> GOWING, Emilia Aylmer (Blake)

2141. GOWING, Clara [Am. 19c]
My chest; or, Ransacking.
Reading, MA: W.E. & J.F. Twombly, 1899. 125p. NUC OCLC
[Misc. poetry]

2142. GOWING, Emilia Aylmer (Blake), Mrs. [Br. 19/20c] ALT: Blake, Emilia Aylmer; Gowing, Mrs. Aylmer
Ballads and poems for recitation.
L: John & Robert Maxwell, 1884. 120p. BL

2143. -----Ballads of the tower and other poems, mostly adapted for recitation.
L: Griffith, Farran, Okeden & Welsh, 1891. 152p. BL
[Incl. a few memorial poems]

2144. -----Boadicea. A play in four acts. Poems for recitation. By Mrs. Aylmer Gowing.
L: Kegan Paul, Trench, Trubner, 1899. 118p. BL OCLC
[Boadicea is an historical tragedy in verse; others are narrative poems & sonnets]

2145. -----The cithern. Poems for recitation.
2 pt. L: John & Robert Maxwell, 1886. 134, 112p. NUC BL OCLC
[Part 2: Several dramatic poems on classical & Biblical themes; sonnets]

2146. -----France discrowned, and other poems.
L: Chapman & Hall, 1874. 91p. BL

2147. -----Sita, and other poems.
L: Elliot Stock, 1895. 104p. BL

2148. GRAHAM, Clementina Stirling, Miss [Br. 1782-1877]
Mystifications.
Edinburgh: Priv. pr., 1859. 108p. NUC BL OCLC
[Incl. songs & ballads of Scotland & Poland, pp. 75-108]

2149. GRAHAM, Grace [Br. 19c]
Lays for the lyre.
L: Priv. pr., 1865. BL

2150. GRAHAM, Isabella Marshall [Am. 1742-1814]
The power of faith: exemplified in the life and writings of Isabella Graham of New York. Comp. Divie Bethune.
NY: J. Seymour, 1816. 411p. NUC BL OCLC
[Incl. devotions and religious poetry.]

2151. GRAHAM, Jean Carlyle [Br. b. 1846]
The child of the bondwoman, and other verses.
L: D. Nutt, 1897. 65p. NUC BL

2152. -----Songs, measures, metrical lines.
L: Kegan, Paul & co., 1893. 123p. BL

2153. GRAHAM, Mary [Am. 19c]
A "fowl" mystery.
Cincinnati, OH: n.p., 1888? 12 l. NUC OCLC
[Humorous poem on an incident in Civil War]

2154. GRAHAME, Agnes Vetch [Br. 19c]
Esther; or, Songs of the captivity, and the Sabbath; a poem.
L: n.p., 1876. BL

GRAHAME, James, co-author see BENGER, Elizabeth Ogilvie

2155. GRANGER, Jane M. C. [Am. b. 1813]
Selected poems.
n.p.: n.p, 1884? 106p. NUC OCLC
[Original misc. poetry]

2156. GRANGER, Lucy Nichols [Am. 19c]
Songs by the way.
Ann Arbor, MI: Register pub. house, 1886. 104p. NUC OCLC

2157. GRANGER, Mary Ethel [Br. 19c] ALT: G., M. E.
Light after darkness. By M.E.G.
L: J. Nisbet, 1885. BL

2158. -----Peace: a thanksgiving after Holy Communion.
L: Sonnenschein & co., 1886. 31p. BL

2159. GRANNISS, Anna Jane [Am. b. 1856]
Sandwort.
Keene, NH: Darling & co., pr., 1897. 60p. NUC OCLC

2160. -----Skipped stitches, verses.
Keene, NH: Darling & co., pr., 1893. 55p. NUC OCLC

2161. GRANT, Anne MacVicar [Br. 1755-1838]
Blue bells of Scotland.
NY & L: White & Allen, 1889. 32p. NUC
[Ballad, with the music.]

2162. -----Dear old songs.
NY: White & Allen, 1889. NUC

2163. -----Eighteen hundred and thirteen: a poem in two parts.
Edinburgh: Pr. by James Ballantyne for Longman, Hurst, Rees, Orme, & Brown, 1814. 146p. NUC BL OCLC

2164. -----The highlanders, and other poems.
Edinburgh: n.p., 1803. 2d ed. L: Pr. C. Whittingham, 1808. 300p. NUC BL OCLC

2165. -----Poems on various subjects.
Edinburgh: Pr. by J. Moir, sold by Longman & Rees; L: Mundell & son, 1803. 447p. NUC BL OCLC

GRANT, Cecília (Havergal) see HAVERGAL, Cecilia

2166. GRANT, Davina [Br. 19c]
Hymns and verses.
Edinburgh: n.p., 1839. BL

2167. GRANT, Eleanor [Br. 19c] ALT: G., E.
Crowning blessings. A selection of poems. By Eleanor Grant.
L: James E. Hawkins, 1888. 24 unnumb. l. BL
[Original religious verse]

2168. GRANT, Emily Fredrica [Br. 19c]
"Looking unto Jesus"; a narrative of the brief race of a young disciple. By her mother, J.T.G. [Judith Towers Grant].
L: J. Nisbet & co., 1865. 138p. NUC BL
[Contains poetry & misc. prose]

2169. GRANT, Gena Fairfield [Am. 19c]
Forget-me-nots. Miscellaneous poems.
Rockland, ME: Courier-Gazette job pr., 1899. NUC OCLC

GRANT, Rev. Johnson, ed. see BELL, Frances Augusta

GRANT, Judith Towers, comp. see GRANT, Emily Fredrica

2170. GRAVES, Adelia Cleopatra (Spencer) [Am. 1821-1895] PSEUD: Aunt Alice
Melodies of heart and home. By Aunt Alice.
St. Louis, MO: Baptist pub. co., c1859. 96p. NUC

2171. GRAVES, Mary Eliot (Dutton) [Am. 19c]
Memorial.
n.p.: n.p., 18--? 20p. NUC
[Also incl. verses by Henry Melzar Dutton]

2172. GRAY, Amy [Am. 19c]
The lily of the valley; or, Margie and I: and other poems.
Baltimore, MD: Kelly & Piet, 1868. 114p. NUC BL OCLC

2173. GRAY, Bessie [Am. 1854-1925]
The angel of prayer.
Boston: L. Prang & co., 1897. 6 l. NUC

2174. -----At the gates of sleep.
Boston: L. Prang & co., 1897. 6 l. NUC OCLC
[Illus. of poppies with verse, by B. Gray & others]

2175. -----Bermuda in June.
Boston: L. Prang & co., 1893. 13 l. NUC

2176. -----A dream of violets.
Boston: L. Prang & co., 1898. 6 l.
NUC

2177. -----Flower beautiful.
Boston: L. Prang, 1896. 8 l. OCLC

2178. -----Nasturtiums bright and gay.
Boston: L. Prang & co., 1897. 7 l.
NUC

GRAY, Mrs. James see GRAY, Mary Ann (Browne)

2179. GRAY, Jane Lewers, Mrs. [Am. 1796-1871]
Selection from the poetical writings of Jane Lewers Gray.
NY: Pr. for priv. dist. by Edward O. Jenkins for A.D.F. Randolph, 1872. 207p. NUC OCLC

2180. GRAY, Mary Ann (Browne), Mrs. James Gray [Br. 1812-1844] ALT: Browne, Mary Ann
Ada, and other poems.
L: Longmans, Rees, Orme, Brown & Green; Hatchard & son; W. Benning, 1828. 277p. NUC BL OCLC

2181. -----The birth-day gift.
L: Hamilton Adams & co.; Liverpool: D. Marples & co., 1834. 184p. NUC BL OCLC

2182. -----The coronal; original poems sacred and miscellaneous.
L: Hamilton, Adams & co.; Liverpool: D. Marples & co., 1833. 183p. BL

2183. -----Ignatia and other poems.
L: Hamilton, Adams; Liverpool: D. Marples & co., 1838. 176p. BL OCLC

2184. -----Mont Blanc, and other poems.
L: Hatchard, 1827. 177p. NUC BL

2185. -----Repentance, and other poems.
L: Longman & co.; Hatchard & son & Saunders & Benning, 1829. 118p. NUC BL OCLC

2186. -----Sacred poetry.
L: Hamilton, Adams & co., 1840. 96p. BL

2187. -----Sketches from the antique: and other poems.
Dublin: W. Curry, jr. & co., 1844. 176p. BL

GRAY, MAXWELL, pseud. see TUTTIETT, Mary Gleed, Miss

GREEN, Anna Katherine see ROHLFS, Anna Katherine (Green)

2188. GREEN, Eliza Craven [Br. 19c]
Sea weeds and heath flowers, or memories of Mona.
L & Liverpool: H. Curphey, 1858. 200p. NUC BL
[Lyrics & poems on the Isle of Man]

2189. GREEN, Kathleen Haydn [Br. 19/20c]
Poems.
L: Dean & son, 1899. 138p. BL

2190. -----The poet's crown, and other verses.
L: Pr. by author for priv. dist., 1895. 54p. NUC

2191. GREEN, M., Mrs. [Br. 19/20c]
Love's romance: or, Jessie Gray. A poem.
L: Eliot Stock, 1882. 15p. BL

2192. GREENE, Aella [Am. 1838-1903]
After night, a summer-place talk, with other poems.
Boston & NY: Lee, Shepard & Dillingham, 1873. 93p. NUC OCLC

2193. -----Conflict and conquest and other poems.
Athol, MA: The Cottager co., pr., 1897. 96p. NUC OCLC

2194. -----Gathered from life and prophetic of another life.
Springfield, MA: C.W. Bryan co., pr., 1893. 228p. NUC OCLC

2195. -----Happy days at Hampton, and other poems.
Springfield, MA: Gill & Hayes, 1872. 98p. NUC OCLC

2196. -----Idyls of freedom.
Florence, MA: Bryant pr. co., 1893. 92p. NUC OCLC

2197. -----Into the sunshine and other poems.
Boston: Lee & Shepard; NY: C.T. Dillingham, 1881. 96p. NUC OCLC

2198. -----The poetical works of Aella Greene.
Holyoke, MA: C.W. Bryan & co., 1886. 167p. NUC OCLC

2199. -----Reminiscence and other poems.

Athol, MA: Cottager pr., 1898. 80p. NUC OCLC

2200. -----Rhymes of Yankee land.
Boston: Lee & Shepard, 1872. 91p. NUC OCLC

2201. -----River, bird and star.
Florence, MA: Bryant pr. co., 1895. 151p. NUC OCLC

2202. -----Stanza and sequel and other poems.
Holyoke, MA: C.W. Bryan & co. pr., 1883. 143p. NUC OCLC

2203. GREENE, Clara Marcelle (Farrar) [Am. 19c] PSEUD: Kendall, Kate
The Magdalen and other poems. By "Kate Kendall".
Portland, ME: B. Thurston & co., 1889. 128p. NUC OCLC

2204. GREENE, E. C., Miss [Am. 19c]
March flowers.
Providence, RI: n.p., 1836. NUC
[Supposed author]

2205. GREENE, Margaret Bromley [Am. 19c]
The rhymed chronicle of the French kings.
NY: C.A. Greene, 1893. 23p. NUC

2206. GREENOUGH, Elizabeth [Am. 19c]
Occasional verses.
Boston?: Priv. pr., 186-? 18p. NUC

GREENOUGH, Mrs. R.S. see GREENOUGH, Sarah Dana (Loring)

GREENOUGH, Mrs. Richard S. see GREENOUGH, Sarah Dana (Loring)

2207. GREENOUGH, Sarah Dana (Loring), Mrs. Richard S. Greenough [Am. 1827-1885] ALT: Greenough, Mrs. R.S.
Mary Magdalene, a poem.
L: Kegan, Paul & co.; Boston: J.R. Osgood & co., 1880. 72p. NUC BL OCLC

2208. -----Mary Magdalene, and other poems.
Boston: Ticknor & co.; L: Chapman & Hall, c1880. 94p. NUC BL OCLC

2209. GREENSTED, Frances [Br. 18c] ALT: G., F.
Fugitive pieces. By F.G.
Maidstone: Pr. for author by D. Chalmers, 1796. 71p. NUC BL
[Poetry, incl. epitaphs, acrostics, lyrics, etc.]

2210. GREENSTREET, Annie Louise (Ashley) [Br. b. 1835] ALT: Ashley, Annie Louise
Heart yearnings after home; and other poems.
Edinburgh: Tract depot; L: Robert L. Allen, 1871. 82p. NUC BL

GREENWELL, Dora, ed. see SOUTHEY, Caroline Anne (Bowles)

2211. GREENWELL, Dora (Dorothy) [Br. 19c]
Camera obscura.
L: Daldy, Isbister, 1876. 108p. NUC BL OCLC

2212. -----Carmina Crucis.
Boston: Roberts bros.; L: Bell & Daldy, 1869. 136p. NUC BL OCLC

2213. -----Home thoughts and home scenes. In original poems by Dora Greenwell and others.
Boston: J.E. Tilton & co., 1865? 35 l.; L & NY: G. Routledge & sons, 1868. NUC
[Ten poems by Greenwell]

2214. -----Poems.
L: William Pickering, 1848. 191p. NUC BL OCLC

2215. -----Poems.
Edinburgh: A. Strahan & co., 1861. 315p. NUC BL OCLC
[Also pub. as: Christina and other poems; expanded ed., 1867. 372p. NUC OCLC]

2216. -----Songs of salvation.
L: A. Strahan & co., 1873. 37p. NUC BL

2217. -----The soul's legend.
L: n.p., 1873. BL

2218. -----Stories that might be true, with other poems.
L: W. Pickering, 1850. 180p. NUC BL OCLC

GREENWOOD, Alice, co-author see BROWN, Annie Johnson-

2219. GREENWOOD, Alice Davis Odekirk [Am. 1851-1936]
Husks and nubbins.
Concord, NH: Rumford press, 1899. 79p. NUC OCLC
[Many in dialect; on farm life in Indiana]

2220. GREER, Laura M. Smith [Am. 19c]

Mother-soul.
San Francisco: n.p., 1899. 30p. NUC OCLC

GREENWOOD, GRACE, pseud. see LIPPINCOTT, Sara J. (Clarke)

2221. GREER, Maria, Mrs. S. Greer [Br. 19c]
The chained Bible; Scriptural sketches, Esther, and other poems.
Dublin: George Herbert; L: Nisbet & co.; Hamilton Adams & co., 1857. 155p.; L: Christian Book society, 1873. BL
[BL also lists under Sarah D. Greer as: The Chained Bible and other poems. Contents are identical.]

2222. GREER, Maria [Br. 19c]
A vision's voice and other poems.
L: Digby & Long, 1897. 62p. BL

GREER, Mrs. S. see GREER, Maria, Mrs.

GREER, Sarah D. see GREER, Maria, Mrs.

2223. GREGG, Lucy Brown [Am. b. 1833]
Poems, in three departments: childhood and youth, religious, and miscellaneous.
Indianapolis, IN: William A. Patton, 1886. 212p. NUC OCLC

2224. GREGORY, Harriet [Br. 19c]
Poems.
Launceston: P.D. Maddox, 1857. 44p. BL

2225. GREGORY, Kate [Am. 19c]
Dreamland hours.
LaFayette, IN: Home Journal, 1899. 126p. NUC OCLC

2226. GREGORY, Pauline [Am. 19c]
Poems and proses.
Kansas City, MO: Ramsey, Millett & Hudson, 1880. 96p. OCLC

GREGORY, Rev. B., comp. see TATHAM, Emma, Miss

GRENVILLE, Anna, Countess Temple see TEMPLE, Anna (Chambers) Grenville-Temple, Countess

GREVILLE-NUGENT, Hon. Mrs. see NUGENT, Hon. Ermengarda Greville-

2227. GREW, Harriet Catherine [Am. 19c]
Memorials of a young Christian.
Philadelphia: Merrihew & Gunn, pr., 1837. 106p. NUC OCLC
[Incl. journal, letters; chiefly poetry]

2228. GREY, Ethel [Am. 19c]
Sunset gleams from the city of the mounds.
St. Louis, MO & NY: John F. Trow, 1852. 182p. NUC OCLC

GREY, CHRISTINA, pseud. see WILSON, Lisa

2229. GREY, F. Elizabeth [Am. 19c]
The passion flower.
n.p.: n.p., c1889. 3p. NUC

2230. GREY, Gertrude [Br. 19c]
Claudius and Eudocia: a tale of the early martyrs. Also Constance, a fragment.
L: W. Tweedie, 1868. 40p. BL OCLC

2231. -----The mother's return; or, New Year's eve. A sketch.
L: n.p., 1876. BL

2232. GREY, GILLIAN, pseud. [Br. 19c]
Tales of the Waveney ... and miscellaneous poems.
L: R.S. Stacy, 1850? 110p. BL
[Descriptive, narrative, misc. poems]

2233. GREY, Rose [Br. 19c]
Double sight. A poem.
L: McClary, 1861. 169p. BL

2234. -----Lays of the turf.
L: Pr. G.M. Nichols, 1863. 62p. NUC

2235. GRIFFIN, Alice McClure [Am. 19c]
Poems.
Cincinnati, OH: Rickey & Carroll, 1864. 126p. NUC OCLC

2236. GRIFFIN, Mary M., Mrs. [Am. 19c]
'Drops from Flora's cup; or, The poetry of flowers with a floral vocabulary.
Boston: G.W. Cottrell & co.; NY: T.W. Strong, 1845. 160p. NUC OCLC

2237. GRIFFITH, Elizabeth Griffith [Br. 1720?-1793] PSEUD: Lady, A
Amana. A dramatic poem. By a lady.
L: Pr. by T. Harrison for W. Johnston, 1764. 54p. NUC BL
[5 acts, blank verse]

GRIFFITH, Mattie see BROWNE, Martha Griffith

2238. GRIFFITHS, Charlotte Mary [Br. 19c]

Gone with the storm, and minor poems.
L: Pr. Cassell, Petter & Galpin, 1874. 97p. NUC BL

2239. GRIFFITHS, J., Miss [Br. 18c]
A collection of juvenile poems, on various subjects.
Warwick: Pr. for the author by J. Sharp, 1784. BL
[Pastorals, imitations of classical forms, written when young.]

2240. GRIFFITHS, Rosa [d. 1877]
A child's verses. Found after her death. In memoriam. [Comp. her sister, H.M. Griffiths].
Birmingham: Priv. pr. by Josiah Allen, 1878. 24p. NUC OCLC
[Lyric and narrative poems; Rose died at 16]

GRIGGS, H.N., Miss <u>see</u> GRIGGS, Helen Augusta

2241. GRIGGS, Helen Augusta [Am. d. 1860] ALT: Griggs, H. N., Miss PSEUD: N., H.
My father's knell: poems, in memory of S.G.
NY: Pr. E.O. Jenkins, 1856. 168p. NUC OCLC

2242. -----Songs for the sorrowing. By H.N.
NY: Phinney, Blakeman & Mason; Buffalo, NY: Breed, Butler & co., 1861. 284p. NUC BL OCLC
[Misc. poetry with religious themes]

2243. GRIGGS, Nellie M. [Am. 19c]
Daily stepping stones.
Richfield Springs, NY: Ibbotson bros. pub., 1889. 15p. NUC OCLC
[Scripture texts and verses for morning & evening of each day of week]

2244. GRIMANI [Grinani BL], Julia C. [Br. 19c] ALT: G., J. C.
Sacred lyrics by J.C.G.
L: John Russell Smith, 1849. 57p. NUC BL

2245. GRIMSTON, Elizabeth (Bernye) [Br. 1563?-1603] ALT: Grymeston, Elizabeth
Miscellanea; meditations; memoratives. [Augmented with addition of other of her meditations. BL].
L: Pr. by Melch. Bradwood for Felix Norton, 1604. 61p. L: Wm. Aspley, 1608? 128p. L: E. Elde for W. Aspley, 1610? NUC BL OCLC
[Short verses & stanzas interspersed in the prose meditations. Incl. "Odes in imitation of the seven penetential Psalms in seven severall kinde of verse."]

2246. GRIMSTONE, Mary Lemon, Mrs. [Br. 19c] PSEUD: Oscar
Cleone, Summer's sunset vision, The confession, with other poems and stanzas. By Oscar.
L: G. & W.B. Whittaker, 1821. 132p. NUC BL

2247. -----Zayda, a Spanish tale, in three cantos; and other poems, stanzas, and canzonets. By Oscar.
L: G. & W.B. Whittaker, 1820. 132p. NUC BL OCLC

GRINANI, Julia C. <u>see</u> GRIMANI, Julia C.

2248. GRISWOLD, Frances Irene (Burge) Smith [Am. 1826-1900] ALT: Smith, F. Burge
Asleep words of comfort to the bereaved. By F. Burge Smith.
NY: I Whittaker, 1871. 149p. NUC
[Poems and stories]

2249. GRISWOLD, Mattie (Tyng), Mrs. [Am. 1840-1909]
Apple blossoms.
Milwaukee, WI: Strickland; Chicago: Jansen, McClurg & co., 1874. 232p. NUC OCLC

2250. GROSE, Caroline Earle [Am. 19c]
Letter, miscellaneous pieces and European journal.
Boston: Geo. H. Ellis, 1888. 349p. NUC OCLC
[Incl. several poems]

2251. GROSS, Adeline E. [Am. 19c]
Polymniana.
Cincinnati, OH: n.p., 1884. 78p. NUC OCLC

2252. GROTE, Harriet Lewin [Br. 1792-1878]
Collected papers in prose and verse.
L: J. Murray, 1862. 293p. NUC BL OCLC
[Poems and essays]

2253. GRUBB, Dorothea [Br. 19c] ALT: G., D.
Gerald Fitzgerald, a tale of the sixteenth century. In five cantos. By D.G.
Waterford: Pr. T. Smith Harvey, 1845. 192p. NUC OCLC

2254. GRUNDY, Emma, Mrs. [Br. 19c]
PSEUD: Lady, A
Poems and translations. By a lady.
L: Pr. for priv. dist. by Manning & Mason, pr., 1841. 108p. NUC BL

GRYMESTON, Elizabeth see GRIMSTON, Elizabeth Bernye

2255. GUBBINS, Charlotte Gibson [Br. 19c] ALT: Gibson, Charlotte
One day's journal; a story of the revenue police, and other poems.
Sligo: Gillmor, 1862. 78p. NUC BL

2256. GUE, Belle Willey [Am. 19/20c]
Interludes; verses.
Chicago: Household Realm press, 1899. 100p. NUC

GUGGENBERGER, Louisa Sarah (Bevington) see BEVINGTON, Louisa Sarah

2257. GUILD, Anne Eliza (Gore), Mrs. James Guild [Am. 1826-1868] ALT: G., A. E.
A.E.G.
Cambridge, MA: John Wilson, 1869. 138p. NUC OCLC
[Contains excerpts of her letters and poetry]

2258. GUILD, Marion Laura (Pelton) [Am. 19/20c]
Song of praise, in memory of Phillip Brooks.
Boston: Frank Wood, pr., 1895. 9p. NUC

GUILD, Mrs. James see GUILD, Anne Eliza (Gore)

2259. GUINEY, Louise Imogen [Am. 1861-1920]
The colours at Cambridge.
Rockland, ME: Courier-Gazette job pr., 1896? 3p. NUC

2260. -----England and yesterday; a book of short poems.
L: G. Richards, 1898. 60p. NUC BL OCLC

2261. -----The martyr's idyl, and shorter poems.
Boston & NY: Houghton, Mifflin & co., 1899. 81p. NUC BL OCLC

2262. -----Nine sonnets written at Oxford.
Cambridge, MA: Priv. pr. by H. Copeland & F.H. Day, 1895. 9p. NUC BL OCLC

2263. -----A roadside harp, a book of verses.
Boston & NY: Houghton, Mifflin & co., 1893. 62p. NUC BL OCLC

2264. -----Songs at the start.
Boston: Cupples, Upham & co., 1884. 110p. NUC BL OCLC

2265. -----The white sail and other poems.
Boston: Ticknor & co., 1887. 133p. NUC BL OCLC

2266. GUINNESS, Jane Lucretia [Br. 19c]
Sketches of nature, comprising views of zoology, botany, and geology, ... illustrated by original poetry.
L: n.p., 1843. BL

2267. GUINNESS, Mrs. John G. [Br. 19c]
Sacred portraiture and illustrations, with other poems.
Dublin: Moore, 1834. 168p. BL OCLC

GUNNING, Mrs. John see GUNNING, Susannah (Minifie)

2268. GUNNING, Susannah (Minifie), Mrs. John Gunning [Br. 1740-1800] ALT: Minifie, Susannah
Virginius and Virginia, a poem in six parts, from the Roman history.
L: n.p., 1792. 65p. NUC BL

2269. GUNTHER, Amelia B. [Br. 19c]
A vision of truth.
L: Copley's broad-thought library, No. 5., 1892. BL

2270. GUPPY, Sarah [Br. 18/19c]
Essays on various subjects ... by Charles De La Garde. To which is added, some poetical pieces by Mrs. Guppy.
2d ed. Bristol: Pr. R. Edwards; L: Sold by T. Hurst, 1800. 103p. BL

GURDON, Lady Camilla see GURDON, Lady Eveline Camilla (Newton)

2271. GURDON, Lady Eveline Camilla (Newton) [Br. 1858-1894] ALT: Gurdon, Lady Camilla
Suffolk tales and other stories. Fairy legends. Poems. Miscellaneous articles.
L & NY: Longmans, Green, 1897. 370p. NUC BL OCLC
[Many reprinted from periodicals, brief stories & literary articles. Verses, pp. 143-155: lyric, humor, religious & descriptive.]

2272. GURNETT, Ann Eliza (Ballard) [Am. 19c] PSEUD: Nobody
Twilight effusions. By Nobody.
Providence, RI: Pr. by John F. Moore, 1850. 56p. NUC
[59 lyric poems, many memorials]

2273. GURNEY, Eliza Paul (Kirkbride) [1801-1881]
Heart utterances at various periods of a chequered life.
n.p.: n.p., 1876? 93p. NUC
[42 poems spanning 1811-1875. Not published.]

2274. GUSTAFSON, Zadel (Barnes) Buddington [Am. 1841?-1917] ALT: Buddington, Zadel Barnes
Meg: a pastoral. And other poems.
Boston: Lee & Shepard, 1879. 280p. NUC BL OCLC

2275. GUTHRIE, Ellen Emma [Br. 1892-1888]
Retrospection. An exile's memories of Skye.
Edinburgh: n.p., 1876. BL
[Memoirs in verse]

2276. GUYTON, Emma Jane (Worboise) [Br. 1825-1887] ALT: Worboise, Emma Jane
Hymns and songs for the Christian Church; and poems. By Emma Jane Worboise.
L: James Clarke & co., 1867. 184p. NUC BL

2277. GWILLIAN, Jane [Br. 19c]
Primrose Hill, a poem: to which are added, The Queen's jubilee, and other ... effusions.
L: n.p., 1838. BL

2278. GWILT, Hannah Jackson [Br. 19c]
The curse, the cross, and the crown.
L: n.p., 1864? BL

2279. -----The heavenly bridegroom with his charge to the ten virgins in Cedron's garden.
L: n.p., 1871. BL

2280. -----Redemptor Mundi.
L: n.p., 1871. BL
[Incl. other poems]

2281. -----Silver moon. Enlarged to commemorate the transit of Venus ... 8th of December, ... 1874.
2d ed. L: n.p., 1874. BL

2282. -----Some account of St. Saviour's, Southwark.
L: Priv. pr., 1865? BL

GWINNETT, Richard, co-author see THOMAS, Elizabeth

2283. GWYN, Laura [Am. 19c]
Miscellaneous poems.
Greenville, SC: G.E. Elford, pr., 1860. 218p. NUC OCLC

H., D. see HASELL, D., Mrs.

H., E. see HADFIELD, Elizabeth Taylor

H., E. see HAGGARD, Ella

H., E., Mrs. see HALL, Mrs. Eardley

H., E.E. see HICKS, Emma Endicott

H., E.L. see HARVEY, Ella Louisa (Spencer)

H., E.S. see HARRINGTON, Elizabeth Still (Pearsall) Stanhope, Countess

H., F.R. see HAVERGAL, Frances Ridley

H., H. see HUNT, Hannah

H., H. see JACKSON, Helen Maria (Fiske) Hunt

H., K. see HEAD, Katherine, Miss

H., M. see HOLFORD, Margaret

H., M.A. see HEDGE, Mary Ann

H., M.W. see HOWIE, Mary Wright

H., R.F. see HILL, Rosa F.

H., T.S. see HENDERSON, Thulia Susannah

2284. HACKELTON, Maria W., Mrs. [Am. 19c]
Jamestown of Pemaquid: a poem.
NY: Hurd & Houghton, 1869. 40p. NUC OCLC

2285. HADFIELD, Elizabeth Taylor [Br. 1818?-1861] ALT: H., E.
Poetical weeds. By E.H.
L: Darton, 1850. 149p. NUC BL OCLC

2286. -----Sprays from the hedgerows.
L: Darton & co., 1850. 222p. NUC BL

2287. HAGAN, Mary Barrett, Mrs. [Am. 19c]
Pictures from Puget Sound.
Seattle, WA: n.p., 1890? 13 l. NUC

2288. HAGGARD, Ella [Br. 1819-1889]
ALT: H., E.
Life and its author: an essay in verse. By E.H.
L & Norwich: Jarrold & sons, 1885. 22p. NUC BL OCLC

2289. -----Myra; or, The rose of the East. A tale of the Afghan War. In nine cantos.
L: Longman, Brown, Green, Longmans & Roberts, 1857. 124p. NUC BL OCLC

2290. HAIGH, Mary J., Mrs. [Am. 19c]
Thoughts in verse.
Schenectady, NY: Daily Union job pr., 1891. 75p. NUC OCLC

2291. HAIGHT, Sarah (Rogers) [Am. 19c] PSEUD: Lady of New York, A
A medley of joy and grief; being a selection of original pieces in prose and verse, chiefly on religious subjects. By a lady of New York.
NY: W.B. Gilley, 1882. 298p. NUC

2292. HAINES, L. Brown [Am. b. 1824]
Life sketches and poems.
Minneapolis, MN: n.p., 1894. 235p. NUC OCLC
[Daughter of Maine sea captain, autobiography & poetry]

2293. HAINES, Phebe [Am. 1804-1882]
Wayside thoughts.
Philadelphia: Stuckey, 1883. 196p. NUC OCLC

2294. HALE, Mrs. [Br. 18/19c]
Poetical attempts.
L: Pr. T. Davison, 1800. 156p. NUC BL OCLC

2295. HALE, C. L., Mrs. [Am. 19c]
Woodland lays, legends and charades.
Philadelphia: Pr. for the author by Lippincott & co., 1868. 282p. NUC OCLC
[Incl. Indian lays, Lays of the plantation, charades & riddles]

2296. HALE, J. A., Mrs. [Br. 19c]
Poetical meditations.
L: n.p., 1871. BL

2297. HALE, Mary Whitwell [Am. 1810-1862]
Poems.
Boston: W.D. Ticknor, 1840. 216p. NUC BL OCLC

2298. HALE, Sarah Josepha (Buell) [Am. 1788-1879] PSEUD: Lady of New Hampshire, A
Alice Ray: a romance in rhyme.
Philadelphia: Pr. A. Scott, 1845. 37p. NUC OCLC

2299. -----Flora's interpreter, and Fortuna Flora.
Boston: Marsh, Capen & Lyon, 1832. 288p. NUC BL
[Rev. & enl. ed. Boston: Sanborn, Carter, Bazin, 1848. 288p.]

2300. -----The genius of oblivion; and other original poems. By a lady of New Hampshire.
Concord, NH: J.B. Moore, 1823. 146p. NUC BL OCLC

2301. -----Harry Guy, the widow's son. A romance of the sea. In verse.
Philadelphia & Boston: B.B. Mussey & co., 1848. 72p. NUC BL

2302. -----Love; or, Woman's destiny. A poem in two parts: with other poems.
Philadelphia: D. Ashmead, 1870. 112p. NUC BL

2303. -----Three hours; or, The vigil of love: and other poems.
Philadelphia: Carey & Hart, 1848. 216p. NUC BL OCLC

2304. HALEY, Alice [Br. 19c] PSEUD: Hughes, Allison
Reed music. Poems. By Allison Hughes.
L: Kegan Paul & co., 1888. BL

2305. HALL, Mrs. Eardley [Br. 19c]
ALT: H., E., Mrs.
The chieftain's daughter; a tale of avarice.
Brighton: n.p., 1856. BL

2306. -----Zelinda. By Mrs. E.H.
L: n.p.; Brighton: Pr. Creasy & Baker, 1850? 47p. BL OCLC

2307. HALL, Edith Macomber, Mrs. Franklin Hall [Am. 19c]
Yesterday and to-day.
Troy, NY: The DeWitt press, c1898. 27 l. NUC

HALL, Mrs. Edward B. <u>see</u> HALL, Louisa Jane (Park)

2308. HALL, Elizabeth Arnold (Spicer) [Am. 19c]

Poems.
Providence, RI: n.p., 1885. 39p. NUC OCLC

2309. HALL, Elizabeth Smith [Am. 19c]
A western tour, and other poems.
Ravenna, OH: Democrat pr., 1865. 24p. NUC

2310. HALL, Elizabeth Sophia [Br. 19c]
Poems on several occasions.
L: Priv. pr. by W. Nichol, Shakespeare press, 1844. 197p. NUC BL OCLC

HALL, Mrs. Franklin <u>see</u> HALL, Edith Macomber

HALL, Gertrude <u>see</u> BROWNELL, Anna Gertrude (Hall)

2311. HALL, Harriet M.M. [Br. 19c]
Voices in verse.
L: H.P. Allenson, 1898. 104p. BL

2312. HALL, Harriet Ware [Am. 19c]
A book for friends.
Boston: Priv. pr. by University press, John Wilson & son, Cambridge, 1888. 68p. NUC OCLC
[Misc. poetry; pub. anon.]

HALL, Harrison, ed. <u>see</u> HALL, Sarah Ewing

HALL, Mrs. James <u>see</u> HALL, Sarah Amelia Maris (Aikin)

2313. HALL, Julia G., Miss [Br. 19c]
The dream of home and other poems.
L: n.p., 1868. BL

2314. HALL, Louisa Jane (Park), Mrs. Edward B. Hall [Am. 1862-1892] ALT: P., L.J.; Park, Louisa Jane
The cross and anchor written for the fair.
Providence, RI: B. Cranston & co., 1844. 31p. NUC OCLC

2315. -----Hannah, the mother of Samuel the prophet and judge of Israel. A sacred drama.
Boston: J. Munroe & co., 1839. NUC
[Dramatic poem, 5 acts]

2316. -----Miriam, a dramatic poem.
Boston: Hilliard, Gray & co., 1837. 124p. NUC BL
[3 scenes, tragedy about early Christians in Rome.]

2317. -----My body to my soul.
Providence, RI: Pr. for priv. circ., 1891. 2p. NUC OCLC

2318. -----Sonnets, stanzas and a crescendo composition.
L: Remington, 1884. 98p. OCLC

2319. -----Verses.
Cambridge: Priv. pr., 1892. 44p. NUC OCLC

2320. HALL, Martha [Am. 19c]
Sacred and entertaining poems.
Boston: n.p., 1854. BL

2321. -----A second portion of sacred and entertaining poems.
Boston: n.p., 1855. BL

2322. HALL, Mary L., Mrs. [Am. b. 1839]
Live coals.
Buffalo, NY: Selkirk, pr., 1878. 116p. NUC OCLC
[Dedicated to the railway conductors' brotherhood.]

2323. HALL, Sarah Amelia Maris (Aikin), Mrs. James Hall [Am. 19c]
Phantasia, and other poems. By Mrs. James Hall.
NY & L: G.P. Putnam, c1848. 144p. NUC OCLC

2324. HALL, Sarah (Ewing) [Am. 1761-1830]
Selections from the writings of Mrs. Sarah Hall, with a memoir of her life. Ed. her son, Harrison Hall.
Philadelphia: H. Hall, 1833. NUC BL OCLC
[Incl. poems, essays, letters, fiction, short story, etc.]

HALLETT, J., ed. <u>see</u> WOOLVEN, Mary

2325. HAM, Elizabeth [Br. b. 1783]
Elgiva; or, The monks. An historical poem with some minor pieces.
L: Baldwin, Cradock & Joy, 1824. 199p. NUC BL

2326. HAM, Marion Franklin [Am. 1867-1956]
The golden shuttle.
NY: Pr. J.J. Little & co., 1896. 128p. NUC OCLC

2327. HAMILTON, Agnes Steuart, Mrs. [Am. b. 1838]
Thoughts and experiences in verse.
Wilmington, DL: Lippincótt press, c1898, 1899. 164p. NUC OCLC

2328. HAMILTON, Anne, Lady [Br. 1766-1846]
The epics of the ton; or, The glories of the great world: a poem, in two books.
L: C. & R. Baldwin, 1807. 269p. NUC BL OCLC

2329. HAMILTON, Annie E. (Holdsworth) Lee-, Mrs. E.J. Lee-Hamilton [Br. 19/20c] ALT: Holdsworth, Annie E.
Forest notes. With Eugene Lee-Hamilton.
L: G. Richards, 1899. 92p. NUC BL OCLC

HAMILTON, Mrs. E.J. Lee- see HAMILTON, Annie E. (Holdsworth) Lee

2330. HAMILTON, Eliza Mary [Br. 1807-1851]
Poems.
Dublin: Hodges & Smith, 1838. 208p. NUC BL OCLC

2331. HAMILTON, Elizabeth, Mrs. [Br. b. 1750] PSEUD: Lady, A
A friend's gift. By a lady.
L: Priv. pr., 1839. 14p. NUC BL OCLC
[Poems incl. occasional verse, odes & elegies; Letters of advice on moral issues]

2332. HAMILTON, Emma (Lyon), Lady [Br. 1761-1815] ALT: Lyon, Emma, Lady
Miscellaneous poems.
Oxford: Pr. J. Bartlett for the author, 1812. 152p. NUC

2333. -----Miscellaneous poems (paraphrases from David's Psalms).
Oxford: Pr. J. Bartlett for the author, 1812. 152p. NUC BL OCLC

HAMILTON, Eugene Lee-, co-author see HAMILTON, Annie E. (Holdsworth) Lee-

HAMILTON, GAIL, pseud. see DODGE, Mary Abigail

HAMILTON, James, ed. see HAMILTON, Janet (Thompson)

2334. HAMILTON, Janet (Thompson) [Br. 1795-1873]
Poems and ballads.
Glasgow: J. Maclehose, 1868. 319p. NUC BL OCLC
[Scottish shoemaker's daughter, learned to write at 50.]

2335. -----Poems and essays of a miscellaneous character on subjects of general interest.
Glasgow: T. Murray & son, 1863. 304p. NUC BL

2336. -----Poems of purpose and sketches in prose of Scottish peasant life in auld langsyne, sketches of local scenes and character.
Glasgow: T. Murray & son, 1865. 299p. NUC BL OCLC
[Sketches are accounts of her neighbors & acquaintences]

2337. -----Poems, essays, and sketches. A selection from the two first volumes ..., with several new pieces. Ed. her son, James Hamilton.
Glasgow: J. Maclehose, 1870. 400p. NUC BL
[Enlarged ed. Glasgow: J. Maclehose, 1880. 512p. NUC OCLC]

HAMILTON, Mrs. Dr. S. see HAMILTON, Sarah Jane, Mrs.

2338. HAMILTON, Sarah, Miss [Br. 19c] PSEUD: Visitor to Leamington Spa, A
The Druid and the Holy King: a lyrical poem. By a visitor to Leamington Spa.
Leamington: n.p., 1838. BL

2339. -----The liberation of Joseph, a sacred dramatic poem, in two parts; The beauties of vegetation, with digressive sketches of Norwich, etc. in four cantos; and other poems.
L: J. Mawman, 1827. 178p. BL OCLC
[Joseph, pp. 1-46; Hymns, 47-76; Misc. poems, 77-104; Beauties, 105-178.]

2340. HAMILTON, Sarah, Miss [Br. 19c] PSEUD: Resident of Sherwood Forest, A
Sonnets, Tour to Matlock, Recollections of Scotland, and other poems. By a resident of Sherwood Forest.
L: J. Mawman, 1825. 260p. BL

2341. HAMILTON, Sarah Jane, Mrs. [Am. 19c] ALT: Hamilton, Mrs. Dr. S.
The angel of the covenant, a poem complete in three books, by Mrs. Dr. S. Hamilton.
Roseburg, OR: Review pub. co., 1886. 63p. NUC OCLC

2342. HAMLETT, Lizzie McDaniel [Am. b. 1842]
The poems of Mrs. Lizzie Hamlett.
Chicago: M.M. Pomeroy, 1876. 345p. NUC OCLC

2343. HAMLIN, Fannie E. [Am. 19c]

Jochebed's trust.
Lock Haven, PA; Philadelphia: Wm. Syckelmoore, pr., 1876. 40p. NUC OCLC

2344. HAMMOND, Mrs. [Br. 19c]
The widow's plea: a collection of poetical pieces.
L: n.p., 1836. BL

2345. HAMMOND, Luranah [Am. b. 1840]
Voices from nature. A volume of original poems.
Milwaukee, WI: Press of the Evening Wisconsin co., 1894. 175p. NUC OCLC

2346. HAMMOND, Mary Crowninshield (Warren), Mrs. Samuel Hammond [Am. 19c]
Letters from a little girl in Paris, written in 1852.
Boston: Priv. pr., 1892. 75p. NUC OCLC
[Includes poetry]

2347. HAMMOND, S., Miss [Br. 19c]
Rustic lays.
Braintree: n.p., 1838. BL

HAMMOND, Mrs. Samuel see HAMMOND, Mary Crowninshield (Warren)

2348. HAMPTON, Lady Laura Elizabeth [Br. 19c]
Musings in verse on the Collects for the Sundays and chief holy days.
L & Hereford: W. Kent & co., 1879. 138p. BL

HANAFORD, Mrs. Joseph H. see HANAFORD, Phebe Ann (Coffin)

2349. HANAFORD, Phebe Ann (Coffin), Mrs. Joseph H. Hanaford [Am. 1829-1921]
From shore to shore, and other poems.
San Francisco: A.L. Bancroft; Boston: B.B. Russell, 1871. 277p. NUC OCLC

2350. -----Our home beyond the tide.
Tonawanda, NY: Chapman & Warner, pr., c1872. 6 l. NUC OCLC

2351. -----Our martyred president ... Abraham Lincoln.
Boston: B.B. Russell & co., 1865. 22p. NUC BL OCLC

2352. HANBURY, Elizabeth Bell [Br. 19c]
Lines, with a brief memoir, on the melancholy death of Ellen Briggs, who was found near Westminster Abbey, and humanely relieved by Elizabeth Wetherall.
L: Pr. for Sherwood, Gilbert & Piper, 1826. 16p. NUC
[Poem on a good Samaritan]

2353. HANCOCK, Anne [Br. 19c]
Sacred songs.
L: n.p., 1857. BL

2354. HANCOCK, Sallie J. [Am. 19c]
Rayon d'amour. Poems.
Philadelphia: J.B. Lippincott & co., 1869. 159p. NUC OCLC

2355. HANDS, Elizabeth [Br. 18c]
The death of Amnon: a poem. With an appendix containing pastorals, and other poetical pieces.
Coventry: Pr. for the author by N. Rollason, 1789. 127p. NUC BL OCLC

HANKEY, Kate see HANKEY, Katherine, Miss

2356. HANKEY, Katherine, Miss [Am. 1834-1911] ALT: Hankey, Kate
Heart to heart. Hymns.
NY: A.D.F. Randolph, 1870. 97p. NUC BL OCLC

2357. -----Lotty's message: a story from real life.
L: n.p., 1867. 14p. BL

2358. -----The mourner's Christmas.
L: W. Macintosh, 1867. 16p. BL

2359. -----The old, old story. Part 1. The story wanted. Part 2. The story told.
NY: E.P. Dutton & co.; L: n.p., 1875. 23p. NUC BL OCLC
[1st Br. ed. 1862; 1879 ed. expanded, The old, old story and other verses. L: n.p.; 200p.]

2360. -----Sahara.
L: n.p., 1875. BL

2361. HANKIN, Mary L. [Br. 19c]
Year by year.
L: T.F. Unwin, 1892. 63p. NUC BL OCLC

2362. HANLEY, Isabella, Mrs. [Br. 19c]
Affection's offering.
Gravesend: n.p., 1868. BL
[Later ed., 1874]

2363. HANNA, Abigail Stanley [Am. 19c]
Withered leaves, from memory's garland.
Providence, RI: A.C. Greene & bros., pr., 1857. 390p. NUC OCLC

[Prose & verse, incl. short fiction, reminiscences, & misc. poetry]

2364. HANNA, Hattie Lloyd [Am. 19c]
Poems and hymns.
Brooklyn, NY: Borden & Cain press, 1880. 65p. NUC

2365. HANNAH, Mary [Br. 19c]
Leaves of poesie.
L: n.p., 1848. BL

2366. -----The rocks of Quidi Vidi.
L: n.p., 1850. BL

2367. HANSBROUGH, Mary Berri (Chapman) [Am. 19/20c]
Lyrics of love and nature.
NY & L: Frederick A. Stokes co., 1895. 226p. NUC

2368. HANSCOM, Alice Emelye [Am. 19c]
Perennia.
Cleveland, OH: Helman-Taylor co., 1898. 62p. NUC OCLC
[Verse on the months, includes a few passages in prose]

2369. HANSFORD, Leah M. P. [Br. 19c]
War contrasted with peace, and other poems.
Weymouth: n.p., 1840. BL

2370. HANSON, Beaulah Kezia, Mrs. James Hanson [Br. 19c]
Poems and tales of social life.
Bradford: James Hanson, 1868. 244p. BL
[7 short stories, pp. 5-188; Misc. poems, pp. 191-229; Poems for children, pp. 233-244]

2371. -----Poetical trifles; or, Thoughts in verse.
Bradford: Pr. B. Walker, 1848. 83p. BL OCLC

2372. HANSON, Mrs. George H. [Br. 19c]
Beauty, an allegory: Eternity, ... with a few minor poems.
L: n.p., 1861. BL

2373. -----A world at war, and a world at peace.
Brighton: n.p., 1872. BL

2374. HANSON, Hannah Maria [Br. 19c]
The sacred mountains and other poems.
L: n.p., 1859. BL

HANSON, Mrs. James see HANSON, Beulah Kezia

2375. HANSON, Martha [Br. 19c]
Sonnets and other poems.
L: J. Mawman, 1809. 2v. NUC BL OCLC

2376. HARBOTTLE, Mrs. [Br. 19c]
Via, a tale of coquet-side: and other poems.
L: n.p., 1856. BL

HARDCASTLE, Mrs., comp. see HARDCASTLE, Eliza Mary

2377. HARDCASTLE, Charlotte [Br. 19c]
Poems.
Brighton: Treacher, 1865. 123p. BL OCLC

2378. -----A song of consolation, and other poems.
L: n.p., 1868. BL

2379. HARDCASTLE, Eliza Mary [Br. 19c]
Memoir of a beloved daughter (E.M. Hardcastle). By a mother, Mrs. Hardcastle.
Leeds: Pr. for the author, 1834. 144p. BL
[Contains hymns & poems]

2380. HARDENBERGH, Marcella V. [Am. 19c]
From heart to heart; poems.
Brooklyn, NY: Orphans' press, Church Charity Foundation, 1880. 121p. NUC OCLC

HARDIN, Mrs. Charles Henry see HARDIN, Mary Barr (Jenkins)

2381. HARDIN, Mary Barr (Jenkins), Mrs. Charles Henry Hardin [Am. b. 1824]
Life and writings of Governor Charles Henry Hardin. By his wife. "A life sketch of Mrs. C.H. Hardin by Wiley J. Patrick."
St. Louis, MO: Buschart bros., 1896. 316p. NUC OCLC
[Incl. 2 poems by her]

2382. HARDWICKE, Elizabeth, Mrs. [19c]
Poems.
Melbourne: Davison, Duncan & co., 1894. 284p. NUC OCLC

HARDY, Mrs. A.S. see HARDY, Mary (Earle)

2383. HARDY, Irene [Am. b. 1841]
Poems.
Oakland, CA: Priv. pr., 1892. 28p. NUC OCLC

2384. HARDY, Mary (Earle), Mrs. A.S. Hardy [Am. 1846-1928]
Three singers.
Chicago: Press of Chapman, 1894. 127p. NUC OCLC

2385. HARDY, Mary Anne (McDowell) Duffus, Lady [Br. 1825?-1891] ALT: Duffus Hardy, Lady
War notes from the Crimea.
L: n.p., 1855. BL

2386. HARDY, Robina Forrester [Br. d. 1891]
Whin-bloom.
Edinburgh: W.P. Nimmo, 1879. NUC BL

2387. -----The wishing well.
L, Edinburgh & NY: Nelson, n.d. 48p. TXU

2388. HARGREAVES, Maud [Br. 19c]
Poems.
L: W. Clowes, 1877. 68p. NUC

2389. HARLOW, Lucie A. [Am. 19c]
A day's fishing; in verse.
Boston: L. Prang & co., c1891. 12 l. NUC

2390. -----A whisper of spring.
Boston: L. Prang & co., 1893. 7 l. NUC

HARNESS, William, ed. see FANSHAWE, Catherine Maria

HARPER, Frances Ellen Watkins, see MONMOUTH, Sarah Elizabeth (Harper)

2391. HARPER, Frances Ellen (Watkins) [Am. 1825-1911] PSEUD: Afton, Effie
Atlanta offering, poems.
Philadelphia: Merrihew & son, pr., 1871. 48p. NUC OCLC

2392. -----Eventide. A series of tales and poems. By Effie Afton.
Boston: Ferridge & co., 1854. 431p. BL
[Fiction & misc. lyric poems, pp. 401-431.]

2393. -----Poems.
Philadelphia: Merrihew & son, pr., 1871. 48p. NUC OCLC

2394. -----Poems on miscellaneous subjects.
Boston: J.B. Yerrinton & son, pr., 1854. 40p. NUC OCLC

2395. -----Sketches of southern life.
Philadelphia: Merrihew & son, pr., 1872. 24p. NUC OCLC
[Depicts life of Aunt Chloe, a former slave, during Reconstruction Days]

2396. -----The sparrow's fall and other poems.
n.p.: n.p., n.d. 22p. NUC
[No title page; one poem on a dying slave, another about the downtrodden of the world.]

2397. HARRADEN, Gertrude [Br. 19/20c]
Saint Hildred, a romaunt in verse.
L: T. Fisher Unwin, 1886. 56p. NUC BL OCLC

HARRIES, Margaret see WILSON, Margaret (Harries) Baron-

HARRIET see WHITE, Harriet

2398. HARRINGTON, Elizabeth Still (Pearsall) Stanhope, Countess of [Br. d. 1912] ALT: H., E.S.; Stanhope, Elizabeth Still (Pearsall), Countess of Harrington
The Norse brothers.
L: n.p., 1875. BL

2399. -----Poems. By E.S.H.
L: H. Sotheran & co., 1874. 67p. NUC BL OCLC

2400. HARRINGTON, Jane Maria Elizabeth [Br. 19c]
Thoughts in prose and verse.
Ryde?: Pr. for priv. circ., 1892. 2v. BL
[V. 2 chiefly poetry; a few brief prose prayers & meditations]

HARRINGTON, KATE, pseud. see POLLARD, Rebecca (Smith)

2401. HARRIS, Alleyne [Br. 19c]
Solitary song.
L: E. Stock, 1891. 227p. NUC BL OCLC

2402. HARRIS, Emelie [Am. 19c]
Corning, and other poems.
Corning, IA: J.C. Burch, 1879. 64p. NUC

2403. HARRIS, Emily Marion [Br. 19c] PSEUD: Estelle
Apples of Eden: a realism. By Estelle.
NY: Minerva pub. co., 1890. 223p. NUC OCLC

2404. -----Verses.
L: Bell & sons, 1881. 149p. BL

2405. HARRIS, Henrietta [Br. 19c]
Poems, on various subjects.

Worcester: The author, 1805. 158p. BL OCLC

2406. HARRISON, Cornelia Rives [Am. 19c]
Bubbles from the Bedford Springs.
Providence, RI: E.L. Freeman & co., pr., 18--? 4p. NUC

2407. HARRISON, Elizabeth [Br. 18c]
A letter to Mr. John Gay, on his tragedy, call'd, The captives. To which is annex'd a copy of verses to the Princess [of Wales], on her patronage of that tragedy.
L: Pr. for the author, 1724. 18p. NUC BL

2408. -----Miscellanies on moral and religious subjects, in prose and verse.
L: Pr. for the author, 1756. 380p. NUC BL OCLC

2409. HARRISON, Jennie M. [Am. 19c]
Leola Leroy, foster sister of Adele.
Cincinnati, OH: R. Clarke & co., pr., 1872. 90p. NUC OCLC

2410. HARRISON, Matilda [Br. 19c]
The poet's wreath, being a selection of poems.
L & Blackburn: Express & Standard Gen. pr. works, 1890. 147p. NUC OCLC

2411. HARRISON, Susannah [Br. 1752-1784]
Songs in the night; by a young woman under deep afflictions.
L: Pr. R. Hawes, sold by T. Vallance & Alexander Hogg, 1780. 153p. NUC BL OCLC

2412. -----A supplement to "Songs in the night.".
Ipswich: Punchard & Jermyn, 1788. 42p. NUC BL OCLC
[1st printing bound with 1783 ed. of Songs.]

2413. HARRISS, Julia Mildred [Am. 19c] PSEUD: Minstrel maiden of Mobile
Wild shrubs of Alabama; or, Rhapsodies of restless hours. By the minstrel maiden of Mobile.
NY: C.B. Norton; Mobile, AL: Carver & Ryland, 1852. 180p. NUC OCLC

HARSTON, Edward, ed. <u>see</u> INGELOW, Jean

HART, Elizabeth Anna <u>see</u> HART, Fanny Wheeler

2414. HART, Fanny Wheeler [19/20c]
ALT: Hart, Elizabeth Anna; Hart, Mrs. Smedley
Harry.
NY: Macmillan & co., 1877. 145p. NUC OCLC

2415. -----Mrs. Jerningham's journal.
L: Macmillan & co., 1869. 141p. NUC BL OCLC

2416. HART, Mary Kerr, Mrs. [Br. 19c]
Heath blossoms: or, Poems written in obscurity and seclusion. With a memoir of the author.
Ballingdon: Pr. W. Hill, 1830? 140p. NUC BL OCLC

HART, Mrs. Smedley <u>see</u> HART, Fanny Wheeler

HARTER, Mrs. Alfred <u>see</u> HARTER, Ethel Maud (De Fonblanque)

2417. HARTER, Ethel Maud (De Fonblanque), Mrs. Alfred Harter [Br. 19/20c] ALT: De Fonblanque, Ethel Maud
A chaplet of love poems.
L: Leonard Smithers, 1899. 129p. NUC BL OCLC

2418. -----Disillusions and other poems.
L: T. Fisher Unwin, 1887. 62p.

2419. -----Poems.
L: Bolton's library, 1880. 90p. BL

2420. HARTER, J. H., Mrs. [Am. 19c]
True religion. A poem ... read at the dedication of Lyceum Hall at Freeville, NY. Aug. 10, 1879.
n.p.: n.p., 1879. 8p. NUC

2421. HARTHILL, Susanna [Br. 19c]
Revolution and other poems.
Edinburgh: n.p., 1850. BL

2422. HARTLEY, Louisa Byam [Br. 19c]
Wild flowers from the Norman Isles.
Jersey: n.p., 1846. BL

2423. HARTWELL, Eugenia N. (Peckham) [Am. 1826-1854]
Poems.
Buffalo, NY: H.M. Lane, 1855. 240p. NUC

2424. HARVEY, Abbie M. [Am. 19c]
Chapel chimes and other poems.
Boston: Silver, Burdett & co., 189-? 18 l. NUC OCLC
[Easter poetry]

2425. -----The discovery of America.
Boston: New England pub. co., 1892.
28p. NUC
[Patriotic masque; incl. songs]

2426. HARVEY, Ella Louisa (Spencer)
[Br. d. 1906] ALT: H., E.L.
A Christmas offering in aid of the industrial school, Richmond. By E.L.H.
Richmond: Priv. pr., 1854. BL

2427. -----The embarkation of the Princess Royal: poem. February 2. 1858. 5p. OCLC

2428. -----Lays and legends of Germany, translated from the German; with other poems.
How: n.p., 1846. 223p. NUC BL

2429. -----The legend of a summer day. A northern dream. By E.L.H.
L: Priv. pr., 1861. BL

2430. -----Songs of the twilight and some ballads and translations. By E.L.H.
Richmond: Priv. pr., 1866. BL

2431. -----Sursum Corda. By E.L.H.
L: n.p., 1862. BL

2432. HARVEY, Ellen T.H. [Am. 19c]
Wilderness and mount. A poem of tabernacles.
Boston: John Bent, 1872. 143p. NUC OCLC

2433. HARVEY, Hannah L. [Br. 19c]
William O'Brien.
n.p.: n.p., 1889. 8p. BL

2434. HARVEY, Jane [Br. 18/19c]
Fugitive pieces.
Newcastle-upon-Tyne: Currie & Bowman, 1841. 109p. NUC BL
[Incl. sonnets, parodies, elegies, epistles, etc., 1 brief prose allegory]

2435. -----Poems on various subjects.
Newcastle-upon-Tyne: Pr. D. Akenhead & sons, 1797. 44p. NUC BL
[Sonnets, pastorals, and other experiments in traditional forms]

2436. HARVEY, Margaret [Br. 19c]
The lay of the minstrel's daughter, a poem in six cantos.
Newcastle upon Tyne: Pr. for the author by J. Marshall, 1814. 244p. NUC BL

2437. HARVEY, Margaret Boyle [Am. d. 1912]
Lower Merion lilies and other poems.
Philadelphia: J.B. Lippincott co., 1887. 129p. NUC OCLC

HARVIER, Evelyn Baker, comp. <u>see</u> SHERWOOD, Mary Elizabeth (Wilson)

HASCALL, Virginia (King), comp. <u>see</u> KING, Sarah A.

2438. HASELL, D., Mrs. [Br. 19c] ALT: H., D.
The rustic muse.
Lancaster: L.W. Willan, 1842. 132p. BL

2439. HASLEWOOD, Frances C. [Br. 19c]
Poetry and fragments of correspondence.
L: W. Skeffington & son, 1878. 71p. NUC BL

2440. HASTINGS, Lady Flora Elizabeth Rawdon- [Br. 1806-1839]
Poems by Lady Flora Hastings. Ed. her sister [Lady Sophia Rawdon-Hastings, aft. Marchioness of Bute].
Edinburgh & L: n.p., 1841. 282p. NUC BL OCLC

2441. HASTINGS, Lucy Webb
Tales and rhymes written by three children [Lucy, Fanny & Platt Hastings] at Soncy, Bermuda Islands.
Washington, D.C.: Brodix pub. co., 1892. 88p. NUC
[Little stories & poems written when these children were between 6 and 11]

HASTINGS, Sally <u>see</u> HASTINGS, Sarah Anderson

2442. HASTINGS, Sarah Anderson [Am. 1773-1812] ALT: Hastings, Sally
Poems on different subjects. To which is added a descriptive account of a family tour to the West, in the year 1800, in a letter to a lady.
Lancaster: W. Dickson for the authoress, 1808. 220p. NUC OCLC

HASTINGS, Lady Sophia Rawdon-, ed. <u>see</u> HASTINGS, Lady Flora Elizabeth Rawdon-

2443. HASTINGS, Sybil [Am. 19c]
Harvestings: sketches in prose and verse.
Boston: W.P. Fetridge & co; NY: J.C. Derby, 1855. 329p. NUC BL OCLC
[Short fictional sketches, c. 30p. each; misc. poems interspersed.]

HATCH, C.L.V.S. see RICHMOND, Cora Linn Victoria (Scott) Hatch Tappen

HATFIELD, Sibella Elizabeth see MILES, Sibella Elizabeth (Hatfield)

2444. HATHEWAY, Mary E.N. [Am. 19c]
In the fields.
Boston: D. Lothrop & co., 1880. 164p. NUC OCLC

2445. HATTERAS, HESPER, pseud. [Br. 19c]
Brittania and Columbia, and other poems.
L: John Camden Hotten; NY: Scribner, Welford & co., 1870. 202p. NUC OCLC

2446. HATTERSLEY, Mary Emma [Br. 19c]
Nehemiah. A poem.
L: n.p., 1877. BL

2447. HATTON, Ann Julia (Kemble), Mrs. Curtis Hatton [Br. 1764-1838] ALT: Kemble, Ann Julia PSEUD: Ann of Swansea
Poetic trifles.
Waterford: Pr. John Bull for the authoress, 1811. 387p. NUC BL
[Incl. sonnets, elegies, imitations of classical forms & other authors, humor, etc. Nearly every genre incl.]

HATTON, Mrs. Curtis see HATTON, Ann Julia (Kemble)

2448. HAVEN, Alice (Bradley) Neal [Am. 1827-1863] ALT: Neal, Alice Bradley
The gossips of Rivertown, with sketches in verse and prose. By Alice B. Neal.
Philadelphia: Hazard & Mitchell, 1850. 327p. NUC BL
[Gossips ...; or, Lessons of Charity, pp. 7-157, 6 short stories. Part 2, Sketches in prose and verse, incl. 10 poems & 7 short stories]

2449. HAVERGAL, Cecilia [Br. 19c]
ALT: Grant, Cecilia Havergal
Easter blessings. With Lily Oakley.
NY: E.P. Dutton, 188-? 12p. NUC

2450. -----Easter praise. With Lily Oakley.
NY: E.P. Dutton; L: E. Nister, n.d. 7, 12p. NUC OCLC

2451. -----From morn till eve.
L: Dean & son, 1892. BL

2452. -----Little singers on land and sea.
NY: Kaufman & Strauss, 188-? 8 l. NUC

2453. -----The master's smile and other poems.
L: Nisbet & co., 1889. 141p. BL

2454. -----Mizpah.
L: Ernest Nister; NY: E.P. Dutton, 1892. 6 unnumb. l. BL
[One poem signed Cecilia Havergal, one unsigned & one by Charlotte Murray]

2455. -----Serving the King. By Cecilia Havergal and others.
NY: T. Nelson & sons, 1888. 32p. NUC BL

2456. HAVERGAL, Frances (Ridley) [Br. 1836-1879] ALT: H., F.R.
Bells across the snow.
NY: E.P. Dutton & co., 1883. 16 l.
L: Castell bros., 1890. NUC BL
[Christmas poetry]

2457. -----Ben Brightboots, and other true stories, hymns and music.
L: Nisbet & Co., 1883. 145p. BL

2458. -----Birthday flowers.
L: Ernest Nister, 1898. BL

2459. -----Birthday hopes.
L: Ernest Nister, 1895. BL

2460. -----Blessings for all.
L: Marshall bros., 1892. BL

2461. -----Christmas sunshine with love and light for the new year.
Boston: H.H. Carter & Karrick, 1886. 18p. NUC

2462. -----Coming to Christ.
Philadelphia: Henry Altemus, 1897. 174p.
[Devotional exercises & hymns]

2463. -----Coming to the King. Hymns by F.R.H. & others.
1886. BL OCLC

2464. -----Compensation, and other devotional poems.
NY: Anson D.F. Randolph & co., 1881. 247p. NUC OCLC

2465. -----An Easter anthem.
L: Ernest Nister, 1895. NUC BL

2466. -----Echoes from the Word for the Christian year.
NY: A.D.F. Randolph & co.; Dutton, 1880. 70p. NUC BL OCLC

2467. -----Fern fronds. Texts and verses for morning and evening.
L: Marcus Ward & co., 1885. BL

2468. -----Footprints, and "living songs." Ed. C. Bullock.
L: Home Words Office, 1883. 90p. BL
[Hymns by FRH; and an essay, "Footprints of FRH" by E.M. Coombe]

2469. -----Forget me nots of promise, texts from scripture and verses.
L: M. Ward & co., 1895. 12 l. NUC BL

2470. -----Fulness of joy.
NY: E.P. Dutton; L: Groombridge & co., 1886. 30p. NUC BL

2471. -----Grasses. Texts and verses for morning and evening.
L: Marcus Ward & co., 1885. BL

2472. -----He is risen.
L: Ernest Nister, 1895. BL

2473. -----I am with thee.
L: Ernest Nister, 1895. BL

2474. -----In the service of the King: poems. With others.
NY: E.P. Dutton, 1888. 32p. NUC OCLC

2475. -----Kept for the Master's use.
Chicago: Donohue; L: J. Nisbet & co., 1879. 42p. Philadelphia: H. Altemus, 1879. 160p. NUC BL OCLC

2476. -----Life chords, comprising Zenith; Loyal responses; and other poems.
L: Nisbet, 1880. 300p. NUC OCLC

2477. -----Life echoes.
L: Nisbet, 1883. 286p. NUC BL

2478. -----Life mosaic; The ministry of song and Under the surface.
L: J. Nisbet, 1879. 315p. NUC

2479. -----Lilies and shamrocks. With Caroline W. Ashby.
L: J. Nisbet, 1883. 84p. NUC BL
[Letters and poems]

2480. -----Lilies from Havergal.
Buffalo, NY: Hayes Lithographing co., 18--? 30p. OCLC

2481. -----Loyal responses; or, Daily melodies for the King's minstrels.
NY: A.D.F. Randolph, 1879? L: J. Nisbet, 1880? 96p. NUC BL OCLC
[Hymns]

2482. -----Many happy returns.
L: Ernest Nister, 1898.

2483. -----The ministry of song.
2d ed. L: Christian Book soc., 1871. 177p. NY: D.C. Lent & co., 1872. 205p. NUC BL OCLC

2484. -----Mizpah.
L: Ernest Nister; NY: E.P. Dutton & co., 1897. 4 unnumb. l. BL

2485. -----Our work and our blessings; or, Under the surface.
NY & L: A.D.F. Randolph, 1874? 296p. NUC BL OCLC
[English ed. pub. as: "Under the surface."]

2486. -----Poems.
NY: E.P. Dutton & co., 1881. 455p. NUC OCLC
[Religious poetry]

2487. -----The poetical works of Frances Ridley Havergal.
NY: Fleming H. Revell; 1885. 855p. NY: E.P. Dutton & co., 1885. 352p. NUC OCLC

2488. -----Precious things.
L: M. Ward & co., 1895. 7 l. NUC
[Religious poetry]

2489. -----Promises.
L: Misch & co., n.d. 2p. NUC

2490. -----Red-letter days; a memorial and birthday book.
NY: A.D.F. Randolph & co., 1882. 320p. NUC BL

2491. -----Religious poems.
Chicago: n.p., 1884. NUC

2492. -----Rose petals. Texts and verses for morning and evening.
L: Marcus Ward, 1885. BL

2493. -----Seaweeds. Texts and verses for morning and evening.
L: Marcus Ward, 1885. BL

2494. -----Silver streams.
L: J.E. Hawkins, 1886. BL

2495. -----Songs of Christmas.
NY: E.P. Dutton, 1885. 16 l. NUC OCLC

2496. -----Songs of the Master's love.
NY: E.P. Dutton; L: J.E. Hawkins, 188-? 16 l. L: Drane, 1885. 32p. NUC BL

2497. -----The sowers.
NY: A.D.F. Randolph & co.; L: Ernest Nister, 188-? 20p. NUC BL
[Religious poetry]

2498. -----Sunbeams from the golden land.
Boston: H.H. Carter & Karrick, 1886. 18p. NUC BL
[Religious verse]

2499. -----Sunshine for life's pathway. Poems for a month by F.R. Havergal and others.
NY: E.P. Dutton, 1886. NUC BL

2500. HAVERGAL, Frances Ridley [Br. 1836-1879]
Swiss letters and Alpine poems. Ed. her sister, Jane Miriam (Havergal) Crane.
L: J. Nisbet & co., 1881. 356p. NY: A.D.F. Randolph & co., 1881. 298p. NUC BL OCLC

2501. -----Talitha Cumi, and other verses. With Caroline W. Ashby. Ed. her sister, Maria Vernon Graham Havergal.
L: Nisbet & co., 1878.

2502. -----Threefold praise and other pieces.
Toronto: Toronto Willard Tract Depository; L: Nisbet & co., 1888. 32p. BL OCLC

2503. -----Under his shadow; the last poems of F.R. Havergal.
L: J. Nisbet, 1879. 212p. NUC BL OCLC

2504. -----Wayside chimes for the months of the year.
L: Hand & Heart pub. office, 1880? 28p. NUC

2505. -----Without carefulness.
NY: A.D.F. Randolph, 18--? 7p. NUC

HAVERGAL, Maria Vernon Graham, ed. see HAVERGAL, Frances (Ridley)

2506. HAVILAND, Margaret Morris [Am. 1865?-1891]
Poems.
NY: Randolph, n.d. 35,42p. NUC

2507. HAWES, Elizabeth, Mrs. [Am. 19c]
The harp of Accushnet: poems, etc.
Boston: Otis, Broaders & co., 1838. 172p. NUC BL OCLC

2508. HAWKE, Hon. Annabelle Eliza Cassandra [Br. 1787-1818]
Babylon: and other poems.
L: William Miller, 1811. 144p. NUC BL OCLC

2509. HAWKEY, Charlotte, Mrs. [Br. 19c]
Neota.
Taunton: Priv. pr., 1871. 256p. BL
[Misc. pieces in verse with personal & family memoirs]

2510. -----The Shakespeare tapestry, woven in verse by C. Hawkey.
Edinburgh & L: W. Blackwood & sons, 1881. 209p. NUC

2511. HAWKINS, Ida Crowen [Am. 19c]
An evergreen wreath, for all sorts and conditions of men.
Brooklyn, NY: C.E. Ogilvie, 1891. 50p. NUC

2512. HAWKINS, Susannah [Br. 19c]
The poetical works of S.H.
Dumfries: n.p., 1829-61. 9v. BL OCLC

2513. HAWKSHAW, Ann, Mrs. [Br. 19c]
Dionysius the Areopagite: with other poems.
L: Jackson & Welford; Manchester: Simms & Dinham, 1842. 194p. NUC BL OCLC

2514. -----Poems for my children.
L: n.p., 1847. BL

2515. -----Sonnets on Anglo-Saxon history.
L: n.p., 1854. BL

2516. HAWORTH, Euphrasia Fanny [Br. 19c]
St. Sylvester's day and other poems.
L: Jeremiah How, 1847. 128p. NUC BL OCLC

2517. HAWTHORN, Margaret [Br. 19c]
Traditionary tales of Roslin Castle and history of M.H. with poems and songs of the glens.
Edinburgh: n.p., 1866. 85p. NUC

HAWTHORNE, EMILY, pseud. see CHARLES, Emily Thornton

2518. HAWTREY, Mrs. [Br. 19c]
Village songs.
L: n.p., 1876. NUC BL

2519. HAY, Emily [Br. 19c]
A wreath of wild flowers; or, Simple effusions of a soldier's daughter.
Eton: Pr. E.P. Williams, 1841. 99p. BL OCLC

HAY, Helen Selina (Sherridan) Blackwood, Countess of Gifford see DUFFERIN and CLANDEBOYE, Helen Selina (Sherridan) Blackwood, Baroness

2520. HAY, M. H., Mrs. [Br. 19c]
The rural enthusiast, and other poems.
L: Longman, Hurst, Rees & Orme, 1808. 168p. NUC BL OCLC

HAY, Rebekah Carmichael see CARMICHAEL, Rebecca

2521. HAYCRAFT, Margaret Scott (Macritchie) [Br. 19/20c] ALT: Macritchie, Margaret Scott
By the sea of Galilee, a poem.
L: Wells Gardner & co., 1882. BL

2522. -----"Crowned with promise," a poem.
L: Religious Tract Society, 1891. BL

2523. -----Drift leaves.
L: Nisbet & co., 1884. 125p. BL

2524. -----Guiding lights.
L: G. Routledge & sons, 1888. BL

2525. -----In quiet resting places.
L: G. Routledge & sons, 1890. BL
[Verses & texts]

2526. -----Songs of peace.
L: Nisbet & co., 1883. 112p. BL

2527. -----Waters of quietness: being daily messages for invalids.
L: J. Nisbet & co., 1881. 96p. BL

2528. -----Wayside chimes.
L: J. Nisbet & co., 1886. 143p. BL

2529. HAYDEN, Caroline A., Mrs. [Am. 19c]
Our country's martyr.
Boston: Dakin & Metcalf, 1865. 23p. NUC OCLC
[Poem on Abraham Lincoln]

2530. HAYDEN, Mabel [Am. 19c]
Cathedral pictures, and other poems.
Washington, DC: Rufus H. Darby, pr., 1889. 32p. NUC

2531. HAYDEN, Susan M. [Am. 19c]
How to cook a husband.
Minneapolis, MN: Pierce & Pierce, 1898. 15p. NUC
[Humorous poem]

2532. HAYES, Catherine E. (Simpson) [Can. 1852-1943] PSEUD: Markwell, Mary
Prairie pot-pourri. By Mary Markwell.
Winnipeg: Stovel, 1895. 186p. NUC
[Incl. poems; a novella: The light of other days; and a Christmas drama for children]

2533. HAYFORD, Alvira [Am. 1805-1883?]
Poems. Ed. her son, Otis Hayford.
Canton, ME: E.N. Carver, pr., 1884. 52p. NUC OCLC

HAYFORD, Otis, ed. see HAYFORD, Alvira

2534. HAYLEY, Harriet [Br. 19c]
Saint Bernard and other poems.
L: Hatchards, 1888. 83p. BL

2535. HAYNES, Caroline [Br. 19c]
The nation's prayer: a poem.
L: n.p., 1872. BL
[On the recovery of the Prince of Wales]

2536. HAYWARD, Amey [Br. 17c]
The female's legacy. Containing divine poems on several choice subjects.
L: n.p., 1699. BL

2537. HAYWARD, Jane Mary [Br. 1825-1894]
Bird notes. Ed. E. Hubbard.
L & NY: Longmans, Green & co., 1895. 181p. NUC BL OCLC
[Diary of a bird watcher; incl. poems]

2538. HAYWARD, Olive Belle (Hull) [Am. 19c]
The cross.
NY: International Art pub. co., 1891. 18p. NUC

2539. HAYWOOD, Annie Winsor [Br. 19c]
Shepherd's tartan, and other poems.
Kirkcaldy: J. & R. Burt; Cupar-Fife: A. Westwood, 1895. 144p. BL OCLC

2540. HAYWOOD, Eliza (Fowler) [Br. 1693-1756] ALT: Heywood, Eliza (Fowler)
Poems on several occasions.
L: D. Browne jr., & S. Chapman, 1725. BL OCLC
[2d ed. bound with the The British Recluse]

2541. HAZARD, Caroline [Am. 1856-1945]
Lenten sonnets.
Riverside, CA?: The Riverside press, 1889. 12 l. OCLC

2542. -----Mission verses.
Santa Barbara, CA: Priv. pr., 1889.
15 l. NUC OCLC

2543. -----Narragansett ballads with songs and lyrics.
Boston & NY: Houghton, Mifflin & co., 1894. 107p. NUC BL OCLC
[Poems based on King Philip's war. Also misc., & some on California.]

2544. -----Three valleys.
n.p.: n.p., 1899? 12p. NUC

2545. HAZARD, Elizabeth Robinson Gibson [Am. 1799-1882]
Autumn musings, and other poems.
Philadelphia: J.B. Lippincott & co., 1874. 128p. NUC OCLC

2546. HAZARD, Gertrude Minturn [Am. 19c]
Farewell.
Boston: Innes & Niles, 1866. 8p. NUC

2547. -----Poems. By Gertrude Minturn Hazard and Anna Peace Hazard.
Philadelphia: Collins, pr., 1873. 87p. NUC OCLC

2548. HAZELWOOD, Hetty [19c]
A garland gathered at morn; a collection of short poems.
Toronto: Hunter, Rose, 1871. 79p. NUC

2549. HEAD, Katherine, Miss [Br. 19c] ALT: H., K.
Sketches in prose and poetry.
L: Smith, Elder & co., 1837. 306p. BL
[30 prose pieces: short essays, descriptive sketches & stories, many relating to Ireland; rest is poetry, incl. lyric, acrostics, elegies, patriotic verse]

HEALD, Sarah Elizabeth Washburn, comp. see WASHBURN, Hannah B.

2550. HEALY, Monica [19c]
Legends of the saints; or, Stories of faith and love.
Dublin: n.p., 1869. BL

2551. HEARD, Josephine D. Henderson [Am. b. 1861]
Morning glories.
Philadelphia: n.p., 1890. 108p. NUC OCLC

2552. HEARN [Hearne BL], Mary Ann [Br. 1834-1909] ALT: Hearne, Mary Anne PSEUD: Farningham, Marianne
Lays and lyrics of the blessed life, consisting of Light from the cross, and other poems. By Marianne Farningham.
L: n.p., 1861. NUC BL OCLC

2553. -----Leaves from Elim.
L: n.p., 1873. BL

2554. -----Poems.
L: n.p., 1865. NUC BL OCLC

2555. -----Songs of sunshine.
L: Clarke & co., 1878. 370p. NUC

2556. -----The summer and autumn of life.
L: n.p., 1876. BL
[Prose & verse]

2557. HEARN, Marianne [Br. 19c]
Echoes from Darenth Vale: tales and truths in prose and verse.
L: Benjamin L. Green, 1858. 168p. BL
[Sacred lyrics, pp. 119-168. 2 long stories: The Unknown Way and "For My Savior," 4 other short religious stories]

HEARNE, Mary Ann see HEARN, Mary Anne

HEARTHSTONE, HETTY, pseud. see FOLLETT, Mary A., Mrs.

2558. HEATH, Clara B. (Sawyer) [Am. b. 1837]
Water lilies, and other poems.
Manchester, NH: Pr. J.B. Clarke, 1881. 224p. NUC OCLC

2559. HEATH, Georgiana L. [Am. 1844-1886]
Anniversary poem.
n.p.: n.p., 1877? NUC

2560. -----Assurance, and other poems.
Boston: D. Lothrop & co., 1886. 158p. OCLC

2561. HEATH, Mary Isaline [Am. 19c]
Thistle-down.
Philadelphia: Alfred J. Ferris, 1899. 31p. NUC OCLC

HEATH, ROSE, pseud. see MCFALL, Anna E. Mays-

2562. HEATON, Eliza Osborn (Putnam) [Am. b. 1816]
Thoughts by the way.
Poughkeepsie, NY: A.V. Haight, pr., 1891. 200p. OCLC
[Religious verse]

2563. HEBRON, Ellen Ellington [Am. 1839-1904]

Faith, or Earthly paradise; and other poems.
Chicago: Pub. for author by the W.T.P.A., 1890. 528p. NUC OCLC

2564. -----Songs from the South.
Baltimore, MD: Eugene R. Smith, c1874. 345p. NUC OCLC
[Misc. poetry, incl. Cornelia. A romance of the [Civil] War; poems in memory of brother]

HEDGE, Marianne see HEDGE, Mary Ann

2565. HEDGE, Mary Ann [Br. 1776-1841] ALT: H., M. A.; Hedge, Marianne
Juvenile poems: a sequel to "Original poems".
3d ed. L: Baldwin, Cradock & Joy; John Poole & son; Colchester: Swinborne & Walter, 1823. 97p. BL

2566. -----The solace of an invalid.
L: 1823; L: J. Hatchard & son, 1825. 253p. TXU
[Prose & verse, incl. devotions & religious poems; approx. half are original]

2567. HEDGELAND, Isabella (Fordyce) Kelly [Br. c1759?-1857] ALT: Kelly, Isabella
A collection of poems and fables.
L: W. Richardson, 1794. 72p. BL

2568. -----Poems and fables on several occasions.
Chelsea: n.p., 1807. 71p. BL

2569. HEMANS, Felicia Dorothea (Browne) [Br. 1793-1835] ALT: Browne, Felicia Dorothea PSEUD: Lady, A
The better land.
L: Hatchards, 1888. 12 unnumb. l. BL OCLC
[Gift book, a song with illustrations]

2570. -----The breaking waves dashed high.
Boston: Lee & Shepard; NY: C.T. Dillingham, 1880. 18 l. NUC OCLC

2571. -----Dartmoor; a poem.
L: Pr. J. Brettell, 1821. 22p. NUC BL

2572. -----The domestic affections, and other poems.
L: T. Cadell & W. Davies, 1812. 172p. NUC BL OCLC

2573. -----Dreams of heaven.
L: Ernest Nister; NY: E.P. Dutton & co., 1891. BL

2574. -----Early blossoms; a collection of poems written between eight and fifteen years of age; with a life of the authoress.
L: J. Allman, 1840. 146p. NUC BL OCLC

2575. -----The forest sanctuary, and other poems.
Edinburgh: W. Blackwood & sons, 1825. 262p. L: J. Murray, 1825. 205p. BL OCLC

2576. -----Hymns and scenes of life; and other poems.
Philadelphia: T.T. Ash, 1835. NUC

2577. -----The last autumn at a favorite residence with other poems: and recollections of Mrs. Hemans. By Mrs. [Rose D'Aguilar] Lawrence.
Liverpool: G. & J. Robinson, 1836. 419p. NUC

2578. -----The league of the Alps, The siege of Valencia, The vespers of Palermo, and other poems.
Boston: Hilliard, Gray, Little & Wilkins, 1826. 480p. NUC OCLC

2579. -----Modern Greece. A poem.
L: John Murray, 1817. 67p. NUC BL OCLC

2580. -----Moral and religious poems.
Edinburgh: W. Blackwood & sons, 1850. 262p. NUC OCLC

2581. -----National lyrics, and songs for music.
Dublin: William Curry jr. & co.; L: Simpkin & Marshall, 1834. 341p. NUC BL OCLC

2582. -----Poems.
L: T. Cadell & W. Davies; Liverpool: Pr. G.F. Harris, 1808. 111p. NUC BL OCLC

2583. -----Records of woman: with other poems.
Boston: Hilliard, Gray, Little & Wilkins, 1828. 253p. NY: Gilley, 1828. 324p. Edinburgh: W. Blackwood; L: T. Cadell, 1828. 320p. NUC BL OCLC
[First pub. in: The forest sanctuary; and other poems. Boston: Hilliard, Gray, Little & Wilkins, 1827. 231p.]

2584. -----The restoration of the works of art to Italy: a poem. By a lady.
Oxford: Pr. W. Baxter, 1816. 23p. NUC BL OCLC

2585. -----The sacred poems of Mrs. Hemans; and the Hebrew melodies of Lord Byron.
NY: Morris & Willis, 1844. 16p. NUC OCLC

2586. -----Scenes and hymns of life, with other religious poems.
L: T. Cadell; Edinburgh: William Blackwood, 1834. 247p. NUC BL OCLC

2587. -----The sceptic; a poem.
L: John Murray, 1820. 38p. NUC BL OCLC
[2d ed. pub. with Stanzas to the memory of the late King. L: J.Murray, 1821. 50p. BL]

2588. -----The siege of Valencia; a dramatic poem. The last Constantine: with other poems.
L: John Murray, 1823. 319p. NUC BL OCLC

2589. -----Songs and lyrics; Scenes and hymns of life, with other poems.
Edinburgh: n.p., 1840. 377p. NUC

2590. -----Songs of the affections, with other poems.
NY: D. Appleton & co., 1826? 128p. Edinburgh: Wm. Blackwood, 1830. 259p. NUC BL OCLC

2591. -----Tales and historic scenes; in verse.
L: J. Murray, 1819. 255p. NUC BL OCLC

2592. HEMENWAY, Abby Maria [Am. 1828-1890] PSEUD: Marie Josephine
The house of gold and the saint of Nazareth. A poetical life of St. Joseph.
Baltimore, MD: Kelly, Piet & co., 1873. 296p. OCLC

2593. -----The mystical rose; or, Mary of Nazareth, the lily of the house of David.
NY: D. Appleton & co., 1865. 290p. OCLC

2594. -----Rosa immaculata; or, The tower of ivory in the house of Anna and Joachim.
NY: P. O'Shea, 1867. 250p. OCLC

2595. HEMPSTEAD, Fay [Am. 1847-1934]
Poems.
Little Rock, AR: Allsopp & Paul, 1898. 307p. OCLC

2596. -----Random arrows.
Philadelphia: J.B. Lippincott & co., 1878. 132p. OCLC

2597. HENDERSON, Mrs. David [Br. 19c]
Highland flora, and other poems.
Edinburgh: D. Douglas, 1889. 108p. BL

2598. HENDERSON, Edith [Br. 19/20c]
ALT: Shields-Aslachsen, Edith Henderson
The democratic Marseillaise.
L: Davis & Mason, 1892. BL

2599. HENDERSON, Elizabeth
Poems.
NY & L: Hanower, 1878. 114p. NUC

2600. HENDERSON, Margaret [Br. 19c]
My garden, and other poems.
Edinburgh: D. Douglas, 1896. 107p. NUC BL

2601. HENDERSON, Mary Eastman, Mrs. [Am. 1818-1890]
Jenny Wade of Gettysburg. In verse.
Philadelphia: J.B. Lippincott & co., 1864. 33p. OCLC

2602. HENDERSON, Thulia Susannah [Br. 19c] ALT: Engall, Thulia Susannah (Henderson); H., T. S.
Olga; or, Russia in the tenth century: an historical poem. By T.S.H.
L: Hamilton, A. & co., 1855. 326p. NUC BL OCLC

HENDRIKS, Rose Ellen <u>see</u> TEMPLE, Rose Ellen (Hendriks)

2603. HENDRIX, Lily Elizabeth Graves [Am. b. 1868]
Fragments: a book of poems. By Lily E.G. Hendrix.
Mexico, MO: Baptist pub. house, 1894. 129p. NUC OCLC

2604. -----Fragments: poems.
St. Louis, MO: Commercial pr. co., 1885. 129p. OCLC

2605. HENNAH, Ann, Mrs. [Br. 19c]
Thirty-one Old Testament narratives, in verse.
Salisbury, Newcastle-on-Tyne: n.p., 1876. BL

2606. -----Twenty-seven New Testament narratives, in verse.
Salisbury, Newcastle-on-Tyne: n.p., 1876. BL

2607. HENNETT, Mrs. [Br. 19c]
Miscellaneous poems, on various subjects.
Spilsby: n.p., 1820. BL

HENRIETTA see NETHERCOTT, Henrietta

HENRIETTA see VALPY, Henrietta F.

2608. HENRY, E., Mrs. [Br. 19c]
Cherished memories of by-gone days.
Portobello: T. Adams, 1888. 168p. BL

2609. -----Poems.
Edinburgh: n.p., 1865. BL

HENRY, M.E. see RUFFIN, Margaret Ellen (Henry)

2610. HENRY, Sarepta Myrenda Irish, Mrs. [Am. 1839-1900]
The marble cross, and other poems.
Chicago: The Woman's Temperance Assn., 1886. 133p. NUC

2611. -----Victoria: with other poems.
Cincinnati, OH: Poe & Hitchcock, 1865. 186p. NUC OCLC
[A dramatic poem]

2612. HENSHAW, Sarah Edwards (Tyler) [Am. 1822-1894]
Rhymes and jingles.
Oakland, CA: Pr. for the family, 1892. 195p. NUC OCLC

2613. HENSLEY, Sophia Margaretta (Almon) [b. 1866]
Poems.
Windsor, NS: Pr. J.J. Anslow, 1889. 17p. NUC OCLC

2614. -----A woman's love letters.
NY: J.S. Tait & sons, 1895. 82 l. NUC

HENTY, Ernest G., co-author see STARKEY, E.A. (Henty)

2615. HENTZ, Caroline Lee (Whiting) [Am. 1800-1856]
Constance of Werdenberg; or, The heroes of Switzerland. A dramatic poem, written for the 'Georgia Citizen'.
n.p.: "Georgia Citizen," 1850. 12p. NUC

2616. -----Human and divine philosophy: a poem, written for the Erosophic society of the U. of Alabama.
Tuscaloosa, Al: Journal & Flag office, 1844. 16p. NUC

2617. -----A poem, read before the Whig Society of Hanover College.
Madison, MA: Pr. at Banner office, 1838. 8p. NUC

2618. HERBERT, Jane Emily [Br. d. 1886?]
The bride of Imael; or, Irish love and Saxon beauty, a poem of the times of Richard the Second.
Dublin: William Curry, jr., 1847. 255p. NUC BL

2619. -----Ione's dream and other poems by Jane Emily Herbert.
n.p.: William Pickering, pr., 1853. NUC BL

2620. -----Poetical recollections of Irish history.
Dublin: n.p., 1842. 208p. NUC BL

HERBERT, John Maurice, ed. see HERBERT, Mary Anne

2621. HERBERT, Mary Anne [Br. 19c]
Poems by the late Mary Anne Herbert.
Ed. John Maurice Herbert.
L: Harrison & son, 1877. NUC

HERBERT, Mary E., co-author see HERBERT, Sarah

HERBERT, Mary (Sidney), Countess of Pembroke see PEMBROKE, Mary (Sidney) Herbert, Countess of

2622. HERBERT, Sarah [1824-1844]
The Aeolian harp; or, Miscellaneous poems. By Sarah and Mary E. Herbert.
Halifax, Nova Scotia; Cambridge, MA: E.G. Fuller & co., 1857. 237p. NUC BL OCLC

2623. HERNAMAN, Claudia Frances (Ibotson)
The crown of life. Verses for holy seasons.
L: Griffith & co., 1886. 260p. BL

2624. HERON, Mary [Br. 18/19c]
The Mandan chief. A tale in verse.
L: n.p., 1845? BL

2625. -----Miscellaneous. Poems by Mary Heron.
Newcastle: Pr. for the author, 1786. 88p. NUC BL

2626. -----Odes on various occasions.
Newcastle: n.p., 1792. BL

2627. -----Sketches of poetry.
Newcastle: n.p., 1786. BL

2628. HERRICK, Stella May [Am. 19/20c]
Thoughtful hours; a book of poems.
Cincinnati, OH: The Literary Shop, 1899. 164p. NUC OCLC

2629. HERRITT, Sarah D. (Hall) [Am. b. 1815]
A keepsake: dedicated to my friends.
Cincinnati, OH: Elm Street pr. co., 1876. 158p. NUC OCLC
[Missionary life; incl. poems]

2630. HERSCHELL, Helen S., Mrs. [Br. 19c]
"Far above rubies." Memoirs of H.S.H. by her daughter. Ed. R.H. Herschell.
L: n.p., 1854. BL
[Incl. The bystander, a poem, by Mrs. Herschell]

HERSCHELL, R.H., ed. see HERSCHELL, Helen S., Mrs.

2631. HERVEY, Eleanora Louisa (Montagu), Mrs. Thomas Kibble Hervey [Br. 1811-1903] ALT: M., E.; Montagu, Eleanora
The band of the sea-kings, a legend of Kingley-Vale, with other poems.
Chichester: William Mason & son; L: Longman, Rees, Orme, Brown, Green & Longman, 1833. 79p. NUC BL

2632. -----Edith of Graystock: a poem. By E.M.
L: Henry Lindsell, 1833. 100p. BL OCLC

HERVEY, Baron John, co-author see MONTAGUE, Mary Seymour

2633. HERVEY, Rosamond [Br. 19c]
Duke Ernest, a tragedy, and other poems.
L: Macmillan & co., 1866. NUC BL
[5 acts]

HERVEY, Mrs. Thomas Kibble see HERVEY, Eleanora Louisa (Montagu)

2634. HEWITT, E. C., Mrs. [Br. 19c]
Meditations on some of the names and covenant characters of Christ. In eighteen poems.
L: n.p., 1830. BL

2635. HEWITT, Mary Elizabeth (Moore) [Am. b. 1807] ALT: Stebbins, Mary Elizabeth (Moore) Hewitt
Poems: sacred, passionate, and legendary.
NY: Lamport, Blakeman & Law, 1854. 196p. NUC BL OCLC

2636. -----The songs of our land, and other poems.
Boston: W.D. Ticknor & co., 1846. 156p. NUC BL OCLC

2637. HEWLETT, Elizabeth, Mrs. William Hewlett [Br. 19c]
The valley of Elah; or, Faith triumphant. A poem by Mrs. William Hewlett.
Oxford: Pr. W. Baxter, 1822. 41p. NUC BL

HEWLETT, Mrs. William see HEWLETT, Elizabeth

2638. HEXT, Julia A. [Am. 19c]
Smiles and tears. Fugitive pieces.
Charleston, SC: Walker & James, 1853. 112p. NUC OCLC
[Some poems written as a girl; incl. occasional & memorial verse]

2639. HEY, Rebecca, Mrs. William Hey [Br. 19c]
Holy places, and other poems.
L: Hatchard, 1859. 163p. NUC BL

2640. -----The moral of flowers.
L: Rees, Orme, Brown, Green, Longman & J. Hatchard; Leeds: M. Robinson, 1833. 179p. NUC BL

2641. -----Recollections of the lakes, and other poems.
L: Tilt & Bogue, 1841. 284p. NUC

2642. -----The spirit of the woods.
L: Longman, Rees, Orme, Brown, Green & Longman, 1837. 306p. NUC BL
[Instructional work on English trees and plants.]

HEY, Mrs. William see HEY, Rebecca

HEYWOOD, Eliza see HAYWOOD, Eliza (Fowler)

2643. HEYWOOD, Eliza Fowler [Br. 19c]
Poems and translations.
Cheltenham: n.p., 1852. NUC

HEYWOOD, Eliza, of Cheltenham see HEYWOOD, Eliza

2644. HEYWOOD, Eliza of Cheltenham [Br. 19c]
Ermangarde, a tale of the twelfth century, Royalist lyrics and other poems.
Cheltenham: n.p., 1837. NUC BL

2645. HIBBARD, Agnes Marilla [Am. 19c]
Dixville notch.
Colebrook, NH: Highland Home, 1899. 27p. NUC OCLC
[Description & history of the area in New Hampshire; legend of an Indian chief.]

HIBBARD, Grace, co-author <u>see</u> COOLBRITH, Ina Donna

2646. HIBBARD, Grace (Porter) [Am. 19/20c] ALT: Hibbard, Helen Grace (Porter)
A collection of wild flowers from California pressed and arranged by Miss E.C. Alexander, with appropriate sonnets specially written by Miss Ina D. Coolbrith and Grace Hibbard of California.
4th ed. San Francisco & NY: Dodge bk. & stationery co., 1898. NUC OCLC

2647. -----Del Monte oaks.
n.p.: n.p., 18--? 12p. NUC OCLC

2648. -----From her window.
San Francisco: n.p., n.d. 12p. NUC OCLC

2649. -----Neath Monterey pines.
n.p.: n.p., n.d. 12p. NUC

2650. -----Wild poppies. Poems.
Buffalo, NY: C.W. Moulton, 1893. 106p. NUC OCLC

HIBBARD, Helen Grace (Porter) <u>see</u> HIBBARD, Grace (Porter)

2651. HICKEY, Emily Henrietta [Br. 1845-1924]
Ancilla Domini: thoughts in verse on the life of the Blessed Virgin.
L: The author, 1848. 38p. BL

2652. -----Michael Villiers, idealist, and other poems.
L: Smith & Elder, 1891. 192p. NUC BL OCLC

2653. -----Poems.
L: E. Mathews, 1896. 55p. NUC BL OCLC

2654. -----A sculptor and other poems.
L: Kegan Paul, Trench & co., 1881. 176p. NUC BL OCLC

2655. -----Verse tales, lyrics and translations.
Liverpool: W. & J. Arnold; L: E. Mathews, 1889. 120p. NUC BL OCLC

2656. HICKOK, Eliza M. [Am. 19c]
Star gleams. Poems.
Boston: George H. Ellis, 1887. 126p. NUC OCLC

2657. HICKS, Emma [Br. 19c]
Church sonnets.
Dorchester: n.p., 1850? BL

2658. HICKS, Emma Endicott [Am. 19c]
ALT: H., E.E.
Verses, by E.E.H.
Cambridge, MA: Riverside press, 1895. 99p. NUC OCLC

2659. HICKS, Maude (Robertson) [Br. 19c]
Flowers from oversea and other verse.
Rugby: G.E. Over, 1893. 69p. NUC BL

HIGGINS, Elsie, co-author <u>see</u> BROWN, Annie Johnson-

2660. HIGGINSON, Ella Rhoads [Am. 1862-1940]
A bunch of western clover.
New Whatcom, WA: Edson & Irish, 1894. 26p. NUC OCLC

2661. -----The snow pearls; a poem.
Seattle, WA: Lowman & Hanford stationery & pr. co., 1897. 10 l. NUC OCLC
[On Puget Sound]

2662. -----When the birds go north again.
NY: The Macmillan co., 1898. 175p. NUC
[Lyrics & sonnets]

2663. HIGGINSON, Mary Potter (Thacher), Mrs. Thomas Wentworth Higginson [Am. 1844-1941]
Such as they are. Poems. With Thomas Wentworth Higginson.
Boston: Roberts bros., 1893. 74p. OCLC

HIGGINSON, T.W., ed. <u>see</u> DICKINSON, Emily

HIGGINSON, Thomas Wentworth, co-author <u>see</u> HIGGINSON, Mary Potter (Thacher)

HIGGINSON, Mrs. Thomas Wentworth <u>see</u> HIGGINSON, Mary Potter (Thacher)

2664. HILDEBRAND, Anna Louisa [Br. b. 1842]
Lays from the land of the Gael.
Belfast: M'Caw, Stevenson & Orr, 1879. 150p. NUC BL OCLC
[Misc. poetry, sonnets & sacred poems.]

2665. -----Western lyrics.
Dublin: McGlashan & Gill, 1872. 190p. NUC BL OCLC

2666. HILES, Mary [Br. 19c]
The deluge, and other poems.

L & Kidderminster: Thomas Pennell, 1828. 146p. BL

2667. HILL, Agnes (Leonard) Scanland [Am. 1842-1917] PSEUD: Myrtle, Molly
Myrtle blossoms. Pub. as: Molly Myrtle.
Chicago: For the authoress by J.C.W. Bailey, 1863. 304p. NUC OCLC

2668. HILL, Elisabeth Lord (Chase) [Am. 1825-1887]
Gleanings: girlhood and womanhood. Printed for private distribution.
Concord, NH: Republican press assoc., 1887. 76p. NUC OCLC
[Memorial volume of poetry & prose sketches]

2669. HILL, Elizabeth [Am. 19c]
My childhood's home and other poems.
Shelbyville, IL: Pr. for the author at Our Best Words office, 1889. 123p. NUC OCLC

2670. HILL, Elizabeth S., Mrs. [Am. 19c]
Elm leaves.
New Haven, CT?: Morehouse, & Taylor, pr., 1892, 1893. 10 l. NUC

2671. HILL, Fidelia S.T. [19c]
Poems. And recollections of the past.
Sydney: Pr. T. Trood, 1840. 66p. NUC BL
["Recollections" are impressions of Australia]

2672. HILL, Isabel [Br. 19c]
Holiday dreams: or, Light reading, in poetry and prose.
L: T. Cadell, 1829. 184p. NUC BL
[Misc. poetry & personal recollections in prose.]

HILL, Isabel <u>see</u> LANDON, Letitia Elizabeth

2673. HILL, Phillipina (Burton) [Br. 18c] ALT: Burton, Phillipina PSEUD: Lady, A
Miscellaneous poems, written by a lady, being her first attempt.
L: Pr. for the author by S. Chandler, 1768. 3v. BL
[Vols. 2 & 3 in prose. Ascribed also to Elisabeth Rolt]

2674. -----Portraits, characters, pursuits and amusements of the present fashionable world, interspersed with poetic flights of fancy.
L: n.p., 1785? 84p. BL
[Satiric poems on society; Flights of fancy are tributes to public figures, Duchess of Devonshire, David Garrick; one poem in praise of country life]

2675. HILL, Mrs. Robert [Br. 18/19c]
A poem, sacred to Freedom: and a poem entitled Beneficence.
Dublin?: n.p., 1800? BL

2676. HILL, Rosa F. [Br. 19c] ALT: H., R. F.
The Lady Ina, and other poems. By R.F.H.
L: Virtue bros. & co., 1865. 236p. BL

2677. HILL, Susie E. [Am. 19/20c]
Heather bells. Poems.
Waterbury, CT: n.p., 1899. 28p. NUC OCLC

HILL-LOWE, Thomas, ed. <u>see</u> LOWE, Helen

2678. HILLS, Caroline Parker [Am. 19c]
A Nantucket hermitage and other poems.
Washington, DC: B.S. Adams, 1895. 64p. NUC OCLC

2679. HILLS, Elise [Br. 19c]
Kebir, and other poems.
Portsmouth: n.p., 1835. BL

2680. HILLS, Emily Malvina [19/20c]
The pictured rocks of Lake Superior. Songs and legends.
Rome: n.p., 1894. 250p. NUC

HIME, Mrs. Maurice Charles <u>see</u> HIME, Rebecca Helena

2681. HIME, Rebecca Helena, Mrs. Maurice Charles Hime [Br. 19/20c]
Brian Boru and the Battle of Clontarf, a ballad.
L: Simpkin, Marshall, 1889. 46p. NUC BL OCLC

2682. HINCKS, Elizabeth [Br. 17c]
The poor widow's mite cast into the Lord's treasury, wherein are contained some reasons in the justification of the meetings of ... Quakers.
L?: n.p., 1671. 47p. NUC BL OCLC

2683. HINDMARSH, Isabella [Br. 1798?-1823]
The cave of Hoonga, a Tongaen tradition, in two cantos, and other poems.

Alnwick: Pr. for the author by W. Davison, 1818. 254p. NUC BL OCLC

2684. HINE, Maude Egerton [Br. 19c]
Poems.
L: Chiswick press, priv. pr., 1885. 84p. NUC BL OCLC

2685. HINES, Nelle (Womack) [Am. 19c]
ALT: Womack, Nelle
Waifs from wild meadows. By Nelle Womack.
Atlanta, GA: Foote & Davies, pr., 1898. 99p. NUC OCLC

HINKSON, Mrs. Henry Albert see HINKSON, Katherine (Tynan)

2686. HINKSON, Katherine (Tynan), Mrs. Henry Albert Hinkson [Br. 1861-1931] ALT: Tynan, Katharine
Ballads and lyrics. By Katharine Tynan.
L: K. Paul, Trench, Trubner & co., 1891. 153p. NUC BL OCLC

2687. -----Cuckoo songs.
L: E. Mathews & J. Lane; Boston: Copelan & Day, 1894. 105p. NUC BL OCLC

2688. -----Louise de la Valliere and other poems.
L: Kegan Paul, Trench & co., 1885. 102p. NUC BL OCLC

2689. -----A lover's breast-knot.
L: E. Mathews, 1896. 49p. NUC BL OCLC

2690. -----Shamrocks.
L: K. Paul, Trench & co., 1887. 197p. NUC BL OCLC

2691. -----The wind in the trees: a book of country verse.
L: Grant Richards, 1898. 104p. NUC BL OCLC

2692. HINSDALE, Laura Fenling [Am. 19c]
Legends and lyrics of the Gulf Coast.
Biloxi, MS: Herald press, 1896. 40p. NUC OCLC
[Gulf of Mexico between New Orleans & Mobile]

2693. HINXMAN, Emmeline [Br. 19c]
Poems.
L: Longman, 1856. 183p. NUC BL OCLC

2694. HIPPISLEY, Ellen (Fitzgerald) [Br. 18/19c]
Hours of idleness, by Gustavus Alexander Butler Hippisley. Printed for private circulation.
L & Beccles: Pr. W. Clowes & sons, c1840. 57p. NUC BL
[In verse; incl. poems by the mother of the author]

HIPPISLEY, Gustavus Alexander Butler, co-author see HIPPISLEY, Ellen (Fitzgerald)

2695. HIRST, Edith H. [Br. 19c]
Round the campfire and other Australian poems.
L: Digby, Long & co., 1892. 70p. BL

2696. HITCHENER, Elizabeth [Br. 19c]
The fire-side bagatelle, containing enigmas on the chief towns of England and Wales.
L: Barlow & Bishop, 1818. 37p. NUC OCLC

2697. -----The weald of Sussex, a poem.
L: Black, Young & Young, 1822. 149p. NUC

2698. HOARD, Margarette A. [Am. 19c]
Ten sonnets and other verses.
NY: Anson D.F. Randolph & co., 1894. 37p. NUC OCLC

2699. HOARE, Sarah [Br. 1777-1856 NUC; 1767-1855 OCLC] PSEUD: Friend to Youth, A
A poem on the pleasures and advantages of botanical pursuits ... and other poems. By a friend to youth [S. Hoare].
Bristol: Pr. Philip Rose, 1825? 134p. NUC BL OCLC

2700. -----Poems on conchology and botany.
L: Simpkin, 1831. 106p. NUC BL OCLC

HOBART-HAMPDEN, Hon. Mrs. Charles see HOBART-HAMPDEN, Lucy Pauline (Wright)

2701. HOBART-HAMPDEN, Lucy Pauline (Wright), Hon. Mrs. Charles Hobart-Hampden [Br. 19/20c] ALT: Wright, Lucy Pauline
The changed cross, and other helpful poems. By the Honorable Mrs. Charles Hobart-Hampden.
L: W.W. Gardner, 1855? 24p. BL OCLC
[New ed. with added poems, 1868]

2702. -----The star and the cloud.
L: William Wells Gardner, 1876. BL
[Religious allegory: "The star" in verse, and "The cloud" in prose]

HOBBS, Mrs. Josiah Howard see HOBBS, Mary E. (Erwin)

2703. HOBBS, Mary E. (Erwin), Mrs. Josiah Howard Hobbs [Am. 19c]
The poems of Mrs. Mary E. Erwin Hobbs; [comp.] her surviving husband, Josiah Howard Hobbs.
Chicago: American publishers' assn., 1891. 201p. NUC OCLC

2704. HOBLYN, Anna Margaret [Br. 19c]
God's omnipresence; the Gospel plan of salvation; and other poems.
L: n.p., 1870. BL

2705. -----Time's "changes." Pilgrims' poems and hymns.
L: n.p., 1863. BL

2706. HOBLYN, Maria Theresa [Br. 19c] PSEUD: Theta
The fisherman's daughter, and Dreams of the past by Theta.
L: William Macintosh, 1869. 31p. BL
[2 narratives in verse]

2707. HOBSON, Martha Sophia (Cooke), Mrs. William Hobson [Br. 19c]
Songs of my leisure hours.
Pr. at the "Guardian" steam-prtg. offices, 1861. 219p. NUC BL OCLC

HOBSON, Mrs. William see HOBSON, Martha Sophia (Cooke)

2708. HODGES, Elizabeth [Br. 19c]
A Christmas carol for mdcccxlvij.
Newcastle,: M.A. Richardson, 1847. BL

2709. -----Soothing thoughts for sorrowing hours.
L: n.p., 1849. BL

2710. HODGES, Laura Jane, Mrs. [Am. 19c]
Panorama of the heart; or, The four prayers of life.
Worcester, MA: Pr. Chas. Hamilton, Palladium office, 1866. 12p. NUC OCLC

HODSON, Margaret (Holford) see HOLFORD, Margaret

2711. HOFFMAN, Martha Lavinia [Am. 1865-1900?]
Berries and blossoms.
Oakland, CA: Pacific press pub. co., 1888. 19p. NUC OCLC

2712. HOFFMAN, Minta Barnette [Am. 19c]
Memorial songs.
St. Louis, MO: Western pr. co., 1877. 95p. NUC OCLC

2713. HOFLAND, Barbara (Wreaks) Hoole [Br. 1770-1844] ALT: Hoole, Barbara
Poems. By Barbara Hoole.
Sheffield: Pr. J. Montgomery, sold by Vernor & Hood, 1805. 256p. NUC BL OCLC

2714. -----A season at Harrogate; in a series of poetical epistles, from Benjamin Blunderhead, esquire, to his mother, in Derbyshire: ... .
Knaresbrough: Pr. G. Wilson, sold by R. Wilson, 1812. 103p. NUC BL OCLC
[Satire]

2715. HOGBEN, Dorothea (Scott) Gotherson [Br. 1611-1680] ALT: Gotherson, Dorothea Scott; Scott, Dorothea
To all that are unregenerated: a call to repentance from dead works ... .
L: n.p., 1661. 125p. NUC OCLC
[Incl. 11 poems of 10-50 lines with religious themes]

2716. HOLAHAN, Martha Eileen [Am. b. 1863]
Nondescript; or, The passionate recluse.
Philadelphia: Press of J.B. Lippincott co., 1889. 106p. NUC OCLC
[Narrative of unrequited love; 7 pts.]

2717. HOLBROOK, Jennie E., Mrs. [Am. 19c]
Ruth Haight, and other poems.
Milwaukee, WI: Cramer, Aikens & Cramer, pr., 1878. 146p. NUC OCLC

2718. HOLCOMBE, Helen J. [Am. 19c]
A rose of yesterday.
NY: n.p., 1894. 110p. NUC

2719. HOLDEN, Frances Gillam [19c]
Her father's darling, and other child pictures.
Sydney: Turner & Henderson, 1887. 96p. NUC

2720. HOLDER, Phebe A. [Am. 19c]
Voices from Lakeview.
Everett, MA: Press of Frank D. Woodbury, 1897. 71p. NUC OCLC

HOLDSWORTH, Annie E. see HAMILTON, Annie E. (Holdsworth) Lee-

2721. HOLFORD, Margaret, Mrs. [Br. 18c]
Gresford Vale, and other poems.
L: Hookham & Carpenter, 1798. 44p. BL

2722. HOLFORD, Margaret [Br. 1778-1852] ALT: H., M.; Hodson, Margaret Holford

Margaret of Anjou: a poem in ten cantos. By Miss Holford.
L: J. Murray, 1816. 474p.
Philadelphia: M. Carey, 1816. 292p.
NUC BL OCLC

2723. -----The past, etc. By Miss Holford.
L: Longman, Hurst, Rees, Orme & Browne; Bath: J. Upham, 1819. 46p.
NUC BL

2724. -----Poems. By Miss Holford.
L: Longman, Hurst, Rees, Orme & Browne, 1811. 117p. NUC BL OCLC

2725. -----Wallace; or, The fight of Falkirk; a metrical romance. By M.H.
L: T. Cadell & W. Davies, 1809. 248p.
NUC BL

2726. HOLL, Louisa Margaret [Br. 19c]
The Indian captive, and other poems.
L: Longman, Orme, Brown & co.; Birmingham: J.C. Barlow, 1839. 103p.
NUC BL

HOLLAND, J., ed. <u>see</u> HUTTON, Mary

HOLLAND, Josiah Gilbert, ed. <u>see</u> SHEPARD, Dolly Ellen (Ring)

2727. HOLLAND, Maud C., Mrs. [Br. 19c]
Verses.
L: E. Arnold, 1898. 66p. BL

2728. HOLLEY, Marietta [Am. 1836-1926] PSEUD: Josiah Allen's wife
The lament of the Mormon wife. A poem.
Hartford, CN: Am. pub. co., 1880. 13 or 16 l. NUC OCLC

2729. -----Poems. By "Josiah Allen's wife."
NY: Funk & Wagnalls, 1887. 216p. NUC OCLC

2730. HOLLINS, Dorothea [Br. 19c]
PSEUD: North, Theophila
The veiled figure and other poems.
L, Edinburgh & Oxford: Williams & Norgate, 1895. 87p. NUC OCLC
[Pub. anon.]

2731. HOLLOWAY, Elvira Haskins [Am. 19c]
Gleanings from the Golden State.
San Francisco: n.p., 1893. 48p. NUC

2732. HOLMES, Alice A. [Am. b. 1821]
Arcadian leaves.
NY: Pudney & Russell, pr., 1858. 122p. NUC OCLC
[Misc. poetry & 2 short stories]

2733. -----Lost vision.
NY: The De Vinne press, 1888. 95p.
NUC OCLC
[On her blindness]

2734. -----Poems.
NY: J.F. Trow, 1849. 53p. NUC OCLC

2735. -----Stray leaves.
NY: C.S. Westcott & co., pr., 1868. 60p. NUC BL OCLC

2736. HOLMES, Ann [Br. 18/19c]
An epic poem on Adam and Eve. With poetry on two ladies in disguise.
Bedale: n.p., 1800. BL

2737. HOLMES, Elizabeth (Emra), Mrs. Marcus H. Holmes [Br. 1804-1843]
A sister's record, or memoir of Mrs. Marcus H. Holmes.
L: Hamilton, Adams & co., 1844. 176p.
BL
[Incl. letters, poems, one short story]

2738. HOLMES, Georgiana (Klingle) [Am. 19c] PSEUD: Klingle, George
Bethlehem to Jerusalem; a new poem.
By George Klingle.
NY: F.A. Stokes & bro., 1888. NUC
[Travel: Palestine; in verse]

2739. -----In the name of the King.
By George Klingle.
NY: F.A. Stokes & bro., 1888. 119p.
NUC OCLC

2740. -----Laus Deo. By George Klingle.
NY: Frederick A. Stokes co., 1893. 86p. NUC

2741. -----Make thy way mine, and other poems. By George Klingle.
NY: White, Stokes, & Allen, 1886. 103p. NUC OCLC

2742. -----Perdita; a book of verses.
By George Klingle.
Buffalo, NY: C.W. Moulton, 1894. 99p.
NUC OCLC

2743. HOLMES, Izette S., Mrs. [Am. 19c]
A collection of miscellaneous poems.
Greenland, NH: Ernest Holmes, pr., 1879. 72p. NUC OCLC

2744. HOLMES, Kate Raworth [Am. 19c]
Pictures from nature and life, poems.
Chicago: A.C. McClurg & co., 1893. 105p. NUC

HOLMES, Mrs. Marcus H. see HOLMES, Elizabeth (Emra)

2745. HOLT, Ellen Frances [Br. 19c]
In memoriam. (In memory of E.F. Holt ... lines written by herself).
n.p.: Priv. pr., 1871. 32p. BL

2746. HOLT, Jane Wiseman [Br. 18c]
A fairy tale inscrib'd, to the Honourable Mrs. W____ with other poems.
L: R. Burleigh, 1717. 30p. NUC BL OCLC

2747. HOLWORTHY, Sophia Matilda [Br. 19c]
Scenes and thoughts from history, with other poems.
L: A. Hall & co., 1856. 152p. BL

2748. HOLYOKE, Maria Ballard [Am. b. 1833]
Violets, early and late. Poems.
Chicago: Mills & Spining, 1886. 211p. NUC OCLC

HOME, Anne see HUNTER, Anne (Home)

HOME, CECIL, pseud. see WEBSTER, Julia Augusta (Davies)

HOME, Hon. James Archibald, ed. see STUART, Lady Louisa

2749. HOMES, Mary Sophie (Shaw) Rogers [Am. b. 1830?] PSEUD: Mayfield, Millie
Progression; or, The South defended. By Millie Mayfield.
Cincinnati, OH: Applegate & co., 1860. 226p. NUC
[Civil War poems]

2750. -----A wreath of rhymes. By Millie Mayfield.
Philadelphia: J.B. Lippincott & co., 1869. 386p. NUC OCLC

HOMESPUN, PRUDENTIA, MRS., pseud. see WEST, Jane, Mrs.

2751. HONEYWOOD, Patty [Br. 19c]
Poems.
L: Kegan Paul, Trench & co., 1883. 99p. NUC BL

2752. HOOBLER, Idella Clarence [Am. 19c]
Poems of the New England coast and others.
Worcester, MA: The author, 1897. 62p. NUC OCLC
[Also pub. as: Souvenir poems of the New England coast and others]

2753. HOOD, Catherine [Br. 19c]
Remonstrance; with other poems.
L: Pr. for the author, 1801. 112p. BL OCLC

2754. HOOD, Isabel [Br. 19c]
Memoirs and manuscripts of Isabel Hood. Comp. Rev. John MacDonald.
2d ed. Edinburgh: n.p., 1844. BL

HOOK, Walter Farquhar, ed. see ALEXANDER, Cecil Frances (Humphreys)

HOOLE, Barbara see HOFLAND, Barbara (Wreaks) Hoole

HOOPER, Edward William, comp. see HOOPER, Ellen H. (Sturgis)

2755. HOOPER, Ellen H. (Sturgis) [Am. 1812?-1848]
Poems.
n.p.: n.p., 184-? NUC

2756. -----Poems.
Boston?: n.p., 1872? 119 l. NUC
[Coll. & priv. pr. author's son, Edward William Hooper]

2757. -----Portfolio of poems.
Boston?: n.p., 187-? 105 l. NUC OCLC
[Coll. & priv. pr. her son, Edward William Hooper.]

2758. HOOPER, Lucy [Am. 1816-1841]
The complete poetical works of the late Miss Lucy Hooper.
NY: Fanshaw, 1848. 402p. NUC OCLC

2759. -----Poetical remains of the late Lucy Hooper, collected and arranged by John Keese.
NY: S. Colman, 1842. NUC BL OCLC

2760. HOOPER, Lucy Hamilton (Jones) [Am. 1835-1893]
Poems. By Lucy Hamilton Hooper.
Philadelphia: J.B. Lippincott & co., 1871. 196p. NUC

2761. -----Poems: with translations from the German of Geibel and others.
Philadelphia: F. Leypoldt, 1864. 96p. NUC OCLC
[33p. of translations; 48 original miscellaneous poems.]

2762. HOPE, Anne Fulton [Br. 1809-1887]
Flowers from an Indian garden.
Dusseldorf: Breidenbach & co., 187-? 1v. NUC

HOPKINS, E.A.W., Mrs. see HOPKINS, Eliza Ann Woodruff, Mrs.

2763. HOPKINS, Eliza Ann Woodruff, Mrs. [Am. 19c] ALT: Hopkins, E. A. W., Mrs.
Little shells from many shores. By Mrs. E.A.W. Hopkins.
San Francisco: Bacon & co., pr., 1872. 300p. NUC OCLC

HOPKINS, Ellice see HOPKINS, Jane Ellice

2764. HOPKINS, Jane Ellice [Br. 1836-1904] ALT: Hopkins, Ellice
Autumn swallows, a book of lyrics.
L: Macmillan, 1883. 283p. NUC BL

2765. HOPKINS, Louisa Parsons (Stone) [Am. 1834-1895]
Breath of the field and shore.
Boston: Lee & Shepard, 1881. 145p. NUC OCLC

2766. -----Easter carols.
Boston: Lee & Shepard, 1888. 32p. NUC

2767. -----Motherhood. A poem.
Boston: Lee & Shepard; NY: C.T. Dillingham, 1881. 44p. OCLC

2768. -----Persephone, an Easter poem.
Boston: n.p., 1888? 15 l. NUC OCLC

HOPKINS, Salem Armstrong see HOPKINS, Saleni (Armstrong), M.D.

2769. HOPKINS, Saleni (Armstrong), M.D. [Am. b. 1855] ALT: Hopkins, Salem Armstrong
Fruit of suffering.
Buffalo, NY: The Peter Paul book co., 1896. 225p. NUC BL OCLC

2770. -----Within the purdah; also, In the Zenana homes of Indian princes, and Heroes and heroines of Zion; being the personal observations of a medical missionary in India.
NY: Eaton & Mains; Cincinnati, OH: Curts & Jennings, 1898. 248p. NUC BL OCLC
[Incl. poems]

2771. HOPKINS, Vira M. Darling [Am. 19c]
Sunny side sketches for young and old.
Elkhart, IN: Mennonite pub. co., 1887. 143p. NUC OCLC
[Poems & short stories]

HOPPER, Nora see CHESSON, Nora Hopper

HOPPUS, Mary A.M. see MARKS, Mary A.M. (Hoppus)

2772. HOPWOOD, D. Caroline (Skene) [Br. 18/19c]
An account of the life and religious experiences of D. Caroline Hopwood, of Leeds, deceased ... To which is added, a collection of pieces in prose and poetry, on various subjects, written by the same author.
Leeds: E. Baines, 1801. 64p. NUC BL

2773. HORN, Kate [Am. 19c]
"Woman's rights," a right good ballad "rightly" illustrating "woman's rights."
Boston: G.P. Reed, 1853. 4p. NUC
[Music & poetry]

2774. HORN, Louise McCloy [Am. 19c]
Songs of the Lakes and other poems.
Cincinnati, OH: Editor pub. co., 1899. 85p. NUC OCLC

HORNBLOWER, Mrs. Francis see HORNBLOWER, Jane Elizabeth (Roscoe)

HORNBLOWER, Jane Elizabeth (Roscoe) see JEVONS, Mary Anne (Roscoe)

2775. HORNBLOWER, Jane Elizabeth (Roscoe), Mrs. Francis Hornblower [Br. 1797-1853] ALT: Roscoe, Jane Elizabeth
Poems.
L: Simpkin, Marshall, & co.; Liverpool: D. Marples, 1843. 216p. NUC BL OCLC

2776. -----Poems, by one of the authors of "Poems for youth, by a family circle."
L: Baldwin, 1820. 66p. NUC BL OCLC
[BL attr. to Hornblower; DNB to Mary Anne Roscoe Jevons]

2777. HORNER, Hattie, Miss [Am. 19c]
Poems.
Topeka, KS: Kansas pub. house, 1885. 69p. BL OCLC

2778. HORSFIELD, Louisa A. [Br. 19c]
The cottage lyre: being miscellaneous poetry.
2d ed. L: n.p., 1862. BL

2779. HORSFORD, Mary L'Hommedieu (Gardiner) [Am. 1824-1855]
Indian legends and other poems.
NY: J.C. Derby; Boston: Phillips, Sampson & co., 1855. 167p. NUC BL OCLC

2780. HORTON, Mary Lambert [Louisa BL] [Am. 19c]
Poetical prose compositions.

Salem, OR: W. & S.B. Ives, 1832. 88p.
NUC BL

2781. HOSFORD, Maud [Am. 19c]
Happy-valley verses.
n.p.: n.p., n.d. 11 l. NUC

2782. HOSMER, Harriet Goodhue [Am. 1830-1908]
Boston & Boston people, in 1850.
Boston: n.p., 1850. 45p. NUC
[A stroll through Boston, in verse]

2783. HOTTINGER, Elisabeth [Am. b. 1876]
Poetry.
n.p.: n.p., n.d. 7p. NUC

2784. HOUGH, E. H., Mrs. [Am. 19c]
PSEUD: Evergreen, Eva
Opening buds: a collection of poems. By Eva Evergreen.
Xenia, OH: Nichols & Fairchild, 1858. 240p. NUC

2785. HOUGHTON, Jane [Br. 19c]
Blossoms of genius.
Liverpool: n.p., 1800? BL

2786. HOUGHTON, Mary Arnald [19c]
Emilia of Lindinau; or, The field of Leipsic. A poem, in four cantos.
Philadelphia & Baltimore, MD: Mathew Carey, 1816. 200p. L: Whittingham & Arliss, 1815. 201p. NUC BL OCLC

2787. HOUK, Eliza Phillips Thruston, Mrs. [Am. b. 1833]
Puritan. A poem in seven cantos.
Cincinnati, OH: Pr. R. Clarke & co., 1868. 94p. NUC OCLC

2788. HOUSH, Esther T. (Stewart) [Am. 19c]
The old and new, a New Year's poem.
Brattleborough, VT: Frank E. Housh, 1886. 19p. NUC OCLC

2789. HOVENDEN, Sophia [Br. 19c]
The hand unseen.
Jerusalem: n.p., 1846. BL

2790. HOWARD, Mrs. [Br. 19c]
Poetry for home and day schools.
L: n.p., 1856. 2 pt. BL

2791. HOWARD, Alice G. [Am. 19c]
Ours.
San Francisco: C.A. Murdock & co., 1890. 30 l. NUC OCLC
[Religious poems]

2792. HOWARD, Lady C. [Br. 19c]
The chapel bell. By Lady ----, a convert from Anglicanism to Catholicity.
Dublin: James Duffy, 1854. 56p. BL

2793. HOWARD, Hattie, Mrs. [Am. 19c]
Later poems.
Hartford, CT: Case, Lockwood & Brainard co., 1887. 108p. NUC OCLC

2794. -----Poems.
Hartford, CT: Case, Lockwood & Brainard co., 1886. 108p. NUC OCLC

2795. HOWARD, Hope [Am. 19c]
The man hunt. An American ballad.
n.p.: n.p., 1859? 8p. NUC

2796. HOWARTH, Ellen Clementine (Doran) [Am. 1827-1899]
Poems.
Newark, NJ: Martin R. Dennis & co., 1868. 112p. NUC BL OCLC

2797. -----The wind harp, and other poems.
Philadelphia: W.P. Hazard, 1864. 244p. NUC BL OCLC

2798. -----Work and song, a poem.
Trenton, NJ: Murphy & Becktel, pr., 1866. 10p. NUC

2799. HOWE, Miss [Br. 19c]
Hours of solitude.
Brighton: n.p., 1846. BL

2800. HOWE, Caroline Dana, Mrs. [Am. d. 1907]
Ashes for flame, and other poems.
Portland, ME: Loring, Short & Harmon, 1885. 100p. NUC OCLC

2801. HOWE, Julia Ward [Am. 1819-1910]
From sunset ridge: poems old and new.
Boston & NY: Houghton, Mifflin & co., 1898. 190p. NUC BL OCLC

2802. -----Later lyrics.
Boston: J.E. Tilton & co., 1866. 326p. NUC BL OCLC

2803. -----Passion flowers.
Boston: Ticknor, Reed & Fields, 1853. 187p. NUC BL OCLC

2804. -----Words for the hour.
Boston: Ticknor & Fields, 1856. 165p. NUC BL OCLC

2805. HOWE, Lucretia T. [Am. 19c]
Home songs and chronicles of the Ellis.

Rumford Falls, ME: Rumford Falls pub. co., 1899. 160p. NUC
[Occasional & memorial poems; Ellis River, ME]

2806. HOWELL, Agnes Rous [Br. 19/20c]
Fifty years after: a tale in verse.
Norwich: G.S. Hanchett, 1880. 87p. BL

2807. -----Sybelle's dream; and other poems on pictures.
Norwich: Fletcher, 1874?, 1899. 94p. BL OCLC

2808. -----Through the woods: a volume of original poems.
L: Hamilton, 1875. 160p. NUC BL

2809. HOWELL, Annie, Mrs. [Br. 19c]
PSEUD: Ephziba
Elim: or, Harrogate in prose and verse. By Mrs. Annie Howell (Ephziba).
Harrogate: R. Ackrill, 1892. 127p. BL
[Descriptions of local sights in prose. Chiefly verse: some occasional and descriptive of Harrowgate, odes and elegies]

2810. HOWELL, Caroline A. [Br. 19c]
Songs for the wilderness.
L: Sold by J. Groom, 18--? 45p. NUC
[Hymns]

2811. HOWELL, Elizabeth (Lloyd) [Am. 1811-1896] ALT: Lloyd, Elizabeth
An appeal for the bondwoman, to her own sex.
Philadelphia: Merrihew & Thompson, pr., 1846. 36p. NUC OCLC
[Anti-slavery]

2812. HOWELL, S. [Br. 19c]
Trifles; a collection of original poems; containing High beach, an historical descriptive sketch; Market day; elegies, odes, songs, etc.
L: Pr. for the author by J. Plummer, 1815. 120p. NUC

2813. HOWIE, Mary Wright [Br. 19c]
ALT: H., M.W.
Memorials of a beloved daughter. A selection from the poetical remains of M.W.H.
Edinburgh: Priv. pr., 1870. 112p. BL

2814. HOWITT, Mary (Botham), Mrs. W. Howitt [Br. 1799-1888]
Ballads and other poems.
L: Longmans, Brown, Green & Longmans, 1847. 394p. NY: Wiley & Putnam, 1847. 270p. NUC BL OCLC

2815. -----Birds and flowers and other country things.
L: Darton & Clark, 1838. 208p. NUC BL OCLC

2816. -----The desolation of Eyam. The emigrant, a tale of the American woods, and other poems. With William Howitt.
L: Wightman & Cramp, 1827. 322p. NUC BL OCLC

2817. -----Fireside verses.
L: Darton & Clark, 1845. 36p. NUC BL OCLC

2818. -----The forest minstral, and other poems. With William Howitt.
L: Baldwin, Cradock & Joy, 1823. 197p. NUC BL OCLC

2819. -----Hymns and fire side verses.
L: n.p., 1859. BL

2820. -----Marien's pilgrimage: a poem.
NY: n.p., 1844. 16p. NUC BL
[Later pub. as: Marion's pilgrimage, a fireside story, and other poems. L: n.p., 1859. BL] [Pub. in the 1844 Poems of Mary Howitt]

2821. -----Pictorial calendar of seasons.
L: n.p., 1854. 567p. TXU

2822. -----The poems of Mary Howitt.
Philadelphia: J. Locken, 1844. 303p. NUC OCLC
[Incl. Mabel on midsummer day; a story of the olden time.]

2823. -----The seven temptations.
L: R. Bentley, 1834. 373p. NUC OCLC
[Dramatic poems]

HOWITT, Mrs. W. <u>see</u> HOWITT, Mary (Botham)

HOWITT, William, co-author <u>see</u> HOWITT, Mary (Botham)

2824. HOWLAND, Sarah Hazard [Am. 1784-1847]
Extracts from the journal of Sarah Howland, and some of the poetry, letters, and other papers preserved by her ... . Comp. Howland Pell.
NY: Priv. pr., 1890. 122p. NUC BL OCLC

2825. HOXTER, Mary E. [Am. 19c]
A few verses ...

n.p.: n.p., 189-? 24p. NUC
[3 pt.: In memoriam, humorous, serious poems]

2826. HOY, Elizabeth [Br. 19c]
Poems.
L: W. Dawson & sons, 1863. 10p. BL

2827. HOYLAND, Alice [Br. 19c]
Original hymns.
L: n.p., 1848. BL

HUBBARD, E., ed. see HAYWARD, Jane Mary

2828. HUBBARD, Janette P. [Am. 1830-1891]
1790. A hundred years. 1890.
Port Huron, MI: Sherman co., pr. 1891? 23p. NUC OCLC
[Cover-title: Centennial. Poem written for Hubbard family centennial]

2829. HUBBELL, Mary E. [Am. 1833-1854]
The memorial; or, The life and writings of an only daughter. By her mother [Martha (Stone) Hubbell].
Boston: J.P. Jewett; Cleveland; OH: H.P.B. Jewett, 1857. 384p. NUC BL OCLC
[Incl. letters, poems, fiction & essays]

2830. HUDSON, Hannah Reba [Am. 19c]
Poems.
Boston: J.R. Osgood & co., 1874. 214p. NUC OCLC

2831. HUDSON, Mary Ann [Br. 19c]
The beacon of hope. Poems on various subjects.
L: n.p., 1860. BL

HUDSON, Mary E. (Clemmer) Ames see AMES, Mary E. (Clemmer)

2832. HUGER, Meta D., Mrs. [Am. 19c]
The Britons. A rhymed history of England, and the Roman, English and German dates, together with general questions.
NY: Brentano's, 1889. 76p. NUC

HUGHES, ALLISON, pseud. see HALEY, Alice

2833. HUGHES, Anne, Mrs. [Br. 18/19c]
Poems.
L: J. Dodsley, 1784. 131p. NUC BL OCLC

2834. HUGHES, Elizabeth Binfield [Br. 19c]
Miscellaneous poems.
L: Church press co., 1869. 43p. BL

HUGHES, F., co-author see HUGHES, S., Miss

2835. HUGHES, F., Miss [Br. 19c]
Poems, sacred and moral.
2d ed. L: Pr. Odell & Ives, 1860. 44p. NUC BL OCLC

HUGHES, Joanna, ed. see ALCOCK, Mary Cumberland

2836. HUGHES, S., Miss [Br. 19c]
Poems on nature and grace. By S. Hughes and F. Hughes.
L: Priv. pr., 1856. BL

2837. HULL, Amelia Matilda [Br. 19c]
Heart melodies and life lights.
L: n.p., 1864. BL

2838. -----Hymns.
South Petherton: Edwin Bennett, 1850? BL

2839. -----Royal musings concerning the King and his work.
L: J.E. Hawkins, 1884. 175p. BL

2840. HULL, Mattie E. (Browne) [Am. 19c]
Wayside jottings. Essays, sketches, poems and songs, gathered from the highways, by-ways and hedges of life.
Des Moines, IA: M. Hull & co., 1888. 208p. NUC OCLC
[Spiritualist & strong believer in all human rights.]

HUMANITAS, pseud., co-author see MOODY, Elizabeth, Miss

HUMBOLT, Gay see NARAMORE, Gay Humbolt

2841. HUME, Elizabeth
At the piano; verses with a Whittier prelude.
Amesbury, MA: n.p., 1894. 15p. NUC OCLC

HUME, Mary C. see HUME-ROTHERY, Mary Catherine

2842. HUME-ROTHERY, Mary Catherine [Br. 1824-1885] ALT: Hume, Mary C.
The bridesmaid, Count Stephen, and other poems.
L: John Chapman, 1853. 362p. NUC BL

2843. -----Normiton: a dramatic poem, in two parts. With other miscellaneous pieces.

L: John W. Parker & son, 1857. 312p.
NUC BL

2844. -----Sappho; a poem.
L: n.p., 1862. BL
[Repr. from the Intellectual Repository]

2845. HUMPHREYS, Eliza [Br. 19c]
Metrical collects, from the Book of Common Prayer.
L: Seeley, Jackson & Halliday, 1856. 137p. NUC
[Pub. anon.]

2846. HUMPHREYS, Jennett [Br. 19/20c]
Home thoughts and home scenes. In original poems by ... J.H. et al.
Boston: J.E. Tilton & co., 1865. NUC
[9 poems by Humphreys; others by Ingelow, & other women.]

HUNT, Caroline, ed. see DE BURGH, Emma Maria (Hunt)

2847. HUNT, Eliza [Br. 19c]
Poems on various subjects.
L: Pr. W. Stevens, 1808. 90p. NUC BL

2848. HUNT, Hannah [Br. 19c] ALT: H., H.
Songs of the spirit. By H.H.
L: F.B. Kitto, 1868. 154p. NUC BL

HUNT, Helen Maria (Fiske) see JACKSON, Helen Maria (Fiske) Hunt

2849. HUNT, Rachel [Am. 19c]
Autumnal fruits and flowers; being the effusions of a reflecting mind in the decline of life.
Philadelphia: Pr. J. Richards, 1843. 166p. NUC OCLC

2850. HUNT, Sara Keables
The two little stockings, and other poems.
NY: Rogers & Sherwood, 1890. 21 f. NUC

HUNTER, Agnes see SEMPLE, Agnes Sophia (Hunter)

2851. HUNTER, Anne (Home), Mrs. John Hunter [Br. 1742-1821] ALT: Home, Anne
Poems.
L: Pr. for T. Payne, by T. Bensley, 1802. 122p. NUC BL OCLC
[Odes, ballads & songs]

2852. -----The sports of the genii.
L: T. Payne, 1804. 16p. NUC BL OCLC

2853. HUNTER, Harriett Eliza [Br. 19c]
The gold mine, and other poems.
L: n.p., n.d. BL

HUNTER, Mrs. John see HUNTER, Anne (Home)

2854. HUNTER, Maggie [Am. 19c]
Pearls of a woman's heart.
Peoria, IL: J.W. Franks & son, pr., 1886. 143p. NUC OCLC

2855. HUNTER, Rachel, Mrs. [Br. 1754-1813]
Poems.
n.p.: n.p., 1802. Summers

HUNTINGTON, Abel, ed. see HUNTINGTON, Cornelia

2856. HUNTINGTON, Cornelia [Am. 1803-1890]
Odes and poems and fragmentary verses; from original manuscripts transcribed from various sources. Ed. Abel Huntington.
n.p.: A. Huntington, c1891. 203p. NUC OCLC

2857. HUNTINGTON, Mary H., Mrs. [Am. 19c]
Fish story. Poem and design.
NY state?: n.p., c1890. 12 l. NUC OCLC

2858. HUNTINGTOWER, Catherine Rebecca (Grey) Talmash, Baroness [Br. 1766/7-1852] ALT: M-----, Lady; Manners, Catherine Rebecca, Lady
Poems.
L: n.p., 1794. BL

2859. -----Poems, by Lady Manners.
L: J. Bell, 1793. 106p. NUC BL OCLC

2860. -----Review of poetry, ancient and modern. A poem. By Lady M-----.
L: J. Booth, 1799. 30p. NUC BL OCLC

2861. HUNTLEY, Anna Miner [Am. 19c]
Poems.
NY: Burr pr. house, 1883. 182p. NUC OCLC

HUNTLEY, Lydia Howard see SIGOURNEY, Lydia Howard (Huntley)

2862. HURD, Annie, Mrs. [Am. 19c]
Little sister. A poem.
n.p.: n.p., 1882. 8p. NUC

2863. HURD, Helen Marr [Am. b. 1839]
Poetical works of Helen Marr Hurd.

Boston: B.B. Russell, 1887. 418p. NUC OCLC

2864. -----Sub montem: Christmas and other poems.
Boston: B.B. Russell, 1890. 15p. OCLC

2865. -----What Christmas brings.
Hallowell, ME: W.F. Marston, 188-? 6p. OCLC
[Sub-montem: Christmas and other poems. Part second.]

2866. HUSKINSON, Eliza [Br. 19c]
Song of the spheres.
L: n.p., 1853. BL

2867. HUSSEY, Mary Bassett [Am. 19c]
Consolation and other poems.
Buffalo, NY & NY: Charles Wells Moulton, 1899. 113p. NUC

2868. HUSTON, Alice H. [Am. 19c]
First at the tomb; an Easter poem.
Baltimore, MD: D.W. Glass & co., 1888. 3 l. NUC

2869. HUSTON, Isabella Pennock (Lukens) [Am. 1822?-1889]
Autumn leaves.
Philadelphia: Pr. Sherman & co., 1873. 181p. NUC OCLC

HUTCHINSON, Ellen Mackay see CORTISSOZ, Ellen Mackay (Hutchinson)

2870. HUTTER, Nannie Langhorne [Am. 19c]
Poems.
Richmond, VA: George M. West, bookseller, 1896. 84p. NUC OCLC

2871. HUTTON, Mary [Br. 19c]
Cottage tales and poems.
Sheffield: J. Blurton, pr., 1842. 104p. BL
[5 short stories; poems are primarily occasional, elegies, addresses]

2872. -----The happy isle; and other poems.
L: n.p., 1836. BL

2873. -----Sheffield Manor, and other poems. Ed. J. Holland.
Sheffield: n.p., 1831. BL

2874. HUTTON, Rebecca Lothrop (Shaw) [Am. 1821-1884]
Poems of affection.
Richmond, IN: n.p., 188-? 68 l. NUC

2875. HUXLEY, Henrietta Anne (Heathorn), Mrs. Thomas Henry Huxley [Br. d. 1915]
Poems of Henrietta A. Huxley, with three of Thomas Henry Huxley.
L: Priv. pr., 1899. 181p. NUC BL
[BL ed. 1913]

HUXLEY, Thomas Henry, co-author see HUXLEY, Henrietta Anne (Heathorn)

HUXLEY, Mrs. Thomas Henry see HUXLEY, Henrietta Anne (Heathorn)

2876. HYDE, Emeline R.
The table of plenty.
NY: n.p., 1877. 1v. NUC

2877. HYDE, Mabel C. [Br. 19c]
Pansies.
L: Swan Sonnenschein & co., 1897. 64p. BL

2878. HYDE, Mary E. [Am. 19c]
A Christmas hymn.
Fall River, MA: Press of J.H. Franklin & co., 1890? 22p. NUC

2879. HYDE, Nancy Maria [Am. 1792-1816]
The writings of Nancy Maria Hyde, of Norwich, Conn., connected with a sketch of her life. Ed. Lydia Howard (Huntley) Sigourney.
Norwich, CT: Russell Hubbard, 1816. 252p. NUC BL
[Diary of a teacher, incl. many orig. verses]

2880. HYGEMA, Effie [Am. 19c]
Thoughts in verse. Poems of duty to God, home on earth, and rest in heaven.
Elkhart, IN: Mennonite pub. co., 1885. 32p. NUC OCLC

2881. HYNEMAN, Rebekah, Mrs. [Am. 19c]
The leper, and other poems.
Philadelphia: A. Hart, 1853. 216p. NUC BL OCLC

I., C.H. see INGLIS, Catherine Hartland

IANTHE, pseud. see EMBURY, Emma Catherine (Manley)

IDAMORE, pseud. see CUTTS, Mary

IDLER, AN, pseud. see BOYD, Nellie

ILIFF, Mrs. Edward H. see ILIFF, Palmer

2882. ILIFF, Palmer, Mrs. Edward H. Iliff [Br. 19c]
Poems upon several subjects.
L: Pub. & sold for author by Vernor, Hood & Sharpe, 1808. 147p. NUC BL OCLC

2883. INGELOW, Jean [Br. 1820-1897]
The complete poems of Jean Ingelow.
Boston: Roberts bros., 1869. 332, 313p. NUC OCLC

2884. -----The high tide on the coast of Lincolnshire, 1571.
Boston: Roberts bros., 1863. 1883. 35 l. NUC BL OCLC

2885. -----The monitions of the unseen, and poems of love and childhood.
Boston: Roberts bros., 1871. 172p. NUC OCLC

2886. -----The new poems of Jean Ingelow, John Greenleaf Whittier [and] Henry Wadsworth Longfellow.
Toronto, Canada: Belford bros., 1876. 161p. NUC OCLC

2887. -----One hundred holy songs, carols, and sacred ballads. Original, and suitable for music.
L: Longmans, Green & co., 1878. 152p. NUC BL

2888. -----Poems.
L: Longmans, Green & co.; Boston: Roberts bros., 1863. 256p. NUC BL OCLC

2889. -----Poems of the old days and the new.
Boston: Roberts bros., 1885. 229p. NUC BL OCLC

2890. -----Poems. Second series.
6th ed. L: Longmans, Green & Co., 1874. Copyright ed. Leipzig: B. Tauchnitz, 1873. 2v. NUC BL OCLC

2891. -----Poems. Third series.
L: Longmans, Green & co., 1885. 248p. NUC BL

2892. -----The poetical works of Jean Ingelow: including the Shepherd lady and other poems.
NY: Lovell, 1863? 520p. NUC OCLC

2893. -----A rhyming chronicle of incidents and feelings. Ed. Edward Harston.
L: Longman, Brown, Green & Longmans, 1850. 264p. NUC BL OCLC
[Under Harston with no mention of Ingelow in OCLC]

2894. -----Songs of seven.
Boston: Roberts bros., 1866. 29p. NUC OCLC

2895. -----Songs of the night watches. [Arranged by Helen S. Childs].
Boston: H.H. Carter & Karrick, 1887. 20p. NUC

2896. -----A story of doom, and other poems.
L: Longmans, Green & co., 1867. 296p. Boston: Roberts bros., 1867. 290p. NUC BL OCLC

2897. INGHAM, Jane Sarson Cooper [Br. 19c] ALT: Ingham, Sarson C. J.
Caedmon's vision, and other poems. By Sarson C.J. Ingham.
L: K. Paul, Trench, 1882. 252p. OCLC

INGHAM, Sarson C.J. see INGHAM, Jane Sarson Cooper

2898. INGLIS, Catherine Hartland [Br. 19c] ALT: I., C.H.
One hundred songs in sorrow and in joy. By C.H.I.
Edinburgh: James Taylor, 1880. 188p. BL

2899. -----Songs in sorrow and songs of joy. By C.H.I.
Edinburgh: James Taylor, 1864. 188p. BL

INGRAM, A.E., Miss, co-author see INGRAM, W., Mrs.

INGRAM, Percy T., co-author see INGRAM, W., Mrs.

2900. INGRAM, W., Mrs. [Br. 19c]
Verses by Mrs. W. Ingram and Miss A.E. Ingram. In: A garland from Hesperides, woven in verse and prose. By Percy T. Ingram.
Grantham: W. Clarke; L: Simpkin, Marshall, Hamilton, Kent & co., 1892. 128p. BL
[7 poems by Mrs. Ingram, narrative & religious lyrics; 16 poems by Miss Ingram, mainly narrative]

INNSLY, OWEN, pseud. see JENNISON, Lucy White

2901. INSTONE, Sarah [Br. 18c]
Poems on several occasions.
Bridgnorth: Pr. & sold by G. Gitton, 1797. 67p. NUC BL

2902. IRIS, pseud. [Br. 19c]
The man of sorrows. Thoughts for holy week.
n.p.: n.p., 1893. BL

2903. IRVINE, Mary Catherine [Br. 19c] PSEUD: Aura
Christabelle. A tale of Christmas, and other poems.
L: Longmans & co., 1875. 28p. BL

2904. -----Heart repose.
L: Simpkin, Marshall & co., 1867. 175p. NUC BL
[A dramatic poem, in three acts. Moral & religious themes, group of 8 odes, in Act III, scene XII]

2905. IRVING, Elizabeth Jane [Br. 19c]
Fireside lays.
Glasgow: Pr. Robert Anderson, 1872. 248p. BL

2906. IRVING, Ethel [Br. 19c]
Helvige; and poems.
L: W. Macintosh, 1872. 155p. BL OCLC
[Drama, three acts, verse]

2907. IRWIN, Anne [Br. 19c]
Combe flowers: poems.
2d ed. rev. L: n.p., 1879. BL

IRVING, MINNA, pseud. see ODELL, Minnie

IRVING, Washington, ed. see DAVIDSON, Margaret Miller, Mrs.

ISA see KNOX, Isa (Craig)

2908. ISAACS, Mrs. [Br. 19c]
The wanderings of fancy, consisting of miscellaneous pieces in prose and verse.
L: C. Chapple, 1812. 286p. BL
[Lyrics and short stories]

ISABEL, pseud. see RITCHIE, Anna Cora (Ogden) Mowatt

2909. ISARD, Elizabeth Ann [19c]
Wayside songs.
Newmarket, Canada: Eva pub. house, the author, 1896. 224p. NUC BL

2910. ISELIN, Sophia [Br. 19c]
My dream book: poems.
First series. L: n.p., 1847. BL

ITA, pseud. see COLLING, Elizabeth

2911. IVERSON, Winifred A. [Br. 19c]
God's touch, and other poems.
L: Marshall bros., 1890. 95p. BL

2912. -----Whispers from the throne, and other verses.
L: E. Stock, 1894. 156p. BL

2913. IVISON, Ursula [Br. 18c]
The retired penitent: a poem.
L: n.p., 1794. BL

2914. IVORY, Bertha May [Am. 19c]
PSEUD: Antonia
A cluster of roses and other poems. By Bertha May Ivory, "Antonia".
St. Louis, MO: Ennis press, 1895. 166p. NUC OCLC

J., J.C. see JONES, Julia Clinton

J., K.H. see JOHNSON, Katherine (Hardenbergh)

2915. J., L.L.D. [Am. 19c] PSEUD: Lady, A
One more river to cross; a national song, composed and sung by a lady.
Cincinnati, OH: John Church, jr., 1862. NUC

J., M.E.M. see JONES, Margaret Elizabeth Mary

J--N, M.J. see JOURDAN, Mary Jane, Mrs.

2916. JACKSON, Caroline L. [Am. 19c]
Wood mosses; poems.
New Haven, CT: Pr. T.J. Stafford, 1867. 84p. NUC OCLC

2917. JACKSON, Mrs. Clement Nugent [Br. 19/20] PSEUD: Jim's Wife
Gordon league ballads for working men and women. By Jim's wife.
L: Skeffington & son, 1897. NUC BL
[Ballads & dramatic stories in verse]

JACKSON, Flo see JACKSON, Trothy Florence Brown

2918. JACKSON, Helen Maria (Fiske) Hunt [Am. 1830-1885] ALT: H., H.; Hunt, Helen Maria (Fiske)
Best. A poem.
Boston: n.p., 1885? NY: Garrett, 1972? NUC

2919. -----A calendar of sonnets.
Boston: Roberts bros., 1886. 13p. NUC OCLC

2920. -----Easter bells, an original poem.
NY: White, Stokes & Allen, 1884. 22p. NUC OCLC

2921. -----The last poems of Helen Jackson.
n.p.: n.p., 1883. NUC

2922. -----My legacy.
Boston: H.H. Carter & Karrick, 1888. 6 l. NUC OCLC

2923. -----Poems.
Boston: Roberts bros., 1886-1888, c1873-1886. 2v. NUC BL OCLC
[V. 1 verses. V. 2 sonnets & lyrics. New & enl. ed., 1887.]

2924. -----Poems.
Boston: Roberts bros., 1892. 266p. NUC OCLC

2925. -----Sonnets and lyrics.
Boston: Roberts bros., 1886. 135p. NUC BL OCLC

2926. -----Spinning. By H.H.
Cliftondale, MA: Coates bros., 1880? 6 l. Boston: D. Lothrop, 188-? 8 l. NUC OCLC

2927. -----The story of Boon.
Boston: Roberts bros., 1874. 28p. NUC OCLC
[Siamese woman martyred in attempt to save husband from King's wrath.]

2928. -----Verses.
Boston: Fields, Osgood & co., 1870. 100p. NUC BL OCLC
[New & enl. ed. Boston: Roberts bros., 1890. 137p.]

2929. JACKSON, Lucy Evelyn [Am. 19c] PSEUD: Edwards, Evelyn
The marriage of the months. By Evelyn Edwards.
Boston: n.p., 1898. 13 l. NUC

2930. JACKSON, Lydia M. [Am. 19c]
Wild rose petals.
Topeka, KS: G.W. Crane pub. co., 1889. 66p. NUC BL OCLC

2931. JACKSON, Trothy Florence Brown [Br. 19c] ALT: Jackson, Flo
Sea dreams. By Flo Jackson.
Hull: Andrews & co., 1893. 24p. NUC BL

2932. JACOB, Catharine, Mrs. [Br. 19c]
Poems.
Southampton: n.p., 1821. BL

2933. JACQUES, Mary J. [Am. 19c]
Dream roses, with madrigals.
Boston: L. Prang & co., c1897. 10 l. NUC OCLC

2934. JAMES, Alice Archer (Sewall) [Am. b. 1870]
Little lyrics.
n.p.: E.J. Appleton, 1890? 23p. OCLC

2935. -----An ode to girlhood and other poems.
NY & L: Harper & bros., 1899. 72p. NUC OCLC

2936. JAMES, Eliza [Br. 19c]
Hours of leisure. Poems.
Durham: n.p., 1807. BL

2937. JAMES, Maria [Am. 1793-1868]
Wales, and other poems.
NY: J.S. Taylor, 1839. 170p. NUC BL OCLC

2938. JAY, KAY, pseud. [Br. 19c]
Rose: a romance of 192-.
Bristol: J.W. Arrowsmith, 1898. 126p. BL

JAY, W.M.L., MRS., pseud. <u>see</u> WOODRUFF, Julia Louisa Matilda (Curtiss)

JEFFERIES, Bradford, co-author <u>see</u> JEFFERIES, Harriet Anne

2939. JEFFERIES, Harriet Anne [Br. 19c]
The widow of Nain, and other poems. By Bradford and Harriet Anne Jefferies.
Manchester: n.p., 1862. BL

2940. JEFFREY, Rosa (Vertner) Johnson [Am. 1828-1894]
The crimson hand and other poems.
Philadelphia: J.B. Lippincott, 1881. 200p. NUC BL OCLC

2941. -----Daisy Dare and baby power: poems.
NY & Philadelphia: Claxton, Remsen & Haffelfinger, 1871. 58p. NUC OCLC
[Daisy Dare is a romance; Baby power is on her own 3 children.]

2942. -----Poems.
Boston: Ticknor & Fields, 1857. 334p. NUC OCLC

2943. JEMMAT, Catherine (Yeo) [Br. 18c] ALT: Jemmatt, Catherine (Yeo)

Miscellanies, in prose and verse.
L: Pr. for the author, 1766. 227p. BL
[Chiefly poetry: occasional, odes, etc. Also incl. An essay in vindication of the female sex and prose sketches.]

JEMMATT, Catherine (Yeo) see JEMMAT, Catherine (Yeo)

2944. JENKINS, Daphne Smith (Giles) [Am. b. 1812] ALT: Giles, Daphne S.
The balm of Gilead. By Daphne S. Giles.
NY: R. Craighead, 1852. 114p. NUC OCLC

2945. -----A collection of scriptural and miscellaneous poems.
Ann Arbor, MI: Cole & Arnold, 1845. 172p. NUC OCLC
[Incl. some prose]

2946. JENKINS, Helen N. (Gerrard) [Am. b. 1836]
Poems.
Bangor, ME: O.F. Knowles & co., pr., c1887. 184p. NUC OCLC

JENKINS, Howard M., comp. see WISTER, Sarah

2947. JENNESS, Caroline Elizabeth [Am. 1824-1857]
Writings of Caroline Elizabeth Jenness. With a memoir ... .
Boston: J. Wilson & son, 1858. 275p. NUC OCLC
[Chiefly prose; incl. lyric poetry, pp. 200-275.]

JENNISON, Lucia White see JENNISON, Lucy White

2948. JENNISON, Lucy [Lucia BL] White [Am. b. 1850] PSEUD: Innsly, Owen
Love poems and sonnets. By Owen Innsly.
Boston: A. Williams & co., 1881. 195p. NUC BL OCLC

JERMYN, Laetitia, comp. see COBBOLD, Elizabeth Knipe

JERVEY, Caroline Howard, co-author see GILMAN, Caroline (Howard)

2949. JERVIS, Marian, Lady [Br. 19c]
Gleanings.
Paris: n.p., 1840. BL

2950. JESSOP, Anne Jane Elizabeth [Br. 19c] ALT: Battersby, Anne Jane Elizabeth (Jessop)
The wreath: or, Thoughts, foreign and indigenous, in verse, forming a varied tissue.
L: Whittaker & co.; York: H. Bellerby & son, 1855. 50p. BL

2951. JEVONS, Mary Anne (Roscoe) [Br. 1795-1845] ALT: Jevons, Mrs., the elder
Poems.
L: Baldwin, Cradock & Joy, 1820. 66p. NUC
[Attr. to her by DNB. BL attr. to Jane Elizabeth (Roscoe) Hornblower]

2952. -----Sonnets, and other poems, chiefly devotional.
Liverpool & L: Simpkin, 1845. 134p. NUC BL OCLC

2953. -----The syrens and other poems.
L: Kent & co., 1879. 46p. NUC BL
[BL attributes to Mary Anne Jevons, the younger]

JEVONS, Mary Anne (Roscoe) see HORNBLOWER, Jane Elizabeth (Roscoe)

JEVONS, Mary Anne, the younger see JEVONS, Mary Anne (Roscoe)

JIM'S WIFE, pseud. see JACKSON, Mrs. Clement Nugent

2954. JOHNSON, Anna Cummings [Am. 1818-1892] PSEUD: Myrtle, Minnie
The myrtle wreath; or, Stray leaves recalled. By Minnie Myrtle.
NY: C. Scribner, 1854. 380p. NUC BL OCLC
[Stories, sketches & poems]

2955. JOHNSON, Elizabeth [Am. 19c]
Reflections in retirement.
Boston: B.H. Greene, 1834. 112p. NUC
[Incl. poetry]

JOHNSON, Elizabeth, co-author see JOHNSON, Lucinda

2956. JOHNSON, Ella M. [Am. 19c]
Daydreams, selections from poems by Ella M. Johnson.
San Francisco: Golden Era co., 1885. 36p. NUC OCLC

2957. JOHNSON, Ella S. [Am. 19c]
Psalm of the stars and other poems.
n.p.: n.p., n.d. 18p. NUC
[16 brief lyric poems in a "souvenir." No imprint]

2958. JOHNSON, Emily Pauline [Can. 1861-1913]

The white wampum.
L: John Lane; Boston: Lamson, Wolffe & co., 1895. 87p. NUC BL OCLC

JOHNSON, Mrs. Herrick <u>see</u> JOHNSON, Katherine (Hardenbergh)

2959. JOHNSON, Katherine (Hardenbergh), Mrs. Herrick Johnson [Am. d. 1907] ALT: J., K.H.
Comfort. By K.H.J.
NY: A.D.F. Randolph & co., 1877. 107p. NUC OCLC

2960. JOHNSON, Laura Winthrop [Am. 1825-1889]
Poems of twenty years.
NY: De W.C. Lent, 1874. 148p. NUC OCLC

2961. JOHNSON, Lucinda [Br. 19c]
Poems. With Elizabeth Johnson of Chapel-town, near Leeds.
Huddersfield: Priv. pr., 1819. BL

2962. JOHNSON, M.O., Mrs. [Am. 19c]
The century-plant, and other poems.
Boston: W.V. Spencer, 1867. 144p. NUC

2963. JOHNSON, Mary F. [Br. 19c]
Original sonnets, and other poems.
L: Longman, Hurst, Rees & Orme, 1810. 160p. BL OCLC

2964. JOHNSON, Mary Kellogg [Am. b. 1836]
Aloha and other poems.
Boston: H.H. Carter & co., 1895. 218p. NUC OCLC

JOHNSON, Samuel, co-author <u>see</u> WILLIAMS, Anna

2965. JOHNSON, Susanna C. [Br. 19c]
New popular rhymes, for Puseyite times.
2d ed. L: n.p., 1843. BL

JOHNSON, William, ed. <u>see</u> BACON, Fanny Elizabeth

2966. JOHNSTON, Ellen [Br. 19c]
Autobiography. Poems and songs.
Glasgow: W. Love, 1867. 232p. NUC BL OCLC
[Cover title: Factory girl's poems]

2967. JOHNSTON, Julia Harriette [Am. 1849-1919]
Bright threads.
NY & Boston: Thomas Y. Crowell & co., 1897. 157p. NUC OCLC
[Misc. poetry; some prose, advice on daily life.]

2968. -----The school of the master, and other religious poems [verses OCLC].
NY: A.D.F. Randolph & co., c1880. 68p. NUC OCLC

2969. JONES, A., Mrs. [Br. 19c]
Poems and songs.
Preston: R. Parkinson & co., 1890. 103p. BL OCLC
[NUC attr. to Amanda Theodosia Jones; BL specifies "of Ashton-on Ribble"]

JONES, Amanda Theodosia <u>see</u> JONES, A., Mrs.

2970. JONES, Amanda Theodosia [Am. 1835-1914]
Poems.
NY: Hurd & Houghton, 1867. 203p. NUC OCLC

2971. -----A prairie idyll, and other poems.
Chicago: Jansen, McClurg & co., 1892. 160p. NUC OCLC

2972. -----Utah and other poems.
2d ed. Buffalo, NY: H.H. Otis, 1861. 309p. NUC OCLC

2973. JONES, Clara Augusta [Am. 19c] ALT: Clara Augusta
Poems. By Clara Augusta.
Philadelphia: J.B. Lippincott, 1873. 161p. NUC OCLC

2974. JONES, Eliza Grew [Am. 1803-1838]
Memoir of Mrs. Eliza G. Jones, missionary to Burmah and Siam.
Philadelphia: Am. Baptist Pub. & Sun. Sch. Soc., 1842. 172p. NUC
[Contains 6 of her poems.]

2975. JONES, Elizabeth C., Mrs. [Am. 19c]
Fugitive poems.
Providence, RI: Smith & Parmenter, pr., 1828. 59p. NUC OCLC

2976. -----Original poems, on different subjects.
Part 2. Providence, RI: n.p., 1821. 47p. NUC

2977. -----Poems on different subjects, original and selected.
Providence, RI: H.H. Brown, pr., 1819. 48p. NUC OCLC

2978. JONES, Gertrude Manly [Am. 19c]
Aunt Charity's 'ligious 'speriences [and] other poems.

Dalton, GA: A.J. Showalter, pr., 1896. 101p. NUC OCLC

2979. JONES, Hannah Watts- [Br. 19c]
PSEUD: British Matron, A
Jackanory. By a British matron.
Bolton: Tillotson & son, 1897? 46p. BL
[Travel to: Dakota, Vancouver, France & Wales; ballad: "The Home-coming of Ednafyd Vychan"]

2980. JONES, Isabel Mary [Br. 19c]
The Christmas bell, and other verses.
Oxford: A.R. Mowbray & co., 1898. 39p. BL

2981. JONES, Julia Clinton [Am. 19c]
ALT: J., J.C.
Amor patriae. Our roll of honor; or, Poems of the Revolution.
NY: G.P. Putnam's sons, 1894. 49p. NUC OCLC
[4 poems in honor of the American Revolution.]

2982. -----Cleopatra. By J.C.J.
San Francisco: The Bancroft co., 1889. 11p. NUC OCLC

2983. -----Story of the ship; and Mechanic art.
San Francisco: The Bancroft co., 1890. 30p. NUC OCLC
[On U.S.S. Charleston, first steel warship built on Pacific coast.]

2984. -----Valhalla. The myths of Norseland, a saga in twelve parts.
San Francisco: Pr. E. Bosqui & co., 1878. 156p. NUC BL OCLC

2985. JONES, Julia P.
Poems.
Philadelphia: MacCalls, 1891. 296p. NUC

2986. JONES, Margaret Elizabeth Mary [Br. 19c] ALT: J., M.E.M.
Jubal; a poem in six cantos. By M.E.M.J.
L: W. Edwards, 1839. 112p. NUC BL

2987. -----Waldenberg; a poem in six cantos. By M.E.M.J.
L: T. Geeves, 1837. 108p. NUC BL

2988. JONES, Maria W. [Am. 19c]
A Quaker love story and other poems.
Chicago: J.L. Regan & co., 1885. 80p. NUC OCLC

2989. JONES, Mary, Miss [Br. 18c]
Miscellanies in prose and verse.
Oxford: Dodsley, 1750. 405p. BL OCLC
[Poetry & literary correspondence; satire on life at court.]

2990. JONES, Mary Amelia [Br. 19c]
Life echoes: a volume of poems.
Shifnal: R. Lowe, 1880. 112p. BL

2991. -----Poems of memory and feeling.
Stafford: n.p., 1854. BL

2992. -----Sunlight in the shade.
Stafford: n.p., 1858. BL

2993. JONES, Mary Elizabeth [Br. 19c]
The lake, and other poems.
L: Simpkin, Marshall & co.;
Liverpool: D. Marples, 1844. 164p. NUC BL

2994. JONES, Mary Elizabeth (Pye) [Br. d. 1834]
Poems.
L: Pr. for author, 1826. 51p. NUC

2995. JONES, Sarah (Liekman) [Br. 19c]
Poems.
Bath: T.B. Tabb, 1862. 144p. BL
[Additional poems by Mr. J. Liekman, her father, pp. 137-144; chiefly religious]

2996. JONES, Sarah Smith [Br. 19c]
My sketch book; or, Gatherings from stray papers in verse and prose.
L: Pr. for the author by Ward & co., 1857. 85p. BL
[Prose: descriptions & meditations. Poems: religious, bereavement.]

2997. JONES, Sophia [Br. 19c]
Poetical sketches.
L: Pr. for the authoress by C. Lowndes, 1808. 80p. BL
[Narrative, odes, 1 sonnet, 1 acrostic, etc.]

2998. JORDAN, Agnes C. [Br. 19c]
Poems social, military and domestic.
L: Houlston, 1862. 111p. BL OCLC

2999. JORDAN, Cornelia Jane (Matthews) [Am. 1830-1888]
Corinth, and other poems of the war.
Lynchburg, VA: Johnson & Schaffter, pr., 1865. 31p. NUC
[This work was publicly burned as "objectionable and incendiary publication" in 1865]

3000. -----Echoes from the cannon, by Cornelia J. Matthews Jordan. Ed. Theresa J. Ambler.

Buffalo, NY: C.W. Moulton, 1899.
207p. NUC OCLC
[Civil War poems]

3001. -----Flowers of hope and memory.
Richmond, VA: A. Morris, 1861. 330p.
NUC OCLC

3002. -----Richmond: her glory and her graves. A poem in two parts.
Richmond, VA: Richmond medical journal pr., 1866. 39p. NUC OCLC

3003. JORDAN, Dulcina Mason [Am. 1833-1895]
Rosemary leaves.
Cincinnati, OH: R. Clarke & co., 1873. 158p. NUC OCLC

3004. JORDAN, Judith, Mrs. [Br. 19c]
The religious breathings and exercises of a mind ... devoted to Jesus of Nazareth.
Shrewsbury: n.p., 1809. BL

3005. JORDAN, Margaret Eileen [Am. b. 1856]
Echoes from the pines.
Portland, ME: McGowan & Young, 1885. 140p. NUC OCLC

3006. JOSEPH, Rosabelle [Br. 19/20c]
Album of acrostics and stray verses.
Swansea: Parry, 1898. 32p. BL

3007. JOSEPHINE, pseud. [Br. 19c]
Marantha: "the Lord is at hand." Poems on the Lord's appearing.
L: Morgan & Chase, 1859. 79p. BL

3008. JOSEPHINE, Katie [19c]
Love's disappointment.
n.p.: n.p., 1886. 16p. NUC OCLC
[Dramatic poem]

JOSIAH ALLEN'S WIFE, pseud. <u>see</u> HOLLEY, Marietta

3009. JOURDAN, Mary Jane, Mrs. [Br. 19c] ALT: J--n, M. J. PSEUD: Lady, A
The Althorp picture gallery, and other poetical sketches. By a lady.
Edinburgh: W. Blackwood, 1836. 163p.
NUC OCLC

3010. -----Mind's mirror; poetical sketches: with minor poems. By M.J. J--n.
Edinburgh: J. Hogg, etc., 1856. 280p.
NUC

3011. JOWITT, Jane [Br. b. 1770]
Memoirs of Jane Jowitt, the poor poetess, aged 74 years ... written by herself.
Sheffield: J. Pearce, 1844. BL OCLC
[Incl. poetry]

3012. JOYNES, Bessie [Br. 19c]
Out of the darkness.
Manchester: Labor press soc. ltd., 189-? 31p. NUC
[Verse & prose parables in first person on love, friendship, faith, etc.]

3013. JOYNES, Lucy [Br. 19c]
Occasional and miscellaneous poems.
Nottingham: Pr. Sutton & son for the author, 1820. 107p. NUC BL

3014. JUDSON, A. C., Mrs. [Am. 19c]
The gospel hope, and other poems.
Rochester, NY: E. Darrow, 1853. 191p.
NUC

3015. -----The world: as it was, is and will be.
Rochester, NY: E. Darrow, 1853. 695p.
NUC OCLC
[First half: philosophical prose with poems interspersed; second half: misc. poems, mostly religious.]

3016. JUDSON, Emily C. (Chubbuck) [Am. 1817-1854] PSEUD: Forester, Fanny
Alderbrook. A collection of Fanny Forester's village sketches, poems, etc.
Boston: W.D. Ticknor & co., 1847. 2v.
NUC BL OCLC

3017. -----The Kathayan slave, and other papers connected with missionary life.
Boston: Ticknor, Reed & Fields, 1853.
186p. NUC BL OCLC
[Tale of slave tortured to death in a Burmese prison; 4 poems, a Burmese legend, and essays on missionary work.]

3018. -----A mound is in the graveyard; or, The missionary mother's lament.
Boston: G.P. Reed & co., c1851. 5p.
NUC BL OCLC
[With music]

3019. -----An olio of domestic verses.
NY: Lewis Colby, 1852. 235p. NUC BL OCLC

JUDSON, Emily C. (Chubbuck), comp. <u>see</u> JUDSON, Sarah (Hall) Boardman

JUDSON, Emily E. (Chubbuck), comp. see CHUBBUCK, Lavinia

3020. JUDSON, Sarah (Hall) Boardman [Am. 1803-1845]
[Missionary biography BL] The memoir of Sarah B. Judson, member of the American Mission to Burmah. By Fanny Forester [Emily E. (Chubbuck) Judson].
Cincinnati, OH: N. Anderson; NY: Sheldon; L: Colby & co.; Aylott & Jones, 1848. 250 or 180p. NUC BL OCLC
[Incl. poems]

JUVENAL, HORACE, pseud. see ROBINSON, Mary (Darby)

K., C., co-author see FORTNUM, Sophia King

K., H. St. A. see KITCHING, H. Saint A., Miss

K., M.A. see KELTY, Mary Ann

K., S. see FORTNUM, Sophia King

3021. KAHN, Ruth (Ward) [Am. b. 1872]
The first quarter.
Author's ed. Cincinnati, OH: Editor pub. co., 1898. 82p. NUC OCLC

3022. -----Gertrude.
Chicago & Cincinnati, OH: Block pub. & pr. co., 1891. 25p. NUC OCLC

3023. KAIL, Mary E., Mrs. [Am. 19c]
Crown our heroes, and other poems.
Washington, DC: Judd & Detweiler, pr., 1887. 159p. NUC OCLC

KATY-DID, pseud. see BLEECKER, Sophia

KATY-DIDN'T, pseud. see BLEECKER, Sophia

3024. KATZENBERGER, Frances Isabelle [Am. 19c]
Westward ho!
Dayton, OH: Pub. for author by Groneweg pr. co., 1895. 22 l. NUC OCLC

3025. KAUTZ, Augusta [Am. 19/20c]
Straggling thoughts among homely duties.
San Francisco: n.p., 1898. 80p. NUC

3026. -----A world my own.
San Francisco: H.S. Crocker, 1896. 56p. NUC OCLC

KAYE, Catherine Parr see PARR, Catherine

3027. KEARY, Eliza [Br. 19c]
At home again, verse.
L & NY: Marcus Ward & co., 1886. 59p. NUC BL OCLC

3028. KEELER, Amelia [Am. 19c] ALT: Amelia of Western N.Y.
Footprints; or, Poems, by Amelia, of Western N.Y.
Binghamton, NY: Pr. @ the Daily Republican office, 1860. 133p. NUC

3029. KEENE, Elizabeth Carolina [Br. 18c]
Miscellaneous poems.
L: Pr. for author & sold by S. Hooper, 1762. 169p. NUC BL OCLC

3030. KEENE, Katherine [Br. 19c]
Voiceless teachers: whence they come, and what they teach.
L: Swan Sonnenschein & co., 1885. 150p. BL
[Poetry & prose, descriptions of flowers]

3031. KEESE, Catherine (Robinson), Mrs. Samuel Keese [Am. 1806-1860]
A memoir of Catherine R. Keese, late of Peru, N.Y. Comprising extracts from her letters and other sketches ... . Ed. her husband, Samuel Keese.
NY: J. Egbert, pr., 1866. 76p. NUC OCLC
[Incl. poems]

KEESE, J., ed. see SMITH, Elizabeth Oakes (Prince)

KEESE, John, comp. see HOOPER, Lucy Hamilton (Jones)

KEESE, Samuel, ed. see KEESE, Catherine (Robinson)

KEESE, Mrs. Samuel see KEESE, Catherine (Robinson)

3032. KEINTON, Martha [Br. 18c]
A poem.
L: Pr. S. Holt, 1716. 6p. NUC BL
[On George I]

3033. KELLEY, Sarah A. (Ulrich) [Am. b. 1842] PSEUD: Bard of Shanty Hill, The
Deserted: a new novel.
NY: n.p., c1886. 4p. NUC
[Autobiographical sketch and poems]

3034. -----Gems from the pen of Mrs. Sarah Ulrich Kelley.

NY: n.p., 1890? 8p. OCLC

3035. -----Selections from gems of poetry by the Bard of Shanty Hill. n.p.: n.p., c1885. 8p. NUC [Nominated for National poetess of the U.S.]

3036. KELLOGG, Sarah Prescott [Am. 1829-1895]
Rhymes for all seasons.
Boston: D. Lothrop & co., 1889 or 1886. 233p. NUC OCLC

3037. KELLY, Ellinor J. [Br. 19c]
Lays and rhymes for hours at sea.
L: n.p., 1875. BL

3038. -----Tattered banners, and other poems.
L: W. Wells Gardner, 1877. 100p. BL

KELLY, Isabella see HEDGELAND, Isabella Kelly

KELLY, M.A.B. see KELLY, Meriba Ada (Babcock)

3039. KELLY, May, Mrs. Tom Kelly [Br. 19c]
Meadowsweat.
L: Von Portheim & co., 1889. 22p. NUC

3040. -----Those were the days.
L: Dean & son, 1890. 24 l. NUC

3041. KELLY, Meriba Ada (Babcock) [Am. 19c] ALT: Kelly, M. A. B., Mrs.
A volume of poems. By Mrs. M.A.B. Kelly.
Boston: J.G. Cupples, 1892. 254p. NUC OCLC

KELLY, Mrs. Tom see KELLY, May

3042. KELTY, Mary Ann [Br. 1789-1873] ALT: K., M. A.
Waters of comfort ... small volume of devotional poetry ... addressed to the thoughtful and suffering.
Cambridge: Macmillan & co., 1856. 190p. NUC BL

KEMBLE, Adelaide see SARTORIS, Adelaide Kemble

KEMBLE, Ann Julia see HATTON, Ann Julia (Kemble)

KEMBLE, Fanny see KEMBLE, Frances Anne

3043. KEMBLE, Frances Anne [Br. 1809-1893] ALT: Butler, Mrs Pierce; Kemble, Fanny
Poems. By Frances Anne Butler (late Fanny Kemble).
Philadelphia: J. Penington, 1844. 152p. L: H. Washbourne; Edinburgh: Oliver & Boyd; Dublin: Machen & co., 1844. 144p. NUC BL OCLC

3044. -----Poems.
Boston: Ticknor & Fields, 1859. 311p. NUC OCLC
[Expanded edition]

3045. -----Poems.
L: E. Moxon & co., 1866. 285p. NUC BL OCLC

3046. -----Poems.
L: R. Bentley & son, 1883. 338p. NUC BL

3047. KENDALL, Harriet [Br. 19/20c]
A lakeland story.
L: J. Walker & co., 1888. BL
["Miniature golden floral series."]

3048. -----Synariss and other poems for recitation.
L: Simpkin, Marshall, Hamilton, Kent & co., 1894. NUC BL

KENDALL, KATE, pseud. see GREENE, Clara Marcelle (Farrar)

3049. KENDALL, May [Br. b. 1861]
Dreams to sell.
L & NY: Longmans, Green & co., 1887. 150p. NUC BL OCLC

3050. -----Songs from dreamland.
L: Longmans, Green & co., 1894. 136p. NUC BL OCLC

3051. -----That very Mab. With Andrew Laing.
L: Longmans, Green, 1885. 215p. OCLC

3052. KENDREW, Mary E. [Br. 19/20c]
Lyra sacra.
L: Stock, 1894. 71p. BL OCLC

3053. KENNEY, Martha [Br. 19c]
Charity: a poem.
Bath: Richard Crutwell, 1823. 15p. BL

KENNEY, Minnie E. see PAULL, Minnie E. (Kenney)

3054. KENTISH, Mrs. [Br. 19c]
Poems on various subjects.
2d ed. Liverpool: Pr. G.F. Harris' widow & bros.; sold by George Crickshank; L: Longman, Hurst, Rees & co.; Edinburgh: A. Constable & co., 1821. 136p. BL OCL

KENTISH MOTHER, A, pseud. see THOMAS, L., Mrs.

3055. KEOGH, Margaret [Br. 19c]
Herculaneum, Pompeii, and other poems.
L: J.L. Cox & son, 1842. 24p. BL

3056. KETCHAM, Minnie Wallace [19c]
Driftwood. Sketches in poetry and prose.
L & NY: F. Tennyson Neely, c1898. 77p. NUC OCLC
[Misc. poetry & short stories about love.]

3057. KETCHUM, Annie (Chambers) Bradford [Am. 1824-1904] ALT: Bradford, Annie Chambers; Chambers-Ketchum, Mrs.
Benny: a Christmas ballad.
NY: S.R. Wells, 1870. 29p. NUC OCLC

3058. -----Christmas carillons, and other poems.
NY: D. Appleton & co., 1888. 205p. NUC OCLC

3059. -----Lotos-flowers, gathered in sun and shadow. By Mrs. Chambers-Ketchum.
NY: D. Appleton & co., 1877. 205p. NUC OCLC

3060. -----War poetry of the South.
NY: Richardson, 1866. 7 sheets. OCLC
[Incl. poems of Mrs. Annie Chambers-Ketchum of Georgetown, KY]

3061. KETTLE, Mary Rosa Stuart [Br. d. 1895] ALT: Kettle, Rosa Mackenzie
Autumn leaves from the Leny Pass.
L: J. Weir, 1880. NUC BL
[Tales & descriptions of Scotland]

3062. -----Christmas berries and summer roses. By Rosa Mackenzie Kettle.
L: J. Weir, 1881. 135p. BL
[Prose & verse]

3063. -----Furze blossoms. Stories and poems for all seasons. By Rosa Mackenzie Kettle.
L: T.F. Unwin, 1892. 316p. BL

3064. -----Summer shade and winter sunshine. Poems.
2d ed. L: Tinsley, 1874. 89p. NUC BL

KETTLE, Rosa Mackenzie see KETTLE, Mary Rosa Stuart

KEY, Amy see CLARKE, Amy (Key)

3065. KEYNE, Ada [Br. 19c]
Spells and voices.
L: n.p., 1865. BL

3066. KIDD, Jane, Mrs. [Br. 19c]
Poems and hymns.
Sheffield: Pr. for author & sold by J. Blackwell, 1827. 216p. NUC BL OCLC

KIDDER, D.P., ed. see MAXWELL, Mary H., Mrs.

3067. KILBURN-BROWN, Helen L. [Am. 19c]
One of the shepherds of Bethlehem. A poem.
Pittsfield, MA: J.B. Harrison, 1883. 14 l. NUC OCLC

3068. -----Trinity chimes and songs of the unseen.
Pittsfield, MA: J.A. Maxim, c1893. 64p. NUC OCLC

3069. KILLICK, Louisa M. [Br. 19c]
A lay of Magdala.
L: n.p., 1868. BL

3070. KILLIGREW, Anne [Br. 1660-1685]
Poems.
L: S. Lowndes, 1686. 100p. NUC BL OCLC

KIMBALL, E.A. see KIMBALL, Emma Adeline, Mrs.

3071. KIMBALL, Emma Adeline, Mrs. [Am. b. 1847] ALT: Kimball, E. A.
Wayside flowers. By E.A. Kimball.
Portland, ME: Hoyt, Fogg & Donham, 1882. 129p. NUC OCLC

3072. KIMBALL, Hannah Parker [Am. b. 1861]
The cup of life and other verses.
Boston: J.G. Cupples co., 1892. 85p. NUC OCLC

3073. -----Soul and sense.
Boston: Copeland & Day, 1896. 89p. NUC OCLC
[Half-title: Oaten Stop Series. IV]

3074. -----Victory and other verses.
Boston: Copeland & Day, 1897. 76p. NUC OCLC

3075. KIMBALL, Harriet McEwen [Br. 1834-1917]
All's well.
NY: A.D.F. Randolph & co., 1887. 6 l. NUC
[Also contains "Homeward," by H.M.]

3076. -----The blessed company of all faithful people.
NY: A.D.F. Randolph & co., 1879. 67p. NUC OCLC
[Religious verse]

3077. -----Hymns.
Boston: E.P. Dutton & co., 1866. 83p. NUC BL OCLC

3078. -----Poems. Complete ed.
NY: A.D.F. Randolph & co., 1889. NUC OCLC

3079. -----Swallow flights. Poems.
NY: E.P. Dutton & co., 1874. 131p. NUC OCLC

KING, Charlotte, co-author <u>see</u> FORTNUM, Sophia King

3080. KING, Charlotte [Br. 18c]
Trifles of Helicon. By Charlotte & Sophia King [Fortnum].
L: n.p., 1798. BL

3081. KING, E., Miss [Br. 19c] PSEUD: Young lady, A
Poems and reflections ... by a young lady.
L: J. Booth, 1815. 143p. NUC BL

3082. KING, Hannah Tapfield [Am. 19c]
An epic poem. A synopsis of the rise of the church of Jesus Christ of Latter-day Saints ... .
Salt Lake City, UT: Pub. at the Juv. Instructor office, 1884. 62p. NUC OCLC

3083. -----Songs of the heart.
Salt Lake City, UT: Star book & job pr. off., 1879. 87p. NUC OCLC

3084. KING, Harriet Barbara [Br. 19c]
The bridal and other poems.
L: n.p., 1844. BL

3085. KING, Harriet Eleanor (Baillie-Hamilton) [Br. 1840-1920]
Aspromonte and other poems.
L: Macmillan & co., 1869. 166p. NUC BL OCLC

3086. -----Ballads of the North, and other poems.
L: K. Paul, Trench, 1887. 158p. NUC BL OCLC

3087. -----A book of dreams.
L: K. Paul, Trench, & co., 1883. 93p. NUC BL OCLC

3088. -----The disciples (J. Ruffini, V. Bassi, A. Milano, Baron G. Nicotera).
2d ed. L: H.S. King & co., 1874. 320p. NUC BL OCLC
[Blank verse narrative.]

3089. -----The prophecy of Westminster and other poems. In honour of Henry Edward, Cardinal Manning.
L: W.B. Whittingham, 1895. 63p. BL OCLC

3090. KING, Harriet Rebecca [Br. 19c]
Metrical exercises upon scripture texts and miscellaneous poems.
L: n.p., 1834. BL

3091. -----Poems.
Salisbury: Brodie & Dowding, 1823. 62p. NUC BL OCLC

3092. -----Thoughts in verse upon scripture texts ... to which are added miscellaneous poems and nursery hymns.
L: n.p. 1842-46. 2v. BL

3093. KING, Mary Ada [Br. 19c]
Poems.
L: n.p., 1850. BL

3094. KING, Maude Egerton (Hine) [Br. 1867-1927]
My book of songs and sonnets.
L: Percival, 1893. 115p. NUC BL OCLC

3095. KING, Sarah [Br. 18c]
The Hiberian Rosciad, by S___ K___.
Dublin: Pr. for the booksellers, 1765. 16p. NUC

3096. KING, Sarah [Br. 19c]
Poems.
L: n.p., 1859. BL

3097. KING, Sarah A. [Am. d. 1884]
The writings of Sarah A. King. Comp. her daughter, Virginia (King) Hascall.
NY: Pr. for priv. circ., Press of Theo L. DeVinne & co., 1884. 141p. NUC OCLC
[Misc. poetry; speeches to Sorosis on philanthropy, etc.]

3098. KING, Sarah Catharine
The garland: poems. With Elvira K. Nelson.
Indianapolis, In: Hasselman, 1883. 221p. OCLC

KING, Sophia, co-author <u>see</u> KING, Charlotte

KING, Sophia see FORTNUM, Sophia King

3099. KINNEY, Elizabeth Clementina (Dodge)
Felicita; a metrical romance.
NY: J.S. Dickerson, 1855. 188p. NUC BL OCLC

3100. -----Poems.
NY: Hurd & Houghton, 1867. 226p. NUC BL OCLC

3101. KINSLEY, Miss [Br. 19c]
The emerald isle; a poem.
Liverpool: Booker & co., 1846. 99p. NUC BL

KIPPIS, Andrew, ed. see WILLIAMS, Helen Maria

3102. KIRCHHOFFER, Julia Georgiana Mary [Br. 19c]
Poems and essays.
Paisley: J. & R. Parlane, 1885. 126p. BL

3103. KIRKLAND, Caroline Matilda (Stansbury) [Am. 1801-1864]
Autumn hours and fireside reading.
NY: Charles Scribner, 1854. 311p. NUC OCLC
[Chiefly essays; incl. 5 short poems]

3104. KIRKPATRICK, Cynthia Cole [Am. b. 1811]
Poems for the times.
Parkersberg, WV: Blair & Gibbens book & job prs., 1865. 28p. NUC

3105. KITCHING, H. Saint A., Miss [Br. 19c] ALT: K., H. St. A.
The last bell tolls! Monody on the death of the Princess Louise.
L: n.p., 1832. BL

KLINGLE, GEORGE, pseud. see HOLMES, Georgiana (Klingle)

3106. KNIGHT, Ann Cuthbert [Br. 19c]
Home: a poem.
Boston: Samuel H. Parker, E. Lincoln, pr., 1806. 144p. Edinburgh: A. Constable & co., 1815. 98p. NUC OCLC
[Supposed author; NUC enters under Greenshields, John Blackwood]

3107. -----A year in Canada, and other poems.
Edinburgh: Pr. J. Ballantyne & co., for Doig & Stirling, 1816. 126p. NUC BL

3108. KNIGHT, Annette F.C. [Br. 19c]
Poems.
L: n.p., 1874. BL

KNIGHT, Cornelia see KNIGHT, Ellis Cornelia

3109. KNIGHT, Elleanor Warner [Am. b. 1799]
A narrative of the Christian experience, life and adventures, trials and labours of Elleanor Knight, written by herself. To which is added a few remarks and verses.
Providence, RI: n.p., 1839. 126p. NUC

3110. KNIGHT, Ellis Cornelia [Br. 1757-1837] ALT: Knight, Cornelia
Additional verses to God save the king. For the Battle of the Nile.
n.p.: n.p., 1800? BL

3112. -----Lines address'd to victory in consequence of the success of Lord Cornwallis and his army against Tippoo Saib.
Parma: Pr. Bodoni, 1793. 6 l. NUC BL OCLC

3113. -----Miscellaneous poems. By Ellis Cornelia Knight, W.R. Spencer, Samuel Rogers and others.
Frogmore Lodge, Windsor: Priv. pr., 1812. BL

3111. -----The battle of the Nile. A pindarick ode to his excellency the Right Honorable Sir William Hamilton.
Vienna: Pr. Widow Alberti, 1800. 13p. NUC

3114. KNIGHT, Leona Annie, Miss [Am. b. 1859]
Book of poems, by Miss Leona A. Knight.
n.p.: n.p., 1889. 260p. NUC

KNIPE, Eliza see COBBOLD, Elizabeth Knipe

3115. KNOWLES, Louisa J. [Am. 19c]
Thoughts in metre.
Milwaukee, WI: Cramer, Aikens & Cramer, 1889. 69p. NUC OCLC

3116. KNOWLES, Marion Miller [Br. 19c]
Fronds from the black's spur.
Melbourne: G. Robertson & co., 18--? 184p. NUC

3117. -----Love, luck and lavender, original poems.
2d ed. Malvern: H. Mullin, n.d. 49p. NUC

3118. -----Songs from the hills.
L: Melville, Mullen & Slade, 1898. 204p. NUC OCLC

3119. KNOWLES, Mary Morris [Br. 1733-1807]
Compendium of a controversy.
L: Pr. C. Stower, 1805. 7p. NUC BL
[On baptism]

3120. -----The Pope's journey to the other worlds, to seek advice against the national assembly of France.
L: J. Ridgway, 1791. 33p. NUC

KNOWLES, Sarah Elizabeth see BOLTON, Sarah Elizabeth (Knowles)

3121. KNOWLTON, Annie I. [Am. 19c]
Good-bye, old South, good-bye!
Worcester, MA: Bullard art pub. co., 1887. 6 l. NUC

3122. -----My lover's love.
Worcester, MA: Bullard art pub. co., 1887. 5 l. NUC

3123. KNOX, Emeline L. [Am. 19c]
Gems from the field of thought; or, A glimpse into mute life.
Utica, NY: T.J. Griffiths, pr., 1891. c1890. 117p. NUC OCLC
[Poems by a deaf mute]

3124. KNOX, Hon. Lucy (Spring-Rice), Mrs. O.N. Knox [Br. 1845-1884/1894]
Four pictures from a life, and other poems.
L: Kegan Paul & co., 1884. 102p. BL

3125. -----Sonnets and other poems by Hon. Mrs. O.N. Knox.
L: Priv. pr. by R. Barrett & sons, 1872. 52p. NUC BL OCLC

3126. KNOX, Isa Craig [Br. 1831-1903]
ALT: Craig, Isa; Isa
The Burns festival. Prize poem recited at the Crystal Palace, January 25, 1859.
L: Bradbury & Evans, 1859. 7p. NUC OCLC

3127. -----Duchessa [Duchess NUC OCLC] Agnes and other poems.
L: Alexander Strahan, 1864. 228p. NUC BL OCLC
[Verse drama]

3128. -----Poems by Isa.
Edinburgh & L: W. Blackwood & sons, 1856. 172p. NUC BL

3129. -----Poems: an offering to Lancashire.
L: E. Faithfull, 1863. 62p. NUC BL OCLC

3130. -----Songs of consolation.
L: Macmillan & co., 1874. 126p. BL

KNOX, Mrs. O.N. see KNOX, Hon. Lucy (Spring-Rice)

3131. KOHAUS, Hannah More, Mrs. [Am. 19c]
Soul-fragrance.
Chicago: F.M. Harley pub. co., 1895. 170p. NUC OCLC

3132. KOPTA, Flora Pauline (Wilson) [Am. 19c]
Bohemian legends and ballads.
Schuttenhofen: A. Jansky, 1890. 63p. NUC OCLC

3133. -----Bohemian legends and other poems.
2d ed. NY: W.R. Jenkins, 1896. 183p. NUC OCLC
[Misc. poetry, most based on Bohemian folk tales]

3134. KOSSITER, Anna M. S. [19c]
Christmas chimes [by] Lilla N. Cushman.
n.p.: n.p., 1880? 11 l. NUC

3135. KUTZ, M. Jennie, Mrs. [Am. 19c]
Wah-ah-see, a legend of the sleeping dew; and other poems.
Chicago: Pub. for the author by S.S. Boyden, 1868. 200p. NUC OCLC

L. see ADAMS, L.B., Miss

L., pseud., co-author see SHORE, Arabella

L. see SHORE, Louisa Catherine

L., pseud. see SWANWICK, Catherine

L., A. see LEE, Abby

L., A.E. see LEE, Ann Elizabeth

L., A.T. see LUNT, Adeline Treadwell (Parsons)

L., E. see LEWIS, Emma

L., E.S. see COLCHESTER, Lady Elizabeth Sophia (Law)

L., E.S. see COLCHESTER, Elizabeth Susan (Law) Abbot, Baroness Colchester

L., Eliz. B.B. see BULWER, Elizabeth Barbara (Lytton)

L., J. see LARNED, Julia

L., L.E. see LANDON, Letitia Elizabeth

L., L.M. see LUSHINGTON, Lucy Maria

L., S.J. see LAWRENCE, S.J., Mrs.

L., W., co-author see LIDDIARD, J.S. Anna (Wilkinson)

LACTILLA, pseud. see YEARSLEY, Ann (Cromartie)

3136. LACY, Fanny Eliza [Br. 19c]
Centenary tribute to Robert Burns.
L: n.p., 1859. BL

3137. -----The labyrinth and the path; a sacred poem.
Chelsea: n.p., 1856. BL

LADD, Mrs. C.M. see LADD, Catharine (Stratton)

3138. LADD, Eleanor Mary [Am. 19c]
Cherry-bloom; or, Bits of verse from summer-land.
Buffalo, NY: The Peter Paul book co., 1896. 22p. NUC

LADY, A, pseud. see ALLARDYCE, Anne Dundas (Blair)

LADY, A, pseud. see ARTHUR, Grace

LADY, A, pseud. see BACON, Eliza Ann (Munroe)

LADY, A, pseud. see BALLANTYNE, Mrs. John

LADY, A, pseud. see BARRAND, Elizabeth

LADY, A, pseud. see BLENNERHASSETT, Margaret Agnew

LADY, A, pseud. see BONHOTE, Elizabeth, Mrs.

LADY, A, pseud. see COCHRANE, Mrs. Alexander

LADY, A, pseud. see COWPER, Frances Maria (Madan)

LADY, A, pseud. see DE KRAFFT, Mary

LADY, A, pseud. see DORSET, Catherine Ann (Turner)

LADY, A, pseud. see ELLIOTT, Charlotte

LADY, A, pseud. see FRANCIS, Ann

LADY, A, pseud. see G., M.

LADY, A, pseud., co-author see GOULD, Hannah Flagg, Mrs.

LADY, A, pseud. see GRIFFITH, Elizabeth Griffith

LADY, A, pseud. see GRUNDY, Emma, Mrs.

LADY, A, pseud. see HAMILTON, Elizabeth, Mrs.

LADY, A, pseud. see HEMANS, Felicia Dorothea (Browne)

LADY, A, pseud. see HILL, Phillipina (Burton)

LADY, A, pseud. see J., L.L.D.

LADY, A, pseud. see JOURDAN, Mary Jane, Mrs.

LADY, A, pseud. see LETCHES, Mrs.

LADY, A, pseud. see LUCAN, Margaret Smith Bingham, Countess of Lucan

LADY, A, pseud. see MARTINEAU, Harriet

LADY, A, pseud. see MONTAGU, Lady Mary (Pierrepont) Wortley

LADY, A, pseud. see NIVEN, Anna Jane (Vardill)

LADY, A, pseud. see O'BRIEN, Mary, Mrs.

LADY, A, pseud. see ORDE, Isabella

LADY, A, pseud. see PERKINS, Elizabeth (Steele)

LADY, A, pseud. see PINCKNEY, Maria Henrietta

LADY, A, pseud. see POYNTZ, Anne B., Mrs.

LADY, A, pseud. see PYE, Jael Henrietta (Mendez)

LADY, A, pseud. see RICHINGS, Rebecca

LADY, A, pseud. see RITSON, Anne, Mrs.

LADY, A, pseud. see ROBINSON, Anne Steele

LADY, A, pseud. see ROLT, Elizabeth

LADY, A, pseud. see SERRES, Olivia (Wilmot)

LADY, A, pseud. see SMITH, Sarah Pogson, Mrs.

LADY, A, pseud. see SPROAT, Nancy Dennis

LADY, A, pseud. see STRINGER, Mrs.

LADY, A, pseud. see THOMAS, Elizabeth

LADY, A, pseud. see TOMLINS, Elizabeth Sophia

LADY, A, pseud. see YOUNG, Mary Julia

LADY, A, pseud. see WINCHILSEA, Anne (Kingsmill) Finch, Countess of

3139. LADY, A., pseud. [19c]
The Christian's wedding ring, containing five letters and a series of poems, written by a lady, with the sincere desire of sowing the seeds of union in the Christian church.
Montreal: Pr. Lovell pr. & pub. co., 1874. NUC

3140. LADY, A., pseud. [Am. 19c]
Esther: a scripture narrative. By a lady. Together with an original poem, by Miss H.F. Gould.
NY: D. Appleton & co., 1835. NUC BL

3141. LADY, A., pseud. [Br. 19c]
An evening walk in the forest: a poem descriptive of forest trees.
L: Jordan & Maxwell, 1807. 36p. TXU

3142. LADY, A., pseud. [Br. 18c]
The fine gentleman's etiquette; or, Lord Chesterfield's advice to his son, versified.
L: T. Davies, 1776. 26p. NUC BL OCLC

3143. LADY, A., pseud. [Br. 19c]
Original sacred poetry. By a lady.
Salisbury: Priv. pr. by F.A. Blake, 1870. 128p. NUC BL

3144. LADY, A., pseud. [Br. 19c]
A peep at the Esquimaux; or, Scenes on the ice. To which is annexed, a polar pastoral.
L: H.R. Thomas, 1825. 58p. NUC BL OCLC

LADY OF BOSTON, A, pseud. see MORTON, Sarah Wentworth (Apthorp)

LADY OF CHARLESTON, S.C., A, pseud. see MURDEN, Eliza (Crawley)

LADY OF ENGLAND, A, pseud. see TUCKER, Charlotte Marie

LADY OF GEORGIA, A, pseud. see DANNELLY, Elizabeth Otis (Marshall)

LADY OF LEXINGTON, A, pseud. see LITTLEFORD, Mrs.

LADY OF NEW HAMPSHIRE, A, pseud. see HALE, Sarah Josepha (Buell)

LADY OF NEW YORK, A, pseud. see HAIGHT, Sarah (Rogers)

LADY OF PHILADELPHIA, A, pseud. see BOTSFORD, Margaret, Mrs.

LADY OF QUALITY, A, pseud. see CHUDLEIGH, Mary (Lee), Lady

LADY OF QUALITY, A, pseud. see DUBOIS, Lady Dorothea (Annesley)

LADY OF RICHMOND, A, pseud. see LITTLEFORD, Mrs.

3145. LAFARGUE, Francis Harriet [Br. 19c]
Leon, and other poems.
L: n.p., 1846. NUC BL

3146. LAFFAN, Bertha Jane (Grundy), Mrs. R.S. DeCourcy Laffan [Am. d. 1912] ALT: Adams, Bertha Leith
A son of jubilee, and other poems.
L: K. Paul, Trench & co., 1887. 77p. NUC BL

LAFFAN, Mrs. R.S. DeCourcy see LAFFAN, Bertha Jane (Grundy)

LAGRANGE, Magdalene I. see MERRITT, Magdalene Isadora (LaGrange)

3147. LAHEE, M.R., Miss [Br. 19c]
Tim Bobbin's centenary. A ghostly conversation in verse. Died July 14th 1786.
Manchester: J. Heywood, 1886. 14p. BL
[On works of Tim Bobbin, pseud. of John Collier, writer in Lancashire dialect]

LAING, Andrew, co-author see KENDALL, May

3148. LAKE, Anne [Br. 19c] PSEUD: Ekalenna
The beauty of holiness and other poems.
Torrington: M.C. Heywood, 1871. 40p. BL

3149. LAKE, Catherine [Br. 19c]
Euterpe; or, The dream of music.
L: n.p., 1852. BL
[Allegory]

LAKE, CLAUDE, pseud. see BLIND, Mathilde

3150. LAMB, Lady Caroline (Ponsonby) [Br. 1785-1828]
Fugitive pieces and reminiscences of Lord Byron ... also some original poetry, letters, and recollections of Lady Caroline Lamb. By Isaac Nathan.
L: Whitaker, Treacher & co., 1829. 196p. BL OCLC

3151. -----Gordon, a tale. A poetical review of Don Juan.
L: Allman, 1821. NUC

3152. -----A new canto.
L: William Wright, 1819. 16p. BL
[Pub. anon. Satire on her critics, on London, on Napoleon]

3153. LAMB, Martha Joanna Reade (Nash) [Am. 1829-1893] PSEUD: Aunt Mattie
The Christmas basket; holiday entertainment (original & selected).
NY: White & Stokes, 1882. 16 l. NUC
[Not intended for children; 2 of the 12 poems are by Lamb.]

3154. -----The Christmas owl. A budget of entertainment. Original and selected.
NY: White & Stokes, 1881. 16 l. NUC
[Intended for all ages.]

3155. LAMBERT, Eliza [Br. 19c]
Poetic strains: or, Thoughts in leisure hours.
Derby: n.p., 1830. BL

LAMBERT, Mary see TUCKER LAMBERT, Mary

3156. LAMBERT, Mary [Am. 19c]
Poems.
San Francisco: Pr. Bancroft co., 1892. 200p. NUC
[Lettered on cover: Rhyming oak leaves]

3157. LAMBERT, Mary H. P. [d. 1921] PSEUD: Luigi
A legend of Lake Leman. By Luigi.
Geneva: Burkhardt, 1885. 28p. NUC

3158. LAMONT, Mrs. Aeneas [Br. 19c]
Poems, and tales in verse.
L: Ogles, Duncan, & Cochran, 1818. 179p. NUC BL

LANDER, META, pseud. see LAWRENCE, Margaret Oliver (Woods)

LANDON, J.T.B., ed. see WATT, Mrs. Francis

3159. LANDON, Letitia Elizabeth [Br. 1802-1838] ALT: L., L.E.; Mrs. George Maclean
A birthday tribute. By L.E.L.
L & Paris: n.p., 1837. BL
[Addressed to Princess Alexandrina]

3160. -----Corinne; or, Italy ... By Madame de Stael. Translated by Isabel Hill; with metrical versions of the odes by L.E. Landon.
L: R. Bentley, 1833. 392p. NY: 1861. BL OCLC
[3d Am. ed. Philadelphia: E.L. Carey & A. Hart, 1836. 2v. in 1. OCLC]

3161. -----The Easter gift, a religious offering. By L.E.L.
L: Fisher, 1832. 47p. NUC BL

3162. -----The fate of Adelaide, a Swiss romantic tale; and other poems.
L: J. Warren, 1821. 154p. NUC BL OCLC

3163. LANDON, Letitia Elizabeth [Br. 1802-1838]
Fisher's drawing room scrapbook ... With poetical illustrations by L.E.L.
L: America [etc.] Fisher, son & co., 1837. 56p. NUC OCLC

3164. -----The golden violet, with its tales of romance and chivalry; and other poems.
L: Longman, Rees, Orme, Brown, & Green, 1827. 310p. NUC BL OCLC

3165. -----The improvisatrice, and other poems by L.E.L.
New ed. L: Longman, Rees, Orme, Brown & Green, 1827. 326p. NUC BL

3166. -----The improvisatrice; and other poems.
L: Hurst, Robinson; Edinburgh: A. Constable, 1824. 327p. NUC BL OCLC

3167. -----Life and literary remains of L.E.L., by Laman Blanchard.

L: H. Colburn, 1841. 2v. NUC OCLC
[Incl. lyric poems & "Castruccio Castrucani; or, The triumph of Lucca. A tragedy." in 5 acts]

3168. -----Miscellaneous poetical works of L.E.L.
L: Saunders & Otley, 1835. 352p. NUC

3169. -----The passion flower.
NY: n.p., 1844. 32p. NUC
[Pub. with N.P. Willis: Sacred poems.]

3170. -----The poetical works of L.E.L.
New ed. L: Longman, Rees, Orme, Brown & Green, 1827. 326p. NUC BL OCLC

3171. -----The poetical works of Miss Landon.
Philadelphia: E.L. Carey & A. Hart, 1838. 348p. NUC OCLC

3172. -----The Venetian bracelet, the lost Pleiad, A history of the lyre, and other poems. By L.E.L.
L: Longman, Rees, Orme, Brown, & Green, 1829. 307p. NUC BL

3173. -----The vow of the peacock, and other poems. By L.E.L.
L: Saunders Otley, 1835. 352p. NUC OCLC

3174. -----The Zenana and minor poems of L.E.L.; with a memoir by Emma Roberts.
L: Fisher, 1839. 297p.

3175. LANG, Fanny Forrester [Am. b. 1848]
Little poems. By Fanny Forrester Lang. Aged nine years.
Boston: Pub. for the authoress. W. White, pr., 1858. 24p. NUC

3176. LANGSTON, C.B., Mrs. [Br. 19c]
The earth. An epic poem.
L: S. Tinsley & co., 1879. 61p. BL

3177. -----Poems.
L: F.V. White & co., 1882. 240p. BL

3178. LANGTON, Millicent [Br. 19c]
Musings of the work-room.
L: J.R. Howe; Leicester: Rowe, 1865. 136p. BL OCLC

LANIER, Aemelia <u>see</u> LANYER, Aemilia

3179. LANYER, Aemilia [Br. 1569-1645]
Salve Deus Rex Judaeorum.
Containing, 1. The passion of Christ. 2. Eve's apologie in defence of women. 3. The teares of the daughters of Jerusalem. 4. The salutation and sorrow of the Virgine Marie.
L: Pr. Valentine Simmes for Richard Bonian, 1611. NUC BL

3180. LARCOM, Lucy [Am. 1824-1893]
At the beautiful gates and other songs of faith.
Boston & NY: Houghton, Mifflin & co., 1892. 117p. NUC BL OCLC

3181. -----The crystal hills. With John Greenleaf Whittier.
Boston: L. Prang & co., 1889. 8p. NUC OCLC
[Cover title: White mountain vistas]

3182. -----Easter gleams.
Boston & NY: Houghton, Mifflin & co., 1890. 45p. NUC OCLC

3183. -----Easter messengers; a new poem of the flowers.
NY: White, Stokes, & Allen, 1886. 24p. NUC OCLC

3184. -----The governor's tree.
Boston: n.p., 1890. 4p. NUC
[Arbor Day poem]

3185. -----An idyll of work.
Boston: J.R. Osgood & co., 1875. 183p. NUC OCLC
[Narrative poem on life of female mill-workers in New Hampshire]

3186. -----The Kansas prize song ... call to Kansas.
Boston: n.p., 1855. NUC
[Won contest for the best song for Kansas immigrants]

3187. -----Lays of the emigrants, as sung by the parties for Kansas, on the days of their departure from Boston, during the spring of 1855.
Boston: A. Mudge & son, 1855. 4p. NUC

3188. -----Poems.
Boston: Fields, Osgood & co., 1869. 275p. NUC BL OCLC

3189. -----Snow bloom and other poems.
Boston: R. Marvin & son, 187-? 22p. NUC

3190. -----Wheaton seminary: a semi-centennial sketch.
Cambridge, MA: Riverside press, 1885. 94p. NUC OCLC

[Incl. a poem & a hymn.]

3191. -----Wild roses of Cape Ann and other poems.
Boston: Houghton, Mifflin, 1881. 272p. NUC BL OCLC

3192. -----A year in heaven.
Boston: n.p., 1892. NUC

3193. LARNED, Augusta [Am. 1835-1924]
In woods and fields.
NY & L: G.P. Putnam's sons, 1895. 157p. NUC OCLC

3194. LARNED, Julia [Am. 19c] ALT: L., J.
The story of a hunchback, and other poems. By J.L.
Chicago?: n.p., 1881. 88p. NUC OCLC
[Also attr. to Walter Cranston Larned]

LARNED, Walter Cranston see LARNED, Julia

3195. LARUE, Eliza W. [Am. 19c]
PSEUD: Diehope
The garland: a collection of juvenile poems.
NY: Stephen H. Latkins, 1824. 97p. NUC OCLC
[Written when author was young. Some previously pub. in newspaper as "Diehope."]

3196. LATHBURY, Mary Artemisia [Am. 1841-1913] PSEUD: Aunt May
The birthday week; pictures and verse.
NY: R. Worthington, 1884. 22 l. NUC OCLC
[Also pub. as "Seven little maids; or, The birthday week," based on "Monday's child is fair of face," etc.]

3197. -----Idyls of the months; poems and drawings.
NY: G. Routledge & sons, 1885. 14 l. NUC OCLC

3198. -----Out of darkness into light. Poems and drawings.
Boston: D. Lothrop, 1878. 21 l. NUC OCLC

3199. LATHRAP, Mary (Torrans) [Am. 1838-1895] ALT: Lathrop, Mary (Torrans)
The poems and written addresses of Mary T. Lathrap ... with a short sketch of her life ... . Comp. & ed. Julia R. Parish.
Bay City, MI: Woman's Christian Temperance Union, 1895. 430p. NUC OCLC

3200. -----Rare gems from the literary works of Mary T. Lathrap.
Bay City, MI: Woman's Christian Temperance Union, 1895. 95p. NUC OCLC
[Misc. poetry; Prose aphorisms on temperance]

3201. -----What means this stone? a poem.
L & NY: Raphael Tuck & son, 1890. 12p. NUC OCLC

LATHROP, Mary (Torrans) see LATHRAP, Mary (Torrans)

LATHROP, Mother Mary Alphonsa see LATHROP, Rose (Hawthorne)

3202. LATHROP, Rose Hawthorne [Am. 1851-1926] ALT: Lathrop, Mother Mary Alphonsa
Along the shore.
Boston: Ticknor & co., 1888. 104p. NUC BL OCLC

LATIMER, E., Miss, ed. see DYSON, Julia A. (Parker)

3203. LATIMER, E., Miss [Am. 19c]
The beautiful.
NY: Baker & Taylor for the author, 1885. 106p. NUC BL OCLC
[Essays on the beautiful; eight original poems]

3204. -----Idyls of Gettysburg.
Philadelphia: George Maclean, 1872. 126p. NUC BL OCLC
[Poems and an essay on the battle]

3205. LATTER, Mary, Mrs. [Br. 1725-1777]
Liberty and interest: a burlesque poem on the present times.
L: J. Fletcher, 1764. 20p. BL OCLC

3206. -----A lyric ode on the birth of His Royal Highness the Prince of Wales.
L: C. Bathurst, 1763. 8p. NUC BL
[George IV, King of Great Britain]

3207. -----A miscellaneous poetical essay in three parts.
L: W. Sandby, 1761. 56p. NUC BL

3208. -----The miscellaneous works in prose and verse, of Mrs. Mary Latter.
Reading: C. Pocock; L: J. Wilkie, 1759. 3 pt. 212p. NUC BL

[(1) epistolary correspondence (2) poems and soliloquies (3) prose poem]

3209. LAURIE, Catherine Ann, Mrs. Simon Somerville Laurie [Br. d. 1895]
In memory of Catherine Ann Laurie, Nairne Lodge, Duddingston Midlothian, who departed this life on the 31st July, 1895. Ed. her husband, Simon Somerville Laurie.
Edinburgh: Priv. pr. by Mrs. R.F. Hamilton Bruce, 1896. 145p. NUC
[Incl. poetry]

3210. LAW, Elizabeth Annie [Br. 19c]
The hyacinth. A collection of poems.
L: The author, 1845. 132p. BL

LAURA MARIA, pseud. see ROBINSON, Mary (Darby)

LAURIE, Mrs. Simon Somerville see LAURIE, Catherine Ann

LAW, Elizabeth Susan see COLCHESTER, Elizabeth Susan (Law) Abbot, Baroness Colchester

3211. LAW, Isabella [Br. 19c]
Winter weavings; poems.
L: Smith, 1863. 179p. NUC BL

3212. LAWFORD, F.G.V., Mrs. [Br. 19/20c] PSEUD: Lillian
Our Queen, and other poems. By Lillian.
L: Digby, Long & co., 1895. 136p. BL

3213. LAWLESS, Hon. Emily [Br. 1845-1913]
Atlantic rhymes and rhythms by E.L.
L?: Pr. S.S. for herself & 4 others, 1898. 101p. OCLC

LAWRENCE, Annie Maria see CLARK, Annie Maria (Lawrence)

3214. LAWRENCE, Bessie [Am. 19c]
PSEUD: Agatha
Thanksgiving, and other poems, by Agatha.
NY: G.P. Putnam's sons, 1880. 101p. NUC OCLC

3215. LAWRENCE, Elizabeth [Am. 19c]
The Inca's bride, a poem.
Memphis, TN: D.O. Dooley & co., 1855. 113p. NUC OCLC
[Pub. with "America; her history & her scenery: a fragment," a poem]

3216. LAWRENCE, Lavinia J. [Am. 19c]
Euthanasia, and other poems.
Philadelphia: Turner & co., 1870. 153p. NUC BL OCLC

3217. LAWRENCE, Margaret Oliver (Woods) [Am. 1813-1901] PSEUD: Lander, Meta
Blossoms of childhood, by a mother.
NY: L. Colby, c1839. 155p. NUC OCLC

3218. -----Fading flowers. By Meta Lander.
Boston: J.E. Tilton & co., 1860. 288p. NUC OCLC

LAWRENCE, Rose D'Aguilar, Mrs., comp. see HEMANS, Felicia Dorothea (Browne)

3219. LAWRENCE, Rose D'Aguilar [Br. 19c]
The last autumn at a favourite residence: with other poems.
L: N. Hailes, 1828. 104p. NUC OCLC

3220. -----The last autumn at a favourite residence: with other poems.
2d ed. Liverpool: n.p., 1829. NUC BL OCLC
[2d ed. has many additions]

3221. LAWRENCE, S.J., Mrs. [Am. 19c]
ALT: L., S.J.
Consolation; or, A winter's gleaning. In a poem. By S.J.L.
Boston: B.B. Russell, 1871. 144p. NUC OCLC

3222. LAWRENCE, Sarah, Miss [Br. 19c]
Poems by Sarah Lawrence.
L: Kinder, 1847. 100p. BL OCLC

3223. LAWSON, Emilie [Am. 19c]
Arkansaw Jackson, his reminiscences of the medical college of the Pacific.
n.p.: n.p., 18--? 7p. NUC

3224. LAWSON, Mary Jane (Katzmann), Mrs. William Lawson [1828-1890]
Frankincense and myrrh, selections from the poems of the late Mrs. William Lawson.
Halifax, N.S.: Morton & co., 1893. 152p. NUC

LAWSON, Mrs. William see LAWSON, Mary Jane (Katzmann)

3225. LAWTON, Hester Annie [Br. 19c]
Elodie, a legend of the Dee, and other poems.
L: Longman, 1847. 227p. NUC BL OCLC

3226. LAYARD, Nina Frances [Br. 19c]
I, myself, and other poems.
L: Simpkin, Marshall, 1893. 118p. BL

3227. -----Poems.
L: Longmans, Green, 1890. 161p. NUC BL OCLC

3228. -----Songs in many moods. By Nina Frances Layard [and] The wandering albatross, etc. by Annie Corder.
L & NY: Longmans, Green, 1897. 126p. NUC BL
[Sep. collections bound together]

3229. LAZARUS, Emma [Am. 1849-1887]
Admetus, and other poems.
NY: Hurd & Houghton, 1871. 229p. NUC BL OCLC
[Trans. from German, pp. 195-229.]

3230. -----Poems and translations. Written between the ages of fourteen and seventeen [sixteen OCLC].
NY: Pr. for priv. circ., 1866. 207p. NUC BL OCLC

3231. -----The poems of Emma Lazarus. Biographical sketch by her sister, Josephine Lazarus.
Boston: Houghton, Mifflin, 1888. 2v. NUC BL OCLC
[Narrative, lyric, & dramatic poems.]

3232. -----Songs of a Semite: the dance to death and other poems.
NY: Office of "The American Hebrew," 1882. 80p. NUC BL OCLC
[The dance to death; historical tragedy in five acts, p. 5-48]

3233. -----The spagnoletto: a drama in verse.
n.p.: n.p., 1876. 56p. NUC OCLC

LAZARUS, Josephine, comp. see LAZARUS, Emma

LEA, GOWAN, pseud. see MORGAN, Mary

3234. LEADBEATER, Mary Shackleton [Br. 1758-1826]
Poems.
Dublin: M. Keene, 1808. 419p. BL OCLC
[Incl. trans. Aenead Bk. XIII]

3235. LEAKEY, Caroline Woolmer [Br. 1827-1881]
Lyra Australis, or, attempts to sing in a strange land.
L: Bickers & Bush, 1854. 298p. NUC BL

3236. LEAN, E.J., Mrs. [Br. 19c]
PSEUD: Spinster, A
Leap year: addressed to the bachelor members of Her Majesty's Rifle Corps; by a spinster.
L: T.C. Newby, 1860. 23p. NUC BL

3237. -----Original poems on various subjects.
Brighton: n.p., 1845. BL

3238. LEAPOR, Mary, Mrs. [Br. 1722-1746]
Poems upon several occasions. Ed. Isaac Hawkins Browne.
L: Pr. J. Roberts, 1748-51. 2v. NUC BL OCLC
[Vol. 2 contains a tragedy in blank verse, The unhappy father]

3239. LEARNED, Lydia [Am. 1730-1792]
A poem on the death of Mr. Abraham Rice, aged 80, and Mr. John Cloyes, aged 41, who were struck with lightning, June 3, 1777, in Framingham. By Lydia Learned, of Framingham.
Boston: Pr. at the Bible & Heart in Cornhill, 1777? 10p.

3240. LEATHLEY, Mary Elizabeth Southwell (Dudley) [Br. 1818-1899]
Verses.
L: Pr. for priv. circ., 1896. 102p. BL

LEAVITT, Mrs. L.M. see LEAVITT, Martha Cornelia

3241. LEAVITT, Martha Cornelia, Mrs. L.M. Leavitt [Am. b. 1841]
Echoes. By Mrs. L.M. Leavitt.
Lewiston, ME: Gordon & Payne, 1885. 192p. NUC

LE BAILLY, Winifred M. (Lucas) see LUCAS, Winifred M.

3242. LECK, Jane [Br. 19c]
Doon lyrics.
Glasgow: Pr. for the author by J. Maclehose, 1894. 182p. NUC BL OCLC

3243. LECKIE, Elizabeth (Horner), Mrs. George Leckie [Br. d. 1856]
The dream of the western shepherd.
Edinburgh: Priv. pr., 1845. BL

3244. -----The guardian: a dramatic poem.
Edinburgh: Edinburgh pr. & pub. co.; L: Smith, Elder & co., 1843. BL
[2 acts]

3245. -----The Hebrew boy. A dramatic poem.
Edinburgh: Edinburgh pr. & pub. co.; L: Smith, Elder & co., 1842. BL
[2 acts]

3246. -----The power of conscience. A dramatic poem.
Edinburgh: Edinburgh pr. & pub. co.; L: Smith, Elder & co., 1841. 27p. BL
[2 acts, music & poetry]

3247. -----The stepmother. A dramatic poem.
Edinburgh: Edinburgh pr. & pub. co.; L: Smith, Elder & co., 1842. BL
[2 acts, music & poetry]

LECKIE, Mrs. George see LECKIE, Elizabeth (Horner)

3248. LECKY, Elizabeth [Br. 19c]
From first to last; or, The current of life. With Susan Lecky.
n.p.: n.p., 18--? 32p. OCLC
[Poems on the seasons & the cycle of life]

LECKY, Susan, co-author see LECKY, Elizabeth

3249. LEE, Ann Elizabeth [Br. 19c]
ALT: L., A.E.
The fruits of the valley (Song of Solomon, chap. VI, ver. ii). By A.E.L.
L: n.p., 1855. BL

LEE, Eleanor Percy (Ward), co-author see WARFIELD, Catherine Ann (Ware)

3250. LEE, Emma (Carter) [Am. 19c]
Poems, by Mrs. Emma Carter Lee, and address, by Walter S. Carter, delivered at the centennial celebration, at Barkhamsted, Litchfield County, Connecticut, Sept. 10, 1879.
NY: S.B. Leverich, pr., 1879. 20p. NUC

3251. LEE, Floride (Clemson) [Am. 1842-1871] PSEUD: de Flori, C.
Poet skies, and other experiences in versification, by C. de Flori.
Baltimore, MD: J.W. Woods, pr., 1868. 72p. NUC OCLC

LEE, Mrs. Frank see LEE, Mary (Chappell)

LEE, HOLME, pseud. see PARR, Harriet

LEE, Ida see MARRIOTT, Ida (Lee)

3252. LEE, Ira, Mrs. [Am. 19c]
The mother's lament.
Providence, RI: Knowles, Anthony & co., prs., 1840. 192p. NUC
[Poems on the death of her daughter]

3253. LEE, Mary Elizabeth [Am. 1813-1849]
The poetical remains of the late M.E. Lee. Ed. S. Gilman.
Charleston, SC: Walker & Richards, 1851. 224p. NUC BL OCLC

3254. LEE, Rebecca [Br. 19c]
Verses, original, and translated from the Italian and French.
L: Hamilton, Adams & co., 1842. 144p. NUC BL OCLC

3255. LEE, Rona [Br. 19c]
The legend of the three sisters. A poem.
L: n.p., 1853. BL

3256. LEE, Sophia [Br. 1750-1824]
A hermit's tale recorded by his own hand and found in his cell.
L: T. Cadell, 1787. 40p. NUC BL OCLC
[Ballad of 156 stanzas on border warfare]

3257. LEECH, Margaret, Miss [Br. 19c]
Poems on various subjects.
L: Pr. Whittingham & Rowland, 1816. 195p. NUC BL

3258. LEECH, Sarah [Br. b. 1809]
Poems on various subjects. With a biographic memoir.
Dublin: Pr. J. Charles, 1828. 72p. NUC

L'ECLAIR, pseud. see ODOM, Mary (Hunt) McCaleb

LEESER, Isaac, ed. see AGUILAR, Grace

LEFANU, Alicia, comp. see SHERIDAN, Frances (Chamberlaine)

3259. LEFANU, Alicia, Miss [Br. 19c]
The flowers; or, the Sylphid queen: a fairy tale, in verse.
L: J. Harris, 1809. 52p. NUC BL OCLC

3260. -----Rosara's chain: or, The choice of life. A poem.
L: Pr. for M.J. Godwin by Joyce Gold, 1812. 108p. NUC BL OCLC

3261. LEFEVRE, Lily Alice (Cooke) [1853/4-1938]
The lion's gate.
Vancouver, B.C.: n.p., 189-? 9p. NUC
[First dated ed. 1895]

3262. LEFROY, Anne (Rickman) [Br. d. 1808]
Carmina domestica; or, Poems on several occasions ... by Mrs. Lefroy

... now printed, with some others, by her son [Christopher Edward Lefroy]. L: Law & Gilbert, 1812. 184p. BL

LEFROY, Christopher Edward, co-author see LEFROY, Anne (Rickman)

3263. LE HARDY, Esther [Br. 19c]
Agabus; or, The last of the Druids: an historical poem.
L: William Pickering, 1851. 156p. NUC BL OCLC
[BL: Incl. notes and The dying Druid, a poem by R.A. Davenport]

3264. LEICESTER, Mary [Br. 19c]
Sung in the shadow. A collection of short poems.
L: L. Lloyd, 1899. 31p. BL

LEIGH, ARBOR, pseud. see BEVINGTON, Louisa Sarah

LEIGH, ARRAN, pseud. see BRADLEY, Katherine Harris

3265. LEIGH, Helen [Br. 18c]
Miscellaneous poems.
Manchester: Pr. C. Wheeler, sold by Mssrs. Clarkes, 1788. 32p. NUC BL

LEIGH, ISLA, pseud. see COOPER, Edith Emma

3266. LEIGHTON, Harriet W. [Am. 19c]
Prairie songs.
Lincoln, NB: H.W. Leighton, pr. by Hoge & Benton, 1898. 138p. NUC OCLC

LEITH, Mrs. Disney see LEITH, Mary Charlotte Julia (Gordon)

LEITH, Mrs. James John Forbes see LEITH, Williamina Helen Stewart Forbes

3267. LEITH, Emily [Br. 19c]
Thoughts and remembrance. Verses.
Glasgow: D. Bryce & son, 1885. 117p. NUC BL OCLC

3268. LEITH, Mary Charlotte Julia (Gordon), Mrs. Disney Leith [Br. 19/20c]
A martyr bishop, and other verses.
L: J. Masters, 1878. 113p. NUC BL

3269. -----Original verses and translations. By Mrs. Disney Leith.
L: J. Masters, 1895. 151p. NUC BL OCLC
[Trans. from Icelandic poetry]

3270. LEITH, Williamina Helen (Stewart) Forbes, Mrs. James John Forbes Leith [Br. 19c]
Whitehaugh; a poem, by W.H.S.F.L., ... addressed to her eldest son, after the demise of his father.
Boulogne-sur-mer: Priv. pr., 1848. BL

LELAND, Frank, comp. see LELAND, Hattie M. (Perkins)

LELAND, Mrs. Frank see LELAND, Hattie M. (Perkins)

3271. LELAND, Hattie M. (Perkins), Mrs. Frank Leland [Am. 1833?-1884]
PSEUD: Ingleby, Kate
Affection's offering by Mrs. Frank Leland. Comp. Frank Leland.
Madison, WI: David Atwood, 1882. 230p. NUC OCLC
[Poems, 2 short prose pieces]

3272. -----Golden thoughts at Ingleside. Gleaned from the life thoughts of Mrs. Frank Leland, "Kate Ingleby." Comp. Frank Leland.
Elkhorn, WI: F. Leland, 1887. 316p. NUC OCLC
[Incl. poetry]

3273. LENNOX, Charlotte (Ramsay) [Am/Br. 1720-1804] ALT: Ramsay, Charlotte PSEUD: Young Lady, A
Philander. A dramatic pastoral.
Dublin: R. Smith, 1758. 36p. L: A. Millar, 1758. 48p. NUC BL OCLC
[Inspired by Il Pastor Fido, 3 acts, verse; 2 songs are by another hand]

3274. -----Poems on several occasions. Written by a young lady.
L: S. Paterson, 1747. 88p. NUC BL OCLC

3275. LE NOIR, Elizabeth Anne (Smart) [Br. 1755?-1841]
Clara de Montfier; a moral tale. With original poems.
Reading: Pr. A.M. Smart for the author, sold by Rivington's, 1808. 3v. BL OCLC
[2d ed., 1819: The Maid of La Vende, or Clara de Montfier. Incl. over 2 dozen songs, hymns, a ballad, beast fable & an allegory. Mostly pastoral in theme]

3276. -----Miscellaneous poems.
L: Pr. for the author, sold by M. Cowslade & co., 1825. 2v. NUC

3277. -----Village anecdotes; or, The journal of a year, from Sophia to Edward. With original poems.

L: Vernor & Hood, 1804. 3v. NUC BL OCLC

3278. LENT, Emma A. [Am. 19c]
The chime of bells.
Albany, NY: Weed, Parsons, & co., 1883. 107p. NUC OCLC

3279. LEONARD, Caroline H. [Am. 19c]
The rose of America: a poem, treating upon portions of the United States' history; to which are added, a few miscellaneous pieces.
Lee, MA: Pr. French & Royce, 1854. 62p. NUC

3280. LEONARD, Carrie, Mrs. [19c]
Gems for the home circle. Original poems.
London, Ontario: n.p., 1869. 150p. NUC

3281. LEONARD, Eliza Lucy [Br. 19c]
The miller and his golden dream.
Wellington: Pr. F. Houlston & son, 1822. 30p. NUC BL

3282. -----The ruby ring; or, The transformations.
L: John Sharpe, 1815. 64p. NUC BL OCLC

3283. LEONARD, Elizabeth C. [Am. 19c]
Poems.
Boston: George H. Ellis, 1889. 107p. NUC OCLC

3284. LEONARD, Mary Hall [Am. 1847-1921]
The story of Portus and songs of the southland.
Buffalo, NY: C.W. Moulton, 1894. 107p. NUC OCLC

3285. LESLIE, Eliza [Am. 1787-1858]
Birth day stories.
Philadelphia: H.F. Anners, 1840. 179p.
[Incl. dramatic dialogue & a poem.]

3286. LESLIE, Eliza A. [Br. 19c]
Stray leaves.
Edinburgh: R. Grant & son, 1866. 138p. BL

3287. LESLIE, Mary Eliza [Br. 19c]
Heart echoes from the East; or, Sacred hymns and sonnets.
L: n.p., 1861. BL

3288. -----Ina, and other poems.
Calcutta: W. Newman & co., 1856. 290p. BL

3289. -----Sorrows, aspirations, and legends from India.
L: n.p., 1858. BL

3290. LETCHES, Mrs. [Br. 18c] PSEUD: Lady, A
Poems on several occasions, by a lady.
Bristol: Pr. Bulgin & Rosser, 1792. 27p. BL OCLC

LETHBRIDGE, Caroline Gifford <u>see</u> PHILLIPSON, Caroline Giffard (Lethbridge)

LEVERING, Sarah R., comp. <u>see</u> BLAKE, Margaret Jane

3291. LEVY, Amy [Br. 1861-1889]
A London plane-tree and other verse.
L: T. Fisher Unwin, 1889. 94p. NUC BL OCLC
[Cameo Series]

3292. -----A minor poet and other verse.
L: T.F. Unwin, 1884. 93p. NUC BL OCLC

3293. -----Xantippe and other verse.
Cambridge: E. Johnson, 1881. 30p. NUC BL OCLC

LEWES, Marian <u>see</u> EVANS, Marian

3294. LEWIS, Eliza Gabriella, Miss [Am. 19c]
Poems.
Brooklyn, NY: Pr. Shannon & co., 1850. 148p. NUC BL OCLC
[Incl. "The outlaw, a dramatic sketch," 3 acts, set in Germany. Misc. poetry.]

3295. LEWIS, Emma [Br. 19c] ALT: L., E.
Night watches; or, The peace of the cross. By E.L.
Philadelphia: Willis P. Hazard, 1853. 248p. NUC BL OCLC
[Misc. poetry, religious]

3296. LEWIS, Emma
Treasures of darkness. By E.L.
Philadelphia: W.P. Hazard, 1854. 252p. NUC BL OCLC

3297. LEWIS, Estelle Anna Blanche (Robinson) [Am. 1824-1880] PSEUD: Lewis, Sarah Anna, Mrs.
The broken trust.
1847.

3298. -----Child of the sea, and other poems. By Mrs. S. Anna Lewis.

NY: G.P. Putnam, 1848. 179p. NUC
[Title poem, a narrative in 4 cantos; Isabella, narrative in 3 cantos; misc. poems]

3299. -----Myths of the minstrel. By Estelle Anna Lewis.
NY: D. Appleton & co., 1852. 95p. NUC BL

3300. -----Records of the heart and other poems. By Sarah Anna Lewis.
NY: D. Appleton & co.; Philadelphia: G.S. Appleton, 1844. 255p. NUC BL OCLC
[Pub. under own name in 1857]

3301. LEWIS, Hannah Jane (Woodman) [Am. b. 1816] ALT: Woodman, H. J., Miss
The language of gems, with their poetic sentiments.
Boston: A. Tompkins & B.B. Mussey, 1845. 160p. NUC OCLC

3302. -----Sibylline verses; or, The mirror of fate. By Miss H.J. Woodman.
Boston: A. Tompkins, 1846. 216p. NUC

3303. -----The poetical works of Mrs. H.J. Lewis.
Boston: Cupples, Upham & co., 1885. 148p. NUC OCLC

3304. LEWIS, Mary [Br. 19c]
Poems and prose.
L: Houlston & Stoneman; Stroud: F.W. Harmer, 1855. 146p. BL
[Poems, primarily religious & nature; 11 short prose pieces, incl. 2 flower legends]

3305. LEWIS, Mary G., Miss [Br. 19c]
Zelinda, a poem; and Cardiff Castle, a dramatic-historical sketch .... By M.G. Lewis.
L: Simpkin & Marshall, 1823. 144p. NUC
[Zelinda, a melodramatic tale in verse; Cardiff Castle, play, 5 scenes, on Henry I of England.]

3306. LEWIS, Mary McFarland [Am. 1828-1893] PSEUD: Meta
Heart echoes, by Meta.
Baltimore, MD: Turnbull bros., 1873. 131p. NUC OCLC

LEWIS, S. Anna, Mrs. see LEWIS, Estelle Anna Blanche (Robinson)

LEWIS, Sarah Anna, Mrs. see LEWIS, Estelle Anna Blanche (Robinson)

3307. LICKBARROW, Isabella [Br. 19c]
A lament upon the death of ... the Princess Charlotte, and Alfred, a vision.
Liverpool: n.p., 1818. BL

3308. -----Poetical effusions.
Kendal: Pr. M. Branthwaite, 1814. 131p. NUC BL OCLC

LIDDELL, Margaret Fraser (Tytler) see TYTLER, Margaret Fraser

3309. LIDDELL, Mary Hannah [Br. 19c]
Poetry: original and select.
York: Robert Sunter, 1850. 240p. NUC BL

LIDDIARD, I.S. Anna (Wilkinson) see LIDDIARD, J.S. Anna (Wilkinson)

3310. LIDDIARD, J. [I. BL] S. Anna (Wilkinson) [Br. 19c]
Kenilworth and Farley Castle; with other poems.
Dublin: Pr. at the Hibernia press office for priv. circ., 1813. 144p. NUC BL

3311. -----Kenilworth: a mask. With: The phantom knight; or, Farley Castle. A chivalric tale.
Dublin: John Cumming; L: Longman, Hurst, Rees, Orme, & Browne, 1815. 112p. BL
[Based on the entertainment presented for Elizabeth I; 3 days' pageants]

3312. -----Mount Leinster; or, The prospect: a poem descriptive of Irish scenery.
L: Longman, Hurst, Rees, Orme & Browne, 1819. 31p. BL OCLC

3313. -----Poems.
Dublin: Pr. at the Hibernia press office, 1810. 100p. NUC BL OCLC

3314. -----The Sgelaighe; or, A tale of old; with a second edition of poems, published in Dublin with additions.
Bath: Pr. Meyler & son, 1811. 184p. NUC BL
[Irish legendary tales, odes, elegies, nature, & poems on the Irish Harp Society]

3315. -----Theodore and Laura: or, Evening after the battle, a tale. An ode on the year 1815. Pub. with: Mount St. Jean, a poem by W[illiam L[iddiard].

Dublin: John Cumming; L: Longman, Hurst, Rees, Orme & Browne, 1816. 72p. BL
[Theodore & Laura pp. 41-56 in verse; ode 57-60]

LIDDIARD, William, co-author <u>see</u> LIDDIARD, J.S. Anna (Wilkinson)

LIEKMAN, J., co-author <u>see</u> JONES, Sarah (Liekman)

3316. LIGHTFOOT, Catherine Anne [Br. 19c]
The Battle of Trafalgar; a poem, in six cantos.
Sevenoaks: Pr. C. Payne; L: Whittaker, Treacher & co., 1883. 148p. NUC BL

LILLIAN, pseud. <u>see</u> LAWFORD, F.G.V., Mrs.

3317. LILLIE, Mrs. R. Shepard [Am. 19c]
Two chapters from the book of my life, with poems.
Boston: J. Wilson & son, 1889. 229p. NUC OCLC

3318. LINCOLN, Jeanie Thomas (Gould) [Am. 1846-1921] ALT: G., Jeanie
A chaplet of leaves. By Jeanie G.
NY: Hurd & Houghton; Cambridge, MA: Riverside press, 1869. 112p. NUC BL OCLC

3319. LINCOLN, Martha D., Mrs. [Am. b. 1838]
Over the lawn to the White House.
Washington, DC: M.D. Lincoln & E. Maynicke, 1893. 20p. NUC BL
[In verse]

LINDSAY, Lady Anne <u>see</u> BARNARD, Anne (Lindsay), Lady

3320. LINDSAY, Caroline Blanche Elizabeth (Fitzroy), Lady [Br. 1844-1912]
The apostle of the Ardennes. By Lady Lindsay.
L: Kegan Paul, Trench, Trubner & co., 1899. 161p. NUC BL OCLC

3321. -----The Christmas of the sorrowful.
L: Kegan Paul & co., 1898. 7p. BL

3322. -----The flower seller and other poems.
L & NY: Longmans, Green, 1896. 187p. NUC BL OCLC

3323. -----The king's last vigil and other poems.
L: K. Paul, Trench, Trubner, 1894. 202p. NUC BL OCLC

3324. -----Lyrics and other poems.
L: K. Paul, Trench, Trubner, 1890. 169p. NUC BL

3325. LINDSAY, Maud J. [Br. 19c]
A Whitsuntide offering.
L: n.p., 1873. BL

3326. LINN, Edith Lenore (Willis) [Am. b. 1865]
Out of the deep; pen pictures in prose and verse.
NY: The Metaphysical pub. co., 1895. 30p. NUC
[5 poems & 5 prose parables]

3327. -----Poems.
Buffalo, NY: C.W. Moulton, 1892. 167p. NUC OCLC

3328. -----Within, above, beyond.
Washington: Beresford, pr., 1899. 11p. NUC

LINWOOD, LOTTIE, pseud. <u>see</u> COOKE, Helen M., Mrs.

3329. LINWOOD, Mary [Br. 1755-1845]
The Anglo-Cambrian; a poem in four cantos.
L: Longman, Hurst, Rees, Orme & Brown, 1818. 94p. NUC BL

3330. LIPPINCOTT, Sara J. (Clarke) [Am. 1823-1904] ALT: Clarke, Sara Jane PSEUD: Greenwood, Grace
Greenwood leaves. Poems.
Boston: Ticknor, Reed & Fields, 1850. 406p. NUC
[Prose primarily. Verse & prose contributions by various authors, signed by initials p. 283-308]

3331. -----Poems, by Grace Greenwood.
Boston: Ticknor, Reed & Fields, 1851. 190p. NUC BL OCLC

3332. -----Shadows on the wall, by Grace Greenwood: a New Year's poem for the patrons of the Saturday Evening Post, January 1, 1885.
n.p.: n.p., 1885. 8p. NUC

3333. LITCHFIELD, Grace Denio [Am. 1849-1949]
Mimosa leaves.
NY: G.P. Putnam's sons, 1895. 112p. NUC BL OCLC

3334. LITCHFIELD, H. Elizabeth [Am. 19c]
Life's web, and other poems.
Bath, ME: R.W. Stearns pr., 1892. 15p. NUC OCLC

3335. LITTELL, Mary V. [Am. 19c]
"Tag."
NY: J.S. Ogilvie, 1899. 41p. NUC OCLC
[Country life, some in dialect]

3336. -----Tramplets.
NY: J.S. Ogilvie pub. co., 1899. 32p. NUC OCLC

3337. LITTLE, Janet [Br. 18c]
Poetical works of Janet Little, the Scotch milkmaid.
Ayr: Pr. J. & P. Wison, 1792. 207p. NUC BL OCLC

3338. LITTLE, Lizzie Mary [Br. 19/20c]
Persephone, and other poems.
Dublin: William McGee, 1884. 115p. NUC BL OCLC

3339. -----Wild myrtle.
L: J.M. Dent & co., 1897. 96p. NUC BL

LITTLE, Sarah <u>see</u> LITTLE, Sophia Louisa (Robbins)

3340. LITTLE, Sophia Louisa (Robbins) [Am. b. 1799] ALT: Little, Sarah
PSEUD: Rowena
The birth, last days, and resurrection of Jesus. Three poems.
Pawtucket, RI: Pr. for the author, 1841. 156p. NUC BL
[Pub. 1889 as: The last days of Jesus and other poems, with the addition of "Pentecost."]

3341. -----The last days of Jesus: a poem.
Pawtucket, RI: Pr. for the author, 1839. NUC BL OCLC

3342. -----Pentecost.
Newport, RI: Davis & Pitman, 1869. 49p. NUC
[Religious dialogue in verse]

3343. -----Poems.
Pawtucket, RI: n.p., 1841. 156p. NUC

3344. LITTLEBOY, Sarah (Edes) [Br. 1795-1870]
Memoranda relating to the late Sarah Littleboy, of Boxwells, Great Berkhampstead. With selection from her poetry and manuscripts.
L: Pr. for priv. circ., 1873. 194p. BL
[Occasional verse]

3345. LITTLEFORD, Mrs. [Am. 19c]
PSEUD: Lady of Lexington, A; Lady of Richmond, A
The wreath: or, Verses on various subjects. By a lady of Lexington.
Lexington, KY: Pr. D. Bradford, 1820. 118p. NUC OCLC
[Pub. 1828 in Richmond, VA, "By a lady of Richmond"]

3346. LITZSINGER, Louisa E. [Am. 19c]
Violets under the snow; a collection of short poems.
Clayton, MO: People's Advocate press, 1898. 73p. NUC

3347. LIVINGSTON, Anne Home (Shippen) [Am. 1763-1841] ALT: Shippen, Anne Home
Sacred records, abridged in verse. Consisting of some of the parables and miracles, the life, death, resurrection and ascension of the Blessed Saviour.
Philadelphia: Pub. for the author by T.S. Manning, 1817. 124p. NUC OCLC

3348. LIVINGSTON, Catherine [Am. 19c]
Poems on several occasions.
L: Pr. for the author, & sold by D. Ogilvy & son, 1797. 46p. NUC
[Note on t.p. suggests Livingston was from New York]

LIVINGSTON, O.M., Mrs. <u>see</u> LIVINGSTON, Ophelia Mead, Mrs.

3349. LIVINGSTON, Ophelia Mead, Mrs. [Am. 19c] ALT: Livingston, O. M., Mrs.
Poems. By Mrs. O.M. Livingston.
Cambridge, MA: Riverside press, 1868. 242p. NUC BL

3350. LLEWELLYN, Mrs. E.V.C. [Am. 19c]
Heavenly dews.
Baltimore, MD: Turnbull bros., 1875. 125p. NUC OCLC

LLOYD, Elizabeth <u>see</u> HOWELL, Elizabeth Lloyd

3351. LLOYD, Jane G. [Am. 19c]
The fountain and the rose by M.G.B.
Philadelphia: Becktold & co., 1883. 13p. NUC OCLC

3352. LLOYD, Mary [Br. 19c]
Brighton, a poem. Descriptive of the place and parts adjacent: and other poems.

L: Pr. for the author, J. Harding, 1809. 88p. NUC BL

3353. LLOYD, Mary Anne [Br. 19c]
The funds and more companies, with technical phrases on stock, or flippancies of the times. In rhyme. 3d ed. L: n.p., 1825. BL

3354. -----Lines on the passions ... To which is added a sonnet to a star.
L: n.p., 1823. BL

3355. -----Lines written on being present at the White Fast, Sept. 15, 1823 ... on the day of atonement.
L: n.p., 1823. BL

3356. -----A manual, consisting of a defence of the Bible in an original manner; with an appendix in prose and verse on many interesting subjects.
L: n.p., 1820. BL

3357. -----Poems. Preceeded by an address to the reader.
L: n.p., 1823. 7 l. BL

3358. -----A poetical prayer for relief to myself and Poyais land and people. Also elegiac verses on departed plants.
L: n.p., 1823. BL

3359. -----A second letter, and two poems, one for Easter day's dinner, the other a description of the ... blue coat school, as the boys appear on Easter Monday.
L: n.p., 1831. BL

3360. -----"Think of Jesus." A poem written for Good Friday.
L: n.p., 1823. BL

3361. -----To the gentlemen of the stock exchange. Lines on the Poyais bonds, 12 August, 1823, being His Majesty's natal day. Lines on a neglected rose tree.
L: n.p., 1823. BL

3362. LLOYD, Sarah Maria [Br. 19c]
Majesty. The lay of the new year. A tribute to the memory of the beloved Princess Charlotte of Saxe Cobourg.
Lowestoft: S. Gowing, 1819. 16p. BL

3363. LLOYD, Sophia Webster, Mrs. [Am. 19c]
Poems.
Cincinnati, OH: Standard pub. co., pr., 1887. 128p. NUC OCLC

3364. LLUELLYN, Eliza Augusta [19c]
Poems.
n.p.: n.p., 18--? 126p. NUC

3365. LOCKE, Jane Ermina (Starkweather) [Am. 1805-1859]
Boston. A poem.
Boston: W. Crosby & H.P. Nichols, 1846. 46p. NUC BL OCLC

3366. -----Daniel Webster: a rhymed eulogy.
Boston & Cambridge, MA: J. Munroe & co., 1854. 24p. NUC BL

3367. -----Miscellaneous poems.
Boston: Otis, Broaders & co., 1842. 300p. NUC BL OCLC

3368. -----The recalled; in voices of the past, and poems of the ideal.
Boston & Cambridge, MA: J. Munroe & co., 1854. 246p. NUC OCLC
[Misc. poetry]

3369. LOCKE, Mary [Br. 18c]
Eugenius; or, Virtue in retirement. A poem.
L: T. Hookham, 1791. 19p. NUC
[Tribute to Edward Taylor, the author's uncle]

3370. LODGE, Harriet (Newell) [Am. b. 1848]
Consider the lilies.
Cliftondale, MA: Coates bros., 1888. 4p. NUC

3371. LOFTUS, Cissie [Am. 19c]
First verses.
NY: The Lotus press, 1895. 30p. NUC

3372. LOGAN, F. A., Mrs. [Am. 19c]
Poems.
Sacramento, CA: n.p., 1883. 47p. NUC

3373. LOGAN, Margaret Ann [Am. 1840-1919]
Sweet alyssum; poems.
Buffalo, NY: C.W. Moulton, 1894. 104p. NUC OCLC

3374. LOGAN, Maria [Br. 19c]
Poems on several occasions.
York: Pr. for the author by Wilson, Spence & Mawman, 1793. 64p. NUC BL

3375. LOGUE, Emily Rose [Am. b. 1876]
At the foot of the mountain.
Philadelphia: H.L. Kilner & co., 1898. 46p. NUC OCLC
[Misc. poetry]

3376. L'OISEAU, Amelie [Am. 19c]

Original rhymes and illustrations of the seventh regiment in camp.
n.p.: n.p., 1897. 16p. NUC OCLC
[Cover title: Seventh in camp]

3377. LOMAX, Judith [Am. 1774-1828]
The notes of an American lyre. By Judith Lomax, a native of the State of Virginia.
Richmond, VA: Pr. Samuel Pleasants, 1813. 70p. NUC OCLC

3378. LONG, Catherine (Walpole), Lady [Br. 1798-1867]
The midsummer souvenir. Thoughts, original and selected.
L: James Nisbet & co., 1846. 138p. NUC BL
[Chiefly poetry, less than half is original]

3379. LONG, Elizabeth W., Mrs. [Am. 19c]
The parallel--a legend and a vision.
Baltimore, MD: n.p., 1848? NUC
[A protest against dissolving the Union of the States]

LONGFELLOW, Henry Wadsworth, co-author see INGELOW, Jean

3380. LONGSTAFF, Mrs. Leam [Br. 19c]
Poems, 1894-98.
L: E. Stanford, 1898. 33p. BL

3381. LONSDALE, Fanny [Br. 19c]
Echoes from Beulah, and Home memories. Hymns and poems.
L: Haughton & co., 1878. 72p. BL
[Religious & memorial poems]

LONSDALE, Henry, comp. see BLAMIRE, Susanna

3382. LOOKUP, Mary Milton [Br. 18c]
Britannia's tears: an elegiack poem, occasioned by the death of His Royal Highness the Prince of Wales; humbly inscribed to His Grace the Duke of Douglas.
Edinburgh: n.p., 1751. 11p. NUC

3383. LOOMIS, Clara J. [Am. 1841-1886]
Verse and prose.
Springfield, MA: C.W. Atwood, pr., 1887. 299p. NUC
[Misc. verse, short stories, personal recollections, brief essays]

3384. LOOMIS, Submit (Chesebrough) [Am. 1807-1892] PSEUD: Golden Rod
Poetry and prose.
NY: G.H. Barnham & co., 1893. 304p. NUC OCLC
[Lyrics & essays]

3385. LORD, Alice Emma (Sauerwein) [Am. 1848-1930]
A symphony in dreamland.
NY: G.P. Putnam's sons, 1882. 90p. NUC OCLC

3386. LORD, H. Augusta [Am. 19c]
Songs of the mosses.
Vineyard Haven, MA: n.p., 1887. NUC

LORRIMER, LAURA, pseud. see SHELTON, Julia Finley

3387. LOTHROP, Harriet Mulford (Stone) [Am. 1844-1924] PSEUD: Sidney, Margaret
The minute man; a ballad of "The shot heard round the world." By Margaret Sidney.
Boston: D. Lothrop & co., 1886. 29p. NUC OCLC

3388. -----On Easter day. By Margaret Sidney.
Boston: D. Lothrop & co., 1886. 15p. NUC

3389. LOUD, Clara [Br. 19c]
The early primrose; poems.
Canterbury: n.p., 1859. BL

3390. -----The ivy branch; poems.
Dover: n.p., 1871. BL

3391. -----The violet: poems.
Canterbury: n.p., 1857. BL

3392. -----Wild rose buds; poems.
Canterbury: n.p., 1865. BL

3393. -----The woodbine: poems.
Canterbury: n.p., 1861. BL

3394. -----A wreath from the woods: poems.
Canterbury: n.p., 1868. BL

3395. LOUD, Marguerite St. Leon (Barstow) [Am. 1812?-1889]
Wayside flowers; a collection of poems.
Boston: Ticknor, Reed & Fields, 1851. 276p. NUC BL OCLC

3396. LOUDON, Jane (Webb), Mrs. John Claudius Loudon [Br. 1807-1858] ALT: Webb, Jane
Prose and verse.
Birmingham: R. Wrightson, 1824. 125p. NUC BL

LOUDON, Mrs. John Claudius see LOUDON, Jane (Webb)

3397. LOUGHERY, Fannie Love [Am. 19c]
Pleasant thoughts or verses.
2d ed. Austin, TX: n.p., 1899. 26p. NUC

3398. -----Pleasant thoughts or verses.
3d ed. Austin, TX: Pr. Augusta M. Loughery, 1898/9? 46p. OCLC

LOUISA, pseud. see BOYD, Elizabeth

LOVER OF HER COUNTRY, A, pseud. see CLARKE, Anne, Miss

LOVER OF NATURE, A, pseud. see CROGGON, Lucy (Emra)

LOVER OF THE FINE ARTS, A, pseud. see BROOKS, Maria A. (Gowen)

LOW, Marie, co-author see WEST, Maud

3399. LOWE, Helen [Br. 19c]
Poems, chiefly dramatic, edited by Thomas Hill-Lowe, Dean of Exeter.
L: Pickering, 1840. 140p. NUC OCLC
[Attr. to Helen Lowe, Thomas's daughter]

3400. -----The prophecy of Balaam, the queen's choice, and other poems.
Exeter: P.A. Hannaford; L: John Murray, 1841. 229p. NUC BL OCLC

3401. -----Taormina, and other poems.
L: T.C. Newby, 1864. 197p. NUC OCLC

3402. -----Zareefa, a tale, and other poems.
L: William Pickering, pr., 1844. 167p. NUC OCLC

3403. LOWE, Martha Ann (Perry) [Am. 1829-1902]
The immortals.
Boston: The Botolph book co., 1899. 38p. NUC OCLC
[Memorial poems]

3404. -----Love in Spain, and other poems.
Boston: W.V. Spencer, 1867. 232p. NUC OCLC
[Incl. campaign song for Lincoln's re-election and elegies on Lincoln]

3405. -----The olive and the pine.
Boston: Crosby, Nichols & co., 1859. 156p. NUC BL OCLC
[Poems about Spain and New England]

3406. -----The story of Chief Joseph.
Boston: D. Lathrop & co., 1881. 40p. NUC
[Versification of a speech by Native American chief]

LOWELL, Mrs. James Russell see LOWELL, Maria (White)

3407. LOWELL, Maria (White), Mrs. James Russell Lowell [Am. 1821-1853]
The poems of Maria Lowell.
Cambridge, MA: Priv. pr., 1855. 68p. NUC BL OCLC

LOWNDES, Thomas, comp. & co-author see DAY, Esther (Milnes)

3408. LUBY, Catherine [Br. 19c]
Father Matthew; or, Ireland as she is; a national poem.
Dublin: S.J. Macken, 1845. 103p. BL

3409. -----The spirit of the lakes; or, Mucruss Abbey. A poem in three cantos.
L: Longman, Hurst, Rees, Orme, & Brown, 1822. 208p. NUC BL OCLC

3410. LUCAN, Margaret Smith Bingham, Countess of Lucan [Br. d. 1814]
PSEUD: Lady, A
Verses on the present state of Ireland, by a lady.
L: Pr. for P. Elmsley, 1778. 20p. NUC OCLC

3411. LUCAS, Alice, Mrs. Henry Lucas [Br. 1851/2-1935]
The Jewish year: a collection of devotional poems for Sabbaths and holidays throughout the year. Translated and composed by A. Lucas.
L & NY: Macmillan, 1898. 187p. NUC BL OCLC

LUCAS, Mrs. Henry see LUCAS, Alice

3412. LUCAS, Winifred M. [Br. b. 1867] ALT: Le Bailly, Winifred M. (Lucas)
Francis and fragments.
L: A. & F. Denny, 1893. 51p. BL

3413. -----Fugitives.
L: J. Lane, 1899. 95p. BL

3414. -----Lana Caprina.
L: Diprose, Bateman & co., pr., 1888. 31p. NUC BL OCLC
[Sonnets & misc. verse]

3415. -----Units.
L & NY: J. Lane, 1896. 78p. NUC BL OCLC
[Misc. poetry]

3416. -----Verses.
L: Squire, 1895. 58p. NUC

3417. LUCE, Hannah Gale [Am. 19c]
Poems. With Samuel Slayton Luce.
Trempealeau, WI: C.A. Leith, 1876. 207p. NUC OCLC
[Her poems pp. 149-207. Lyrics, narratives & Civil War poems]

LUCE, Mrs. Joel see LUCE, Phebe

3418. LUCE, Nancy [Am. 1820-1890]
A complete edition of the works of Nancy Luce, of West Tisburg, Dukes county, Mass.
New Bedford, MA: Fessenden & Baker, pr., 1871. 12p. NUC OCLC
[Poems, religious works]

3419. -----Poor little hearts.
n.p.: n.p., 1860. 16p. NUC
[Incl. in A complete edition ...]

3420. LUCE, Phebe, Mrs. Joel Luce [Am. 19c]
Maternal admonition, or the orphan's manual: by Mrs. Phebe Luce, to her children, supplementary to a work, entitled Vicissitudes of life; or the history of Mrs. Phebe Luce.
Cooperstown, NY: Pr. for the author by H. & F. Phinney, 1819. 96p. NUC
[Contains poems]

LUCE, Samuel Slayton, co-author see LUCE, Hannah Gale

3421. LUDERS, Catharine [Am. 19c]
Voices in the wilderness.
Philadelphia: C. Luders, 1884. 220p. NUC OCLC

LUIGI, pseud. see LAMBERT, Mary H.P.

3422. LUKE, Jemima (Thompson), Mrs. S. Luke [Br. 1813-1906] ALT: Thompson, Jemima
The sweet story of old.
L: Religious Tract Society; J.E. Hawkins, 1889. 164p. BL OCLC

3423. LUKE, Mamie [Am. 19c]
Curious couplets; showing some of the beauties and capabilities of the English language.
Brooklyn, NY: M. Luke, c1881. 3p. NUC OCLC

3424. -----The demon of drink. A poem.
NY: n.p., c1881. NUC

3425. -----In memoriam. Our late president [Garfield]. A tribute.
n.p.: n.p., c1881. 3p. NUC

3426. -----Lights o' Gotham!
NY: n.p., c1882. NUC

3427. -----The passing of Gotham's glory. A day dream.
Brooklyn, NY: n.p., c1883. NUC

3428. -----What then? Something all men should ponder.
Brooklyn, NY: n.p., c1886. NUC

3429. -----Who? A series of metrical queries, with responses.
Brooklyn, NY: n.p., c1885. NUC

3430. -----Why, and why not?
Brooklyn, NY: n.p., c1882. NUC

LUKE, Mrs. S. see LUKE, Jemima (Thompson)

3431. LUKENS, Susan [Am. d. 1873]
Gleanings at seventy-five.
Philadelphia: Porter & Coates, 1873. 216p. NUC OCLC

LUNDIE, Mrs. J.C., comp. see DUNCAN, Mary (Lundie)

LUNDIE, Mary see DUNCAN, Mary (Lundie)

LUNDY, Benjamin, comp. see CHANDLER, Elizabeth Margaret

3432. LUNT, Adelina Treadwell (Parsons), Mrs. George Lunt [Am. 19c]
ALT: L., A.T.
Old age. 1883-1796=87.
Boston: n.p., 1883. NUC

3433. -----Old age. 1884-1796=88.
Bridgewater?: n.p., 1884. NUC

3434. -----Old age. 1886-1796=90.
n.p.: n.p., 1886. NUC

3435. -----Old age. 1881-1796=85. By A.T.L.
Bridgewater: n.p., 1881. NUC

3436. -----To C.F. Bradford, on his eightieth birthday.
n.p.: n.p., n.d. NUC

3437. -----To one who knoweth.
Boston: n.p., c1885. NUC

LUNT, Mrs. George see LUNT, Adeline Treadwell (Parsons)

3438. LUQUER, Eloise Elizabeth [Am. 1834-1894]

The poems.
NY: Gilliss press, 1894. 55p. NUC OCLC

3439. LUSHINGTON, Henrietta (Prescott), Lady [Br. d. 1875]
Poems.
L: Priv. pr. by Spottiswoode & co., 1877. 235p. NUC BL

3440. -----The sea spirit and other poems.
L: 1850.

3441. LUSHINGTON, Lucy Maria [Br. 19c] ALT: L., L. M.
Verses by L.M.L.
Maidstone: Pr. for priv. circ. by F. Bunyard, 1880. 100p. NUC BL OCLC

3442. LUTTON, Anne [Br. 1791-1881]
Poems on moral and religious subjects.
Dublin: J.O. Bonsall, 1829. 208p. NY: G. Lane & P.P. Sanford, 1842. 136p. NUC BL OCLC

3443. LUTWYCHE, Elizabeth, Mrs. [Br. 19c]
The broken vase; or, Scattered flowers. Collected.
Lyme: n.p., 1840. BL
[Chiefly occasional verse; incl. prose sketches]

LYNCH, Anne Charlotte see BOTTA, Anne Charlotte (Lynch)

LYNCH, Mrs. Henry see LYNCH, Theodora Elizabeth (Foulks)

3444. LYNCH, Theodora Elizabeth (Foulks), Mrs. Henry Lynch [Br. 1812-1885] PSEUD: Personne
Lays of the sea and other poems. By Personne.
L: n.p., 1846. BL

3445. -----Lays of the sea and other poems. By Mrs. Henry Lynch.
2d ed. L: Seeleys, 1850. 223p. OCLC

3446. -----Songs of the evening-land and other poems.
L: n.p., 1861. BL

3447. LYON, Anna E. West- [Am. 19c]
My first harvest; or, The leisure hours of a youthful poet.
Niagara Falls, NY: The author, 1893. 160p. NUC OCLC

LYON, Emma, Miss see HAMILTON, Emma (Lyon), Lady

LYTHWYN, EDDA, pseud. see SCRAMM, Emma I.

3448. LYTTON, Rosina Anne Doyle (Wheeler) Bulwer-Lytton, Baroness [Br. 1802-1882] ALT: Bulwer, Rosina Doyle (Wheeler), Baroness Lytton
Life of Rosina, Lady Lytton, with numerous extracts from her MS autobiography and other original documents, published in vindication of her memory. By Louisa Devey.
L: Swan, Sonnenschein, Lowrey & co., 1887. 432p. NUC BL OCLC MB
[Letters of Lady Lytton & newspaper articles of the time. Brief poems by Lady Lytton.]

M., pseud. see GILLETTE, Florence Lilian

M., A.W. see MITCHELL, Agnes (Woods)

M., B. see MAC ANDREW, Barbara (Miller)

M., E. see HERVEY, Eleanora Louisa (Montagu)

M., E.H. see MAIR, Elizabeth Harriet (Siddons)

M., E.J. see MARSHALL, E.J., Mrs.

M., H., co-author see KIMBALL, Harriet McEwen

M., I.A. see MERRYWEATHER, I.A., Mrs.

M., L.H. see MARVIN, Lydia H., Mrs.

M., M. see COLVILLE, Elizabeth (Melville), Lady Colville of Culross

M., M.A. see MAC DONALD, Almeda Evans

M., M.A. see MERRY, M.A., Mrs.

M., M.N. see MEIGS, Mary Noel (Bleecker) MacDonald

M----, Lady see HUNTINGTOWER, Catherine Rebecca (Grey) Talmash, Baroness

3449. MABON, Agnes Stuart [Br. 19c]
Homely rhymes, etc. from the banks of the Jed.
Paisley: J. & R. Parlane, 1887. 270p. BL

3450. MC ABOY, Mary R. (Thornton) [Am. 19c]
Roseheath poems.
Cincinnati, OH: R. Clarke & co., 1884. 176p. NUC OCLC

3451. MACALPINE, Mary [Br. 19c]
The traitor lake, and other poems.
Greenock, Scotland: W. Hutchison, 1895. 106p. NUC BL OCLC

3452. MAC ANDREW, Barbara (Miller) [Br. 19c] ALT: M., B.
Elijah, and other poems. By B.M.
L & NY: T. Nelson, 1880. 142p. NUC BL OCLC

3453. -----Ezekiel, and other poems, by B.M.
NY: A.D.F. Randolph; NY & L: T. Nelson & sons, 1871. 249p. NUC BL OCLC

3454. MAC ARTHUR, Mary, Mrs. James MacArthur [Br. 19c]
The necropolis: an elegy. And other poems. By Mrs. James MacArthur.
Glasgow: D. Bryce, 1842. 165p. NUC BL

MAC ARTHUR, Mrs. James <u>see</u> MAC ARTHUR, Mary

3455. MACAULAY, Beata Elizabeth [Br. 19c]
The Newtown rats: an Isle of Wight legend.
L: Sampson Low, son, & Marston, 1869. 1v. NUC
[Incl. other poems]

3456. MACAULEY, Elizabeth Wright [Br. 1785?-1837]
Mary Stuart.
L: Macauley, 1823. 138p. BL OCLC

3457. -----Poetical effusions; consisting of The birth of friendship, The birth of affection, and The birth of sensibility.
L: n.p., 1812. 140p. BL OCLC

3458. MAC CARTHY, Charlotte [Br. 18c]
The fair moralist; or, Love and virtue.
L: B. Stichall, etc., 1745, 1746. 220p. BL
[Fiction, poetry and moral tract]

3459. -----News from Parnassus, or political advice from the nine muses to His Grace, the D--- of B---. A poem.
Dublin: Pr. S. Powell, 1757. 8p. BL

3460. MC CARTHY, Kate [Am. 19c]
Centennial gleanings.
NY: The Catholic pub. soc., 1876. NUC BL
[Short poems by K. McCarthy, M. Mosher and 4 others]

3461. MACCARTHY, Mary Stanislaus, Sister [Br. 1849-1897]
Songs of Sion.
Dublin: Browne & Nolan, 1898. 160p. NUC BL OCLC

3462. MAC CLELLAN, Kate [Am. 19c]
In memoriam: K.M.
Brooklyn, NY: n.p., 1870? 79p. NUC
[Incl. selections from her prose and poetry.]

MC CLURG, Mrs. Gilbert <u>see</u> MC CLURG, Mary Virginia (Donaghe)

MC CLURG, M. Virginia (Donaghe) <u>see</u> MC CLURG, Mary Virginia (Donaghe)

3463. MC CLURG, Mary Virginia (Donaghe), Mrs. Gilbert McClurg [Am. 1858-1931] ALT: McClurg, M. Virginia (Donaghe); McClurg, Virginia Donaghe
Colorado favorites.
NY: Francis Hart & co., pr., 1882. 19p. NUC

3464. -----A Colorado wreath.
Colorado Springs, CO: J. O'Brien, 1899. 12p. NUC OCLC
[Nine poems, each describing a Colorado plant]

3465. -----Seven sonnets of sculpture.
Boston: Soule photograph co., 1889. 17p. NUC

MAC COLL, Mary Jemima <u>see</u> SCHULTE, Mary Jemima (MacColl)

MAC CONKEY, Harriet E. (Bishop) <u>see</u> BISHOP, Harriet E.

3466. MC CONNELL, Marion Delana (Daniel) [Am. 19c] ALT: Daniel, Marion Delana
Sheaves of song by Marion Delana Daniel.
NY: The Peter Paul book co., 1895. 100p. NUC OCLC

3467. MC CONNELL, Sara J. [Am. 19c]
Selections of poems and prose.
Pittsburgh; PA: P.F. Smith, 1893. 16, 40p. NUC
[Misc. poetry, a short story, and two brief essays.]

MC CORD, Adelaide see MENKEN, Adah Isaacs

MC CORD, Mrs. David James see MC CORD, Louisa Susannah (Cheves)

3468. MC CORD, Louisa Susannah (Cheves), Mrs. David James McCord [Am. 1810-1879/80]
My dreams.
Philadelphia: Carey & Hart, 1848. 211p. NUC BL

3469. MC COY, Kittie C., Mrs. [Am. 19c]
Buds and blossoms. A collection of original poems.
Pontiac, MI: Gazette pub. house, 1886. 228p. NUC OCLC

3470. MAC COY, Mary [Br. 19c]
A poem in answer to an anonymous pamphlet: in three letters, called friendly hints to Catholic emancipation.
Belfast: n.p., 1813. BL
[12 p. satiric poem]

3471. MC CUE, Rebecca L. [Am. 19c]
Poems entitled flowers of spring.
Minneapolis, MN: Irish Standard job pr. co., 1888. 110p. NUC OCLC

3472. MC CULLOUGH, N. N., Mrs.
...Centennial hymn of the Northwest territory.
Springfield, IL: Springfield pr. co., 1887. 24p. NUC
[Verses & narrative on growth of the area]

MC D., M. see MAC DERMOTT, Mary

3473. MAC DERMOTT, Mary [Br. 19c]
ALT: McD., M.
Lays of love.
Dublin: n.p., 1859. BL

3474. -----My early dreams. By M. McD.
Belfast: Finlay, 1832. 228p. BL OCLC
[Poems, short stories & essays]

3475. MAC DONALD, Almeda Evans, Mrs. M.A. Macdonald [Am. 19c] ALT: M., M. A.
A dream of another country. By M.A.M.
Philadelphia: Reformed Episcopal pub. soc., 1886. 47p. NUC

3476. -----Poems.
NY: Carleton; L: S. Low, son & co., 1871. 64p. Philadelphia: Treager & Lamb, pr., 1889. 264p. NUC OCLC

MAC DONALD, Elizabeth Roberts see MAC DONALD, Jane Elizabeth Gostwycke (Roberts)

3477. MAC DONALD, Jane Elizabeth Gostwycke (Roberts) [Am. 1864-1922]
ALT: MacDonald, Elizabeth Roberts
Northland lyrics. With William Carman Roberts and Theodore Roberts.
Boston: Small, Maynard & co., 1899. 86p. NUC OCLC

MAC DONALD, Rev. John, comp. see HOOD, Isabel

MAC DONALD, Mrs. M.A. see MAC DONALD, Almeda Evans

MAC DONALD, Mary Noel see MEIGS, Mary Noel (Bleecker) MacDonald

MAC DOUGAL, Margaret Armour see ARMOUR, Margaret

3478. MC DOUGALL, Frances Harriet (Whipple) Greene [Am. 1805-1878]
The genius of American liberty: a patriotic poem.
San Francisco: B. Todd & co., 1867. 32p. NUC OCLC

3479. MC DOWELL, Kate Goldsboro [Am. 19c]
Unfolding leaves of tender thought.
Louisville, KY: J.P. Morton & co., 1898. 112p. NUC OCLC

3480. MC DOWELL, Katherine Sherwood (Bonner) [Am. 1849-1883] ALT: Bonner, Katherine Sherwood; Bonner, Sherwood PSEUD: Atom, An
The radical club. A poem, respectfully dedicated to "the infinite." By an atom.
Boston: The Times pub. co., 1876. 14p. NUC OCLC
[Parody of Poe's The Raven]

MACE, Frances L. see MACE, Frances Parker (Laughton)

3481. MACE, Frances Parker (Laughton) [Am. 1836-1899] ALT: Mace, Frances L.
Hesperus (The evening star). Cantata for female voices, words by Frances L. Mace. Composed by John Hyatt Brewer.
Boston: A.P. Schmidt, 1894. 23p. NUC

3482. -----Legends, lyrics and sonnets.
Boston: Cupples, Upham & co., 1883. 192p. NUC OCLC

3483. -----A poem by Frances L. Mace. Read at the closing lesson of the class in literature, April 13, 1880.
n.p.: n.p., 1880. 4 l. NUC
[Caption title: The scholar's realm.]

3484. -----Under pine and palm.
Boston: Ticknor & co., 1888. 222p. NUC OCLC
[Poetry about Maine & California]

3485. MC FALL, Anna E. Mays [Am. 19c]
PSEUD: Heath, Rose
Poems of fact and fiction, by Rose Heath.
Cincinnati, OH: Editor pub. co., 1898. 90p. NUC OCLC

3486. -----Too much for the colonel.
Buffalo, NY: Charles Wells Moulton, 1893. 20p. OCLC

3487. MAC FARLANE, A., Mrs. [Br. 19c]
Minor poems.
L: n.p., 1842. BL

3488. -----Prayer. A poem.
L: n.p., 1840. BL

3489. MC GILL, Anna [Br. 19c]
Some Madonnas of poetry.
Somerset: n.p., 1898. NUC

3490. MAC GREGOR, Helen [Br. 19c]
The burial of Wellington: a dirge.
L: S. Coburn & co., 1853. 8p. BL

3491. -----Lays from history and romance. With translations from the German, and other poems.
L: Wertheim, Mackentosh & Hunt, 1862. 119p. BL

3492. -----Lays of the Crimea.
L: Longmans & co., 1855. 16p. BL

3493. MAC GREGOR, Jane [Br. 19c]
Redeeming love, and other poems.
Edinburgh: n.p., 1862. BL

3494. MACHAR, Agnes Maule [Am. 19c]
Easter poems: Easter lilies, by Agnes Maule Machar; an Easter poem, by Mrs. L.C. Whiton.
Boston: D. Lothrop co., c1889. NUC

3495. MACHELL, Margaret, Mrs. [Br. 19c]
Epitaphs and thoughts for a village churchyard.
2d ed. Stockton: Jennett & co., 1858. 27p. NUC BL
[Some original, some collected from var. cemeteries]

3496. -----Poems and translations.
L: J.W. Parker & son, 1856. 244p. BL

3497. MC HENRY, Jennie Taylor [Am. 1832-1914]
Forget-me-not. A collection of poems.
Louisville, KY: Bradley & Gilbert, 1867. 83p. NUC

3498. MC ILVAIN, Clara (Lowell) [Am. 1836-1881]
Echoes of the past: poems. Ed. her daughter, Lottie [Charlotte] (McIlvain) Moore.
Louisville, KY: J.P. Morton & co., 1890. 262p. NUC OCLC

MACK, Robert Ellice, comp. see BLAND, Edith (Nesbit)

MACKAY, Catherine Edith Macaulay see MARTIN, Catherine Edith Macaulay (Mackay)

3499. MACKAY, Elizabeth D. [Am. 19c]
Poems and hymns.
Elgin, OH: MacDonald, 1843. 77p. NUC BL

3500. MACKAY, Jessie [1864-1938]
The sitter on the rail, and other poems.
Christchurch, New Zealand: Simpson & Williams, 1891. 77p. NUC BL OCLC

3501. -----The spirit of the Rangatira and other ballads.
Melbourne: G. Robertson, 1889. 111p. NUC

3502. MACKAY, Margaret, Mrs. [Br. 19c]
"Thoughts redeemed:" or, Lays of leisure hours.
Edinburgh: W.P. Kennedy; L: Hamilton, Adams & co., 1854. 197p. NUC BL

3503. MC KEAN, May Field [Am. 19c]
"Behold, He goeth before you;" a legend of the risen Lord.
Boston: J.H. Earle, 1895. 155p. NUC OCLC
["Founded upon a legend told by an old monk to Russell H. Conwell while in Jerusalem in 1868"]

3504. -----Ruth, the gleaner.
Philadelphia: A.J. Rowland, 1897. 60p. NUC
[Retelling of Biblical story; blank verse]

3505. MAC KEEVER, Harriet Burn, Miss [Am. 1807-1886]

Twilight musings and other poems.
Philadelphia: Willis P. Hazard, 1857.
263p. NUC

3506. MACKELLAR, Mary (Cameron) [Br. 1834-1890]
Poems and songs, Gaelic and English.
Edinburgh: Maclachlan & Stewart, 1880. 140p. NUC BL

3507. MACKENZIE, Lucie Ada [Am. 19c]
Rose: a tale of the Indian River, and other poems.
NY: Pr. for the author, 1891. 64p. NUC

3508. -----The two ladies of the lake; A tale of Florida. Also, The song of two rivers.
NY: Pr. for the author, 1893. 107p. NUC OCLC

3509. MACKEY, Mary, Mrs. [Br. 19c]
The scraps of nature. A poem.
L: n.p., 1810. BL

3510. MC KINNEY, Ida Scott (Taylor) [Am. 19c] ALT: Taylor, Ida Scott
A fortress of strength ... selected verses and texts and original poems. By Ida Scott Taylor.
Paris & NY: Raphael Tuck & sons, 189-? 80p. NUC OCLC

3511. -----Look up, lift up; Selected hymns, texts and original verses.
NY: Mount & Eaton; Cincinnati, OH & Chicago: Cranston & Curts, 189-? 78p. NUC

3512. -----The story of Columbus told in rhyme. With Martha Capps Oliver.
L: R. Tuck & sons, 1893? NUC

3513. MC KINNEY, Kate (Slaughter) [Am. b. 1857] PSEUD: Katydid
Katydid's poems, with a letter by Jno. Aug. Williams.
Louisville, KY: Pr. by the Courier-Journal pr. co., 1887. 113p. NUC

3514. MACKINTOSH, Margaret [Br. 19c]
The cottager's daughter; a tale founded on facts, betwixt 1685 and 1688. To which are added miscellaneous ... pieces ... songs.
Edinburgh: Pr. H. & J. Pillans, 1836. 335p. NUC BL OCLC

3515. MC LANATHAN, Mary Leland [Am. 19c]
As at this time. A Holy week and Easter musing.
NY: A.D.F. Randolph & co., 1884. 12 l. NUC

3516. -----Three kings: a Christmas legend of long ago.
NY: A.D.F. Randolph & co., c1886. 30 l. NUC

3517. MACLAURIN, Mary [Br. 19c]
Poems.
Haddington: Priv. pr., 1812. BL

3518. MACLEAN, Anna Jane [Br. 19c]
Conviction: a poem.
Dublin: n.p., 1851. BL

MACLEAN, Mrs. George <u>see</u> LANDON, Letitia Elizabeth

3519. MAC LEAN, Jean [Br. d. 1897]
God my exceeding joy. A sketch of the trials, labours, and triumphs of the late Miss Jean MacLean. Comp. her twin sister, Margaret [MacLean].
2d ed. L: Parsmore & Alabaster, 1899. 233p. BL
[Incl. poems]

3520. -----"Tongues, as of fire." A pentecostal message.
L: Marshall bros., 1896. BL

3521. MACLEAN, Kate Seymour [19c]
The coming of the princess, and other poems.
Toronto: Hunter, Rose & co., 1881. 175p. NUC OCLC

MACLEAN, Letitia Elizabeth (Landon) <u>see</u> LANDON, Letitia Elizabeth

MAC LEAN, Margaret, comp. <u>see</u> MAC LEAN, Jean

3522. MC LEAN, Mary Irene [Am. 19c]
Songs in darkness.
Jackson, MI: Hunt & Bridgman, 1889. 54p. NUC OCLC

3523. MACLENNAN, Anne [Br. 19c]
Poems: sacred and secular.
Edinburgh: Pr. for priv. circ., 1884. 68p. BL

3524. MACLINTOCK, Agnes C. [Br. 19c]
The broken plough, and other poems.
2d ed. Glasgow: C. Glass & co., 1877. 56p. BL

3525. MC MASTERS, Julia Russell (Bowers) [Am. 1821-1879]
Silver pictures.
Philadelphia: H. Cowperthwait & co., 1856. 64p. NUC BL OCLC
[Verses on a lost child; incl. other poems]

3526. MC MILLAN, Elva Irene [Am. 19c]
Lyrics of the West.
NY & L: G.P. Putnam's sons, 1899.
225p. NUC BL OCLC

3527. MACMULLAN, Mary Anne [Br. 19c]
Britain; or, Fragments of poetical aberration.
L: n.p., 1818. BL

3528. -----The crescent, a national poem. To commemorate the ... victory at Algiers.
L: n.p., 1816. BL

3529. -----Dioramic sketches.
L: n.p., 1853. BL

3530. -----The Naiad's wreath.
L: n.p., 1816. BL

3531. MC NINCH, Maggie [Am. 19c] ALT: Maggie
Wayside flowers, gathered by "Maggie."
Richmond, VA: Whittet & Shepperson, 1880. 116p. NUC
[Poems & prose sketches: Civil War, nature, country life]

3532. MACNIVEN, Hope [19c]
The bard of Clutha, and other poems.
Ingersoll, Ontario: P.S. Gurnett, 1873. 82p. NUC

3533. M'CORD, Louisa S. (Cheves), Mrs. David James McCord [Am. 1810-1879]
My dreams. Volume of poetry.
Philadelphia: Carey & Hart, 1848.
211p. BL OCLC

3534. MC PHERSON, Lydia (Starr) [Am. 1827-1903]
Reullura, a book of poems.
Buffalo, NY: Author's ed, C.W. Moulton, 1892. 95p. NUC
[Misc. poetry]

3535. MC QUEEN, Annie C. [Am. 19c]
All for thy happy day.
NY: n.p., 1888. NUC

3536. -----"Alleluia" songs of joy.
NY: n.p., 1888. NUC

3537. -----Altar flowers.
NY: n.p., 1888. NUC

3538. -----Among the grasses.
NY: Hard & Parsons, 1888. 5 l. NUC

3539. -----The birds' Christmas.
NY: n.p., 1887. NUC

3540. -----Birthday gems.
NY: n.p., 1889. NUC

3541. -----Birthday wishes.
NY: Hard & Parsons, 1889. 5 l. NUC

3542. -----Bitter-sweet emblems for Christmas-tide.
NY: n.p., 1887. NUC

3543. -----Breezes waft my Christmas greeting.
NY: n.p., 1888. NUC

3544. -----The brooklet's Christmas song.
NY: Hard & Parsons, 1887. 6 l. NUC

3545. -----Christmas bells.
NY: n.p., 1887. NUC

3546. -----A Christmas blossom.
NY: n.p., 1887. NUC

3547. -----Christmas echoes from the woodland.
NY: n.p., 1889. NUC

3548. -----Christmas gladness.
NY: n.p., 1887. NUC

3549. -----Christmas heralds.
NY: n.p., 1887. NUC

3550. -----A Christmas lay.
NY: n.p., 1887. NUC

3551. -----A Christmas leaf.
NY: Hard & Parsons, 1887. NUC

3552. -----A Christmas message.
NY: n.p., 1887. NUC

3553. -----Christmas music.
NY: Hard & Parsons, 1887. NUC

3554. -----Christmas peace.
NY: n.p., 1892. NUC

3555. -----A Christmas prayer.
NY: Hard & Parsons, 1887. NUC

3556. -----A Christmas sunbeam.
NY: n.p., 1887. NUC

3557. -----A Christmas token.
NY: n.p., 1887. NUC

3558. -----A Christmas visitor.
NY: n.p., 1887. NUC

3559. -----Crystal thoughts.
NY: n.p., 1887. 12p. NUC

3560. -----Crystals for birthday hours.
NY: n.p., 1887. NUC

3561. -----Dawn of Christmas day.
NY: n.p., 1887. NUC

3562. -----Easter bells.
NY: n.p., 1888. NUC

3563. -----Easter blossoms.
NY: n.p., 1888. NUC

3564. -----Easter tide.
NY: n.p., 1888. NUC

3565. -----Easter tidings: "Christ is risen."
NY: n.p., 1888. NUC

3566. -----Fair Eastertide.
NY: n.p., 1888. NUC

3567. -----For Christmas weal.
NY: n.p., 1889. NUC

3568. -----Frost fancies.
NY: n.p., 1889. NUC

3569. -----A glimpse of Christmas woodland.
NY: n.p., 1887. NUC

3570. -----Hallelujah! Song of angels.
NY: n.p., 1888. NUC

3571. -----Happy Christmas-time.
NY: n.p., 1887. NUC

3572. -----Heart echoings.
NY: n.p., 1887. 16p. NUC

3573. -----Heavenly messengers.
NY: n.p., 1889. NUC

3574. -----Heigh-o! for the Christmas-tide.
NY: n.p., 1887. NUC

3575. -----The heralding angel.
NY: n.p., 1889. NUC

3576. -----Holiday joys.
NY: n.p., 1887. NUC

3577. -----Holly berries.
NY: n.p., 1887. NUC

3578. -----Joyous Easter voices.
NY: n.p., 1888. NUC

3579. -----Lily-bells ring a birthday chime.
NY: n.p., 1889. NUC

3580. -----The little Christmas rover.
NY: n.p., 1887. NUC

3581. -----Memories sweet for thy birthday.
NY: Hard & Parsons, 1888. 5 l. NUC

3582. -----Message of joy.
NY: n.p., 1889. NUC

3583. -----Messengers of joy.
NY: n.p., 1887. NUC

3584. -----Queen of the snow.
NY: n.p., 1887. NUC

3585. -----Rejoicings of Eastertide.
NY: n.p., 1888. NUC

3586. -----Ripples of Christmas song.
NY: n.p., 1889. NUC

3587. -----A song of Easter gladness.
NY: n.p., 1888. NUC

3588. -----Songs of the seasons.
NY: n.p., 1889. NUC

3589. -----Sweet strains for Christmas-tide.
NY: n.p., 1889. NUC

3590. -----Under the mistletoe.
NY: n.p., 1887. NUC

3591. -----Violets.
NY: n.p., 1888. NUC

3592. -----Violets greeting.
NY: n.p., 1889. NUC

3593. -----Waiting the Christmas-tide.
NY: n.p., 1887. NUC

3594. -----Where Christmas berries grow.
NY: n.p., 1887. NUC

3595. -----White-winged bearers of birthday joy.
NY: n.p., 1889. NUC

3596. -----Woodland greeting.
NY: n.p., 1889. NUC

3597. MACREADY, Catherine Frances Birch [Br. 1835-1869]
Cowl and cap; or, The rival churches: and minor poems.
L: E. Moxon & co., 1865. 189p. NUC BL

3598. -----Devotional lays.
L: n.p., 1868. BL

3599. -----Leaves from the Olive Mount. Poems.
L: Chapman, 1860. 136p. NUC BL OCLC

MACRITCHIE, Margaret Scott <u>see</u> HAYCRAFT, Margaret Scott (Macritchie)

3600. MADAN, Judith (Cowper) [Br. 1701-1781]
Abelard to Eloisa. Letters of Abelard and Eloisa ... To which are now added, the poems of Eloisa to Abelard by Mr. [Alexander] Pope. And Abelard to Eloisa by Mrs. Madan.
L: n.p., 1773. BL OCLC
[Various other editions]

3601. -----The progress of poetry.
L: J. Dodsley, 1783. 24p. NUC

3602. MADDOCKS, Mrs. [Br. 19c]
Cottage similies, or, Poems on domestic occasions, designed for those in humble life.
L: n.p., 1829. BL

3603. -----The female missionary advocate.
L: n.p., 1827. BL
[Poetic dialogue on missionary life]

3604. MADISON, Rebecca W. [Am. 19c]
Life. Questionings. Why?
Manchester, NH: Pr. John B. Clarke, 1887. 6p. NUC

3605. -----A waste-basket, containing poems.
Manchester, NH: n.p., 1889. 8p. NUC

3606. -----Whisperings of my muse.
Manchester, NH: n.p., 1887. 12p. NUC

3607. MAGEE, Annie Houser [Am. 19c]
In the fields; a collection of the poems of A.H. Magee.
Port Austin, MI: A. Magee, 1893. 187p. NUC OCLC

MAGGIE <u>see</u> MC NINCH, Maggie

3608. MAGIE, Lizzie [Am. 19c]
My betrothed, and other poems.
Washington, D.C.: Brodix pub. co., 1892. 29p. NUC

3609. MAGRATH, Anne Jane [Br. 19c]
Blossoms of genius: poems on various subjects.
Dublin: n.p., 1834. BL

3610. MAHONY, Agnes [Br. 19c]
A minstrel's hours of song; or, Poems.
L: William Pickering, 1825. 174p. BL OCLC

3611. MAINWARING, Miss [Br. 19c]
The slaves of Zanquebar; and other poems.
Birmingham: n.p., 1826. BL

3612. MAIR, Elizabeth Harriet (Siddons) [Br. d. 1876] ALT: M., E. H.
Recollections of the past, a series of letters by E.H.M.
Edinburgh: Priv. pr. by R. & R. Clark, 1877. 102p. NUC BL OCLC
[Incl. poems]

3613. MAITLAND, Ella Fuller [Br. 19c] ALT: M., E.F.
Parva.
Edinburgh: W. Blackwood & sons, 1886. 80p. NUC BL OCLC

3614. MAITLAND, Ellinor J.S. [Br. 19c]
Poems.
L & Cambridge: n.p., 1863. NUC BL

3615. MAITLAND, Frances Sara Fuller [Br. 19c] ALT: Colquhoun, Frances Sara Fuller Maitland
Rhymes and chimes.
L: Macmillan & co., 1876. 56p. BL

3616. MAJOR, Elizabeth [Br. 17c]
Honey on the rod; or, A comfortable contemplation for one in affliction; with sundry poems.
L: Pr. T. Maxey, 1656. 212p. NUC BL OCLC
[Dialogue of Soul and Consolation, in prose; religious poems]

3617. MAKEEVER, Idael [Am. 19c]
Golden rod and dialect poems.
n.p.: n.p., 1898. 88p. NUC

3618. -----Prairie flowers and meadow grasses.
Stromsburg, NE: n.p., 1899. 91p. NUC OCLC
[Incl. sonnets, lyrics & a short story: "In the shadow of Bohemia"]

3619. MALLARD, Harriet [Am. 19c]
Bible evergreens for Christmas.
NY: Baker & Godwin, pr., 1872. 71p. NUC

3620. -----Thoughts of heaven.
NY: Baker & Godwin, pr., 1867. 48p. NUC

3621. MALLETT, Mrs. [Br. 19c]
Consolation.
L: n.p., 1861. BL

3622. -----The maid of the isle.
L: n.p., 1834. BL
[2 narrative poems & misc. lyrics]

MALLOY, Louise see MALLOY, Marie Louise

3623. MALLOY, Marie Louise [Am. 19/20c] ALT: Malloy, Louise
The prince's wooing. A dramatic poem. By Louise Malloy.
Baltimore, MD: American job pr. office, 1894. 31p. NUC

3624. MALONEY, Mary Teresa, Mrs. [Am. b. 1839]
The legend of Nonnenwerth, and other poems.
San Jose, CA: J.J. Owen, 1876. 126p. NUC OCLC

MANLEY, Emma Catherine see EMBURY, Emma Catherine (Manley)

MANN, NELLIE A., pseud. see MANVILLE, Helen Adelia (Wood)

MANNERS, Catherine Rebecca, Lady see HUNTINGTOWER, Catherine Rebecca (Grey) Talmash, Baroness

3625. MANNERS, Mary Emmeline (Rackham) [Br. 1858-1941]
Aunt Agatha Ann and other verses.
L: J. Clarke, 1897. 88p. BL OCLC

3626. -----The bishop and the caterpillar ... and other pieces.
2d ed. L: J. Clarke, 1893. 92p. NUC OCLC
[Humorous verses for recitation. Suitable for all ages.]

3627. MANNING, Carrie C., Mrs. [Am. b. 1839]
Heart echoes, from the shadowy land of the blind. A collection of brief poems.
Charles City, LA: n.p., 1890.
[Predominately original verse]

3628. MANNING, Eliza F. [Br. 19c]
Delightful Thames.
L: Sampson & Low & co., 1886. 29p. BL

3629. MANNING, Jessie (Wilson) [Am. b. 1855]
The passion of life.
Cincinnati, OH: R. Clarke & co., 1887. 75p. NUC

3630. MANSELL, Mrs. [Br. 19c]
Flowers by the wayside, for little pilgrims; Katy, a tale of the litany and other poems.
Glasgow: Pr. William MacKenzie, 1876. 76p. NUC BL
[Flowers, pp. 1-42, & Katy, pp. 43-48, for young people. Misc. poems, pp. 49-76 for more general audience]

3631. MANSFIELD, Charlotte [Br. b. 1881]
Flowers of the wind.
L: Elkin Mathews, 1899. 53p. BL

3632. MANVILLE, Helen Adelia (Wood) [Am. b. 1839] PSEUD: Mann, Nellie A.
Heart echoes. By Helen A. Manville (Nellie A. Mann).
NY: S.R. Wells & co., 1875. 169p. NUC OCLC

3633. MANWARING, Miss [Br. 19c]
The slaves of Zanquebar; and other poems.
Birmingham: n.p., 1826. BL

3634. MARCHBANK, Agnes [Br. 19c]
Songs of labour, home and country.
Auchterarder: Tovani & co., 1892. 41p. BL

3635. MAREAN, Emma (Endicott) [Am. 1854-1936]
Eighteen.
Boston: Pr. George B. Wilcox, 1894. 33p. NUC OCLC

MARIA see WESTON, Maria D., Mrs.

3636. MARIA SOPHIA [Br. 19c]
The grave of the suicide; The parting kiss; and other poems.
L: n.p., 1824. BL

MARIE see SKIDMORE, Harriet Marie

MARIE JOSEPHINE, pseud. see HEMENWAY, Abby Maria

MARINE, ULTRA, pseud. see PARHAM, Helena Beatrice Richenda, Mrs.

3637. MARK, Amy [Br. 19c]
The sea king's daughter and other poems. With Gertrude M. Bradley.
Birmingham: G. Napier, 1895. 44p. NUC BL OCLC

3638. MARKS, Mary A. M. (Hoppus) [Br. 19/20c] ALT: Hoppus, Mary A. M.
The tree of knowledge.
Guildford: Billing & sons, 1896. 64p. NUC BL

MARKWELL, MARY, pseud. see HAYES, Catherine E. (Simpson)

MARR, Fannie H. see MARR, Frances Harrison

3639. MARR, Frances Harrison [Am. b. 1835] ALT: Marr, Fannie H.
Heart-life in song. By Fannie H. Marr.
Boston; Baltimore: Turnbull, 1874. 165p. NUC OCLC

3640. -----Songs of faith.
Warrenton, VA: n.p., n.d. 55p. NUC

3641. -----Virginia, and other poems. By Miss Fannie H. Marr.
Philadelphia: Sherman & co., pr., 1881. 152p. NUC OCLC

MARRIOTT, Mrs. C.B. see MARRIOTT, Ida (Lee)

3642. MARRIOTT, Frances Smith [Br. 19c]
The votive offering.
L: E. Faithfull, 1862. 152p. OCLC

3643. MARRIOTT, Ida (Lee), Mrs. C.B. Marriott [Br. 19/20c] ALT: Lee, Ida
The bush fire and other verses.
2d ed. L: Sampson, Low & co., 1897. 62p. BL OCLC

3644. MARSDEN, Elizabeth Anne Reynolds Rogerson [Br. 19c]
Leisure musings of a busy life; or, Poems of youth and age.
Leeds: A. Megson & sons, 1885? 90p. BL

3645. MARSH, Caroline (Crane), Mrs. George P. Marsh [Am. 1816-1901]
Wolfe of the knoll, and other poems. By Mrs. George P. Marsh.
NY: C. Scribner; L: Sampson Low, son, & co., 1860. 327p. NUC BL OCLC

3646. MARSH, Catherine M. [Br. 1818-1912]
Memory's pictures.
L: James Nisbet & co., 1871. BL

MARSH, Mrs. George P. see MARSH, Caroline (Crane)

MARSH, Priscilla, ed. see BOWDEN, Hannah (Marsh)

3647. MARSHALL, Anna P. [Am. 19c]
Ben Hazzard's guests.
Boston: Animal Rescue League, 1890? 12p. NUC OCLC

3648. MARSHALL, Augusta Eliza, Lady [Br. 19c]
Helig's warning; a Cymric legend of the seventh century.
L: n.p., 1854. BL

3649. -----Odds and ends.
L: n.p., 1853. BL

3650. -----A Prince of Wales long ago; a Bardic legend of the twelfth century.
L: Whittaker, 1855. 160, 21p. NUC BL

3651. MARSHALL, E.J., Mrs. [Br. 19c] ALT: M., E.J.
A memorial of E.J.M.
Oxford: Pr. for priv. circ., 1856. 51p. NUC BL
[Poems by her]

3652. MARSTON, Hannah [Am. 19c]
Hymns and poems on death. With a letter from a father to his children.
Parsonfield, ME: n.p., 1827. 62p. NUC

3653. MARTIN, Catherine Edith Macaulay (Mackay) [Br. 19/20c] ALT: Mackay, Catherine Edith Macaulay PSEUD: C., M.
The explorers and other poems. By M.C.
Melbourne: George Robertson, 1874. 270p. NUC BL

3654. MARTIN, Margaret (Maxwell) [Am. 19c]
Religious poems. By Mrs. M. Martin.
Nashville, TN: The author, 1858. 234p. NUC OCLC

3655. -----Sabbath-school offerings; or, True stories and poems. Ed. T.O. Summers.
Nashville, TN: Southern Methodist pub. house, 1879. 210p. NUC

3656. MARTIN, Martha [19/20c]
Poem-miniatures.
Montreal: Guertin pr. co., 1899. 61p. NUC BL

3657. MARTIN, Sarah, Miss [Br. 1791-1843]
Selections from the poetical remains of ... Miss S. Martin.
Yarmouth: n.p., 1845. BL

3658. MARTINEAU, Harriet [Br. 1802-1876] PSEUD: Lady, A
Addresses; with prayers and original hymns, for the use of families and schools. By a lady.
L: Rowland Hunter, 1826. 152p. NUC BL

[Contains twelve hymns.]

MARVIN, Abijah Perkins, ed. see WAKEFIELD, Nancy Amelia Woodbury (Priest)

MARVIN, JENNIE, pseud. see FRENCH, Myriam Bedell, Mrs.

3659. MARVIN, Lydia H., Mrs. [Am. 19c] ALT: M., L.H.
Christmas thoughts and carol. By L.H.M.
Brooklyn, NY: n.p., 1889. 13p. NUC

3660. -----Sweet peas, an idyl of memory, love, and hope. By L.H.M.
Brooklyn, NY: n.p., 1888. 16p. NUC
[Poem in memory of her grandparents]

3661. MARVIN, Lydia Hooper [Am. 19c]
The eight beatitudes.
Hartford, CT: Pr. at the Church press, 1873. 24p. NUC
[One poem on each beatitude by the daughter of Wm. Henry Lewis, D.D. on his 70th birthday]

MARY see ST. JOHN, Mary

3662. MARY EDITH, Sister [Am. 19c]
The palace of Shushan and other poems.
Milwaukee, WI: The Young Churchman co., 1891. 68p. NUC

MARY EUGENIA see BROWN, Mary Eugenia

3663. MARZIALS, Emilie Louise [Br. 19c]
Poems.
2 pt. L: Pr. C. Whiting, 1864. 59, 16 p. NUC BL

3664. MASHAM, Damaris (Cudworth), Lady [Br. 1658-1708]
A discourse concerning the love of God.
L: A. & J. Churchil, 1696. 126p. NUC BL OCLC

3665. -----Occasional thoughts in reference to a virtuous or Christian life.
L: n.p., 1700. BL

3666. MASKELL, Eliza [Br. 19c]
Gospel themes: a series of sacred poems.
L: n.p., 1860. BL

3667. -----Moral tales, in verse.
L: n.p., 1847. BL

3668. -----Poetical musings, on religious and sacred subjects.
L: Pub. for author by Darton & Clark, 1845. 72p. NUC BL

3669. -----The poetical treasury, a series of sacred poems.
L: n.p., 1842. BL

3670. -----A sacred offering, containing various pieces on religious subjects, in prose and verse, etc.
L: n.p., 1849. BL

3671. MASON, Mrs. [Am. 19c]
Ellegaic [sic] poems, sacred to friendship.
Greenwich, MA: John Howe, 1803. 12p. NUC OCLC
[NUC note attrib. to Catherine George (Ward) Mason]

3672. MASON, Caroline Atherton (Briggs) [Am. 1823-1890] ALT: Briggs, Caroline Atherton
Fremont's proclamation.
Fitchburg, MA: n.p., 1862. 1p. NUC

3673. -----The lost ring, and other poems. By Caroline A. Mason.
Boston & NY: Houghton, Mifflin & co., 1891. 194p. NUC BL
[OCLC attributes to Caroline Atwater Mason, but intro. specifies Caroline Atherton (Briggs) Mason.]

3674. -----Utterance; or, Private voices to the public heart. A collection of home-poems. By Caroline A. Briggs.
Boston: Phillips, Samson, & co., 1852. 255p. NUC BL OCLC

MASON, Caroline Atwater see MASON, Caroline, Atherton (Briggs)

3675. MASON, Catharine George (Ward) [Br. b. 1787] ALT: Ward, Catherine George
The dandy family, or, The pleasures of a ball night.
L: n.p., 1815. BL

3676. -----Miscellaneous poems.
L: Pr. for the author by Joyce Gold, 1820. 84p. NUC BL OCLC

3677. -----Poems.
Edinburgh: J. Moir, 1805. 43p. NUC BL

3678. -----Poems.
Coventry: n.p., 1812. 60p. BL
[Expanded version of 1805 ed.]

3679. -----A tributary poem on the death of ... the Princess Charlotte of Saxe-Coburg.
L: n.p., 1817. BL

3680. MASON, Ellen (Huntley) Bullard [Br. 19c]
Our mother's prayer. In: Mason, Francis. A cenotaph.
NY: n.p., 1851. p. 186-87. NUC

3681. -----A song of the famine.
Rangoon: n.p., 1874. NUC BL

3682. MASON, Flora Louise [Am. 19c]
Nine muses. Charades.
Taunton, MA: Press of G.L. Hoyt, 1895. 6 l. NUC

MASON, Mrs. George <u>see</u> MASON, Susanna (Hopkins)

3683. MASON, Marie [d. 1881]
In memoriam. Poems.
n.p.: n.p., 1881? 126p. NUC BL OCLC

3684. MASON, Mary Augusta [Am. 19c]
With the seasons.
NY: A.D.F. Randolph co., 1897. 110p. NUC OCLC

MASON, Rachel, comp. <u>see</u> MASON, Susanna (Hopkins)

3685. MASON, Ruth [Br. 19c]
Poems.
Cross-Hills: R. Smith, 1850? 12p. BL

3686. MASON, Susanna (Hopkins), Mrs. George Mason [Am. 1748-1805]
Selections from the letters and manuscripts of the late Susanna Mason, with a brief memoir of her life by her daughter, Rachel [Mason].
Philadelphia: Rackliff & Jones, 1836. 312p. NUC BL OCLC
[Incl. poems]

3687. MASSEY, Lucy (Fletcher) [Br. 19c] ALT: Fletcher, Lucy
Figures of the true.
L: Skeffington & son, 1890. 70p. BL

3688. -----The inner life. Hymns on "the imitation of Christ" by Thomas a Kempis.
Oxford & L: James Parker & co., 1871. 102p. NUC BL OCLC
[Original poems]

3689. -----Songs of the noontide rest.
L & Cambridge: Macmillan & co., 1875. 158p. BL
[Lyric poetry]

3690. MASSEY, Susanna [Am. 19c]
God's parable and other poems.
NY: G.P. Putnam's sons, 1895. 143p. NUC BL OCLC

3691. -----Verses for Christmas.
Philadelphia: J.B. Lippincott, 1885. 14 l. NUC OCLC

3692. MASSON, Phoebe Ann, Miss [Br. 19c]
Legends of the Dunbars, and other poems. By one of their descendents.
L: Priv. pr. by Stewart & Murray, 1854. 347p. NUC BL OCLC

3693. -----Sir Ninian; a tale of chivalry; and other poems.
L: Pr. Smith, Elder & co., 1860. 530p. NUC BL OCLC

3694. MASTERS, Mary [Br. 1694?-1771/1759 OCLC]
Familiar letters and poems on several occasions.
L: Pr. for the author by D. Henry & R. Cave, 1755. 336p. NUC BL OCLC

3695. -----Poems on several occasions.
L: Pr. T. Browne for the author, 1733. 267p. NUC OCLC

3696. MATHER, Dora Mary [Br. 19c]
Poetic meditations.
L: n.p., 1876. BL

MATHERS, Helen Buckingham <u>see</u> REEVES, Helen Buckingham (Mathers)

3697. MATHESON, Annie [Br. 1853-1924]
Love triumphant, and other new poems.
L: Innes, 1898. 114p. NUC BL

3698. -----Love's music, and other poems.
L: S. Low, Marston, 1894. 94p. NUC BL

3699. -----"The religion of humanity" and other poems.
L: Percival & co., 1890. 184p. NUC BL

3700. -----Selected poems, old and new.
L: Henry Frowde, 1899. 152p. NUC BL OCLC

MATHEWS, Charles, ed. <u>see</u> MATHEWS, Eliza Kirkham (Strong)

MATHEWS, Mrs. Charles <u>see</u> MATHEWS, Eliza Kirkham (Strong)

3701. MATHEWS, E., Miss [Br. 19c]
The orphan boy; or, How little John was reclaimed.
L: S.W. Partridge, 1863. 16p. BL

3702. MATHEWS, Eliza Kirkham (Strong), Mrs. Charles Mathews [Br. d. 1802] ALT: Strong, Elizabeth Kirkham
Poems.
Doncaster: n.p., 1802. BL

3703. -----Poems. By Elizabeth Kirkham Strong, of Exeter.
Exeter: Pr. J. M'Kenzie & son, 1796. 63p. NUC

3704. -----Poems. By the late Mrs. Charles Mathews. Ed. Charles Mathews.
Doncaster: Sheardown, 1802. 115p. NUC BL OCLC

3705. MATHEWS, J. A., Mrs. [19c]
PSEUD: Wanda
Three years in Purgatory; short stories, poems and acrostics (dedicated to Montreal) by Wanda.
NY: n.p., 1899? 72p. NUC

3706. MATHIS, Juliette Estelle [Am. 19c]
Songs and sonnets.
San Francisco: C.A. Murdock & co., 1899. 112p. NUC OCLC

MATILDA see EDWARDS, Matilda Caroline (Smiley)

3707. MATSON, Anna [Am. 19c]
The city that a cow kicked over.
Chicago: A.H. Andrews & co., 1881. 20p. NUC OCLC
[On Chicago fire of 1871]

3708. MATSON, Cora Adele [Am. 19c]
As the cardinal flower.
Fulton, NY: Fred Bennett, 1890? 117p. NUC OCLC

3709. MATTESON, Frances F., Mrs. [Am. 19c]
The fragment; or, Letters and poems.
Rome, NY: A. Sandford, pr., 1855. 144p. NUC

3710. -----The wild poet's rest; or, A short series of essays, meditations, poems, etc.
Rome, NY: Pickard & Carr, pr., 1852. 110p. NUC BL

3711. MATTESON, O.S., Mrs. [Am. 19c]
The centennial flight of the king of the air; a poetical description of the battles of the revolutionary war, with the places and dates of their occurrence; as seen by that grand old bird, the American eagle. In two cantos.
Chicago: Hazlitt & Reed, pr., 1875. 118p. NUC

3712. MATTHEW, Mary H., Mrs. [Am. b. 1816]
Mother's souvenir, composed in the 71st year of her age.
San Francisco: Griffith & sons, 1887. 76p. NUC OCLC
[Chiefly domestic poems]

3713. MATTHEWS, Elizabeth [Br. 19c]
Original hymns and moral poems ... By E. Matthews and R. Matthews.
2d ed. L: n.p., 1835. BL

MATTHEWS, R., co-author see MATTHEWS, Elizabeth

MAWR, ETA, pseud. see COLLING, Elizabeth

3714. MAXIM, Rose [Am. 1850-1898]
Autumn leaves.
North Cambridge, MA: Pub. by the author, 1890. 93p. NUC

3715. MAXWELL, Caroline [Br. 19c]
Feudal tales, being a collection of romantic narratives and other poems.
L: T. Hookman & E.T. Hookman, 1810? 116p. BL OCLC

MAXWELL, Mrs. John see MAXWELL, Mary Elizabeth (Braddon)

3716. MAXWELL, Mary Elizabeth (Braddon), Mrs. John Maxwell [Br. 1837-1915] ALT: Braddon, Mary Elizabeth
Garibaldi, and other poems.
L: Bosworth & Harrison, 1861. 318p. NUC BL

3717. MAXWELL, Mary H., Mrs. [Am. 1815-1891]
Johnny wine; or, The history of the temperance house. Ed. D.P. Kidder.
NY: Lane & Scott, 1849. 45p. NUC

3718. -----Knack and luck, and Harry Lee.
NY: 1850.
[Two tales in verse]

3719. -----The water lily. Ed. D.P. Kidder.
NY: Lane & Scott, 1848. 24p. NUC OCLC

3720. -----A will and a way. A temperance story. In verse. Ed. D.P. Kidder.
NY: Carlton & Porter; Lane & Scott, 1852. 95p. NUC OCLC

3721. MAY, Caroline [Am. b. 1820?]
Lays of memory and affection, the seasons and the sea, the beatitudes.
NY: A.D.F. Randolph & co., 1888. 281p. NUC BL OCLC

3722. -----Poems.
NY: Carleton, 1865. 223p. NUC OCLC

3723. MAY, Celeste (Ball) [Am. b. 1850]
Sounds of the prairie.
Topeka, KS: G.W. Crane & co., pr., 1886. 182p. NUC BL OCLC

MAY, EDITH, pseud. see DRINKER, Anna

3724. MAY, Edith J. [Emily Juliana BL] [Br. 19c]
Poems.
Philadelphia: Butler, 1852. 218p. NUC BL

3725. MAY, Emily Jane [Br. 19c]
Compensation, and other poems.
L: Elliot Stock, 1865. 187p. BL OCLC

MAY, Emily Juliana see MAY, Edith J.

3726. MAY, Julia Harris [Am. 1833-1912]
Songs from the woods of Maine.
NY: G.P. Putnam's sons, 1894. 139p. NUC BL OCLC

3727. MAY, Lilian [Am. 19c]
Poems.
Harrisburg, PA: n.p., 1852. 99p. NUC OCLC

3728. MAY, Lizzie [Br. 19c]
Twilight hours; their memories and yearnings. A selection of poems.
L: n.p., 1859. BL
[Original misc. lyrics]

MAY, MARGARET, pseud. see TUCKER, Margaretta Ames

MAY, MORNA, pseud. see BICKFORD, Lelia B.

MAYFIELD, MILLIE, pseud. see HOMES, Mary Sophie (Shaw) Rogers

3729. MAYLIN, Anne Walter [Am. 1806-1889]
Lays of many hours.
Philadelphia: H. Hooker, 1847. 168p. NUC BL OCLC

3730. MAYNARD, Hon. Julia Augusta [Br. 19c]
Eight of our Lord's parables paraphrased, and other poems.
L: n.p., 1858. BL

3731. -----Poems.
L: n.p., 1845. BL

3732. MAYNARD, Mary [Br. 19c]
Poems.
L: Smith, Elder, 1851. 188p. BL OCLC

MAYO, Amory Dwight, comp. see MAYO, Sara Carter (Edgarton)

MAYO, Mrs. Amory Dwight see MAYO, Sara Carter (Edgarton)

MAYO, Sara Carter (Edgarton), comp. see SCOTT, Julia H. (Kinney)

3733. MAYO, Sara Carter (Edgarton), Mrs. Amory Dwight Mayo [Am. 1819-1848]
Selections from the writings of Mrs. Sarah C. Edgarton Mayo: with a memoir by her husband [Amory Dwight Mayo].
Boston: A. Tomkins, 1849. 432p. NUC OCLC
[Incl. poetry & short fiction]

3734. -----Language and poetry of flowers.
L & Edinburgh: n.p., 1848. BL

3735. MEAD, Jane M. [Am. 19c]
The old homestead.
n.p.: n.p., 1853? NUC

3736. MEARS, Amelia Garland [Br. 19c]
Idylls, legends and lyrics.
L: Kegan Paul, Trench, Trubner & co., 1890. 277p. NUC BL

3737. MEDINI, Frances Roena, Mme. [Am. b. 1856] ALT: Roena, F.
Edalaine: a metrical romance.
NY: G.W. Dillingham, 1892. 254p. NUC OCLC

3738. -----Love's hymnal, sonnets.
Cambridge, MA: Pr. H.O. Houghton & co., 1896. 45 l. NUC OCLC

3739. MEDLEY, Sarah [Br. 19c]
Original poems, sacred and miscellaneous.
Liverpool: Pr. J. Smith for W. Robinson, 1807. 228p. NUC BL

3740. MEETKERKE, Cecilia Elizabeth [Br. 19c]
Songs of evening.
L: L. Booth, 1863. 132p. NUC BL

3741. MEIGS, Mary Noel (Bleecker) MacDonald [Am. 19c] ALT: M., M. N.; McDonald, Mary Noel
Hark! a burst of heavenly music.
NY: n.p., n.d. 3p. NUC
[Christmas verse]

3742. -----Poems. By Mrs. Mary Noel McDonald.
NY: Pudney, Hooker, & Russell, pr., 1844. 208p. NUC OCLC

MEIGS, Mary Noel (Bleecker) Macdonald, comp. see BLEECKER, Sophia

MEL, MARY, pseud. see BENNETT, Mary E.

MELBOURNE, GRACE, pseud. see BARKER, Alice J., Mrs.

MELISSA, pseud. see BRERETON, Jane

MELVILL, Elizabeth see COLVILLE, Elizabeth (Melville), Lady Colville of Culross

3743. MELVIN, Fannie Bosworth [Am. 19c]
An Indian idyl.
n.p.: n.p., 1898. 11 l. NUC OCLC

3744. MENKEN, Adah Isaacs [Am. 1835-1868] ALT: McCord, Adelaide
Infelicia.
Philadelphia: J.B. Lippincott, 1868. 126p. NY: H.L. Williams; L & Paris: John Camden Hotten, 1868. 141p. NUC BL OCLC

3745. MENTEATH, Mrs. A. Stuart [Br. 19c]
Lays of the kirk and covenant.
Edinburgh: Johnston & Hunter, 1850. 152p. NUC BL OCLC

3746. MERCEDES, Sister [Am. b. 1846]
Wild flowers from "The mountainside." Poems and dramas.
Philadelphia: J.B. Lippincott & co., 1885. 260p. NUC
[5 verse plays; misc. poems]

3747. MERCUR, Anna Hubbard, Mrs. [Am. 19c]
The Christmas star.
NY: A.E. Chasmar, 1882. 1p. NUC
[With music]

3748. -----Cosmos and other poems.
Buffalo, NY & NY: P. Paul & bro., 1893. 215p. NUC OCLC

3749. -----Crusaders of '61.
n.p.: n.p., 1875? NUC
[No imprint, C.W. Moulton Collection]

3750. MEREDITH, Harriet R. [Am. 19c]
Sketches, life thoughts and incidents.
Philadelphia: J.B. Lippincott & co., 1881. 179p. NUC OCLC
[Mostly poetry; incl. a few short fictional parables]

3751. MERIDEN, Kate [Am. 19c]
Leaves from Hemlock Valley. A collection of poems and stories.
NY: James Miller, 1872. 104p. NUC OCLC

3752. MERING, Ann S. [Am. 19c]
Songs in the night, and musings of an invalid.
Cincinnati, OH: Pr. for the author by William Doyle, 1855. 62p. NUC OCLC

3753. MERIWETHER, Lida (Smith) [Am. b. 1829]
One or two? By two sisters. With L[ucy] Virginia (Smith) French.
St. Louis, MO: Meriwether bros., 1883. 228p. NUC OCLC

MERIWETHER, Lide (Smith), co-author see FRENCH, Lucy Virginia (Smith)

3754. MERRITT, Magdalene Isadora (LaGrange) [Am. b. 1864] ALT: LaGrange, Magdalene I.
Songs of the Helderberg; poems. By Magdalene I. LaGrange.
Albany, NY: Boyd's Albany pr. co., 1893. 126p. NUC OCLC

3755. MERRY, M. A., Mrs. [Br. 19c] ALT: M., M. A.
Poems by M.A.M.
Guilden Morden: Priv. pr. at the Vickerage, 1850. BL

MERRY, Mrs. Robert see COWLEY, Hannah (Parkhouse)

MERRY, Robert, co-author see COWLEY, Hannah (Parkhouse)

3756. MERRYWEATHER, I. A., Mrs. [Br. 19c] ALT: M., I. A.
The hermit of Eskdaleside, and other poems. By I.A.M.
Whitby: R. Kirby, 1833. 136p. NUC BL OCLC

3757. MESSENGER, Lillian (Rozell) [Am. 1843-1921]
Fragments from an old inn.
NY & L: G.P. Putnam's sons, 1885. 123p. NUC OCLC
[Misc. verse; prose: aphorisms, description of the inn & of a friend.]

3758. -----"In the heart of America."
Richmond, VA: J.L. Hill pr. co., 1896. 15 l. NUC OCLC
[Poem read at the Atlanta exposition.]

3759. -----The southern cross, and other poems.
Buffalo, NY: C.W. Moulton, 1891. 42p. NUC OCLC

3760. -----Threads of fate.
Washington, D.C.: The author, 1873. 227p. NUC

3761. -----The vision of gold, and other poems.
NY & L: G.P. Putnam's sons, 1886. 156p. NUC

META, pseud. see LEWIS, Mary McFarland

3762. MEYLER, Mary [Br. 19c]
Hours of solitude: or, Thoughts in verse.
Bath: Meyler & son, 1849. 82p. BL

3763. MEYNELL, Alice Christiana Gertrude (Thompson) [Br. 1847-1922] ALT: Thompson, Alice Christina
Other poems.
L: Priv. pr., 1896. 16p. NUC BL

3764. -----Poems.
L: Elkin Mathews & John Lane, 1892. 72p. NUC BL

3765. -----Preludes. By A.C. Thompson.
L: H.S. King & co., 1875. 84p. NUC BL

3766. MEYRICK, Geraldine [Am. 19c]
Songs of a fool.
San Jose, CA: n.p., 1895. 16 l. NUC

MICHENER, Amanda, comp. see MICHENER, Frances Lavinia

3767. MICHENER, Amanda (Pyle) [Am. 19/20c]
Naphtali; or, The young bondman.
Philadelphia: J.B. Lippincott co., 1889. 161p. NUC
[Narrative poem]

3768. -----Whisperings of the spirit, by Amanda Pyle Michener and My heart life, by Annie E. Michener.
Philadelphia: J.B. Lippincott, 1895. 360p. OCLC

MICHENER, Annie E., co-author see MICHENER, Amanda (Pyle)

MICHENER, Fannie L. see MICHENER, Frances Lavinia

3769. MICHENER, Frances Lavinia [Am. 1866-1882] ALT: Michener, Fannie L.
The prose and poetical works of Fannie L. Michener. With a memoir by Amanda Michener.
Philadelphia: J.B. Lippincott & co., 1884. 386p. NUC OCLC
[Short stories written when 10-13 years of age; 78 poems, chiefly narrative, written before her death at 16]

3770. MILBURN, Mrs. William Henry [Am. 19c]
Poems of faith and affection.
NY: Hurd & Houghton; Boston: E.P. Dutton & co., 1866. 103p. NUC BL

MILES, Mrs. Alfred see MILES, Sibella Elizabeth (Hatfield)

3771. MILES, Sibella Elizabeth (Hatfield), Mrs. Alfred Miles [Br. 1800-1882] ALT: Hatfield, Sibella Elizabeth
Fruits of solitude, or prose and poetic compositions; consisting of sketches of natural and moral scenery; Tales, essays, and meditations. By Sibella Elizabeth Hatfield.
L: Longman, Rees, Orme, & Brown; Whittaker, Treacher & Arnott, 1831. 212p. BL
[Primarily poetry; 3 brief prose essays]

3772. -----Leisure evenings; or, Records of the past. A collection of prose and poetical miscellanies. By Mrs. Alfred Miles.
L: Geo. Phipps, 1860. 166p. BL
[Chiefly poetry: lyric, dramatic, occasional, philosophical. Four essays and one short story]

3773. -----Moments of loneliness, or prose and poetic efforts, on various subjects and occasions. By Sibella Elizabeth Hatfield.
L: Simpkin & Marshall, 1829. 204p. BL
[Chiefly poetry; 2 essays and 1 short story, "The last of the Druids"]

3774. -----The wanderer of Scandinavia; or, Sweden delivered, in five cantos, and other poems.
L: Sold by Longman & co., 1826. 2v. NUC BL OCLC

MILLARD, James Henry, comp. see WESTWOOD, Lucy Bell

MILLER, Alice Maud (Duer), co-author see DUER, Caroline King

3775. MILLER, Anna (Riggs), Lady [Br. 1741-1781]
On novelty: and on trifles and triflers.
Bath: R. Crutwell, 1778. 17p. BL

3776. -----Poetical amusements.
Bath: L. Bull, n.d. 150p. BL
[Pub. for "Benefit of the pauper-charity of that city;" went into 4 eds.]

3777. -----Poetical amusements at a villa near Bath.
2d ed. L: Edward & Charles Dilly, 1776-1781. 4v. BL OCLC
[Contains enigmas, riddles, poems on set topics: harmony, beauty, etc. By Miller and friends, incl. Anna Seward]

3778. MILLER, Elvira Sydnor [Am. 19c]
Songs of the heart.
Louisville, KY: J.P. Morton & co., 1885. 144p. NUC OCLC

MILLER, Ellen Clare see PEARSON, Ellen Clare (Miller)

3779. MILLER, Emily Clark (Huntington) [Am. 1833-1913]
From Avalon, and other poems.
Chicago: A.C. McClurg & co., 1896. 75p. NUC OCLC

3780. -----Songs from the nest.
Chicago: Kindergarten Literature, 1894. 85p. NUC OCLC
[Poems on motherhood & babies]

3781. MILLER, Fannie de C. [Am. 19c]
In the redwoods.
San Francisco: F. Eastman & co., pr., 1895. 18p. NUC OCLC

MILLER, George, co-author see MOODY, Elizabeth, Miss

3782. MILLER, Lotta [Am. 19c]
Flowers from the kitchen garden; miscellaneous poems.
Oil City, PA: Derrick pub. co., 1894. 48p. NUC

3783. MILLER, Marion Mills, Mrs. [Am. b. 1864]
The man sent of God. A poem.
NY: n.p., 1899. 7p. NUC
[Poem based on funeral oration for Henry George.]

3784. -----Parnassus by rail.
NY: G.P. Putnam's sons, 1891. 105p. NUC OCLC
[Railroad poetry]

3785. MILLER, Mary Morgan [Am. 19c]
Poems. With a memoir of her life, by her sister, Lydia M. Chase.
Columbus, OH: William G. Hubbard, 1885. 92p. NUC OCLC

3786. MILLER, Minnie (Willis) Baines- [Am. b. 1845]
The pilgrim's vision, an allegory.
Cincinnati, OH: Cranston & Stowe, 1891. 121p. NUC
[Poem discussing the questioning of religion by science.]

3787. MILLIGAN, Sophia [Br. 19c]
Original poems, with translations from Scandinavian and other poets.
L: Hurst & Blackett, 1856. 338p. NUC BL

MILLER, Rev. John, co-author see TRUBSHAW, Susanna

MILLS, Elizabeth Willesford see BORRON, Elizabeth Willesford (Mills)

3788. MILLS, Joanna Eames (Dana) [Am. 1823-1893]
Old and new and other poems.
Boston: Columbian pr. co., 1893. 90p. NUC BL OCLC

3789. -----Remembrance of my mother, and some of my own poems.
Boston: A. Williams & co., 1881. 94p. NUC OCLC
[Mostly misc. poetry by Mills. Incl. her mother's reminiscences and a few letters. Her mother's name not given.]

3790. MILNE, Christian (Ross) [Br. b. 1773]
Simple poems on simple subjects. By Christian Milne, wife of a journeyman ship carpenter, in Footdee, Aberdeen.
Aberdeen: n.p., 1805. BL

3791. MILNE, Frances Margaret (Tener) [Am. b. 1846]
A cottage gray, and other poems.
Buffalo, NY: Charles Wells Moulton, 1895. 79p. NUC OCLC

3792. -----For today, poems.
Boston: Arena pub. co., 1893. 137p.
NUC OCLC

MINSTREL MAIDEN OF MOBILE, pseud. <u>see</u> HARRISS, Julia Mildred

3793. MITCHELL, Agnes (Woods) [Am. 19c] ALT: M., A.W.
The smuggler's son and other tales and sketches in prose and verse. By A.W.M.
Philadelphia: H. Hooker, 1842. 300p. NUC BL OCLC
[Intended for "improvement of the young," but the short stories are not childlike. Misc. poetry incl.]

3794. MITCHELL, Catharine [Am. 19c]
The downfall of Jerusalem, and other poems.
Philadelphia: n.p., 1845. 90p. NUC

3795. -----The minstrel's bride; or, The shepherd of Hazel Glen.
Philadelphia: J.B. Lippincott co., 1859. 237p. NUC OCLC

3796. MITCHELL, Mrs. E.A. Newman [Am. 19c]
Consolations, written and compiled.
Juda, WI: The author, 1897. 144p. NUC OCLC
[About 68 original poems with selections from other poets.]

3797. MITCHELL, Elizabeth Harcourt (Rolls) [Br. 19c] ALT: R., E. H.; Rolls, Elizabeth Harcourt
The ballad of Sir Rupert: a ghost story. By E.H.R.
Monmouth: T. Farror, 1855. BL

3798. -----The battle of Trafalgar. A ballad.
L: J. Masters & co., 1887. 11p. NUC BL

3799. -----First fruits. Poems. By E.H.R.
L: Hurst & Blackett, 1857. 108p. NUC BL OCLC

3800. -----Wild thyme; verses.
L: n.p., 1861. NUC BL

3801. MITFORD, Mary Russell [Br. 1787-1855]
Christina, the maid of the south seas; a poem.
L: Pr. A.J. Valpy for F.C. & J. Rivington, 1811. 332p. NUC BL OCLC

3802. -----Dramatic scenes, sonnets, and other poems.
L: G.B. Whittaker, 1827. 392p. NUC OCLC

3803. -----Narrative poems on the female character, in the various relations of life. V. 1.
L & NY: Eastburn, Kirk & co., 1813. 206p. NUC BL OCLC
[No other vols. pub.]

3804. -----Poems.
L: Pr. A.J. Valpy, sold by Longman, Hurst, Rees, & Orme, 1810. 144p. NUC BL OCLC

3805. -----Poems.
2d ed. with considerable additions.
L: Pr. A.J. Valpy, sold by F.C. & J. Rivington, 1811. 257p. NUC OCLC

3806. -----Watlington Hill; a poem.
L: Pr. A.J. Valpy, 1812. 11p. NUC BL OCLC

3807. MOE, Adelaide T. [Am. 19c]
The old fountain inn, and other poems.
Philadelphia: J.B. Lippincott & co., 1875. 123p. NUC OCLC

MOI-MÊME, pseud. <u>see</u> COVENTRY, Mary

MOIISE, Penina <u>see</u> MOISE, Penina, Miss

3808. MOIR, Ellen Beatrice (Pearson) [Br. 1875-1899]
In memoriam Ellen Beatrice Moir.
Glasgow: University press, 1899. 69p. NUC
[Contains her meditations & poems]

3809. MOISE, Penina, Miss [Am. 1797-1880] ALT: Moiise, Penina
Fancy's sketch book.
Charleston, SC: J.S. Burges, 1883. [1833 OCLC] 159p. NUC OCLC

3810. -----Hymns written for the use of Hebrew congregations.
Philadelphia: W.W. Jones, 1856. 214p. OCLC

MOLESWORTH, Richard, Viscount, ed. <u>see</u> MONK, Mary (Molesworth)

3811. MOLLINEUX, Mary (Southworth) [Br. 1648-1695]
Fruits of retirement; or, Miscellaneous poems, moral and divine, being some contemplations, letters, etc. written on variety of subjects and occasions. By Mary

Mollineux, late of Liverpool, deceased. To which is prefixed, some account of the author.
L: Pr. T. Sowle, 1702. 174p. NUC BL OCLC

MONCK, Mary (Molesworth) see MONK, Mary (Molesworth)

3812. MONCKTON, Charlotte Penelope [19c]
Lines. Written on several occasions.
n.p.: n.p., 1806. 59p. NUC

MONCKTON-ARUNDELL, Vere, Viscountess see GALWAY, Vere (Gosling) Monckton-Arundell, Viscountess

3813. MONK, Hon. Mary (Molesworth) [Br. d. 1715] ALT: Monck, Mary (Molesworth)
Marinda. Poems and translations upon several occasions. Ed. & pub. her father, Lord Molesworth [Richard, Viscount Molesworth].
L: Pr. J. Tonson, 1716. 156p. NUC BL OCLC

MONMOUTH, Mrs. J.E. see MONMOUTH, Sarah Elizabeth (Harper)

3814. MONMOUTH, Sarah Elizabeth (Harper), Mrs. J.E. Monmouth [Am. 1829-1887] PSEUD: Afton, Effie
Eventide, a series of tales and poems. By Effie Afton.
Boston: Fetridge, 1854. 431p. NUC BL OCLC
[BL assigns this pseud. and work to Frances Ellen Watkins Harper, NUC to Monmouth.]

3815. MONROE, Harriet [Am. 1860-1936]
Commemoration ode written by Harriet Monroe at the request of the Committee on ceremonies and delivered at the dedication of the World's Columbian exposition on the 400th anniversary of the discovery of America.
Chicago: Pr. for author by Rand, McNally & co., 1892. 15p. NUC OCLC
[Also called: "The Columbian ode"]

3816. -----A poem written on the occasion of the centenary of Georgetown convent of the Visitation. Read before the alumnae on Wednesday, May 31, in the year of our Lord 1899.
Georgetown, D.C.: n.p., 1899. 8p. NUC

3817. -----Valeria and other poems.
Chicago: Pr. for the author at the De Vinne press, 1891. 287p. NUC OCLC

MONTAGU, Eleanora see HERVEY, Eleanora Louisa (Montagu)

3818. MONTAGU, Lady Mary (Pierrepont) Wortley [Br. 1689-1762] ALT: Montague, Lady Mary (Pierrepont) Wortley PSEUD: Lady, A
An elegy to a young lady, in the manner of Ovid ... with an answer: by a lady.
L: J. Roberts, 1733. 8p. NUC BL OCLC

3819. -----The poetical works. Ed. I. Reed.
L: J. Williams, 1768. 109p. BL NUC OCLC

3820. -----Six town eclogues, with some other poems.
L: M. Cooper, 1747. 48p. NUC BL OCLC
[First pub. as a pirated ed., Court Poems; by a lady of quality. L: Pub. by Curll, 1716]

3821. -----Verses address'd to the imitator [A. Pope] of the first satire of the second book of Horace. By a lady
L: J. Roberts, 1733. 7p. BL OCLC
[Satire on Alexander Pope addressed to him by Lady MWM & Lord Hervey (John, Baron Hervey BL)]

MONTAGUE, Lady Mary (Pierrepont) Wortley see MONTAGU, Lady Mary (Pierrepont) Wortley

3822. MONTAGUE, Mary Seymour [Br. 18c] PSEUD: Lady, A
An original essay on woman, in four epistles. Written by a lady.
L: Pr. A. Bridgman, 1771. 55p. NUC BL

3823. MONTEFIORE, Dora B. [Br. 19/20c]
"Singings through the dark": poems.
L: S. Low, Marston & co., 1898. 76p. NUC BL

MONTGOMERY, Hon. Mrs. Alfred see MONTGOMERY, Fanny Charlotte (Wyndham)

3824. MONTGOMERY, Carrie Frances (Judd) [Am. b. 1858]
Heart whisperings.
Oakland, CA: Office of Triumphs of Faith, 1897. 73p. NUC OCLC

3825. -----The heavenly babe; a Christmas carol.
Beulah, CA: Office of Triumphs of Faith, 1880? 11p. NUC

3826. -----Lilies from the vale of thought.
Buffalo, NY: H.H. Otis, 1878. 109p. NUC OCLC
[Poems written between ages 14-19]

3827. -----Zaida Eversey; or, Life two-fold.
Buffalo, NY: H.H. Otis, 1881. 234p. NUC OCLC

3828. MONTGOMERY, Eleanor Elizabeth [19/20c]
Songs of the singing shepherd.
Wanganui, New Zealand: A.D. Willis, 1885. 162p. NUC BL OCLC

3829. MONTGOMERY, Fanny Charlotte (Wyndham), Hon. Mrs. Alfred Montgomery [Br. 1820-1893] ALT: Wyndham, Fanny Charlotte
Poems.
L: Rivington, 1846. 134p. NUC BL

3830. -----Truth without prejudice.
n.p.: n.p., 1842. BL

MONTGOMERY, James, co-author see BENGER, Elizabeth Ogilvie

3831. MONTOLIEU, Mrs. [Br. 19c]
The enchanted plants, fables in verse. Inscribed to Miss Montolieu and Miss Julia Montolieu.
L: Pr. T. Bensley, 1800. NUC OCLC
[Written for her daughters]

MOODIE, Mrs. John Wedderburn Dunbar see MOODIE, Susanna (Strickland)

3832. MOODIE, Susanna (Strickland) [Br. 1803-1885] ALT: Strickland, Susanna
Enthusiasm, and other poems.
L: n.p., 1831. BL

3833. MOODY, Elizabeth, Miss [Br. 18c]
Anna's complaint; or, The miseries of war. In: War, a system of madness ... by Humanitas [George Miller].
Edinburgh: n.p., 1796. 64p. BL

3834. -----Poetic trifles.
L: Pr. H. Baldwin & son, for T. Cadell & W. Davies, 1798. 186p. NUC BL OCLC

3835. MOORE, Ada F., Mrs. [Am. 19c]
Under the pines.
Milwaukee, WI: West, 1875. 204p. NUC OCLC

3836. MOORE, Adelaide [Am. 19c]
Drift-weed of idle moments.
NY: Photo-gravure co., 1885? 48p. NUC
[On t.p.: Souvenir. Poems and reviews of her performances in Shakespearean roles]

MOORE, C.J., pseud. see MOORE, Clara Sophia (Jessup) Bloomfield-

MOORE, Charlotte (McIlvain), ed. see MC ILVAIN, Clara (Lowell)

3837. MOORE, Clara Sophia (Jessup) Bloomfield- [Am. 1824-1899] PSEUD: Moreton, Clara; Ward, H.O.; Moore, C.J.
Gondaline's lesson; The warden's tale; Stories for children, and other poems.
L: C. Kegan Paul & co., 1881. 226p. NUC BL OCLC

3838. -----Poems. A chapter from the modern pilgrim's progress. Slander and gossip.
Philadelphia: Pr. for priv. circ., 1882. 105p. NUC BL
[Last two parts are prose.]

3839. MOORE, Ella Maude (Smith) [Am. b. 1849] ALT: Moore, Maude
Songs of sunshine and shadow, by Maude Moore.
Boston: D. Lothrop, c1880. 230p. NUC OCLC

3840. MOORE, Jane [Br. 19c]
Staleybridge "in ye olden times," etc.
Manchester: J. Heywood, 1888. 32p. BL

3841. -----Wild flowers of song; a miscellaneous collection of songs and poems.
Manchester: J. Heywood, 1880. 128p. NUC

3842. MOORE, Jane Elizabeth (Gobeil) [Br. b. 1738]
Genuine memoirs of Jane Elizabeth Moore, late of Bermondsey, in the county of Surrey. Written by herself: containing the singular adventures of herself and family. Her sentimental journey through Great Britain; specifying the various manufactures carried on at each town. To which is prefixed a poetic index.
L: Logographic press, 1785? 3v. NUC BL
[Autobiography and poems]

3843. MOORE, Jane Elizabeth [Br. 18c]
Miscellaneous poems on various subjects.
L: n.p., 1796. BL

3844. MOORE, Julia A. (Davis) [Am. 1847-1920]
Centennial, 1876. The sentimental song book.
Grand Rapids, MI: C.M. Loomis, pr., 1876. 66p. NUC OCLC

3845. -----The death of Brigham Young.
Cleveland, OH: J.F. Ryder, 1877. 2p. NUC

3846. -----A few choice words to the public, with new and original poems, by Julia A. Moore. Written by the author. Her second book.
Grand Rapids, MI: C.M. Loomis, pr., 1878. 55p. NUC OCLC

3847. -----The sweet singer, of Michigan. Later poems of Julia A. Moore.
Grand Rapids, MI: Eaton, Lyon & co., 1878. 90p. NUC BL

MOORE, Lottie (McIlvain), ed. see MCILVAIN, Clara (Lowell)

3848. MOORE, Marinda Branson, Mrs. [Am. 19c]
Songs of love and liberty. Comp. a North Carolina lady.
Raleigh, NC: Branson & Farrar, 1864. 62p. NUC OCLC

3849. MOORE, Mary Ann [Am. 19c]
Musings of a blind and partially deaf girl.
Philadelphia: J.B. Lippincott & co., 1873. 144p. NUC OCLC
[Verse and prose]

MOORE, Maude see MOORE, Ella Maude (Smith)

MOORE, Mollie E. see DAVIS, Mary Evelyn (Moore)

3850. MORE, Hannah [Br. 1745-1833]
PSEUD: Z.
The bad bargain: or, The world set up to sale.
L: Sold by J. Marshall, 1796. 7p. NUC BL OCLC

3851. -----Bible rhymes, on the names of all the books of the Old and New Testament: with allusions to some of the principal incidents and characters.
Boston: Wells & Lilly, 1821. 72p. NUC BL

3852. -----Bishop Bonner's ghost.
Strawberry Hill: Pr. Thomas Kirgate, 1789. 4p. NUC BL OCLC
[Satire]

3853. -----Florio: a tale for fine gentlemen and fine ladies: and, The Bas bleu; or, Conversation: two poems.
Dublin: Colles, White, Byrne, Cash, Heery, McKenzie, & Moore, 1786. 95p. NUC BL

3854. -----The harvest home. A hymn of praise for the abundant harvest of 1796, after a year of scarcity in England. By Z.
n.p.: n.p., 1796. NUC

3855. -----Ode to Dragon, Mr. Garrick's house-dog, at Hampton.
L: T. Cadell, 1777. 14p. NUC OCLC

3856. -----Poems.
L & Philadelphia: Pr. Young, Stewart & M'Culloch, 1785. 24p. NUC

3857. -----Sacred dramas; chiefly intended for young persons, the subjects taken from the Bible. To which is added: Sensibility, a poem.
L: n.p., 1782. BL
[On Old Testament subjects, in verse]

3858. -----Slavery, a poem.
L: T. Cadell, 1788. 20p. NUC BL OCLC

3859. -----St. Eldred of the bower, and The bleeding rock, two legendary tales.
L: n.p., 1776. BL

3860. MOREHEAD, Lovinia M. (Espy) [Am. 1818-1900]
Autumn leaves gathered for a few friends.
NY: A.D.F. Randolph, & co., 1883. 135p. NUC OCLC

3861. MOREHOUSE, Carrie Warner, Mrs. [Am. 19c]
The legend of Psyche, and other verses.
St. Johnsbury, VT: C.T. Walter, 1889. 98p. NUC OCLC

MORETON, CLARA, pseud. see MOORE, Clara Sophia (Jessup) Bloomfield

MORFITT, John, co-author see PICKERING, Mrs.

3862. MORGAN, Harriette Pain [Br. 19c]

The parting gift, and other poems.
L: W. Poole, 1879. BL

3863. MORGAN, Libbie S. [Am. 19c]
Poems.
Cincinnati, OH: Standard pub. co., 1888. 130p. OCLC

MORGAN, Lyttleton F., comp. see MORGAN, Susan Rigby (Dallam)

MORGAN, Mrs. Lyttleton F. see MORGAN, Susan Rigby (Dallam)

3864. MORGAN, Martha M. (Stout), Graham [Am. b. 1825]
Journey across the plains in the year 1849, with notes of a voyage to California by way of Panama. Also some spiritual songs, etc.
San Francisco: Pioneer press, 1864. 31p. NUC OCLC
[Also pub. as: A trip across the plains]

3865. MORGAN, Mary [Br. 19/20c]
PSEUD: Lea, Gowan
Marguerites. By Mary Morgan (Gowan Lea).
L: Haas & co., 1898. 71p. NUC BL

3866. -----Poems and translations.
Montreal: J.T. Robinson, 1887. 195p. NUC
[Misc. original poetry & sonnets. Trans. from German & French poetry]

3867. -----Woodnotes in the gloaming. Poems and translations.
Boston: Cupples & Hurd, 1889. 195p. NUC

3868. MORGAN, Susan Rigby (Dallam), Mrs. Lyttleton F. Morgan [Am. d. 1887]
Poems of Mrs. Lyttleton F. Morgan; with a memoir by her husband.
Baltimore, MD: D.H. Carroll for priv. circ., 1888. 336p. NUC

3869. MORGAN, Sydney (Owenson), Lady [Br. c1782/3-1859] ALT: O., S.; Owenson, Sydney
The lay of an Irish harp; or, Metrical fragments.
L: Pr. for Richard Phillips, by T. Bensley, 1807. 199p. NUC BL OCLC

3870. -----The Mohawks; a satirical poem with notes.
L: H. Colburn, 1822. 164p. NUC OCLC

3871. -----Poems.
Dublin: Pr. Alex Stewart; L: Pr. Mr. Philips, 1801. 157p. NUC BL

3872. MORINSKI, Georgina J. [Am. 19c]
"Return to me again," a very popular ballad, written and composed for, and respectfully dedicated to Lady H. d'Orsay. Sung with great eclat by Henry Russell.
NY: S.C. Jollie's; New Orleans, LA: Charles Horst, 1850? 5p. NUC

3873. MORISON, Hannah [Am. 19c]
Poems on various subjects.
Newry: Pr. A. Wilkinson, 1817. 210p. NUC

MORISON, Jean see CAMPBELL, Jean (Morison)

3874. MORRIS, Eliza F. [Br. 19c]
Life lyrics.
L: Kent & co.; Worcester: J. Grainger, 1866. 143p. BL OCLC

3875. -----The voice and the reply.
L: n.p., 1858. BL

3876. MORRIS, Florence Ada [Am. 19c]
Destruction of the battle ship "Maine." An original poem.
Epping, NH: n.p., 1898. 20 l. NUC

MORRIS, Madge see WAGNER, Madge (Morris)

3877. MORRIS, Margaret H. [Am. 19c]
PSEUD: S., F.M.
Heavenly dawn. Original and selected pieces. By Margaret H. Morris.
Philadelphia: Claxton, Remsen & Haffelfinger, 1879. 402p. NUC
[14 original poems; selections include: Home Life, Nature, & Heaven. Original pieces signed: F.M.S.]

3878. -----A praise-meeting of the birds.
Philadelphia: Edward S. Morris, 1878. 38p. NUC OCLC
[Composed for Heavenly Dawn, but pub. separately first.]

3879. MORRISON, Sarah Parke [Am. 1833-1916]
A monody: to a father's memory.
Cambridge, MA: Riverside press, 1891. 48p. NUC OCLC

MORSE, Samuel Finley Breese, ed. see DAVIDSON, Lucretia Maria

3880. MORTON, Eliza Happy [Am. 1855-1916]
Still waters; or, Dreams of rest. A collection of sacred poems.
Portland, ME: Hoyt, Fogg & Donham, 1881. 208p. NUC OCLC

[All original]

3881. MORTON, Harriet (Cave) [Br. 19c] ALT: Cave, Harriet
Jubilee echoes. A poem in celebration of the fifty years reign of Queen Victoria 1837-1887.
L: James E. Hawkins, 1887. BL

3882. -----Mary of Garway farm; or, The despised warning.
L: S.W. Partridge & co., 1868. 30p. NUC
[Temperance verse]

3883. -----May blossoms; Lines on the Jubilee of Her Majesty the Queen.
L: W. Kent & co., 1869. 32p. BL

3884. -----Milly's mission; or, Harry and his mother. A ballad.
L: S.W. Partridge & co., 1869. 30p. NUC BL
[Temperance]

3885. MORTON, Jessie D.M. [Br. 19c]
Clarkson Grey; and other poems.
Edinburgh: n.p., 1866. BL
[2d ed. L: Houlston & Wright, 1867. 139p. NUC]

3886. MORTON, Sarah Wentworth (Apthorp) [Am. 1759-1846] PSEUD: Lady of Boston, A; Philenia
Beacon Hill. A local poem, historic and descriptive. Book I. Published according to act of Congress.
Boston: Pr. Manning & Loring for the author, 1797. 56p. NUC BL OCLC

3887. -----My mind and its thoughts, in sketches, fragments and essays.
Boston: Wells & Lilly, 1823. 295p. NUC BL OCLC
[Misc. poetry; prose aphorisms, & essays.]

3888. -----Ouabi; or, The virtues of nature. An Indian tale. In four cantos. By Philenia, a lady of Boston.
Boston: Pr. I. Thomas & E.T. Andrews, 1790. 51p. NUC BL OCLC

3889. -----Reanimation. A hymn for the Humane Society.
Boston?: n.p., 181-. NUC

3890. -----The virtues of society. A tale, founded on fact.
Boston: Pr. Manning & Loring, for the author, 1799. 46p. NUC OCLC

3891. MOSHER, Ada A. [Am. 19c]
From fallow fields.
Baltimore, MD: John Murphy & co., 1897. 104p. NUC OCLC

MOSHER, M., co-author <u>see</u> MCCARTHY, Kate

MOSSCOCKLE, Rita Frances, Mrs. <u>see</u> COCKLE, Rita Frances Moss-, Mrs.

3892. MOTE, Eliza, Mrs. [Br. 19c]
Passing thoughts amid life's work and life's tears; or, Poems sacred and moral.
L: Partridge & co., 1883. 61p. BL

3893. MOTT, Mrs. Isaac Henry Robert [Br. 19c]
Sacred melodies, preceded by an admonitory appeal to the Right Honourable Lord Byron, with other small poems.
L: n.p., 1824. BL

3894. MOULDING, Sarah, Mrs. [Br. d. 1871]
A brief sketch of the life of Mrs. Moulding ... Chiefly derived from her own letters. Comp. Henry Smith.
L: W. Hunt & co., 1872. 78p. BL
[Spent last 16 years in St. Alban's Union Workhouse; includes poems]

3895. MOULTON, Ellen Louise (Chandler) [Am. 1835-1908] ALT: Chandler, Ellen Louise; Moulton, Louise Chandler
At the wind's will, lyrics and sonnets.
L: Macmillan & co.; Boston: Little, Brown & co., 1899. 171p. NUC BL OCLC

3896. -----In the garden of dreams: lyrics and sonnets.
Boston: Roberts bros.; L: Macmillan, 1890. 170p. NUC BL OCLC

3897. -----Poems.
Boston: Roberts bros., c1877. 153p. NUC BL OCLC

3898. -----Swallow flights.
Boston: Roberts bros.; L: Macmillan & co., 1878. 140p. NUC BL OCLC
[Repr. of 1877 vol. with ten new poems]

3899. -----This, that and the other. By Ellen Louise Chandler.
5th ed. Boston: Phillips, Samson & co.; NY: J.C. Derby, 1854. 412p. NUC OCLC
[Stories, essays and poems]

MOULTON, Louise (Chandler) see MOULTON, Ellen Louise (Chandler)

3900. MOULTON, Sarah H. [Br. 19c]
The sepulchre of Lazarus, recollections of Scotland, and other poems.
L: Saunders & Otley, 1842. 135p. NUC BL

MOULTRIE, Rev. Gerard, co-author see MOULTRIE, Mary Dunlop

3901. MOULTRIE, Mary Dunlop [Br. 1837-1866]
Hymns and lyrics for the seasons and saints' days of the church. With her brother, Rev. Gerard Moultrie.
L: J. Masters, 1867. 433p. NUC BL OCLC

3902. MOUNTAIN, Annie [Br. 19c]
The legend of St. Helier.
Jersey: C. LeFeuvre, 1863. 16p. NUC

3903. -----Old and new Sarum; Addison's birthplace; and Stonehenge; by Annie Mountain. Selected from Wiltshire ballads, by the same.
Salisbury: n.p., 1862. 26p. BL

3904. -----"A wreath of rue," for Lent; and the sacred lake.
Toronto: n.p., 1873. 49p. NUC

MOWATT, Anna Cora (Ogden) see RITCHIE, Anna Cora (Ogden) Mowatt

3905. MOWER, Sarah S. [Am. 19c]
The snow drop; a holiday gift.
Hallowell, ME: Masters, Smith, pr., 1851. 160p. NUC OCLC

3906. MUCHMORE, Jennie [Am. 19c]
Poems. Hillside violets.
Des Moines, IA: Iowa pr. co., 1888. 223p. NUC OCLC

3907. MUDIE, Miss [Br. 19c]
Poems on various subjects, and fragmentary pieces, &c., &c., &c.
L: T.W. Grattan, 1848? 130p. BL
[Narrative & lyric poems on wide variety of topics]

MUENSTER, Mrs. Alfred M. see MUNSTER, Mary C.F. (Monck)

3908. MUIR, Janet Kelso [Br. 19c]
Lyrics and poems of nature and life.
Paisley: J. & R. Parlane, 1878. 247p. BL OCLC

MULHOLLAND, Rosa see GILBERT, Rosa (Mulholland), Lady

MULOCK, Dinah Maria see CRAIK, Dinah Maria (Mulock)

3909. MULVANY, Alicia A. [Br. 19c]
Landmarks of a long life. Verses found subsequent to the writer's death.
Dusseldorf: Pr. for priv. circ., 1897. 108p. BL

3910. -----Notes on the journey.
n.p.: n.p., 1897. 174p. BL
[Religious verse]

3911. MUNDAY, Lurania A. H. [Am. b. 1828]
Acacian lyrics and miscellaneous poems.
St. Louis, MO: Pr. at the office of the Cumberland Presbyterian, 1857. 183p. NUC OCLC
[Masonic poetry]

3912. MUNGER, Victoria (Spencer) [Am. 19c]
Gems of thought.
Springfield, MA: Clark W. Bryan & co., pr., 1889? 207p. NUC OCLC
[Primarily religious poems.]

3913. MUNSTER, Mary C. F. (Monck), Mrs. Alfred M. Munster [Br. c1835-1892] ALT: MUENSTER, Mrs. Alfred M.
Waifs and strays. Verses. By Mrs. Alfred M. Munster.
L: M. Ward, 1879. 196p. NUC BL OCLC

3914. MUNRO, Emilia [Br. 19c]
Rossale: a tale. Ceilia and Nora; or, the warning; and other pieces in rhyme.
Aberdeen: G. & R. King, 1851. 338p. NUC BL

3915. MURDEN, Eliza (Crawley) [Am. 19c] ALT: Crawley, Eliza PSEUD: Charleston, S.C., A Lady of; Young Lady of Charleston, A
The little match girl: a poem by a lady of Charleston, S.C.
Charleston, SC: Fogartie's bk. depository; Philadelphia: J.B. Lippincott & co., c1870. 22p. NUC OCLC

3916. -----Miscellaneous poems, by a lady of Charleston, South Carolina.
Charleston, SC: Pr. & pub. for author by P. Hoff, 1826. 217p. NUC BL OCLC

3917. -----Poems, by a young lady of Charleston.
Charleston, SC: Pr. J. Hoff, 1808. 112p. NUC

3918. MURPHY, Anna [Br. 19c]
A short account of a few of the most remarkable trees and plants; to which are added, miscellaneous poems.
L: The author, 1808. 140p. NUC BL
[Binder's title: Farmer's boy.]

3919. MURPHY, Eveleen (Stanley), Mrs. H. Murphy [Am. 19c]
Since the war in the sunny South. Sketches and poems by Mrs. H. Murphy.
Norfolk, VA: Green, Burke & Gregory, pr., 1890. 128p. NUC OCLC

MURPHY, Mrs. H. <u>see</u> MURPHY, Eveleen (Stanley)

3920. MURRAY, Ann [Br. 18c]
Poems on various subjects.
L: Pr. for the author, 1779. 147p. NUC BL OCLC

MURRAY, Charlotte <u>see</u> HAVERGAL, Cecilia

3921. MURRAY, Charlotte [Br. 19/20c]
Cared for and kept (a birthday poem).
L: Castell bros., 1892. BL

3922. -----Earth's messages.
L: Tuck & sons, 1893. BL

3923. -----Eon the good, and other poems.
L: J. Nisbet & co., 1896. 125p. BL

3924. -----"Faith" from the Epistle to the Hebrews. Poems.
L: R. Tuck & sons, 1890. BL

3925. -----For the Master's sake; a text book for a month.
NY: E.P. Dutton; L: E. Nister, 189-. NUC
[Murphy ed. and wrote some of the poems]

3926. -----He careth.
L: R. Tuck & sons, 1891. BL

3927. -----His holy will.
L: Marshall bros., 1892. BL

3928. -----In the Father's hand.
L: 1891. BL
[Verses]

3929. -----Leaves a-glow. Verses.
NY & Munich: Art Lithographic pub. co., 188-. 24p. NUC

3930. -----The Lord reigneth. A poem.
L: Religious Tract Society, 1891. BL

3931. -----The Master Himself. A poem.
L: Religious Tract Society, 1891. BL

3932. -----Messages from the Master; and other poems.
L: S.W. Partridge & co., n.d. NUC

3933. -----More "messages."
Stirling: Drummonds Tract dept., 1886. BL

3934. -----On the heights or onward! upward! A poem.
L: Art Lithographic pub. co., n.d. NUC

3935. -----Safely home. A word to the bereaved.
NY & Chicago: F.H. Revell co., 1891. 12p. NUC

3936. -----Songs of trust and triumph, verses.
n.p.: n.p., 189-. NUC

3937. -----Sunny life, poems.
n.p.: n.p., n.d. NUC

3938. -----Wardlaugh: or, "Workers together."
L: S.W. Partridge, 1899. BL

3939. -----The wheel of life. A poem.
L: Religious Tract Society, 1890. BL

3940. -----When morning breaks. An Easter parable.
L: Ernest Nister, 1895. BL

3941. -----Won't you?
NY: Art Lithograph pub. co., n.d. 8p. NUC

3942. MURRAY, Joanna Gregory [Br. 19c]
Poems.
Edinburgh: Pr. for priv. circ., 1894. 225p. BL

3943. MURRAY, Judith (Sargent) [Am. 1751-1820] PSEUD: Constantia
The gleaner. A miscellaneous production. By Constantia.
Boston: Pr. I. Thomas & E.T. Andrews, 1798. 3v. NUC BL OCLC
[Collection, mostly original. Incl. 2 5-act plays & poems, but primarily prose letters to a periodical, The Gleaner.]

3944. MURRY, Ann [Br. 18c]
Poems on various subjects.

L: Pr. for the author, 1779. 147p.
NUC BL OCLC

MUSE OF CUMBERLAND, THE, pseud. see BLAMIRE, Susanna

MYRTLE, MAY, pseud. see DUGAN, Annie A. (Stevens)

MYRTLE, MINNIE, pseud. see JOHNSON, Anna Cummings

MYRTLE, MOLLY, pseud. see HILL, Agnes (Leonard) Scanland

N., H., pseud. see GRIGGS, Helen Augusta

N., H. see NOKES, Harriet

3945. NADEN, Constance Caroline Woodhill [Br. 1858-1889]
The complete poetical works of Constance Naden.
L: Bickers, 1894. 22p. NUC BL OCLC

3946. -----A modern apostle; The elixir of life; The story of Clarice; and other poems.
L: K. Paul, Trench, 1887. 177p. NUC BL OCLC

3947. -----Songs and sonnets of springtime.
L: Kegan Paul, Trench, 1881. 171p.
NUC BL OCLC

3948. NAIRNE, Carolina (Oliphant), Baroness [Br. 1766-1845] ALT: Oliphant, Carolina
The land o' the leal, and other songs.
L: W. Scott, n.d. 128p.

3949. -----Lays of Strathearn.
L: R. Addison & co., 1846. Edinburgh: Paterson & sons; L: Hutchings & sons, c1880. 1860 OCLC 104p. NUC OCLC
[Incl. music by Finlay Dun]

3950. -----Life and songs of the Baroness Nairne, with a memoir and poems of Caroline Oliphant the younger [1807-1831]. Ed. the Rev. Charles Rogers.
L: C. Griffin & co.; Edinburgh: J. Grant, 1896. 303p. NUC BL OCLC

3951. -----Life and songs with a memoir and poems of Caroline Oliphant. Ed. Rev. Charles Rogers.
2d ed. L: C. Griffith & co., 1869. 206p. NUC BL OCLC
[Enlarged ed.]

3952. NAPIER, Catherine, Mrs. [Br. 19c]
The city of the world.
L: Priv. pr., 1845. 53p. BL

3953. -----The lay of the palace.
L: J. Ollivier, 1852. 19p. NUC BL

3954. -----A month at Oostcamp.
L: Dolman; Bruges: The Albion Library, 1844. 98p. BL
[Misc. prose and verse. Poems, narrative & descriptive of Flanders, Elegy for Lord Byron, brief prose introductions.]

3955. NARAMORE, Gay (Humbolt) [Am. 19c] ALT: Humbolt, Gay PSEUD: Burr Lington, D.L.L.
Poems.
Cambridge, MA: Riverside press, 1865. 104p. BL NUC OCLC

3956. -----Poems and letters to Don Brown by Gay Humboldt, alias Burr Lington, D.L.L.
Albany, NY: E.H. Bender, 1857. 252p. BL NUC
[Pub. in 1865 as: Poems. 2d ed. enlarged, 1866. BL]

3957. -----Queen Loo, and other poems.
Philadelphia: J.B. Lippincott & co., 1873. 82p. NUC OCLC

3958. NASH, Caroline [Br. 19c]
Reflections on the value of the scriptures: and other poems.
L: F. Clemence, 1852. 100p. BL
[Religious verse]

3959. -----The sacred bee; and other poems. Ed. F. C[lemence].
L: F. Clemence, 1850. 96p. BL
[Title poem, pp. 1-49, description of books of the Bible. Misc. poems, pp. 53-96, also chiefly religious.]

3960. NASON, Emma Caroline (Huntington)
The tower, with legends and lyrics.
Boston & NY: Houghton, Mifflin & co., 1895. 141p. NUC BL
[Misc. poetry]

3961. -----White sails.
Boston: D. Lothrop co., 1888. 162p.
NUC OCLC

NATHAN, Isaac, comp. see LAMB, Lady Caroline (Ponsonby)

3962. NAYLOR, R. S., Mrs. [Am. 19c]
Affection's tribute. Original poems.
Oskaloosa, IA: Central book concern, 1874. 87p. NUC OCLC

NEAL, Alice (Bradley) see HAVEN, Alice (Bradley) Neal

3963. NEALDS, Adeline Martha, Mrs. Charles Nealds [Br. 19c]
Poems. By Mrs. Charles Nealds.
L: Rivington, 1829. 140p. BL OCLC

NEALDS, Mrs. Charles see NEALDS, Adeline Martha

3964. NEALE, Susanna [Br. 19c]
Temperance songs.
L: Bevington & co., 1886. 16p. NUC BL

3965. NEALY, Mary E. [Am. 19c]
The orphan's appeal. Written for the national fair for the soldiers' and sailors' orphans' home.
Washington, D.C.: n.p., 1866? 4p. NUC

3966. NEEDHAM, Elizabeth Annabel [Annable NUC & OCLC], Mrs. George C. Needham [Br. b. 1844]
Leisure moments; or, The breathings of a poetic spirit.
L: J. Blackwood & co., 1889. 172p. BL

3967. -----Poetic paraphrases.
L: J.E. Hawkins, 1890. 91p. NUC BL

NEEDHAM, Elizabeth Annable see NEEDHAM, Elizabeth Annabel

NEEDHAM, Mrs. George C. see NEEDHAM, Elizabeth Annabel

3968. NEGREPONTE, Mary P. [Br. 19c]
Io and other verse.
L: Kegan Paul, Trench, Trubner & co., 1891. 64p. NUC BL

NELSON, Elvira K., co-author see KING, Sarah Catharine

3969. NELSON, Esther [Br. 19c]
Island minstrelsy: comprising Old King Death, and other poems.
L: n.p., 1839. BL

3970. NELSON, Flora Birdsall [Am. 19c]
Songs of the reapers ... composed and edited by Flora B. Nelson [& others].
Lafayette, IN: n.p., c1896. 158p. NUC
[Hymns by Flora and Fannie Birdsall and other evangelists.]

NESBIT, Edith see BLAND, Edith (Nesbit)

NESBIT, Edith Bland, co-author see WOOD, Helen J.

3971. NETHERCOTT, Henrietta [Br. 19c]
ALT: Henrietta
Poetical pieces on religion and nature.
Dublin: n.p., 1856. BL

3972. -----The traveller's dream, and other poems.
Dublin: John Robertson; L: Simpkin, Marshall, & co., 1858. 192p. NUC BL

NETTIE see CLARK, Jeanette R.

3973. NEWALL, Mrs. [Br. 19c]
Poems.
Manchester: Priv. pr., 1885. 115p. BL

3974. NEWCASTLE, Margaret (Lucas) Cavendish, Duchess of [Br. 1623-1673]
ALT: Cavendish, Margaret (Lucas), Duchess of Newcastle
The cavalier and his lady: selections from the works of the first Duke and Duchess of Newcastle. Ed. Edward Jenkins.
L: Macmillan & co., 1872. 287p. NUC OCLC
[Incl. poetry]

3975. -----Letters and poems.
L: n.p., 1676. BL

3976. -----Nature's pictures drawn by Fancie's pencil ... being several feigned stories ... some in verse, some in prose, some mixt, and some by dialogues.
L: J. Martin & J. Allestrye, 1656. 404p. NUC BL

3977. -----Nature's pictures drawn by Fancie's pencil ... ----.
2d ed. L: Pr. A. Maxwell, 1671. 718p. NUC OCLC

3978. -----Philosophical letters. Contains one poem: "Eternal God, infinite deity."
L: n.p., 1664. 542p. NUC BL OCLC

3979. -----Philosophicall fancies. Prose and verse.
L: J. Martin & J. Allestrye, 1653. 94p. BL OCLC

3980. -----Poems and fancies.
L: J. Martin & J. Allestrye, 1653. 214p. NUC BL OCLC

[3d ed. Pub. as: Poems: or several fancies in verse.]

3981. -----The world's olio.
L: J. Martin & J. Allestrye, 1655. 216p. NUC BL OCLC
[Contains 2 poems: "But I would have this monarchy I make" and "Of all my works this work which I have writ."]

3982. NEWCOMB, Florence Ward (Danforth) [1845-1919]
The carnival of Venice and other poems.
L & NY: F.T. Neely, 1897. 172p. NUC OCLC

3983. NEWELL, Bernice E. [Am. 19/20c]
The mountain.
Tacoma, WA: W.D.C. Spike & co., 1890. 11 l. NUC

3984. NEWMAN, Sarah [Br. 19c]
Poems, on subjects connected with Scripture.
Alton: Pr. & sold by W. Pinnock, 1811. 60p. NUC BL

3985. NEWTON, Emily [Am. 19c]
Poems.
n.p.: Pr. for priv. circ., 1896. 66p. NUC OCLC
[Pub. as a memorial vol.]

3986. NICHOLAS, Ann Susannah [Br. 19c] ALT: Nichols, Anne Susanna
Journal of a very young lady's tour from Canonbury to Aldborough, through Chelmsford, Sudbury, and Ipswich; and back through Harwich, Colchester, etc. Sept. 13-21, 1804.
L: Nichols, 1804. 16p. BL OCLC

NICHOLL, M.A. see NICHOLL, Mary Anne

3987. NICHOLL, Mary Anne [19c] ALT: Nicholl, M. A. PSEUD: Stella
Lays from the west. By Stella.
Winnipeg, Manitoba: Free press print, 1884. 103p. NUC

3988. NICHOLLS, Louisa Hannah (Drake) [Am. d. 1852]
Poems.
NY: C.S. Francis & co., 1857. 110p. NUC OCLC

3989. NICHOLS, Alice S. [Am. 19c]
One night in a mountain camp. A sketch. With Charles W. Bacon.
Boston: S.E. Cassino, 1886. 22p. NUC OCLC
[Incl. poems]

NICHOLS, Anne Susanna see NICHOLAS, Ann Susannah

3990. NICHOLS, Catherine, Mrs. R.S. Nichols [Am. 19c] PSEUD: Old Prairie Hen, An
Wild flowers of the West; or, Gleanings from the stubble, by an old prairie hen.
Chicago: H.H. Frary, pr., 1874. 170p. NUC OCLC

3991. NICHOLS, Katherine S. [Am. 19c]
The bells, and other poems.
Haverhill, MA: E.H. Nichols, 1889. 175p. NUC OCLC

3992. -----In sunset land.
Haverhill, MA: E.H. Nichols, 1889. 203p. NUC OCLC

3993. NICHOLS, Lucy Adda [Am. 19/20c]
Eastward bound. A poem.
Nashville, MI: News print, n.d. 15p. NUC

3994. -----The traveler and poet, and other poems.
Charlotte, MI: Pr. J. Saunders & co., 1875. 130p. NUC

NICHOLS, Mrs. R.S. see NICHOLS, Catherine

3995. NICHOLS, Rebecca Shepard (Reed) [Am. 1819-1903]
Bernice: or, The curse of Minna, and other poems.
Cincinnati, OH: Shepard & co., 1844. 216p. NUC OCLC

3996. -----Sing to me softly, my sister. Words by Mrs. R.S. Nichols. Music by O.V. Waterman.
Boston: n.p., 1856? 5p. NUC

3997. -----Songs of the heart and the hearthstone.
Philadelphia: Thomas, Cowperthwait & co.; Cincinnati, OH: J.F. Desilver, 1851. 319p. NUC OCLC

3998. NICHOLSON, Eliza Jane (Poitevent) [Am. 1849-1896] PSEUD: Rivers, Pearl
Lyrics. By Pearl Rivers.
Philadelphia: J.B. Lippincott & co., 1873. 131p. NUC OCLC

3999. NICHOLSON, Ellen Corbett [Br. 19c]
Poems. By James and Ellen C. Nicholson.
L: Hamilton, Adams & co., 1880. 217p. BL

4001. -----Willie Waugh, and other poems. By James and Ellen C. Nicholson.
Edinburgh: J. Menzies, 1884. 250p. BL OCLC

4002. NICHOLSON, Isabella [Br. 19c]
Songs of the soul.
L: J. Nisbet & co., 1885. 100p. BL

NICHOLSON, James, co-author see NICHOLSON, Ellen Corbett

4003. NICHOLSON, Kathleen Monica [Am. 19c]
Whispers of the pines.
Chicago: J.S. Hyland, 1898. 131p. NUC OCLC

4004. NICOLAS, Sarah (Davison), Lady [Br. 19c] PSEUD: Soldier's Daughter, A
The cairn; a gathering of precious stones from many hands.
L: G. Bell, 1846. 254p. NUC BL OCLC
[Poems, anecdotes, essays, etc. Preface signed "a soldier's daughter." Incl. some works by others, but predominately original.]

4005. NIVEN, Anna Jane (Vardill) [Br. 1781-1852 [1749-1811?] PSEUD: Lady, A
The pleasure of human, a poem.
L: Pr. for Longman, Hurst, Rees, Orme & Brown by James Ballantyne & co., 1812. 100p. NUC OCLC

4006. -----Poems and translation, from the minor Greek poets and others; written chiefly between the ages of ten and sixteen, by a lady.
2d ed. L: Longman, Hurst, Rees & Orme; sold by J. Asperne & T. Becket, 1809. 198p. NUC OCLC

4007. NOAKES, Mary Anne [Br. 19c]
Poems from scripture. Isaac and Ishmael, and Ahab, king of Israel.
L: n.p., 1840. BL

NOBODY, pseud. see GURNETT, Ann Eliza (Ballard)

4008. NOEL, Caroline Maria [Br. 1817-1877] ALT: Noel, Charlotte Margaret
The name of Jesus and other verses, for the sick and lonely.
2d ed. L: Wertheim, Macintosh & Hunt, 1861. 87p. NUC BL OCLC

NOEL, Charlotte Margaret see NOEL, Caroline Maria

4009. NOKES, Harriet [Br. 1830-1895] ALT: N., H.
The home wreath and other poems.
L: Longman, Brown, 1857. 131p. NUC BL

4010. NOOTH, Charlotte [Br. 19c]
Original poems, and a play.
L: Longman, Hurst, Rees, Orme, & Brown, 1815. 156p. NUC BL OCLC
["Clara; or, The nuns of charity"; 5 acts, verse]

NORMA, pseud. see BROOKS, Mary Elizabeth (Aiken)

NORMANBY, Marquess of, co-author see WHARTON, Lady Anne (Lee) [Mrs. BL]

4011. NORRIS, Frances B. [Am. 19c]
The drunkard's catechism and creed, and the rumseller's commandments. To which are added poetical selections from newspapers published 25 years ago, now out of print.
Hyannis, MA: Pr. E. Coombs, 1858. 24p. NUC

4012. -----Reasons for hating strong drink, and a plea for suffering humanity, that the plague may be stayed.
Boston: W. & E. Howe, pr., 1859. 18p. NUC OCLC

NORTH, THEOPHILA, pseud. see HOLLINS, Dorothea

4013. NORTHAMPTON, Margaret (Clephane) Compton, Marchioness of [Br. d. 1830] ALT: Compton, Margaret Clephane), Marchioness of Northampton
Irene, a poem in six cantos. Ed. Spencer Joshua Alwyne Compton, Marquis of Northampton.
L: Pr. Mills, Jowett & Mills, 1833. 206p. NUC BL OCLC
[Also incl. misc. poems]

NORTHAMPTON, Spencer Joshua Alwyne Compton, Marquis of, ed. see NORTHAMPTON, Margaret (Clephane) Compton, Marchioness of

4014. NORTON, Caroline Elizabeth Sarah (Sheridan), Hon. Mrs. George Chappel Norton [Br. 1808-1877] ALT: Stirling-Maxwell, Caroline Elizabeth Sarah (Sheridan) Norton, Lady
The centenary festival.
L: C.W. Reynell, 1859. 8p. NUC BL
[Verses on Robert Burns. Repr. from The Daily Scotsman.]

4015. -----The child of the islands. A poem.
L: Chapman & Hall, 1845. 239p. NUC BL OCLC

[Plea for the poor, addressed to the Prince of Wales]

4016. -----The coquette, and other tales and sketches, in prose and verse.
L: E. Churton, 1835. 2v. NUC OCLC

4017. -----The dream and other poems.
L: Henry Colburn, 1840. 301p. NUC BL OCLC

4018. -----Kate Bouverie, and other tales and sketches, in prose and verse.
Philadelphia: E.L. Carey & A. Hart; Boston: W.D. Ticknor, 1835. 2v. NUC BL OCLC

4019. -----The lady of La Garaye.
NY: A.D.F. Randolph, 1861. 115p.
Cambridge: n.p., 1861. 153p. NUC BL OCLC

4020. -----Lines.
L: Saunders & Otley, 1840. 4p. BL
[On Queen Victoria]

4021. -----Poems.
Boston: Allen & Ticknor, 1833. 148p. NUC BL OCLC

4022. -----The sorrows of Rosalie. A tale. With other poems.
L: John Ebers & co., 1829. 136p. NUC BL OCLC

4023. -----Tales and sketches, in prose and verse.
L: E. Churton, 1850. 188p. NUC

4024. -----The undying one and other poems.
L: H. Colburn & R. Bentley, 1830. 272p. NUC BL OCLC

4025. -----A voice from the factories. In serious verse.
L: J. Murray, 1836. 40p. NUC

4026. NORTON, Eliza Bland (Smith) Erskine, Hon. Mrs. [Br. 19c] ALT: Erskine, Esme Steuart, Hon. Mrs.
Alcon Malanzore; a Moorish tale. By Mrs. Esme Steuart Erskine.
Brussels: Pr. Auguste Wahlen, 1815. 193p. NUC BL OCLC
[Rhymed, in 5 cantos]

4027. -----Isabel, a tale, in two cantos; and other poems. By the Hon. Mrs. Esme Steuart Erskine.
L: Pr. for James Ridgway, by T. Robinson, 1814. 148p. NUC BL OCLC

NORTON, Hon. Mrs. George Chapple see NORTON, Caroline Elizabeth Sarah (Sheridan)

4028. NORTON, Mary [19c]
The ministry of flowers, and other poems.
Toronto: W. Briggs, 1890. 110p. NUC

4029. NORTON, Sarah Goodsell (Wolcott) [Am. 1790-1822?]
The two sisters' poems and memoirs. With Eliza Wolcott [1795-1832].
New Haven, CT: Baldwin & Treadway, pr., 1830. NUC

NOVA SCOTIAN, A, pseud. see FRAME, Elizabeth

4030. NOWELL, Sarah Allen [Am. 19c]
Poems.
Boston: A. Tompkins, 1850. 208p. NUC

4031. NUGENT, Hon. Ermengarda Greville- [Br. 19c] ALT: Greville-Nugent, Hon. Mrs.
The rueing of Gudrun and other poems.
L: D. Bogue, 1884. 109p. NUC BL

O., S. see MORGAN, Sydney (Owenson), Lady

4032. OAKEY, Emily Sullivan [Am. 1829-1883]
At the foot of Parnassus.
Albany, NY: D.R. Niver, 1883. 216p. NUC OCLC

OAKLEY, Lily, co-author see HAVERGAL, Cecilia

4033. OATES, Charlotte Mann Beaumont [Br. 19c]
Miscellaneous poems, songs and rhymes.
Bradford: J.S. Toothill, 1898. 400p. NUC BL OCLC

4034. OBERHOLTZER, Sara Louisa (Vickers) [Am. 1841-1930]
Come for arbutus, and other wild bloom.
Philadelphia: J.B. Lippincott & co., 1882. 147p. NUC OCLC

4035. -----Daisies of verse.
Philadelphia: J.B. Lippincott & co., 1886. 152p. NUC OCLC

4036. -----Souvenirs of occasions.
Philadelphia: J.B. Lippincott & co., 1892. 152p. NUC OCLC

4037. -----Violet Lee, and other poems.
Philadelphia: J.B. Lippincott & co., 1873. 143p. NUC OCLC

4038. O'BRIEN, Charlotte Grace [Br. 1845-1909]
Lyrics.
L: Kegan Paul & co., 1886. 115p. BL

4039. -----A tale of Venice: a drama. And lyrics.
Dublin: M.H. Gill & sons, 1880. 138p. BL
[4 acts, verse. Misc. poems, pp. 93-138, incl. songs, poems on nature & on Ireland]

4040. O'BRIEN, Mary, Mrs. [Br. 18c] PSEUD: Lady, A
The pious incendiaries; or, Fanaticism display'd; a poem, by a lady.
L: Pr. for author & sold by S. Hooper, 1785. 100p. NUC BL

4041. -----The political monitor; or, Regent's friend. Being a collection of poems, published in England during the agitation of the Regency.
Dublin: Pr. for author by W. Gilbert, 1790. 10, 51p. NUC BL

4042. O'CONNOR, Ruth A. [19c]
Wild flowers.
NY: Catholic pub. soc.; L: Burns & Oates, 1885. 100p. NUC OCLC
[Misc. poetry & prose: 3 short stories, brief essays]

4043. ODELL, Minnie [Am. 19c] PSEUD: Irving, Minna
Songs of a haunted heart, by Minna Irving.
NY, Chicago, San Francisco: Belford, Clarke & co., 1888. 221p. NUC OCLC

4044. O'DOHERTY, Mary Anne (Kelly) [Br. 1826-1910] PSEUD: Eva
Poems by "Eva" of "The Nation".
San Francisco: P.J. Thomas, 1877. 275p. NUC OCLC
[Originally pub. in The Dublin Nation & other journals, 1846-48.]

4045. ODOM, Mary (Hunt) McCaleb [Am. 19c] PSEUD: L'Eclair
Lenare, a story of the Southern Revolution, and other poems. By L'Eclair.
New Orleans, LA: Bouvain & Lewis, book & job prs., 1866. 107p. NUC OCLC

4046. -----Poems.
NY: G.P. Putnam's sons, 1884. 300p. NUC

4047. O'DONNELL, Jessie Fremont [Am. 1860-1897]
Heart lyrics.
NY & L: G.P. Putnam's sons, 1887. 111p. NUC BL OCLC

4048. O'DONOGHUE, Marian Adele (Longfellow) [Am. 1849-1924]
The lily of the resurrection.
Boston: H.H. Carter, 1885. 17p. NUC OCLC

4049. -----Snow crystals.
Boston: H.H. Carter & Karrick, 1885. 15p. NUC OCLC

4050. O'DONOGHUE, Nannie Power (Lambert) [Br. b. 1858] ALT: O'Donoghue, Mrs. Power
Spring leaves; poems.
3d ed. L: Charles J. Skeet, 1877. 287p. NUC

O'DONOGHUE, Mrs. Power <u>see</u> O'DONOGHUE, Nannie Power (Lambert)

O'DONOVAN, Mary Jane (Irwin) <u>see</u> ROSSA, Mary Jane (Irwin) O'Donovan

4051. OESTERREICHER, Jane, Baroness [Br. 19/20c]
Light and darkness, and other poems.
L: Bickers & son, 1899. 60p. BL

OFFICER'S WIFE, AN, pseud. <u>see</u> FRASER, Susan

OFFLEY, Mrs. <u>see</u> TRENCH, Melesina (Chenevix) St. George

4052. OGDEN, Eva L. [Br. 19c]
The maid of honour.
The Queen's gift series. L: n.p., 1883. 16p. BL

OGILVY, Mrs. David <u>see</u> OGILVY, Eliza Ann Harris (Dick)

OGILVY, Donald, co-author <u>see</u> OGILVY, Dorothea Maria

4053. OGILVY, Dorothea Maria [Br. 19c]
My thoughts. Poems.
Aberdeen: D. Wyllie & son; Edinburgh & L: W. Blackwood & sons, 1870. 316p. BL

4054. -----Poems. With Donald Ogilvy.
Aberdeen: n.p., 1865. BL

4055. -----Poems.
2d ed. Edinburgh: n.p., 1873. BL

4056. OGILVY, Eliza Ann Harris (Dick), Mrs. David Ogilvy [Br. 19c]
A book of Highland minstrelsy. By Mrs. D. Ogilvy.
L: G.W. Nickisson, 1846. 272p. NUC BL OCLC
[Ballads]

4057. -----Poems of ten years (1846-1855).
L: Bosworth, 1856. 341p. BL OCLC

4058. -----Traditions of Tuscany, in verse.
L: n.p., 1851. BL

4059. OGILVY, Georgiana (Bosonquet), Mrs. L. Ogilvy [Br. 19c]
The nun of Enzklosterle. A legend of the Black Forest, in six songs.
L: n.p., 1864. 77p. NUC BL

OGILVY, Mrs. L. see OGILVY, Georgiana (Bosonquet)

4060. OGLE, Margaret [Br. 18c]
Mordecai triumphant: or, The fall of Haman, prime minister of state to King Ahasuerus. An heroic poem.
L: n.p., 1742. BL
[Satire on Sir Robert Walpole]

4061. O'HARE, Teresa Beatrice [Am. 19c]
Songs at twilight.
Columbus, OH: Columbus pr. co., 1897. 80 l. NUC OCLC

4062. OKE, Eliza, Mrs. [Br. 19c]
Sacred poems on various subjects.
L: n.p., 1834. BL

4063. O'KEEFFE, Adelaide D. [Br. 1776-1855]
National characters exhibited in forty geographical poems.
Lymington & L: Darton & Harvey, 1818. 139p. NUC BL

4064. -----A trip to the coast; or, Poems descriptive of various interesting objects on the sea-shore.
L: Darton, Harvey & Darton, 1819. 157p. NUC BL OCLC

OLD PRAIRIE HEN, AN, pseud. see NICHOLS, Catherine, Mrs.

4065. O'LEARY, Ellen [Br. 1831-1889]
Lays of country, home, and friends.
Dublin: Sealy, Bryers & Walker, 1890. 155p. NUC BL OCLC

4066. -----Songs and ballads. Ed. William Butler Yeats.
n.p.: n.p., 1892. 6p. NUC BL

OLIPHANT, Carolina see NAIRNE, Carolina (Oliphant), Baroness

OLIPHANT, Caroline, the younger, co-author see NAIRNE, Carolina (Oliphant), Baroness

4067. OLIVER, Alicia B. [Br. 19c]
Sunbeams. By Alicia B. Oliver, Hackney.
L: Pr. for priv. circ., 1872. 57p. NUC BL

OLIVER, Martha Capps, co-author see MCKINNEY, Ida Scott (Taylor)

4068. OLSEN, Sophia B., Mrs. [Am. 19c] ALT: Sophia
The fall of Chicago.
NY: T.F. Leslie & co.'s typography, 1871. 8p. NUC OCLC
[On the Chicago fire]

4069. -----The whited sepulchre. By Sophia.
Nashua, NH: Moore & Langley, letter-press prs., 1869. 48p. NUC OCLC
[On an insane asylum.]

ONE OF THE SMALL FRY OF THE LAKES, pseud. see BARKER, Miss

4070. O'NEILL, Mrs. Francis [Br. 19c]
Poetical essays; being a collection of satirical poems, songs and acrostics.
L: n.p., 1802. BL

4071. O'NEILL, Henrietta Bruce [Br. 19c]
Nugae canorae: A collection of poems.
Dublin: J. McGlashan, 1847. 263p. NUC BL OCLC

4072. OPIE, Amelia (Alderson) [Br. 1769-1853]
The black man's lament; or, How to make sugar.
L: Harvey & Darton, 1826. 25 l. BL OCLC

4073. -----Elegy to the memory of the late Duke of Bedford; written on the evening of his interment.
L: T.N. Longman & O. Rees, 1802. 16p. NUC BL OCLC

4074. -----The father and daughter, a tale, in prose: with An epistle from the maid of Corinth to her lover, and other poetical pieces.

L: Pr. Davis, Wilks, & Taylor, sold by Longman & Rees, 1801. 244p. NUC BL OCLC

4075. -----Lays for the dead.
L: Longman, Rees, Orme, Brown, Green, & Longman, 1834. 144p. NUC BL OCLC

4076. -----Memorials of the life of Amelia Opie; selected and arranged from her letters, diaries and other manuscripts. Ed. Cecelia Lucy Brightwell.
Norwich: Fletcher & Alexander, 1854. 409p. NUC BL OCLC
[Incl. a dozen poems; biography incorporating many of her letters.]

4077. -----Poems.
L: Pr. for T.N. Longman & O. Rees by Taylor & Wilks, 1802. 192p. NUC BL OCLC

4078. -----The warrior's return, and other poems.
L: Longman, Hurst, Rees, and Orme, 1808. 185p. Philadelphia: Bradford & Inskeep, 1808. 191p. NUC BL OCLC

4079. ORDE, Isabella [Br. 19c] PSEUD: Lady, A
Poems. By a lady.
Portobello: n.p., 1839. BL

ORINDA, pseud. <u>see</u> PHILIPS, Katherine (Fowler)

ORINTHIA, pseud. <u>see</u> TEFT, Elizabeth

4080. ORME, Cornelia J. [Am. 19c] PSEUD: Rustic, Ruth
Forget-me-nots from dew drop dale. By Ruth Rustic.
Washington, D.C.: Taylor & Maury, 1855. 212p. NUC OCLC

4081. ORMOND, M. Georgia [Am. 19c]
Glimpses.
Toledo, OH: n.p., 1888. 68p. NUC OCLC

4082. ORNE, Caroline Frances [Am. 1818-1905]
In memoriam. E.H. Brabrook.
Cambridge, MA: n.p., 1880. 3p. NUC

4083. -----Morning songs of American freedom.
Boston: A. Williams and co., 1876. 89p. NUC OCLC

4084. -----Sweet auburn and Mount Auburn, with other poems.
Cambridge: J. Owen, 1844. 196p. NUC BL OCLC

4085. ORRED, Meta [Br. 19/20c]
Ave all' anima mia.
L: Smith, Elder & co., 1880. 57p. BL

4086. -----Berthold and other poems.
L: Smith, Elder & co., 1878. 257p. NUC BL

4087. -----A dream-alphabet and other poems.
L: Smith, Elder & co., 1888. 113p. NUC BL

4088. -----Poems.
L: Smith, Elder & co., 1874. 145p. BL OCLC

4089. ORTON, May, Mrs. [Am. 19c]
Custer's last battle, a poem.
Detroit, MI: Friesema bros. pr. co., 1891. 8p. NUC

OSCAR, pseud. <u>see</u> GRIMSTONE, Mary Lemon, Mrs.

4090. OSGOOD, Azalia Aldrich, Mrs. [Am. 19c]
Campaign poem, Requital. For 1888.
n.p.: n.p., 1888. 17p. NUC

4091. -----In memoriam--Gen. U.S. Grant.
Portland, OR: G.H. Himes, 1886. 54p. NUC

4092. OSGOOD, Frances Sargent (Locke) [Am. 1811-1850] PSEUD: Florence
The casket of fate.
L: C. Whittingham, 1839. 79p. NUC BL

4093. -----The cries of New York with 15 illustrations drawn from life by distinguished artist.
NY: n.p., 1846. NUC

4094. -----Driving home the cows. With Kate Putnam Osgood.
Boston: D. Lothrop, 1871? 7 l. NUC OCLC
[Civil War poem]

4095. -----A letter about the lions.
NY: Putnam, 1849. 24p. NUC

4096. -----Lines to Mr. Dodson, engraver of the plate of female contributors to Graham's Magazine.
Boston & Brooklyn, NY: Elzevir Press, 1885. NUC

4097. -----Osgood's poetical works, containing a choice collection of sacred and miscellaneous poems, and songs, ballads and floral fancies.

NY: Benjamin & Young, 1840. 43p. NUC OCLC

4098. -----Philosophical enigmas; a series of poetical enigmas.
L: Rock, 183-? NUC

4099. -----Poems.
NY: Clark & Austin, 1846. 252p. NUC OCLC

4100. -----Poems.
Philadelphia: n.p., 1850. BL
[A different collection]

4101. -----A wreath of wild flowers from New England.
L: E. Churton, 1838. 364p. NUC BL OCLC
[Verse; includes "Elfrida, a dramatic poem in 5 acts]

OSGOOD, Frances Sargent (Locke), co-author see OSGOOD, Kate Putnam

4102. OSGOOD, Kate Putnam [Am. 1842-1912]
Driving home the cows. With Frances Sargent (Locke) Osgood.
Boston: D. Lothrop, 1871? 7 l. NUC OCLC
[Civil War poem]

4103. O'SHERIDAN, Mary Grant [Am. 19/20c]
Conata. A collection of poems.
Madison, WI: D. Atwood, pr., 1881. 103p. NUC OCLC
[Misc. poetry, incl. several trans. from German.]

4104. OSSOLI, Sarah Margaret (Fuller), Marchesa d' [Am. 1810-1850]
ALT: Fuller, Margaret
Life without and life within; or, Reviews, narratives, essays and poems. Ed. her brother, Arthur B. Fuller.
Boston: Brown, Taggard & Chase, 1859. 424p. NUC BL OCLC

OTHEMAN, Edward, comp. see PICKARD, Hannah Maynard (Thompson)

4105. OVERINGTON, Lily [Br. 19c]
Random rhymes and Christmas chimes.
L: Digby, Long & co., 1895. 288p. BL

OWEN, Mrs. A.L. see OWEN, Nellie (Huggins)

4106. OWEN, Frances Browning [Am. 19c]
Columbian and other poems.
Ann Arbor, MI: 1893. 141p.

4107. OWEN, Frances Mary (Synge) [Br. 1842-1883] ALT: F.; Synge, Frances Mary
Essays and poems. By Frances Mary Owen.
L: J. Bumpus, 1887. 252p. NUC

4108. -----Trefoil. Verses by three, namely: * [Frances E. Steele-Graves, aft. Bowen-Graves], "E." [Miss E. Synge] and "F".
L: Longmans, Green, 1868. 112p. NUC BL

4109. OWEN, Gabrielle M. [Br. 19c]
Poems.
L: n.p., 1888. 39p. NUC

4110. OWEN, Isabel Burnard [Br. 19c]
Poems.
L: n.p., 1857. BL

OWEN, Mrs. James, co-author see BROWN, Annie Johnson-

4111. OWEN, Nellie (Huggins), Mrs. A.L. Owen [Am. 19c]
"Elmwood" ... During the war, and My old battered canteen. (Dedicated to the reunion of the United Confederate Veterans at Richmond, VA, June 30, July 1 & 2, 1896).
Richmond, VA: Southern Eng. co., 1896. 15p. NUC CCLC
["My battered canteen," poem, 3p., in pamphlet on Owen's family's experiences in Civil War]

OWENSON, Sydney see MORGAN, Sydney (Owenson), Lady

4112. OWER, Jane Frazer, Mrs. [Br. 19c]
Poems and songs.
L: n.p., 1862. BL

P., A. see PENNY, Anne (Christian)

P., A.E. see POLGLASE, Ann Eaton

P., A.M. see PORTER, Anna Maria

P., C.H. see PARISH, C.H., Miss

P., J.W. see PITCAIRN, Janet Wyld

P., K.L. see PARSONS, Katherine Loomis

P., L.J. see HALL, Louisa Jane (Park)

P., S.F., ed. see PECKHAM, Mary Chase (Peck)

P., S.S. see PUGH, Sarah S.

4113. PACKARD, Hannah James [Am. 1815-1831]
The choice: a tragedy; with miscellaneous poems.
Boston: L.C. Bowles, 1832. 22, 142p. NUC OCLC
[3-act play, misc. poems & 1 short story]

4114. PACKARD, Mary F., Mrs. [Am. 1804-1863]
Miscellaneous poems, with a biographical sketch of the author.
NY: Curtiss & Childs, 1867. 54p. NUC

4115. PACKMAN, Anne [Br. 19c]
Songs for all seasons.
L: L. Lloyd, 1899. 46p. BL

4116. PAGAN, Isabel [Br. 19c]
A collection of songs and poems on several occasions.
Glasgow: n.p., 1803. BL

PAGE, Amie S. see PAGE, E. Amie (Simonton)

PAGE, Ann see CHILD, Anne Page

4117. PAGE, Ann Maria, Mrs. [Br. 19c]
Poems.
L: n.p., 1864. BL

4118. PAGE, E. Amie (Simonton) [Am. 19c] ALT: Page, Amie S.
At the gates of light and other poems. By Amie S. Page.
San Francisco: William Doxey, 1893. 204p. NUC OCLC

4119. -----Christmas tide.
Boston: n.p., 1881. 8p. Boston: L. Prang & co., 1889. 12p. NUC OCLC

4120. PAGE, Jean Hooper [19c]
Through fields and fallow.
NY & L: F. Tennyson Neely, 1897. 155p. NUC OCLC

4121. PAINE, Louise Mason (Akerman) [Am. 19c]
Flower bells.
Providence, RI: Press of Kellogg pr. co., priv. pr., 1883. 34 l. NUC OCLC

4122. PAINTER, Lydia Ethel (Farmer) [Am. 1842-1909] PSEUD: X., G.E.
The chatelaine, by G.E.X.
Buffalo, NY: Peter Paul book co., 1897. 211p. NUC OCLC
[Prose allegory, epigrams, philosophical reflections; poems, original & selected]

4123. -----The rosary, by G.E.X.
Cleveland, OH: Pr. Fenton & Stair, 1899. NUC OCLC
[62p. poems, chiefly love poetry; Incl. allegorical play, "The rose tree," 29p.]

4124. PALFREY, Sara Hammond [Am. 1823-1914] PSEUD: Foxton, E.
The blossoming rod, and other poems.
Boston: Cupples, Upham & co., 1886. 174p. NUC
[3 parts: Poems of the War of the Rebellion; The churchyard; Misc. poems]

4125. -----The chapel and other poems, Christo et Ecclesiae by E. Foxton.
NY: G.P. Putnam's sons, 1880. 130p. NUC
[Misc. poetry]

4126. -----Old times and new.
Boston: W.B. Clarke co., 1899. 49p. NUC OCLC

4127. -----Pre'mices, by E. Foxton.
Boston: Ticknor & Fields, 1855. 196p. NUC BL OCLC
[2 narrative poems: Hilda: a love song and The Princess' bath; misc. poems]

4128. -----Sir Pavon and St. Pavon, by E. Foxton.
n.p.: n.p., 1867. 85p. NUC

4129. PALMER, Ann [Br. 1806-1834]
Extracts from the diary of Ann Palmer ... a Christian in humble life ... With G.P. Richards.
3d ed. Exeter: n.p., 1838. BL
[Incl. poems]

4130. PALMER, Ellen [Br. 19/20c]
The temptation of Job, and other poems.
L: G. Phillip & son, 1882. 124p. BL

4131. PALMER, Georgiana Maria [Br. 19c]
Miscellaneous poems.
Liverpool: n.p., 1844. BL

4132. PALMER, Mary [Am. 1775-1800]
Miscellaneous writings on religious subjects: together with some extracts

from a diary. The whole written during six years of lingering sickness.
Windsor, VT: Pr. A. Spooner, 1807. 119p. NUC
[Incl. poems]

PALMER, Phoebe, ed. see COX, Lydia Noyes

4133. PALMER, Phoebe (Warrell), Mrs. Walter Charles Palmer [Am. 1807-1874]
A mother's gift; or, A wreath for my darlings. Poems.
NY: W.C. Palmer, jr.; L: F.F. Longley, 1875. 241p. NUC OCLC

PALMER, Mrs. Walter Charles see PALMER, Phoebe (Warrell)

4134. PALMERTON, Ann [Am. b. 1800]
The alarming state of the world.
Rochester, NY: Pr. for the author, 1859. 302p. NUC OCLC
[Primarily religious; includes poems]

4135. PANTON, Jane Ellen (Frith) [Br. 1848-1923]
Country sketches in black and white.
L: David Bogue, 1882. 313p. BL
[Descriptions of nature in prose; sonnet for each month]

4136. PARDOE, Julia S. H. [Br. 1806-1862]
The nun, a poetical romance and two others.
L: Longman, Hurst, Rees, Orme, Browne & Green, 1823. 228p. NUC

4137. PARDON, Emma L. [Am. 19c]
The organist. A poem of the New Year.
n.p.: n.p., 1894. 18p. NUC

PARHAM, H.B. Richenda, Mrs. see PARHAM, Helena Beatrice Richenda, Mrs.

4138. PARHAM, Helena Beatrice Richenda, Mrs. [Br. 19c] ALT: Parham, H. B. Richenda, Mrs. PSEUD: Marine, Ultra
The contents of a Madeira mail-bag, or, island etchings. By Ultra Marine.
L: Moran & co., c1885. 129p. BL
[Incl. poetry]

4139. PARISH, C.H., Miss [Br. 19c] ALT: P., C.H.
Enoch Arden (continued), by C.H.P.
Teignmouth: n.p., 1866. 12p. NUC OCLC
[Continuation of Tennyson's poem]

PARISH, Julia R., comp. & ed. see LATHRAP, Mary (Torrans)

4140. PARK, Elisabeth [Am. 19c]
Miriam; a dramatic poem.
2d ed. Boston: H.P. Nichols & co., 1838. 122p. TXU
[1st ed. 1837. 2d ed. incl. corrections. 3 long scenes on early Christians in Rome.]

PARK, Louisa Jane see HALL, Louisa Jane (Park)

4141. PARKER, Caroline Eustis (Roberts) [Am. 19c]
The old kitchen fire, and other poems.
NY: American tract soc., 1869. 96p. NUC OCLC

4142. PARKER, Emma J. [Br. 19c]
Summer sonnets, and other verses.
L: Grant Richards, 1898. 57p. NUC BL OCLC

4143. PARKER, Frances (Talbot), Countess of Morley [Br. 1781-1857]
PSEUD: Spruggins, Richard Sucklethumkin
The flying burgomaster: a legend of the Black Forest.
L: F. Morley, 1832. 14p. NUC BL

4144. -----The nose, a poem in six stanzas ... dedicated to all unmarried ladies, who may profit by the example of Dorothy Spruggins.
L: n.p., 1831. 8p. BL

4145. -----Portraits of the Spruggins family, arranged by Richard Sucklethumkin Spruggins, esq.
L: n.p., 1829. 41 l. NUC OCLC

4146. PARKER, Harriet B. [Am. 19c]
Christmas chimes.
Newton, MA: n.p., 1885. 10p. NUC

4147. -----The creeds of the bells.
Newton, MA: n.p., 1885. 10p. NUC

4148. PARKER, Maria Hildreth [Am. 19c]
Poems and stories.
Lowell, MA: Stone, Huse & co., pr., 1876. 224p. NUC OCLC

4149. -----Stray thoughts, or poems.
Boston: Cupples, Upham & co., 1885. 196p. NUC OCLC

4150. PARKER, Mary (Saltonstall), Mrs. W.P. Parker [Am. 19/20c]

At the squire's in old Salem.
Salem, MA: I.K. Annable, 1897. 25p. NUC OCLC
[Verse description]

4151. -----A metrical medley for the months.
Salem, MA: I.K. Annable, 1897. 28p. NUC

4152. -----Salem scrap book.
Salem, MA: M.S. Parker & S.E.C. Oliver, press of A.N. Webb & co., 1896. 14 l. NUC OCLC
[Narrative and humorous poems on Salem's past]

4153. -----Tempt ye appetite with salads.
Salem, MA: Mrs. W.P. Parker, 1895. 15p. NUC

4154. PARKER, R., Miss [Am. 19c]
The harp of genius; sacred to the cause of truth and righteousness.
Lowell, MA: Pr. for the author, 1845. 12p. NUC
[Religious poetry and prose essays.]

4155. -----The tree of life, containing moral and religious subjects, calculated to benefit and interest.
Lowell, MA: n.p., 1844. 24p. NUC
[Poems & prose]

4156. PARKER, Sarah [Br. 19c]
Miscellaneous poems. Second edition ... with ... additions.
Glasgow: n.p., 1856. BL

4157. -----The opening of the sixth seal; and other poems.
Ayr: n.p., 1846. BL

PARKER, Mrs. W.P. <u>see</u> PARKER, Mary Saltonstall

PARKES, Bessie Rayner <u>see</u> BELLOC, Bessie Rayner (Parkes)

4158. PARKINSON, Amy [1859?-1938]
"In His keeping:" words of sustaining from the source of all strength; with kindred thoughts in verse.
Toronto: Upper Canada tract soc., 1897. 37p. NUC BL

4159. -----Love through all; a voice from a sick room. Thoughts for each day.
Toronto: Endeavor Herald pub. co., 1893. 38p. NUC

4160. PARKS, Martha A., Mrs. [Am. 19c]
Echoes.
Chicago: Church, Goodman, & Donnelley, 1865. 45p. NUC OCLC
[About Abraham Lincoln]

4161. PARMELEE, Helen Louisa (Beck) [Am. 1821-1863]
Hymns for the sick-room.
NY: A.D.F. Randolph, 1860. 130p. NUC OCLC

4162. -----Poems religious and miscellaneous. By the late Helen L. Parmelee.
NY: A.D.F. Randolph, 1865. 112p. NUC BL

4163. PARMINTER, Anne, Mrs. [Br. 19c]
The votive wreath, and other poems.
L: Pr. for the authoress & sold by J. Bulcock, 1826. 158p. NUC BL OCLC

4164. PARMINTER, Jane [Br. 19c]
Poems.
L: A.H. Bailey, 1872. 256p. NUC

4165. PARR, Catherine [Br. 18c] ALT: Kaye, Catherine (Parr)
The feast of Madain, and other poems.
Norwich: Goose & co., 1881. 184p. BL

4166. PARR, Harriet [Br. 1828-1900] PSEUD: Lee, Holme
Country stories, old and new. In prose and verse. By Holme Lee.
L: Smith, Elder & co., 1872. 2v. NUC BL
[Narrative & misc. poetry. Mostly short fiction]

4167. PARR, Olive Katherine [Br. b. 1874] PSEUD: Mary Aquinas
Poems. By Mary Aquinas.
L: R. & T. Washbourne; NY: Benziger, 1899. 61p. NUC BL OCLC

PARRIS, Miss, comp. <u>see</u> PARRIS, Hephzibah

4168. PARRIS, Hephzibah [Br. 1833-1850]
Memoirs of Mary and Hephzibah Parris, and a brief memoir of Miriam Parris. By their sister [Miss Parris].
L: n.p., 1858. BL
[Incl. letters & poems by Hephzibah]

4169. PARRY, Fannie [Am. 1840-1860]
Wayside gleanings. A collection of the miscellaneous writings of Fannie Parry.
Providence, RI: H.L. Hastings, 1861. 163p. NUC

[Incl. letters & poems]

4170. PARSONS, Eliza Dwight (Willard) [Am. 1790-1855]
Poems, on various subjects.
Troy, NY: Pr. F. Adancourt, 1826. 255p. NUC BL OCLC

4171. PARSONS, Elizabeth Mary (Rocker) [Br. 1812-1873]
The end of the pilgrimage and other poems.
L: n.p., 1859. BL

4172. -----Routine; or, A tale of the Goodwin Sands, etc., etc., poems.
L: Westerton, 1861. 134p. OCLC

4173. PARSONS, Gertrude (Huxt) [Br. 1812-1891]
Rhymes, grave and gay, chiefly by Mrs. Parsons.
L: n.p., 1864. BL

4174. PARSONS, Katherine Loomis [Am. d. 1930] ALT: P., K.L.
Poems, by K.L.P.
Richmond, VA: J.W. Randolph & English, 1889. 94p. NUC OCLC

4175. PARSONS, Letitia [Br. 19c]
Verses, hymns, and poems.
L & Cranbrook: n.p., 1806-08. 2 pt. BL

4176. -----Verses, hymns and poems, on various subjects; composed under a long series of affliction and deprivation of sight.
Kent: Sold by T. Coe, 1815. 88,42p. NUC

4177. PARSONS, Mary [Br. 19c]
Cries out of the depths. Poems on sacred subjects.
L: n.p., 1819. 310p. NUC BL

4178. PASMORE, Bertha [Br. 19c]
Grannie's posey.
Exeter: Flying Post, 1898. BL
[Incl. other poems]

4179. PATON, Ida [Br. 19c]
The forcing of the Khaibar Pass with other poems.
Greenock: Pr. for the author, 1897. 173p. BL

PATRICK, Wiley J., comp. <u>see</u> HARDIN, Mary Barr (Jenkins)

4180. PATRICKSON, Margaret [Br. 19c]
Miscellaneous poems.
L: Pr. R. Taylor & co., for R. Faulder, 1806. 2v. NUC BL

4181. PATTERSON, Jane (Lippitt) [Am. b. 1829]
Buena Vista windows.
Boston: James H. West co., 1899. 60p. NUC OCLC

PATTERSON, Lizzie <u>see</u> PATTERSON, Rachel Elizabeth

4182. PATTERSON, Minnie Ward [Am. 19c]
Pebbles from old pathways.
Chicago: C.J. Burroughs & co., 1875. 204p. NUC OCLC

4183. PATTERSON, Rachel Elizabeth [Am. b. 1820] ALT: Patterson, Lizzie
Songs in affliction: a collection of miscellaneous poems, written during seasons of protracted illness. By Lizzie Patterson.
Baltimore, MD: Pr. Sherwood & co., 1852. 55p. NUC

4184. PATTON, Abby Hutchinson, Mrs. [Am. 1829-1892]
A handful of pebbles.
Cambridge, MA: Riverside press, 1891. 57p. NUC OCLC
[Observations, aphorisms in prose, by a concert singer and abolitionist. 6 poems interspersed.]

4185. PATTON, Ellen (Young) [Am. 19c]
Mignonette.
Atchinson, KS: Press of Haskell & son, 1883. 200p. NUC OCLC
[3 parts: Songs of Hope, Miscellaneous, & Child's Department]

PAULL, Mrs. George A. <u>see</u> PAULL, Minnie E. (Kenney)

4186. PAULL, Minnie E. (Kenney), Mrs. George A. Paull [Am. 1859-1895] ALT: Kenney, Minnie E.
The chimes of Amsterdam and other poems.
NY: A.D.F. Randolph & co., 1890. 68p. NUC OCLC

4187. PAYNE, Clara [Br. 19c]
A loyal garland. From tributary thoughts.
L: n.p., 1874. BL

4188. PAYSON, Hannah W. [Am. 19c]
Poems.
Boston: H.R. Whateley, 1895. 91p. NUC OCLC

PEABEE, JAY, pseud. <u>see</u> BURGE, Julia P.

PEACE, Mrs. M.S. see PEARCE, Mrs. M.S.

4189. PEACOCK, Mabel Geraldine Woodruffe [Br. 1855?-1920]
North Lincolnshire dialect: tales and rhymes in the Lindsey folk-speech.
Brigg: George Jackson & son; L: George Bell & sons, 1886. 136p. NUC BL OCLC

4190. PEACOCK, Mary Woodruffe [Br. 19c]
Poems.
Hull: William Andrews; L: Simpkin, Marshall, Hamilton, Kent, 1893. 82p. NUC BL

4191. PEACOCKE, Georgiana [Br. 19c]
Rays from the Southern Cross.
L: H.S. King & co., 1876. NUC BL

4192. PEARCE, [Peace BL OCLC] Mrs. M.S. [19c]
The convict ship and other poems.
Greenock, Newfoundland: R.A. Baird, 1850. 264p. NUC BL OCLC

4193. PEARSON, Ann (Henderson), Mrs. William Fenwick Pearson [Br. 19c]
The grateful remembrance; in letters of advice to an absent niece.
Hexam: n.p., 1816. BL
[Letters of advice introduce poems describing the virtues of country people]

4194. -----Miscellaneous pieces.
Hexam: n.p., 1834. BL
[Chiefly lyric poems]

4195. PEARSON, Ellen Clare (Miller) [Br. 19c] ALT: Miller, Ellen Clare
A dream of a garden and other poems.
Manchester & L: John Heywood, 1894. 62p. NUC BL OCLC

4196. PEARSON, Susanna [Br. 18c]
Poems, dedicated, by permission, to the Right Honourable the Countess Fitz-William.
Sheffield: Pr. J. Gales, 1790. 68p. NUC BL OCLC

PEARSON, Mrs. William Fenwick see PEARSON, Ann (Henderson)

4197. PEAT, Anne, Miss [Br. 19c]
Lines ... on the birth of the young prince.
Edinburgh: n.p., 1856. BL
[On Prince Napoleon Eugene Louis John Joseph]

4198. -----New Year's Day, 1857 (-1859).
Edinburgh?: n.p., 1857-1859. BL

4199. -----Poems by Miss A. Peat.
Edinburgh: n.p., 1854. BL

4200. PECKHAM, Lucy (Gore) Creemer [Am. b. 1842]
Sea moss; poems by Dr. Lucy Creemer Peckham.
Buffalo, NY: C.W. Moulton, 1891. 89p. NUC

4201. PECKHAM, Mary Chase (Peck) [Am. 1839-1892]
Mrs. Mary Chace Peckham. Reprinted from the Unitarian, June, 1892.
NUC
[Printed as pamphlet. Incl. 10 of her poems.]

4202. -----"Windfalls gathered only for friends," and other poems.
Memorial edition. Ed. S.F.P. [Stephen F. Peckham].
Buffalo, NY: C.W. Moulton, 1894. 176p. NUC BL OCLC
[Cover title: Gathered Windfalls]

4203. PECKHAM, P. Annetta, Mrs. [Am. 19c]
Cuttings: selected from the writings of Mrs. P. Annetta Peckham.
San Francisco: Amanda M. Slocum, pr., 1877. 71p. NUC OCLC
[Incl. lyric poems and prose essays]

PECKHAM, Stephen F., ed. see PECKHAM, Mary Chase (Peck)

4204. -----Welded links.
Chicago: P. Annetta Peckham, 1875. 116p. NUC OCLC
[New, rev. & ext. ed. NY: Pub. by author, 1898. 297p. Misc. poetry on social, domestic & religious subjects by temperance lecturer.]

4205. PEILE, H., Mrs. [Br. 19c]
A tablet of juvenile memory.
L: n.p., 1836. 2 pt. BL
[Juvenile author]

4206. PEIRSON, Lydia Jane (Wheeler) [Am. 1802-1862]
Forest leaves, and other poems.
Philadelphia: Lindsay & Blakiston, 1845. 264p. NUC BL OCLC

4207. -----The forest minstrel. Ed. Rev. B.S. Schneck.
Philadelphia: J.W. Moore; Harrisburg, PA: W.O. Hickok, 1846. 264p. NUC BL OCLC

[Religious verse by a woman from the Alleghenies]

4208. PEMBERTHY, E., Mrs. [Am. 19c]
The history of Cornwall, the life of a hermit (known to the author), and other poems.
Galena, IL: H.H. Houghton & co., 1856. 17p. NUC

4209. PEMBERTON, Harriet Louisa Childe- [Br. 19/20c] ALT: Childe-Pemberton, Harriet Louisa
Dead letters, and other narrative and dramatic pieces.
L: Ward, Locke & co., 1896. 125p. BL OCLC

4210. -----In a Tuscan villa and other poems.
L: Griffith, Farran & co., 1890. 143p. BL

4211. -----Original readings and recitations. "Prince," a story of the American war, and other ... poems.
L: Ward & co., 1883. 79p. BL

4212. PEMBROKE, Mary (Sidney) Herbert, Countess of [Br. 1561-1621] ALT: Herbert, Mary (Sidney), Countess of Pembroke; Sidney, Mary
Astrophel. A pastoral elegy upon the death of ... Sir Philip Sidney ... By Edmund Spenser, the Countess of Pembroke, and others. In: Colin Clouts come home againe.
L: William Ponsonbie, 1595. 79p. NUC BL OCLC

4213. -----A dialogue between two shepherds, Thenot and Piers, in praise of Astrea. In: A poetical rhapsody. Ed. Francis Davison.
L: J. Nichols, 1823. 3v. OCLC

4214. -----A poem on our Savior's passion. From an unpublished manuscript in the British Museum.
L: J. Wilson, 1862. 32p. NUC BL

4215. -----The psalms of David translated into divers and sundry kindes of verse ... begun by ... Sir Philip Sidney, and finished by the ... Countess of Pembroke, his sister. Ed. S.W. Singer.
Chiswick: C. Whittingham for R. Triphook, 1823. NUC BL OCLC

4216. -----To the angell spirit of Sir P. Sidney. In Samuel Daniel: Whole works in poetrie, 1623.
L: Simon Waterson, 1623. OCLC

4217. PENDLETON, Charlotte [Am. 19c]
PSEUD: Charlton
Easter song.
NY: E.P. Dutton & co., 1892. 15p. NUC

4218. -----Songs of the year and other poems by "Charlton".
Cincinnati, OH: Robert Clarke, 1875. 178p. OCLC

4219. PENNEFATHER, Catherine King [Br. 1818-1893]
Homeward journey: a selection of poems by Mrs. P. and others.
L: J.E. Hawkins, 1887. 16 l. NUC BL

4220. PENNELL, Alice Isabel [Am. 19c]
Pearls.
Springfield, MA: Springfield print & binding co., 1890. 112p. NUC OCLC

4221. -----Silver cloud.
Springfield, MA: Springfield print co., 1887. 99p. NUC OCLC

4222. PENNINGTON, Marianne [Br. 19c]
Poems.
Hertford: n.p., 1847. BL

4223. PENNY, Anne (Hughes) Christian, Mrs. Peter Penny [Br. 1731-1784] ALT: P., A.; Christian, Mrs. Thomas
An elegy, on the death of the most Honourable Francis Russell, marquis of Tavistock. [Signed A.P.].
n.p.: n.p., 1767. 3p. NUC

4224. -----An invocation to the genius of Britain.
L: Pr. for the author & sold by J. Dodsley in Pall Mall, 1778. 15p. NUC OCLC
[Attrib. to Anne Penny]

4225. -----Poems, with a dramatic entertainment.
L: Pr. for the author, 1771. 220p. NUC BL OCLC

PENNY, Mrs. Peter see PENNY, Anne (Hughes) Christian

4226. PENNYMAN, Lady Margaret (Anger) [Br. 1688-1733]
Miscellanies in prose and verse, by ... Lady Margaret Pennyman, containing, i. Her late journey to Paris ... ii. Poems on several occasions, with familiar letters to a friend. Published from her original manuscripts. To which are annexed some other curious pieces.

4 pt. L: E. Curll, 1740. NUC BL OCLC

PERCY, FLORENCE, pseud. see ALLEN, Elizabeth Ann (Chase) Akers

PERDITA, pseud. see ROBINSON, Mary (Darby)

4227. PERKIN, Ana [Am. 19c]
Pen-leaves.
n.p.: C. Lezius, pr., 1892. 18p. NUC
[Poems & prose opinions]

4228. PERKINS, Annie Stevens [Am. 19c]
Thoughts of peace.
Boston: James H. Earle, 1892. 93p. NUC OCLC

4229. PERKINS, Elizabeth (Steele) [Br. 19c] ALT: Perkins, Miss Steele PSEUD: Lady, A
The botannical and horticultural meeting; or, Flora and Pomona's fete. A poem ... By a lady. From notes by John Quill.
Birmingham: Beilby, Knott, & Beilby, 1834. 27p. NUC BL OCLC
[BL: By Miss Steele Perkins, or rather, Mrs. E.S. Perkins]

4230. -----Flora's fancy fete or floral characteristics. A poem, illustrative of the language and sentiment of flowers.
Brighton: n.p., 1839. BL
[Sequel to Flora and Pomona's Fete]

4231. PERKINS, Elmira (Johnson) [Am. 1814-1896] PSEUD: Elvira
Harp of the willows; by Elvira.
Boston: Pr. for the author by G.C. Rand & Avery, 1858. 144p. NUC OCLC
[Also attr. to Judith Grant Perkins]

PERKINS, Judith Grant see PERKINS, Elmira (Johnson)

PERKINS, Miss Steele see PERKINS, Elizabeth (Steele)

4232. PERRING, E., Mrs. [Br. 19c]
Domestic hours; poems.
L: n.p., 1841. BL

4233. PERROTT, Frances, Mrs. [Br. 19c]
A collection of poems and songs. By the late Mrs. F. Perrott.
Newcastle-upon-Tyne: n.p., 1800? BL

PERRY, Alice see PERRY, Mary Alice

4234. PERRY, Anna M. [Am. 19/20c]
"In the presence," and other verses.
NY: Thomas Whittaker, 1889. 72p. NUC OCLC

4235. PERRY, Charlotte Augusta [Am. b. 1848] ALT: Perry, Carlotta
Carlotta Perry's poems.
Chicago, NY & San Francisco: Belford, Clarke & co., 1888. 240p. NUC OCLC

PERRY, Ella Cabot see PERRY, Lilla (Cabot)

4236. PERRY, Emeline [Am. 19c]
Poems. With a memorial.
Indianapolis, IN: Press of Levey bros. & co., 1893. 58p. NUC OCLC

4237. PERRY, Emily Ross [Am. 19c]
"Minnehaha, laughing water."
Minneapolis, MN: n.p., 1889. 16p. NUC OCLC

4238. PERRY, Lilla (Cabot) [Am. 19/20c] ALT: Perry, Ella Cabot
The heart of the weed.
NY & Boston: Houghton, Mifflin & co., 1886. 105p. NUC OCLC
[Sonnets & other lyrics]

4239. -----Impressions; a book of verse.
Boston: Copeland & Day, 1898. 81p. NUC OCLC

4240. PERRY, Mary Alice [Am. 1854-1883] ALT: Perry, Alice
A teacher's poems ... published as a tribute of love ... by her brothers, H.K. and C.W. Perry. By Alice Perry.
Manistee, MI: H.K. & C.W. Perry, 1898. 163p. NUC OCLC

4241. PERRY, Nora [Am. 1831-1896]
After the ball, and other poems.
Boston: J.R. Osgood, 1875. 192p. NUC BL OCLC

4242. -----Her lover's friend and other poems.
Boston: Houghton, Osgood, 1880. 183p. NUC BL OCLC

4243. -----Lyrics and legends.
Boston: Little, Brown, 1891. 142p. OCLC

4244. -----New songs and ballads.
Boston: Ticknor, 1887. 196p. NUC BL OCLC

4245. PERRY, Susan Teall, Mrs. [Am. 19c]
Little poems in a mother's life.

Chicago: M. Warren, 1877. 125p. NUC OCLC

PERSONNE, pseud. see LYNCH, Theodora Elizabeth (Foulks)

4246. PETER, Mary L., Mrs. [Am. 19c]
A century of presidents of the United States from George Washington, 1789, to Benjamin Harrison, 1889, with important events that occurred during each administration. In verse.
Buffalo, NY: Mary L. Peter, 1892. 39p. NUC OCLC

4247. -----Names of the presidents of the United States, from 1789 to 1889, in rhyme.
n.p.: n.p., 1891. 3 l. NUC

PETERS, PETRESIA, pseud. see ALDRICH, Julia Carter

PETERS, Phillis (Wheatley) see WHEATLEY, Phillis

4248. PETERSON, Mattie J. [Am. 1866-1947]
Little Pansy, a novel, and miscellaneous poetry. Introduction by Richard Walser.
Wilmington, NC: Messenger steam job print, 1890. 54p. Charlotte, NC: McNally & Loftin, NUC OCLC

4249. PETRE, Lady Catherine (Howard) [Br. 1832-1882]
Hymns and verses.
L: Burns & Oates, 1884. 181p. NUC BL

4250. -----Sacred verses.
L: n.p., 1864. 80p. BL

4251. PETRIE, Essie [Am. 19c]
Gennesaret.
Montgomery, AL: Barrett & Brown, 1881. 1v. NUC OCLC

PETRIE, Mary Louisa Georgina see WILSON, Mary Louisa Georgina (Petrie) Carus

4252. PFEIFFER, Emily Jane (Davis) [Br. 1827-1890]
Flowers of the night.
L: Trubner, 1889. NUC BL
[Poems. Incl. translations from Heine p. 117-138]

4253. -----Gerard's monument; and other poems.
L: Trubner, 1873. 186p. NUC BL OCLC

4254. -----Glan-Alarch, his silence and song.
L: King, 1877. 256p. NUC BL

4255. -----Margaret; or, The motherless.
L: Hurst & Blackett, 1861. 159p. NUC BL

4256. -----Poems.
L: Strahan & co., 1876. 150p. NUC BL

4257. -----Quarterman's grace and other poems.
L: C.K. Paul, 1879. 144p. NUC BL

4258. -----The rhyme of the lady of the rock, and how it grew.
L: K. Paul, Trench, & co., 1884. 184p. NUC BL
[Travel in Scottish highlands; narrative poem based on true event written as entertainment while waiting out the rain.]

4259. -----Sonnets & songs.
New ed. L: C. Kegan Paul, 1880. 103p. NUC OCLC

4260. -----Sonnets revised and enlarged.
L: Field & Tues.; NY: Scribner & Walford, 1886. 115p. NUC BL OCLC

4261. -----Under the aspens: lyrical and dramatic.
2d ed. L: K. Paul, Trench & co., 1881. 1882. 311p. NUC BL OCLC
[Incl.: "The Wynnes of Wynhavod, a drama of modern life, in 5 acts;" 4 narrative poems; sonnets & songs.]

PHELAN, Charlotte Elizabeth (Browne) see TONNA, Charlotte Elizabeth (Browne) Phelan

4262. PHELPS, Mrs. [Br. 19c]
The Suttee, and other poems.
Thame: Bradford, 1831. 76p. BL OCLC

4263. PHELPS, Adaliza (Cutter) [Am. 1823-1852]
The life of Christ, and other poems.
Boston: J.P. Jewett & co.; Cleveland OH: Jewett, Proctor, & Worthington, 1852. 286p. NUC OCLC

PHELPS, Elizabeth Stuart see WARD, Elizabeth Stuart (Phelps)

4264. PHELPS, Jessie Adeline (Cole) [Am. b. 1864]
Poems.
Denver, CO: F.W. Wood & co., pr., 1885. 291p. NUC OCLC
[Colorado poetry]

PHELPS, Samuel Merrick, co-author see GILBERT, Harriette Eliza (Phelps)

PHILANTHEA, pseud. see DEVERELL, Mary, Mrs.

PHILANTHROPOS, pseud. see CLARKE, Anne, Miss

PHILENIA, pseud. see MORTON, Sarah Wentworth (Apthorp)

4265. PHILIPPART, C., Mrs., Mrs. John Philippart [Br. 19c]
Muscovy: a poem in four cantos: with notes, historical and military: also several detached pieces.
L: P. Martin, etc., 1813. 159p. NUC BL OCLC
[Napoleonic wars]

4266. -----La Puebla's tree.
L: n.p., 1813. BL

4267. -----Victoria.
L: n.p., 1813. BL

PHILIPPART, Mrs. John see PHILIPPART, C., Mrs.

4268. PHILIPPS, Janetta [Br. 19c]
Poems.
Oxford: Priv. pr. by Collingwood & co., 1811. 67p. NUC BL OCLC

4269. PHILIPS, Joan [Br. 17c] PSEUD: Ephelia
Female poems on several occasions. By Ephelia.
L: Pr. William Downing for James Courtney, 1679. 112p. NUC BL OCLC
[2d ed. with extra leaves containing poems by Rochester & others. L: For James Courtenay, 1682. 169p. BL]

4270. PHILIPS, Katherine (Fowler) [Br. 1631-1664] PSEUD: Orinda
The crooked six-pence. With a learned preface.
L: R. Dodsley, 1743. 24p. NUC BL

4271. -----Poems by the most deservedly admired Mrs. Katherine Philips, the matchless Orinda. To which is added M. Corneille's Pompey and house tragedies. With several other translations out of French.
L: Pr. J.M. for H. Herringman, 1667. 112p. NUC BL OCLC

4272. -----Poems. By the incomparable, Mrs. K.P.
L: Pr. J.G. for Rich, Marriott, 1664. 242p. NUC BL
[Pirated ed., suppressed]

4273. PHILLIPS, Catherine (Payton) [Br. 1727-1794]
The happy king: a sacred poem. With occasional remarks ... address to George the Third.
6 pt. L: n.p., 1794. BL

4274. PHILLIPS, Charlotte [Br. 19c]
Echoes of life. Poems.
Manchester: Priv. pr., 1871. 175p. BL

4275. -----The shower of pearls. A collection of poetry, original and selected.
L & Peterborough: n.p., 1855. BL

4276. PHILLIPS, Clarinda (Hardman) [Am. 1835-1866]
Poetry and prose.
Newcastle, PA: Pr. E.S. Durham, 1867. 140p. NUC
[Misc. poetry; prose recollections and thoughts.]

4277. PHILLIPS, Elizabeth (Springer) [Am. b. 1840]
Mother's poems.
Maquoketa, IA: E.G. Chown, 1897. 118p. NUC

4278. PHILLIPS, Sarah A. [Br. 19c]
Pen and ink sketches.
Shrewsbury: Watson & son, pr., 1898. 50p. BL
[Songs & poems]

4279. PHILLIPS, Susan K. [Br. 19c]
The last poems of Susan K. Phillips.
L: Grant Richards, 1898. 133p. NUC BL OCLC

4280. -----On the seaboard, and other poems.
L: Macmillan & co., 1878. 296p. NUC BL OCLC

4281. -----Told in a coble and other poems.
Leeds: J.S. Fletcher & co., 1884. 147p. NUC OCLC

4282. -----Verses and ballads.
L: Pr. J.E. Taylor, 1865. 267p. NUC OCLC

4283. PHILLIPSON, Caroline Giffard (Lethbridge) [Br. 19c] ALT: Lethbridge, Caroline Gifford
Eva, a romance in rhyme; and other poems.
L: n.p., 1857. BL

4284. -----Lonely hours, poems, new edition, enlarged.
L: J. Moxon, 1856. 393p. NUC BL

4285. -----Mental flights. A volume of verse political and sentimental.
L: n.p., 1871. BL

4286. -----Poems.
L: n.p., 1849. BL

4287. -----A song in prose to the Westminster owl, on the criticism of the "Westminster review," of July 1856, on "lonely hours," poems.
L: J. Moxon, 1856. 15p. NUC

4288. -----Songs on Italy: and other poems.
L: n.p., 1862. BL

PHILOMATH, pseud. see DOUGLAS, Sarah

PHILOMELA, pseud. see ROWE, Elizabeth (Singer)

PHILPOT, L.C., Miss, ed. see W., E.A., Miss

4289. PHIPPS, Elvira Anna [Br. 19c]
Memorials of Clutha; or, Pencilings on the Clyde.
L: C. Armand for the author, 1841. 107p. NUC BL
[Travel narrative; includes poems]

PIATT, John James, co-author see PIATT, Sarah Morgan (Bryan)

4290. PIATT, Sarah Morgan (Bryan) [Am. 1836-1919]
Child's world ballads. Three little emigrants. A romance of Cork Harbour, 1884, &c.
Cincinnati, OH: Robert Clarke & co.; L: Elliot Stock, 1887. 55p. NUC BL OCLC
[Poems on children]

4291. -----Child's world ballads. (Second series) and other poems.
Westminster: A. Constable & co., 1895. 120p. BL

4292. -----The children out-of-doors, a book of verse, by two in one house. With John James Piatt.
Cincinnati, OH: R. Clarke & co., 1885. 88p. NUC BL OCLC
[Poems on children]

4293. -----Dramatic persons and moods, with other new poems.
Boston: Houghton, Osgood & co., 1880. 96p. NUC BL OCLC

4294. -----An enchanted castle, and other poems: pictures, portraits and people in Ireland.
L & NY: Longmans, Green & co., 1893. 98p. NUC BL OCLC

4295. -----In primrose time, a new Irish garland.
NY & Boston: Houghton Mifflin & co.; L: Kegan Paul, Trench, 1886. 70p. NUC BL OCLC

4296. -----An Irish garland.
Edinburgh: D. Douglas, 1884. 62p. NUC BL OCLC

4297. -----An Irish wild-flower, etc.
NY: F.A. Stokes co.; L: T. Fisher Unwin, 1891. 38p. NUC BL OCLC

4298. -----The nests at Washington, and other poems. With John James Piatt.
NY: W. Low; L: S. Low, son & co., 1864. 150p. NUC OCLC

4299. -----Poems.
L & NY: Longmans, Green & co., 1894. 2v. NUC BL OCLC

4300. -----Poems in company with children.
Boston: D. Lothrop & co., 1877. NUC BL OCLC
[Pub. in 1882 as: A book about baby. Poems on children.]

4301. -----_____. (Second series) and other poems.
Westminster: A. Constable & co., 1895. 120p. BL

4302. -----That new-world, and other poems.
Boston: J.R. Osgood & co., 1877. 130p. NUC OCLC

4303. -----A voyage to the Fortunate Isles and other poems.
Boston: J.R. Osgood & co., 1874. 180p. NUC BL OCLC

4304. -----The witch in the glass, etc.
L: Elliot Stock, 1888. 101p. NUC BL OCLC

4305. -----A woman's poems.
Boston: J.R. Osgood & co., 1871. 127p. NUC OCLC

4306. PICKARD, Hannah Maynard (Thompson), Mrs. Humphrey Pickard [Am. 1812-1844]

Memoir and writings of Hannah Maynard Pickard, late wife of Rev. Humphrey Pickard. Comp. Edward Otheman.
Boston: David H. Ela, pr., 1845. 250p. NUC OCLC
[Incl. poems, prose sketches for children]

PICKARD, Mrs. Humphrey see PICKARD, Hannah Maynard (Thompson)

4307. PICKARD, Kate E.R. [Am. 19c]
Flowers from a private garden, gathered for friends.
n.p: n.p., 1868. 43 ff. NUC

4308. PICKENS, Anna E., Mrs. [Am. 19c]
Wayside wildings.
Somerville, MA: Somerville journal print, 1884. 104p. NUC

4309. PICKERING, Amelia [Br. 18c]
The sorrows of Werter; a poem.
L: T. Cadell, 1788. 69p. NUC BL OCLC
[Founded on Goethe]

PICKERING, Mrs. I. see PICKERING, Priscilla (Pointon)

4310. PICKERING, Priscilla (Pointon), Mrs. I. Pickering [Br. c1740-1801]
ALT: Pointon, Priscilla; Poynton, Priscilla
Poems; on several occasions.
Birmingham: Pr. for the author by T. Warren, 1770. 108p. NUC BL OCLC

4311. -----Poems ... To which are added poetical sketches by the author [John Morfitt], and translator [Joseph Weston], of Philotoxi Ardenae. Ed. Joseph Weston.
Birmingham: Pr. E. Piercy, 1794. 183p. NUC BL OCLC
[Her poems, occasional, elegiac, misc., pp. 1-68]

4312. PICKERSGILL, Mrs. [Br. 19c]
Tales of the harem.
L: Longman, Rees, Orme, Browne & Green, 1827. 191p. BL
[Four narrative poems: The witch of Himlaya; The cave of Gulistan; The Hetaeria; The Indian maid.]

4313. PIERCE, Elizabeth, Mrs. [Br. 19c]
Village pencillings, in prose and verse.
L: W. Pickering, 1842. NUC BL
[Descriptive sketches, short stories and poems]

4314. PIERS, Sarah, Lady [Br. d. 1720]
George for Britain: a poem.
L: Bernard Lintott, 1714. 44p. NUC BL OCLC

4315. PIERSON, B.A., Mrs. [Am. 19c]
The lost fairy bird. A poem.
Toledo, OH: Blade print & paper co., 1874. 23p. NUC OCLC

4316. PIERSON, Cornelia Louisa (Tuthill) [Am. 1820-1870] PSEUD: Young Lady, A
Christian ornaments; or, Spirit of the church.
Boston: n.p., 1844. NUC

4317. -----Wreaths and branches for the church, by a young lady.
Boston: n.p., 1842. NUC OCLC

4318. PIGGOTT, Isabel [Br. 19c]
A tribute of praise and thanksgiving ... in remembrance of February 27, 1872.
L: Charles H. Clarke, 1872. 12p. BL
[On the recovery of the Prince of Wales]

4319. PIGOTT, Jean Sophia [Br. 19c]
A royal service, and other poems.
L: n.p., 1877. BL

PIKE, Sarah Leigh see PYKE, Sarah Leigh

PILKINGTON, Mrs. J. see PILKINGTON, Mary (Hopkins)

PILKINGTON, Jane see PILKINGTON, Mary (Hopkins)

4320. PILKINGTON, Laetitia (Van Lewen), Mrs. Matthew Pilkington [Br. 1712-1750]
The celebrated Mrs. Pilkington's jests: or, The cabinet of wit and humour. To which is now first added, a great variety of bon mots, witticisms, and anecdotes of the inimitable Dr. Swift ... The whole forming the most brilliant collection of quaint jokes, facetious puns, smart repartees, entertaining tales in verse and prose, epigrams, epitaphs, conundrums, etc., now extant.
L: W. Nicoll, 1751. 116p. NUC BL OCLC

4321. -----Memoirs of Mrs. Laetitia Pilkington, wife to the Rev. Mr. Matthew Pilkington. Written by herself. Wherein are occasionally

interspersed, all her poems; with anecdotes of several eminent persons, living and dead.
Dublin: Pr. for author, 1748. 2v. NUC BL OCLC

4322. PILKINGTON, Mary (Hopkins), Mrs. J. Pilkington [Br. 1766-1839]
Miscellaneous poems.
L: T. Cadell, jr. & W. Davies, 1796. 2v. 2d ed. L: Verner & Hood, 1799. 2v. NUC BL OCLC
[NUC & OCLC attrib. to Jane Pilkington, though dedication signed: "M. Pilkington."]

4323. -----Original poems.
L: Pr. for author by Vernor, 1811. 191p. BL OCLC
[Tales in verse, elegiac & misc. poems, many addressed to various friends]

PILKINGTON, Mrs. Matthew see PILKINGTON, Laetitia (Van Lewen)

4324. PILLSBURY, L.B., Mrs. [Am. 19c]
The legend of the old mill and other poems.
Somerville, MA: Pr. E.D. Pillsbury, 1888. 139p. NUC OCLC

PIM, Mrs. Edward Bedford see PIM, Sophia Soltau (Harrison)

4325. PIM, Sophia Soltau (Harrison), Mrs. Edward Bedford Pim [Br. 1799-1885]
Job, and fugitive pieces.
L: Gee & co., 1885. BL
[Meditation on Job; anagrams, verses on Ireland]

4326. PIMM, Frances [Br. 19c]
Earth and its story: ----- Book V.
Worthing & L: C.H. Loveday, 1874. 40p. BL

4327. -----Earth and its story: changes, chances and results, from time past and present.
Worthing: C.H. Loveday, 1877. 57, 396p. BL

4328. -----The sea king; or, The death of Sir Humphrey Gilbert.
Worthing: n.p., 1873. BL

4329. PINCKNEY, Maria Henrietta [Am. 19c] PSEUD: Lady, A
Essays, religious, moral, dramatic and poetical. By a lady.
Charleston, SC: A.E. Miller, 1818. 242p. NUC OCLC

4330. PINDAR, Susan [Am. 19c]
Poems.
NY: J.A. Jenkins, 186-. NUC

4331. PINKERTON, Jane L., Mrs. [Am. 19c]
Religious and miscellaneous poems.
Coshocton, OH: Pr. for the author by B.E. Drone, 1848. 218p. NUC OCLC

4332. PINKNEY, Jane Vaughn [Br. 19c]
Patchwork poems and antediluvian rhymes.
L: C.H. Clarke, 1885. 112p. NUC BL

4333. PIRTLE, Jane Anne, Mrs. [Am. 19c]
Scattered poems.
Pittsburgh, PA: J. Eichbaum & co., 1882. 30p. NUC

4334. PITCAIRN, Janet Wyld [Br. 19c]
ALT: P., J. W.
The shepherd, and other verses. By J.W.P.
Edinburgh & L: Oliphant, Anderson & Ferrier, 1889. 102p. BL

4335. -----The shepherd, and other verses. By J.W.P.
New ed. rev. & enlarged. Edinburgh & L: Oliphant, Anderson & Ferrier, 1897. 134p. BL

4336. PITMAN, Alice A. [Br. 19c]
Tales from fairy-land. The maid with the golden hair.
L: G.J.W. Pitman, 1895. 2 l. BL
[Verses for recitation; Title page advertizes another such work: Tales from London life.]

4337. PITTMAN, Jeannie L., Mrs. [Am. 19c]
Poems.
Brooklyn, NY: n.p., 1892. 22 l. NUC

4338. PIZEY, Susannah [Br. 19c]
Poems.
L: Rackham, 1817. 80p. BL OCLC

4339. PLAKE, Kate, Mrs. [Am. b. 1838]
The captured mother and the stolen child.
L: n.p., 1871. 24p. NUC
[Pamphlet on how her child was taken from her and her own confinement in an asylum. Contains 6 poems.]

4340. PLATO, Ann [Am. 19c]
Essays; including biographies and miscellaneous pieces, in prose and poetry.
Hartford, CT: Pr. for author, 1841. 122p. NUC BL OCLC

[Author was black woman from CT. Essays on religion, education, nature, etc., 19 poems]

4341. PLEASANTS, Mrs. Joseph [Am. 19c]
Cinderella, The widow of Nain, and The resurrection of Lazarus, in rhyme. Composed for the benefit of the Sanitary Fair.
Philadelphia: n.p., 1864. 16p. NUC OCLC

4342. PLEASANTS, Julia [Am. 1827?-1886] ALT: Creswell, Julia Pleasants
Apheila; and other poems. By two cousins of the South, Miss Julia Pleasants and Thomas Bibb Bradley.
NY: C. Scribner, 1854. 272p. NUC BL OCLC

4343. PLOMLEY, Mary Ann [Br. 19c]
Rural lays.
L: n.p., 1826. BL

PLUMLEY, Mrs. Frank <u>see</u> PLUMLEY, Lavinia Lucretia (Fletcher)

4344. PLUMLEY, Lavinia Lucretia (Fletcher), Mrs. Frank Plumley [Am. 1848-1906]
The isle of rest. The ... poem was prepared by Mrs. Plumley to be read at an impromptu social entertainment designed to "while away" an evening in camp.
North Hero, VT: n.p., 1890. 8p. NUC
[Camp Grand View, North Hero, VT]

4345. POCKLINGTON, Mrs. Thorston [Br. 19c]
Alphabetical chips. Ancient and modern.
York: n.p., 1885. BL
[Satirical & political verses on the alphabet]

4346. POE, Anna H. [Am. 19c]
Poems and stories.
Springfield, IL: Her sister, Marianna Poe Brown, 1893. 145p. NUC

POINTON, Priscilla <u>see</u> PICKERING, Priscilla (Pointon)

4347. POLGLASE, Ann Eaton [Br. 19c] ALT: P., A.E.
The shipwreck; a tale of Arabia: and other poems. By A.E.P.
L: Hamilton & Adams, 1827. 252p. NUC BL OCLC

4348. POLLARD, Josephine [Am. 1834-1892]
Co-education.
NY: G.F. Birmingham & co., 1883. 42p. NUC BL OCLC
[Feminist poem in 4 sections: Helpmate, Slave, Toy & Equal]

4349. -----The decorative sisters, a modern ballad.
NY: A.D.F. Randolph & co., 1881. 34p. NUC BL OCLC

4350. -----Vagrant verses.
NY: Phillips & Hunt; Cincinnati, OH: Cranston & Stowe, 1886. 216p. NUC

4351. POLLARD, Rebecca (Smith) [Am. 1831-1917] PSEUD: Harrington, Kate
Centennial and other poems. By Kate Harrington.
Philadelphia: J.B. Lippincott & co., 1876. 252p.
[Poems selected from the writings of Professor N.R. Smith, father of the author, pp. 233-252]

4352. -----In memoriam. Maymie. April 6, 1869. By Kate Harrington.
Keokuk, IA: Constitution bk. & job office, Gate City pr. & pub. house, 1870. 60p. NUC

4353. -----Lionel Lightfoot, a temperance poem. By Kate Harrington.
Keokuk, IA: Constitution Bk. & job office, Gate City pr. & pub. house, 1876. 52p. NUC OCLC

4354. POMEROY, Mary Stella [Am. 19c]
Songs of the heart.
Milwaukee, WI: Cramer, Aikens & Cramer, pr., 1877. 200p. NUC OCLC

4355. PONSONBY, Catherine, Mrs. [Br. 19c]
Lays of the lakes, and other poems of description and reflection.
Glasgow: n.p., 1850. BL

4356. PONSONBY, Lady Emily Charlotte Mary [Br. 1817-1877]
Mary Gray and other tales and verses.
L: G. Hoby, 1852. 248p. BL OCLC

4357. POOLE, Eva L. (Travers) Evered [Br. 19c] ALT: Evered Poole, Mrs.; Travers, Eva L.
Left alone with Jesus and other poems.
L: Nisbet & co., 1890. 115p. BL

4358. -----"Lonely? No, not lonely" and other poems.
2d ed. L: J. Nisbet & co., 1881. 133p. BL

4359. POOLE, Fanny Huntington (Runnells) [Am. 1863-1940]
A bank of violets, verses.
L & NY: G.P. Putnam's sons, 1895. 76p. NUC BL OCLC

4360. POOLE, Hester Martha (Hunt) [Am. 1833-1932]
Christmas wanderings.
NY: Hard & Parsons, 1887. 5 l. NUC

4361. -----Moss fancies.
NY: Hard & Parsons, 1887. 5 l. NUC
[Cover-title: Moss fancies for Christmas-tide.]

POPE, Alexander, co-author see MADAN, Judith (Cowper)

4362. POPE, Marion (Manville) [Am. b. 1859]
Over the divide: and other verses.
Philadelphia: J.B. Lippincott & co., 1888. 190p. NUC OCLC

4363. POPE, Mary E. (Foote) [Am. 19c]
Poems.
Philadelphia: J.B. Lippincott & co., 1872. 150p. NUC OCLC

PORDEN, Eleanor Anne see FRANKLIN, Eleanor Anne (Porden)

4364. PORTER, Anna Maria [Br. 1780-1832] ALT: P., A.M. PSEUD: Young lady, A
Ballad romances and other poems.
L: Longman, Hurst, Rees, Orme & Brown, 1811. 196p. NUC BL OCLC

4365. -----Original poems on various subjects, by a young lady, 18 years of age.
L: T. Caddell, 1798? 91p. NUC OCLC

4366. PORTER, Elizabeth [Br. 19c]
The borderland of dreams.
Cambridge: University press, 1895. 67p. NUC OCLC
[24 lyric poems]

4367. PORTER, Maria S. (Alley) [Am. 1832-1904]
Recollections of Louisa May Alcott, John Greenleaf Whittier, and Robert Browning, together with several memorial poems.
Boston: For the author by the New Magazine corp., 1893. 59p. NUC BL OCLC
[Incl. 3 memorial poems by Porter]

4368. PORTER, Mel-inda Jennie, Mrs. [Am. 19c]
Valkyria, chaplets of Mars.
NY: W.B. Smith & co., 1881. 133p. NUC OCLC

4369. PORTER, Rose [Am. 1845-1906]
Christmas blessings: joy, light, glory, hope, love, faith, cheer, peace, praise.
Boston: D. Lothrop & co., 1886. 12 l. NUC

4370. -----Winged songs: an Easter jubilee.
NY: A.D.F. Randolph, 1883. 35p. NUC
[Anthology with some orig. religious verse]

4371. PORTER, Sarah, Mrs. [Am. 18c]
The royal penitent. In three parts. To which is added, David's lamentation over Saul and Jonathan. By Mrs. Sarah Porter. Of Plymouth in New Hampshire.
Concord, NH: Pr. George Hough, 1791.
Newburyport: Pr. G.J. Osborne, 1793. 21p. NUC OCLC
[Rhymed narratives based on David & Bathsheba]

POSTGATE, Isa J. see POSTGATE, Isabella J.

4372. POSTGATE, Isabella J. [Br. 19/20c] ALT: Postgate, Isa J.
A Christmas legend; and other verses.
L: Simpkin, Marshall & co., 1889. 121p. BL

4373. -----Little Saint Cyril, and other poems.
Oxford & L: Mowbray & co., 1896. 82p. BL

4374. -----Songs of rest, by Isa J. Postgate.
NY: Art Lithographic pub. co.; L: Artistic Lithographic co., 18--? 12p. NUC

4375. POTTER, Elizabeth Claghorn [Am. d. 1879]
Patience and hope.
New Bedford, MA: n.p., 1879? 6p. OCLC

4376. -----Poems.
New Bedford, MA: n.p., 1879. 4 l. NUC

4377. POTTS, Anna H. [Br. 19c]
Simple poems for national and Sunday schools.
Cambridge: Pr. at the Univ. press, 1852. 36p. BL
[Language is simple; many poems on poor cottagers]

4378. -----Sketches of character. And other pieces in verse.
L: John W. Parker; Cambridge: Deighton; Macmillan & co., 1849. 213p. NUC BL
[Misc. lyrics, occasional verse; incl. tributes to L.E.L. & Mrs. Hemans]

4379. POTTS, Ellen, Mrs. [Br. 19c]
Bardrick, the King of the Teign. A lay of South Devon. In ten cantos.
L: Provost & co., 1869. 76p. NUC BL OCLC

4380. POTTS, Ethelinda Margaretta (Thorpe) [Br. 19c]
Moonshine (I. Sketches in England and Wales, 1814. II. Miscellaneous trifles, 1814).
L: Longman, Hurst, Rees, Orme & Brown, 1814. 2v. NUC BL
[Chiefly verse]

4381. -----Moonshine (III. Unconnected trifles, and appendix, 1835).
2d ed. L: David Simmons & co., 1832-1835. NUC BL
[Chiefly verse]

4382. -----To my grandchildren.
L: n.p., 1835? NUC

4383. POTTS, Eugenia Dunlap, Mrs. [Am. 19c]
The song of Lancaster, Kentucky. To the statesmen, soldiers, and citizens of Garrard County.
Cambridge, MA: Riverside press, 1876. 135p. NUC OCLC

4384. POUCHER, Emma E. [Am. 19c] ALT: E., E.L.
Life and dreams, poems. By E.L.E.
NY: G.W. Dillingham, 1895. 159p. NUC

4385. POULTER, Louisa Frances [Br. 19c] PSEUD: Spero
Imagination; a poem. In two parts.
L: J. Hatchard & son, 1820. 103p. NUC BL

4386. -----Imagination; a poem, in two parts. With other poems.
L: Saunders, 1841. 151p. NUC BL

4387. -----Poems, by Spero.
L: F. Straker, pr., 1858. 176p. NUC

4388. POWEL, Esther [Br. 19c]
The story of a life, and other poems.
L: Digby & Long, 1892. 56p. BL

4389. -----Vox Rumana.
L: Jarrold & sons, 1896. 38p. BL

4390. POWELL, Anne [Br. 19c]
Clifton, Caractacus, Boadicea, and other pieces.
Bristol: Albion press, pr. by Wansbrough & Saunders, 1821. 122p. NUC BL OCLC

POWER, Anna Marsh see POWER, Susan Anna

4391. POWER, Marguerite A. [Br. 1815-1867]
Virginia's hand, a poem.
L: n.p., 1860. BL

4392. POWER, Susan Anna [Am. 1813-1877] ALT: Power, Anna Marsh
Cinderella. With her sister, Sarah Helen (Power) Whitman [1803-1878].
Providence, RI: Hammond, Angell & co., pr., 1867. 12p. NUC OCLC
[In verse]

4393. -----Dissolving views.
Providence, RI: Hammond, Angell & co., pr., 1868. 11p. OCLC

4394. -----The garnered years: annals of the decade.
Providence, RI: Hammond, Angell, & co., pr., 1870. 17p. NUC
[Poems, for 1859, 1860, & 1861, which recount major national events. Cover says: "originally published as New Year's addresses."]

4395. -----The sleeping beauty. With Sarah Helen (Power) Whitman.
Providence, RI: Hammond, Angell & co., pr., 1868. 14p. NUC BL OCLC
[Verse]

4396. POWERS, O.A., Mrs. [Am. 19c]
High-toned sprees: a temperance poem.
Middletown, NY: Hill & Slauson, pr., c1873. 36p. NUC OCLC

4397. -----Long live America.
Philadelphia: J.B. Lippincott & co., 1882. 16p. NUC
[Temperance poems]

4398. -----The maple dell of '76.
Philadelphia: J.B. Lippincott & co., 1878. 93p. NUC OCLC
[Record of domestic troubles, in verse]

4399. POWLEY, Mary [Br. 1812-1882]
Echoes of old Cumberland. Poems and translations.

L: Bemrose & sons, 1875. 250p. NUC BL OCLC

4400. POYAS, Catherine Gendron [Am. 1813-1882]
The Huguenot daughters, and other poems.
Charleston, SC: J. Russell, 1849. 167p. NUC

4401. -----In memory of the Rev. C.P. Gadsden, rector of St. Luke's Church, Charleston, S.C.
Charleston, SC: Holmes' book house, 1871. 6p. NUC OCLC

4402. -----Years of grief, and other poems.
Charleston, SC: Walker, Evans, & Cogswell, pr., 1869. 242p. NUC OCLC

POYNTON, Priscilla <u>see</u> PICKERING, Priscilla (Pointon)

4403. POYNTZ, Anne B., Mrs. [Br. 18c]
PSEUD: Lady, A
Je ne scai quoi: or, a collection of letters, odes, etc. Never before published. By a lady.
L: n.p., 1769. 112p. NUC BL
[Satirical letters, character sketches, odes]

PRAIRIE BIRD, pseud. <u>see</u> WELLMAN, Mary Ward (Bryant)

4404. PRATT, Harriet Agatha (Lethbridge), Mrs. Henry F.A. Pratt [Br. 19c]
Poems.
L: Pr. for the authoress by W.H. Dalton, 1843. 80p. BL OCLC

PRATT, Mrs. Henry F.A. <u>see</u> PRATT, Harriet Agatha (Lethbridge)

4405. PRATT, Reba (Beebe) [Am. b. 1856]
The sheaf of a gleaner; poems. Nil desperandum.
Salt Lake City, UT: Jos. Hyrum Parry & co., 1886. 90p. NUC OCLC

PRENTICE, George D., comp. <u>see</u> CHITWOOD, Mary Louisa

4406. PRENTISS, Caroline (Edwards) [Am. b. 1872]
Fleeting thoughts.
NY: G.P. Putnam's sons, 1893. 128p. NUC BL OCLC

4407. -----Sunshine and shadow.
NY: G.P. Putnam's sons, 1896. 175p. NUC BL

PRENTISS, E. <u>see</u> PRENTISS, Elizabeth (Payson)

4408. PRENTISS, Elizabeth (Payson), Mrs. G.L. Prentiss [Am. 1818-1878]
ALT: Prentiss, E.
Religious poems.
NY: A.D.F. Randolph, 1873. 200p. NUC BL OCLC
[Pub. as: "Golden hours" in 1874.]

PRENTISS, Mrs. G.L. <u>see</u> PRENTISS, Elizabeth (Payson)

4409. PRESCOTT, Henrietta [Br. 19c]
Poems. Written in Newfoundland.
L: Saunders & Otley, 1839. 311p. NUC BL OCLC

4410. PRESTON, Margaret (Junkin) [Am. 1820-1897]
Beechenbrook; a rhyme of the war.
Richmond, VA: J.W. Randolph, 1865. 64p. NUC BL OCLC

4411. -----Cartoons.
Boston: Roberts bros., 1875. 240p. NUC BL OCLC

4412. -----Centennial poem for Washington & Lee University, Lexington, Virginia, 1775-1885.
NY & L: G.P. Putnam's sons, 1885. 24 l. NUC OCLC

4413. -----Colonial ballads, sonnets, and other verses.
NY & Boston: Houghton, Mifflin & co., 1887. 259p. NUC BL OCLC

4414. -----Epithalamium, 1878. October 10th.
Lexington, VA: n.p., 1878? 8p. NUC OCLC

4415. -----For love's sake; poems of faith and comfort.
NY: A.D.F. Randolph, 1886. 142p. NUC BL OCLC

4416. -----Old song and new.
Philadelphia: J.B. Lippincott & co., 1870. 312p. NUC OCLC
[Ballads, sonnets, religious verse & poems based on Hebrew & Greek stories]

4417. -----Semi-centennial ode for the Virginia Military Institute, Lexington, VA (written at the request of the Board of Visitors).
L & NY: G.P. Putnam's sons, 1889. 26 l. NUC OCLC

4418. -----The young ruler's question.
Philadelphia: Presbyterian board of pub., 1869. 14p. NUC
[Poem on Jesus Christ]

4419. PRICE, Alicia [Br. 19c]
Sacred poems.
Dublin: W. Curry, 1843. 61p. BL

4420. PRICE, Charlotte A. [Br. 19c]
Poems and lyrics for idle hours.
L: F.V. White & co., 1881. 244p. BL

4421. PRICHARD, M., Mrs. [Br. 19c]
The siege of Pembroke, and other poems.
L: T. Hatchard, 1851. 119p. BL OCLC

PRIDEAUX, Fanny Ann <u>see</u> PRIDEAUX, Fanny Ash

4422. PRIDEAUX, Fanny Ash [Ann OCLC] (Ball), Mrs. Frederick Prideaux [Br. d. 1894]
Claudia.
L: Smith, Elder & co., 1865. 223p. BL OCLC
[5 pt. epic of Roman Britain and early Christianity]

4423. -----The nine days' queen. A dramatic poem. By Mrs. Frederick Prideaux.
L: Bell & Daldy, 1869. 244p. BL OCLC
[Four acts, blank verse, on Lady Jane Grey]

4424. -----Philip Molesworth: and other poems. By Mrs. Frederick Prideaux.
L: S. Low, Marston, Searle, & Rivington, 1886. 257p. OCLC

PRIDEAUX, Mrs. Frederick <u>see</u> PRIDEAUX, Fanny Ash

PRIME, Frederick, jr., ed. <u>see</u> PRIME, Lydia (Hare)

PRIME, Mrs. Frederick <u>see</u> PRIME, Lydia (Hare)

4425. PRIME, Lydia (Hare), Mrs. Frederick Prime [Am. 1818-1883]
In memory of L.H.P. Ed. her son, Frederick Prime, jr.
NY: D. Appleton & co., 1884. 208p. NUC OCLC
[Mem. vol. of her poems: Narrative, domestic, incl. some written as a child]

4426. PRIMROSE, Lady Diana [Br. 17c]
A chain of pearle, or a memorial of the peerles, graces, and heroick vertues of Queene Elizabeth, of glorious memory. Composed by the noble Lady, Diana Primrose.
L: Thomas Paine, sold by P. Waterhouse, 1630. NUC BL
[Dorothy Berry, in the preface, calls Diana "the prime-rose of the muses nine"]

4427. PRINCEPS, Elizabeth Louisa Slater [Br. 19c]
Variety, a novel. With poetry.
L: W. Fearman, Library, 1820. 3v. BL
[Incl. "The pilgrim: a legendary tale," V3, pp. 135-224, a gothic ballad with songs interspersed, some verses in the text of the novel.]

PRINGLE, Caroline (Tounley) <u>see</u> TOUNLEY, Caroline

4428. PROBYN, May [Br. 19c]
A ballad of the road, and other poems.
L: W. Satchell & co., 1883. 127p. NUC BL

4429. -----Pansies. A book of poems.
L: E. Mathews, 1895. 65p. NUC BL OCLC

4430. -----Poems.
L: W. Satchell & co., 1881. 78p. NUC BL

4431. PROCTER, Adelaide Anne [Br. 1825-1864]
A chaplet of verses.
L: Longman, Green, Longman & Roberts, 1862. 126p. NUC BL OCLC
[Published for the benefit of the Providence Row Night Refuge for Homeless Women and Children.]

4432. -----The complete poetical works, with an introduction by Charles Dickens.
Boston & NY: Houghton, Mifflin, & co., 1899. 257p. NUC BL OCLC

4433. -----Legends and lyrics, a book of verses.
L: Bell & Daldy, 1858-61. 2v. NUC BL OCLC

4434. -----The lost chord and other favorite poems.
Boston: Lothrop, 1884. 25 l. NUC BL

4435. -----The message.
L: Ernest Nister; NY: E.P. Dutton, 1892. 12p. BL OCLC

4436. -----The year's blessing.
L: Ernest Nister, 1895. BL

4437. PROCTOR, Edna Dean [Am. 1829-1923]
Poems.
NY: Hurd & Houghton; Boston: E.P. Dutton & co., 1866. 140p. NUC OCLC

4438. -----Poems.
Boston & NY: Houghton Mifflin & co., 1890. 257p. NUC OCLC

4439. -----The song of the ancient people.
Boston & NY: Houghton Mifflin & co., 1892. 69p. NUC
[Narrative on the Zuni culture]

4440. PROWETT, Miss [Br. 19c]
Poems written by a father and daughter. With J.A. Prowett.
L: n.p., 1845. 433p. BL

PROWETT, J.A., co-author <u>see</u> PROWETT, Miss

PROWSE, Mrs. I.S. <u>see</u> PROWSE, Marianne (Jeffery)

4441. PROWSE, Marianne (Jeffery), Mrs. I.S. Prowse [Br. 19c]
Poems. By Mrs. I.S. Prowse.
L: Smith, Elder, & co., 1830. 183p. NUC BL OCLC

4442. PUGH, Sarah S. [Br. 19c] ALT: P., S.S.
Poems addressed to various literary characters. By S.S.P.
Weymough: Pr. for the author by G. Kay, 1827. 111p. NUC OCLC

4443. PUMPELLY, Mary Hollenback (Welles) [Am. 1803-1879]
Poems.
NY: C. Scribner, 1852. 76p. NUC BL OCLC

4444. PURDY, Amelia V. [Am. 19c]
First fruit.
Pittsburg & Harrisburg, PA: B. Singerly, pr., 1875. 308p. NUC OCLC

4445. PURVIS, Tacy (Townsend) [Am. 19c]
Abi Meredith, by Tacy Townsend.
Philadelphia: Friends' book assoc., 1878. 107p. NUC OCLC

4446. PUTNAM, Effie Douglass [Am. 19/20c]
Margaret and the singer's story.
Boston: Cupples & Hurd, 1888. 103p. NUC OCLC

4447. PUTNAM, Irene [Br. 19c]
Songs without answer.
NY & L: G.P. Putnam's sons, 1896. 93p. NUC BL OCLC
[Nature poems]

PYE, Mrs. Hampden <u>see</u> PYE, Jael Henrietta (Mendez)

4448. PYE, Jael Henrietta (Mendez), Mrs. Hampden Pye [Br. d. 1782] PSEUD: Lady, A
Poems. By a lady.
L: n.p., 1767. 36, 40p. NUC BL
[2d ed. L: J. Walter, 1772.]

4449. -----Poems. By a lady.
L: n.p., 1771. BL
[A different work]

4450. PYE, Mary Elizabeth [Br. d. 1834]
Poems on several occasions.
Stoke Poges: Pr. at Stoke Park, 1802. 40p. NUC

4451. PYER, Catherine Smith [Br. 19c]
Songs of freedom.
L: n.p., 1849. BL

4452. -----Wild flowers; or, Poetic gleanings from natural objects.
L: n.p., 1844. BL

4453. PYKE, Sarah Leigh [Br. 18/19c] ALT: Pike, Sarah Leigh PSEUD: Serena
Eighty village hymns.
Taunton: n.p., 1832. BL

4454. -----Israel, a juvenile poem. By Serena.
Bath: Pr. R. Crutwell for the author, 1795. 2v. BL
[Biblical epic, story of Exodus by a Juvenile author.]

4455. -----The triumph of Messiah.
Exeter: n.p., 1812. BL

PYLADES, pseud., co-author <u>see</u> THOMAS, Elizabeth

4456. PYPER, Mary [Br. b. 1795]
Hebrew children. Poetic illustrations of Biblical character.
Edinburgh: n.p., 1858. BL

4457. -----Sacred poems.
Edinburgh: Elliot, 1865. 107p. NUC

4458. PYPER, Mary [Br. 19c]
Sacred poems.
Edinburgh: Elliot, 1865. 107p. NUC

4459. -----Select pieces.
Edinburgh: n.p., 1847. BL

QUACKENBOS, G.P., ed. see BULLOCK, Cynthia

4460. QUIGLEY, Catharine [Br. 19c]
The microscope; or, Village flies, in three cantos. With other poems, never before published.
Monoghan: n.p., 1819. 114p. NUC BL

4461. -----Poems.
Dublin: Pr. T. Courtney, 1813. 192p. NUC BL

4462. QUINN, Minnie [Am. 19c]
May blossoms: poems.
Atlanta, GA: Dodson's pr. office., 1885. 128p. NUC OCLC

4463. -----"Under the roses.".
Atlanta, GA?: n.p., 1881? 46p. NUC OCLC

4464. -----Violets. Poems.
Atlanta, GA: James P. Harrison & co., 1879. NUC

4465. R., A. [Br. 18c] PSEUD: Young Lady, A
Select contemplations and meditations. To which are added divine poems ... Written by a young lady in her retirement.
L: J. Oswald, 1739. 216p. NUC BL OCLC

R., A.M. see RICHARDS, Anna Matlack

R., C. see REEVE, Clara

R., C.A. see ROWLAND, Catherine Anne

R., E.D. see BIANCIARDI, Elizabeth Dickinson (Rice)

R., E.H. see MITCHELL, Elizabeth Harcourt (Rolls)

R., E.L. see RAYMOND, Ellen Louisa

R., F., co-author see REDDIN, Mary Gertrude

R., L.N. see RANYARD, Ellen Henrietta (White)

R., M. see RIDDELL, Maria (Woodley)

R., M.A. see ROBERTS, Mary Ann

R., M.G. see REDDIN, Mary Gertrude

R., M.H., co-author see RENSHAW, F.M.

R.R., comp. see WRIGHT, Hannah Mary

4466. RADCLIFFE, Ann (Ward) [Br. 1764-1823]
Gaston de Blondeville, or the Court of Henry III keeping festival in Ardenne, a romance. St. Alban's Abbey, a metrical tale; with some poetical pieces ... To which is prefixed a memoir of the author, with extracts from her journals.
L: H. Colburn; H.C. Carey & I. Lea, 1826. 4v. NUC BL OCLC
[Vols. 3 & 4 have half-title: "The posthumous works of Mrs. Radcliffe"]

4467. -----The mysteries of Udolpho, a romance interspersed with some pieces of poetry.
L: G.G. & J. Robinson, 1794. 4v. NUC BL OCLC

4468. -----The poems of Mrs. Ann Radcliffe.
L: J. Smith, 1816. 118p. NUC BL OCLC

4469. -----The poetical works of Ann Radcliffe.
L: Pub. for H. Colburn by R. Bentley, 1834. 2v. NUC BL OCLC
[Incl. St. Alban's Abbey, a metrical romance with other misc. poems. Complete poetic works.]

4470. -----The romance of the forest; interspersed with some pieces of poetry.
L: T. Hookham & J. Carpenter, 1791. 3v. NUC BL OCLC

4471. -----A Sicilian romance.
L: T. Hookham, 1790. 2v. NUC BL OCLC

4472. RADCLIFFE, Mary Ann, Mrs. [Br. 18/19c]
The memoirs of Mrs. Mary Ann Radcliffe: in familiar letters to her female friend.
Edinburgh: Pr. for the author, 1810. 544p. NUC BL
[Incl. poetry and a tract, "The Female Advocate"]

4473. RADCLIFFE, Mira M. [Br. 19c]
Ina, and other poems.
Liverpool: n.p., 1841. BL

4474. RADFORD, Dollie Maitland [Br. b. 1858]

Good night.
L: D. Nutt, 1895. 40 l. NUC BL OCLC

4475. -----A light load.
L: Elkin Mathews, 1891. 64p. NUC BL OCLC

4476. -----Songs and other verses.
L: John Lane; Philadelphia: J.B. Lippincott & co., 1895. 93p. NUC BL OCLC

4477. RAEBURN, Mrs. [Br. 19c]
Poems.
Edinburgh: n.p., 1887. NUC

4478. RAINE, Rosa [Br. 19c]
Floreat Ecclesia. A manual of church poesy.
L: John Hughes, 1851. 106p. BL
[Original religious verse. Written to awaken Christians to the needs of the poor and the oppressed]

4479. RALSTON, Harriet Newell (Jackson) [Am. 1828-1920]
Columbus and Isabella. The immortals. A souvenir centennial poem.
Washington, DC: H.N. Ralston, 1893. 39p. NUC BL OCLC

4480. -----The spectral feast.
Washington, DC: Press of the National Republican pr. co., 1878. 14p. NUC
[Temperance poetry]

RAMSAY, Charlotte see LENNOX, Charlotte (Ramsay)

4481. RAMSEY, Vienna G. (Morrell) [Am. b. 1817]
A censer; poems.
Boston: Morning Star pub. house, 1896. 278p. NUC OCLC

4482. -----A legend of the White Hills, and other poems.
Boston: D. Lothrop & co.; Dover, NH: G.T. Day & co., 1872. 190p. NUC OCLC

4483. RAND, Martha Agnes [Am. 19c]
The legend of a thought, and other verses.
Chicago: Pr. Rand, McNally & co., 1889. 53p. NUC OCLC

RANDALL, Alice Elizabeth (Sawtelle), co-author see SAWTELLE, Mary Anna

4484. RANKIN, Sarah Burlingame (Lapham) [Am. 19c]
Centennial poem.
Peoria, IL: n.p., 1876. 24p. NUC OCLC

4485. -----Climbing poems.
Baltimore, OH: Turnbull bros., 1874. 200p. NUC OCLC

4486. -----A grand[d]aughter's poem.
Peoria, IL?: n.p., 1877. 8p. OCLC

4487. -----Mariamne, queen of the Jews, Genesis, Tree of life (to Edison), The fairies, Centennial songs, and other poems.
Cincinnati, OH: Press of Robert Clarke & co., 1884. 191p. NUC OCLC
[Narrative, lyric & occasional poetry]

4488. RANYARD, Ellen Henrietta (White) [Br. 1810-1879] ALT: R., L. N.
The borderland [border land BL]: and other poems. Olive leaves. Myrtle leaves. Ivy leaves. Cypress leaves. By L.N.R.
2d ed. L: J. Nisbet & co., 1876. 243p. NUC BL

4489. -----Leaves from life.
L: S. Bagster, 1855. 250p. NUC BL

4490. RATHBONE, Hannah Mary (Reynolds) [Br. 1748-1878]
The strawberry girl, with other thoughts and fancies in verse.
L: Longman, Brown, Green, Longmans & Roberts, 1858. 103p. BL OCLC

4491. RAY, Henrietta Cordelia [Am. d. 1916]
Lincoln; written for the occasion of the unveiling of the freedman's monument in memory of Abraham Lincoln, April 14, 1876.
NY: Press of J.J. Little & co., 1893. 11 l. NUC

4492. -----Sonnets.
NY: Press of J.J. Little & co., 1893. 29p. NUC OCLC

RAY, HETTIE J., pseud. see CURTIS, Harriet J., Mrs.

4493. RAYMOND, Ellen Louisa [Br. 19c] ALT: R., E.L.
Eden: and other poems. By E.L.R.
L: n.p., 1867? BL

4494. READ, Harriette Fanning, Miss [Am. 19c]
Dramatic poems; Medea, Erminia, and the New world.
Boston: W. Crosby & H.P. Nichols, 1847, 1848. 297p. NUC BL OCLC
[All three are 5-act tragedies]

4495. READ, Jane Maria [Am. b. 1853]
Between the centuries, and other poems.
Boston: Henry A. Young & co., 1887. 205p. NUC OCLC

READ, M.S., Mrs. see READ, Mary Sabina, Mrs.

4496. READ, Mary Sabina, Mrs. [Am. 19c] ALT: Read, M.S., Mrs.
The wild flower.
Portland, ME: S.H. Colesworthy, 1848. 96p. NUC OCLC

4497. READER, Emily E. [Br. 19c]
Echoes of thought. A medley of verse.
L: Longmans & co., 1889. 146p. NUC BL

4498. -----Priestess and queen. A tale of the white race of Mexico.
L & NY: Longmans, Green & co., 1899. 306p. NUC BL OCLC

4499. -----Voices from flowerland. Original couplets ... A birthday book and language of flowers.
NY: n.p., n.d. L: Longmans & co., 1884. NUC BL

4500. READER, Sarah [Br. 19c]
Cowley; and other poems.
L: Priv. pr., 1870. BL OCLC

4501. REAVIS, Rebecca (Morrow) [Am. 19c]
The builders; a souvenir poem: The Saint Louis Exhibition and Music Hall and its builders.
St. Louis, MO: Becktold & co., 1884. 33p. NUC OCLC

4502. -----The course of empire and other poems.
St. Louis, MO: n.p., 1886. 32p. NUC OCLC

4503. -----A home offering. "Consider the lilies," and other poems.
St. Louis, MO: Becktold & co., 1883. 54p. NUC OCLC

RECTOR'S WIFE, THE, pseud. see GOODALL, Harriot Annabella

4504. REDDIN [Rettin OCLC], Mary Gertrude [Br. 19c] ALT: R., M.G.
Memories. By M.G.R.
Dublin: M. & S. Eaton, 1887. 376p. NUC

4505. -----Sunday evenings at Loretto. By M.G.R.
Dublin: M. & S. Eaton, 1881. 248p. NUC OCLC
[Saints' lives in verse]

4506. -----A wreath of wild flowers by M. and F.R. Poems.
Dublin: W. Powell, 1875. 196p. NUC

REDNAXELA, pseud. see CROPPER, Hon. Mrs.

4507. REED, Alice [Br. 19c]
When my ship comes home. With Graham Clifton Bingham.
L: Ernest Nister, 1891. BL

4508. REED, Anna Medora (Morrison) [Am. 1850-1921]
The earlier poems of Anna M. Morrison. Revised and arranged by herself.
San Francisco: A.L. Bancroft & co., 1880. 86p. NUC OCLC

4509. -----The later poems of Anna Morrison Reed.
San Francisco: J. Stuart & co., 1891. 55p. NUC OCLC

4510. -----The latest and later poems of Anna Morrison Reed.
San Francisco: Hicks-Judd co., 1896. 85p. NUC OCLC

4511. REED, Hattie Almira [Am. 19c]
The Rocky Mountains at sunset, and other poems.
Boston: B.B. Russell; San Francisco: A.L. Bancroft & co., 1873. 216p. NUC OCLC

REED, I., ed. see MONTAGU, Lady Mary (Pierrepont) Wortley

4512. REES, Maria Isabella Irwin [Br. 19c]
The forest house and other poems.
L: n.p., 1850. BL

4513. REESE, Lizette Woodworth [Am. 1856-1935]
A branch of May. Poems.
Baltimore, MD: Cushings & Bailey, 1887. 42p. NUC OCLC

4514. -----A handful of lavender.
Boston & NY: Houghton, Mifflin & co.; Portland, ME: T.B. Mosher, 1891. 100p. NUC BL OCLC

4515. -----A quiet road.
Boston & NY: Houghton, Mifflin & co., 1896. 79p. NUC OCLC

4516. REEVE, Anna [Br. 19c]
Euterpe Montana and other poems.
L: S.W. Partridge, 1885. 192p. NUC BL OCLC

4517. -----Lights and shadows. Poems.
L: S.W. Partridge, 1882. 248p. BL

4518. REEVE, Clara [Br. 1729-1807] ALT: R., C.
Original poems on several occasions. By C.R.
L: Pr. T.J. Pasham for W. Harris, 1769. 107p. NUC BL OCLC

4519. REEVE, Mary Ann [Br. 19c]
Lays from the West.
Odiham: H. Gotelee, 1865. 88p. NUC BL

4520. REEVES, Eliza [Br. 18c]
Poems on various subjects.
L: Pr. for the author & sold by C. Dilley, 1780. 224p. NUC BL OCLC

4521. REEVES, Helen Buckingham (Mathers), Mrs. Henry Reeves [Br. 19/20c] ALT: Mathers, Helen Buckingham
The token of the silver lily.
L: R. Bentley, 1877. 170p. NUC BL

REEVES, Mrs. Henry see REEVES, Helen Buckingham (Mathers)

4522. RENNIE, Eliza [Br. 19c]
Poems.
L: B.E. Lloyd & son, 1828. 182p. NUC BL

4523. RENO, Lydia M. [Am. b. 1831]
Early buds.
Boston & Cambridge: J. Munroe & co., 1853. 309p. NUC BL

4524. RENOU, Sarah [Br. 19c] ALT: R., S.
The temple of truth. A poem in five cantos.
L: n.p., 1818. BL
[Allegory]

4525. RENSHAW, F. M. [Br. 19c]
Verses by two sisters, F.M. and M.H.R. [Mary H. Renshaw].
Glasgow: J. Maclehose, 1893. 178p. NUC

RENSHAW, Mary H., co-author see RENSHAW, F.M.

RENTON, Gertrude see WEAVER, Baille Gertrude (Renton) Dunn

4526. RE QUA, Harriet (Warner) [Am. 19c]
Stones for the temple; or, Gaining the summit. Poems.
Rochester, NY: E.R. Andrews, 1885. 217p. NUC OCLC

4527. -----Ziona: the bride of the King, and miscellaneous poems.
Chicago & NY: Fleming H. Revell, 1889. 226p. NUC

RESIDENT OF SHERWOOD FOREST, A, pseud. see HAMILTON, Sarah, Miss

4528. RESKELLY, Katharine Jane (Waylen) [Br. 1843-1893]
A selection from the poems of the late Mrs. K.J. Reskelly; also a biographical sketch by one of her brothers, and obituary notices by various contributors. Ed. her husband.
Newnham, Gloucs.: Pr. for priv. circ., 1894. 210p. NUC BL OCLC

RETTIN, Mary Gertrude see REDDIN, Mary Gertrude

4529. REYNOLDS, Celia M. [Am. 19c]
Looking upward; or, Poems of the Christian life.
NY: n.p., 1887. 318p. NUC

4530. RHOADS, Rachel, Mrs. [Am. 19c]
Poems: a series of tales in verse, with a variety of lyrical productions on chosen themes.
Philadelphia: J.B. Lippincott & co., 1863. 348p. NUC BL

4531. RHODES, Henrietta [Br. 19c]
Poems and miscellaneous essays.
Brentford: Priv. pr. by P. Norbury, 1814. 80p. NUC BL
[Odes, lyrics and "Sir Edric, a legendary tale." Essays on horticulture & Stonehenge]

RHODES, Katharine Augusta see WARE, Katharine Augusta (Rhodes)

RICE, Elizabeth Dickinson see BIANCIARDI, Elizabeth Dickinson (Rice)

4532. RICH, Caroline Webster D. (Stockbridge), Mrs. Thomas Hill Rich [Am. 19c] ALT: Strout, C.W.D., Mrs.
Golden-rod, and some other verses. By Caroline W.D. Rich.
Buffalo, NY: Peter Paul book co., 1895. 11p. NUC OCLC
[Misc. poetry]

4533. -----Happenings.
Auburn, ME: Lakeside press, 1888. 9 l. NUC

4534. -----Poem written for the centennial celebration of the town of Turner, Maine.
Portland, ME: Pr. B. Thurston & co., 1886. 14p. NUC

4535. -----A summer idyl. By Mrs. Thomas Hill Rich.
Lewiston, ME: Journal pub. house, 1882. 6 l. NUC

4536. RICH, Helen (Hinsdale) [Am. b. 1827]
A dream of the Adirondacks, and other poems.
NY: G.P. Putnam's sons, 1884. 171p. NUC OCLC

4537. -----Murillo's slave and other poems.
Chicago: Rand, McNally & co., 1897. 196p. NUC OCLC

4538. RICH, Mary W. [Am. 19c]
Verses.
Boston: Spooner, 1896. 73p. NUC

RICH, Mrs. Thomas Hill <u>see</u> RICH, Caroline Webster D. (Stockbridge)

4539. RICHARDS, Anna Matlack [Am. 19c] ALT: R., A.M.
Dramatic sonnets. By A.M.R.
Newport, RI: Richards bros., 1881. 65 l. NUC
[65 sonnets]

4540. -----Letter and spirit; dramatic sonnets of inward life.
Boston: J.G. Cupples, 1891. 111 l. NUC BL OCLC
[57 sonnets, revision of Dramatic sonnets.]

4541. RICHARDS, Elizabeth Barnes [Am. 19c]
The heart's streamlet; or, Buds from memory's store house.
Worcester, MA: Hervey & co., 1856. 168p. NUC
[Chiefly by Richards]

RICHARDS, G.P., co-author <u>see</u> PALMER, Ann

4542. RICHARDS, Laura Elizabeth (Howe) [Am. 1856-1943]
L.E.R.
Gardiner, ME: n.p., 1886? 23p. NUC
[Narrative & lyric poetry]

4543. RICHARDS, Lydia Platt [Am. 19c]
American monodies.
Franklin, OH: Editor pub. co., 1899. 126p. NUC
[Narrative poems of the Wild West, a Pawnee Indian legend, etc.]

4544. RICHARDS, Susan [Am. 19c]
Poetry. Wayside thoughts, a collection of poems on various subjects, sacred, special, and tributary, with some few thoughts in prose.
Oakland, CA: Pacific Press pub. house, 1883. 202p. NUC OCLC
[Misc. poetry; Prose is a fictional sketch of Grandma in heaven, & other thoughts]

4545. RICHARDSON, Amanda Cranwill [Am. 19c]
Scattered leaves; poems from a collection of poems lost during the war.
Louisville, KY: John P. Morton & co., 1895. 96p. NUC OCLC
[Mostly occasional poems from personal recollections.]

RICHARDSON, C.E., Mrs. <u>see</u> RICHARDSON, Caroline E.

4546. RICHARDSON, Caroline E., Mrs. George G. Richardson [Br. 1777-1853]
ALT: Richardson, C.E., Mrs.
Poems. By Mrs. George G. Richardson.
Edinburgh: Cadell, 1828. 227p. NUC BL OCLC

4547. RICHARDSON, Charlotte Caroline (Smith) [Br. 1775-1850?]
Harvest, a poem, in two parts; with other poetical pieces.
L: Pr. for the author by W. Thorne, 1818. 112p. NUC BL OCLC

4548. -----Isaac and Rebecca.
L: n.p., 1817. BL

4549. -----Ludolph; or, The light of nature, a poem.
L: Sherwood, 1823. 127p. NUC BL

4550. -----Poems written on different occasions. To which is prefixed some account of the author, together with the reasons which have led to their publications. Ed. Catherine (Harrison) Cappe.
York: Pr. T. Wilson & R. Spence, 1806. 127p. NUC BL OCLC

4551. -----Poems [chiefly composed during the pressure of severe illness].

2d ed. York: n.p., 1806-09. 2v. BL
[Expanded ed. of poems]

4552. -----Waterloo. A poem ... to which is added truth, a vision.
L: n.p., 1815. BL

RICHARDSON, Mrs. George G. see RICHARDSON, Caroline E.

4553. RICHARDSON, Harriette Potter [Am. 19c]
Easter; verses from Fairleigh Cottage.
Providence, RI: n.p., 1884? 12p. NUC OCLC

4554. -----Happy New Year.
Providence?: n.p., n.d. 12 l. 8p. NUC

4555. -----Merry Christmas. Rural rhymes from Fairleigh Cottage.
Providence, RI: n.p., n.d. 13 l. NUC

4556. -----Sylva.
Providence, RI: n.p., n.d. 14 l. 10p. NUC

4557. RICHARDSON, Margaret [Br. 19c]
The buds of hope; a collection of miscellaneous poems.
L: Mitchell & son, 1839. 218p. NUC BL

4558. RICHARDSON, Marian [Br. 19c]
The talk of the household; poems.
L: n.p., 1865. BL

4559. RICHARDSON, Mary E., Mrs. [Am. 19c]
Heart blossoms. Poems.
Memphis, TN: Boyle & Chapman, 1874. 165p. NUC OCLC

4560. RICHEY, Isabel Grimes [Am. b. 1863]
A harp of the West.
Buffalo, NY: C.W. Moulton, 1895. 72p. NUC OCLC

4561. RICHINGS, Rebecca, Miss [Br. 19c] PSEUD: Lady, A
Elijah: a poem. By a lady.
L: L.B. Seeley, 1818. 47p. BL

4562. RICHMOND, Cora Linn Victoria (Scott) Hatch Tappen [Am. 1840-1923] ALT: Hatch, C.L.V.S.; Tappen, C.L.V.
Hesperia. By Cora L.V. Tappan.
Cambridge, MA: H.O. Houghton & co., 1871. 235p. NUC OCLC
[122p. allegorical poem. Second half of vol.: "Ouina," a narrative poem to the American Indian. RPB has 13 unpub. poems "of Ouina, through the mediumship of Mrs. Cora L.V. Richmond."]

4563. -----Six lectures, including invocations and poems, delivered by Mrs. Cora L.V. Richmond.
Chicago: Gilbert & Griffin, 1877. 94p. RPB

4564. -----Spiritual sermons.
n.p.: n.p., n.d. RPB
[Addresses on spiritualism, interspersed with impromptu poems on subjects suggested by the audience.]

4565. RICHMOND, Elizabeth Yates [Am. 19c]
Poems of the western land.
Milwaukee, WI: The author, 1878. 192p. NUC OCLC

4566. RICHMOND, Mary Elizabeth [Br. b. 1853]
Roundels, sonnets and other verses.
Edinburgh: Priv. pr., 1898. NUC

RICHMOND LADY, A, pseud. see WINSTON, Charles P., Mrs.

4567. RICHTER, Ann, Mrs. [Br. 19c]
The nun, and other poems.
Hull: Goddard, 1841. 184p. BL OCLC

4568. RICKER, Charlotte E., Miss [Am. 19c]
Buds.
Boston: Goodwin & Drisko, 1881. 104p. NUC OCLC

RICKEY, Anna S. see ROBERTS, Anna Smith (Rickey)

4569. RICKOFF, Bertha Monroe [Am. 19c]
Ohio, a poem for the centennial celebration, 1888.
Cincinnati, OH: Rob't. Clarke & co., 1888. 13 l. NUC OCLC
[Read at the banquet of the Ohio Society of New York, at Delmonico's April 7, 1888]

4570. RICORD, Elizabeth Stryker [Am. 1788-1865]
Zamba, or The insurrection. A dramatic poem, in five acts.
Cambridge, MA: J. Owen, 1842. 139p. BL OCLC
[History of Martinique]

4571. RIDDELL, Charlotte, Mrs. J.H. Riddell [Br. 1832-1906] PSEUD: Hawthorne, Rainey; Trafford, F.G.

City and suburb; a novel. With her sister-in-law, Eliza Lawson (Cowan). 2d ed. L: C.J. Skeet, 1861. 3v. NUC BL

4572. RIDDELL, Maria (Woodley) [Br. 1772?-1808] ALT: R., M.
The metrical miscellany: consisting chiefly of poems hitherto unpublished.
L: T. Cadell & W. Davies, 1802. 224p. NUC BL OCLC
[Original & selected. At least 9 poems by Riddell.]

RIDPATH, John Clark, ed. see BOLTON, Sarah Tittle (Barrett)

4573. RIGDEN, Martha [Br. 19c]
By a way they knew not; being memorials of blind Fanny Winton, etc.
L: The book society; George Stoneman, 1873. BL
[Incl. poems]

4574. RIGG, Caroline [Br. 1824-1889]
In memoriam. Caroline Rigg. Born May 14th, 1824. Died December 17, 1889.
L: Pr. for priv. circ. by Hazel, Watson & Viney, 1892. BL
[Incl. poems]

RILEY, James Whitcomb, co-author see BOLTON, Sarah Tittle (Barrett)

4575. RIMMERT, Jane [Br. 19c]
Recollections and poems.
L: Pr. for the author by Chiswick press, 1825. 55p. NUC BL OCLC
[Narrative & lyric poems]

4576. RIPLEY, Mary A. [Am. 1831-1893]
Hymn. Written for the quarter-centennial services at the Lafayette St. Presbyterian Church.
Buffalo, NY: n.p., 1870. 1 l. NUC

4577. -----Poems.
Rochester, NY: Adams & Ellis, 1867. 151p. NUC OCLC

4578. RITCHIE, Anna Cora (Ogden) Mowatt [Am. 1819-1870] ALT: Mowatt, Anna Cora (Ogden) PSEUD: Isabel
Pelayo; or, The cavern of Covadonga. A romance. By Isabel.
NY: Harper & bros., 1836. 204p. NUC BL OCLC
[In 6 cantos]

4579. RITCHIE, Mrs. Carnegy [Br. 19c]
Poems, serious and comic.
Edinburgh: Pr. W. Burness, for priv. circ., 1861. 111p. NUC BL

4580. RITCHIE, Maria Kate [Br. 19c]
Love and hatred, and other poems.
Edinburgh: n.p., 1865. BL

4581. RITSON, Anne, Mrs. [Br. 19c]
PSEUD: Lady, A
Exercises for the memory ... .
L: J. & E. Wallis, 1813. 107p. TXU
[In verse]

4582. -----The poetical chain, consisting of miscellaneous poems.
L: n.p., 1811. BL

4583. -----A poetical picture of America, being observations made, during a residence of several years, at Alexandria, and Norfolk, in Virginia; illustrative of the manners and customs of the inhabitants: and interspersed with anecdotes, arising from a general intercourse with society in that country, from the year 1799 to 1807. By a lady.
L: Pr. for author by W. Wilson, 1809. 177p. NUC OCLC

4584. RITTENHOUSE, Laura J. [Am. 19c]
Out of the depths.
Brattleboro, VT: Frank E. Housh, 1886. 18 l. NUC OCLC
[Narrative]

4585. RITTER, Frances Malone (Raymond) [Am. 1830-1890] ALT: Ritter, Fanny Raymond-
Songs and ballads. By Fanny Raymond-Ritter.
NY: F.W. Christern, 1887. 128p. NUC OCLC

RITTER, Fanny Raymond- see RITTER, Frances Malone (Raymond)

4586. RITTER, Mary Louise [Am. 19c]
Sheaves.
Cambridge, MA: Pr. at Riverside press, by H.O. Houghton & co., 1872. 134p. NUC OCLC

RIVERS, PEARL, pseud. see NICHOLSON, Eliza Jane (Poitevent)

4587. ROBARTS, Lilla W. [Am. 19c]
A sheaf for winter birds.
Atlanta, GA: J.P. Harrison & co., pr., 1885. 15p. NUC

4588. ROBBINS, Caroline A. [Am. 19c]
Poems and an anti-slavery drama in prose and verse.
Providence, RI: J.A. & R.A. Reid, pr., 1876. 82p. NUC OCLC
[Poetry honors John Brown & other abolitionists; religious.]

4589. ROBERTS, Anna Smith (Rickey) [Am. 1827-1858] ALT: Rickey, Anna S.
Forest flowers of the West. By Anna S. Rickey.
Philadelphia: Lindsay & Blakiston, 1851. 138p. NUC OCLC

4590. ROBERTS, Betsey Ann (Smith) [Am. 19c]
Original poems.
Patchogue, NY: Patchogue Advance pr., 1893. 163p. NUC OCLC

4591. -----What an old horse said.
Patchogue, NY: Pr. at the office of the "Advance," 1876. 10p. NUC OCLC

4592. ROBERTS, Elizabeth Piddocke [Br. 19c]
Miscellaneous poems.
L: Darton & Clarke, 1845. 167p. NUC BL OCLC

4593. ROBERTS, Ellen, Miss [Br. 19c]
Heathen fables in Christian verse.
L: James Nisbet & co., 1860. 156p. BL
[Based chiefly on Aesop's fables, mainly, but not exclusively for younger readers]

4594. -----Verses by the wayside, and rhymes for the nursery.
L: J. Nisbet & co., 1864. 182p. NUC BL
[Memorial vol., preface dated 1863 indicates many were previously suppressed as too personal. Nature poems & children's verse]

4595. ROBERTS, Emma [Br. 1794?-1840]
Oriental scenes, dramatic sketches and tales, with other poems.
Calcutta: N. Grant, 1830. 263p. NUC BL OCLC

ROBERTS, Emma, comp. see LANDON, Letitia

4596. ROBERTS, Harriet Alicia [Br. 19c]
Forest thoughts. 2 ser.
L: E. Palmer & son, 1852. BL

4597. ROBERTS, Maggie [Am. 19c]
PSEUD: Strebor, Eiggam
Shadows and silver sprays. By Eiggam Strebor.
NY: J.F. Trow & son, 1875. 123p. NUC OCLC

4598. -----The shot heard round the world; or, From the birth of the republic. By Eiggam Strebor.
NY: Lange, Little & co., 1876. 94p. NUC OCLC
[Pub. same year as: "Great battles of the Republic"]

4599. ROBERTS, Mrs. Martyn [Br. 19c]
The spiritual creation, or soul's new birth. A poem in seven books.
L: W. Pickering, 1843. 170p. NUC BL OCLC

4600. ROBERTS, Mary, Sister [Br. 1788-1864] PSEUD: Young Lady, A
Flowers of the matin and even song; or Thoughts for those who rise early.
L: Grant & Griffith, 1845. 192p. NUC BL OCLC

4601. -----The royal exile; or, Poetical epistles of Mary, Queen of Scots, during her captivity in England: with other original poems. By a young lady. Also by her father, The life of Queen Mary.
L: Longman, 1822. 2v. NUC BL OCLC
[DNB attr. to Mary Roberts of Sheffield, 1763-1848, a cousin of this writer. "Life of Queen Mary" to Samuel Roberts, her father]

4602. ROBERTS, Mary [Am. 19c]
Voices from the woodlands, descriptive of forest trees, ferns, mosses, and lichens.
L: Reeve & Benham, 1850. 368p. TXU
[Stories & poetry, mostly original]

4603. ROBERTS, Mary Ann [Br. 19c]
ALT: R., M.A.
Early buds and autumn leaves, gathered by M.A.R.
Sheffield: Pr. Thomas Stannard Algar, 1862. 102p. BL
[Occasional, Biblical, one dramatic dialogue.]

4604. ROBERTS, R., Miss [Br. d. 1788]
Albert; Edward and Laura; and The hermit of Priestland; three legendary tales.
L: T. Cadell, 1783. 68p. NUC BL OCLC
[Gothic tales & 1 occasional poem added.]

4605. ROBERTS, Sarah [Am. 19c]
The voice of the grass. By Sarah Roberts.
Boston: L. Prang & Co., 1887. 263p. [102p. OCLC, 16 l. NUC] NUC OCLC

ROBERTS, Sarah see BOYLE, Sarah Roberts

4606. ROBERTS, Susan Birdsall [Am. 19c]
Short poems.

Elmira, NY: Empire pr. house, 1891. 116p. NUC OCLC

ROBERTS, Theodore, co-author see MACDONALD, Jane Elizabeth Gostwycke (Roberts)

ROBERTS, William Carman, co-author see MACDONALD, Jane Elizabeth Gostwycke (Roberts)

4607. ROBERTSON, Agnes Heatley [Br. 1837-1886]
Extracts from the diary, letters, and miscellaneous writings of Agnes Heatley Robertson.
Glasgow: James Maclehose & sons, 1895. 377p. NUC

4608. ROBERTSON, Eliza Frances [Br. 1771-1805]
Consolatory verses of the late E.F. Robertson. With some account of the life and character of the author. To which are added observations ... on her very remarkable case.
L: Jones & Bumford, 1808. NUC BL
[Poems written by her while in Fleet Prison for debt, pp. 107-173. Elegies & misc. verse]

4609. -----Dividends of immense value; and my claim on others evidenced by indisputable authorities. To which is added a poetical epistle, to a friend.
L: Pr. for the author by J. Cundee, 1801. 36p. BL OCLC

4610. ROBERTSON, Janet Logie [Br. 19c]
New songs of innocence.
Edinburgh: Macniven & Wallace; L: David Stat, 1889. 109p. NUC BL

ROBINSON, A. Mary F. see DUCLAUX, Agnes Mary Frances (Robinson)

4611. ROBINSON, Anne Steele [Am. 19c] PSEUD: Lady, A
Poetic reveries. By a lady.
Baltimore, MD: F. Lucas, jr., 1848. 171p. NUC OCLC

4612. ROBINSON, Edith W. [Br. 19c]
The lay of Saint Jucundas: a legend of York.
L: Swan Sonnenschein, Lowrey & co., 1887. 27 l. NUC BL
[Humorous narrative]

4613. ROBINSON, Ellen, Mrs. [Br. 19c]
Poem written on the death of the Rev. T. Spencer, in four parts.
Liverpool: Mollison, 1811. 31p. NUC BL

4614. -----Poems on different subjects.
Liverpool: n.p., 1814. 32p. NUC

4615. -----The power, wisdom and goodness of God displayed in the works of creation and redemption: a poem.
Liverpool: n.p., 1816. BL

4616. -----A tribute of sorrow and affection to the memory of a beloved son, ... who was ... drowned ... Sept. 23, 1821. Embellished with engravings by the late T. Robinson, the ... subject of the following lines.
Liverpool: n.p., 1821? 16p. NUC BL

4617. ROBINSON, Emma [Br. 1814-1890]
Epithalamium in honour of the marriage of their Royal Highnesses the Prince and Princess of Wales.
L: C. Westerton, 1863. BL

4618. ROBINSON, Lucy Catlin (Bull) [Am. 1861-1903] ALT: Bull, Lucy Catlin
A child's poems from October to October, 1870-1871. By Lucy Catlin Bull.
Hartford, CT: Case, Lockwood & Brainard, priv. pr., 1872. 171p. NUC OCLC
[Written when author was 9 or 10. Incl. 3 plays: Rolling Stone ..., Spilled Milk, & Victor]

4619. ROBINSON, Mary (Darby) [Br. 1758-1800] PSEUD: Juvenal, Horace; Laura Maria; Perdita
Ainsi va le monde, a poem. Inscribed to Robert Merry, esq. by Laura Maria.
L: Pr. J. Bell, 1790. 15p. NUC

4620. -----Captivity; a poem, and Celadon and Lydia; a tale.
L: T. Becket, 1777. 48p. NUC BL OCLC

4621. -----Elegaic verses to a young lady on the death of her brother; who was slain in the late engagement at Boston.
L: J. Johnson, 1776. 17p. NUC

4622. -----Lyrical tales.
L: T.N. Longman & O. Rees, 1800. 218p. NUC BL OCLC

4623. -----Memoirs of the late Mrs. Robinson, written by herself. With

some posthumous pieces. Ed. her daughter, Mary Elizabeth Robinson.
L: R. Phillips, 1801. 4v. NUC BL OCLC
[V. 1-2. Memoirs. V.3. The sylphid, satiric prose fiction. Jasper, a fragment, an unfinished novel. The Savage of Aveyron, a narrative poem. V.4. The progress of liberty, a poem in 2 books.]

4624. -----Modern manners; a poem, in two cantos. By Horace Juvenal.
L: Pr. for author, sold by James Evans, 1793. 32p. NUC

4625. -----Monody to the memory of Sir Joshua Reynolds, late president of the Royal Academy.
L: Pr. J. Bell, 1792. 16p. NUC BL OCLC

4626. -----Monody to the memory of the late Queen of France, Marie Antoinette.
L: Pr. T. Spilsbury & sold by J. Evans, 1793. 27p. NUC BL

4627. -----Ode to the harp of the late accomplished and amiable Louisa Hanway.
L: Pr. J. Bell, 1793. 8p. NUC OCLC

4628. -----Poems.
L: C. Parker, 1775. 134p. NUC

4629. -----Poems.
L: Pr. J. Bell, 1791-93. 2v. NUC OCLC
[Many previously pub. in The Oracle under signatures of Laura, Laura Maria, Oberon, etc. Odes, elegies, stanzas & sonnets.]

4630. -----Poems, by Mrs. Mary Robinson. A new ed.
L: Pr. T. Spilsbury & son; sold by J. Evans, n.d. 266p. NUC

4631. -----The poetical works of the late Mrs. Mary Robinson: including many pieces never before published. Ed. her daughter, Mary Elizabeth Robinson.
L: R. Phillips, 1806. 3v. NUC BL OCLC
[Also pub. L: Jones & co., 1824. 232p. NUC OCLC]

4632. -----Sappho and Phaon. In a series of legitimate sonnets, with thoughts on poetical subjects, and anecdotes of the Grecian poetess.
L: Pr. S. Gosnell, for the author, & sold by Hookham & Carpenter, 1796. 82p. NUC BL OCLC

4633. -----Sight, The cavern of woe, and Solitude. Poems.
L: Pr. T. Spilsbury & son, 1793. 32p. NUC BL OCLC

4634. -----The songs, chorusses, etc. in The Lucky escape, a comic opera as performed at the Theatre-Royal in Drury Lane.
L: Pr. for the author, 1778. 19p. NUC BL OCLC

ROBINSON, Mary Elizabeth, ed. <u>see</u> ROBINSON, Mary (Darby)

4635. ROBINSON, Mary Elizabeth, Miss [Br. d. 1818]
The wild wreath.
L: Mercier, R. Phillips, 1804. 228p. NUC BL OCLC
[Tales, in verse; written by herself and others]

4636. ROBY, Mary K. [Br. 19c]
Children and their thoughts.
L: n.p., 1862. BL

4637. -----Story of a household, and other poems.
Cambridge: n.p., 1862. BL

4638. RODGERS, Vincentia, Miss [Br. 19c]
Cluthan and Malvina; an ancient legend. With other poems.
Belfast: F.D. Finlay, 1823. 102p. NUC BL

ROENA, F. <u>see</u> MEDINI, Frances Roena, Mme.

4639. ROGERS, Alice M. [Am. 19c]
Whiter than snow; poems.
Buffalo, NY: Peter Paul book co., 1896. 230p. NUC OCLC

4640. ROGERS, Eliza [Br. 19c]
Poems.
L: Hurst & Blackett, 1857. 164p. NUC BL

4641. ROGERS, Emma [Br. 19c]
The forget-me-not; or, The troubador's vow, and other tales in prose and poetry.
L: Hatchards, 1883. NUC

4642. ROGERS, Mrs. Joseph [Br. 19c]
Poetical fragments.
L: n.p., 1874. 84p. NUC BL

4643. ROGERS, Mary Eliza [Br. 19c]
My vis-a-vis; or, Harry's account of his courtship, and other poems.

L: Bell & Daldy, 1865. 145p. BL OCLC

ROGERS, Rev. Charles, ed. see NAIRNE, Carolina (Oliphant), Baroness

ROGERS, Samuel, co-author see KNIGHT, Ellis Cornelia

4644. ROHLFS, Anna Katherine (Green), Mrs. Charles Rohlfs [Am. 1846-1935]
ALT: Green, Anna Katherine
The defence of the bride, and other poems.
NY: G.P. Putnam's sons, 1882. 124p. NUC BL OCLC

ROHLFS, Mrs. Charles see ROHLFS, Anna Katherine (Green)

4645. ROLFE, Ann, Mrs. [Br. 19c]
Miscellaneous poems for a winter's evening.
Colchester: Pr. J. Chaplin, 1840? 120p. NUC BL

4646. ROLLESTON, Frances [Br. 1781-1864]
Lights and shadows on the sunny side of Skiddaw.
Keswick: M. Pailey; L: F. & J. Rivington, 1859. BL
[Poems, chiefly original]

4647. -----The pilgrimage of Harmonia. A legend of youth.
L: James Nisbet & co., 1874. BL

4648. ROLLINS, Alice Marland (Wellington) [Am. 1847-1897]
From snow to sunshine.
NY: F.A. Stokes & bros. 1889. 8 l. NUC

4649. -----My welcome beyond, and other poems.
NY: Dodd, Mead & co.; New Haven, CT: Judd & White, 1877. 194p. NUC OCLC

4650. -----The ring of amethyst.
NY: G.P. Putnam's sons, 1878. 108p. NUC OCLC
[Poems]

4651. -----The story of Azron.
NY: Press of J.J. Little, 1895. 21 l. NUC OCLC

ROLLS, Elizabeth Harcourt see MITCHELL, Elizabeth Harcourt (Rolls)

4652. ROLLS, Mrs. Henry [Br. 19c]
The home of love, a poem.
L: n.p., 1817. BL

4653. -----Legends of the North; or, The feudal Christmas; a poem.
L: W. Simpkin & R. Marshall, 1825. 272p. NUC BL

4654. -----Moscow. A poem.
L: Pr. J. Valpy; sold by Law & Whittaker, 1816. 31p. BL
[On Napoleon's destruction of Moscow]

4655. -----A poetical address to Lord Byron.
L: W. Hone, 1816. 8p. NUC

4656. -----Sacred sketches from scripture history.
L: Sold by Law & Whittaker, 1815. NUC BL
[With other religious poems]

ROLT, Elisabeth see HILL, Phillipina (Burton)

4657. ROLT, Elizabeth [Br. 18c]
PSEUD: Lady, A
Miscellaneous poems.
L: Pr. for the author & sold by H. Turpin, 1768. 54p. BL
[Incl. satire, odes, occasional, pastoral "Dialogue between the dead and the living."]

4658. -----Miscellaneous poems, written by a lady.
L: Pr. for the author by S. Chandler, 1768. 3v. NUC BL
[NUC attr. to Philippina (Burton) Hill. BL has 1 vol. work which lists author on t.p. as Elizabeth Rolt of Chesham, Bucks. See entry above.]

ROOTSEY, Samuel, co-author see TURNER, Margaret

ROSCOE, Jane Elizabeth see HORNBLOWER, Jane Elizabeth (Roscoe)

4659. ROSE, Heloise Durant [19c] ALT: Durant, Heloise
Dante: a dramatic poem.
L: K. Paul, Trench & co., 1889. 136p. NUC BL OCLC
[In three acts & a prologue]

4660. -----Pine needles; or, Sonnets and songs.
NY & L: G.P. Putnam's sons, 1884. 160p. NUC OCLC

ROSE MATILDA, pseud. see DACRE, Charlotte

4661. ROSEBOOM, Jane [Am. 19c]
The lawgiver and other poems.

Hillsdale, MI: The author, 1873. 216p. NUC OCLC

4662. -----Poems on various subjects. Hillsdale, MI: The author, 1869. 199p. NUC OCLC

4663. ROSHER, Ethel Margaret [Br. 19c]
Poems.
L: Kegan Paul & co., pr. for priv. circ., 1896. 62p. BL OCLC

4664. ROSLING, Eliza [Br. 19c]
Verses.
L: Barrett, priv. pr., 1863. 47p. BL OCLC

ROSLYN, pseud. <u>see</u> SINCLAIR, Margaret A.

4665. ROSS, Dora [Br. 19c]
Christmas joy and peace. A poem.
L: Religious Tract Society, 1896. BL

4666. -----Heavenly visitants.
L: Religious Tract Society, 1896. BL

4667. -----Risen to glory: an Easter poem.
NY: Art Lithographic pub. co.; L: Artistic Lithographic co., 189-. 8p. OCLC

4668. ROSS, Nancy, Mrs. [Am. 19c]
The angel band. Poems.
Oil City, PA: Pr. the Oil City Derrick, 1893. 97p. NUC

4669. ROSSA, Mary Jane (Irwin) O'Donovan [Am. b. 1845] ALT: O'Donovan, Mary Jane (Irwin)
Irish lyrical poems. By Mrs. O'Donovan (Rossa).
NY: P.M. Haverty, 1868. BL
[Dedicated to her husband, Jeremiah, sentenced to life in prison for his "devotion to the cause of Ireland"]

4670. ROSSETTI, Christina Georgina [Br. 1830-1894]
The face of the deep: a devotional commentary on the Apocalypse.
L: Soc. for Promoting Christian Knowledge; NY: E. & J.B. Young & co., 1892. 552p. NUC OCLC
[Includes poems.]

4671. -----Goblin market and other poems.
Cambridge: Macmillan, 1862. 192p. NUC BL OCLC

4672. -----Maude; a story for girls.
L: J. Bowden, 1897. 80p. Chicago: H.S. Stone & co., 1897. 122p. NUC BL OCLC
[prose and verse]

4673. -----Monna innominata, sonnets and songs.
Portland, ME: T.B. Mosher, 1899. 93p. NUC OCLC

4674. -----New poems by Christina Rossetti, hitherto unpublished or uncollected. Ed. William Michael Rossetti.
NY & L: Macmillan & co., 1896. 397p. NUC OCLC

4675. -----Outlines for illuminating. Consider. A poem.
NY: n.p., 1866. BL

4676. -----A pageant, and other poems.
Boston: Roberts bros., 1881. 208p. L: Macmillan, 1881. 198p. NUC BL OCLC

4677. -----The prince's progress and other poems.
L: Macmillan & co., 1866. 216p. NUC BL OCLC

4678. -----Verses ... dedicated to her mother.
L: Priv. pr. at G. Polidori's, 1847. 66p. NUC BL OCLC
[Written between ages 12 to 16]

ROSSETTI, William Michael, ed. <u>see</u> ROSSETTI, Christina Georgina

4679. ROSSITER, Mary [Br. 19c]
The gathered lily and other poems.
L: n.p., 1873. BL

4680. -----Mildred Gower, and other poems.
L: n.p., 1875. BL

4681. ROUSE, T., Miss [Br. 19c]
Naomi; a dramatic poem, and other pieces.
L: Hamilton, Adams, 1845? [1850? BL] 90p. NUC BL OCLC

4682. -----Poems, by Miss T. Rouse of Cley.
Holt: J. Shalders, 1840. 156p. NUC BL

4683. ROWBOTHAM, Elizabeth F. A. [Br. 19c]
Harps of Zion; a collection of poems.
Edinburgh: n.p., 1875. BL

4684. ROWDEN, Frances Arabella [Br. 19c]

The pleasures of friendship. A poem, in two parts.
L: Pr. A.J. Valpy, sold by Longman, Hurst, Rees & Orme, 1810. 139p. NUC BL OCLC

4685. -----Poetical introduction to the study of botany.
L: Pr. T. Bensley, 1801. 167p. NUC BL OCLC

4686. ROWE, Elizabeth (Singer), Mrs. Thomas Rowe [Br. 1674-1737] PSEUD: Philomela
A collection of divine hymns and poems upon several occasions: by the E. of Roscommon, J. Dryden, Mr. Dennis, Mr. Norris, Mrs. Katherine Phillips, Philomela and others.
L: J. Baker, 1709. 216p.
[First pub. 1704 as: Divine hymns and poems in several occasions. NUC]

4687. -----Friendship in death; in twenty letters from the dead to the living. To which are added letters moral and entertaining, in prose and verse.
L: n.p., n.d. 292p. NUC BL

4688. -----Friendship in death ... .
3d ed. L: T. Worrall, 1733-34. 70, 138, 125, 129p. NUC BL OCLC
[NUC note on 1731 ed. says "written originally by Madam Dacier; trans. by R. Bundy." Dublin: n.p., 1731.]

4689. -----The hermit; a poem.
Philadelphia: n.p., 1753. 8p. NUC

4690. -----The history of Joseph. A poem. In eight books.
L: T. Worrall, 1736. 78p. NUC BL OCLC

4691. -----Letters on various occasions, in prose and verse.
L: T. Worrall, 1729. 218p. NUC OCLC

4692. -----Letters moral and entertaining, in prose and verse.
L: T. Worrall, 1729-31. NUC OCLC

4693. -----The poetical works of ... including the history of Joseph. In ten books and an account of her life and writings.
L: W. Suttaby & C. Carroll, 1804. 261p. TXU

4694. -----The miscellaneous works in prose and verse of Mrs. Elizabeth Rowe. The greater part now first published, ... from her original manuscripts, by Mr. Theophilus Rowe.
L: R. Hett & R. Dodsley, 1739. 2v. NUC BL OCLC
[Also incl., following a sep. title page, dated 1739, her husband, Thomas Rowe's poems] [Incl. trans. from Tasso; 2 pastorals, 2 letters in verse, verses, last letter & will.]

4695. -----Philomela: or, Poems by Mrs. E. Singer.
2d ed. L: E. Curll, 1737. 184p. NUC BL OCLC
[Preface by Elizabeth Johnson. A reprint of her poems on several occasions, 1736.]

4696. -----Poems on several occasions. Written by Philomela.
1st ed. L: John Dunton, 1696. 12, 72, 69p. NUC BL OCLC

4697. ROWE, Hannah [Br. 18c]
A Pindaric poem. Consisting of versified selections from the Revelation of St. John.
L: James Evans, 1789. 48p. BL

4698. ROWE, M. F., Mrs. [Am. 19c]
The Master's messenger; or, Gospel truths in rhyme. Collection of spiritual songs and short poems, principally devoted to the subject of scriptural holiness.
San Francisco: Jos. Winterburn & co., pr., 1884. 97p. NUC OCLC

ROWE, Theophilus, comp. see ROWE, Elizabeth (Singer)

ROWE, Thomas, co-author see ROWE, Elizabeth (Singer)

ROWE, Mrs. Thomas see ROWE, Elizabeth (Singer)

ROWENA, pseud. see LITTLE, Sophia Louisa (Robbins)

4699. ROWLAND, Catherine Anne [Br. 19c] ALT: R., C.A.
Happy hours; or, Affection's whispers. Miscellaneous poems, domestic and sacred. By C.A.R.
L: n.p., 1861. BL

4700. ROWLES, Charlotte [Br. 19c]
Eastern scenes in early ages.
L: n.p., 1835. BL

4701. -----Nadaber, a tradition: with other poems. With Martha Rowles.
L: n.p., 1829. BL

ROWLES, Martha, co-author see ROWLES, Charlotte

4702. ROWLEY, Frances A., Mrs. [Am. 19c]
Poems for the times: devoted to woman's rights, temperance, etc.
Cincinnati, OH: Miami pr. & pub. co., 1871. 317p. NUC OCLC

4703. ROWLEY, Mary S. [Am. 19c]
Froth and foam.
Rochester, NY: Union & Advertiser co., pr., 1888. 85p. NUC OCLC
[Incl. dramatic poem, rhymed comedy about modern love.]

4704. ROWSON, Susanna (Haswell), Mrs. William Rowson [Br./Am. c1762-1824]
Miscellaneous poems.
Boston: Pr. for the author by Gilbert & Dean, State Street ... sold by W.P. & L. Blake, Cornhill bros., 1804. 227p. NUC BL OCLC
[Contains poems from: Poems on various subjects]

4705. -----A trip to Parnassus, or, The judgment of Apollo on dramatic authors and performers. A poem.
L: Pr. John Abraham, 1788. 26p. NUC

ROWSON, Mrs. William see ROWSON, Susanna (Haswell)

4706. RUDDY, Ella Augusta (Giles) [Am. b. 1851] ALT: Giles, Ella A.
Flowers of the spirit. By Ella A. Giles.
Chicago: Charles H. Kerr & co., 1891. 93p. NUC OCLC

4707. RUDE, Ellen Sergeant [Am. b. 1838]
Magnolia leaves, poems.
Buffalo, NY: C.W. Moulton, 1891. 123p. NUC

4708. RUDLAND, Mary [Br. 1854-1871]
ALT: Rudland, Rosetta Mary
Mary Rudland: her sketches in prose and verse. Ed. her father, Robert Rudland.
L: John Snow & co., 1873. BL
[Lyric poems, 6 school essays, 5 short stories, 3 of which are for children]

RUDLAND, Rosetta Mary see RUDLAND, Mary

RUFFIN, Mrs. Frank G. see RUFFIN, Margaret Ellen (Henry)

4709. RUFFIN, Margaret Ellen (Henry), Mrs. Frank G. Ruffin [Am. d. 1941]
ALT: Henry, M.E.
Drifting leaves. By M.E. Henry.
NY: The Catholic pub. soc.; L: Burns & Oates, 1884. 46p. NUC OCLC

4710. RUNCIE, Constance Owen (Faunt Le Roy) [Am. 1836-1911]
Poems, dramatic and lyric.
NY: G.P. Putnam's sons, 1888. NUC OCLC
[Dramatic poems for reading only.]

4711. RUNNELLS, Eliza B. (Dade) [Am. 19c]
The wreath of love.
NY: Pub. for the authoress, 1852. 162p. NUC OCLC

4712. RUSSELL, Caroline [Br. 19c]
The English captive.
Lincoln: Bradbury & Dent, 1823. 112p. BL
[Captured by French privateer, imprisoned in Holland; incl. poems]

4713. RUSSELL, Caroline E. [Am. 19c]
Blossoms of thought.
Boston: Arena pub. co., 1895. 87p. NUC OCLC
[Devotional prose, 15 religious poems]

4714. RUSSELL, Kate (Pyer) [Br. 19c]
Wayside leaves. Poems various.
L: J. Snow & co., 1880. 60p. BL

RUSTIC, RUTH, pseud. see ORME, Cornelia J.

4715. RUTHERFORD, Eliza [Br. 19c]
Maternal sketches; with other poems.
L: Holdsworth & Bell, 1832. 176p. NUC OCLC

4716. RUTLAND, Jane [Br. 19c]
Poems, grave and gay, from the Finchley Woods.
L: n.p., 1865. BL

4717. RUTSON, Charlotte Fanny [Br. 19c]
Some verses.
L: Priv. pr., 1887? 78p. BL

4718. RYAN, Eliza, Mrs. [Br. 19c]
Poems on several occasions.
Dublin: n.p., 1816. BL

RYAN, Eva, comp. see ALLERTON, Ellen Palmer, Mrs.

4719. RYAN, Margaret [Br. 19/20c]
Songs of remembrance.
Dublin: M.H. Gill, 1889. 136p. NUC BL OCLC

[Poems appeared in The Irish Monthly, chiefly lyrics]

4720. RYAN, Mary C. [Am. 19c]
Poems.
NY: John B. Alden, 1890. 62p. NUC OCLC
[Cover title: Poems of hope]

RYVES, Eliza see RYVES, Elizabeth

4721. RYVES, Elizabeth [Br. 1750-1797] ALT: Ryves, Eliza
Dialogue in the Elysian fields between Caesar and Cato.
L: n.p., 1784. BL

4722. -----The Hastiniad; a heroick poem in three cantos.
L: J. Debrett, 1785. 21p. NUC BL OCLC
[Satire on Warren Hastings and his wife]

4723. -----Ode to ... Lord Milton, infant son of Earl Fitzwilliam.
L: n.p., 1787. BL

4724. -----Ode to the Rev. Mr. Mason. By Eliza Ryves.
L: J. Dodsley, Pall Mall, 1780. 15p. NUC BL

4725. -----Poems on several occasions.
L: Pr. for the author & sold by J. Dodsley, 1777. 176p. NUC BL OCLC
[Incl. The prude: a comic opera. 3 acts]

4726. RYVES, F., Mrs. [Br. 19c]
Cumbrian legends, or, Tales of other times: dedicated to Her Royal Highness, the Princess Charlotte of Wales.
Edinburgh: Pr. for the author, 1812. 184p. NUC BL OCLC

S., MISS, pseud. see STOCKDALE, Mary R.

S., A. see SHIPTON, Anna

S., Mrs. C.N see STREATFEILD, Sophia Charlotte

S., E. see SCUDDER, Eliza

S., E. see STRUTT, Elizabeth

S., E.M. see STEWART, Elizabeth M., Miss

S., E.S.G. see SAUNDERS, Emily Susan Goulding

S., F.M. see SUTCLIFFE, Frances Mary

S., F.M., pseud. see MORRIS, Margaret H.

S., I., co-author see EVANS, Margaret Freeman

S., M. see SMEDLEY, Menella Bute

S., M. see SMITH, Mary

S., M.C. see SPARKS, Mary Crowninshield (Silsbee)

S., M.E. see SIMPSON, Mary E.

S., M.E.W. see SHERWOOD, Mary Elizabeth (Wilson)

S., M.J.M. see SWEAT, Margaret Jane (Mussey)

S., M.P. see SWAIN, M.P., Miss

S., S. see SHEPPARD, Sarah, Miss

S., S.G. see STOCK, Sarah Geraldina

4727. S...., Lady [Br. 19c]
Sacred mountains and waters versified. By Lady S... .
2d ed. L: Jas. Burns, 1841. 32p. NUC BL

S---, Elizabeth see SMITH, Elizabeth

4728. SAFFERY, Maria Grace (Andrews) [Br. 1772-1858]
Poems on sacred subjects.
L: Hamilton, Adams, & co.; Edinburgh: Waugh & Innes, 1834. 206p. NUC BL OCLC

4729. ST. AUBYN, Mary [Br. 1813-1838]
The deformed, Jessy Bell, and other poems.
L: W. Pickering, 1842. 190p. NUC BL OCLC

4730. -----Poems.
Torquay: Pr. E. Cockrem, 1837. 36p. OCLC

ST. GEORGE, Melesina (Chenevix) see TRENCH, Melesina (Chenevix) St. George

4731. ST. JOHN, Mary [Br. 19c] ALT: Mary

Elrauna: a legend of the 13th century in four cantos, with notes. By Mary. Dublin: W.H. Tyrell [Tyrreli NUC], 1815. 124p. NUC BL OCLC

4732. SALWAY, Charlotte Maria (Birch) [Br. 19c] ALT: Birch, C. M.
Reveries of song. By C.M. Birch.
L: Bell & Daldy, 1871. 156p. BL OCLC
[Lyrics & a narrative poem in 5 pts.: Delphine]

4733. SAMUDA, Miss [Br. 19c]
Bertha Devreux: an incident in the Wars of the Roses.
L: Richard Bentley, 1866. 114p. BL

SANDBACH, Mrs. Henry Roscoe <u>see</u> SANDBACH, Margaret Roscoe

4734. SANDBACH, Margaret Roscoe, Mrs. Henry Roscoe Sandbach [Br. 1812-1852]
Aurora, and other poems. By Mrs. H.R. Sandbach.
L: William Pickering, 1850. 157p. NUC BL OCLC

4735. -----Giuliano de' Medici; a drama ... with other poems.
L: W. Pickering, 1842. 213p. NUC BL OCLC
[5 acts, on his assassination; misc. poetry]

4736. -----Poems.
L: W. Pickering, 1840. 121p. NUC BL OCLC

4737. SANDERS, Charlotte Elizabeth [Br. 18c]
Poems on various subjects.
L: Pr. at the Logographic press, sold by Messrs. Wilkie, 1787. 200p. NUC BL

4738. SANDERS, Eliza Whitfield, Miss [Br. 1832?-1846]
Poems: chiefly devotional.
L: Pr. for priv. circ., Maurice & co., 1850. 33p. NUC

4739. SANDERS, Maria Ruth [Br. 19c]
Original rhymes.
L: W. & T. Piper, 1851. 104p. NUC BL
[A separate work; incl. 3 essays in prose]

4740. -----Original rhymes on various subjects.
L: Roberts & Blatch, 1833. 211p. NUC BL

4741. SANDERSON, A., Mrs. [Br. 19c]
A letter addressed to the officers of the Army of England, containing a valuable discovery, wherby victory may be obtained without bloodshed. Also War in the West; or 400 pound weight of coin lost; a poem.
North Shields: n.p., 1819. BL

4742. -----A poem ... inscribed to ... the Queen [Caroline].
North Shields: Pr. for the author by J.K. Pollock, 1820. 7p. NUC BL

4743. -----Poems on various subjects.
North Shields: n.p., 1819. BL

4744. SANDERSON, Amanda Cary [Am. 19c]
Echoes along the shore.
Kansas City, MO: Hudson-Kimberly pub. co., 1889. 214p. NUC OCLC
[Poems on the creation, the fall, and redemption]

4745. SANFORD, Katharine I. [Am. 19c]
A new book of charades.
NY: James T. White & co., 1896. 53p. RPB
[Puzzle rhymes.]

4746. SANFORD, Mary Fred, Mrs. [Am. 19c]
For you and me are these scattered leaves regathered.
Great Barrington, MA: Pr. for priv. circ., 1879? 104p. NUC OCLC
[Misc. poetry; prose incl. travel notes & essays]

4747. SANGSTER, Margaret Elizabeth (Munson) [Am. 1838-1912]
Easter bells; poems.
NY: Harper & bros., 1897. 143p. NUC OCLC

4748. -----Home and heaven: a book of thoughts and sketches.
Boston: American Tract Soc., 1868. 1v. BL NUC
[Chiefly religious; poems and short stories]

4749. -----On the road home; poems.
NY: Harper & bros., 1893. 144p. NUC OCLC

4750. -----Poems of the household.
Boston: J.R. Osgood & co., 1882. 259p. NUC BL OCLC

4751. SANTLEY, Mary McDermott, Mrs. [Am. 19/20c]
An elect lady.
Cleveland, OH: n.p., 1892. 2p. NUC
[Poem on Susanna Wesley]

4752. -----Margery Rae.
Cleveland, OH: n.p., 1892. 2p. NUC
[Temperance verse]

4753. SARGANT, Alice [Br. 19/20c]
A book of ballads.
L: Elkins Mathews, 1898. 46p. NUC BL OCLC

4754. -----Master death, mocker and mocked.
L: J.M. Dent & co., 1899. 32p. BL

4755. SARGANT, Jane Alice [Br. 19c]
PSEUD: Englishwoman, An
Britannia's appeal.
L: n.p., 1836. 4p. BL
[Poem on the war between England and America]

4756. -----Extracts from the pilgrimage of St. Caroline; with notes, by an Englishwoman.
L: W. Wright, 1821. 87p. NUC BL
[Satire on Queen Caroline with other misc. verse satires]

4757. -----Sonnets, and other poems.
L: n.p., 1817. 120p. NUC BL

4758. SARGEANT, Anne Maria [Br. 1809/10-1852]
The Isle of Wight, and other poems.
L: n.p., 1832. BL

4759. SARGENT, Mary [Am. 19c]
Easter morn. A poem.
Plaistow?, NH: n.p., 1882. NUC

4760. SARTORIS, Adelaide (Kemble) [Br. 1814?-1878/9] ALT: Kemble, Adelaide
Past hours. Ed. May E. Gordon.
L: R. Bentley & sons, 1880. 2v. NUC BL OCLC
[Tales and poems]

4761. SATCHELL, Agnes F. [Br. 19c]
Miscellaneous poems.
Antigua: n.p., 1852. BL

4762. SAUNDERS, Emily Susan Goulding [Br. 19c] ALT: S., E.S.G.
David. A poem. By E.S.G.S.
L: n.p., 1880. 45p. BL

4763. -----Esther.
L: n.p., 1870. 8p. BL

4764. -----Ezra.
L: n.p., 1869. 4p. BL

4765. -----Jacob. A poem, by E.S.G.S.
L: E. Edey, 1889. 46p. BL

4766. -----Missionary-pictures. By E.S.G.S.
L: n.p., 1871. 24p. BL

4767. -----Nehemiah: or, The memory of God.
Ipswich: n.p., 1874. BL

4768. -----The new Christian year; or, Thoughts on the present lectionary. By E.S.G.S.
L: George Stoneman, 1891. 253p. BL

4769. -----The rivers, rocks and mountains of the Bible. By E.S.G.S.
L: n.p., 1866. 20p. BL

4770. -----Thistle-down. By E.S.G.S.
L: n.p., 1866. 53p. BL

4771. -----The three-fold cord: faith, hope and love.
L: W.B. Whittingham & co., 1879. 27p. BL

4772. SAUNDERS, Mary [Br. 19c]
Songs, sonnets, and miscellaneous poems of John and Mary Saunders.
L: n.p., 1838. BL

4773. SAVAGE, Anna [Br. 19c]
Angel visits. Poems.
L: Longman, Brown, Green & Longmans, 1845. 172p. NUC BL

4774. SAVAGE, M., Mrs. [Br. 18c]
Poems on various subjects and occasions.
L: C. Parker, 1777. 2v. NUC BL

SAVORY, Martha <u>see</u> YEARDLEY, Martha (Savory)

4775. SAWTELLE, Mary Anna [Am. b. 1861]
An olio of verse. With Alice Elizabeth (Sawtelle) Randall [1865-1909].
NY: Knickerbocker press; L: G.P. Putnam's sons, 1895. 52p. NUC BL OCLC

4776. SAWYER, Anna, Mrs. [Br. 19c]
Poems on various subjects. ... With notes, historical and explanatory.
Birmingham: Pr. for the author by Swinney & Hawkins, 1801. 84p. NUC BL OCLC

SAWYER, Mrs. C.B. <u>see</u> SAWYER, Elizabeth E. Turner

SAWYER, Caroline Mehitabel (Fisher), comp. <u>see</u> SCOTT, Julia H. (Kinney)

4777. SAWYER, Elizabeth E. Turner, Mrs. C.B. Sawyer [Am. 1822-1900]
The singing brook.
Chicago: Justitia pub. co., 1891. 5 l. NUC OCLC

4778. SAWYER, Harriet Adams, Mrs. [Am. 19c]
A song of the Christ.
Boston: D. Lothrop co., 1893. 40p. NUC OCLC

4779. SAXBY, Jane Euphemia (Browne) [Br. 19c] ALT: Browne, Jane Euphemia
The dove and the cross and other thoughts in verse.
L: J. Nisbet, 1857. 136p. NUC BL OCLC

4780. -----The voice of the bird.
L: Seeley, Jackson & Halliday, 1875. 71p. BL

4781. SAXBY, Jessie Margaret (Edmondston) [Br. 1842-1940]
Glamour from Argyllshire.
Edinburgh & Inverary: John Rodger, 1874. 54p. BL OCLC
[Chiefly poetry]

4782. -----Heim-land and heim-folk.
Edinburgh: R. & R. Clark, 1892. 85p. NUC OCLC
[Prose sketches and poems of the Shetland Islands.]

4783. -----Lichens from the old rock.
Edinburgh: W.P. Nimmo, 1868. 188p. NUC OCLC

4784. SAYER, Frances Anne [Br. 19c]
Gold and tinsel, with other poems.
L: n.p., 1873. BL

4785. SAYERS, Frances H. [Br. 19c] PSEUD: Cecil, Lady Frances H.
Paradise found, and other poems. By Lady Frances H. Cecil.
L: J. Nisbet & co., 1882. 68p. BL

4786. SCAIFE, Elizabeth, Miss [Br. 1817-1842]
Poems on various subjects. By the late Miss Elizabeth Scaife.
Liverpool: W. Grapel, 1846. 235p. NUC BL OCLC

4787. SCHENCK, Jessie (Glenn) [Am. 19c] ALT: Glenn, Jessie
Poems. By Jessie Glenn.
Pottsville, PA: Bannan & Ramsey, 1871. 168p. NUC OCLC

4788. SCHEYER, Lena [Br. 19c]
"In memoriam." The widow and the orphans' cry.
L: n.p., 1884. BL

4789. SCHIMMELPENNINCK, Mary Anne (Galton) [Br. 1778-1856]
Asaph; or, The Hernhutters, being a rhythmical sketch of the principal events ... in the modern history of the Church of Unitas Fratrum commonly called Moravians.
L: Ogle, Tunon & co., 1822. 140p. NUC BL
[Poem on Moravian history. Hymns interspersed.]

SCHNECK, Rev. B.S., ed. see PEIRSON, Lydia Jane (Wheeler)

4790. SCHRACK, Annie M. [Am. 19c]
Wayside gleanings.
Providence, RI: Standard pr. co., 1896. 20 l. NUC OCLC
[18 lyrics]

4791. SCHUELLERMANN, Carrie V. [Am. 19c]
Buds and blossoms.
Philadelphia: J.B. Lippincott co., 1890. 75p. NUC OCLC

4792. SCHULTE, Mary Jemima (MacColl) [Am. b. 1847] ALT: MacColl, Mary Jemima
Bide a wee, and other poems.
Buffalo, NY: Peter Paul & bro., 1880., c1879. 103p. NUC OCLC

4793. SCOONES, Emily, Mrs. [Br. 19c]
A poem, written on the sermon preached by ... C.H. Spurgeon, from the words "His name shall be called wonderful." Isaiah ix.16.
L: n.p., 1858. BL

4794. SCOT, Elizabeth (Rutherford), Mrs. Walter Scot [Br. 1729-1789]
Alonzo and Cora (from Marmontel's Incas of Peru); with other original poems, principally elegaic ... To which are added letters in verse, by [Thomas] Blacklock and [Robert] Burns.
L: Bunney & Gold, 1801. 168p. NUC BL OCLC

SCOT, Mrs. Walter see SCOT, Elizabeth (Rutherford)

4795. SCOTT, Catharine Amy (Dawson) [Br. 19/20c] ALT: Dawson, C. Amy; Dawson-Scott, C. A.
Idylls of womanhood.
L: Heinemann, 1892. 120p. NUC BL OCLC

4796. -----Sappho.

L: Kegan Paul, Trench & co., 1889. 210p. NUC BL

4797. SCOTT, Christabel [Br. 19c]
PSEUD: Sheila
Iona: a romance of the West.
L: E. Stock, 1896. 204p. BL

4798. -----Sketches from nature: a book of verses. By Sheila.
L: Kegan Paul & co., 1891. 101p. BL

SCOTT, Dorothea see HOGBEN, Dorothea (Scott) Gotherson

4799. SCOTT, Elizabeth, Miss [Br. 19c]
Specimens of British poetry. Chiefly selected from authors of high celebrity, and interspersed with original writings.
Edinburgh: Pr. James Ballantyne & co., 1823. 395p. NUC BL OCLC
[Anthology of famous 18 & 19c poets with poems by Scott]

4800. SCOTT, Honoria [Br. 19c]
Amatory tales of Spain, France, Switzerland and the Mediterranean: containing The fair Andalusian; Rosolia of Palermo; and The Maltese portrait: interspersed with pieces of original poetry.
L: J. Dick, 1810. 4v. NUC BL OCLC

4801. SCOTT, Jane M. [Br. 19c]
Sir Ralph de Fynes, and other ballads and poems.
L: T. Richardson & son, 1865. 83p. BL

4802. SCOTT, Mrs. John [Br. 19c]
Thoughts in verse.
L: n.p., 1846. BL

4803. SCOTT, Julia H. (Kinney) [Am. 1809-1842]
Memoir of Mrs. Julia H. Scott; with her poems and selections from her prose. Comp. Caroline Mehitabel (Fisher) Sawyer.
Boston: A. Tompkins, 1853. 432p. NUC BL OCLC

4804. -----Poems ... together with a brief memoir, by Miss Sarah Carter Edgarton [Mayo].
Boston: A. Tompkins & B.B. Mussey, 1843. 216p. NUC OCLC
[Misc. poems, all by Scott.]

4805. SCOTT, Maria L. (Doud) [Am. 1828-1870] PSEUD: Vale, Ella
Autumn leaves.
Des Moines, IA: Mills & co., 1880. 251p. NUC OCLC
[Nature & memorial poems; previously pub. in newspaper under pseud., Ella Vale]

4806. SCOTT, Mary, Miss [Br. 1774-1788]
The female advocate; a poem occasioned by reading Mr. Duncome's Feminead.
L: Pr. for the author & sold by Wm. Flexney, 1770. 35p. NUC BL OCLC

4807. -----Messiah: a poem in two parts.
Bath: Pr. R. Cruttwell, 1788. 55p. NUC BL OCLC

4808. SCOTT, Rebecca [Br. 19c]
Echoes from Tyrconnel: a collection of legendary and other poems.
Londonderry: J. Colhoun, 1880. 215p. NUC BL

4809. -----A glimpse of spring: a prize poem, Gertrude's dower: and other poems.
Dublin: n.p., 1870. BL

SCOTT, Sir Walter, ed. see BARNARD, Anne (Lindsay), Lady

SCOTT, Walter, ed. see SEWARD, Anna

4810. SCRAMM, Emma I. [Am. 19c]
PSEUD: Lythwyn, Edda
Glismont. A tale in verse. By Edda Lythwyn.
Chicago: H.J. Smith & Simon, 1897. 348p. NUC

4811. SCUDDER, Eliza [Am. 1821-1896]
ALT: S., E.
Hymns and sonnets. By E.S.
Boston: Lockwood, Brooks & co., 1880. 50p. NUC BL OCLC

4812. SEARLE, Ann Amelia [Br. 19c]
Lasting happiness. Poems.
L: n.p., 1866. BL

4813. SEATON, Rose [Br. 19/20c]
Romances and poems.
L: Simpkin, Marshall, Hamilton, Kent & co., 1891. 119p. NUC BL OCLC
[Primarily poetry. Incl. Andromeda, 2 pt. dramatic poem; Fleurette, gothic romance, 5 cantos and other narrative & lyric poems.]

4814. SEDGWICK, Catherine Maria [Am. 1789-1867]
A beautiful spirit set free.
L: n.p., 1869. BL

4815. -----A distick for disturbed districts.
L: R. Washbourne, 1869. 8p. BL

4816. SEDGWICK, Susan Ann Livingston (Ridley) [Am. 1789-1867]
Alida: or, Miscellaneous sketches of incidents during the late American War ... with poems.
3d ed. NY: The author, 1841. 244p. NUC OCLC

4817. -----Founded on fact. By an unknown author ... .
3d ed. NY: The author, 244p. NUC OCLC

4818. SEELY, Catherine [Am. 1799-1838]
Memoir of Catherine Seely, late of Darien, Connecticut.
NY: Collins bros. & co., 1843. 140p. NUC OCLC
[Incl. poetry]

4819. SELDEN, Almira [Am. 19c]
Effusions of the heart.
Bennington, VT: Pr. Darius Clark, 1820. 152p. NUC BL OCLC
[Incl. poems & 2 plays: "Naomi," 5 scenes, verse; "The Irish exiles in America," 5 scenes, prose]

4820. SELLON, Martha Ann [Br. 19c]
The Caledonian comet elucidated.
L: Rivington, 1811. NUC BL
[A reply in verse to "The Caledonian comet," a satire on Sir Walter Scott by John Taylor.]

4821. -----Individuality; or, The causes of reciprocal misapprehension: in six books.
L: R. Baldwin, 1814. 438p. NUC BL

4822. SEMPLE, Agnes Sophia (Hunter) [Br. 19c] ALT: Hunter, Agnes Sophia
Miscellanies, designed chiefly for the benefit of female readers. By A.S. Hunter.
L: Vernor, Hood, & Sharpe, 1810. 198p. BL
[2d ed. rev. & enlarged. Harwick: n.p., 1811. BL]

4823. SERGEANT, Emily Frances Adeline [Br. 1851-1904]
Poems ... With an introduction by Adeline [Jane (Hall) Sergeant].
L: Hamilton, Adams & co., 1866. 86p. BL

4824. SERGEANT, Emma Louisa [Br. 19c]
Co-operation. A poem.
L: W. Strange, 1832. 27p. BL

SERGEANT, Jane (Hall), comp. see SERGEANT, Emily Frances Adeline

4825. SERGEANT, Jane (Hall) PSEUD: Adeline
Missionary lays; and other poems. By Adeline.
L: J. Mason, 1848. 136p. NUC BL

4826. -----Scenes in the West Indies; and other poems. By Adeline.
2d ed. L: J. Mason, 1849. 130p. NUC BL

4827. SERRANO, Mary Jane (Christie) [Am. d. 1923]
Destiny, and other poems.
NY: G.P. Putnam's sons, 1883. 189p. NUC BL OCLC

SERRES, Mrs. J.T. see SERRES, Olivia (Wilmot)

4828. SERRES, Olivia (Wilmot), Mrs. J.T. Serres [Br. 1772-1834] ALT: W.S.--, Olivia PSEUD: Cumberland, Princess of; Lady, A
Flights of fancy, or, Poetical effusions, by a lady ... .
L: Pr. J. Long, 1791. 46p. NUC
[L: Pr. D.N. Shury for J. Ridgway, 1805. DNB]

4829. SEWALL, Harriet Winslow [Am. 1819-1889]
Poems. Ed. Ednah Dow Littlehale Cheney.
Cambridge, MA: Riverside press, 1889. 124p. NUC OCLC

SEWARD, Anna, co-author see MILLER, Anna (Riggs), Lady

4830. SEWARD, Anna [Br. 1742-1809] PSEUD: Swan of Litchfield, The
Blindness, a poem.
Sheffield: J. Montgomery, 1806. NUC BL

4831. -----Elegy on Captain Cook. To which is added, an Ode to the sun.
L: J. Dodsley, 1780. 23p. NUC BL OCLC

4832. -----Llangollen vale, with other poems.
L: G. Sael, 1796. 48p. NUC BL OCLC

4833. -----Louisa, a poetical novel, in four epistles.
Dublin: n.p., 1774. 86p. Lichfield: J. Jackson & G. Robinson, 1784. 95p. NUC BL

4834. -----Miss Seward's enigma.

L: R. Theobald, 1855. 10p. BL
[Riddle in couplets, with prose explanation.]

4835. -----Monody on Major Andre. By Miss Seward ... to which are added, letters addressed to her by Major Andre, in the year 1769. Republished with elegy on Capt. Cook in 1817.
Lichfield: J. Jackson, 1781. 47p. NUC BL OCLC

4836. -----Ode on General Eliott's return from Gibralter.
L: T. Cadell, 1787. 11p. NUC BL

4837. -----Original sonnets, on various subjects; and odes paraphrased from Horace.
L: G. Sael, 1799. 179p. NUC BL OCLC

4838. -----Poem to the memory of [Anna (Riggs)] Lady Miller.
L: G. Robinson, 1782. 20p. NUC BL OCLC

4839. -----Poems ... To which are added, Letters addressed to her by Major Andre in the year 1769.
5th ed. Dublin: Pr. P. Byrne C. Jackson, 1781. 69p. NUC OCLC

4840. -----The poetical works of Anna Seward, with extracts from her literary correspondence. Ed. Walter Scott.
Edinburgh: J. Ballantyne & co., 1810. 3v. NUC OCLC

SEWELL, Mrs. George see SEWELL, Mary (Young)

4841. SEWELL, Mary (Wright) [Br. 1797-1884]
The children of Summerbrook; scenes of village life described in simple verse.
L: Jarrold, 1859. 100p. NUC BL

4842. -----Church ballads.
2 ser. L: J.T. Hayes, 1868, 69. BL
[Each issued separately in paper covers, 18-20 pp., 25 issues in all, hymns incl. in some of the numbers. Ballads written to illustrate a particular festival or doctrine. Church Review: "Sure to be popular with children and the poor"]

4843. -----Homely ballads for the working man's fireside.
L: Jarrold & sons, 1858. 121p. NUC BL

4844. -----Homely ballads; and stories in verse.
L: Jarrold & sons, 1870? 127, 132p. BL OCLC
[18 numbers pub.]

4845. -----Isabel Grey: or, the mistress didn't know.
L: Smith, Elder, 1861. 22p. BL OCLC
[Repr. 1870 with Katie, the young nurse girl.]

4846. -----The little forester and his friends. A ballad of the olden time.
L: Jarrold, 1866. 101p. BL OCLC

4847. -----The little shoes.
Norwich: S. Jarrold, 18--. 12p. NUC
[A ballad.]

4848. -----The lost child: a ballad of English life.
L: n.p., 1865. NUC BL

4849. -----"Our Father's care." A ballad.
L: Jarrold & sons, 1870? 30p. BL

4850. -----Pictures and ballads of London life.
L: Jarrold, 1870. 25p. NUC OCLC

4851. -----Poems and ballads. With memoir by Miss E.B. Bayly.
L: Jarrold, 1886. 2v. NUC BL

4852. -----The rose of Cheriton. A ballad.
L: Jarrold, 1868? 91p. NUC BL
[Also pub. as: The rose of Cheriton, a temperance ballad.]

4853. -----Village children at home.
3d ed. L: n.p., 1861. BL

4854. -----Village children at school.
3d ed. L: n.p., 1861. BL

4855. -----A vision of the night.
L: Jarrold & sons, 187-? [1882. BL] 41p. BL OCLC

4856. SEWELL, Mary (Young), Mrs. George Sewell [Br. 19c] ALT: Young, Mary
Horatio and Amanda, a poem. By a young lady.
L: Robson, 1777. 20p. BL
[Attr. Mary Julia Young NUC OCLC]

4857. -----Innocence: an allegorical poem. By Miss Mary Young.
L: J. Evans, 1790. 16p. NUC BL OCLC
[Also attributed to Mary Julia Young]

4858. -----Poems and essays. By Mrs. G. Sewell.
Chertsey: R. Wetton, 1809. 3v. NUC BL OCLC
[Primarily misc. poetry. Essays on moral and religious subjects.]

4859. -----Poems. By Mrs. G. Sewell.
Egham & Chertsey: Pr. W. Wetton & sons, 1803. 265p. NUC BL OCLC

4860. -----Poems. By Mrs. George Sewell.
2d ed. Egham: Wetton & sons, 1805. 2v. NUC BL OCLC

SEYMOUR, Charlotte, Duchess of Somerset <u>see</u> SOMERSET, Charlotte Seymour, Duchess of

SEYMOUR, Frances (Thynne), Duchess of Somerset <u>see</u> SOMERSET, Frances (Thynne) Seymour, Duchess of

4861. SHANNON, Mary Eulalie (Fee) [Am. 1824-1855] ALT: Eulalie
Buds, blossoms, and leaves: poems. By Eulalie.
Cincinnati, OH: Moore, Wilstach & Keyes, 1854. 194p. NUC OCLC

4862. SHARP, Katherine Dooris [Am. 19/20c]
Eleanor's courtship and the songs that sang themselves.
Cincinnati, OH: R. Clarke & co., 1888. 162p. NUC OCLC
[Narrative, lyric & meditative poetry]

4863. SHARPE, Matilda [Br. 19c]
The journey to paradise; or, Flight of the soul to its maker. A heavenly day dream set down by Matilda Sharpe.
L: Christian Life Office, 1899. 49p. BL
[TP: Never forget, ye rising generation. Religious allegory]

4864. SHATTUCK, Harriet Clark [Am. b. 1801]
Miscellaneous poems.
Lowell, MA: Abijah Watson, pr., 1840. 48p. NUC

4865. SHAW, Fanny [Br. 19c]
Rhymes and readings for the dales.
Leeds: B.W. Sharp, 1866. 72p. BL
[Religious poetry; a few prose meditations]

4866. SHAW, Gertrude E. [Br. 19c]
Forget-me-nots.
L: M. Ward & co., 1895. BL

4867. -----Friendship's tribute.
NY; L; Munich; Berlin: Art Lithographic pub. co., 189-? 12p. NUC OCLC

SHAW, Henry, ed. <u>see</u> DUNN, Sarah Jane

4868. SHAW, Louisa [Br. 19c]
The isle of the deathless; with minor poems. Also, Spare moments, or Thoughts in prose.
L: Simpkin, Marshall & co., 1850. 165,31p. BL OCLC

4869. -----Zuleika; and other poems.
Leamington: Taylor, Clover & co.; Warwick: Henry Sharpe, 1846. BL
[Narrative poem in 3 cantos; misc. lyrics, domestic & on solitude]

4870. SHEARER, Flora MacDonald [Am. 19c]
The legend of Aulus.
San Francisco: W. Doxey, 1896. 95p. NUC BL OCLC
[Also incl. ballads, sonnets, & misc. verse]

SHEILA, pseud. <u>see</u> SCOTT, Christabel

4871. SHELBY, Helen [Am. 19c]
Poems.
NY: Van Fleet, pr., 1891. 150p. NUC OCLC

4872. SHELLEY, Elizabeth [Br. 1794-1831] PSEUD: Cazire
Original poetry by Victor and Cazire [Percy Bysshe Shelley and Elizabeth Shelley]. Ed. Richard Garnett.
L & NY: John Lane, 1898. 66p. NUC BL
[1st pub. 1810.]

4873. SHELLEY, Mary Wollstonecraft (Godwin), Mrs. Percy Bysshe Shelley [Br. 1797-1851]
The choice. A poem on Shelley's death. Ed. Harry Buxton Forman.
L: Pr. for editor, for priv. distrib., 1876. 14p. NUC BL OCLC

SHELLEY, Mrs. Percy Bysshe <u>see</u> SHELLEY, Mary Wollstonecraft (Godwin)

SHELLEY, Percy Bysshe, co-author <u>see</u> SHELLEY, Elizabeth

4874. SHELLOCK, Sarah [Br. 19c]
A voice from a cottage; or, Thoughts in verse.
Ipswich: n.p., 1858. BL

4875. SHELTON, Ada Stewart [Am. 19/20c]

Easter lilies.
NY: J. Pott & co., 1892. 9 l. NUC

4876. -----Song of the Indian River.
Buffalo, NY: Matthews-Northrup co., c1890. 12p. NUC OCLC
[Indian River, Florida]

4877. SHELTON, Julia Finley [Am. 19c]
PSEUD: Lorrimer, Laura
A voice from the South. By Laura Lorrimer.
Nashville, TN: Southern Methodist pub. house, 1882. 249p. NUC OCLC

SHEPARD, D. Ellen Goodman see SHEPARD, Dolly Ellen (Ring)

4878. SHEPARD, Dolly Ellen (Ring) [Am. 1820-1853] ALT: Shepard, D. Ellen Goodman; Goodman, Mrs Haskell C.
Cut-flowers: a collection of poems. By Mrs. D. Ellen Goodman Shepard. Ed. Josiah Gilbert Holland.
Springfield, MA: Bessey & co., 1854. 168p. NUC OCLC
[Narrative & lyric poems]

4879. SHEPHERD, Mrs. [Br. 19c]
Poems.
L: n.p., 1807. BL

4880. SHEPPARD, Sarah, Miss [Br. 19c] ALT: S., S.
Illustrations of scripture, the Hebrew converts, and other poems. By S.S.
L: John Hatchard & son, 1837. 271p. BL OCLC

SHEPPART, J., comp. see STEELE, Anne, Mrs.

4881. SHERIDAN, Frances (Chamberlaine), Mrs. Thomas Sheridan [Br. 1724-1766]
Memoirs of the life and writings of Mrs. F. Sheridan ... and selections from the works of Mrs. Sheridan, by her granddaughter, Alicia Lefanu.
L: G. & W.B. Whittaker, 1824. 435p. NUC BL OCLC
[Incl. Ode to patience]

SHERIDAN, Mrs. Thomas see SHERIDAN, Frances (Chamberlaine)

4882. SHERMAN, Anna F. McNeill [Am. 19c]
Poems for the deaf mutes. With John Sherman.
Pasadena, CA: News pub. co., 1895. 11p. OCLC

SHERMAN, John, co-author see SHERMAN, Anna F. McNeill

4883. SHERRICK, Fannie Isabel [Am. 19c]
Love or fame; and other poems.
St. Louis, MO: W.S. Bryan, 1880. 152p. NUC OCLC

4884. -----Star-dust.
Chicago, NY & San Francisco: Belford, Clarke & co., 1888. 176p. NUC OCLC

4885. SHERWIN, Elizabeth [Br. 19c]
Poems.
Wolverhampton: Joseph Bridgen, 1851. 97p. NUC OCLC

4886. SHERWOOD, Ann [Br. 19c]
Verses of a past age.
Ipswich: n.p., 1872. NUC

SHERWOOD, Mrs. John see SHERWOOD, Mary Elizabeth (Wilson)

SHERWOOD, Kate (Brownlee) see SHERWOOD, Katherine Margaret (Brownlee)

4887. SHERWOOD, Katherine Margaret (Brownlee) [Am. 1841-1914] ALT: Sherwood, Kate Brownlee
Albert Sidney Johnston Memorial poem: written by invitation ... for the unveiling ceremonies of the General Albert Sidney Johnston equestrian statue ... at New Orleans, April 6, 1887.
Toledo, OH: n.p., 1887. 4p. NUC OCLC

4888. -----Camp-fire, Memorial-day, and other poems.
Chicago: Jansen, McClurg & co., 1885. 212p. NUC OCLC

4889. -----Dream of the age, a poem of Columbia.
Washington, DC: National Tribune, 1893. 85p. NUC OCLC

4890. -----Poem written for Forsyth post, no. 15, G[rand] A[rmy of the] R[epublic].
Toledo, OH: Montgomery & Vrooman, steam job pr., 1878. 4p. NUC

4891. SHERWOOD, Mary Elizabeth (Wilson), Mrs. John Sherwood [Am. 1830-1903] ALT: S., M.E.W.
Poems, by M.E.W.S. Comp. Evelyn Baker Harvier.
NY: George M. Allen co., 1892. 75p. NUC

SHIELDS-ASLACHSEN, Edith Henderson see HENDERSON, Edith

SHINDLER, Mrs. Mary Dana see SHINDLER, Mary Stanley Bunce (Palmer) Dana

4892. SHINDLER, Mary Stanley Bunce (Palmer) Dana [Am. 1810-1883] ALT: Dana, Mary S. B.
The parted family, and other poems.
NY: Dayton & Saxton; Boston: Saxton & Pierce, 1842. 312p. NUC BL OCLC

4893. SHIPLEY, Mary Elizabeth [Br. b. 1842]
The legend of St. Christopher, and other poems.
L: n.p., 1877. BL

SHIPPEN, Anne Home see LIVINGSTON, Anne Home (Shippen)

4894. SHIPTON, Anna [Br. 19c] ALT: S., A.
The angel guest. "A word to him that is weary."
L: Morgan & Chase, 1873. NUC BL

4895. -----The brook in the way: original hymns and poems.
3d ed. L: Morgan, 1864. 174p. NUC BL OCLC

4896. -----The hearing heart (I Kings iii 9).
L: James Nisbet & co., 1890. 104p. BL
[Devotional prose, with accounts of personal experience, religious poems interspersed.]

4897. -----Poems.
NY: Crowell, 18--. NUC OCLC

4898. -----Precious gems for the Saviour's diadem.
L: William Yapp, 1862. BL
[Poems & prose meditations]

4899. -----The watch-tower in the wilderness.
NY: T.Y. Crowell; L: Morgan & Scott, 1874. 176p.; 160p. BL OCLC

4900. -----Waymarks of my pilgrimage, poems.
L: n.p., 1877. BL

4901. -----Whispers in the Psalms. Hymns and meditations.
L: n.p., 1855.
[2d ed., 1858, augmented]

SHORE, Arabella, comp. see SHORE, Louisa Catherine

4902. SHORE, Arabella [Br. 19c] ALT: A.
Elegies and memorials. By A. & L. [Arabella & Louisa Catherine Shore].
L: Kegan Paul, Trench, Trubner, 1890. 53p. NUC BL

4903. -----Fra Dolcino, and other poems. By A. & L. [Arabella & Louisa Catherine Shore].
L: Smith Elder & co., 1870. 326p. BL

4904. -----Gemma of the isles, a lyrical drama, and other poems. By A. & L. [Arabella & Louisa Catherine Shore].
L: Saunders & Otley, 1859. 194p. NUC BL

4905. -----Poems by A. & L. [Arabella & Louisa Catherine Shore].
L: Lane, 1897. 215p. NUC OCLC

4906. -----War lyrics. By A. & L. [Arabella & Louisa Catherine Shore].
L: Saunders, 1855. 48p. NUC BL OCLC

SHORE, Louisa Catherine, co-author see SHORE, Arabella

4907. SHORE, Louisa Catherine [Br. 1824-1895] ALT: L.
Poems. Comp. Arabella Shore.
L & NY: J. Lane, 1896. 215p. NUC BL OCLC
[Selection of her unpublished verse.]

4908. SHOREY, L., Mrs. [Br. 19/20c]
The broken angel and other poems.
L: G. Stoneman, 1892. 80p. BL

SHORTER, Mrs. Clement see SHORTER, Dora May (Sigerson)

4909. SHORTER, Dora May (Sigerson), Mrs. Clement Shorter [Br. d. 1918] ALT: Sigerson, Dora May
Ballads and poems.
L: J. Bowden, 1899. 123p. NUC BL OCLC

4910. -----The fairy changeling, and other poems.
L & NY: John Lane, 1898. 100p. NUC BL OCLC

4911. -----My lady's slipper, and other verses.
NY: Dodd, Mead & co., 1899. 157p. NUC

4912. -----Verses.
L: Eliot Stock, 1893. 134p. NUC BL OCLC

SHORTFELLOW, HENRY WANDSWORTH, pseud. see CLARKE, Mary Victoria (Novello) Cowden-

4913. SHORTT, Mary Lesingham Dicken [Br. 19c]
Lines and lays for wedding days.
L: Eyre & Spottiswoode, 1885. 288p. BL

4914. SHRIMPTON, Amelia [Br. 19c]
Stray thoughts 'midst busy scenes: a book of religious and moral poetry. With Sarah Shrimpton.
L: n.p., 1862. BL

SHRIMPTON, Sarah, co-author see SHRIMPTON, Amelia

4915. SHUEY, Lillian (Hinman) [Am. 1853-1921]
California sunshine.
Oakland, CA: Pacific press pub. co., 1888. 122p. NUC OCLC
[On the seasons, in memoriam & on the San Joaquin]

4916. SHULTZ, M. Genevieve [Am. 19c]
A few rhymes.
Batavia, NY: Her brother, 1893. 30p. NUC

4917. SHUTE, Anna Clara [Br. 19c]
Posthumous poems.
L: Chapman & Hall, 1875. 304p. NUC BL OCLC
[Incl. trans. of 7 German poems]

SIDNEY, MARGARET, pseud. see LOTHROP, Harriet Mulford (Stone)

SIDNEY, Mary see PEMBROKE, Mary (Sidney) Herbert, Countess of

SIDNEY, Sir Philip, co-author see PEMBROKE, Mary (Sidney) Herbert, Countess of

4918. SIDNEY, Violet E. [Br. 19c]
Waima, and other verses.
L: E. Stock, 1898. 88p. BL

SIGOURNEY, Mrs. C. see SIGOURNEY, Lydia Howard (Huntley)

SIGOURNEY, Lydia Howard (Huntley), ed. see HYDE, Nancy Maria

4919. SIGOURNEY, Lydia Howard (Huntley), Mrs. C. Sigourney [Am. 1791-1865] ALT: Huntley, Lydia Howard
The coronal; or, Tales and pencillings in poetry and prose.
L & Edinburgh: T. Nelson, 1848. 237p. NUC BL

4920. -----The daily counsellor.
Hartford, CT: Brown & Gross, 1859. 402p. NUC
[A poem for every day of the year. For devotional use]

4921. -----Gleanings.
Hartford, CT: Brown & Gross; NY: D. Appleton & co., 1860. NUC

4922. -----Illustrated poems.
Philadelphia: Carey & Hart, 1849. 408p. NUC OCLC

4923. -----Lays from the West: poems. Collected and arranged by ... J. Belcher.
L: T. Ward & co., 1834. 102p. NUC BL OCLC

4924. -----Lays of the heart, with Oriska and other poems.
L: n.p., 1835? BL

4925. -----Letters of life.
NY: D. Appleton & co., 1866. 414p. NUC BL OCLC
[Her autobiography; incl. poems, many prev. pub.]

4926. -----Letters to my pupils: with narrative and biographical sketches.
NY: R. Carter & bros., 1851. 341p. NUC BL OCLC
[Letters, essays, sketches, one short story & poems]

4927. -----The man of Uz, and other poems.
Hartford, CT: Williams, Wiley & Waterman, 1862. 276p. NUC OCLC
[Biblical narrative based on Job; "The rural life in New England," 3 cantos; 62 poems in memoriam.]

4928. -----Past meridian.
NY: D. Appleton & co.; Boston: J.P. Jewett & co., 1854. 239p. NUC BL OCLC
[Prose & poetry on old age]

4929. -----Pleasant memories of pleasant lands.
Boston: J. Munroe & co., 1842. 368p. NUC OCLC
[Incl. description in verse of Great Britain]

4930. -----Pocahontas, and other poems.
L: R. Tyas, 1841. 308p. NY: Harper & bros., 1841. 281p. NUC BL OCLC

4931. -----Poems.
Boston: Samuel G. Goodrich, 1827. 228p.

4932. -----Poems.
Philadelphia: Key & Biddle, 1834. 288p. NUC BL OCLC

4933. -----Poems.
1842. 256p.
[Religious poems]

4934. -----Poems by the author of Moral pieces.
Boston: S.G. Goodrich, 1827. 228p. NUC OCLC

4935. -----Poems for the sea.
Hartford, CT: H.S. Parsons & co., 1850. 152p. NUC BL OCLC

4936. -----Poems: religious and elegiac.
L: R. Tyas, 1841. 352p. NUC BL OCLC

4937. -----The poetical works of Mrs. L.H.S. Ed. F.W.N. Bayley.
L: G. Routledge, 1850. 236p. NUC OCLC

4938. -----Poetry for seamen.
Boston: J. Munroe & co., 1845. 63p. NUC BL
[Enlarded ed. pub. as: The sea and the sailor.]

4939. -----Sayings of the little ones and poems for their mothers.
Buffalo, NY: Phinney & co.; NY: Ivison & Phinney, 1855. 262p. NUC OCLC

4940. -----Scenes in my native land.
Boston: J. Munroe & co., 1845. 319p. NUC OCLC
[Prose & verse. Atlantic states description and travel.]

4941. -----Traits of the aborigines of America. A poem.
Cambridge, MA: Hilliard & Metcalf, pr., 1822. 284p. NUC BL OCLC
[In 5 cantoes]

4942. -----Voice of flowers.
Hartford, CT: H.S. Parsons & co., 1846. 123p. NUC OCLC
[Gift book]

4943. -----Water-drops.
NY & Pittsburg, PA: Robert Carter, 1848. 275p. NUC OCLC
[Verse & prose; temperance fiction]

4944. -----Weeping willow.
Hartford, CT: H.S. Parsons, 1847. 128p. NUC OCLC
[Poetry on death]

4945. -----The western home, and other poems.
Philadelphia: Parry & McMillan, 1854. 359p. OCLC NUC

4946. -----Zinzendorff, and other poems.
NY: Leavitt, Lord & co.; Boston: Crocker & Brewster, 1835. 300p. NUC BL OCLC

4947. SILSBEE, Marianne Cabot (Devereux) [Am. 1812-1889]
The modern Phoenix. Pub. anon.
Boston?: n.p., 1868? 43p. NUC OCLC
[An account of the Ladies' Club, Boston]

4948. SIMMONS, Anna Wilson [Am. 19c]
Heart whispers.
Denver, CO: The Merchants pub. co., 1895. 142p. NUC OCLC

4949. SIMPSON, Jane Cross (Bell) [Br. 1811-1886] PSEUD: Gertrude
April hours. By Gertrude.
Edinburgh: William Blackwood & sons, 1838. 224p. BL

4950. -----The consumptive, by Gertrude.
Hartford, CT: Press of Case, Tiffany, 1850. 70p. NUC OCLC
[Fiction with some verse]

4951. -----Linda and other poems.
Edinburgh: Edmonston & co.; Glasgow: James Maclehose, 1879. 248p. BL
[DNB as: Picture poems and Linda. A collection of her works.]

4952. -----Linda, or beauty and genius: a metrical romance.
Glasgow: n.p., 1859. BL

4953. SIMPSON, Mary E. [Br. 19c] ALT: S., M.E.
Cast thy burden on the Lord.
L: W. Poole, 1880. BL

4954. SINCLAIR, Anna M., Mrs. [Am. 19c]
Poems of the heart.
n.p.: n.p., 1887? 102p. NUC OCLC

4955. SINCLAIR, Carrie Bell [Am. b. 1839]
Poems.
Augusta, GA: H.D. Norrell, 1860. 160p. NUC OCLC

4956. SINCLAIR, Catherine [Br. 1800-1864]
Scotch courtiers and the court.

Edinburgh: W. Whyte & co., 1842. 121p. NUC BL
[A poem, occasioned by the queen's visit to Scotland]

4957. SINCLAIR, Margaret A. [Br. 19c] PSEUD: Roslyn
Echoing oars, or "Waitemata" and other verses. By Roslyn.
Auckland: Pr. at Star off., 18--? 26p. NUC

4958. -----The Huia's homeland, and other verses. By Roslyn.
L: E. Stock, 1897. 214p. BL OCLC

4959. SINCLAIR, May [Br. 1865-1946]
Essays in verse.
L: Kegan Paul, Trench, Trubner & co., 1891. 86p. NUC BL

SINGER, S.W., ed. <u>see</u> PEMBROKE, Mary (Sidney) Herbert, Countess of

4960. SKELTON, Edith [Br. 19c]
All good things come to those who wait.
L: Griffith Farran & co., 1884. 32p. BL

4961. -----The crucial test, and other poems.
L: Griffith Farran & co., 1889. 128p. NUC BL

4962. -----"Folded wings," and other poems.
L: Griffith Farran & co., 1880. 64p. BL

4963. SKELTON, Eliza [Br. 19c]
A voice around [round NUC].
2d ed. L: Dean & son, 1868. 252p. NUC BL
[Long religious poem; prose meditations]

4964. SKELTON, Sophia [Br. 19c]
Arnold of Brescia, a dramatic poem.
L: Simpkin, Marshall & co., 1866. 123p. BL
[Historical tragedy. 5 acts. Not intended for performance]

4965. -----The bride of the Nile ... and other poems.
L: Simpkin & Marshall, 1865. BL

4966. -----Saul; a dramatic poem.
L: Simpkin & Marshall, 1864. 86p. BL
[5 acts, Biblical themes, not intended for performance]

4967. SKENE, Felicia Mary Frances [Br. 1821-1899]
The isles of Greece, and other poems.
L: n.p., 1843. BL

SKIDDY, Ellen Mary, co-author <u>see</u> SKIDDY, Mary Angela

4968. SKIDDY, Mary Angela [Br. 19c]
Miscellaneous poems; by Mary Angela Skiddy and her mother, Ellen Mary Skiddy.
Cork: Henry & Coghlan, 1866. 104p. NUC OCLC

4969. SKIDMORE, Harriet Marie [Am. 1837-1904] ALT: Marie
Beside the western sea: a collection of poems.
NY: P. O'Shea, 1877. 536p. NUC OCLC
[Cover title: Poems of Marie. Incl. 4 plays in verse, religious poetry]

4970. -----Lines written in memory of Mrs. Catherine S. (Oliver) Tobin. Died Nov. 7, 1882, aged 26 years, 4 months.
San Francisco: Bosqui Eng. & pr. co., 1882? 12 l. OCLC

4971. SLAUGHTER, Elvira Sydnor (Miller) [Am. 19/20c]
Songs of the heart.
Louisville, KY: John P. Morton, c1885. 144p. NUC OCLC

4972. SLAUGHTER, Linda Warfel, Mrs. [Am. b. 1850]
Early efforts.
Philadelphia: J.W. Daughaday & co., 1868. 136p. NUC

4973. SLEIGH, Isabella, Mrs. [Br. 19c]
Poems, moral and religious, by the late Mrs. Sleigh ... To which is prefixed a prefatory address ... including a few sketches of her history and character, by her husband.
Barnstaple: n.p., 1819. BL

4974. SLOCUM, Grace Leila [Am. b. 1865]
The vision of the Madonna.
NY: Thomas Whittaker, 1899. 23p. NUC OCLC

4975. SMALLPIECE, Anna Maria [Br. 19c]
Original sonnets, and other small poems.
L: n.p., 1805. BL

4976. SMEDLEY, Menella Bute [Br. 1820-1877] ALT: S., M.

Child-nature.
L: Strahan & co., 1869. 294p. NUC

4977. -----Lays and ballads from English history. By S.M.
L: James Burns, 1842-1848. NUC BL OCLC

4978. -----The story of Queen Isabel, and other verses. By M.S.
L: Bell & Daldy, 1863. 111p. NUC BL OCLC
[Title poem, pp. 1-47 gothic narrative; other narrative & misc. poems, tribute to Cavour & poems on Garibaldi]

4979. -----Two dramatic poems.
L: Macmillan & co., 1874. 346p. NUC BL
[Blind love, a dramatic poem; Cyril: four scenes from a life, with other poems.]

4980. SMITH, Adele Crofton [Br. 19/20c]
Lyrics.
L: Jarrold & sons, 1899. 72p. BL

SMITH, Annie Lenthal, co-author see BALLARD, Julia Perkins (Pratt)

4981. SMITH, Annie Rebekah (Spalding) [Am. 1828-1855]
Home here, and home in heaven; with other poems.
Rochester, NY: Advent Review off., 1855. 112p. NUC OCLC

4982. -----Poems: with a sketch of the life and experience of Annie R. Smith. By Mrs. Rebekah Smith.
Manchester, NH: John B. Clarke, pr., 1871. 152p. NUC OCLC
[Predominately poems by the compiler, but incl. 14 previously unpub. poems by A.R. Smith.]

4983. SMITH, Bithiah, Mrs. [Br. 19c]
PSEUD: Clergyman's Wife, A
The poetical keepsake. By a clergyman's wife.
L: n.p., 1857. BL
[Original poems: religious & secular]

SMITH, C. Fox see SMITH, Cicely Fox

4984. SMITH, Caroline [Am. 19c]
Haverhill in eclipse; or, Scenes at midnight.
Newburyport: Wm. H. Huse, pr., 1870. 12p. NUC
[Narrative satirical poem. Sold for benefit of the Old Ladies Home Assn.]

4985. SMITH, Catharine Barnard [Br. 19c]
Poems.
L & Cambridge: Macmillan, 1868. 182p. NUC BL OCLC

4986. SMITH, Charlotte (Turner) [Br. 1749-1806]
Beachy Head, with other poems.
L: Pr. for author; sold by J. Johnson, St. Paul's Church yd., 1807. 219p. NUC BL OCLC

4987. -----Elegiac sonnets and other essays.
L: J. Dodsley, 1784. 26p. NUC BL OCLC
[Fifth ed., 2 v. 1789-97, adds more poems.]

4988. -----The emigrants, a poem, in two books.
L: T. Cadell, 1793. 68p. NUC BL OCLC

4989. SMITH, Cicely Fox [Br. 1882-1954] ALT: Smith, C. Fox
The foremost trail. By C. Fox Smith.
L: Sampson, Low, Marston & co., 1899. 87p. NUC BL OCLC

4990. -----Songs of Greater Britain and other poems.
Manchester: Sherratt & Hughes, 1899. 119p. NUC BL OCLC

4991. SMITH, Mrs. Eldridge J. [Am. 19c]
Songs of the morning. By Mrs. Eldridge Smith.
Washington, DC: Brown & McElfresh, pr., 1889. 30p. NUC

4992. -----Which? By Mrs. Eldridge Smith.
Washington, DC: n.p., 1886. 3p. NUC

4993. SMITH, Eliza Roxey (Snow) [Am. 1804-1887] ALT: Snow, Eliza R.
Poems, religious, historical, and political.
V. 1. Liverpool: F.D. Richards, 1856. 270p. V. 2. Salt Lake City, UT: Pr. at Latter-day Saints pr. & pub. est., 1877. 284p. NUC BL OCLC

4994. SMITH, Elizabeth [Br. 18c]
The brethren, a poem: paraphrased from part of the history of Israel and his family.
Birmingham: Pr. for the author by Pearson & Pollason, 1787. 158p. NUC BL OCLC

4995. -----Israel; a poem in four books.

Birmingham: Pr. for the authoress by Brown & Bentley, 1789. 118p. NUC BL

4996. SMITH, Elizabeth [Br. 1776-1806] ALT: S---, Elizabeth
Fragments in prose and verse. By a young lady lately deceased. Ed. Henrietta Maria Bowdler.
L: Richard Cruttwell; Dublin: Graisberry & Campbell for W. Watson, 1808. 232p. NUC BL OCLC

4997. SMITH, Elizabeth [Br. 18c]
Life review'd; a poem ... To which is added an elegy on the late Rev. Mr. S. Walker.
Exeter: B.Thorn, 1780. 132p. NUC BL

4998. SMITH, Elizabeth [Br. 19c]
Poems of Malvern, and other subjects.
Worcester: n.p., 1829. BL

4999. SMITH, Elizabeth Budd [Am. 19c]
The poems of Elizabeth Budd Smith.
Philadelphia: Priv. pr., 1891. 170p. NUC
[Misc. poems, some on Civil War]

5000. SMITH, Elizabeth Oakes (Prince), Mrs. Seba Smith [Am. 1806-1893]
The keepsake: a wreath of poems and sonnets. By Mrs. Seba Smith.
NY: Leavitt & co., 1849. 204p. NUC OCLC

5001. -----The poetical writings of Elizabeth Oakes Smith. First complete edition.
NY: J.S. Redfield, 1845. 204p. NUC OCLC

5002. -----The sinless child, and other poems. Ed. J. Keese.
NY: Wiley & Putnam; Boston: W.D. Ticknor, 1843. 177p. NUC BL OCLC

5003. SMITH, Emeline Sherman, Mrs. [Am. b. 1823]
The fairy's search, and other poems.
NY: Nafis & Cornish; St. Louis, MO: Nafis, Cornish & co., 1847. 128p. NUC OCLC

5004. -----Poems and ballads.
NY: Rudd & Carleton, 1859. 336p. NUC OCLC

5005. SMITH, Emily Lee [Am. 19c]
A Trinity Sunday in Hawthorne.
Pittsburgh, PA: n.p., 1876. 3p. NUC

5006. SMITH, Emma Pow, Mrs. [Am. 1848-1901]
Jets of truth; or, Revolutionary spokes in the wheel of progress.
San Francisco: Brunt & Fisher, pr. & pub., 1886. 112p. NUC OCLC
[53 poems: patriotic, moral, temperance]

SMITH, F. Burge see GRISWOLD, Frances Irene (Burge) Smith

SMITH, G., ed. see BUTLER, Anne

5007. SMITH, Grace, Mrs. [Am. 18c]
The dying mother's legacy. Or the good and heavenly counsel of that eminent and pious matron, Mrs. Grace Smith. Taken from her own mouth a little before her death, by the minister of that town where she died ...
Boston: Timothy Green, 1712. 12p. NUC
[Incl. poems]

5008. SMITH, Hannah [Am. 19c]
The life of Christ. A poem.
Brooklyn, NY: n.p., 1895. 13p. NUC

5009. SMITH, Hannah H., Mrs. [Am. 18/19c]
Selections from the poems of Mrs. Hannah H. Smith. Ed. her daughter, Julia Evalina Smith.
Hartford, CT: Case, Lockwood & Brainard co., c1881. 55p. NUC OCLC

5010. SMITH, Harriette [Br. 19c]
Irene Floss, and other poems.
L: n.p., 1878. BL

5011. SMITH, Jane Luella (Dowd) [Am. b. 1847] ALT: Dowd, J. Luella; Smith, Luella Dowd
Flowers from foreign fields.
Buffalo, NY: Peter Paul book co., 1895. 72p. RPB
[Misc. poetry]

5012. -----Wayside leaves. By J. Luella Dowd.
NY: G.P. Putnam's sons, 1879. 201p. NUC OCLC
[Orig. poetry, essays, & short stories]

5013. -----Wind flowers.
Chicago: Charles H. Kerr, 1887. 235p. NUC OCLC

5014. SMITH, Jeanie Oliver (Davidson) [Am. 1836-1925]
The Christ; a poetical study of His life from advent to ascension. With O.C. Auringer.
NY: G.P. Putnam, 1899. 106p. NUC OCLC

5015. -----Christmas day.
Johnstown, NY: n.p., 189-? 3p. NUC

5016. -----Day lilies.
NY & L: G.P. Putnam's sons, 1888. 321p. NUC OCLC

5017. SMITH, Jennie M. [Br. 19c]
Poems.
Bury St. Edmund's: Bury Post & Suffolk Standard co., 1888. 100p. BL

SMITH, Julia Evalina, ed. see SMITH, Hannah H., Mrs.

5018. SMITH, Lizzie [Am. 19c]
A tribute to Theodore; who died August 29, 1860 .... .
Salem, MA: York & Lunt, pr., 1860. 15p. NUC

5019. SMITH, Lizzie H. [Br. 19c]
Poems of a dairymaid.
Paisley: J. & R. Parlane, 1898. 131p. NUC OCLC

5020. SMITH, Lucy [Br. 19c]
The convict's grave, scenes from Uncle Tom's cabin, and other poems.
Shrewesbury: n.p., 1853. BL

SMITH, Luella (Dowd) see SMITH, Jane Luella (Dowd)

5021. SMITH, Lydia B. [Br. 19c]
Bianca, and other poems.
L: n.p., 1838. BL

5022. -----Songs of Granada and the Alhambra, with other poems.
L: Saunders & Otley, 1836. 231p. NUC BL

5023. SMITH, Martha A., Mrs. [Am. 19c]
Poems.
Brooklyn, NY: Pr. for the author, 1881. 132p. NUC OCLC

5024. -----Poems.
Brooklyn, NY: Pr. for the author, 1883. 107p. NUC OCLC

5025. -----Poems.
Brooklyn, NY: Pr. for the author, 1892. 148p. NUC OCLC

5026. SMITH, Mary [Br. 1822-1889]
ALT: S., M.
The autobiography of Mary Smith, schoolmistress and non-conformist. A fragment of a life. With letters from Jane Welsh and Thomas Carlyle.
L: Bemrose & sons, 1892. 2v. NUC BL OCLC
[V. 2 contains her poems]

5027. -----Poems. By M.S.
L: n.p., 1860. BL

5028. -----Progress, and other poems ... by M.S.
L: n.p., 1873. BL

5029. SMITH, Mary [Am. 19c]
Poems and essays.
Mobile, AL: Motor pr. works, 1888. 64p. NUC OCLC

5030. SMITH, Mary A. [Am. 19c]
His face and her face.
NY: Pr. at 433 8th Ave., 1881. 19p. NUC

5031. SMITH, Mary E. [Am. 19c]
Conselumbia; or, The carnival of the states.
Keene, NH: Press of Sentinel pr. co., c1893. 48p. NUC

5032. SMITH, Mary Elizabeth, Miss [Br. 19c]
Moscha Lamberti: or, a deed done has an end. A romance.
L: n.p., 1849. BL

5033. SMITH, Mary Louise (Riley) [Am. 1842-1927] ALT: Smith, May Riley
Cradle and armchair. By May Riley Smith.
NY: A.D.F. Randolph & co., 1893. 131p. NUC OCLC

5034. -----A gift of Gentians, and other verses. By May Riley Smith.
NY: A.D.F. Randolph, 1882. 106p. NUC OCLC

5035. -----His name. By May Riley Smith.
NY: A.D.F. Randolph & co., c1887. 5 l. NUC

5036. -----The inn of rest. Later poems. By May Riley Smith.
NY: A.D.F. Randolph, 1888. 35p. NUC OCLC

5037. -----Lilies and violets for Easter day. By May Riley Smith.
NY: A.D.F. Randolph & co., 1886. 8 l. NUC

5038. -----Sometime, and other poems. By May Riley Smith.
NY: A.D.F. Randolph & co., 1885. 6 l. E.P. Dutton, 1893. 167p. NUC OCLC

5039. -----Tired mothers.

NY: A.D.F. Randolph & co., 1895. 5 l. NUC

5040. -----Your birthday.
NY: A.D.F. Randolph & co., c1886. 9 l. NUC

SMITH, May Riley see SMITH, Mary Louise (Riley)

SMITH, Minerva C. see SMITH, Minna Caroline

5041. SMITH, Minna Caroline [Am. 1860-1929] PSEUD: Californian, A
Gold stories of '49; by a Californian.
Boston: Copeland & Day, 1896. 52p. NUC OCLC
[3 narrative poems. Minna Caroline Smith & Minerva C. Smith both penciled on t.p. OCLC also attr.: Nüima Smith.]

5042. -----In fruitful lands, and other poems.
Boston: Cupples, 1885. 55p. NUC OCLC

SMITH, Professor N.R., co-author see POLLARD, Rebecca (Smith)

SMITH, Nüima see SMITH, Minna Caroline

SMITH, Rebekah, co-author & comp. see SMITH, Annie Rebekah (Spaulding)

5043. SMITH, Sara (Henderson) [Am. d. 1884]
Christmas-day anthem.
NY: A.D.F. Randolph & co., 1885. 7 l. NUC

5044. -----Easter day.
NY: A.D.F. Randolph & co., 1886. 7 l. NUC

5045. -----Up to the light, with other religious and devotional poems.
NY: A.D.F. Randolph & co., 1884. 108p. OCLC

5046. SMITH, Sarah Louisa P. (Hickman) [Am. 1811-1832]
Poems.
Providence, RI: A.S. Beckwith, 1829. 250p. NUC BL OCLC

5047. SMITH, Sarah Pogson, Mrs. [Am. 19c] PSEUD: Lady, A
The Arabian: or, The power of Christianity.
Philadelphia: n.p., 1844. 56p. NUC
[Narrative of conversion of an Arab to Christianity]

5048. -----Daughters of Eve, by a lady.
Schnectady, NY: Pr. G. Ritchie, 1826. 91p. NUC OCLC

5049. SMITH, Sarah S. [Am. 19c]
Amaranth blooms; a collection of embodied poetical thoughts.
Utica, NY: J.W. Fuller, 1853. 199p. NUC OCLC

SMITH, Mrs. Seba see SMITH, Elizabeth Oakes (Prince)

5050. SMITH, Sophia Mary [Br. 19c]
The Eastern princess, and other poems: together with Walberg; or, Temptation: a drama.
L: Simpkin, Marshall & co., 1844. 338p. BL
[Walberg is historical drama of the Reformation, 3 acts]

5051. SMITH, Mrs. T. [Br. 19c]
Poetic flowers.
2d ed. Geneva: J.J.L. Sestie, pr., 1824. 26p. BL

SMYTH, Rev. Edward, comp. see DAVIDSON, Margaret

5052. SMYTH, Florida (Watts) [Am. 19/20c]
The varied grace of nature's face.
St. Louis, MO: E.E. Carveras, pr., 1895. 119p. NUC OCLC
[European travel in verse]

SMYTHIES, Mrs. Gordon see SMYTHIES, Harriet Maria Gordon

5053. SMYTHIES, Harriet Maria Gordon, Mrs. Gordon Smythies [Br. 1838-1883]
The bride of Siena. A poem.
L: Saunders & Otley, 1835. 124p. NUC BL OCLC

5054. -----Incurable! Or, the suffering family. A poem ... written in aid of the friends of the Royal Hospital for Incurables.
L: n.p., 1863. BL

5055. -----The prince and the people. A poem.
L: n.p., 1854. BL

5056. -----Sebastopol. A poem.
L: n.p., 1854. BL

5057. SNELL, Mina Sloane, Miss [Am. b. 1841]
Essays, short stories and poems ... including a short sketch of the author's life.

Chatham: Banner steam pr., 1881. 162p. NUC BL

SNOW, Eliza R. see SMITH, Eliza Roxey (Snow)

5058. SNOW, Elizabeth [Br. 19c]
A bouquet of wild flowers.
L: Priv. pr., 1843. 54p. BL OCLC
[28p. poem on flowers, misc. songs & lyrics]

5059. SNOW, Florence Lydia [Am. b. 1861]
The lamp of gold.
Chicago: Way & Williams, 1896. 121p. NUC OCLC

SNOW, Laura Anne (Barter) see BARTER, Laura Anne

5060. SNOWDEN, Eleanor [Br. 19c]
The maid of Scio, a tale of modern Greece. In six cantos.
Dover: Pr. G. Chapman, 1829. 128p. BL OCLC

5061. -----The Moorish queen: a record of Pompeii; and other poems.
L: n.p., 1831. BL

SOLARI, Catherine Hyde see GOVION BROGLIO SOLARI, Catherine Hyde, Marquise de

SOLDIER'S DAUGHTER, A, pseud. see NICOLAS, Sarah (Davison), Lady

5062. SOLOMONS, Rosa J. [Br. 19/20c]
Facts and fancies.
Dublin: William M'Gee; L: Simpkin, Marshall & co., 1883. 140p. NUC BL OCLC
[All poetry]

5063. SOMERS, Eliza [Br. 18/19c]
Elegy on the death of a favourite terrier.
n.p.: n.p., 1802. 3p. BL

5064. SOMERSET, Charlotte Seymour, Duchess of [Br. 19c] ALT: Seymour, Charlotte Duchess of Somerset
The powers of imagination, a poem. In three parts. Written at the age of sixteen.
L: T.N. Longman & O. Rees, 1803. 130p. NUC OCLC

5065. SOMERSET, Frances (Thynne) Seymour, Duchess of [Br. 1699-1754] ALT: Seymour, Frances (Thynne), Duchess of Somerset
The story of Inkle and Yarrico. A most moving tale [By Sir Richard Steele] from the Spectator. Attempted in veres [sic] by the Right Hon. the Countess of ****.
L: J. Cooper, 1738. 16p. BL

SOMERSET, Lady Henry see SOMERSET, Isabella Caroline (Somers-Cocks)

5066. SOMERSET, Isabella Caroline (Somers-Cocks), Lady Henry Somerset [Br. 1851-1921]
Our village life. Words and illustrations by Lady Henry Somerset.
L: S. Low, Marston, Searle & Rivington, 1884. 36p. NUC BL

SOPHIA see OLSEN, Sophia B., Mrs.

5067. SOUDER, Emily Bliss (Thacher) [Am. 19c]
An appeal for the floating church, and other poems.
Philadelphia: King & Baird, pr., 1851. 83p. NUC OCLC

5068. -----Leaves from the battlefield of Gettysburg; a series of letters from a field hospital; and national poems.
Philadelphia: C. Sherman, son, & co., 1864. 144p. NUC OCLC

5069. SOUTHALL, Eliza Allen [Br. 1823-1851]
Portions of the diary, letters and other remains of Eliza Southall. Selected by William Southall.
Birmingham: Priv. pr. by White & Pike, 1855. 141p. NUC BL OCLC
[Incl. poems]

SOUTHALL, Isabel, co-author see EVANS, Margaret Freeman

SOUTHALL, William, comp. see SOUTHALL, Eliza Allen

SOUTHCOAT, Joanna see SOUTHCOTT, Joanna

5070. SOUTHCOTT, Joanna [Br. 1750-1814] ALT: Southcoat, Joanna
Songs of Moses and the Lamb. Poems.
L: Chambers, pr., 1804. 352p. NUC OCLC

5071. SOUTHERN, Isabella J. [Br. 19c]
Sonnets, and other poems.
L: W. Scott, 1891. 260p. NUC BL OCLC

SOUTHESK, The Earl of, ed. see ELLIOT, Lady Charlotte

5072. SOUTHEY, Caroline Anne (Bowles), Mrs. Robert Southey [Br. 1786-1854] ALT: Bowles, Caroline Anne
Autumn flowers and other poems.
Boston: Saxton, Peirce & co.; NY: Saxton & Miles, 1844. 132p. NUC

5073. -----The birth-day; a poem, in three parts: to which are added, occasional verses.
L & Edinburgh: W. Blackwood & sons, 1836. 288p. NUC BL OCLC

5074. -----Ellen Fitzarthur. A metrical tale.
L: Longman, Hurst, Rees, Orme, & Brown, 1820. 134p. NUC BL OCLC

5075. -----The floral wreath of autumn flowers.
4th ed. L: Auburn: Derby, Miller, 1848. 128p. NUC OCLC

5076. -----The poetical works of Caroline Bowles Southey.
Edinburgh & L: W. Blackwood & sons, 1867. 304p. NUC BL OCLC

5077. -----Robin Hood. With Robert Southey.
L & Edinburgh: William Blackwood & sons, 1847. 248p. NUC BL OCLC

5078. -----Solitary hours.
L: T. Cadell; Edinburgh: W. Blackwood, 1826. 236p. NUC BL OCLC
[Misc. poems, short stories & essays]

5079. -----Tales of the factories.
L & Edinburgh: W. Blackwood, 1833. 85p. NUC BL

5080. -----The widow's tale, and other poems.
L: Longman, Hurst, Rees, Orme, & Brown, 1822. 222p. NUC BL OCLC

SOUTHEY, Robert, co-author see SOUTHEY, Caroline Anne (Bowles)

SOUTHEY, Mrs. Robert see SOUTHEY, Caroline Anne (Bowles)

SPALDING, Louise (Billings) see SPALDING, Lucy Horatia (Billings)

5081. SPALDING, Lucy Horatia (Billings) [Am. 19c] ALT: Spalding, Louise Billings
The ruined statues and other poems. By Louise Billings Spalding.
Philadelphia: J.B. Lippincott & co., 1871. 155p. NUC BL OCLC

5082. SPALDING, Susan Marr, Mrs. [Am. 19c]
The wings of Icarus.
Boston: Roberts bros., 1892. 111p. NUC BL OCLC

5083. -----Winter roses.
Philadelphia: A. Edward Newton & co., 1888. 24p. NUC OCLC

5084. SPARKS, Mary Crowninshield (Silsbee) [Am. 1809-1887] ALT: S., M.C.
Hymns, home, Harvard. By M.C.S.
Boston: A. Williams & co., 1883. 295p. NUC
[Divided into 3 themes]

5085. SPAULDING, E.A., Mrs. [Am. b. 1811]
Bric-a-brac: fugitive pieces.
Boston: Pr. for the author, 1886. 128p. NUC OCLC
[Incl. autobiography, poems & essays]

5086. SPEARING, Annie Belle, Mrs. [Am. b. 1858]
Poems.
Bangor, ME: C.H. Glass & co., pr., 1893. 132p. NUC OCLC

5087. SPECHT, Rachel [Br. 17c] ALT: Speight, Rachael
Certain quaeres to the bayter of women in mouzell.
L: Pr. N. Okes for T. Archer, 1617. 14, 38p. NUC
[Special t.p. in "A mouzell for Melastomus ..."]

5088. -----Mortalities memorandum, with a dream prefixed, imaginary in manner, reall in matter.
L: E. Griffin for J. Bloome, 1621. 38p. BL

5089. -----A mouzell for Melastomus: the cynicall bayter of, and foule mouthed barker against Evahs sex; or An apologeticall answere to that irreligious and illiterate pamphlet, made by Io. Sw[etnam], and by him intituled, the arraignement of women.
L: N. Okes for T. Archer, 1617. 38p. NUC BL

SPEIGHT, Rachael see SPECHT, Rachel

SPENCE, Mrs. George see SPENCE, Sarah

5090. SPENCE, Sarah, Mrs. George Spence [Br. 18/19c]
Poems and a meditation.
Colchester: Pr. for author by Swinborne & Walter, 1821. BL

[2 long poems, 2 brief prose meditations]

5091. -----Poems, and miscellaneous pieces.
Bury St. Edmund's: Pr. for author by P. Gedge, 1795. 130p. NUC BL
[Incl. short prose meditations]

5092. SPENCER, Alla (Hubbard) [Am. 1860-1889]
A souvenir: posthumous writings of Alla Hubbard Spencer.
NY: J.B. Alden, 1890. 120p. NUC OCLC
[Incl. poetry & prose essays]

5093. SPENCER, Mrs. Canning [Br. 19c]
Early and late recollections.
L: n.p., 1853. BL
[Reminiscences; 65 p. of poems]

5094. SPENCER, Emily B. [Am. 19c]
Prose and poetry.
Salt Lake City, UT: Star bk. & job pr. off., 1880. 88p. OCLC
[Religious]

5095. -----The rose of Deseret.
Salt Lake City, UT: n.p., 1887. 100p. NUC OCLC
[Poetry & prose on Mormonism]

SPENCER, W.R., co-author see KNIGHT, Ellis Cornelia

5096. SPENCER, Mrs. Walter [Br. 18/19c]
Commemorative feelings; or, Miscellaneous poems.
L: White, 1812. 163p. NUC BL OCLC
[Mostly poetry, a few prose sketches]

5097. -----Miscellaneous poems. Frogmore Lodge.
Windsor: Pr. E. Harding, 1812. 90p. NUC

5098. -----Poetical trifles: or, Miscellaneous poems on various subjects.
L: n.p., 1781. BL

SPENSER, Edmund, co-author see PEMBROKE, Mary (Sidney) Herbert, Countess of

SPERANZA, pseud. see WILDE, Jane Francesca (Elgee), Lady

SPERO, pseud. see POULTER, Louisa Frances

SPHINX, pseud. see FOX, Sarah Hustler

5099. SPICER, Isabella [Br. 19c]
The gem of Christian peace, and other poems.
L: n.p., 1886. BL

SPINSTER, A, pseud. see LEAN, E.J., Mrs.

5100. SPIRE, Caroline [Br. 19c]
The blind girl; being the true history of Eliza Grove. A poem. To which are added the Bride of the Lamb, and the Prisoner in the dungeon.
L: Gadsby, 1870. 32p. BL
[3 narrative poems]

5101. SPOFFORD, Harriet Elizabeth (Prescott) [Am. 1835-1921]
Ballads about authors.
Boston: D. Lothrop co., 1887. 111p. NUC BL OCLC

5102. -----In Titian's garden and other poems.
Boston: Copeland & Day, 1897. 108p. NUC BL OCLC

5103. -----Poems.
Boston & NY: Houghton, Mifflin & co., 1882. 172p. NUC BL OCLC

5104. SPOONER, Mary A., Mrs. [Am. 19c]
Gathered leaves.
NY: G.P. Putnam, c1848. 180p. NUC OCLC
[90 lyric poems: occasional, memorial, nature, misc.]

5105. SPRAGUE, Achsa W., Miss [Am. 19c]
I still live: a poem for the times.
Oswego, NY: Oliphant, 1862. 19p. NUC OCLC

5106. -----The poet and other poems.
Boston: W. White & co., 1865. 304p. NUC BL OCLC

5107. SPRATT, Mrs. George [Br. 19c]
The language of birds, containing [comprising OCLC] poetic and prose illustrations of the most favourite cage-birds.
L: Saunders & Otley, 1837. BL OCLC

5108. SPRINGER, Rebecca (Ruter) [Am. 1832-1904]
Songs by the sea.
Chicago & NY: Fleming H. Revell, c1889. 10, 169p. NUC OCLC
[Sea poetry]

5109. SPROAT, Nancy Dennis [Am. 1766-1827] PSEUD: Lady, A
Poems on different subjects. By a lady.
Boston: West & Richardson, 1813. 117p. NUC OCLC

5110. -----Village poems.
NY: Wood, 182-? [1830? BL] 67p. NUC BL

5111. SPROULE, Harriet Letitia [Br. 19c]
Poems, etc.
L?: n.p., 1820? 216p. BL
[Hymns, odes & religious verse]

5112. SPURGEON, Elizabeth Georgiana [Br. 19c]
Evergreens: being selections from the poetic works of E.G. Spurgeon.
L: n.p., 1860. BL

SPRUGGINS, RICHARD SUCKLETHUMKIN, pseud. <u>see</u> PARKER, Frances (Talbot), Countess of Morley

SQUIRRELL, Elizabeth <u>see</u> SQUIRRELL, Mary Elizabeth

5113. SQUIRRELL, Mary Elizabeth [Br. b. 1838] ALT: Squirrell, Elizabeth
The autobiography of Elizabeth Squirrell of Shottisham, and selections from her writings ... .
L: Simpkin, Marshall & co., 1853, 1858. 298, 300p. NUC BL OCLC
[Incl. 31 poems; blind & deaf woman]

STANHOPE, Elizabeth Still (Pearsall), Countess of Harrington <u>see</u> HARRINGTON, Elizabeth Still (Pearsall) Stanhope, Countess

5114. STANIFORTH, Amy Susanna [Br. 19c]
Australia and other poems.
Melbourne: Wilson & co., 1863. 252p. BL

5115. STANLEY, Mrs. [Br. 19c]
Tales and poems.
L: J. Booth, 1818. BL
[4 short stories; 18 poems]

5116. STANLEY, Mrs. D. [Br. 18c]
Sir Philip Sidney's Arcadia, moderniz'd by Mrs. Stanley.
L: n.p., 1725. 511p. NUC BL OCLC

5117. STANWOOD, Eunice H. [Am. 19c]
The true perfection which God requires attainable on earth.
Boston: McDonald & Gill, Office of the Christian Witness, 1885. 235p. NUC OCLC
[Poem on Book of Job]

5118. STAPLETON, Miss [Br. 19c]
Apples of gold by starlight.
L: n.p., 1873. BL
[Bible text and poem on it for each day of year and readings for Easter]

5119. -----Apricot Golding of Sunnyside.
L: n.p., 1866. BL

5120. -----The fisherman's family.
L: n.p., 1864. BL

5121. -----Jasper, the man who never cared what people said.
L: n.p., 1865. BL

5122. -----The life of Christ.
L: Williams & Norgate, 1876. 256p. BL OCLC

5123. -----The pastor of Silverdale and other poems.
2d ed. L: n.p., 1867. BL

5124. -----The two doctors, or, making a good thing of it here and thereafter.
L: n.p., 1865. BL

5125. -----Youth and age.
L: n.p., 1864. BL

5126. STARKE, Mariana [Br. 1762?-1838]
The beauties of Carlo-Maria Maggi paraphrased. To which are added sonnets by Mariana Starke.
Exeter: Pr. for the author by S. Wodner, 1811. 51p. NUC BL OCLC

5127. STARKEY, E. A. (Henty), Mrs. Edward Starkey [Br. 19c]
Australian idylls and bush rhymes ... . By ... Ernest G. Henty and E.A. Starkey.
L: Digby & Long, 1896. 79p. NUC BL

STARKEY, Mrs. Edward <u>see</u> STARKEY, E.A. (Henty)

5128. STARR, Eliza Allen [Am. 1824-1901]
Poems.
Philadelphia: H. McGrath, 1867. 224p. NUC BL OCLC

5129. -----Songs of a lifetime.
Chicago: Pub. by author, 1887. 400p. NUC OCLC

STEBBINS, Mary Elizabeth (Moore) Hewitt see HEWITT, Mary Elizabeth (Moore)

5130. STEBBINS, Sarah (Bridges) [Am. 19c]
Galgano's wooing, and other poems.
NY: G.W. Dillingham, 1890. 185p. NUC OCLC

5131. STEEL, M., Mrs. [Br. 19c]
Early days and riper years.
L: n.p., 1850. BL

5132. -----Hymns and verses. A revised edition.
L: n.p., 1855? BL

5133. -----Pathetic and religious poems.
Saxmundham: n.p., 1834. BL

5134. STEELE, Anna Caroline (Wood) [Br. 19c] PSEUD: C.
Thoughts versified. By C.
Braintree: E. & C. Joscelyne, 1860. BL

5135. STEELE, Anne, Mrs. [Br. 1717-1778] PSEUD: Theodosia
Hymns, psalms, and poems. By A. Steele. With memoir by J. Sheppart.
L: D. Sedgwick, 1863. 271p. NUC BL OCLC

5136. -----Poems on subjects chiefly devotional ... . By Theodosia.
L: J. Buckland & J. Ward, 1760. 2v. NUC BL OCLC

5137. -----Poems on subjects chiefly devotional. A new edition. To which is added a third volume consisting of miscellaneous pieces.
Bristol: Pr. W. Pine, sold by T. Cadell, T. Mills, T. Evans, J. Buckland & J. Johnson, 1780. 3v. BL OCLC

5138. -----The works of Mrs. Anne Steele. Comprehending poems ... and miscellaneous pieces. By Theodosia.
Boston: Munroe, Francis & Parker, 1808. 2v. NUC BL OCLC
[Hymns, occasional poems, psalms, misc. poems, and essays, mostly religious]

5139. STEELE, Elizabeth Anne [Br. 19c]
Fire side musings, or thoughts in verse.
Bury St. Edmunds: n.p., 1857. BL

5140. STEELE, Sarah [Br. 19c]
Eva, an historical poem, with illustrative notes, accompanied by some lyric poems.
Dublin: Pr. for the author by J. Jones, 1816. 101p. NUC BL

STEELE-GRAVES, Frances E., co-author see OWEN, Frances Mary (Synge)

5141. STEERS, Fanny [Br. 19c]
The ant-prince, a rhyme.
L: W. Pickering, 1847. 42p. NUC BL OCLC
[Beast fable]

5142. -----The last links are broken.
L: D'Almaine & co., 18--? 5p. NUC OCLC
[Ballad; Music by E.J. Loder]

STELLA, pseud. see NICHOLL, Mary Anne

STELLA OF LAKAWANNA, pseud. see WATRES, Harriet Gertrude (Hollister)

5143. STEPHENS, Ann Sophia (Winterbotham) [Am. 1810?/1813?-1886]
Lily. In memoriam.
NY: J.J. Little & co., 1884. 37p. NUC

5144. STEPHENS, Eliza Jane [Am. 19c]
Poems.
Seymour, CT: W.C. Sharpe, 1895. 22p. NUC OCLC

5145. STEPHENS, Harriet Marion (Ward) [Am. 1823-1858]
Home scenes and home sounds; or, The world from my window.
Boston: Fetridge & co., 1854. 288p. NUC OCLC
[Short stories and poems]

STEPNEY, Catherine Pollok Manners, Lady see HUNTINGTOWER, Catherine Rebecca (Grey) Talmash, Baroness

STERNDALE, MARY, pseud. see STOCKDALE, Mary R.

STERNE, STUART, pseud. see BLOEDE, Gertrude

5146. STETSON, Grace Ellery (Channing) [Am. 1862-1937]
Sea drift; poems.
Boston: Small, Maynard & co., 1899. 90p. NUC OCLC

5147. STEVENS, Beulah Rose, Mrs. [Am. 19c]
The seasons in Florida, and other poems.

Bartow, FL: Courier-informant steam pr., 1891. NUC

5148. STEVENS, Flora Ellice [Am. 19/20c]
Leaves, a collection of poems.
Kansas City, MO: Ramsey, Millett & Hudson, 1882. 74p. NUC

5149. STEVENSON, Edith [Br. 19c] ALT: Edith
The Yetts o' Muckart; or, The famous pic-nic and the brilliant barn-ball.
Edinburgh: n.p., 1872. NUC BL

5150. STEWART, Beatrice [Br. 19c]
Silent hours poems ... . First series.
Eton: R.I. Drake, 1894. 32p. BL

5151. STEWART, Elizabeth [Br. 19c]
Anaya, the prophetess of Miwar. A poem. Pt. 1. Cantos 1 & 2.
L: n.p., 1838. BL
[No more published]

5152. STEWART, Elizabeth M., Miss [Br. 19c] ALT: S., E.M.
The rival roses. A poem. Addressed to Miss O'Neil and Miss Sommerville, of the Theatre Royal, Covent Garden.
L: Handy, 1819. 8p. NUC

5153. -----The shrine, or sketches of sacred biography, in verse.
L: The author, 1834. 111p. BL

5154. -----Stories of the Christian schools.
NY: The Catholic pub. soc. co.; L: Burns & Oates, 1882. 189p. NUC BL
[Verse & prose, incl. The cloister of Nazareth, and other poems.]

5155. STEWART, Jessie [Br. 19c]
Ode to Dr. Thomas Percy, Lord Bishop of Dromore; occasioned by reading the reliques of ancient English poetry.
Edinburgh: Mundell & son; L: Longman & Rees, 1804. 38p. NUC

5156. STEWART, Jessie Fremont, Miss [Am. 19c]
After sunset: poetical gems.
Springfield, IL: n.p., 1891. 135p. NUC

5157. STEWART, Maria L. [Am. 19c]
Glimpses of cadet life at West Point; from the candidate to the graduate; a poem.
n.p.: n.p., 1882. 61p. NUC OCLC

5158. -----Our little brown house; a poem of West Point.
NY: F. Kalkoff, jr., 1880. 15 l. NUC OCLC

5159. STICKNEY, Julia (Noyes) [Am. b. 1830]
One hundred sonnets.
Groveland, MA: Ambrose & co., pr., 1894. 100p. NUC OCLC

5160. -----Poems on Lake Winnipesaukee.
Haverhill, MA: C.C. Morse & son, pr., 1884. 32p. NUC OCLC

STICKNEY, Sarah <u>see</u> ELLIS, Sarah (Stickney)

STIRLING-MAXWELL, Caroline Elizabeth Sarah (Sheridan) Norton <u>see</u> NORTON, Caroline Elizabeth Sarah (Sheridan)

5161. STOCK, Sarah Geraldina [Br. 1839-1898] ALT: S., S.G.
The brighter day. Poems by S.G.S. and E.H. Thompson.
L: J.E. Hawkins, 1889. BL

5162. -----Joy in sorrow.
2d ed. L: J.F. Shaw & co., 1884. 56p. BL

5163. -----Life abundant and other poems.
L: J.F. Shaw & co., 1892. 254p. BL

5164. STOCKALL, Harriett [Br. 19c]
Poems and sonnets.
L: n.p., 1879. NUC BL

5165. -----Poems. Second series.
L: Simpkin, Marshall & co., 1886. 184p. BL

5166. STOCKDALE, Jane [Br. 19c]
Streams from the fountain, sacred and sympathetic writings in prose and verse.
Kendal: Thompson bros., 1886. BL
[Religious poems introduced by brief prose meditations]

5167. STOCKDALE, Mary [Br. 19c]
Miscellaneous poems, by Mary Stockdale: published at various times and collected in 1826.
L: S. Gosnell, pr., n.d. NUC
[The wedding ring.]

5168. STOCKDALE, Mary R. [Br. 18/19c] PSEUD: S., Miss; Sterndale, Mary
The Christian poet's lament over the Christian statesman.
L: John Stockdale, 1812. 21p. NUC

5169. -----The effusions of the heart; poems.
L: John Stockdale, 1798. 160p. NUC OCLC

5170. -----The family book, or children's journal ... from the French of Berquin. Interspersed with poetical pieces written by the translator, Miss Stockdale.
L: J. Stockdale, 1798. 294p. BL

5171. -----The mirror of the mind. Poems by Miss Stockdale.
L: Stockdale, 1810. 2v. NUC BL OCLC
[V. 1 includes autobiography]

5172. -----The mother and child; a poem.
L: M. Stockdale, 1818. 28p. NUC

5173. -----A shroud for Sir Samuel Romilly: an elegy.
L: M. Stockdale, 1818. 33p. NUC BL OCLC
[Also pub. as: A plume for Sir Samuel Romilly]

5174. -----The widow and her orphan family. An elegy.
L: J. Stockdale, 1812. 19p. NUC BL

5175. -----A wreath for the urn; an elegy on the Princess Charlotte; with other poems.
L: M. Stockdale, 1818. 22p. NUC BL

5176. STODDARD, Elizabeth Drew (Barstow), Mrs. Richard Henry Stoddard [Am. 1823-1902]
Poems.
Boston & NY: Houghton, Mifflin & co., 1895. 164p. NUC OCLC

STODDARD, Mrs. Richard Henry <u>see</u> STODDARD, Elizabeth Drew (Barstow)

5177. STOKES, Catherine [Br. 19c]
Poems, on subjects religious, moral (addenda on Christmas Day).
Salisbury: Pr. J.A. Gilmour, 1818. 78p. NUC BL

5178. STONE, Cara Elizabeth (Hanscom) Whiton- [Am. b. 1831]
A cycle of sonnets. Ed. Mabel Loomis Todd.
Boston: Roberts bros., 1896. 93p. NUC OCLC

5179. -----Sonnets, songs, laments.
Boston: J.G. Cupples, 1891. 184p. NUC

5180. STONE, Catherine [Br. 19c]
The voice of mercy.
Guildford: Billing & sons, 1884. 77p. BL

5181. STONE, Elizabeth [Br. 19c]
Three incidents, strictly true.
Worthing: n.p., 1873. 8p. BL
[Religious poetry]

5182. STONE, Katherine Mary [Br. 19c]
Our flag, a lay of the Pontifical Zouaves; and other poems.
L: Burns & Oates; Dublin: M.H. Gill & son, 1878. 123p. NUC BL

5183. STONE, Mary K.A. [Am. 19c]
"As thy days," and other verses.
NY: James Pott & co., 1893. 32p. NUC OCLC

5184. STONEHEWER, Agnes [Br. 19c]
Monacella: a poem.
L: n.p., 1876. BL

5185. STOPFORD, Octavia [Br. 19c]
Sketches in verse, and other poems.
Hull: Wilson, 1826. 142p. NUC BL

5186. STOWE, Harriet Elizabeth (Beecher) [Am. 1811-1896]
Light after darkness. Religious poems.
L: S. Low & Marston, 1867. 105p. NUC BL OCLC

5187. -----Religious poems.
1st ed. Boston: Ticknor & Fields, 1867. 107p. NUC BL OCLC

5188. STRACHAN, Mary [Br. 19c]
Muirland rhymes.
Strathaven: Pr. N.W. Bryson, 1899. 100p. NUC OCLC

5189. STREATFEILD, Sophia Charlotte [Br. 19/20c] ALT: S., Mrs C. N.
Above these clouds. Words of comfort for mourners.
L: Skeffington & son, 1899. 36p. BL

5190. -----Hymns and verses on the collects. By Mrs. C.N.S.
L: Longmans, Green & co., 1866. 97p. BL

5191. -----Hymns on the love of Jesus and the home above.
L: Skeffington & son, 1875. BL

5192. -----The story of the Good Shepherd. A service of song.
L: Skeffington & son, 1873. BL

5193. -----Words of comfort for the sick and suffering.

L: n.p., 1875. BL
[Prose & verse]

STREBOR, EIGGAM, pseud. see ROBERTS, Maggie

5194. STRICKLAND, Agnes [Br. 1796-1874]
Demetrius: a tale of modern Greece; in three cantos; with other poems.
L: J. Fraser, 1833. 171p. NUC BL

5195. -----Floral sketches, fables and other poems.
L: Effingham Wilson, 1836. 155p. NUC BL OCLC

5196. -----Historic scenes and poetic fancies.
L: Henry Colburn, 1850. 400p. NUC BL OCLC
[Retellings in prose of Charles I's captivity, & misc. poetry]

5197. -----Monody upon the death of the Princess Charlotte of Wales.
L: J. Ridgway, 1817. BL
[Pub. anon.]

5198. -----The sea side offering.
Edinburgh: n.p., 1856. BL

5199. -----The seven ages of woman and other poems.
L: Hurst, Chance & co., 1827. 152p. NUC BL OCLC

5200. -----Worcester Field; or, The cavalier. A poem in four cantos, with historical notes.
L: Longman, Rees, Orme, Browne & Green, 1826. 163p. NUC BL OCLC

STRICKLAND, Susanna see MOODIE, Susanna (Strickland)

5201. STRINGER, Mrs. [Br. 19c] PSEUD: Lady, A
The chain of affection ... . By a lady.
Richmond: Priv. pr., 1830? BL
[Moral poem in couplets; 2 lyrics]

STRONG, Elizabeth Kirkham see MATHEWS, Eliza Kirkham (Strong)

5202. STRONG, Mary E., Mrs. [Am. 19c]
Her mission. By the mother of Grace Strong. Composed in memory of Grace Strong, by her blind mother.
Columbus, OH: W.G. Hubbard & co., 1888. 108p. NUC

STROUT, C.W.D., Mrs. see RICH, Caroline Webster D. (Stockbridge)

5203. STRUTT, Elizabeth [Br. 19c]
ALT: S., E.
The story of Psyche. With a classical enquiry into the signification and origin of the fable.
L: n.p., 1852. 53p. BL OCLC

5204. -----A wreath for the altar of the new church.
Bury St. Edmunds: Priv. pr., 1842. BL

5205. STRYKOR, Cornelia [Am. 19c]
PSEUD: Ailenroc
Ailenroc's book. Composed of poems and stories.
Nashville, TN: Gospel Advocate pub. co., 1899. 205p. NUC

5206. STUART, E.G., Mrs. [Br. 19c]
The calling of the sea and other poems.
L: W.G. Wheeler, 1891. 64p. BL

5207. STUART, Helen Montagu [Br. 19c]
The message home and other poems.
L: n.p., 1878. BL

5208. STUART, Jane Isabella [Br. 19c]
Songs and verses.
L: Sonnenschein & co., 1886. 156p. BL

5209. STUART, Lady Louisa [Br. 1757-1851]
Lady Louisa Stuart. Selections from her manuscripts. Ed. Hon. James Archibald Home.
Edinburgh: D. Douglas, 1894. 308p. NY & L: Harper & bros., 310p. NUC BL OCLC
[Incl. 2 long poems: The Fairies' frolic & The diamond robe, or The maniac]

5210. -----Stuartiana; or, Bubbles blown by and to some of the family of Stuart. Comp. William Stuart.
Menabilly: Priv. pr. by Jonathan Rushleigh, 1857. BL
[Incl. poems by Lady Louisa]

STUART, William, comp. see STUART, Lady Louisa

5211. STUART-WORTLEY, Lady Emmeline Charlotte Elizabeth (Manners) [Br. 1806-1855] ALT: Wortley, Lady Emmeline Charlotte Elizabeth Manners (Stuart)
The Great Exhibition. Honour to labour, a lay of 1851.
L: n.p., 1851. BL

5212. -----Hours at Naples, and other poems.

L: n.p., 1837. BL

5213. -----Impressions of Italy and other poems.
L: Saunders, 1837. NUC BL

5214. -----Jairah, a dramatic mystery; and other poems.
L: J. Rickerby, 1840. 380p. NUC BL
[2 acts]

5215. -----The knight and the enchantress; with other poems.
L: n.p., 1835. BL

5216. -----Lays of leisure hours.
L: n.p., 1838. 2v. BL

5217. -----London at night; and other poems.
L: Longman, Rees, Orme, Brown, Green & Longman, 1834. 12p. NUC BL

5218. -----The maiden of Moscow: a poem in twenty-one cantos.
L: n.p., 1842. BL

5219. -----On the approaching close of the Great Exhibition, and other poems.
L: n.p., 1851. BL

5220. -----Poems.
L: Murray, 1833. 278p. NUC BL OCLC

5221. -----Queen Berengaria's courtesy, and other poems.
L: J. Rickerby & J. Hatchard & son, 1838. 3v. NUC BL OCLC

5222. -----The slave and other poems, English and Spanish.
L: T. Bosworth, 1853. 126p. NUC

5223. -----Sonnets written chiefly during a tour through Holland, Germany, Italy, Turkey and Hungary.
L: J. Rickerby, 1839. 230p. NUC BL

5224. -----Travelling sketches in rhyme.
L: n.p., 1835. 116p. NUC BL

5225. -----The village churchyard; and other poems.
L: n.p., 1835. NUC BL

5226. -----The visionary; a fragment, with other poems.
2 pt. L: n.p., 1836-39. BL

5227. STURM, Olga Louise, Mrs. [Am. 19c]
Wayside flowers, poems.
Cleveland, OH: Household realm co., 1894. 56p. NUC OCLC

5228. STURT, Anne Barnard [Br. 1793-1872]
Reminiscences of our mother.
L: Pr. Unwin bros. for priv. circ., 1873. 284p. NUC BL OCLC
[Incl. poetry, stories, religious writings]

SUFFOLK VILLAGER, A, pseud. see COWELL, Elizabeth Susan

SUMMERS, T.O. see MARTIN, Margaret (Maxwell)

5229. SUNTER, J. Pauline, Mrs. [Am. 19c]
All around the year.
Boston: n.p., 188-91. 2v. NUC

5230. -----A birthday greeting.
NY: Hard & Parsons, 1888. 7 l. NUC

5231. -----Christmas greetings.
NY: Ford & Parsons, 1886. 29p. NUC

5232. -----The greeting.
NY: Hard & Parsons, 1886. 15 l. NUC OCLC

5233. -----A happy New Year to you.
Boston: Lee & Shepard, 1889. 10 l. NUC

5234. -----A message for you.
NY & L: The Art Lithographic pub. co., 1891? 24p. NUC OCLC

5235. -----A song for Christmas morning.
Munich & NY: The Art Lithographic pub. co., 188-? 12 l. NUC OCLC

5236. -----Wandering winds.
Boston: S.E. Cassino, 1888. 10 l. NUC

5237. SUSANNA, pseud. [Br. 18c]
Poems by Susanna.
L: Pr. L. Wayland, for Charles Dilly, 1789. 31p. NUC BL

5238. SUTCLIFF, Anne Hirst [Br. 1767-1800]
Poems.
Sheffield: Iris off.; pr. by James Montgomery, 1800. 32p. NUC BL

5239. SUTCLIFFE, Alice [Br. 17c]
Meditations of man's mortalitie. Or, A way to true blessedness ... . The second edition, enlarged.

L: Pr. B. Alsop & T. Fawcet for Henry Seyle, 1634. NUC BL
[Prose & poetry]

5240. SUTCLIFFE, Frances Mary [Br. 19c] ALT: S., F.M.
Long Tom, otherwise, Thomas Long.
L: George Wightman, 1836. 16p. BL

5241. -----Mount Pleasant and Pleasant Row.
L: James Nisbet & co., 1838. 31p. BL

5242. -----The squire and his man; or, The way to get up in the world.
L: J.C. Bridgewater, 1839. 20p. NUC BL

5243. SUTFIN, M.A., Mrs. [Am. 19c]
Wayside gleanings.
Jackson, MI: Pub. for the author by A.H. Brown, 1883. 84p. NUC OCLC

5244. SUTHERLAND, Jane Gunn [Br. 19c] PSEUD: Una
Lays of the Luri; and other rhymes. By "Una."
Keighley: E. Craven, 1885. BL
[Narrative & lyric poems]

5245. SWAIN, M.P., Miss [Am. 19c] ALT: S., M. P.
Mara; or, A romance of the war. A poem. By M.P.S.
Selma, AL: Mississippian steam bks. & job off., 1864. 80p. NUC OCLC

5246. SWAIN, Sarah, Mrs. [Br. 19/20c]
1893. Song for the people ... On the occasion of the Princess Mary of Teck's alliance with ... the Duke of York.
Barbados: n.p., 1893. BL

5247. -----Birthday song for her Brittanic Majesty Victoria ... 24th May, 1893.
Barbados: n.p., 1893. BL

5248. -----A record of the loss of the "Victoria."
Barbados: n.p., 1893. BL

5249. SWAINE, C. Jennie, Mrs. [Am. 19c]
Legends and lilies: a souvenir.
Concord, NH: Republican press assoc., 1893. 207p. NUC OCLC
[Lyric poems; nature]

SWAN OF LITCHFIELD, THE, pseud. <u>see</u> SEWARD, Anna

5250. SWANWICK, Catherine [Br. 19c] PSEUD: L.
Legends, parables and lyrics.
L: E.T. Whitfield, 1875. 295p. OCLC

5251. -----Poems, by L.
L: E.T. Whitfield, 1858. 119p. NUC

5252. -----Poems. By L.
L: E.T. Whitfield, 1858. 119p. NUC

5253. -----Poems. By L.
2d ed. 3d ser. L: E.T. Whitfield, 1858-1860. 155p. NUC BL

5254. -----Poems: narrative and dramatic.
L: E.T. Whitfield, 1872. 208p. NUC

SWAYNE, George Carless, co-author <u>see</u> SWAYNE, Margaret Sarah

5255. SWAYNE, Margaret [Br. 19c]
A true tale of the sea, and other verses.
L: Chapman & Hall, 1899. 60p. BL

5256. SWAYNE, Margaret Sarah [Br. 19c]
Poems. With George Carless Swayne.
Darmstadt: n.p., n.d. BL

5257. SWEAT, Margaret Jane (Mussey) [Am. b. 1823] ALT: S., M.J. M.
Verses by M.J.M.S.
Portland, ME: Lakeside press, 1890. 158p. NUC

5258. SWEETMAN, Elinor [Br. 19/20c]
Footsteps of the God, and other poems.
L: G. Bell, 1893. 98p. NUC BL OCLC

5259. -----Pastorals, and other poems.
L: J.M. Dent & co., 1899. 92p. NUC BL OCLC

5260. SWIFT, Frances Elizabeth (Chase) [Am. 19c] PSEUD: Fales, Fanny
Hearth songs, and on the wing.
Boston: n.p., c1899. 28,22p. NUC OCLC

5261. -----Legend of Long Pond; or, Lake of the Golden Cross.
Boston: A. Mulge & sons, 1885. 8p. NUC
[On Indian girl forsaken by her lover.]

5262. -----Rhymes of Falmouth.
Falmouth, MA?: n.p., c1892. 29 l. NUC OCLC

5263. -----Soul songs.
Boston: Press of Lewis F. Clarke, 1895. 25p. NUC OCLC

5264. -----Voices of the heart. By Fanny Fales.
Boston: B.B. Mussey & co., 1853. 120p. NUC OCLC

5265. SWIFT, Julia M. [Am. 19c]
Christmas chimes and other poems.
Philadelphia: Claxton, Remsen & Haffelfinger, 1877. 96p. NUC OCLC

5266. -----Field flowers.
Philadelphia: Claxton, Remsen & Haffelfinger, 1872. 196p. NUC OCLC

5267. SWINGLE, Emma F. [Am. 19c]
Muskingum melodies.
Columbus, OH: Hann & Adair, pr., 1897. 199p. NUC OCLC

5268. SWINNEY, Jane [Br. 18c] PSEUD: Young Lady, A
A collection of poems, by a young lady.
L & Rochester: Pr. Gillman & Etherington, 1792. 200p. NUC BL

5269. SWINTON, Minna Maynard [Br. 19c]
A lay of Montrose and other verses.
Guildford: "Surrey Advertiser" off., 1877. 36p. BL

5270. SWISHER, Bella French, Mrs. [Am. 1837-1894]
Florecita.
NY: John B. Alden, 1889. 106p. NUC OCLC

5271. -----The sin of Edith Dean.
NY: J.B. Alden, 1890. 96p. NUC OCLC

SYKES, Lady see SYKES, Mrs. S.

5272. SYKES, Mrs. S. [Br. 19c] ALT: Sykes, Lady
Hymns and poems on moral subjects.
L: n.p., 1815. BL

5273. SYMMONS, Caroline [Br. 1789-1803]
Poems, by Caroline Symmons and Charles Symmons. Ed. Charles Symmons.
L: J. Johnson & co., 1812. NUC BL

5274. -----The raising of Jairus' daughter. A poem ... [By Francis Wrangham] to which is annexed a short memoir, interspersed with a few poetical productions of the late Caroline Symmons.
L: J. Mawman, 1804. 45p. NUC BL OCLC

SYMMONS, Charles, co-author & ed. see SYMMONS, Caroline

SYNGE, Bertha, co-author see BROWN, Annie Johnson-

SYNGE, E., Miss, co-author see OWEN, Frances Mary (Synge)

SYNGE, Frances Mary see OWEN, Frances Mary (Synge)

T., B.L. see TOLLEMACHE, Beatrix Lucia Catherine (Egerton)

T., F. see TROLLOPE, Frances (Milton)

T., F.L. see TURNBULL, Francese Hubbard (Litchfield)

T., H. Mary see TEULON, H. Mary

T., K.N. see TRASK, Kate (Nichols)

T., L. see THOMAS, L., Mrs.

T., L.N. see TODRIG, Louise N., Mrs.

T., M. see TEESDALE, M., Mrs.

T., M.A. see TINCKER, Mary Agnes

T., M.A. see TOWNSEND, Mary Ashley (Van Voorhis)

T., M.F. see TYTLER, Margaret Fraser

TADEMA, Laurence Alma see ALMA-TADEMA, Laurence, Miss

5275. TADLOCK, Clara Moyse, Mrs. [Am. 19c]
A California idyl.
n.p.: n.p., 1893. 7p. NUC OCLC

5276. -----Holiday souvenir no. 5, 1897-1898.
n.p.: n.p., 1898? 11p. NUC
[Christmas poetry]

5277. -----Solomon Grinder's Christmas eve and other poems.
Boston: D. Lothrop & co., 1885. 204p. NUC OCLC
[Title poem long narrative, others misc.]

5278. TAGGART, Cynthia [Am. 1801-1849]
Poems.
Providence, RI: Cranston & Hammond, 1834. 98p. NUC BL OCLC

5279. TALBOT, Catherine [Br. 1721-1770]

Essays on various subjects.
2d ed. L: J. & F. Rivington, 1772.
2v. BL NUC OCLC
[Tales, essays, poems]

5280. -----The works of the late Mrs. Catherine Talbot. A new edition.
L: Pr. J., F. & C. Rivington, 1780.
336p. NUC BL OCLC
[On conduct of life. Incl. essays, letters, dialogues, prose pastorals, allegories & poetry]

5281. TALCOTT, Hannah Elizabeth (Bradbury) Goodwin [Am. 1827-1893]
Elizabeth and the roses. A legend of Hungary.
Boston: Cupples, Upham & co., 189-?
19p. NUC

TALLEY, Susan Archer <u>see</u> WEISS, Susan Archer (Talley)

5282. TANEY, Mary Florence [Am. 19c]
Kentucky pioneer women, Columbian poems and prose sketches.
Cincinnati, OH: R. Clarke & co., 1893. 99p. NUC OCLC
[Poems on Kentucky frontier life]

5283. TANNER, Clara (Coulthard) [Br. 19c] ALT: Coulthard, Clara
The fringed cloud and Woman, two short poems.
L: C. Becket, 1853. 8p. BL

5284. -----Poems.
Bath: W. Pocock; L: Simpkin, Marshall & co., 1842. 131p. BL

5285. -----Prayers and hymns. To which is added, The Millenium: a poem.
L: Aylott & Jones, 1845. 106p. BL

5286. -----Rhymes for an hour. Poems on several occasions.
L: Simpkin, Marshall & co., 1842.
120p. BL

5287. -----The vision of the blue isle. A poem.
Bath: Birns & Goodwin; L: Simpkin, Marshall & co., 1840. 16p. BL

5288. TANNER, Mary J. [Am. 19c]
A book of fugitive poems.
Salt Lake City, UT: Pr. J.C. Graham & co., 1880. 128p. NUC OCLC

TAPPEN, C.L.V. <u>see</u> RICHMOND, Cora Linn Victoria (Scott) Hatch Tappen

5289. TATHAM, Emma, Miss [Br. 1830-1855]
The dream of Pythagoras and other poems.
L: n.p., 1854; 2d ed. L: Longman & co.; Edinburgh: Oliver & Boyd, 1854.
216p. NUC BL OCLC

5290. -----The dream of Pythagoras.
5th ed. L: n.p., 1872. BL
[Contains additional pieces and a memorial by Rev. B. Gregory.]

5291. -----Etchings and pearls: or, A flower for the grave of Emma Tatham. By Mrs. J. Cooke Westbrook.
2d ed. L: n.p., 1837. BL
[Incl. some of her poems]

5292. -----On the ocean of time.
L: Hodder & Stoughton, 1892. BL

TAYLOR, Ann (Martin), co-author <u>see</u> TAYLOR, Jane

5293. TAYLOR, Clare [Br. d. 1778]
Hymns composed chiefly on the death and sufferings of Christ, and redemption through his blood.
L: n.p., 1859. 60p. NUC BL
[Pub. 1865 as: Hymns composed chiefly on the Atonement of Christ, and redemption through his blood. L: D. Sedgwick, 1865. 60p. NUC BL]

5294. TAYLOR, Elizabeth (Colpeper) [Br. 1749-1836]
Memoir of Mrs. Elizabeth Taylor, late of Saffron-Walden, by her daughter, Mrs. H.E. Webster, with many of her unpublished poems.
4th ed. L: n.p., 1849. BL

5295. TAYLOR, Ellen [Br. 18c]
Poems.
Dublin: G. Draper, 1792. 14p. NUC BL
[Taylor was known as: The Irish cottager]

5296. TAYLOR, Emily [Br. 1795-1872]
Poetical illustrations of passages of Scripture.
Wellington & L: F. Houlston & son, 1826. 78p. NUC BL

5297. -----The visions of Las Casas, and other poems.
L: Taylor & Hessey, 1825. 122p. NUC BL

5298. TAYLOR, Mrs. Enoch [Am. 19c]
A-naughty-biography and other poems.
Cincinnati, OH: R. Clarke & co., pr., 1878. 153p. NUC OCLC
["Naughty" was the nickname of the author.]

5299. TAYLOR, Hannah Harris [Br. 1784-1812]
Memoir of Hannah Taylor, extracted from her own memorandums.
York: W. Alexander, 1820. 168p. NUC BL OCLC
[Incl. poetry]

TAYLOR, Ida Scott see MCKINNEY, Ida Scott (Taylor)

TAYLOR, Isaac, ed. see TAYLOR, Jane

5300. TAYLOR, J.M., Mrs. [Am. 19c]
Mott's party, and other poems.
Holmesburg, PA: W.F. Knott, 1872. 50p. NUC OCLC

5301. TAYLOR, Jane [Br. 1783-1824]
The family pen. Memorials, biographical and literary of the Taylor family of Ongar. Ed. Isaac Taylor.
L: Jackson, Walford & Hodder, 1867. 2v. NUC BL OCLC
[Prose & verse; also incl. writings of Ann (Martin) Taylor]

5302. -----Memoirs and poetical remains of the late Jane Taylor with extracts from her correspondence. Comp. Isaac Taylor.
L: B.J. Holdsworth, 1825. 2v. NUC BL OCLC

5303. -----Writings of Jane Taylor.
Boston: Perkins & Marvin, 1832. 5v. NUC
[Memoirs, correspondence & poetry]

5304. TAYLOR, Janette L. Plass [Am. 19c]
Violet leaves.
Vassar, MI: Pioneer steam pr. off., 1880. 31p. NUC OCLC

5305. TAYLOR, Margaret Scott [Br. 19c]
'Boys together,' and other poems.
L: Kegan Paul & co., 1884. 220p. BL

5306. TAYLOR, May [Am. 19c]
Poems.
Chicago: Priv. pr. by R.R. Donnelley, 1896. 52p. NUC OCLC

5307. TEESDALE, M., Mrs. [Br. 19c]
ALT: T., M.
Poems by M.T. Ed. her children.
Edinburgh & L: Pr. Ballantyne, Hanson, & co., for priv. circ., 1888. 99p. [102p. BL] NUC BL OCLC

5308. TEETZEL, Frances Grant, Mrs. [Am. 19c]
Poems; vagrant fancies.
Milwaukee, WI: Pub. by the author, 1893. 68p. NUC OCLC

5309. TEFT, Elizabeth [Br. 18c]
PSEUD: Orinthia
Orinthia's miscellanies: or a compleat collection of poems never before published.
L: n.p., 1747. 159p. NUC BL

5310. TELFORD, Sarah [Br. 19c]
Miscellaneous poems.
Durham: n.p., 1848. BL

5311. TEMPLE, Anna (Chambers) Grenville-Temple, Countess [Br. d. 1777] ALT: Chamber, Anna; Grenville, Anna, Countess Temple
Poems by Anna Chamber, Countess Temple.
Strawberry Hill: n.p., 1764. 34p. NUC BL OCLC

5312. -----Verses sent to Lady Charles Spencer, with a painted taffety, occasioned by saying she was low in pocket and could not buy a new gown.
Strawberry Hill: Pr. Thomas Kingate, 1764? 1 l. NUC BL

5313. TEMPLE, Augusta [Br. 19c]
A birthday posy for young and old. Verses, songs, stories, plays.
L: Masters & co., 1889. 297p. BL

5314. TEMPLE, Laura Sophia [Br. 18/19c]
Lyric and other poems.
L: Longman, Hurst, Rees, & Orme, 1808. 145p. NUC BL OCLC

5315. -----Poems.
L: R. Phillips, 1805. 192p. NUC BL

5316. -----The siege of Zaragoza, and other poems.
L: William Miller, 1812. 150p. NUC BL OCLC

5317. TEMPLE, Rose [Br. 19c]
Parliamentary reminiscences.
Norwood: J. Platt, 1886. 70p. BL
[Satires on M.P.'s, incl. Lord Randolph Churchill]

5318. TEMPLE, Rose Ellen (Hendriks) [Br. 19c] ALT: Hendriks, Rose Ellen
Chit chat: a poem. In twelve cantos.
L: Kent & Richards, 1849. 140p. NUC BL

5319. -----The poet's souvenir of amateur artists.

L: n.p., 1856. BL

5320. -----The wild rose, with other poems.
L: n.p., 1847. BL

5321. TEMPLER, Caroline B.
Tales by the flowers. By Caroline B. Templer.
L: n.p., 1861. BL

TENELLA, pseud. see CLARKE, Mary Bayard (Devereux)

TERRY, Rose see COOKE, Rose Terry

5322. TESKE, T. Alcliffe, Mrs. [Am. 19c]
Heart echoes.
Hartford, CT: T. Alcliffe Teske, 1887. 64p. NUC OCLC

5323. -----Songs of love.
Hartford, CT: Press of the Plimpton mfg. co., 1894. 44p. NUC

5324. TEULON, H. Mary [Br. 19c] ALT: T., H. Mary
Blossoms in the shade.
L: n.p., 1863. BL

5325. -----Fruits of the valley.
L: n.p., 1865. BL

5326. THACKERAY, Rose E. [Br. 19c]
Pictures of the past; or, Rhythmical recollections of a foreign tour, to which are added some miscellaneous pieces.
Norwich: Pr. Fletcher & son, 1876. 148p. NUC OCLC
[84 poems, on European travel, sacred poems, & misc.]

5327. -----Social sketches, in verse.
L: T. Cautley Newby, 1868. 144p. BL OCLC

5328. THATCHER, Mary [Br. 19c]
Isis. A divine poem.
L: J. Handyside, 1854. 38p. BL

5329. THAXTER, Celia (Leighton) [Am. 1836-1894]
Among the isles of Shoals.
Boston: J.R. Osgood & co., 1873. 184p. NUC BL OCLC

5330. -----The cruise of the Mystery and other poems.
Boston: Houghton, Mifflin, 1886. 121p. NUC BL OCLC

5331. -----Drift-weed.
Boston: Houghton, Osgood, & co., 1879. 152p. NUC BL OCLC

5332. -----Idyls and pastorals; a home gallery of poetry and art.
Boston: D. Lothrop & co., 1886. 58p. NUC OCLC

5333. -----My lighthouse, and other poems. Illustrated by author.
Boston: L. Prang & co., 1890. 8p. NUC

5334. -----Poems.
Boston & NY: Hurd & Houghton, 1872. 86p. NUC BL OCLC

5335. -----Verses.
Boston: D. Lothrop co., 1891. 54p. NUC OCLC

THAYER, Mrs. C.M. see THAYER, Caroline Matilda (Warren)

5336. THAYER, Caroline Matilda (Warren) [Am. 19c] ALT: Thayer, Mrs. C.M.
Poems on various occasions.
Ravenna, OH: Pr. at the office of the Ohio Star, 1840. 32p. NUC OCLC

5337. -----Religion recommended to youth, in a series of letters addressed to a young lady, to which are added: "Poems on various occasions."
NY: T. Bakewell, 1817. 139p. NUC BL OCLC

THEODOSIA, pseud. see STEELE, Anne, Mrs.

THETA, pseud. see HOBLYN, Maria Theresa

THICKNESSE, Ann (Ford) see THICKNESSE, Anne (Ford)

5338. THICKNESSE, Anne [Ann NUC] (Ford) [Br. 1737-1824] ALT: Ford, Anne
A letter from Miss F--d, addressed to a person of distinction with a new ballad to an old tune. Sent to the author by an unknown hand.
L: n.p., 1761. 47p. NUC BL OCLC
[Attr. to Thicknesse. Supposedly addressed to William Villiers, Earl of Jersy]

5339. THISTLETHWAYTE, Grace [Br. 19c]
Hymns and other compositions. By Grace Thistlethwayte ... between the age of ten and twelve years.
L: n.p., 1840. BL

THOMAS, CAROLINE, pseud. see DORR, Julia Caroline (Ripley)

5340. THOMAS, Edith Matilda [Am. 19c]
Babes of the year.
NY: F.A. Stokes & bro., 1888. 13 l.
NUC OCLC
[Poems on children]

5341. -----Children of autumn.
NY: F.A. Stokes & bro., 1888. 4 l.
NUC
[The children of the seasons series.]

5342. -----Children of spring.
NY: F.A. Stokes & bro., 1888. 4 l.
NUC
[The children of the seasons series.]

5343. -----Children of summer.
NY: F.A. Stokes & bro., 1888. NUC
[The children of the seasons series.]

5344. -----Children of winter.
NY: F.A. Stokes & bro., 1888. 4 l.
NUC
[The children of the seasons series.]

5345. -----Fair shadow land.
NY: Houghton, Mifflin & co., 1893.
130p. NUC BL OCLC

5346. -----Heaven and earth; an antiphon.
NY: F.A. Stokes & bro., 1889. 12 l.
NUC

5347. -----The inverted torch.
Boston & NY: Houghton, Mifflin & co., 1890. 94p. NUC BL OCLC

5348. -----Lyrics and sonnets.
Boston & NY: Houghton, Mifflin, & co., 1887. 136p. NUC BL OCLC

5349. -----A New Year's masque, and other poems.
Boston & NY: Houghton, Mifflin & co., 1885. 138p. NUC BL OCLC

5350. -----Tiny folk of sunny days.
Ill. by Maud Humphrey.
NY: Frederick A. Stokes & bro., 1889. 7 l. NUC
[Also incl. in: Babes of the nations.]

5351. -----A winter swallow, with other verse.
NY: C. Scribner's sons, 1896. 120p.
NUC OCLC

THOMAS, Mrs. Edward see THOMAS, Jane (Hamilton)

THOMAS, Mrs. Edward see THOMAS, Jane (Pinhorn)

5352. THOMAS, Elizabeth [Br. 1677-1731] PSEUD: Corinna; Lady, A
The metamorphosis of the town: or, a view of the present fashions. A tale: after the manner of Fontaine.
2d ed. L: J. Wilford, 1730. 40p. NUC BL OCLC
[Incl. Swift's Journal of a modern lady. 4th ed. L: J. Wilford, 1743. 62p. NUC BL]

5353. -----Miscellany poems on several subjects.
L: T. Combes, 1722. 295p. NUC OCLC
[Later pub. as: Poems on several occasions, by a lady]

5354. -----Pylades and Corinna: or, Memoirs of the lives, amours, and writings of Richard Gwinnett ... and Mrs. Elizabeth Thomas, junior.
L: n.p., 1731-32. NUC BL OCLC
[Letters & misc. pieces in prose & verse, incl. love poems]

5355. -----Serious poems, comprising The Churchyard, Village Sabbath, Deluge.
L: Whittaker, Treacher & co., 1831.
276p. BL

5356. THOMAS, Elizabeth, Mrs. [Br. 19c]
The confession; or, The novice of St. Clare, and other poems.
L: W. Simpkin & R. Marshall, 1818.
88p. BL

5357. -----The convert. A tale of real life.
L: n.p., 1840. 13p. BL

5358. -----The Georgian; or, The Moor of Tripoli, and other poems.
L: C.A. Bartlett, 1847. 127p. BL

5359. THOMAS, Emily, Lady [Br. 19c]
The faithful hound. A true tale in verse.
2d ed. L: n.p., 1863. BL

5360. THOMAS, J. R., Mrs. [Br. 19c]
Poems.
L: n.p., 1846. BL

5361. THOMAS, Jane (Hamilton), Mrs. Edward Thomas [Am. 19c]
Autumnal leaves, elegaic and other poems.
L: W. Walker & co., 1860. 200p. NUC BL

5362. -----Poems by Mrs. Thomas.
L: Hatchard & son, 1846. 292p. BL

5363. -----Primroses by a river's brim: poems.
L: n.p., 1865. BL

5364. -----Thoughts, in verse, on the principal festivals and holy days of the Church of England.
Pt. 2. Bristol: Ch. of England Tract Soc.,no. 24, 1847. 47p. NUC

5365. -----Tranquil hours; poems.
L: n.p., 1838. BL

5366. THOMAS, Jane (Pinhorn), Mrs. Edward Thomas [Br. d. 1871]
The commemoration ode, written for the 300th anniversary of the birth of Shakespeare ... poetry by Mrs. Edward Thomas, music by Alfred Gilbert.
L: Addison & Lucas, 1864. 20p. NUC

5367. THOMAS, L., Mrs. [Br. 19c] ALT: T., L. PSEUD: Kentish Mother, A
Hollingbourne. By L.T.
Maidstone: W.S. Vivish, 1881. 13p. BL
[On the Village of Haur; written in 1851 to preserve its history]

5368. -----Lines to Kentish children, by a Kentish mother.
Maidstone: R.T. Nicholson, 1875. 10p. BL
[On beauties & history of Kent for Kentish people]

5369. THOMAS, Mary Pettus [Am. b. 1857]
Maudine Lariven.
Chicago: Scroll pub. & literary syndicate, c1899. 58p. NUC

5370. THOMAS, Rose Haig [Br. 19/20c]
Pan: a collection of lyrical poems.
L: Bliss, Sands & co., 1897. 94p. BL

5371. THOMPSON, Ann Stuart [Br. 19c]
Miscellaneous poems.
L: Hamilton, Adams & co., 1864. 294p. NUC BL

5372. THOMPSON, Annie [Am. 19/20c]
Simplicity unveiled, poems.
Indianapolis, IN: Douglass & Carlon, pr., 1880. 104p. NUC OCLC

THOMPSON, E.H., co-author <u>see</u> STOCK, Sarah Geraldina

5373. THOMPSON, Eliza, Miss [Br. 18c]
Poems on various subjects.
L: n.p., 1787. BL

5374. THOMPSON, Jane (Tonge), Mrs. Pickey Thompson [Am. 19c]
Solitary musings.
Washington, D.C.: n.p., 1826? 19p. NUC OCLC
[5 poems, occasional & memorial]

5375. THOMPSON, Louise [Am. d. 1889?]
Works of Louise Thompson: poetry and prose. Ed. her mother, M.A. Thompson.
Cincinnati, OH: Standard pub. co., 1889. 193p. NUC OCLC
[Chiefly lyric & narrative verse; incl. 2 short stories]

THOMPSON, Jemima <u>see</u> LUKE, Jemima (Thompson)

THOMPSON, M.A., ed. <u>see</u> THOMPSON, Louise

5376. THOMPSON, Martha F. [Am. 19c]
Fables in verse.
Haverhill, MA: Chase bros., c1888. 28p. NUC

5377. THOMPSON, Maude Louise [Am. 19c]
Reflections in poems.
Ogden, UT: n.p., 1895. 22p. NUC

THOMPSON, Mrs. Pickey <u>see</u> THOMPSON, Jane (Tonge)

5378. THOMPSON, Rachel, Miss [Br. 19c]
In honour to a Triune God. Original poems.
Malmesbury: N. Riddick, 1890. 69p. BL

THOMSON, Mrs. A.T. <u>see</u> THOMSON, Katherine (Byerley)

5379. THOMSON, Katherine (Byerley), Mrs. A.T. Thomson [Br. 1797-1862]
Allaooddeen, a tragedy, and other poems.
L: Smith, Elder, Thomson, 1880. 230p. NUC

5380. THORNDYKE, E.P., Mrs. [Am. 19c]
Astrea, or goddess of justice.
San Francisco: Amanda M. Slocum, pr., 1881. 104p. NUC OCLC
[Poems & prose essays on "Womanhood," "Woman and Man," etc.]

5381. THORNTON, Carrie Alice (Esmond) [Am. 1846-1887]
Mrs. Carrie Alice Thornton, ne Esmond, born May 16th, 1846. Died January 2nd, 1887.
Richmond, VA: E. Waddey, pr., 1887. 102p. NUC OCLC

[Memorial volume of her poems]

5382. THORNTON, Fairelie [Br. 19c]
Work for Jesus. Poems.
L: S.W. Partridge & co., 1884. 112p.
BL

THORPE, Rosa (Hartwick) see THORPE, Rose (Hartwick)

5383. THORPE, Rose [Rosa BL] (Hartwick) [Am. 1850-1939]
"Curfew must not ring tonight."
Boston: Lee & Shepard, c1882. 26p.
NUC BL OCLC

5384. -----Ringing ballads including "Curfew must not ring to-night."
Boston: D. Lothrop co., 1887. 115p.
NUC OCLC

5385. -----Temperance poems.
Pentwater, MI: L.M. Hartwick, 1887.
21p. NUC

5386. -----The yule log: a cluster of Christmas selections for holiday times. Poems.
Chicago: F.H. Revell, c1881. 20 l.
L: John Walker & co., 188-? 10 l.
NUC OCLC

5387. THRELFALL, Evelyn Agnes, Lady [Br. 19/20c]
Starlight songs.
L: Kegan Paul, Trench, Trubner & co., 1895. 98p. NUC BL

5388. THRELFALL, Jennette [Br. 19c]
Sunshine and shadow. Poems.
L: n.p., 1873. BL

5389. THROOP, Anne [Am. 19c]
Whisperings of a wind-harp. With a prose poem introduction by Sadakichi Hartman.
NY: n.p., 1897. 26p. NUC BL

5390. THURSTON, Julia Grace [Am. 19c]
Threads of song.
Chicago: E.A. Weeks & co., c1893.
123p. NUC OCLC

5391. THURTELL, Mary Gordon (Bartrum) [Br. 1821-1857]
In memoriam. Extracts from the scrapbook of Mary Gordon Thurtell.
Swaffham: E.A. Simpson, 1857. 29p. BL
[Religious, nature, & occasional verse]

5392. THWAITES, Clara [Br. 19c]
Songs for labour and leisure.
L: J. Nisbet & co., 1885. 152p. BL

5393. TICKNER, Caroline [Br. 1866-1937]
The old house at home.
L: E. Nister, 1891. BL

5394. TIERNAN, Mary Anne [Br. 19c]
Monody on the death of ... the Princess Charlotte of Wales. To which is added: Desolation, a dream.
2d ed. L: Pr. for the author by Sherwood, Neely & Jones, 1818. 23p.
BL
[Desolation, a dream vision in verse.]

5395. TIERNEY, Catherine A. [Am. 19c]
Dreamland stars and other poems.
NY: Clark & Story, pr., c1894. 66p.
NUC

5396. TIFFANY, Esther Brown [Am. b. 1858]
The angel at the sepulchre.
Boston: L. Prang & co., c1889. 9p.
NUC
[Dramatic poem in 2 scenes.]

5397. TIFFANY, Olive E. Fairbanks [Am. 19/20c]
Floral poems and others.
Kansas City, MO: Hudson-Kimberly pub. co., 1893. 94p. NUC OCLC

TIGHE, Mrs. Henry see TIGHE, Mary (Blachford)

5398. TIGHE, Mary (Blachford), Mrs. Henry Tighe [Br. 1772-1810]
Mary, a series of reflections during twenty years.
Dublin?: n.p., 1811. 35p. NUC
[Chiefly verse, sonnets & occasional. Prose recollection of a dream.]

5399. -----Psyche, with other poems, by Mrs. Henry Tighe.
L: Longman, Hurst, Rees, Orme, & Brown, 1811. 314p. NUC BL OCLC

5400. -----Psyche: or, the legend of love.
L: Pr. for James Carpenter by C. Whittingham, 1795, 1805. 214p. NUC BL OCLC

5401. TILBURY, Caroline [Br. 19c]
Candlewicks. A year of thoughts and fancies.
L: E. Stock, 1897. 96p. BL

5402. TILLERY, Anne Vyne [Am. 19/20c]
Dream verses.
Rocky Mount, NC: Transcript press, 18--? 52p. NUC OCLC

5403. TILLEY, Harriet Meston [Br. 19c]
Blossoms of thought. Poems.
L: n.p., 1850. BL

5404. TILLEY, Lucy Evangeline [Am. 1859-1890]
Little rhymes in brown.
Westerly, RI: George C. Champlin, pr., 1886. 24p. NUC OCLC

5405. -----Verses.
n.p.: n.p., 188-. 65p. NUC

5406. TILLOTSON, Mary Ella (Tillotson) [Am. b. 1816]
Poems on miscellaneous topics ... .
Philadelphia: Burket McFetridge, pr., 1887. 319p. NUC OCLC

5407. TILT, Julia [Br. 19c]
Arundel Castle and other poems.
L: n.p., 1849. BL

5408. -----Historical ballads illustrative [instructive NUC] of the history of England, with other poems.
L: E. Churton, 1852. 176p. NUC BL OCLC

5409. -----Lays of Alma, and other poems.
L: L. Booth, 1856. 176p. NUC OCLC

5410. -----Poems and ballads.
2d ed. L: Churlton, 1847. 158p. BL OCLC

5411. TIMBURY, Jane [Br. 18c]
The history of Tobit; a poem. With other poems on various subjects.
L: The author, 1787. 60p. NUC BL

5412. -----The story of Le Fevre ... put into verse by J. Timbury.
L: R. Jameson, 1787. 31p. NUC BL
[From: Tristram Shandy]

5413. TIMLOW, Caroline E. [Am. 19c]
Poems.
Buffalo, NY: Peter Paul & bro., 1891. 208p. NUC OCLC

5414. TINCKER, Mary Agnes [Am. 1831-1907] ALT: T., M.A.
Autumn leaves; verse and story.
NY: W.H. Young & co., 1899. 291p. NUC OCLC
[Short stories, with a few poems interspersed]

5415. -----Xariffia's poems. By M.A.T.
Philadelphia: J.B. Lippincott & co., 1870. 262p. NUC
[Attributed to Tincker by Cushing; also attrib. to Mary Ashley Townsend NUC]

5416. TINDAL, Henrietta Euphemia (Harrison) [Br. d. 1879]
Lines and leaves.
L: Chapman & Hall, 1850. 128p. BL OCLC

5417. -----Rhymes and legends ... with a prefatory memoir.
L: R. Bentley & son, 1879. 279p. BL OCLC

5418. TINSLEY, Annie (Turner), Mrs. Charles Tinsley [Br. 19c] ALT: Turner, Annie
The children of the mist, The conqueror, and other poems.
L: Lutz, 1827. 212p. BL
[OCLC enters under Annette Turner]

5419. -----Lays for the thoughtful and the solitary.
L: Longman & co., 1848. 156p. BL

TINSLEY, Mrs. Charles <u>see</u> TINSLEY, Annie (Turner)

5420. TIPPER, Elizabeth [Br. 17c]
The pilgrim's viaticum; or, The destitute, but not forlorn. Being a divine poem, digested from meditations upon the Holy Scriptures.
L: Thomas Ballard, 1698. 83p. NUC BL

TIRWIT, Elizabeth, Lady <u>see</u> TYRWHITT, Elizabeth, Lady

5421. TITTERINGTON, Sophie Bronson [Am. b. 1846]
Folded hands. Poetry. "They also serve who only stand and wait."
NY: American Tract Soc., c1878. 303p. NUC

TODD, Mabel Loomis, ed. <u>see</u> DICKINSON, Emily

TODD, Mabel Loomis, ed. <u>see</u> STONE, Cara Elizabeth (Hanscom) Whiton-

5422. TODD, Susan Hill, Mrs. [Am. 19c]
Occasional poems: a New Year's offering.
Boston: W. Crosby & H.P. Nichols, 1851. 215p. NUC BL

5423. TODRIG, Louise N., Mrs. [Am. 19c] ALT: T., L.N.
The ballad of the good ship, Sarah Sands.

Buffalo, NY: Carrell & Nisell, 1884. 11p. NUC OCLC

5424. -----Golden rod. By L.N.T. Buffalo, NY: Steam pr. house of Bigelow bros., 1881. 24p. NUC OCLC

5425. TOKE, Emma [Br. 19c]
Poems.
L: Pr. for priv. circ., 1866. 308p. BL OCLC

5426. TOLAND, Mary Bertha McKenzie, Mrs. [Am. 1825?-1895]
Aegle and the elf. A fantasy.
Philadelphia: J.B. Lippincott co., 1887. 55p. NUC OCLC
[In verse]

5427. -----Atlina, queen of the floating isle.
Philadelphia: J.B. Lippincott co., 1893. 34p. NUC OCLC
[Atlantis]

5428. -----Eudora, a tale of love.
Philadelphia: J.B. Lippincott co., 1888. 110p. NUC OCLC

5429. -----The Inca princess. An historical romance.
Philadelphia: J.B. Lippincott co., c1885. 96p. NUC BL OCLC
[In 5 cantos]

5430. -----Iris: the romance of an opal ring.
Philadelphia: J.B. Lippincott co., 1879. 95p. NUC BL OCLC

5431. -----Legend of Laymore, a poem.
Philadelphia: J.B. Lippincott co., 1890. 61p. NUC OCLC

5432. -----Onti Ora. A metrical romance.
Philadelphia: J.B. Lippincott & co., 1881. 117p. NUC OCLC

5433. -----Sir Rae. A poem.
Philadelphia: J.B. Lippincott & co., 1877. 77p. NUC OCLC

5434. -----Tisayac of the Yosemite.
Philadelphia: J.B. Lippincott co., 1890. 52p. NUC
[Indians of the Yosemite valley]

5435. TOLLEMACHE, Beatrix Lucia Catherine (Egerton), Hon. Mrs. Lionel Tollemache [Br. d. 1926] ALT: T., B.L.
Engelberg, and other verses.
L: Percival & co., 1890. 129p. NUC BL OCLC

5436. -----Safe studies. With Hon. Lionel Arthur Tollemache.
L: Pr. C.F. Hodgson, 1884. 429p. BL OCLC

TOLLEMACHE, Hon. Lionel Arthur, co-author see TOLLEMACHE, Beatrix Lucia Catherine (Egerton)

TOLLEMACHE, Hon. Mrs. Lionel see TOLLEMACHE, Beatrix Lucia Catherine (Egerton)

5437. TOLLET, Elizabeth [Br. 1694-1754]
Poems on several occasions. With Anne Boleyn to King Henry VIII, an epistle.
L: John Clarke, 1755. 238p. NUC BL OCLC

5438. TOMKINS, Mrs. Daniel [Br. 19c]
Twilight-verses.
L: Jarrold & sons, 1886. 199p. BL
[Based on accompanying texts]

5439. TOMKINS, Zitella E. [Br. 19c]
Sister Lucetta and other poems.
L: Kegan Paul, Trench & co., 1887. 113p. NUC BL OCLC

TOMLINS, E., co-author see TOMLINS, Elizabeth Sophia

5440. TOMLINS, Elizabeth Sophia [Br. 1763-1828] PSEUD: Lady, A
Tributes of affection, with The slave; and other poems. By a lady and her brother [E. Tomlins].
L: Pr. H. & C. Baldwin for T.N. Longman, 1797. 143p. BL
[18 pieces, incl. The slave, anti-slavery narrative, signed S., or Eliza. Also sonnets, odes, a fairy interlude & ballads]

5441. TOMLINSON, A.W., Mrs. [Am. 19c]
The summer land, and other poems.
Cincinnati, OH: Elm Street pr. co., c1899. 167p. NUC

5442. TOMS, Mary F., Mrs. [Am. 19c]
Sacred gems.
Hartford, CT: Press of the Case, Lockwood & Brainard co., 1888. 226p. NUC OCLC

TOMSON, GRAHAM R., pseud. see WATSON, Rosamund (Ball) Marriott

5443. TONGE, Eliza, Mrs. [Br. 19c]
Poetical trifles.
Cheltenham: n.p., 1832. BL

5444. TONKIN, Sarah Eliza [Br. 19c]
Rostherne Mere, and other poems.
Manchester: Palmer & Howe, 1866.
224p. NUC BL OCLC

5445. TONNA, Charlotte Elizabeth (Browne) Phelan [Br. 1790-1849] ALT: Browne, Charlotte Elizabeth; Charlotte Elizabeth; Phelan, Charlotte Elizabeth (Browne)
The convent bell, and other poems. By Charlotte Elizabeth.
NY: J.S. Taylor & co., 1845. 78, 121, 146p. NUC BL
[Incl. Izram & Osric]

5446. -----Izram: a Mexican tale, and other poems.
L: James Nisbet, 1826. 230p. NUC BL

5447. -----Osric, a missionary tale: with The garden, and other poems. By Charlotte Elizabeth.
Dublin: W. Curry, jr. & co., 1826. 2v. NUC BL OCLC

5448. -----Posthumous and other poems.
L: Seeley, Burnside & Seeley, 1846. 256p. BL NUC

5449. -----A visit to St. George's Chapel, Windsor, on the evening succeeding the funeral of his late Royal Highness the Duke of York.
L: J. Dennett, 1827. 7p. BL

5450. TOOGOOD, Harriet, Mrs. [Br. 19c]
Poems and ballads.
L: n.p., 1879. BL

5451. -----The summer lake. A collection of poems.
L: n.p., 1852. BL

TOULMIN, Camilla Dufour <u>see</u> CROSLAND, Camilla Dufour (Toulmin)

5452. TOUNLEY, Caroline [Br. 18c]
ALT: Pringle, Caroline Tounley
A collection of short poems by James, George, Caroline, and other members of the family of the Tounleys of Ramsgate.
Ramsgate: Burgess, pr., 1785. BL
[80 pieces in all. Only two signed: "Deaf as a post," Caroline; "On my recovery," Catherine Scott. Most are occasional & relate to family matters]

TOUNLEY, George, co-author <u>see</u> TOUNLEY, Caroline

TOUNLEY, James, co-author <u>see</u> TOUNLEY, Caroline

5453. TOVANI, Elizabeth, Mrs. [Br. 19c]
Stray thoughts. A collection of short poems by Mrs. E. Tovani.
L: n.p., 1862. BL

5454. TOWLE, Mary Louise (Whelpley) [Am. 1825-1898]
Harbor lights.
Napa, CA?: n.p., 1898? 9p.
[5 religious poems not incl. in her other pub. work.]

5455. -----Where is heaven? and other poems.
San Francisco: Bancroft co., 1890. 48p. NUC BL OCLC

5456. TOWNSEND, Eliza [Am. 1789-1854]
Poems and miscellanies, selected from the writings of Miss Eliza Townsend. Printed, but not published.
Boston: Press of G.C. Rand & Avery, 1856. 355p. NUC
[Misc. poetry, and The wife of Seaton; or, The siege of Berwick, historical tragedy, 5 acts.]

5457. TOWNSEND, Elizabeth Fawcett [Am. 19c]
Poems.
Philadelphia: n.p., 1860. 462p. NUC

TOWNSEND, Mary Ashley <u>see</u> TINCKER, Mary Agnes

5458. TOWNSEND, Mary Ashley (Van Voorhis) [Am. 1832-1901] ALT: T., M. A.; Ashley, Mary PSEUD: Xariffa
The captain's story.
Philadelphia: J.B. Lippincott & co., 1874. 47p. NUC OCLC

5459. -----Distaff and spindle; sonnets.
Philadelphia & L: J.B. Lippincott co., 1895. 3p. NUC BL OCLC

5460. -----Down the bayou and other poems.
Boston: J.R. Osgood & co., 1882. 230p. NUC BL OCLC

5461. -----A poem.
New Orleans: n.p., 1881. 14p. NUC

5462. -----A poem, written for the dedication of the Harvard memorial library.
New Orleans?: n.p., 1888? 3p. NUC

5463. -----The World's Cotton Centennial Exposition: poem.
New Orleans: L. Graham & son, pr., 1885. 10p. NUC OCLC

5464. TOWNSEND, Mary Elizabeth, Mrs. [Br. 19c]
So tired and other verses.
L: Rivingtons, 1882. 48p. BL
[New & enl. ed. L & NY: Longmans, Green & co., 1894. 51 p. NUC BL]

5465. TRASK, Kate (Nichols) [Am. 1853-1922] ALT: Trask, Katrina; T., K.N.
Colorado leaves. By K.N.T.
n.p.: n.p., 1878. 85p. OCLC

5466. -----Sonnets and lyrics.
NY: A.D.F. Randolph & co., 1894. 103p. NUC OCLC

5467. -----Under King Constantine.
NY: A.D.F. Randolph, 1892. 129p. L: K. Paul, Trench, Trubner, 1893. 129p. NUC BL OCLC

TRASK, Katrina see TRASK, Kate (Nichols)

TREBUTIEN, G.S., ed. see CAREY, Harriet Mary, Mrs.

5468. TREFUSIS, Elizabeth, Miss [Br. 1763?-1808]
Poems and tales.
L: S. Tipper, 1808. 2v. NUC BL OCLC
[All poetry; tales are narrative poems.]

5469. TREGELLES, Jane M. [Br. 19c]
Childhood's memories, and other poems.
Darlington: A.E. Tregelles, 1890. 88p. BL

TRELAWNY, Anne see GIBBONS, Anne (Trelawny)

5470. TRENCH, Melesina (Chenevix) St. George [Br. 1768-1827]
The assize ball; or, Lucy of the moor.
L: J. Hatchard, 1820. 16p. NUC
[Also attr. Mrs. Offley NUC]

5471. -----Aubrey. In five cantos.
Southhampton: Pr. T. Baker for I. Fletcher, 1818. 78p. NUC OCLC

5472. -----Campaspe, an historical tale, and other poems.
Southhampton: Priv. pr. by T. Baker, 1815. 40p. NUC BL OCLC

5473. -----Ellen: a ballad, founded on recent fact, and other poems.
Bath: Pr. R. Cruttwell, 1815. 48p. NUC OCLC
[Vol. incl. Campaspe]

5474. -----Laura's dream; or, The moonlanders.
L: J. Hatchard, priv. pr., 1816. 47p. NUC BL OCLC
[Vol. incl. Campaspe & Ellen]

5475. -----Lines on reading the last canto of Childe Harold.
Southhampton: T. Baker, 1818? 7p. NUC OCLC

5476. -----A monody on the death of Mr. Grattan.
L: J. Ridgway, 1820. 8p. NUC
[At end, p. [9]: Sonnet on seeing children dance]

5477. -----The remains of the late Mrs. Richard Trench, being selections from her journals, letters, and other papers. Ed. her son, the Dean of Westminster, Richard Chenevix Trench.
L: Parker, son & Bourn, 1862. 525p. NUC BL
[Incl. lyrics & sonnets]

TRENCH, Mrs. Richard see TRENCH, Melesina (Chenevix) St. George

TRENCH, Richard Chenevix, ed. see TRENCH, Melesina (Chenevix) St. George

5478. TREVANION, Ada [Br. 19c]
Poems.
L: Smith, Elder & co., 1858. 178p. NUC BL OCLC

5479. TREVELYAN, Frances Anne [Br. 19c]
Quarr Abbey, or, The mistaken calling: a tale of the Isle of Wight in the XIII century.
L: Rivingtons; Oxford: W.R. Bowden; Ryde: Gibbs, Wagner, 1862. 56p. NUC BL OCLC
[Gothic narrative]

5480. TREVELYAN, Paulina (Jermyn), Lady [Br. 1816-1866]
Selections from the literary and artistic remains of Paulina Jermyn Trevelyan, first wife of Sir Walter Calverley Trevelyan. Ed. D. Wooster.
L: Longmans, Green & co., 1879. 239p. NUC BL OCLC
[Incl. lyric & narrative poems, one short story, "A story of modern Rome," & misc. essays & drawings]

5481. TREVOR, Albinia [Br. 19c]
The widow's tale; or, The sacrament in the forest.
L: n.p., 1871. BL

5482. TRINDER, Mrs. W.H. [Br. 19c]
Voices of home and nature.
L: Bosworth, 1861. 184p. BL OCLC

5483. TRITTON, Ethel Harriet [Br. 19c]
Spiritual songs.
L: Pr. for priv. circ., 1886. 95p. BL

5484. TROLLOPE, Frances Eleanor (Ternan) [Br. 19c]
Prologue ... written to be spoken before a play acted by children for the benefit of sick or forsaken children.
L: n.p., 1888. 3p. BL

5485. TROLLOPE, Frances Milton [Br. 1780-1863] ALT: T., F.
The mother's manual; or, Illustrations of matrimonial economy. An essay in verse. By F.T.
L: Treuttel & Wurtz & Richter, 1833. 82p. NUC BL OCLC

TROTTER, Catherine see COCKBURN, Catherine (Trotter)

5486. TROTTER, Elizabeth Hill [Br. 19c]
Cindabright; or, The fatal flowers. A fairy tale, with minor poems.
Kensington: Pr. & sold by John Wild, 1838. 145p. BL
[Cindabright, pp. 1-99 is allegorical dramatic poem. Minor poems incl. odes, patriotic verse. One prose dream vision.]

TRUBSHAW, Anne, co-author see TRUBSHAW, Susanna

TRUBSHAW, M., co-author see TRUBSHAW, Susanna

5487. TRUBSHAW, Susanna [Br. 19c]
Poems.
Stafford: R. & W. Wright, 1863. 66p. BL

5488. -----Way-side inns.
Stafford: R. & W. Wright, 1874. 98p. BL
[Poems, prose sketches and essays. Incl. three by Rev. John Miller. 9 poems by her mother, M. Trubshaw, one by her brother, Thomas Trubshaw, 3 by her sister, Anne Trubshaw; rest by Susanna]

TRUBSHAW, Thomas, co-author see TRUBSHAW, Susanna

5489. TRUESDELL, Amelia Woodward [Am. 1839-1912]
A California pilgrimage, by one of the pilgrims.
San Francisco: S. Carson & co., 1884. 125p. NUC OCLC
[Poetry describing old missions of California]

5490. -----The song of the flag.
San Francisco: William Doxey, c1898. 8 leaves. NUC OCLC

5491. TRUESDELL, Helen, Mrs. [Am. 19c]
Poems.
Cincinnati, OH: E. Morgan, 1852. 203p. NUC BL OCLC
[3d ed. Cincinnati, OH: E. Morgan, c1853. 212 p. OCLC]

TRUMBULL, TRUMAN, pseud. see GAY, E. Jane

5492. TUCK, Elizabeth
Vallis Vale and other poems.
L: Sold by Longman, Hurst, 1823. 102p. NUC BL

5493. TUCKER, Charlotte Marie [Br. 1821-1893] PSEUD: E., A.L.O.
Glimpses of the unseen. Poems. By A.L.O.E. [A Lady of England].
Edinburgh: Gall, n.d. 108p. NUC BL

5494. -----Hymns and poems. By A.L.O.E.
L: T. Nelson & sons, 1868. 158p. NUC BL

5495. -----The white shroud, and other poems. By A.L.O.E.
Edinburgh: Gall & Inglis, 185-? 108p. NUC

5496. TUCKER, Florence [Br. 19c]
Songs of the heart.
L: n.p., 1876. BL

5497. TUCKER, Margaretta Ames [Am. 1836-1906?] PSEUD: May, Margaret
Driftwood, and other poems by Margaret May.
Boston: H.H. Carter & co., 18--? 20p. NUC OCLC

5498. -----Pools in the sand, by Margaret May.
Boston: L. Prang & co., 1893. 12p. NUC OCLC

5499. TUCKER LAMBERT, Mary Eliza (Perine) [Am. b. 1838] ALT: Lambert, Mary
Cogitots. By Mary Lambert.
Oakland, CA: n.p., n.d. 46p. NUC
[Poems and essays]

5500. -----Loewe's bridge, a Broadway idyl. In verse.
NY: M. Doolady, 1867. 78p. NUC OCLC

5501. -----Poems.
NY: M. Doolady, 1867. 216p. NUC BL OCLC

5502. -----La Rabida; a California Columbian souvenir poem.
San Francisco: Bancroft co., c1893. 3p. NUC

5503. TUCKEY, Mary B. [Br. 19c]
The wrongs of Africa; a tribute to the anti-slavery cause. Published for Glasgow Ladies Emancipation Society.
Glasgow: George Gallie, 1838. 31p. NUC BL OCLC

5504. TUITE, Eliza Dorothea, Lady [Br. 19c]
Miscellaneous poetry.
3d ed. Bath: n.p., 1841. BL

5505. -----Poems. By Lady Tuite.
L: T. Cadell, jr., 1796. 199p. NUC BL OCLC

TUPPER, Ellin Isabelle, co-author see TUPPER, Mary Frances

5506. TUPPER, Ellin Isabelle [Br. 19c]
Poems, translated from the Swedish and original.
L: S.W. Partridge, 1872. 196p. NUC BL OCLC

TUPPER, Margaret Eleanora, co-author see TUPPER, Mary Frances

TUPPER, Margaret Eleanora see TUPPER, Margaret Elenora

5507. TUPPER, Margaret Elenora [Br. b. 1840]
The scent of the heather, and other writings in prose and poetry. Ed. Miss Lolo Julia Bissicks.
L: Leadenhall press, Simpkin, Marshall & co.; NY: C. Scribner's sons, 1895. 215p. NUC BL OCLC
[Memorial vol., incl. 4 short love stories, misc. lyrics, narr. poems & sonnets.]

5508. -----Touches of human love.
L: S.W. Partridge; NY: Nelson & Phillips, 1877. 240p. NUC BL
[12 short stories & prose sketches. Rest is lyric, narrative & misc. poetry]

5509. TUPPER, Mary Frances [Br. b. 1828]
Poems by three sisters.
L: Hatchard, 1864. 207p. NUC BL
[Mary Frances, Ellin Isabelle, and Margaret Eleanora Tupper]

TURELL, Ebenezer, ed. see TURELL, Jane (Colman)

TURELL, Mrs. Ebenezer see TURELL, Jane (Colman)

5510. TURELL, Jane (Colman), Mrs. Ebenezer Turell [Am. 1708-1735]
Memoirs of the life and death of the pious and ingenious Mrs. Jane Turell, chiefly collected from her own manuscripts. Ed. Ebenezer Turell.
Boston: N.E., 1735. 72p. NUC BL
[Poetry, letters & notes from her diaries]

TURNBULL, Mrs. see BARTHOLOMEW, Anne Charlotte (Turnbull)

TURNBULL, Anne Charlotte see BARTHOLOMEW, Anne Charlotte Turnbull

5511. TURNBULL, Francese Hubbard (Litchfield), Mrs. Lawrence Turnbull [Am. d. 1927] ALT: T., F.L.
Marguerite's vow. By F.L.T.
Baltimore, OH: I. Friedenwald, 1882. 80p. NUC

TURNBULL, Mrs. Lawrence see TURNBULL, Francese Hubbard (Litchfield)

TURNER, Annette see TINSLEY, Annie (Turner)

TURNER, Annie see TINSLEY, Annie (Turner)

5512. TURNER, Eliza Sproat [Am. 1826-1903]
Confidential.
Philadelphia: n.p., n.d. 6p. NUC
[New Century Guild]

5513. -----Out-of-door rhymes.
Boston: J.R. Osgood & co., 1872. 187p. NUC BL OCLC

5514. TURNER, Frances [Br. 19c]
Devotional breathings in verse.

L: n.p., 1852. BL

5515. TURNER, Juliana Frances [Am. 19c]
The harp of the beech woods. Original poems.
Montrose, PA: Adam Waldie, 1822. 156p. NUC BL

5516. TURNER, Margaret [Br. 19c]
A poem upon the importance of the study of botany. In: Samuel Rootsey, Syllabus of a course of botanical lectures ... .
Bristol: n.p., 1818. BL

5517. TURNER, Mary Elizabeth Whitney [Am. 19c]
Garnered thoughts.
Natick, MA: Bulletin job pr., c1892. 43p. NUC OCLC

5518. TURNER, Maud E. Kirby [Br. 19c]
"Dream love;" and other poems.
Walsall: W. Henry Robinson, 1895. 40p. BL

TUTHILL, Mrs. Jackson Villiers see TUTHILL, Jane Ann Villiers

5519. TUTHILL, Jane Ann Villiers, Mrs. Jackson Villiers Tuthill [Br. 19c]
Songs of past hours.
L: Saunders & Otley, 1852. 136p. NUC BL

5520. TUTTIETT, Mary Gleed, Miss [Br. 1847-1923] PSEUD: Gray, Maxwell
The forest chapel and other poems. By Maxwell Gray.
L: W. Heinemann, 1899. 128p. NUC BL

5521. -----Lays of the dragon slayer. By Maxwell Gray.
L: Bliss, Sands & Foster, 1894. 192p. NUC BL OCLC
[Based on the Nibelungenlied]

5522. -----Westminster chimes and other poems. By Maxwell Gray.
L: Paul, Trench, Trubner, 1890. 202p. NUC BL OCLC

5523. TUTTLE, Augusta B. [Am. 19c]
Memories.
Kenduskeag, ME: E.H. Boyington, pr., 1878. 12p. NUC OCLC

5524. TUTTLE, Emma Rood [Am. 1839-1916]
Blossoms of our spring. With Hudson Tuttle.
Boston: W. White & co., 1864. 328p. NUC

5525. -----From soul to soul.
NY: M.L. Holbrook & co., 1890. 222p. NUC OCLC

TUTTLE, Hudson, co-author see TUTTLE, Emma Rood

5526. TWEDDELL, Elizabeth (Cole), Mrs. George Markham Tweddell [Br. b. 1833] ALT: Tweddell, Florence Cleveland (Cole) PSEUD: Cleveland, Florence
Rhymes and sketches to illustrate the Cleveland dialect, by Mrs. G.M. Tweddell (Florence Cleveland).
Stokesley, Yorkshire: Tweddell, 1875. 84p. NUC BL OCLC
[Yorkshire dialect]

TWEDDELL, Florence Cleveland (Cole) see TWEDDELL, Elizabeth (Cole)

TWEDDELL, Mrs. George Markham see TWEDDELL, Elizabeth (Cole)

5527. TWENTYMAN, Elizabeth Ann [Br. 19c]
Poems.
Carlisle & L: n.p., 1868. NUC BL

TWO SISTERS OF THE WEST, pseud. see WARFIELD, Catherine Ann (Ware)

5528. TYLECOATE, Elizabeth Margaret Beaufort, Miss [Br. 19c]
Holy seasons. With Thomas Tylecoate.
L: Longmans, Green & co., 1867. 143p. BL

TYLECOATE, Thomas, co-author see TYLECOATE, Elizabeth Margaret Beaufort, Miss

5529. TYLER, Josephine [Am. 19c]
Ben's Isabella; a narrative poem in thirteen cantos.
Buffalo, NY: C. W. Moulton, 1895. 157p. NUC OCLC

5530. -----Lyret; or, The opened pathway.
Boston: D. Lothrop & co.; Dover, NH: G.T. Day & co., 1875. 84p. NUC OCLC
[Gothic narrative]

TYNAN, Katharine see HINKSON, Katherine (Tynan)

5531. TYRWHITT, Elizabeth, Lady [Br. 16c] ALT: Tirwit, Elizabeth Lady
Morning and evening prayer, with divers Psalmes Himnes and meditations. Made by the Lady Elizabeth Tirwit.

L: H. Middelton for C. Barker, 1574. BL

5532. TYTLER, Margaret Fraser [Br. 19c] ALT: Liddell, Margaret Fraser (Tytler); T., M.F.
Hymns and sketches in verse.
L: Harvey & Darton, 1840. BL

ULLIE see AKERSTROM, Ullie R.

5533. ULLMAN, Daisy [Am. 19c]
The dude book.
Chicago: Pr. R.R. Donnelley & sons co., 1897. 40p. OCLC
[Christmas greeting to subscribers to the `Dude,' pub. by Daisy Ullman from ages 10 to 13]

UNA, pseud. see FORD, Mary Anne (McMullen)

UNA, pseud. see SUTHERLAND, Jane Gunn

5534. UNDERDOWN, Emily [Br. 19c]
PSEUD: Chester, Norley
Dante vignettes by Norley Chester.
L: Elliot Stock, 1895. 31 l. NUC BL
[Sonnets]

5535. -----Songs and sonnets by Norley Chester.
L: E. Stock, 1899. 13p. NUC BL

5536. UNDERHILL, Caroline [Am. 19c]
The year's chorus, Margery, and other poems.
NY: Tibbals & Whiting, 1865. 129p. NUC

5537. UPTON, Catherine, Mrs. [Br. 18c]
The siege of Gibraltar from the 12th of April to the 27th of May, 1781. To which is prefixed some account of the blockade.
L: The authoress, 1781. 23p. NUC BL
[Incl. 20p. poem, "Address to Aeolus"]

V., pseud. see CLIVE, Caroline Archer (Wigley)

5538. VAIL, Jennie Van Sickler, Mrs. A.L. Vail [Am. 1838-1892]
Poems. By Mrs. A.L. Vail.
Philadelphia: n.p., 1893. 54p. NUC OCLC

VALE, ELLA, pseud. see SCOTT, Maria L. (Doud)

5539. VALE, VIOLET, pseud. [Br. 19c]
Home blossoms. By Violet Vale.
L: Dunmill, 1879. 55p. BL OCLC

5540. VALENTINE, Carolyn Syron [Am. 1855-1931]
The flag that won.
Cranford, NJ: C.S. Valentine, c1898. 46p. NUC OCLC

5541. VALPY, Henrietta F. [Br. 19c]
ALT: Henrietta
Autumnal leaves. By Henrietta.
L: James Cochrane & co., 1834. 154p. NUC BL

5542. VAN ALLEN, Jane A. [Am. 19c]
One hundred poems.
NY: J.S. Ogilvie, 1890. 160p. NUC
[On Scripture texts]

VAN ALSTYNE, Frances Jane (Crosby) see CROSBY, Frances Jane

5543. VAN AULEN, Mary Elizabeth [Am. 19c]
Home thoughts.
Chicago: Knight & Leonard, 1884. 62p. NUC OCLC

5544. VAN LOON, Hannah, Mrs. [Am. 19c]
Miscellaneous poems.
Towanda, PA: Bradford repub. pr. house, 1880. 143p. NUC OCLC

5545. VAN NADA, L. Belle [Am. 19c]
Poems.
Indianapolis, IN: Carlon & Hollenbeck, pr., 1881. 151p. NUC OCLC

5546. VAN NORMAN, Ina E. Wood, Mrs. [Am. 19c]
Minnewaska, a legend of Lake Mohonk ... and other lyrical poems.
Chicago: Donohue & Henneberry, c1897. 243p. NUC BL OCLC

VANE, HARLEY, pseud. see BASS, Cora C.

VANNAH, Kate see VANNAH, Letitia Katherine

5547. VANNAH, Letitia Katherine [Am. 1855-1933] ALT: Vannah, Kate
From heart to heart.
Boston: J.G. Cupples, 1893. 108p. NUC OCLC

5548. -----Verses.

Philadelphia: J.B. Lippincott & co., 1883. 117p. NUC OCLC

5549. VARIAN, Elizabeth Willoughby (Tracy) [Br. b. 1830?] PSEUD: Finola
Never forsake the ship, and other poems. By Finola.
Dublin: MacGlashen & Gill, 1874. 98p. NUC BL OCLC

5550. -----Poems. By Finola.
Belfast: n.p., 1851. 128p. NUC BL

5551. -----The political and national poems of Finola.
Dublin: M.H. Gill & son, 1877. NUC

VARLEY, Isabella <u>see</u> BANKS, Isabella (Varley) Linnaeus

5552. VASEY, G., Mrs. [Br. 19c]
Midnight reflection, and other poems.
L: n.p., 1827. BL

5553. VAUGHAN, Virginia [Br. d. 1913]
Heaven and earth.
L: Chiswick press, 1877? 57p. NUC
[Prelude to unpub. lyric drama: Adam and Eve, a new Paradise Lost]

5554. -----The new era; a dramatic poem.
L: Chapman & Hall, 1880. 238p. NUC BL OCLC
[Allegorical poem in 4 scenes]

5555. -----Orpheus and the sirens: a drama in lyrics.
L: Chapman & Hall, 1882. 241p. NUC
[Dramatic poem]

5556. VEEDER, Emily Elizabeth (Ferris) [Am. b. 1841]
In the garden and other poems.
Philadelphia & L: J.B. Lippincott co., 1895. 104p. NUC OCLC

VEEL, Mary Colbourne- <u>see</u> COLBORNE-VEEL, Mary

5557. VELEY, Margaret [Br. 1843-1887]
A marriage of shadows and other poems.
L: Smith, Elder, 1888. 149p. NUC BL OCLC

5558. VERNEY, Frances Parthenope (Nightingale), Lady [Br. 1819-1890]
Essays and tales. Comp. Margaret Maria (Williams-Hay) Verney, Lady.
L: Simpkin, Marshall & co., 1891. 635p. BL
[Incl. a few early poems]

VERNEY, Margaret Maria (Williams-Hay), Lady, comp. <u>see</u> VERNEY, Frances Parthenope (Nightingale), Lady

VERY, Jones, co-author <u>see</u> FORMAN, Emily Shaw

5559. VERY, Lydia Louisa Anna [Am. 1823-1901]
Poems.
Andover, MA: Pr. W.F. Draper, 1856. 222p. NUC OCLC

5560. -----Poems and prose writings.
Salem, MA: Salem press pub. & pr. co., 1890. 432p. NUC OCLC
[2/3 misc. poetry. Prose: allegories, travel notes, nature.]

5561. VIALLS, Mary Alice [Br. 19c]
Music fancies, and other verses.
Westminster: A. Constable, 1899. 128p. BL OCLC

VIARDOT-GARCIA, Michelle Ferdinande Pauline <u>see</u> GARCIA, Pauline Viardot

VICTOR, pseud., co-author <u>see</u> SHELLEY, Elizabeth

5562. VICTOR, Frances Auretta (Fuller) Barritt [Am. 1826-1902]
The new Penelope. Stories and poems.
San Francisco: A.L. Bancroft co., pr., 1877. 349p. NUC OCLC
[Sketches based on life in Oregon. Misc. poems.]

5563. -----Poems of sentiment and imagination: with dramatic and descriptive pieces. With Metta Victoria Fuller [Victor].
NY: A.S. Barnes & co., 1851. 264p. NUC OCLC

VICTOR, Metta Victoria (Fuller), co-author <u>see</u> VICTOR, Frances Auretta (Fuller) Barritt

5564. VISHER, Julia Sargent [Am. 19c]
A christening gift.
Chicago: E.M. Colvin, 1892. 24p. NUC

VISITOR TO LEAMINGTON SPA, A, pseud. <u>see</u> HAMILTON, Sarah, Miss

VON K., CAMILLA K., pseud. <u>see</u> WOOD, Mary Camilla (Foster) Hall

5565. VORSE, H. Ellen, Mrs. [Am. 19c]
Poems.
Wellesley Hills, MA: Pr. Charles M. Eaton, 187-? 16p. NUC OCLC

5566. VOX, CLARA, pseud. [Br. 19c]
San(n)itation: an epic and dramatic poem in two parts: by Clara Vox.
L: Vickers; Wandsworth: Cooke & Cooke, 1876. 116p. BL
[Pt. 1: Epic, heroic couplets. Pt. 2: Play, also heroic couplets, 2 acts, satire on women's health organizations.]

5567. VYSE, Maud J. [Br. 19c]
The poetic year and other poems.
L: H.R. Allenson, 1896. 68p. BL OCLC

W., Lady see WALLACE, Eglantine (Maxwell), Lady

W., A., Mrs. see WEAMYS, Anna

W., A., Mrs. see WILSON, Ann, Mrs.

W., A.C.L. see WATERSTON, Anna Cabot Lowell (Quincy)

W., A.D.T. see WHITNEY, Adeline Dutton (Train)

W., A.L. see WARING, Anna Laetitia

W., A.M. see WOOD, Ann Maria (Michell)

W., E. see WALLACE, Eglantine (Maxwell), Lady

W., E. see WATERHOUSE, Elizabeth

W., E. see WEATHERHEAD, Emma

5568. W., E. A., Miss [Br. 19c]
"Words heard in quiet." Searchings "out of the Book of the Lord" and fragments of letters and poems. Ed. Miss L.C. Philpot.
L: n.p., 1870. BL

W., E.D. see DOWDEN, Elizabeth Dickinson (West)

W., E.P. see WOLFERSTAN, Elizabeth Pipe (Jervis)

W., F.M. see WARD, F.M., Mrs.

W., H.M. see WAITHMAN, Helen Maud

W., H.M. see WILLIAMS, Helen Maria

W., J., Mrs. see WILLIAMSON, J., Mrs.

W., M. see WEYLAR, Maria

W., M. see WINTER, Mary

W., M.A. see WARD, Marie A.

W., M.B. see WATERMAN, Mary Bissell

W., M.E. see WARDWELL, Mary E.

W., S. see WARING, S., Miss

W., S. see WATTS, Susannah

W., S.A. see WHITE, S.A., Miss

W.S.--, Olivia see SERRES, Olivia (Wilmot)

5569. WADE, C.J., Mrs. [Br. 19c]
My childhood's days, and other poems.
L: Tweedie, 1867. 100p. BL OCLC

5570. WADSWORTH, Caroline Louisa [Br. 19c]
Songs and poems.
Birmingham: n.p., 1872. BL

5571. -----Temperance songs and poems.
Birmingham: n.p., 1873. BL

5572. -----Wayside flowers.
Birmingham: n.p., 1874. BL

5573. -----Wild buds from Parnassus.
Birmingham: n.p., 1872. BL

5574. WAGNER, Madge Morris [Am. 1862-1924] ALT: Morris, Madge
At San Diego Bay. By Madge Morris.
San Diego, CA: Golden Era co., 1898. 6 l. NUC OCLC

5575. -----Debris, selections from poems. By Madge Morris.
Sacramento, CA: Crocker & co., pr., 1881. 98p. NUC OCLC

5576. -----Poems. By Madge Morris.
San Francisco, CA: Golden Era co., 1885. 134p. NUC OCLC

5577. WAISBROOKER, Lois Nichols [Am. b. 1826]
Mayweed blossoms.
Boston: W. White & co., 1871. 264p. NUC OCLC
[Poems & stories]

5578. WAITE, Barbara [Am. 19c]
The fir-tree.
NY: A.D.F. Randolph & co., 1891. 6 l. NUC

5579. WAITHMAN, Helen Maud [Br. 19c]
ALT: W., H.M.

Ballad of the legend of Forrabury Bells.
L: Ernest Nister, 1890. BL

5580. -----Charybdis and other poems.
L: Eden, Remington & co., 1891. 176p. NUC BL OCLC

5581. -----The season's souvenir.
L: Ernest Nister; NY: E.P. Dutton & co., 1890. BL

5582. -----A woodland song.
L: E. Nister, 1891. BL

5583. -----Year in year out, a book of the months.
L: E. Nister; NY: E.P. Dutton & co., 1890. 36p. NUC BL OCLC

5584. WAKEFIELD, Nancy Amelia Woodbury (Priest) [Am. 1836-1870]
Over the river, and other poems. Ed. Abijah Perkins Marvin.
Boston: Lee & Shepard; NY: C.T. Dillingham, 1883. 391p. NUC OCLC

5585. WALBEY, Clara, Mrs. [Br. 19c]
Thoughts in metre.
L: n.p., 1860. BL

5586. WALCOT, Charlotte [Br. 19c]
The conflict. A sketch.
Ludlow: n.p., 1848. BL

5587. WALCOTT, Josephine, Mrs. [Am. 19c]
World of song.
Cambridge, MA: Pr. at the Riverside press, c1878. 157p. NUC OCLC
[Poems on California; religious lyrics]

5588. WALDO, Elmina R. Ballon, Mrs. [Am. 1810-1856] ALT: Waldo, E. R.B.
Castle Bute; or, A tale of the sixteenth century. A novelette. By E.R.B. Waldo.
Somerville, MA: E. Tufts, 1846. 30p. NUC OCLC
[Narrative poem]

WALDO, E.R.B. <u>see</u> WALDO, Elmina R. Ballon, Mrs.

5589. WALDO, Flora [Am. 19c]
Poems.
Milwaukee, WI: King-Fowle-McGee co., 189-? 85 l. NUC

5590. WALDRON, Adelaide Cilley [Am. 1843-1909]
On Christmas day.
Worcester, MA: Bullard Art pub. co., 1888. 7 l. NUC OCLC

5591. -----On fancy's wing.
n.p.: n.p., c1890. 7 l. NUC

WALKER, Annie Louisa <u>see</u> COGHILL, Annie Louisa (Walker)

5592. WALKER, Bettina [Br. d. 1893]
Songs and sonnets.
L: R. Bentley & son, 1893. 99p. BL

5593. WALKER, Marie Woodruff [Am. 19c] PSEUD: Esdaile, Clifton
The Bedouin prince. By Clifton Esdaile.
NY: Hosford & sons, 1889. 65p. NUC

5594. -----A romance of the willow. By Marie Woodruff Walker (Clifton Esdaile).
NY: Hosford & sons, 1892. 74p. NUC OCLC
[On Chinese willow ware]

5595. WALKER, Marion, Miss [Br. 19c]
Leaves from the backwoods.
Montreal: n.p., 1862. BL

WALKER, Mary <u>see</u> BAILEY, Mary Walker

5596. WALL, Annie Carpenter [Am. b. 1859]
Some scattered leaves.
Buffalo, NY: Charles Wells Moulton, c1893. 41p. NUC OCLC

5597. WALLACE, E.D., Mrs. [Am. 19c]
England's last queen. A poem for parlor and office.
NY: T.F. Leslie & co.'s typography, 1871. 11p. NUC OCLC

5598. WALLACE, Eglantine (Maxwell), Lady [Br. d. 1803] ALT: W., E.; W., Lady
A letter to a friend, with a poem called The ghost of Werter. By Lady ----.
L: Hookham; J. Debrett, 1787. 26p. NUC OCLC

5599. WALLIS, Hannah [Br. 18c]
The female's meditations; or, Common occurrences spiritualized, in verse.
L: n.p., 1787. NUC BL

5600. WALTER, Carrie Stevens [Am. 1846-1907]
Rose-ashes.
San Francisco: C.A. Murdock & co., 1890. 85p. NUC OCLC

5601. WALTERS, Sophia Lydia [Br. 19/20c]
The brook: a poem.

L: n.p., 1879. BL

5602. -----A dreamer's sketchbook.
L: n.p., 1879. BL

5603. -----Lostrata. A poem.
L: E. Stock, 1890. 167p. NUC BL

WALTON, ELLIS, pseud. see COTTON, Mrs. F. Percy

WALTON, MRS. ELLIS, pseud. see COTTON, Mrs. F. Percy

WANDA, pseud. see MATHEWS, J.A., Mrs.

5604. WARD, Miss [Br. 19c]
The buried bride, &c.
L: Simpkin, Marshall & co.; Southampton: W. Sharland, 1840? 173p. BL
[A drama in verse, founded on D.M. Manni's novel "La Sepotta viva." With other poems]

5605. WARD, Caroline [Br. 19c]
Practical illustrations of the virtues. Part I, Faith.
L: Smith, Elder & co., 1839. 148p. BL

WARD, Catherine George see MASON, Catharine George (Ward)

5606. WARD, Elizabeth Stuart (Phelps), Mrs. H.D. Ward [Am. 1844-1911] ALT: Phelps, Elizabeth Stuart
A lost winter.
Boston: D. Lothrop & Co., 1889. 15 f. NUC

5607. -----Poetic studies.
Boston: J.R. Osgood & co., 1875. 141p. NUC BL

5608. -----Songs of the silent world, and other poems.
Boston & NY: Houghton, Mifflin & co., 1884. 155p. NUC BL OCLC

5609. WARD, F. M., Mrs. [Am. 19c]
ALT: W., F.M.
The heart, the mind, the soul. By F.M.W.
NY: A.D.F. Randolph & co., 1887. 17p. NUC

WARD, Mrs. H.D. see WARD, Elizabeth Stuart (Phelps)

5610. WARD, Hetta Lord (Hayes) [Am. 1815-1842]
Memoir of Mrs. Hetta L. Ward, with selections from her writings.
Boston: Pr. T.R. Marvin, 1843. 136p. NUC OCLC
[Incl. 3 poems plus brief essays & letters]

5611. WARD, Lydia (Avery) Conley [Am. 1845-1924]
Love songs.
Chicago: Wind-Tryst press, 1899. 59p. NUC OCLC

5612. -----Under the pines, and other verses.
Chicago: Way & Williams, 1895. 104p. NUC OCLC

5613. WARD, Mabella Ann [Br. 19c]
Kate Dashaway: an autobiography of a "fast" young lady. A burlesque novelette. Also, the Queen Bee.
L: n.p., 1865. BL
[In verse. Queen Bee is a poem for children]

5614. WARD, Marie A. [Am. 19c] ALT: W., M.A.
Our Dorothy. By M.A.W.
NY: F. Warne & co., 1893. 21p. NUC

5615. WARD, Mary [Br. 19c]
Original poetry.
Bath: Pr. Hazard & Binns, 1807. 187p. NUC BL

5616. WARDLAW, Elizabeth (Halket), Lady [Br. 1677-1727]
Hardyknute, a fragment of an antient Scots poem.
Glasgow: Pr. & sold by R. Foulis, 1748. 27p. NUC BL OCLC
[In Scottish dialect, a narrative poem]

5617. WARDLE, Charlotte [Br. 19c]
Norway: a poem.
L: J. Ridgway, 1814. 17p. NUC BL

5618. -----St. Aelian's, or the cursing well. A poem.
L: n.p., 1814. 112p. NUC BL OCLC

5619. WARDWELL, Mary E. [Am. 19c]
ALT: W., M.E.
Thistledown. By M.E.W.
Philadelphia: Bradley & co., 1884. 55p. NUC

5620. WARE, Katharine Augusta (Rhodes) [Br. 1797-1843] ALT: Rhodes, Katharine Augusta
Power of the passions; and other poems.
L: William Pickering, 1842. 148p. NUC BL OCLC

5621. WARE, Mary [Br. 19c]

Poems.
L: T. Cadell & W. Davies, 1809. 230p.
NUC BL
[Original & translations]

5622. WARFEL, Linda [Am. 19c]
Early efforts.
Philadelphia: J.W. Daughday & co., 1868. 136p. NUC BL OCLC

5623. WARFIELD, Catherine Ann (Ware) [Am. 1816-1877] PSEUD: Two sisters of the West
The Indian chamber and other poems. By two sisters of the West [With Mrs. Eleanor Percy (Ware) Lee; 1820-1849].
NY: Pr. for the authors, 1846. 264p.
NUC OCLC

5624. -----The wife of Leon, and other poems. By two sisters of the West [With Eleanor Percy (Ware) Lee].
NY: D. Appleton & co.; Philadelphia: G.S. Appleton, 1844. 256p. NUC BL OCLC
[2d ed. rev. Cincinnati, OH: E. Morgan & co., 1845, c1843. 268p.]

5625. WARING, Anna Laetitia [Br. 1823-1910] ALT: W., A.L.
Additional hymns.
L: n.p., 1858. BL

5626. -----Hymns and meditations.
4th ed. L: W. & F.G. Cash; Dublin: James McLashan & J.B. Gilpin, 1854. 83p. NUC BL OCLC
[1st ed. pub. 1850]

5627. WARING, Catherine W. [M. NUC] [Br. 19c]
Annuals and perennials, or, seed-time and harvest.
L: Joseph Masters, 1853. 68p. NUC BL
[Religious poems]

5628. WARING, Clara Ingersoll [Am. 19c]
Faun-Fa: a story of the Catskill Mountains, in four parts.
Detroit, MI: Ostler pr. co., 1889. 147p. NUC OCLC
[Poetry about Indians]

5629. WARING, S., Miss [Br. 19c] ALT: W., S.
The minstrelry of the woods; or, Sketches and songs connected with the natural history of some of the most interesting British and foreign birds.
L: Harvey & Darton, 1832. 227p. NUC BL OCLC
[50 poems and prose essays on ornithology]

5630. -----The wild garland; or prose and verse illustrative of English wild flowers and forest trees.
L: n.p., 1837. BL
[Poems signed S. or L.]

WARING, Susanna <u>see</u> BOONE, Susanna (Waring)

WARNE, E.A., comp. <u>see</u> WARNE, Emoline Ann

5631. WARNE, Elizabeth [Br. 19c]
Dusky rambles.
L: n.p., 1879. BL
[Lyrics]

5632. WARNE, Emoline Ann [Br. b. 1850]
A brief narrative of the lives of Ephraim Angell and Emoline Ann Warne. By E.A. Warne.
Yeovil: "Western Gazette" works, 1886. 54p. BL
[Account of a blind brother & sister, incl. poems & hymns]

5633. -----Lines composed ... on the occasion of Her Majesty's jubilee, June 1887.
Yeovil: "Western Gazette" works, 1887. 4p. BL

WARNE, Ephraim Angell, co-author <u>see</u> WARNE, Emoline Ann

5634. WARREN, Mary A. [Am. 19c]
Poems.
Alton, IL: Alton Courier steam press pr., 1855. 80p. NUC OCLC

5635. WARREN, Mercy Otis [Am. 1728-1814]
Poems, dramatic and miscellaneous.
Boston: Pr. I. Thomas & E.T. Andrews, 1790. 252p. NUC BL OCLC

5636. WASHBURN, Hannah B. [Am. 1820-1894]
An old family. By Sarah Elizabeth Washburn Heald.
Orange, NJ: n.p., 1882. 48p. NUC OCLC
[Incl. poems by Mrs. Hannah B. Washburn]

5637. WASHBURN, Jean Bruce [Am. 19c]
Blossoms of thought.
San Francisco: Golden Era co., 1886. 325p. NUC OCLC

5638. -----Yo Semite. A poem.
San Francisco: A. Roman & co., 1871. 15p. NUC BL OCLC
[Yosemite valley]

5639. WASHINGTON, Lucy Hall (Walker) [Am. b. 1835]
Columbia, and other poems.
Buffalo, NY: C.W. Moulton, 1893. 154p. NUC OCLC

5640. -----Echoes of song.
Springfield, IL: E.S. Walker, 1878. 200p. NUC OCLC
[Poems on her children, patriotic & temperance verse. Incl. poems for children]

5641. -----Memory's casket.
Buffalo, NY: C.W. Moulton, 1891. 154p. NUC OCLC

WASON, H.L. see WASON, Harriet L. (Castle)

5642. WASON, Harriet L. (Castle) [Am. d. 1904] ALT: Wason, H.L.
Legend of the grand caverns at Manitou, and other songs.
Denver, CO: n.p., 1899. 40p. OCLC

5643. -----Letters from Colorado. By H.L. Wason.
Boston: Cupples & Hurd, 1887. 158p. NUC OCLC

5644. WASSELL, Mary Ann [Br. 19c]
The rivals: or, The general investigation.
L: n.p., 1815. BL
[Narrative of rival suitors]

5645. -----The rivals: or, the general investigation.
5th ed. Cheltenham: n.p., 1859. BL
[With additional poems]

5646. WATERHOUSE, Elizabeth [Br. 19c]
Verses.
Newbury: T. Hawkins, 1897. 55p. NUC OCLC

5647. WATERHOUSE, L. G., Mrs. [Am. 19c]
The "sleeping gianters," and other poems.
Sacramento, CA: Globe pr. co., 1873. 22p. NUC OCLC

WATERMAN, Catherine Harbeson see ESLING, Catherine Harbeson (Waterman)

5648. WATERMAN, Mary Bissell [Am. 1836-1889] ALT: W., M.B.
"Gathered fragments." Easter, Christmas, and other poems.
Utica, NY: Daniel Waterman, 1889. 56p. NUC OCLC

5649. WATERS, Gay [Am. b. 1856]
The poetical works of Gay Waters. Including the Wicota.
Cincinnati, OH: Standard pub. co., 1887. 153p. NUC OCLC
[Poetry on Dakota Indians]

5650. WATERSTON, Anna Cabot Lowell (Quincy), Mrs. R.C. Waterston [Am. 1812-1899] ALT: W., A.C.L.
Verses. By A.C.L.W.
Boston: Pr. J. Wilson & son, 1863. 74p. NUC OCLC

WATERSTON, Mrs. R.C. see WATERSTON, Anna Cabot Lowell (Quincy)

5651. WATKINS, H., Miss [Br. 19c]
Poems on a variety of subjects. With Miss J.P. Watkins.
Bath: Pr. Meyler & son, sold by G. Robinson, 1812. 136p. NUC BL OCLC

WATKINS, J.P., Miss, co-author see WATKINS, H., Miss

WATRES, H.G. see WATRES, Harriet Gertrude (Hollister)

5652. WATRES, Harriet Gertrude (Hollister) [Am. b. 1821] ALT: Watres, H.G. PSEUD: Stella of Lakawanna
Cobwebs, by H.G. Watres (Stella of Lakawanna).
Boston: D. Lothrop & co., c1886. 219p. NUC OCLC
[Lyrics on misc. topics; songs]

5653. WATROUS, Sophia, Miss [Am. 19c]
The gift; or, miscellaneous poems.
Montpelier, VT: E.P. Walton & sons, 1841. 172p. NUC OCLC

5654. WATSON, Adelaide H. [19c]
Poems.
n.p.: n.p., 1867. 35p. NUC
[Cover title: Fancies]

5655. WATSON, Amy Ann [Br. 19c]
Poems on select passages of Scripture.
L: Jackson Walford & Hodder, 1863. 64p. NUC BL

5656. WATSON, Eleanor [Br. 19c]
Faith Graeme, and other poems: sacred and miscellaneous.
L: n.p., 1870. BL

5657. WATSON, Emily Rowley [Br. 19c]
The lament of Billy Villy.
L: Raphael Tuck & sons, 1894. BL

5658. WATSON, Mrs. Howard [Br. 19/20c]
Bridal lays.
Ormskirk: n.p., 1893. 6p. BL

5659. WATSON, Rosamund (Ball) Marriott [Am. 1863-1911] PSEUD: Tomson, Graham R.
The bird-bride, a volume of ballads and sonnets. By Graham R. Tomson.
L & NY: Longmans, Green & co., 1889. 136p. NUC BL OCLC

5660. -----The patch work quilt. By Graham R. Tomson.
L: E. Nister; NY: Dutton, 1891. 15p. NUC BL

5661. -----A summer night, and other poems. By Graham R. Tomson.
L: Methuen & co., 1891. 83p. NUC BL OCLC

5662. -----Tares, a book of verses.
Portland, ME: Thomas B. Mosher, 1898. 26p. NUC BL

5663. -----Vespertilia, and other verses.
L: John Lane; Chicago: Way & Williams, 1895. 110p. NUC BL OCLC

5664. WATSON-TAYLOR, Lady Hannah Charlotte (Hay) [Br. 1818-1887]
Memories and musings.
L: Priv. pr. at the Elzevir press, 1876. 98p. NUC
[Misc. poetry]

5665. WATT, Mrs. Francis [Br. 19c]
Poems. Ed. J.T.B. Landon.
L: Whittaker, 1853. 206p. BL OCLC

WATTS, Alaric Alfred, co-author <u>see</u> WATTS, Anna Mary (Howitt)

5666. WATTS, Anna Mary (Howitt) [Br. 1824-1884]
Aurora: a volume of verse. With Alaric Alfred Watts.
L: Henry S. King & co., 1875. 266p. NUC BL OCLC

5667. WATTS, Mary [Br. 19c]
The sculptor of Florence: and other poems.
L: Lewis & son, 1856. 95p. NUC BL

WATTS, Susanna <u>see</u> WATTS, Susannah

5668. WATTS, Susannah [Br. d. 1842] ALT: W., S.; Watts, Susanna
Chinese maxims, translated from the Oeconomy of human life [of R. Dodsley] into heroic verse. In seven parts.
Leicester: Pr. John Gregory, 1784. 72p. BL OCLC
[Each part deals with a different duty: The individual, woman, religion, etc.]

5669. -----Elegy on the death of the Princess Charlotte Augusta of Wales.
Leicester: I. Cockshaw, jr., 1817. 24p. NUC BL

5670. -----Hymns and poems of Mrs. S.W., with a few recollections of her life.
Leicester: J. Waddington, 1842. 71p. BL

5671. -----The insects in council, addressed to entomologists, with other poems.
L: Hurst, Chance, & co., 1828. 72p. NUC BL

5672. -----Original poems and translations, particularly Ambra, from Lorenzo de'Medici, chiefly by S.W.
L: F. & C. Rivington, 1802. 144p. NUC BL OCLC

WEAMES, Anna <u>see</u> WEAMYS, Anna

5673. WEAMYS, Anna [Br. 17c] ALT: W., A. Mrs; Weames, Anna
A continuation of Sir Philip Sydney's Arcadia.
L: Pr. Wm. Bentley, sold by T. Heath, 1651. 199p. NUC BL OCLC

5674. WEATHERHEAD, Emma [Br. 19c] ALT: W., E.
Leaves from Hazelwood.
L: Pr. for priv. circ., 1894. 52p. BL

5675. WEAVER, Baille Gertrude (Renton) Dunn [Br. 19/20c] ALT: Renton, Gertrude; Weaver, Gertrude Renton PSEUD: Colmore, G.
Poems of love and life. By G. Colmore.
L: Gay & Bird, 1896. 103p. BL OCLC

5676. -----Points of view, and other poems. By G. Colmore.
L: Gay & Bird, 1898. 181p. NUC BL OCLC

WEAVER, Gertrude (Renton) <u>see</u> WEAVER, Baille Gertrude (Renton) Dunn

5677. WEBB, Laura S., Mrs. [Am. 19c]
Custer's immortality. A poem, with biographical sketches of the chief

actors in the late tragedy of the wilderness.
NY: N.Y. Evening Post steam presses, 1876? 72p. NUC OCLC

5678. -----Heart leaves.
Mobile, AL: Pr. at the Daily Register bk. & job off., 1868. 135p. NUC
[Chiefly poetry, much of it on the fallen South; 2 essays]

5679. -----A requiem for Lee.
New Orleans, LA: Pelican press, 18--. 32p. NUC
[Civil War poem]

5680. WEBSTER, Miss [Br. 1785-1803]
A poem on that important subject, repentance. Wrote by Miss Webster, on her death-bed, etc.
Leeds: E. Bains, 1803? 8p. BL
[3 poems]

5681. WEBSTER, Ann [Br. 19c]
Solitary musings.
L: n.p., 1825. 19p. BL OCLC

WEBSTER, Augusta <u>see</u> WEBSTER, Julia Augusta (Davies)

5682. WEBSTER, Elizabeth Hedge [Am. b. 1822]
Clover blossoms.
Boston: Pr. W.G. Crawford, 188-? 224p. NUC
[Misc. poetry & brief prose essays, many on women's rights]

WEBSTER, Mrs. H.E., comp. <u>see</u> TAYLOR, Elizabeth (Colpeper)

5683. WEBSTER, Julia Augusta (Davies) [Br. 1837-1894] ALT: Webster, Augusta PSEUD: Home, Cecil
Blanche Lisle and other poems. By Cecil Home.
L & Cambridge: Macmillan & co., 1860. 168p. NUC BL OCLC

5684. -----A book of rhyme.
L: Macmillan, 1881. 146p. NUC BL OCLC
[Rural poems]

5685. -----Dramatic studies.
L & Cambridge: Macmillan & co., 1866. 165p. NUC BL OCLC
[Narrative poems]

5686. -----In a day: a drama.
L: Kegan Paul, Trench, 1882. 93p. NUC BL OCLC

5687. -----Lilian Gray. By Cecil Home.
L: Smith, 1864. 48p. NUC BL OCLC

5688. -----Mother and daughter. An uncompleted sonnet sequence. To which are added seven, (her only other) sonnets.
L & NY: Macmillan & co., 1895. 51p. NUC BL

5689. -----Portraits.
L: Macmillan & co., 1870. 161p. NUC BL OCLC

5690. -----The sentence, a drama.
L: T.F. Unwin, 1887. 138p. NUC OCLC

5691. -----A woman sold and other poems.
L & Cambridge: Macmillan & co., 1867. 288p. NUC BL OCLC

5692. -----Yu-pe-ya's lute: a Chinese tale in English verse by A.W.
L: Macmillan & co., 1874. 64p. NUC BL OCLC
["Found in the Choix de coutes et nouvelles traduits du Chinois par Theodore Pavre"]

5693. WEDDERBURN, Margaretta [Br. 19c]
Mary, Queen of Scots. An historical poem, with other miscellaneous pieces, etc.
Edinburgh: n.p., 1811. NUC BL

5694. WEED, Emily Stuart [Am. 19c]
Twilight echoes.
Buffalo, NY: C.W. Moulton, 1890. 160p. NUC

5695. WEEDEN, Howard, Miss [Am. 19c]
Bandanna ballads.
NY: Doubleday & McClure co., 1899. 90p. NUC OCLC

5696. -----Shadows on the wall. By H. Weeden.
Huntsville, AL & NY: M. Stolz & co., c1898. 31p. NUC OCLC

5697. WEEDEN, Jane E. [Am. 19c]
Los Angeles, a descriptive poem.
Los Angeles: n.p., 1884. 4 l. NUC OCLC

5698. -----San Francisco. A descriptive poem.
n.p.: n.p., 1884. 4p. OCLC

5699. WEEKS, Della Jerman [Am. 19c]
Legends of the war.
Boston: Mudge & son, pr., 1863. 63p. NUC OCLC

[Civil War]

WEEKS, Mrs. Lyman Horace see WEEKS, Reba J. (Kaplinger)

5700. WEEKS, Reba J. (Kaplinger), Mrs. Lyman Horace Weeks [Am. 19c]
Sunlight and shadow.
Boston: L. Prang & co., 1889. 14p. NUC

5701. -----Twilight fancies.
Boston: L. Prang & co., 1889. 6 l. NUC

5702. WEISS, Susan Archer (Talley) [Am. b. 1835] ALT: Talley, Susan Archer
Poems.
NY: Rudd & Carleton, 1859. 183p. NUC OCLC

5703. WEITZEL, Sophie Winthrop [Am. 19c]
From time to time: a book of verse. By S.W. Weitzel.
NY: A.D.F. Randolph, 1892. 64p. NUC BL OCLC

5704. WELBY, Amelia Ball (Coppuck) [Am. 1819/21-1852] ALT: Amelia
The evening skies. A poem.
n.p.: n.p., n.d. NUC

5705. -----Gems of poetry.
2d ed. Philadelphia: Bryson & Cooper, 1851. 224p. NUC OCLC

5706. -----Poems, by Amelia.
Boston: A. Tompkins, 1845. 259p. NUC BL OCLC

5707. WELCH, Ann [Am. 18/19c]
Fruits of retirement. A collection of pieces in prose and poetry.
Downingtown, PA: Pr. Charles Mowry, 1816. 47p. NUC
[Poems, mostly religious, written 1781-1814. No prose included.]

5708. WELCH, Lydia Stuart (Edwards) [Am. d. 1882]
In memoriam. Lydia Stuart Welch, died February 5, 1882.
Detroit, MI: n.p., 1882? 199p. NUC OCLC
[Contains poems]

5709. WELLER, Mary-Ann [Br. 19c]
Pastoral and descriptive poems.
Birmingham: n.p., 1802. BL

5710. WELLINGTON, Caroline Louisa (Fisher) [Am. 1843-1879]
Leaflets along the pathway of life. Ed. her sister, Sarah C. Fisher.
Boston: Mills, Knight & co., c1883. 274p. NUC OCLC
[Incl. sonnets, songs, reminiscences, patriotic, etc.; all poems]

5711. WELLMAN, Mary Ward (Bryant) [Am. c1825-1891] PSEUD: Prairie Bird
Poems, and other thoughts, suggested upon the death of Hon. Daniel Webster. By Prairie Bird, a lady of Massachusetts.
Boston: The author, 1853. 17p. NUC OCLC

5712. WELLS, Anna Maria (Foster) [Am. 1795?-1868]
The floweret: a gift of love.
Boston: T.H. Carter, c1840. 72p. NUC

5713. -----Poems and juvenile sketches.
Boston: Carter, Hendee & Babcock, 1830. 104p. NUC BL
[1st half adult poetry; 2nd half poems on bereavement for children.]

5714. WELLS, Elizabeth [Br. 19c]
Poems and dialogues in various subjects.
L: F.C. & J. Rivington, 1812. 146p. BL OCLC

5715. WELLS, Ella Maria Wilson [Am. 1866-1880]
Ella's life and poems. Ed. L.F.G.
Norfolk,, VA: W.N. Grubb, pr., 1880. 48p. NUC OCLC

5716. WELLS, Ellen Harriet [Br. 19c]
A selection of sacred and other poems by the late Ellen Harriet Wells.
L: G.J.W. Pitman, 1891. 120p. BL OCLC

5717. WELLS, Elvenah C. (Raymond), Mrs. G.C. Wells [Am. 1826-1869]
Lingering sounds from a broken harp. Ed. her husband, Rev. G.C. Wells.
Albany, NY?: S.R. Gray, 1869. 254p. NUC OCLC
[Devotional prose, but incl. about 6 poems]

5718. WELLS, Emmeline Blanche (Woodward) [Am. 1828-1921]
Musings and memories; poems.
Salt Lake City, UT: G.Q. Cannon & sons co., 1896. 304p. NUC OCLC

WELLS, Mrs. G.C. see WELLS, Elvenah C. (Raymond)

WELLS, Rev. G.C., ed. see WELLS, Elvenah C. (Raymond)

WENTWORTH, Milly, co-author see DUCKWORTH, Eleanor

5719. WERNER, Alice [Br. 1859-1935]
A time and times. Ballads and lyrics of East and West.
L: T.F. Unwin, 1886. 157p. NUC BL OCLC

WEST, Elizabeth see DOWDEN, Elizabeth Dickinson (West)

5720. WEST, Florence D., Mrs. [Am. 19c]
The marble lily and other poems.
n.p.: Priv. ed., 1878. 53p. NUC OCLC

WEST, Mrs. Frederick see WEST, Theresa Cornwallis J. (Whitby)

5721. WEST, Jane, Mrs. [Br. 1758-1852] PSEUD: Homespun, Prudentia, Mrs.
An elegy on the death of the Right Honourable Edmund Burke.
L: T.N. Longman, 1797. 19p. BL OCLC

5722. -----The humours of Brighthelmstone.
L: Pr. for the author, 1788. 15p. NUC BL

5723. -----Miscellaneous poems, and a tragedy.
York: Sold by R. Faulder, pr. by W. Blanchard, 1791. 127p. NUC BL
[Incl.: Edmund, surnamed Ironside, 5 acts, verse]

5724. -----Miscellaneous poetry. Written at an early period of life.
L: W.T. Swift, 1786. 44p. NUC BL OCLC
[Elegies, odes, & 1 narrative poem]

5725. -----The mother; a poem, in five books.
L: n.p., 1809; 2d ed. L: Longman, Hurst & co., 1810. 242p. NUC BL OCLC

5726. -----Poems and plays.
L: Pr. C. Whittingham for T.N. Longman & Rees, 1799-1805. 4v. NUC BL OCLC
[Incl.: Adela, tragedy, 5-acts. Nine elegies, 10 sonnets, & misc. poetry.]

5727. WEST, Maud [Br. 19c]
Through woodland and meadow, and other poems. With Marie Low.
L: E. Nister, 1891. 24 l. NUC BL

5728. WEST, Theresa Cornwallis J. [I. NUC] (Whitby), Mrs. Frederic West [Br. 1805?-1886]
Frescoes and sketches from memory.
Edinburgh: Gall & Inglish, 1855. BL

WESTBROOK, Mrs. J. Cooke, comp. see TATHAM, Emma, Miss

5729. WESTBROOK, Mrs. J. Cooke [Br. 19c]
Little Lillie's prayer: a ballad.
L: n.p., 1871. BL

5730. WESTBROOK, Mary Ann [Br. 19c]
Songs of the isle, seaside musings, etc.
Sandown: Taylor & Mearman, 1880? 44p. BL

5731. WESTON, Amanda [Am. 19c]
May-flowers. A selection of poems.
NY: L.C. Matlack, 1850. 202p. NUC OCLC
[Misc. original poetry]

5732. WESTON, Emma Gertrude [Am. 19c]
The old home and other poems.
Concord, NH: Republican press assn., 1895. 91p. NUC OCLC

5733. -----Songs from the hills.
Concord, NH: Republican press assoc., 1897. 84p. NUC OCLC

WESTON, Joseph, ed. see PICKERING, Mrs.

5734. WESTON, Maria D., Mrs. [Am. 19c] ALT: Maria
The fatal excursion. By Maria.
Boston: White & Potter; Pawtucket, RI: R.W. Potter, 1847. 24p. NUC OCLC
[Incl. 3p. poem recounting fatal accident]

5735. -----Susan's visit; or, A week spent in the country. By Maria.
Boston: White & Potter, 1847. 23p. NUC
[Narrative poetry]

5736. WESTWOOD, Lucy Bell [Br. 1832-1850]
The poetical remains of Lucy Bell Westwood: with some account of her life by the Rev. James Henry Millard.
L: Simpkin, Marshall & co., 1850. 119p. NUC BL
[Nature, temperance poems]

5737. WETHERALD, Agnes Ethelwyn [Am. 1857-1940]
The house of trees and other poems.
Boston & NY: Lamson, Wolffe & co., 1895? 94p. NUC

5738. WETHERBEE, Emily Greene [Am. 1839-1897]
The bridal.
n.p.: n.p., 1885? 5 l. NUC

5739. -----A crystal wedding.
Lawrence, MA: n.p., 1884. 6 l. NUC

5740. -----A golden wedding.
Lawrence, MA: n.p., 1885. 10 l. NUC

5741. -----Poems and addresses.
Lawrence, MA: The Lawrence pub. co., 1898. 163p. NUC OCLC
[Incl. addresses for Memorial Day & on Patriotism]

5742. WEYLAR, Maria [Br. 18c] ALT: W., M.
Reveries du coeur, or feelings of the heart. Attempted in verse by M.W.
L: Pr. for the author, sold by Messrs. Dodsley, 1770. NUC BL

5743. WEYMOUTH, Sarah [Br. 19c]
Rural poems; with other fugitive pieces.
L: G.B. Whittaker, 1827. 99p. NUC BL

5744. WHARTON, Anne (Lee), Lady [Mrs. BL] [Br. 1632?-1685]
Examen miscellaneum. Consisting of verse and prose.
L: n.p., 1702. BL

5745. -----The temple of death, a poem; written by the Marquess of Normanby ... To which is added several poems of the Honourable Madam Wharton.
L: Tho. Warren for Francis Saunders, 1693. 273p. BL

5746. -----Whartoniana: or, Miscellanies, in verse and prose.
L: n.p., 1727. NUC

5747. WHARTON, Edith Newbold (Jones) [Am. 1862-1937]
Verses.
Newport, RI: C.E. Hammett, jr., 1878. 38p. NUC OCLC

WHATELEY, Mary <u>see</u> DARWALL, Mary (Whateley)

5748. WHEATLEY, Phillis [Am. c1753?-1784] ALT: Peters, Phillis Wheatley
An elegaic poem on the death of ... Reverend ... George Whitefield.
Boston: Pr. & sold by Ezekiel Russell & John Boyles, 1770. 8p. NUC OCLC

5749. -----An elegy ... to the memory of ... Dr. Samuel Cooper. By Phillis Peters.
Boston: E. Russell, 1784. 8p. NUC OCLC

5750. -----Liberty and peace, a poem. By Phillis Peters.
Boston: Pr. Warden & Russell, 1784. 4p. NUC

5751. -----Memoir and poems of Phillis Wheatley, a native African and a slave to Mr. John Wheatley of Boston.
Boston: G.W. Light, 1834. 103p. NUC BL OCLC

5752. -----Poems on various subjects religious and moral.
L: Pr. for A. Bell & sold by Messrs. Cox & Berry; Boston: n.p., 1773? 124p. NUC BL OCLC

WHEELER, Ella <u>see</u> WILCOX, Ella Wheeler

5753. WHEELER, Esther Gracie (Lawrence) [Am. 19c]
Stray leaves from Newport.
Boston: Cupples & Hurd, 1888. 195p. NUC BL OCLC
[Verse & short stories]

5754. WHEELER, Euretta, Mrs. [Am. 19c]
More truth than poetry.
Binghamton, NY: O.R. Bacon, pr., 1891. 64p. NUC

5755. WHEELER, Kate Louise [Am. 19c]
Home poems.
Nashua, NH: Telegraph pub. co., 1897. 137p. NUC OCLC

5756. WHITAKER, Lily C. [Am. b. 1850] PSEUD: Adidnac
Donata and other poems. By Adidnac.
Baltimore, MD: J.B. Piet, 1881. 96p. NUC OCLC

5757. WHITAKER, Mary Scrimgeour (Furman) [Am. 1820-1906]
Poems.
Charleston, SC: J.B. Nixon, pr., 1850. 296p. NUC BL OCLC

5758. WHITE, Harriet [Br. 19c] ALT: Harriet
Verses, sacred and miscellaneous. By Harriet.
L: n.p., 1853. BL

5759. WHITE, Ida L. [Br. 19c]

The three banquets and prison poems.
L: Swan, Sonnenschein & co., 1890.
198p. NUC BL
[White was a Socialist]

5760. WHITE, Isabella [Br. 19c]
The lovers of the mountain, and other poems.
Brechin: Pr. D. Burns, 1869. 51p. NUC
[Narrative]

5761. WHITE, S.A., Miss [Am. 19c]
ALT: W., S.A.
What is a flower to thee? By S.A.W.
Watertown, MA: Pr. Fred G. Barker, 1886. 7 l. NUC OCLC

5762. WHITEFORD, Isabella [Br. 19c]
Poems.
Belfast: William M'Comb, 1860. 297p. NUC

5763. WHITEHEAD, Emma [Br. 19c]
The romance of the city: or, legends of London.
L: Pub. for the authoress, 1854.
308p. NUC BL OCLC
[Primarily narrative verse]

5764. WHITELOCK, Louise Clarkson [Am. 1865-1928] ALT: Clarkson, Lida
The gathering of the lilies.
Philadelphia: J.L. Sibole & co., 1877. 32 l. NUC OCLC

5765. -----Heartsease and happy days.
NY: E.P. Dutton & co., c1882. 47p. NUC OCLC
[Paintings of flowers with original verses]

5766. -----Indian summer; autumn poems and sketches. Comp. L. Clarkson.
NY: E.P. Dutton & co.; L: Griffith, Farran, 1881. 52/55p. BL OCLC
[Sketches & some of the poems by Clarkson]

5767. -----The rag fair and other reveries. Poems.
Philadelphia: F.W. Robinson & co., 1879. 35 l. NUC OCLC

5768. -----Violet among the lilies, a sequel to "Violet with eyes of blue." By L. Clarkson.
NY: E.P. Dutton & co., c1885. 17p. NUC OCLC

5769. -----Violet, with eyes of blue!
Philadelphia: J.L. Sibole; Baltimore, MD: A. Hoen & co., pr., 1876. 14 l. NUC OCLC

5770. WHITEMAN, Elizabeth Horsley [Br. 19c]
A seaside story, and other poems.
L: Bell & Daldy, 1870. 163p. NUC BL OCLC

5771. -----Sonnets and other poems.
2d issue. L: n.p., 1865. BL

5772. WHITEMAN, Susan Godfred (Hooker) [Am. 1838-1928]
Wakefield Standley. A story of the flag.
Carrolton, MO: Carroll Record, 1888.
190p. NUC OCLC
[Civil War, narrative]

5773. WHITESIDE, L.T., Mrs. [Am. 19c]
Freedom's banner.
Long Bottom, OH: n.p., 1867. 47p. NUC

5774. WHITING, Lilian [Br. 1859-1942]
From dreamland sent.
Cambridge, MA: Roberts bros., 1899.
133p. NUC BL OCLC
[New ed., expanded, L: Sampson, Low & co., 1899. 167p. BL]

WHITMAN, Sarah Helen (Power), co-author see POWER, Susan Anna

5775. WHITMAN, Sarah Helen (Power) [Am. 1803-1878]
Hours of life, and other poems.
Providence, RI: G.H. Whitney, 1853.
227p. NUC BL OCLC

5776. -----Poems.
Boston: n.p., 1878. Boston: Houghton, Osgood & co., 1879. 261p. NUC BL OCLC

5777. WHITNEY, Adeline Dutton (Train) [Br. 1824-1906] ALT: W., A. D.T.
Daffodils.
Boston & NY: Houghton, Mifflin & co., 1887. 132p. BL

5778. -----Footsteps on the seas; a poem. By A.D.T.W.
Boston: Crosby, Nichols & co., 1857.
50p. NUC OCLC

5779. -----Holy-tides: seven songs of Advent, Christmas, etc.
Boston: Houghton, Mifflin & co., 1886. BL

5780. -----Mother Goose for grown folks.
NY: Rudd & Carleton, 1860. 111p. NUC BL OCLC

5781. -----Pansies "... for thoughts."

Boston: J.R. Osgood & co., 1859, c1872. 111p. NUC BL OCLC
[Enlarged ed. Boston: Houghton, Mifflin, 1882. 204p. BL]

5782. WHITNEY, Anne [Am. 1821-1915]
Poems.
NY: D. Appleton & co., 1859. 191p. NUC BL OCLC

5783. WHITNEY, Hannah [Br. 19c]
Sabbaths in the wood; or, The husband reclaimed: a poem.
L: n.p., 1847. BL

5784. WHITNEY, Helen Hay [Am. 1875-1944]
Some verses.
Chicago & NY: Herbert S. Stone, 1898. 72p. L: Duckworth, 1898. 71p. NUC OCLC

5785. WHITNEY, Isabella [Br. 16c]
A sweet nosgay, or pleasant posye: contayning a hundred and ten phylosophicall flowers.
L: n.p., 1573. BL

WHITON, Mrs. L.C., co-author see MACHAR, Agnes Maule

5786. WHITTEN, Martha Elizabeth (Hotchkiss) [Am. b. 1842]
Author's edition of Texas garlands.
Austin, TX: Triplett & Hutchins, 1885. 364p. NUC OCLC
[Began publishing at 15; collection includes: domestic, memorial, lyric poems; poems on Texas]

5787. -----The drunkard's wife: poem.
Austin, TX: Hutchings pr. house, 1887. 8p. NUC OCLC

5788. WHITTEN, Mary Delano [Am. 1822-1841]
Blossom of Rocky Nook; or, Life and writings of Mary Delano Whitten, 1822-1841. Ed. Sara Hall Browne [Brown OCLC].
Boston: Oliver L. Perkins, 1850. 179p. BL OCLC
[Incl. poems]

5789. WHITTIER, Elizabeth Hussey [Am. 1815-1864]
Hazel blossoms and works. By John Greenleaf Whittier.
Boston: J.R. Osgood, 1874. 133p. NUC BL OCLC
[Her poems p. 101-133]

5790. WHITTIER, Ida Celia [Am. 19c]
Poems.
Chicago & NY: W.B. Conkey co., c1897. 72p. NUC

WHITTIER, John Greenleaf, co-author see INGELOW, Jean

WHITTIER, John Greenleaf, co-author see LARCOM, Lucy

WHITTIER, John Greenleaf, co-author see WHITTIER, Elizabeth Hussey

WHITTLESEY, Oscar Columbus, co-author see WHITTLESEY, Sarah Johnson Cogswell

5791. WHITTLESEY, Sarah Johnson Cogswell, Miss [Am. 1825-1896]
Heart-drops from memory's urn.
NY: A.S. Barnes & co., 1852. 342p. NUC OCLC

5792. -----Spring buds and summer blossoms, by S.J.C. Whittlesey; and Idle hours, by Oscar Columbus Whittlesey.
Philadelphia: Pr. J.B. Lippincott co., 1889. 250p. NUC OCLC

5793. WHITWORTH, Laura A. [Br. 19c]
Glimpses "beyond the veil." Poems spiritual, and songs earthly.
L: W.H. Beer & co., 1884. 95p. BL

WIDOWED WIFE, A, pseud. see DERENZY, Margaret Graves

WIGAN, A. Cleveland, ed. see GODWIN, Catherine Grace (Garnett)

5794. WIGHT, Lucy M. [Am. d. 1894]
The harp of my loved one. Poetry by L.M.W.; music by G.G.
Boston: A. Mudge & son, 1859. NUC

5795. WIGHTMAN, Margaret Theresa [Br. 19c]
The faithful shepherd, and other poems.
Edinburgh & Glasgow: n.p., 1876. BL

5796. WIGLESWORTH, Esther [Br. 1827-1904]
Hymns of the holy feast.
L: J. Masters, 1859. 48p. BL

5797. -----The second advent: a poem.
L: G.J.W. Pitman, 1879. 16p. BL OCLC

5798. -----Songs of perseverance. A manual of devotional verse.
L: J. Nisbet, 1885. 94p. BL OCLC

5799. -----Verses for the Sundays and holidays of the Christian year.

L: Joseph Masters, 1863. 210p. NUC BL

5800. -----Verses on the liturgy.
4th ed. L: G.J.W. Pitman, 1894. 35p.
OCLC
[Bound with The Second Advent]

5801. WIGMORE, Annie [Am. 19c]
Dreams of the first and twentieth century.
Buffalo, NY: Matthews-Northrup co., 1898. 94p. NUC BL
[Short stories, essays & poetry]

5802. WILBRAHAM, Frances M. [Br. 19c]
Hal, the barge boy. A sketch from life.
L: Christian Knowledge soc., 1883. 73p. BL

5803. -----Perils in the mine. A colliery tale in verse.
L: n.p., 1863. BL

5804. WILBUR, Jennie Aurelia, Mrs. [Am. 19c]
Songs of the West.
Chicago: Charles E. Pomeroy, 1866. 300p. NUC OCLC

5805. WILBY, Maria A., Mrs. [Br. 19c]
A cry from the opprest: and other poems.
L: n.p., 1838. BL

5806. WILCOX, Ella (Wheeler) [Am. 1855(1850 OCLC)-1919] ALT: Wheeler, Ella
The birth of the opal.
NY: Jaques & Marcus, c1886. 3p. NUC

5807. -----Custer, and other poems.
Chicago: W.B. Conkey co., 1896. 134p. NUC BL OCLC

5808. -----Drops of water: a selection of temperance poems and recitations.
NY: Nat'l. Temperance soc. & pub. house, 1872. 132p. NUC BL OCLC

5809. -----An erring woman's love.
Chicago: W.B. Conkey co.; NY: American pub.; Lovell, Coryell & co., c1892. 157p. NUC OCLC

5810. -----How Salvator won, and other recitations.
NY: E.S. Werner, 1891. 160p. Chicago: W.B. Conkey co., 1895. 160p. NUC OCLC
[Poems & one prose story.]

5811. -----Maurine.
Milwaukee, WI: Cramer, Aikens & Cramer, 1876. 224p. NUC

5812. -----Maurine, and other poems.
Chicago: Jansen, McClurg & co., 1882. 254p. NUC BL OCLC

5813. -----Poems of passion.
Chicago: Belford, Clarke & co., 1883. 160p. NUC BL OCLC

5814. -----Poems of pleasure.
NY & Chicago: Belford, Clarke & co., 1888. 158p. NUC BL OCLC

5815. -----Shells.
Milwaukee, MN?: Hauser & Storey, 1873. 206p. NUC OCLC

5816. -----The song of the sandwich.
NY: George M. Allen co., 1893. 29 l. NUC OCLC

5817. -----Three women.
Chicago & NY: W.B. Conkey co., 1897. 194p. NUC
[1905 BL]

WILD-BIRD, pseud. <u>see</u> FRINK, Almira Louisa Corey

5818. WILDE, Jane Francesca (Elge), Lady [Br. 1826-1896] PSEUD: Speranza
Poems. By Speranza.
Dublin & L: J. Duffy, 1864. 233p. NUC BL OCLC

5819. -----Ugo Bassi: a tale of the Italian revolution.
L: n.p., 1857. 115p. BL

5820. WILKES, Ann [Br. 19c]
Poems, on subjects temporal and divine.
Birmingham: n.p., 1808. BL

5821. WILKINS, Adela [Br. 19/20c]
Verses for song.
L: Remington & co., 1890. 31p. BL

WILKINS, Mary Eleanor <u>see</u> FREEMAN, Mary Eleanor (Wilkins)

5822. WILKINSON, Janet W. [Br. 19c]
Sketches and legends amid the mountains of North Wales: in verse.
L: T. & W. Boone, 1840. 134p. NUC BL OCLC
[Lyric & narrative poems]

5823. WILKINSON, Mary Anderson [Am. 19c]
Sunshine and shadow.
Baltimore, MD: Turnbull bros., 1873. 191p. NUC

WILKINSON, Sarah <u>see</u> COWELL, Elizabeth Susan

5824. WILLAN, Rhoda Maria [Br. 19c]
The flower girl and other poems.
L: Thomas Miller, 1843. 116p. NUC BL OCLC

5825. WILLARD, Emma C. (Hart) [Am. 1787-1870]
The fulfillment of a promise.
NY: White, Gallaher & White, 1831. 124p. NUC OCLC

5826. WILLARD, Florence J., Mrs. [19c]
A life idyll.
Hamilton, Ontario: A. Lawson, 1869. 92p. NUC OCLC

5827. WILLIAMS, Miss [Br. 19c]
Dependance, a poem.
L: n.p., 1815? BL

5828. WILLIAMS, A. [Br. 18c]
Original poems and imitations.
L: Pr. for the author & sold by W. Harris, 1773. 191p. NUC BL

5829. WILLIAMS, Anna [Br. 1706-1783]
Miscellanies in prose and verse.
L: T. Davies, 1766. 184p. NUC BL OCLC
[Essays in verse, odes, misc. poetry, a fairy tale & a translated play. Incl. some pieces by Dr. Samuel Johnson.]

5830. WILLIAMS, Anna M. [Am. 19c]
Two fisher-lads and other poems.
NY: n.p., 1888. 33p. NUC

5831. WILLIAMS, Catherine M. [Br. 19c]
Tales of Glendevon, and other poems.
L: n.p., 1830? BL

5832. WILLIAMS, Catherine Read (Arnold) [Am. 1790-1872]
Original poems on various subjects.
Providence, RI: Pr. H.H. Brown, 1828. 107p. NUC BL OCLC

5833. WILLIAMS, Gertrude M. [Br. 19c]
The snow-wreath and other tales and poems.
L: Charing Cross pub. co., 1876. 80p. BL OCLC

WILLIAMS, Harriette Sophia, co-author
see WILLIAMS, Sarah Anne

5834. WILLIAMS, Helen Maria [Br. 1762-1827] ALT: W., H.M. PSEUD: Young Lady, A
The charter, lines addressed ... to her nephew, Athanase C.L. Coquerel, on his wedding day.
Paris: n.p., 1819. 8p. NUC BL

5835. -----Edwin and Eltruda. A legendary tale. By a young lady. Ed. Andrew Kippis.
L: T. Cadell, 1782. 31p. NUC BL

5836. -----A farewell, for two years, to England. A poem.
L: T. Cadell, 1791. 15p. NUC BL

5837. -----Julia: a novel interspersed with some poetical pieces.
Dublin: Chamberlaine & Rice; L: T. Cadell, 1790. 2 v. NUC BL OCLC
[Poems incl. as if written by heroine.]

5838. -----An ode on the peace.
L: T. Cadell, 1783. 20p. NUC BL OCLC

5839. -----Ode to peace.
L: n.p., 1786? BL

5840. -----Peru, a poem. In six cantos.
L: T. Cadell, 1784. 95p. NUC BL OCLC

5841. -----A poem on the bill lately passed for regulating the slave trade.
L: T. Cadell, 1788. 23p. NUC BL

5842. -----Poems.
L: Pr. A. Rivington & J. Marshall for T. Cadell, 1786. 2v. NUC BL OCLC
[2d ed. L: T. Cadell, 1791. 2 v. NUC BL OCLC]

5843. -----Poems on various subjects ... .
L: G. & W.B. Whittaker, 1823. 298p. NUC BL

5844. -----Poems, moral, elegant and pathetic ... including original sonnets.
L: E. Newbery, 1801. 220p. NUC BL OCLC

5845. -----Verses addressed by H.M.W. to her two nephews, on Saint Helen's day.
Paris: n.p., 1809. BL

5846. WILLIAMS, Jane [Br. 1806-1885]
PSEUD: Ysgafell
Celtic fables, fairy tales and legends, chiefly from ancient Welsh originals. Versified.
L: Pr. T. Brettell, 1862. 47p. NUC BL OCLC

5847. WILLIAMS, Jane [Br. 19c]
Miscellaneous poems.
Brecknock: n.p., 1824. BL

5848. WILLIAMS, Jenny Perkins [Am. 19c]
Scattered verses and letters gathered again.
NY: French & Wheat, pr., c1869. 64p. NUC

WILLIAMS, Jno. Aug., co-author see MCKINNEY, Kate (Slaughter)

5849. WILLIAMS, Maria L. [Am. 19c]
Heart-thoughts: a collection of home poems.
Boston: Charles H. Crosby, 1859. 141p. NUC

5850. WILLIAMS, Mary St. Clair, Mrs. [Br. 19c]
Floral and other poems.
Welshpool: The authoress, 1872. 151p. NUC BL

5851. WILLIAMS, Sarah [Br. 1814-1868]
Twilight hours: a legacy of verse.
L: Strahan, 1868. 300p. NUC BL OCLC

5852. WILLIAMS, Sarah Anne [Br. 19c]
The first note of the lyre. With Harriette Sophia Williams.
L: n.p., 1845. BL

5853. WILLIAMS, Sarah Johanna [Br. 19c]
Sherwood Forest, a poem.
Nottingham: Pr. G. Stretton, 1832. 38p. NUC BL

5854. WILLIAMSON, Effie [Br. 19c]
The tangled web: poems and hymns.
Edinburgh: R. Williamson, 1883. 160p. OCLC

5855. WILLIAMSON, J., Mrs. [Br. 19c] ALT: W., J., Mrs.
Hymns for the household of faith, and lays of the better land.
L: Wertheim, Macintosh & Hunt, 1861. 419p. NUC BL

5856. WILLIAMSON, Julia May [Am. 1859-1909] PSEUD: Bell, Lura
The choir of the year. By Lura Bell.
Farmington: Chronicle off., 1875. 76p. NUC OCLC
[Misc. poems arr. under seasonal & humorous headings]

5857. -----Echoes of time and tide.
Augusta, ME: Pub. for the author by the press of T.F. Murphy, 1878. 118p. NUC OCLC
[Historical & legendary, lyric, occasional, pathetic & humorous, descriptive & misc.]

5858. -----Star of hope, and other songs. By Lura Bell.
Augusta, ME: J.M. Williamson, 1891. 63p. NUC
[Lyrics & sonnets]

5859. WILLING, Mrs. Charles [Am. 19c]
Genevieve of Brabant. A legend in verse.
Philadelphia: J.B. Lippincott & co., 1879. 127p. NUC BL OCLC

5860. -----Persephone and other poems.
Philadelphia: J.B. Lippincott & co., 1881. 95p. NUC OCLC

5861. WILLIS, Ellen H. [Br. 19c]
"I left it all with Jesus," and other poems.
L: n.p., 1875. BL

WILLOUGHBY, Hon. Mrs. see WILLOUGHBY, Eliza Mary (Gordon Cumming), Baroness Middleton

5862. WILLOUGHBY, Eliza Mary (Gordon Cumming), Baroness Middleton [Br. d. 1922] ALT: Willoughby, Hon. Mrs.
Ballads by the Lady Middleton.
L: Kegan Paul, 1878. 86p. NUC BL OCLC

5863. -----On the north wind, thistledown. By the Hon. Mrs. Willoughby.
L: King, 1874. 251p. BL OCLC

5864. WILLOUGHBY, Julia [Br. 19c]
A child's poetic thoughts.
Leeds: John Smith, Henry Inchbold, 1868. 152p. BL
[Author had just turned 14 at time of pub. Incl. many historical themes & ballads]

5865. WILLS, Ruth [Br. 19c]
Lays of lowly life.
L: n.p., 1861. BL

5866. -----Lays of lowly life.
2d series. L: James Nisbet & co., 1868. 131p. NUC BL

5867. WILLSON, Elizabeth Conwell (Smith) [Am. 19c]
Poems.
Cambridge, MA: n.p., 1866. 79p. NUC

5868. -----The voice of a sea-shell.
Cambridge, MA: Pr. priv., 1866. 139p. NUC

5869. WILMORE, Sarah [Br. 19c]
The progress and comforts of religion; an essay, in blank verse.
Stourport: Pr. G. Nicholson, 1820. 66p. NUC BL OCLC

5870. WILMOT, Barbarina, Baroness Dacre [Br. 1767-1854] ALT: Brand, Barbarina Ogle Wilmot, Baroness Dacre
Dramas, translations and occasional poems.
L: John Murray, 1821. 2v. BL OCLC

5871. WILSON, Ann, Mrs. [Br. 18/19c] ALT: W., A., Mrs.
Jephthah's daughter, a dramatic poem.
L: W. Flexney, 1783. 55p. NUC BL
[5 acts, verse]

5872. -----Teisa: a descriptive poem of the River Teese, its towns and antiquities.
Newcastle Upon Tyne: n.p., 1778. BL

5873. -----Zadok the Israelite.
Carlisle: n.p., 1837. BL
[Religious poem]

5874. WILSON, Annie, Lady, Mrs. James Glenny Wilson [Br. 19/20c] PSEUD: Austral
Poems by Austral.
Adelaide: J. Williams, 1873. 73p. NUC BL

5875. -----Themes and variations.
L: Griffith, Farran, Okeden & Welsh, 1889. 88p. NUC BL OCLC

WILSON, Mrs. Ashley Carus <u>see</u> WILSON, Mary Louisa Georgina (Petrie) Carus

5876. WILSON, Caroline (Fry) [Br. 1787-1846] ALT: Fry, Caroline; F., C.
Death; and other poems.
L: Ogle, Duncan & co., 1823. 110p. NUC BL OCLC

5877. -----History of England in verse.
Turnbridge Wells: Priv. pr., 1802. BL

5878. -----The listener.
L: n.p., 1830. 2v. BL

5879. -----The listener in Oxford. By C.F.
n.p.: n.p., 1839. BL

5880. -----Serious poetry.
L: Ogle, Duncan & co., 1822. 116p. NUC OCLC

5881. WILSON, Cynthia Corwin (Hannon) [Am. b. 1843]
Doves' wings.
Springfield, IL: H.W. Rokker pub. co., 1890. 40p. NUC

5882. WILSON, Eliza, Mrs. Robert Wilson [Br. 19c]
New Zealand and other poems. By Mrs. Robert Wilson.
L: J. Masters, 1851. 172p. NUC BL

5883. WILSON, Florence [Br. 19c]
Boudoir-lyrics.
L: n.p., 1844. BL

5884. WILSON, Harriette [Br. 1786-1846] PSEUD: Wittol, Horatius Cocles
English society in Brussels described, or letters in rhyme addressed to his cousin by Horatius Cocles Wittol.
Paris & L: Baudry, 1825. 167p. NUC

5885. WILSON, Ibbie McColm, Mrs. [Am. 1834-1908]
The fate of the leaf.
Baltimore, MD: Cushing & co., 1891. 47p. NUC OCLC

WILSON, Mrs. James Glenny <u>see</u> WILSON, Annie, Lady

5886. WILSON, Lisa [Br. 19c] PSEUD: Grey, Christina
Verses. By Lisa Wilson (Christina Grey).
L: Bliss, Sands, 1896. 111p. NUC BL OCLC

5887. WILSON, Lizzie [Am. 1835-1858]
Poems. With a biography.
Louisville, KY: Hull & bro., 1860. 200p. NUC OCLC

5888. WILSON, Margaret (Harries) Baron-, Mrs. Cornwell Baron-Wilson [Br. 1797-1846] ALT: Harries, Margaret
Astarte, a Sicilian tale; with other poems. By Miss Harries.
2d ed. L: C. Chapple, 1818. 236p. NUC BL

5889. -----The cypress wreath: a collection of original ballads and tales in verse.
L: Smith, Elder, 1828. 159p. NUC OCLC

5890. -----Hours at home. A collection of miscellaneous poems.
L: n.p., 1826. BL

5891. -----Melancholy hours; a collection of miscellaneous poems.
L: John Richardson, 1816. 186p. NUC

5892. -----Poems.
L: n.p., 1831. BL

5893. -----A volume of lyrics. By Mrs. Cornwell Baron-Wilson.
L & Edinburgh: H. Cunningham, 1840. 407p. NUC BL

5894. WILSON, Mary [Br. 19c]
Poems.
Manchester: T. Powlson, 1844. 60p. BL

5895. WILSON, Mary Louisa Georgina (Petrie) Carus, Mrs. Ashley Carus Wilson [Br. 19/20c] ALT: Petrie, Mary Louisa Georgina
Tokiwa and other poems.
L: Hodder & Stoughton, 1895. 357p. BL OCLC

5896. WILSON, May Hayden Taylor [Am. 19c]
Verses ... October, 1871 - January, 1895.
Baltimore, MD: J.S. Bridges, 1899. 63p. NUC

WILSON, Mrs. Robert <u>see</u> WILSON, Eliza

5897. WILSON, Susanna [Br. b. 1798]
Familiar poems, moral and religious.
L: Darton, Harvey & co., 1814. 161p. NUC BL OCLC

5898. WINCHILSEA, Anne (Kingsmill) Finch, Countess of [Br. 1661-1720] ALT: Finch, Anne (Kingsmill), Countess of Winchilsea PSEUD: Lady, A
Miscellany poems on several occasions, written by a lady.
L: Pr. for John Barber & sold by John Morphen, 1713. 390p. NUC BL OCLC

5899. -----The spleen, a Pindarique ode. By a lady.
L: Pr. & sold by H. Hills, 1709. 16p. NUC BL OCLC

5900. WINDLE, Catherine Forrester (Ashmead) [Am. 19c]
Fallings from a lady's pen.
Philadelphia: Lindsay & Blakiston, 1849. 85p. NUC BL

5901. WINFORD, Miss [Br. 18c]
Hobby-horses: read at Bath-Easton.
L: The author, 1780. 16p. BL
[Satiric verse]

5902. WING, Amelia Kempshall [Am. b. 1837]
Brooklyn fancies.
Brooklyn, NY: Press of Geo. Tremlett, 1890. 70p. NUC OCLC

5903. WINGROVE, Ann [Br. 18/19c]
Letters, moral and entertaining.
Bath: n.p., 1795. BL
[Essays, short stories and poems]

5904. WINN, Edith Lynwood [Am. 1868-1933]
Cadences.
Buffalo, NY: C.W. Moulton, 1898. 67p. NUC BL
[Misc. prose & poems]

5905. WINSCOM, Jane (Cave) [Br. c1754-1813] ALT: Cave, Jane
Poems on various subjects, entertaining, elegiac, and religious ... with a few select poems by other authors.
Winchester: Pr. J. Sadler, 1783. 150p. NUC BL OCLC

5906. WINSER, Lilian [Br. 19c]
Lays and legends of the Weald of Kent.
L: Elkin Mathews, 1897. 77p. NUC BL OCLC
[Poems based on legend, some in dialect.]

5907. WINSTON, Mrs. Charles P., [Am. 19c] PSEUD: Richmond Lady, A
"Cousin Tommie!" A parody, by a Richmond lady.
Richmond, VA: C.F. Johnston, 1885. 8p. NUC OCLC

5908. WINSTON, Rosalie Stuart Bankhead, Mrs. [Am. b. 1836]
Pilate's question: or, What is truth?
Richmond, VA: Walford & son, 1885. 134p. NUC OCLC
[Poems and short fiction]

WINTER, A., ed. <u>see</u> WINTER, Mary

5909. WINTER, Mary [Br. 19c] ALT: W., M.
The ice-bound ship, The sleeping beauty, and other poems. Ed. T.R. & A. Winter.
L: Bosworth & Harrison, 1860. 149p. NUC BL

WINTER, T.R., ed. <u>see</u> WINTER, Mary

5910. WINTHROP, Augusta Clinton [Am. 19c]
"The bugle-call" and others.
Boston: Clarke & co., 1889. 130p. NUC

5911. -----"Scribbles." Verses.
n.p.: Barnet, Warren, 1884. 70p. NUC

5912. -----"Under the cedar" and others.

Boston: Clarke & Carruth, 1888. 77p. NUC

WISTER, Sally see WISTER, Sarah

5913. WISTER, Sarah [Am. 1761-1804] ALT: Wister, Sally
Amusing scenes of the Revolution. Journal of a young lady ... . n.p.: n.p., n.d. NUC
[Journal 1777-1779; incl. poems. Pub. 1902 as Sally Wister's journal. Philadelphia: Ferris & Leach, 1902. NUC]

5914. WITHERS, Emma [Am. 19c]
Wildwood chimes.
Cincinnati, OH: R. Clarke & co., 1891. 135p. NUC OCLC
[Chiefly nature poetry]

5915. WITMAN, Frederica K. [Am. 19c]
"Dose poys."
Washington, DC: Press of J.F. Sheiry, 1893. 65p. NUC

5916. -----Legend of the mound.
Harrisburg, PA: L.S. Hart, 1878. 39 l. NUC OCLC
[On Indians]

WITTOL, HORATIUS COCLES, pseud. see WILSON, Harriette

WOLCOTT, Eliza, co-author see NORTON, Sarah Goodsell (Wolcott)

5917. WOLCOTT, Julia Anna [Am. 19c]
Song-blossoms.
Boston: Arena pub. co., 1895. 262p. NUC OCLC

5918. WOLF, Margaret Isabel [Am. 19c]
Songs of "Cuba libre," a remembrance of the heroes of the Maine.
Dayton, OH: n.p., 1898. 16p. NUC

5919. WOLFERSTAN, Elizabeth Pipe (Jervis) [Br. b. 1763] ALT: W., E.P.
The enchanted flute, with other poems; and fables from La Fontaine.
L: n.p., 1823. BL

5920. -----Eugenia: a poem in four cantos.
L: n.p., 1824. BL

5921. -----Flora and Pomona's fete; or, The origin of botanical and horticultural meetings. A poem after the Butterfly's Ball.
Stroud: n.p., 1872. BL

5922. -----Golden rules.
L: R. Hastings, 1841. 46p. NUC

5923. WOLVERTON, Sarah Suter, Mrs. [Am. 19/20c]
Primroses.
Buffalo, NY: C.W. Moulton, 1895. 122p. NUC

WOMACK, Nelle see HINES, Nelle (Womack)

5924. WOOD, Adelaide [Br. 19c]
Wild blossoms; a collection of poems.
L: David Smith, 1854. 74p. BL

5925. WOOD, Ann Maria (Michell) [Br. 19c] ALT: W., A.M.
Verses and translations. By A.M.W.
L: Pr. for priv. circ., 1836. 7v. BL
[Also pub. as: Verses, with imitations and translations (from Lucian's Dialogues)]

5926. WOOD, Helen J. [Br. 19c]
The beautiful world and other poems, by Helen M. Waithman and Ethel Dawson.
L: E. Nister, 1890. 24 l. NUC BL

5927. -----A birthday wreath.
L: Ernest Nister, 1888. BL

5928. -----Funny friends, humorous stories of animals, with verses.
L: E. Nister, 1889. NUC

5929. -----Happy months.
L: Ernest Nister; NY: E.P. Dutton, 1889. BL

5930. -----Lilies round the Cross. With Edith Bland Nesbit.
L: Ernest Nister, 1889. BL

5931. WOOD, M. Elva [Am. 19c]
The crowned cross and other poems.
NY: n.p., 1870. 205p. NUC

5932. -----Songs of the noon and night.
NY: D. Appleton & co., 1866. 251p. NUC OCLC

5933. WOOD, Mary Camilla (Foster) Hall [Am. 19c] PSEUD: Von K., Camilla K.
Sea-leaves. By Camilla K. Von K.
Santa Barbara, CA: Independent pr., 1887. 178p. NUC OCLC

5934. WOOD, Mary Walpole [Am. 19c]
During a life-time; verses.
Chicago: Thomas P. Halpin, 1893. 351p. NUC OCLC

5935. WOODARD, Hannah A. [Am. 19c]
Noah's dove; a collection of essays and poems. By Mrs. H.A. Woodard.
Newark, NJ: Jennings & Hardham, 1872. 88p. NUC OCLC

5936. WOODBRIDGE, Susan Augusta [Am. b. 1819]
The heavenly alchymist and other poems.
NY: A.D.F. Randolph & co., 1892. 181p. NUC

5937. WOODBURY, Josephine Curtis (Battles) [Am. d. 1930]
Echoes.
NY & L: G.P. Putnam's sons, 1897. 124p. NUC BL

5938. WOODCOCK, Mrs. Henry [Br. 19c]
Laura, a tale.
L: Pr. Thomas Davison, sold by John Murray, 1820. 47p. NUC BL OCLC

WOODLAND, WAIF, pseud. see BLAIR, C.P., Mrs.

WOODMAN, H.J., Miss see LEWIS, Hannah Jane (Woodman)

5939. WOODROOFFE, Anne Cox [Br. 1766-1830]
The first prayer, in verse.
New ed. L: Bell & Daldy, 1855. 30p. BL

5940. WOODROOFFE, Sophia [Br. 19c]
Buondelmonte, the Zingari, Cleanthes, and The court of Flora: four dramatic poems. Posthumously Ed. Rev. G.S. Faber.
L: Seeley, Burnside & Seeley, 1846. 173p. BL
[Not intended for performance. Misc. poems pp. 151-173.]

5941. -----Lethe, and other poems. Posthumously Ed. Rev. G.S. Faber.
L: Seeley, Burnside & Seeley, 1844. 229p. NUC BL

5942. -----Sacred lays; or a legacy to the young.
Winchester: n.p., 1854. BL

5943. WOODRUFF, Belle C. [Am. 19c]
A collection of wild flowers.
Buffalo, NY: C.W. Moulton, 1894. 52p. NUC OCLC
[Misc. poetry]

5944. WOODRUFF, Julia Louisa Matilda (Curtiss) [Am. 1833-1909] PSEUD: Jay, W.M.L., Mrs.
The daisy-seekers. By W.M.L. Jay.
NY: E.P. Dutton & co., c1886. 31p. NUC OCLC

5945. -----Life's sunny side. By W.M.L. Jay.
NY: E.P. Dutton & co., 1886. 32p. NUC
[Bible texts & original verse]

5946. WOODS, Cecelia Frederica [Br. 19c]
Spring flowers of the mind.
L: n.p., 1848. BL
[Narrative & lyric poems]

5947. WOODS, Charlotte Elizabeth, Mrs. R.W. Woods [Br. 19c]
An every-day life.
n.p.: Leadenhall press, 1895. BL
[Poetry; short stories; inspirational essays]

5948. -----Gatherings.
L: Leadenhall press, 1890. BL
[Poetry & essays]

5949. -----"Have ye read it?" Look sharp! By Mrs. R.W. Woods.
L: Leadenhall press; Simpkin, Marshall, Hamilton, Kent & co.; NY: Charles Scribner's sons, 1894. 235p. BL
[Prose reflections with poems interspersed]

5950. WOODS, Kate (Tannatt) [Am. 1838-1910]
Grandfather Grey.
Boston: Lee & Shepard; NY: C.T. Dillingham, 1892. c1891. 19 l. NUC OCLC
[Poem recollecting Grandfather Grey's youth]

5951. -----Poems.
Salem, MA: n.p., 1890. 1v. NUC

5952. -----The wooing of Grandmother Grey.
Boston: Lee & Shepard; NY: C.T. Dillingham, 1890. 39p. NUC OCLC
[Companion poem to Grandfather Grey.]

5953. WOODS, Margaret Louisa (Bradley) [Br. 1856-1945]
Aeromancy, and other poems.
L: Elkin Mathews, 1896. 40p. NUC BL OCLC

5954. -----Lyrics and ballads.
L: Richard Bentley & son, 1889. 100p. NUC BL OCLC

5955. -----Lyrics.

Oxford: Pr. H. Daniel, 1888. 59p. NUC BL OCLC

5956. -----Songs.
Oxford: Daniel, 1896. 28p. NUC BL OCLC

5957. -----Wild justice.
L: Smith, Elder & co., 1896. 87p. NUC BL OCLC
[A dramatic poem]

WOODS, Mrs. R.W. see WOODS, Charlotte Elizabeth

5958. WOODWARD, C.A., Mrs. [Am. 19c]
Heaven and Hell; or, A vision of the judgment day, from an orthodox standpoint.
Lawrenceburg, IN: S. Chapman, pr., 1878. 36p. NUC

5959. WOODWARD, Helen, Miss [Br. 19c]
Beauty and other poems.
Exeter: J. Townsend; H.S. Eland, 1874. 99p. NUC

5960. -----My poetic sketch book; or lays of past hours.
Bath: n.p., 1848. BL

5961. WOODWARD, Mary Anna [19c]
Old rhymes for old friends.
Cambridge: Press of J. Wilson & son, 1874. 43p. NUC

5962. WOODWARD, Mary C. (Sloan) [Am. b. 1833]
Roses and thorns.
Dayton, OH: Press of the United Brethren pub. house, 1894. 153p. NUC OCLC

5963. WOOLFORD, Bessie E. [Am. 19c]
Purple asters and golden rod, and other poems.
Cincinnati, OH: Press of Robert Clarke & co., 1888. 48p. NUC

5964. WOOLSEY, Sarah Chauncey [Am. 1835-1905] PSEUD: Coolidge, Susan
A few more verses. By Susan Coolidge.
Boston: Roberts bros., 1889. 257p. NUC OCLC

5965. -----Verses. By Susan Coolidge.
Boston: Roberts bros., 1880. 181p. NUC OCLC

5966. WOOLSON, Constance Fenimore [Am. 1840-1894]
Two women: 1862. A poem.
NY: D. Appleton & co., 1877. 92p. NUC OCLC

5967. WOOLVEN, Mary [Br. 19c]
The utterance of the heart: consisting of letters, poetry, etc. Ed. J. Hallett.
L: n.p., 1842. BL

WOOSTER, D., ed see TREVELYAN, Paulina (Jermyn), Lady

WORBOISE, Emma Jane see GUYTON, Emma Jane (Worboise)

5968. WORDSWORTH, Barbara [Br. 19c]
Jacob's ladder.
L: Wyman, 1880. 173p. NUC BL
[Short stories in prose and verse]

5969. WORDSWORTH, Dame Elizabeth [Br. 1840-1932]
In doors and out. Poems.
L: Hatchards, 1881. 131p. NUC

5970. -----St. Christopher and other poems.
L: Longmans, Green & co., 1890. 285p. BL OCLC

5971. WORKMAN, Helen (Chaffee) [Am. b. 1868]
Leisure lines.
Franklin, OH: Editor pub. co., 1895. 56p. NUC OCLC

5972. WORTH, Anne (Sadler), Mrs. William Worth [Br. 1776-1813]
Poems, moral and sacred. By A.W. Ed. her husband, William Worth.
Macclesfield: Pr. J. Wilson & sold by Baynes, 1813. 40p. NUC BL

5973. WORTH, Susannah [Br. 19c]
Poems.
L: n.p., 1851. BL

WORTH, William, ed. see WORTH, Ann (Sadler)

WORTH, Mrs. William see WORTH, Ann (Sadler)

WORTLEY, Lady Emmeline Charlotte Elizabeth Manners (Stuart) see STUART-WORTLEY, Lady Emmeline Charlotte Elizabeth (Manners)

WRANGHAM, Francis, co-author see SYMMONS, Caroline

5974. WRAY, Angelina W. [Am. 19/20c]
ALT: Wray, Angie W.
Tales and poems.

New Brunswick, NJ: J. Heidingsfeld, c1890. 251p. NUC OCLC

WRAY, Angie W. see WRAY, Angelina W.

WREN, JENNY, pseud. see ATKINSON, Jane

5975. WRIGHT, Eliza Jane [Br. 19c]
Navigation, and other poems.
Manchester: J. Harrison & son, 1854. 97p. BL

5976. WRIGHT, Elizabeth Cox [Am. 19c]
Lichen tufts, from the Alleghanies.
NY: M. Doolady, 1860. 228p. NUC OCLC
[Lyric, humorous, narrative poems; short essays on nature]

5977. WRIGHT, Hannah Mary [Br. 1840-1872]
The Ruthwell cross and other remains of the late Hannah Mary Wright. With brief memoir of the author [signed R.R.].
Edinburgh: James Taylor; L: Hamilton Adams & co., 1873. 160p. NUC BL
[Essay on & trans. of The dream of the Rood, pp. 17-45. Rest incl. 6 prose stories, sketches & misc. poems.]

5978. WRIGHT, Jean [Am. 19/20c]
As light as air.
Louisville, KY: Flexner & Staadeker, 1892. 34p. NUC

WRIGHT, Lucy Pauline see HOBART-HAMPDEN, Lucy Pauline (Wright)

5979. WRIGHT, Mary Bestwick [Br. 19c]
The cypress wreath: a collection of poems.
L: Pr. for the author, & sold by W. Hextall, H. Buck, etc., 1828. 256p. BL OCLC

5980. WROTH, Mary (Sidney), Lady [Br. c1586-1640]
The Countess of Mountgomerie's Urania. Written by the Right Honourable the Lady Mary Wroath ... Neece to the ever famous and renowned Sir Phillips Sidney, Knight ... .
L: Ioh Marriott & Iohn Grismand, 1621. 558p. NUC BL
[Pastoral romance interspersed with poems and a collection of sonnets]

5981. WYATT, Gertrude [Br. 19c]
PSEUD: Young Lady, A
Miscellaneous poems. By a young lady.
L: C.F. Cock, 1829. 100p. NUC BL

5982. WYKE, Anne [Br. 19c]
Bertha; a tale of the Waldenses; and other poems.
Shrewsbury: C. Hulbert, 1830. 140p. NUC BL OCLC

5983. WYKE, Elizabeth [Am. 19c]
The prophet of the Alleghany Mountains, a missionary tale, and other poems.
Ironbridge: G.M. Smith, 1847. 115p. NUC OCLC

5984. WYLIE, Lollie Belle [Am. 19/20c]
Legend of the Cherokee rose, and other poems.
Atlanta, GA: James P. Harrison & co., pr., 1887. 111p. NUC OCLC

WYNDHAM, Fanny Charlotte see MONTGOMERY, Fanny Charlotte (Wyndham)

5985. WYNNE, Frances [Br. 19/20c]
Whisper!
L: K. Paul, Trench, Trubner & co., 1890. 61p. NUC BL OCLC

X., G.E., pseud. see PAINTER, Lydia Ethel (Farmer)

XARIFFA, pseud. see TOWNSEND, Mary Ashley (Van Voorhis)

Y., A. see YEARSLEY, Ann (Cromartie)

Y., M.J. see YOUNG, Mary Julia

5986. YATES, Jenny [Am. 19c]
Fragments.
Baltimore, MD: Bond & co., 186-? 132p. NUC

5987. YEARDLEY, Martha Savory [Br. 1781-1851] ALT: Savory, Martha PSEUD: Smith, Mrs.
Inspiration, a poetical essay.
L: John & Arthur Arch, 1805. 19p. NUC BL OCLC

5988. -----Life's vicissitudes: or winter's tears. Original poems.
L: Pr. for the author, 1809. NUC BL

5989. -----An original wreath of forget-me-not; presented to those who love to reflect on heavenly things.
L: Harvey, 1829. NUC BL

5990. -----Poetical sketches on Scripture characters.
L: Charles Gilpin, 1848. NUC BL

5991. -----Poetical tales, founded on facts.
L: Darton & Harvey, 1808. 148p. BL OCLC

5992. YEARSLEY, Ann (Cromartie) [Br. 1752-1806] ALT: Y., A. PSEUD: Lactilla
An elegy on Marie Antoinette ... Queen of France. With a poem on the last interview between the King of Poland and Loraski.
Bristol: Pr. J. Radhall, 1795? 15p. NUC BL

5993. -----A poem on the inhumanity of the slave-trade.
L: G.G.J. & J. Robinson, 1788. 30p. NUC BL

5995. -----Poems on various subjects, by A.Y.
L: G.G.J. & J. Robinson, 1787. 168p. NUC BL

5994. -----Poems on several occasions.
3d ed. L: T. Cadell, 1785. 100p. NUC BL

5996. -----Reflections on the death of Louis XVI.
Bristol: Pr. for the author, 1793. 8, 8p. NUC BL

5997. -----The rural lyre.
L: G.G.J. & J. Robinson, 1796. 142p. NUC BL

5998. -----Stanzas of woe.
L: G.G.J. & J. Robinson, 1790. 30p. NUC BL

YEATS, William Butler, ed. see O'LEARY, Ellen

5999. YORKE, Harriet [Br. 19c]
The self-exiled, and other poems.
Cambridge: n.p., 1850. BL

6000. YOUNG, Amy Cripps [Br. 19c]
Thoughts and dreamings.
L: Simpkin, Marshall & co., 1896. 152p. BL
[33 religious poems. Prose meditations & allegories]

6001. YOUNG, Anna M.N. [Br. 19c]
Poems.
Glasgow: n.p., 1858. BL

YOUNG, Carrie F., ed. see B., E.M.

6002. YOUNG, Charlotte [Br. 19c]
The world's complaint, and other poems.
L: Pub. for the author by Grant & Griffin, 1847. 92p. NUC BL

6003. YOUNG, Jane [Br. 19c]
Songs and verses.
L: H.R. Allenson, 1896. 96p. BL

6004. YOUNG, Julia Evelyn (Ditto) [Am. 1857-1915]
The story of Saville: told in numbers.
East Aurora, NY: Roycroft pr. shop, 1897. 101p.

6005. -----This then is the story of Glynne's wife told in numbers.
East Aurora, NY: Roycroft pr. shop, 1896. 143p. NUC OCLC

6006. -----Thistle down poems.
Buffalo, NY: P. Paul & bro., 1893. 157p. NUC

YOUNG, Mary see SEWELL, Mary (Young)

YOUNG, Mary Julia see SEWELL, Mary (Young)

6007. YOUNG, Mary Hulett [Hullett OCLC] Greene, Mrs. [Am. 19c]
Forest leaves and three; or, Genevra's tower. By Mary Hulett Young.
Cambridge, MA: Pr. H.O. Houghton & co., 1887. 246p. NUC OCLC
[Misc. poems]

6008. YOUNG, Mary Julia [Br. 1760?-1821] ALT: Y., M.J. PSEUD: Lady, A; Young Lady, A
Adelaide and Antoine; or, The emigrants: a tale.
L: Pr. J.P. Coughlan, sold by J. Debrett, 1793. 14p. NUC OCLC
[French Revolution]

6009. -----Genius and fancy; or, Dramatic sketches. By a lady.
L: H.D. Symonds & J. Gray, 1791. 48p. NUC BL

6010. -----Horatio and Amanda, a poem. By a young lady.
L: Robson, 1777. 20p. NUC OCLC

6011. -----Poems.
L: n.p., 1798. BL
[Pub. as: The metrical museum. Part I. L: n.p., 1801.]

6012. YOUNG LADY, A, pseud. [Br. 19c]
Eloise, and other poems on several occasions, by a young lady.
Leith: Pr. for the author, & sold by James Burnet, etc., 1815. 181p. OCLC

6013. YOUNG LADY, A.
Miscellaneous poems. By a young lady.
Bath: R. Cruttwell, 1828. NUC

YOUNG LADY, A, pseud. see KING, E., Miss

YOUNG LADY, A, pseud. see LENNOX, Charlotte (Ramsay)

YOUNG LADY, A, pseud. see PIERSON, Cornelia Louisa (Tuthill)

YOUNG LADY, A, pseud. see PORTER, Anna Maria

YOUNG LADY, A, pseud. see R., A.

YOUNG LADY, A, pseud. see ROBERTS, Mary, Sister

YOUNG LADY, A, pseud. see SEWELL, Mary (Young)

YOUNG LADY, A, pseud. see SWINNEY, Jane

YOUNG LADY, A, pseud. see WILLIAMS, Helen Maria

YOUNG LADY, A, pseud. see WYATT, Gertrude

YOUNG LADY, pseud. see YOUNG, Mary Julia

YOUNG LADY OF CHARLESTON, S.C., A, pseud. see MURDEN, Eliza (Crawley)

6014. YOUNGS, Ella Sharpe [Br. 19c]
Apotheosis of Antinous, and other poems.
L: K. Paul, Trench & co., 1887. 213p. NUC BL

6015. -----A heart's life, Sarpedon, and other poems.
L: Kegan Paul, Trench & co., 1884. 166p. NUC BL

6016. -----Osman & Emineh.
L: Spottiswoode & co., 1879. 85p. NUC BL

6017. -----Paphus and other poems.
L: K. Paul, Trench & co., 1882. 158p. NUC BL OCLC

6018. YOUNGS, Jennie M. [Am. 19c]
Nature and tree songs.
Chicago & Buffalo, NY: The Wyatt co., 1899. 8p. NUC
[With music]

YSGAFELL, pseud. see WILLIAMS, Jane

Z., pseud. see MORE, Hannah

APPENDIX

CHRONOLOGICAL LISTING

1475-1599

Dowriche

Tyrwhitt

Whitney, I.

1600-1699

Barker, J.; Bateman, S.B.; Behn; Bradstreet, A.D.

Chudleigh, M.L.; Colville, E.M.

D'Anvers, A.

Evelyn, M.

Fage, M.

Grimston, E.B.

Hayward, A.; Hincks, E.; Hogben

Killigrew, A.

Lanyer, A.

Major, E.; Masham; *Mollineux

Newcastle, M.L.C.

Pembroke, M.S.H.; Philips, J.; Philips, K.F.; Primrose, Lady D.

Rowe, E.S.

Specht, R.; Sutcliffe, A.

Tipper, E.

Weamys, A.; Wharton, A.L.; Wroth, M.S.

1700-1749

Adams, J.; Aubin, P.

Barber, M.; (Behn); Boyd, E.; Boyle, Lady H.; Brereton, J.

Carter, E.; Centlivre, S.F.C.; Chandler, M.; Charke, C.C.; Chudleigh, M.L.; *Cockburn; Collier, M.

Dixon, S.; Drummond; (Dutton, A.); Dyke, A.

Egerton, S.F.

Gentlewoman, A.;

Harrison, E.; Haywood, E.F.; Holt, J.W.

Keinton, M.

*Leapor, M.; Lennox, C.R.

MacCarthy, C.; Masham; Masters, M.; (Mollineux); Monk; Montagu, Lady M.P.W.

Ogle, M.

Pennyman, Lady M.A.; (Philips, K.F.); Piers, S.; Pilkington, L.V.L.

R., A.; Rowe, E.S.

Smith, G.; Somerset, F.T.S.; Stanley, Mrs. D.

Teft, E.; Thomas, E.; Turell

Wardlaw; (Wharton, A.L.); Winchilsea

1750-1799

Alcock, M.C.; Allen, L.; Anna Maria; Arthur, G.; Atwater, E.M.

Bangs, E.M.; Barbauld, A.L.A.; Barnes, E.; Benger, E.O.; Bentley, E.; Betham, M.M.; Beverley, C.; Birkett, M.; Blackett, M.D.; *Blamire; Bland, E.N.; Bleecker, A.E.S.; Bowman, A.; Brand, H.; Brewster, M.W.; Brittle, E.; Brooke, F.M.; Bryan, M.M.; Bryton, A.; Burnside, H.M.; Burrell, S.R.

Carmichael, R.; Carter, E.; Celesia; Chantrell; Chapone; Chappel, S.; Christian, A.; Clark, E.L.; Cobbold,

E.K.; (Cockburn, C.T.); Collier, M.; Cooper; Cooper, M.S.; Cowley, H.P.; Cowper, F.M.M.; Curtis, A.; Cutts

Darling, E.; Darwall, E.; Darwall, M.W.; Davidson, M.; Day, E.H.; Day, E.M.; Defleury; Deverell, M.; Dornford; DuBois, Lady D.A.; Dunlap, J.

Edwards, Miss; Edwards, A.M.; Eliza; Evans, M.

Falconar; Farrell, S.; Fell, E.; Fenno; Forman, E.S.; Fortnum, S.K.; Francis, Ann; Francis, A.G.

Garrard; Gilding, E.; Gooch; Graves, M.E.D.; Greensted; Griffith, E.G.; Griffiths, J.; Gunning, S.M.

Hands, E.; Harrison, C.R.; Harrison, E.; Harrison, S.; Harvey, J.; Havergal, F.R.; Hedgeland, I.F.K.; Heron, M.; Hibbard, G.P.; Hill, P.B.; Holford, M.; Howell, C.A.; Hughes, A.; Huntingtower, C.R.G.T.

Instone; Ivison

Jemmat, C.Y.; Jones, Mary

Keene, E.C.; King, C.; King, S.; Knight, E.C.; Knowles, M.M.

Lady, A; Latter, M.; Lawson, E.; (Leapor); Learned, L.; Lecky, E.; Lee, S.; Leigh, H.; Lennox, C.R.; Letches; Little, J.; Livingston, C.; Lluellyn, E.A.; Locke, M.; Logan, M.; Lookup, M.M.; Lucan, M.S.B.

MacCarthy, C.; Madan, J.C.; Masters, M.; Mathews, E.K.S.; Miller, A.R.; Montagu, Lady M.P.W.; Montague, M.S.; Moody, E.; Moore, J.E.; More, H.; Morton, S.W.A.; Murray, A.; Murray, J.S.; Murry, A.

O'Brien, M.

Pearson, S.; Penny, A.H.C.; Phillips, C.P.; Pickering, A.; Pickering, P.P.; (Pilkington, L.V.L.); Pilkington, M.H.; Porter, A.M.; Porter, S.; Postgate, I.J.; Poyntz; Pye, J.H.M.; Pyke, S.L.

Radcliffe, A.W.; Reeve, C.; Reeves, E.; Roberts, R.; Robinson, M.D.; Rolt; Rowe, E.S.; Rowe, H.; Rowson, S.H.; Ryves, E.

Sanders, C.E.; Savage, M.; *Scot, E.R.; Scott, M.; Serres, O.W.; Seward, A.; Sewell, M.W.; Sewell, M.Y.; *Sheridan, F.C.; Shipton, A.; Sinclair, M.A.; Smith, C.T.; Smith, E.; Spence, S.; Spencer, Mrs. W.; Steele, A.; Steers, F.; Stockdale, M.R.; Susanna; Swinney, J.

Talbot, C.; *Taylor, C.; Taylor, E.; Temple, A.C.G.T.; Thicknesse; Thompson, E.; Tighe, M.B.; Tillery; Timbury; (Tollet, E.); Tomlins, E.S.; Tounley, C.; Tucker, M.A.; Tuite, E.D.

Upton, C.

Wallace, E.M.; Wallis, H.; Warren, M.O.; Watts, S.; Webb, L.S.; West, J.; Weylar; Wheatley, P.; Williams, A.; Williams, Anna; Williams, H.M.; Wilson, A.; Winford; Wingrove, A.; Winscom, J.C.; Wister, S.

Yearsley, A.C.; Young, M.J.

<u>1800-1825</u>

Allen, B.J.; Ames, J.; Andrews, H.; Appleton, E.; Atwater, E.M.

B---n; Baillie, J.; Baillie, M.; Balfour, M.; Bangs, E.M.; Bannerman, A.; *Barbauld, A.L.A.; Barker; Barker, J.; Barnard, A.L.; Barrell, P.; Bath, E.; Bayfield, E.G.; Bell, A.S.; *Bell, F.A.Benger, E.O.; Bentley, E.; Betham, M.M.; Beverley, E.; Birch, E.; Bishop, M.; Blanchard, A.; Bland, E.N.; Blease; Blennerhassett; Bonhote; Botsford, M.; Bowdler, H.M.; Bowen, M.; Bowman, A.; Brettell; Bristow, A.; Brooks, M.A.G.; Brown, E.; Brown, M.; Browning, E.B.; Bryan, M.; Bryan, M.M.; Burnside, H.M.; Burton, M.

Campbell, D.P.; Candler; Cannon, M.M.; Capp, M.E.; Capper; Cassan; Caulfeild, F.S.; Chalmers, M.; Champion de Crespigny; Chapone; Clark, E.; Clarke, A.; Clarke, Anne; Cobbold, E.K.; Cockle, M.; Collins; Cooper, C.; Cope, H.; Costello, L.S.; Cowley, H.P.; Croker, M.S.; Crowther; Currie, H.; Cursham, M.A.; Curties

D.; Dacre, C.; Dark, M.; Darling, E.; Darling, P.R.; Darwall, E.; *Davidson, L.M.; Davies, E.; Davis, M.A.; Davis, Mary Anne; *Dawson, J.F.; (Day, E.M.); DeHumboldt, C.; DeKrafft; *Denning; Derenzy; Devereux, R.; Devonshire, G.S.C.;

DeWitt, S.L.; Dickinson, E.B.; Dixon, C.E.; Dodsworth; Dorset, C.A.T.; Downing, H.; Dunlop, F.E.; Dunnett; Dunsterville; (Dutton, A.)

Earle; Edgar; Edgworth, T.; Edridge, R.; Edwards, M.B.B.; Eliza; Elizabeth; Elliot; Elliott, M.B.; Evans, M.; Ewing, H.

Fairbrother; Fentiman, C.; Finch, B.; Fletcher, E.D.; Fordyce, H.; Forman, E.S.; Fortnum, S.K.; Francis; Francis, E.S.; Francis, S.L.; Franklin, E.A.P.; Fraser, S.

Gardiner, S.H.; Geary, E.; Gibbs, A.; Godwin, C.G.G.; Gomersall; Gooch; Gore, C.G.F.M.; Gorrington, E.S.; Govion Broglio Solari; Graham, I.M.; Grant, A.M.; Graves, M.E.D.; Grimstone; Guppy

Hale; Hale, S.J.B.; Ham, E.; Hamilton, A.; Hamilton, E.L.; Hamilton, S.; Hanson, M.; Harris, H.; Harrison, C.R.; Harvey, M.; Hastings, S.A.; Hatton, A.J.K.; Havergal, F.R.; Hawke, Hon. A.E.C.; Hay, M.H.; Hedge, M.A.; Hedgeland; Hemans, F.D.B.; Hennett; Hewlett, E.; Hibbard, G.P.; Hill, Mrs. R.; Hindmarsh; Hitchener; Hoare, S.; Hofland, B.W.H.; Holford, M.; Holmes, A.; Hood, C.; Hopwood; Hornblower, J.; Houghton, J.; Houghton, M.A.; Howell, C.A.; Howell, S.; Howitt, M.B.; Hunt, E.; Hunter, A.H.; Hunter, R.; Hyde, N.M.

Iliff; Isaacs

Jacob, C.; James, E.; Jevons, M.A.R.; Johnson, L.; Johnson, M.D.; Jones, E.C.; Jones, S.; Jordan, J.; Joynes

Kenney, M.; Kentish; King, E.; King, H.R.; Knight, A.C.; Knight, E.C.; Knowles, M.M.; Knowles, Mary Morris

Lady, A; Lamb, Lady C.P.; Lamb, Lady L.M.C.P.; Lamont; Landon, L.E.; Larue; Lawson, E.; Leadbeater; Lecky, E.; Leech, M.; Lefanu, A.; Lefroy; LeNoir, E.A.S.; Leonard, E.L.; Lewis, M.G.; Lickbarrow; Liddiard; Linwood, M.; Littleford; Livingston, A.H.S.; Lloyd, Mary; Lloyd, M.A.; Lloyd, S.M.; Lluellyn; Lomax, J.; Loudon, J.W.; Luby; Luce

Macauley, E.W.; Maccoy, M.; Mackey, M.; Maclaurin; Macmullan; Mahony, A.; Maria Sophia; Mason; Mason, C.G.W.; *Mason, S.H.; Mathews, E.K.S.; Maxwell, C.; Medley, S.; Milne, C.R.; Mitford, M.R.; Monckton; Montolieu; More, H.; Morgan, S.O.; Morison, H.; Morton, S.W.A.; Mott; Murden, E.; Murphy, A.

Newman, S.; Nicholas, A.S.; Niven, A.J.V.; Nooth, C.; Norton, E.B.S.E.; *Norton, S.G.W.

O'Keeffe, A.D.; O'Neill, Mrs. F.; Opie

Pagan; Palmer, M.; Pardoe; Parsons, L.; Parsons, M.; Patrickson, M.; Pearson, A.H.; (Pembroke, M.S.H.); Perrott; Philippart, C.; Philipps, J.; Pilkington, M.H.; Pinckney, M.H.; Pizey; Porter, A.M.; Postgate, I.J.; Potts, E.M.T.; Poulter; Powell, A.; Princeps; Pye, M.E.; Pyke, S.L.

Quigley, C.

Radcliffe, A.W.; Radcliffe, M.A.; Renou; Rhodes, H.; Richardson, C.C.S.; Richings; Riddell, M.W.; Rimmert; Ritson, A.; Roberts, M.; Robertson, E.F.; Robinson, E.; Robinson, M.D.; Robinson, M.E.; Rodgers, V.; Rolls, Mrs. H.; Rowden, F.A.; (Rowe, E.S.); Rowson, S.H.; Russell, C.; Ryan, E.; Ryves, F.

St. John, M.; Sanderson, A.; Sargant, J.A.; Sawyer, A.; Schimmelpennick; (Scot, E.R.); Scott, E.; Scott, H.; Selden, A.; Sellon; Semple, A.S.H.; Seward, A.; Sewell, M.W.; Sewell, M.Y.; Shepherd; (Sheridan, F.C.); Shipton, A.; Sigourney, L.; Sinclair, M.A.; Sleigh, I.; Smallpiece; Smith, C.T.; Smith, E.; Smith, Mrs. T.; Somers, E.; Somerset, C.S.; Southcott, J.; Southey, C.; Spence, S.; Spencer, Mrs. W.; Sproat, N.D.; Sproule; Stanley; Starke, M.; Steele, A.; Steele, S.; Steers, F.; Stewart, E.M.; Stewart, J.; Stockdale, M.R.; Stokes, C.; Strickland, A.; Sutcliff, A.H.; Sykes; Symmons, C.

Taylor, E.; Taylor, H.H.; Taylor, J.; Temple, L.S.; Thayer, C.M.W.; Thomas, E.; Tiernan; Tighe; Tillery; Trefusis; Trench, M.C.S.G.; Tuck, E.; Tucker, M.A.; Turner, J.F.; Turner, M.

Ward, M.; Wardle, C.; Ware, M.; Wassell; Watkins, H.; Watts, S.; Webb, L.S.; Webster; Webster, A.; Wedderburn; Welch, A.; Weller, M.A.; Wells, E.; West, J.; Wilkes, A.;

Williams; Williams, H.M.; Williams, J.; Wilmore; Wilmot, B.; Wilson, C.F.; Wilson, H.; Wilson, M.H.B.; Wilson, S.; Wolferstan; Woodcock; Worth, A.S.

Yeardley, M.S.; Young Lady, A

1826-1850

A.; *Abbott, M.P.B.; Abdy, M.S.; Acton, E.; Acton, H.; Adams, S.F.F.; Aguilar; Alexander, C.F.H.; Allen, C.; Allen, E.; Allen, Elizabeth; Allen, H.B.; Allingham; Allom; Andrews, M.J.; Archbold; Arthington, M.; Avery, R.J.; Ayre, E.G.

Bacon, E.A.M.; Bacon, M.A.; Bailey, M.W.; Baillie, J.; Baker, E.A.; Balfour, C.L.L.; Ballantyne, Mrs. J.; Balmanno; Banks, I.V.; Barland, K.; Barnard, F.C.; Barnes, C.M.S.; Bartholomew, A.C.T.; Bartholomew, J.M.; Bassett, M.; Beale, A.; Bearcroft; *Beardsley; Beattie, A.; Bell; (Bell, F.A.); Belt; Bennet, G.; Bennison, D.M.L.; Bentley, E.; Berry, S.; Bevan, E.F.A.; Beverley, E.; Biller; Bingham, F.L.; Bingham, J.M.; Blake, L.D.; (Blamire, S.); Boddington; Bond, Mrs. H.; Boone, S.W.; Borron, E.W.M.; Botta; Bourke; Bourne, J.; Bourne, M.A.; Boutelle; Bowen, M.; Bowes, E.; Boyle, M.L.; Bradburn, E.W.; Bradnack; Bragg, J.; Bristow, A.; Britton, F.; Bronte, C.; Brooks, M.E.A.; Brown, E.; Brown, M.E.; Browne, F.; Browne, F.E.; Browning, E.B.; Bruce, C.A.B.; Bruce, J.; Budgett, M.E.; Bullock, C.; Bulmer; Bulwer; Burder, S.M.; Burgess, E.; Burnell, H.P.; Butler, A.; Butler, H.

Caird, E.; Campbell, A.R.; Capadose; Carey, E.S.; Carnes, H.; Carney, J.A.F.; Carrington, E.; Carter, A.P.; Carter, M.A.; Cartwright, F.D.; Cary, A.; Caulfeild, F.S.; Caulkins, F.M.; Caulton, I.; Chadwick; Chalenor; Chandler, E.M.; Chapman, M.W.; Charnock, M.A.E.; Chetwynd; Cheves, E.W.F.; Child, A.P.L; Child, F.; Child, L.M.F.; Clarke, A.; Clemans, S.I.; Clephane; Clive, C.A.W.; Cochrane; Cockle, M.; Cocks, S.; Colchester, E.S.L.A.; Colchester, Lady E.S.L.; Coldwell; Collier, M.; Collier, M.L.; Colling, M.M.; Colthurst; Conkey; Conyngham; *Cook, A.G.; Cook, E.; Cookson, M.A.; Coombe, S.M.; Cooper, M.G.; Cope, H.; Cory, E.; Courtney, M.; Cowell, E.S.; Cox, L.N.; Croggon; Crosland, C.D.T.; Cross, S.; Curling, M.A.; Currie, M.M.L.S.; Cursham, M.A.; Cushing, E.L.F.

Dallor; Daman; Daniels, E.K.T.; Dash, M.; (Davidson, L.M.); Davidson, M.M.; Davies, E.; Davis, J.M.; Davis, M.A.; (Dawson, J.F.); Dawson, M.A.; Day, J.; DeCrespigny, C.; DeCrespigny, H.C.; DeHumboldt, C.; (Denning, E.); Derenzy; DeWindt; Dewolf, A.; Dickinson, E.B.; Dimond; Dinnies, A.P.S.; Dixon, C.E.; Dixon, J.; Dixon, L.; Dixon, S.; Dodd, M.A.H.; Dodge, H.M.; Dorsey, A.H.M.; Downing, H.; Downing, M.; Dowson, S.; Drury, A.H.; Dufferin and Clandeboye; Duncan, M.L.

Edmond, A.M.C.; Edwards; Ella; Ellen; Ellet; Elliot, A.; Elliott, C.; Elliott, J.A.M.; Elliott, M.B.; Ellis, S.S.; Embury, E.C.M.; Esling; Espenser; Evans, A.

Fairweather, M.; Falkner, R.A.P.; Fallow; Fanshawe, C.M.; Fire-fly, F.; Fisher, E.; Fisher, S.; Fitzgerald, S.A.; Fletcher, M.J.J.; Fletcher, M.; Flinders; Fogg, M.M.R.; Follen, E.L.C.; Forbes-Leith; *Foster, H.W.; Frampton, L.C.; Frank, M.; Frankland; Fraser, J.D.; Fry, H.J.; Fullerton, Lady G.C.L.G.; Furlong

Gammage; Gardiner, M.L.; Gardiner, S.H.; Gardner, E.P.; Garland, E.; Garnier, E.; Garrett, A.; Garton, A.; Gascoigne; Geldart; Genevieve; Gervis; Gibbons, A.T.; Gilbert, A.T.; Gilbert, E.; Gilbert, H.E.P.; Gilchrist; Gilman, C.H.; Godwin, C.G.G.; Goldie, E.M.; Gooch; Goodall, H.A.; Gordon, M.M.B.; Goss, A.J.; Gould, H.F.; Grant, D.; Gray, M.A.B.; Greene, E.C.; Greenwell, D.D.; Grew; Grey, G.; Griffin, M.M.; Grimani; Grubb, D.; Grundy, E.; Guinness, J.L.; Guinness, Mrs. J.G.; Gurnett, A.E.B.; Gwillian, J.

Hadfield, E.T.; Hale, M.W.; Hale, S.J.B.; Hall; Hall, E.S.; Hall, L.J.P.; Hall, S.E.; Hamilton, E.M.; Hamilton, E.; Hamilton, S.; Hammond; Hammond, S.; Hanbury, E.B.; Hannah, M.; Hansford, L.M.P.; Hanson, B.K.; Hardcastle, E.M.; Hart, M.K.; Harthill; Hartley, L.B.; Harvey, E.L.S.; Harvey, J.; Hasell, D.; Hastings, Lady F.E.R.; Haven, A.B.N.; Hawes, E.; Hawkins, S.; Hawkshaw;

Haworth, E.F.; Hay, E.; Head, K.; Hemans, F.D.B.; Hentz; Herbert, J.E.; *Herbert, S.; Heron, M.; Hervey, E.L.M.; Hewitt, E.C.; Hewitt, M.E.M.; Hey, R.; Heywood, E.; Hickey, E.H.; Hicks, E.; Hiles, M.; Hill, F.S.T.; Hill, I.; Hills, E.; Hoare, S.; Hodges, E.; Holl; Holmes, A.A.; Holmes, E.E.; Hood, I.; Hooper, E.H.S.; Hooper, L.; Hornblower, J.E.R.; Horton, M.L.; Hosmer; Hovenden; Howe; Howell, E.L.; Howitt, M.B.; *Howland, S.H.; Hoyland; Hull, A.M.; Hunt, R.; Hutton, M.

Ingelow, J.; Iselin

James, M.; Jenkins, D.S.G.; Jervis, M.; Jevons, M.A.R.; Johnson, E.; Johnson, S.C.; Jones, E.G.; Jones, E.C.; Jones, M.E.M.; Jones, M.E.; Jones, M.E.P.; Jourdan, M.J.; Jowitt; Judson, E.C.C.; Judson, S.H.B.

Kemble, F.A.; Keogh, M.; Kidd, J.; King, H.B.; King, H.R.; King, M.A.; Kinsley; Kitching, H.S.A.; Knight, E.W.

Lady, A; Lafargue; Lamb, Lady C.P.; Lambert, E.; Landon, L.E.; Law, E.A.; Lawrence, R.D.; Lawrence, S.; Lawton, H.A.; Lean, E.J.; Leckie, E.H.; Lee, I.; *Lee, M.E.; Lee, R.; Leech, S.; Leith, W.H.S.F.; Leslie, E.; Lewis, E.G.; Lewis, E.A.B.R.; Lewis, H.J.W.; Liddell, M.H.; Lippincott; Little, S.L.R.; Lloyd, M.A.; Locke, J.E.S.; Long, C.W.; Long, E.W.; Lowe, H.; Luby, C.; Lushington, H.P.; Lutton, A.; Lutwyche; Lynch; Lynch, T.

Macarthur, M.; McCord, L.S.C.; MacDermott; MacFarlane, A.; Mackay, E.D.; Mackintosh, M.; M'cord, L.S.C.; Maddocks; Maddocks; Magrath; Mainwaring; Mallett; Manwaring; Marston; Martin, S.; Martineau; Maskell; Mason, R.; (Mason, S.H.); Matthews, E.; Maxwell, M.H.; Maylin; Maynard; Mayo, S.C.E.; Meigs, M.N.B.M.; Menteath; Merry, M.A.; Merryweather, I.A.; Meyler, M.; Miles; Miles, S.E.; Mitchell, A.W.; Mitchell, C.; Mitford, M.R.; Montgomery, F.C.W.; Moodie; Morinski; Moulton, S.H.; Mudie; Murden, E.

*Nairne, C.O.; Napier, C.; Nash, C.; Nealds; Nelson, E.; Nichols, R.S.R.; Nicolas, S.D.; Noakes, M.A.; Northampton, M.C.C.; Norton, C.E.S.S.; (Norton, S.G.W.); Nowell, S.A.

Ogilvy, E.A.H.D.; Oke; O'Neill, H.B.; Opie; Orde; Orne; Osgood, F.S.L.; *Ossoli

Packard, H.J.; Palmer, A.; Palmer, G.M.; Park, E.; Parker, F.T.; Parker, R.; Parker, S.; Parminter; *Parris; Parsons, E.D.W.; Pearce; Pearson, A.H.; Peile; Peirson, L.J.W.; Pennington, M.; Perkins, E.S.; Perring, E.; Phelps; Phillipson, C.G.L.; Phipps; Pickard, H.M.T.; Pickersgill; Pierce, E.; Pierson, C.L.T.; Pinkerton, J.L.; Plato; Plomley, M.A.; Polglase; Ponsonby, C.; Potts, A.H.; Potts, E.M.T.; Poulter, L.F.; Poyas, C.G.; Pratt, H.A.L.; Prescott, H.; Price, A.; Prowett; Prowse, M.J.; Pugh, S.S.; Pyer, C.S.; Pyke, S.L.; Pyper, M.

(Radcliffe, A.W.); Radcliffe, M.M.; Read, H.F.; Read, M.S.; Rees, M.I.I.; Rennie, E.; Richardson, C.E.; Richardson, M.; Richter, A.; Ricord; Ritchie, A.C.O.M.; Roberts, E.P.; Roberts, E.; Roberts, Mrs. M.; Roberts, M.; Robinson, A.S.; Rolfe, A.; Rossetti; Rouse, T.; Rowles, C.; Rutherford, E.

S....; Saffery; St. Aubyn, M.; Sandbach, M.; Sandbach, M.R.; Sanders, E.W.; Sanders, M.R.; Sargant, J.A.; Sargeant, A.M.; Saunders, M.; Savage, A.; Scaife; Scott, Mrs. J.; Scott, J.H.K.; Sedgwick, S.A.L.R.; Seely, C.; Sergeant, E.L.; Sergeant, J.H.; Shattuck; Shaw, L.; *Shelley, E.; Sheppard, S.; Shindler, M.S.B.P.D.; Sigourney; Sigourney, L.; Simpson, J.C.B.; Sinclair, C.; Skene; Smedley, M.B.; Smith, E.; Smith, E.O.P.; Smith, E.S.; Smith, L.B.; Smith, M.E.; Smith, S.L.P.H.; Smith, S.P.; Smith, S.M.; Smythies, H.M.G.; Snow, E.; Snowden, E.; Southey; Southey, C.; Spratt; Steel, M.; Steers, F.; Stewart, E.; Stewart, E.M.; Stopford; Strickland, A.; Stringer; Strutt; Stuart-Wortley, Lady; Sutcliffe, F.M.

Taggart, C.; Tanner, C.C.; Tatham, E.; Taylor, E.C.; Taylor, E.; (Taylor, J.); Telford, S.; Temple, R.E.H.; Thayer, C.M.W.; Thistlethwayte; (Thomas, E.); Thomas, J.R.; Thomas, J.H.; Thompson, J.T.; Tilley, H.M.; Tilt; Tindal; Tinsley; Tinsley, A.; Tonge, E.; Tonna, C.E.B.P.; Trollope, F.M.; Trotter, E.H.; Tucker, C.M.; Tuckey, M.B.; Tuite; Tytler

Valpy, H.F.; Vasey

Walcot, C.; Waldo, E.R.B.; Ward; Ward, C.; Ward, H.L.H.; Ware, K.A.R.; Warfield, C.A.W.; Waring, S.; Watrous; Watts, S.; Welby, A.B.C.; Wells, A.M.F.; Weston, A.; Weston, M.D.; Westwood, L.B.; Weymouth, S.; (Wheatley, P.); Whitaker, M.S.F.; Whitney, H.;Whitten, M.D.; Wilby, M.A.; Wilkinson, J.W.; Willan, R.M.; Willard, E.C.H.; Williams, C.M.; Williams, C.R.A.; Williams, S.A.; Williams, S.J.; Wilson, A.; Wilson, C.F.; Wilson, F.; Wilson, M.H.B.; Wilson, M.; Windle; Wolferstan; Wood, A.M.M.; *Woodrooffe, A.C.; Woodrooffe, S.; Woods, C.F.; Woodward, H.; Woolven; Wright, M.B.; Wyatt, G.; Wyke, A.; Wyke, E.

Yeardley, M.S.; Yorke, H.; Young, C.; Young Lady, A

1851-1875

Abbott, M.; (Abbott, M.P.B.); Adams, A.O.; Adams, C.A.V.B.; Adams, L.B.; Agnew, E.C.; Agnew, Emily C.; Aitken, C.K.; Akerman, L.W.; Alexander, A.W.; Alexander, C.F.H.; Alice Georgina; Alice Margaret; Allardyce, A.D.B.; Allen, E.A.C.A.; Allen, E.C.A.; Allenby; Allingham, H.M.; Allnut; Almy; Anderson, M.J.; Anderson, M.C.; Andrew; Ansell, M.; Arabel; Archer, M.A.; Arey, H.E.G.; Armstrong, F.C.; Arnold, E.C.S.; Arnold, H.S.F.; Arthington, M.; Ashe, C.; Ashley, F.E.; Ashton, K.; Astley, G.E.; Atherton, M.; Atkinson, J.; Atkinson, M.E.; Atteridge, M.E.

B****, R.; Bacon, M.A.; Bahn, R.; Bailey, E.R.; Baillie, E.C.C.; Baillie, J.; Baker, G.M.A.; Baker, S.S.T.; Balcomb, A.; Ball, A.M.; Ball, C.A.R.; Ballantyne, J.B.; Banks, I.V.L.; (Barbauld, A.L.A.); Barbour, M.F.; Barclay, K.; Barker, E.H.; Barker, H.A.; Barland, K.; Barnard, C.A.; Barnard, E.; Barnett, H.O.R.; Barr, C.; Barrand, E.; Barrett, A.B.; Baskin, M.; Bassett, M.; Batchelor, H.; Batham, L.; Batley; Baxter, L.; Bayne, E.; Bell, E.M.; Bell, H.; Belloc, B.R.P.; Benn, M.; Bennet, G.; Bennett, A.R.G.; Bennett, E.T.B.; Bennett, M.E.; Benson, E.; Bethell, E.M.; Bewsher; Bickford, L.B.; Bigelow, M.A.P.; Bigelow, M.A.H.T.; Bigg, L.; Bishop, H.E.; Bishop, M.J.; Black, E.J.; Blackwell, A.; Blagden; Blake, E.M.; Blake, N.; (Blamire, S.); Bleecker, S.; Blevins, L.; Blind, M.; Bloede, G.; Bloomfield-Moore; Blount, A.R.; Blyton, E.; Boate, Mrs. W.; Bogart; Boies; Bolton, S.E.K.; Bolton, S.T.B.; Bond, A.; Booker, E.; Boot, C.; Booth, M.H.C.; Borthwick, J.L.; Bourne, I.; Bowden, H.M.; Bowen, H.M.G.; Bowles, E.; Bowles, Mrs. G.C.; Bowman, A.; Bowman, H.; Boyes; Boyle, E.; Bradlee, L.H.; Bradley, K.H.; Bradstreet, A.; (Bradstreet, A.D.); Bragg, J.; Braikenridge, I.M.; Brainard, M.; Brett, H.; Bridges, S.; Bristol, A.C.; Bromfield; Brooke, E.T.; Brooks, C.E.; Brooks, S.W.; Brotherton, M.I.I.; Brown, C.L.; Brown, M.E.; Browne, F.; Browne, F.E.; Browne, I.; Browne, M.G.; Browning, E.B.; Bruce, Mrs. H.; Bruce, J.; Buckley, S.A.; Budgett, M.E.; Bull, L.C.; Bullock, C.; Burbank, M.M.; Burge, J.P.; Burman, E.E.; Burnside, H.; Burr, S.E.; Bush, B.; Butler, J.H.; Butt, G.; Button, S.S.

Cabell; Cairns; Campbell, A.G.; Campbell, E.A.; Campbell, E.; Campbell, Mrs. G.; Campbell, J.M.; Campbell, J.H.L.; Campbell, N.W.; Canby, M.T.; Cantrell; Carey, H.M.; Carmichael, S.E.; Carnes, H.; Carr, H.; Carshore; Carter, A.P.; Cary, A.; Cary, M.E.; Cary, P.; Castlen; Caulfeild, S.F.A.; Caulkins; Caulton, I.; (Centlivre, S.F.C.); Chafa; Chambers, E.C.; Charles, E.R.; Chase, M.M.; Chatterton; Chetwynd, M.A.; Child, F.; Child, L.M.F.; Chitwood, M.L.; Chubbuck, L.; Churchill, A.L.; Clapp, S.F.P.; Clark, A.E.; Clark, I.G.; Clarke, A.K.; Clarke, M.B.D.; Clarke, M.V.N.C.; Clay, G.; Cleaveland, E.H.J.; Clephane, A.J.D.M.; Cleveland, M.A.; Clive, C.A.W.; Cobbin, M.E.; Cobbold, D.; Colchester, E.S.L.A.; Coles, C.L.; Collet, F.; Colling, E.; Colthurst, E.; Condon, L.G.; Congdon; Conyngham; (Cook, A.G.); Cook, E.; Cooke, E.H.; Cooke, H.M.; Cooke, Mrs. M. A.; Cooke, R.T.; Cooke, S.I.W.; Cooper, M.G.; Copcutt; Corf; Cornish; Cornwallis, C.F.; Corstorphan; Corwin, J.H.; Costello, L.S.; Cowdery; Cowell, C.B.C.; Coxe, E.C.; Craig, C.P.; Craik, D.M.M.; Cranch; *Crawford, A.A.; Crawford, M.; Creswick, M.; Crewdson, J.F.; Crisfield; Croggon, L.E.; Croly; Cropper; Crosby, F.J.; Crosland,

C.D.T.; Cross, A.C.; Cross, E.D.; Cruger, E.; Crute, S.S.; Cull, M.; Culley, E.; Culsha; Cummins, M.; Currie, M.M.L.S.; Curtiss, A.A.; Cutts, M.; Czarnecki

Dale, A.; Dana, E.A.F.; Daniel, M.A.; Dannelly, E.O.M.; Darby, E.; Daughter of Kentucky, A; David, E.M.; Davie, E.; Davies, E.; Dawes, S.E.; Day, H.; Deane, E.S.R.; Debenham; Deblaquiere; Debney, E.E.; DeBurgh, E.M.H.; DeBurgh, M.; DeGeer; DeLesdernier; Denver, M.C.; DePaton; DeVere; DeWolf, A.; Dickinson, H.A.; Dickinson, M.L.; Dickson, E.D.; Dobell, E.M.F.; Dodge, M.B.C.; Donnelly, E.C.; Dorr, J.C.R.; Dorsey, A.H.M.; Doten, E.; Doudney, S.; Douglas; Douglas, B.; Dowling, P.; Down, E.; Downing, M.A.; Downing, S.E.C.; Dranfield, B.; Dring; Drinker; Drummond, Hon. A.; Drury, A.H.; Drury, S.; Duckworth; Duff, A.J.W.; Dufferin and Clandeboye; Duncan, M.B.M.; Duniway, A.J.S.; Dunn, C.A.; Dunn, S.J.; Dunn, W.; Dupe; Dyson, J.A.P.

Eastman, E.G.; Eberle, E.; Eckley; Edis; Edmond, A.M.C.; Edwards, A.A.B.; Edwards, M.C.S.; Elemjay, L.; Eliza; Ellet, E.; Elliott, C.; Elliott, E.E.S.; Ellis, S.S.; Ellison, A.; Ely, C.E.; Embury, E.C.M.; Emerson, E.R.; Emerson, N.S.; Eta; *Evans, Anne; Evans, E.H.S.; Evans, M.; Ewing, Martha; Eyton, E.C.

Fackrell; Fairbanks, C.; (Fanshawe, C.M.); Farmer, P.; Farquhar; Felkin; Fellows, Mrs. F.P.; Field, H.D.D.; Fields, A.A.; Fisher, F.E.; Fitz-simon; Fleming, K.; Florenz; Foot, A.J.; Foot, R.; Ford, Mrs. A.; Ford, E.E.F.; Ford, M.A.M.; Forrest, A.; Forrester, E.; Forsayth, F.J.; Fotherby; Fowler, L.F.; Fox, E.; Fox, Emma; Fox, S.H.; Frame, E.; Frank, M.; Freeman, E.C.; Fremont, A.A.; French, E.W.; French, L.V.S.; Fry, M.P.; Fullerton, E.; Fullerton, Lady G.C.L.G.

Gage, F.D.B.; Gangloff; Gardner, C.E.; Garrison, E.; Gascoigne; Gay, E.J.; Gay, M.A.H.; Gaye, S.; Gemmer, C.M.; Gibbs, A.S.; Gilbert, M.J.; Giles, D.S.; Gill, D.M.; Gilman, C.H.; Gimson; Gladding, E.N.; Glazebrook, H.A.; Goddard, J.B.; (Godwin, C.G.G.); Godwin, E.A.; Goodluck; Goodwin, C.G.; Gordon, H.; Gordon, M.A.; Gordon, R.; Gorton, C.M.R.; Gould, H.F.; Gould, S.; Gould, T.; Goulstone, S.; Goulter; Gowing, E.A.B.; Graham, C.S.; Graham, G.; Grant, E.F.; Gray, A.; Gray, J.L.; Green, E.C.; Greene, A.; Greenough, E.; Greenstreet, A.L.A.; Greenwell, D.D.; Greer, M.; Gregory, H.; Grey, E.; Grey, G.; Grey, R.; Griffin, A.M.; Griffiths, C.M.; Griggs, H.A.; Griswold, F.I.B.S.; Griswold, M.T.; Grote, H.L.; Gubbins, C.G.; Guild, A.E.G.; Guyton, E.J.W.; Gwilt, H.J.; Gwyn, L.

Hackelton; Haggard, E.; Hale, C.L.; Hale, J.A.; Hale, S.J.B.; Hall; Hall, E.S.; Hall, J.G.; Hall, M.; Hamilton, J.T.; Hanaford, P.A.C.; Hancock, A.; Hancock, S.J.; Hankey, K.; Hanley, I.; Hanna, A.S.; Hanson, B.K.; Hanson, Mrs. G.H.; Hanson, H.M.; Harbottle; Hardcastle, C.; Hardy, M.A.M.D.; Harper, F.E.W.; Harrington, E.S.P.S.; Harrison, J.M.; Harriss, J.M.; Hart, F.W.; Hartwell, E.N.P.; Harvey, E.L.S.; Harvey, E.T.H.; Hastings, S.; Hatteras; Havergal, F.R.; Hawkey, C.; Hawkshaw; Hawthorn, M.; Hayden, C.A.; Haynes, C.; Hazard, E.R.G.; Hazard, G.M.; Hazelwood, H.; Healy, M.; Hearn M.A.; Hearn, M.; Hemenway, A.M.; Henderson, M.E.; Henderson, T.S.; Henry, E.; Henry, S.M.I.; Herbert, J.E.; (Herbert, S.); Herschell, H.S.; Hervey, R.; Hewitt, M.E.M.; Hext; Hey, R.; Heywood, E.F.; Hildebrand; Hill, A.L.S.; Hill, R.F.; Hinxman, E.; Hobart-Hampden ; Hoblyn, A.M.; Hoblyn, M.T.; Hobson, M.S.C.; Hodges, L.J.; Holmes, A.A.; Holt, E.F.; Holworthy, S.M.; Homes, M.S.S.R.; (Hooper, E.H.S.); Hooper, L.H.J.; Hope, A.F.; Hopkins, E.A.W.; Horn, K.; Horsfield; Horsford; Hough, E.H.; Houk; Howard; Howard, Lady C.; Howard, H.; Howarth, E.C.D.; Howe, J.W.; Howell, A.R.; Howie, M.W.; Howitt, M.B.; Hoy, E.; Hubbell, M.E.; Hudson, H.R.; Hudson, M.A.; Hughes, E.B.; Hughes, F.; Hughes, S.; Hull, A.M.; Hume-Rothery; Humphreys, E.; Humphreys, J.; Hunt, H.; Huskinson; Huston, I.P.L.; Hyneman

Ingelow, J.; Inglis, C.H.; Irvine, M.C.; Irving, E.J.; Irving, E.

J.; Jackson, C.L.; Jackson, H.M.; Jefferies, H.A.; Jeffrey, R.V.J.; Jenkins, D.S.G.; Jenness, C.E.; Jessop, A.J.E.; Johnson, A.C.; Johnson, L.W.; Johnson, M.O.; Johnston, E.; Jones, A.T.; Jones, C.A.; Jones, M.A.; Jones, S.L.;

Jones, S.S.; Jordan, A.C.; Jordan, C.J.M.; Jordan, D.M.; Josephine; Jourdan, M.J.; Judson, A.C.; Judson, E.C.C.

Keeler, A.; Keese, C.R.; Kelly, E.J.; Kelty; Kemble, F.A.; Ketchum, A.C.B.; Kettle, M.R.S.; Keyne; Killick; Kimball, H.M.; King, H.E.B.H.; King, S.; Kinney, E.C.D.; Kirkland, C.M.S.; Kirkpatrick, C.C.; Knight, A.F.C.; Knox, Hon. L.S.R.; Knox, I.C.; Kutz

Lacy, F.E.; Lady, A; Lady, A; Lake, A.; Lake, C.; (Landon, L.E.); Lang, F.F.; Langton, M.; Larcom, L.; Latimer, E.; Law, I.; Lawrence, E.; Lawrence, L.J.; Lawrence, M.O.W.; Lawrence, S.J.; Lazarus, E.; Leakey, C.W.; Lean, E.J.; Lee, A.E.; Lee, F.C.; (Lee, M.E.); Lee, R.; LeHardy, E.; Leonard, C.H.; Leonard, C.; Leslie, E.A.; Leslie, M.E.; Lewis, E.; Lewis, E.A.B.R.; Lewis, M.; Lewis, M.M.; Lincoln, J.T.G.; Lindsay, M.J.; Lippincott; Little, S.L.R.; Littleboy; Livingston, O.M.; Llewellyn; Locke, J.E.S.; Loud, C.; Loud, M.S.L.B.; Lowe, H.; Lowe, M.A.P.; Lowell, M.W.; Luce, N.; Lukens, S.; Lynch, T.

MacAndrew, B.M.; Macaulay, B.E.; MacClellan, K.; MacDermott, M.; Macdonald, A.E.; McDougall, F.H.W.G.; Macgregor, H.; Macgregor, J.; Machell; McHenry, J.T.; Mackay, M.; Mackeever, H.B.; Maclean, A.J.; McMasters, J.R.B.; MacMullan, M.A.; MacNiven; Macready, C.F.B.; Maitland, E.J.S.; Mallard, H.; Mallett; Manville, H.A.W.; Marr, F.H.; Marriott, F.S.; Marsh, C.C.; Marsh, C.M.; Marshall, A.E.; Marshall, E.J.; Martin, C.E.M.M.; Martin, M.M.; Marvin, L.H..; Marzials; Maskell, E.; Mason, C.A.B.; Mason, E.H.B.; Massey, L.F.; Masson, P.A.; Mathews, E.; Matteson, F.F.; Matteson, O S.; Maxwell, M.E.B.; Maxwell, M.H.; May, C.; May, E.J.; May, E.J.; May, L.; Maynard; Maynard, M.; Mead, J.M.; Meetkerke, C.E.; Menken, A.I.; Mercur; Meriden, K.; Mering; Messenger, L.R.; Meynell, A.; Milburn; Miles, S.E.; Milligan, S.; Mitchell, C.; Mitchell, E.H.R.; Moe, A.T.; Moise, P.; Monmouth, S.E.H.; Moore, A.F.; Moore, M.B.; Moore, M.A.; Morgan, M.M.S.G.; Morris, E.F.; Morton, H.C.; Morton, J.D.M.; Moulding, S.; Moulton, E.L.C.; Moultrie, M.D.; Mountain, A.; Mower, S.S.; Munday, L.A.H.; Munro, E.

(Nairne, C.O.); Napier, C.; Naramore, G.H..; Nash, C.; Naylor, R.S.; Nealy, M.E.; Nethercott, H.; (Newcastle, M.L.C.); Nicholls, L.H.D.; Nichols, C.; Nichols, L.A.; Nichols, R.S.R.; Nicholson, E.J.P.; Noel, C.M.; Nokes, H.; Norris, F.B.; Norton, C.E.S.S.

Oberholtzer, S.L.V.; Odom, M.H.M.; Ogilvy, D.M.; Ogilvy, E.A.H.D.; Ogilvy, G.B.; Oliver, A.B.; Olsen, S.B.; Opie; Orme, C.J.; Orred; Osgood, F.S.L.; Osgood, K.P.; (Ossoli); Owen, F.M.S.; Owen, I.B.; Ower, J.F.

Packard, M.F.; Page, A.M.; Palfrey, S.; Palmer, P.W.; Palmerton, A.; Parish, C.H.; Parker, C.E.R.; Parker, S.; Parks, M.A.; Parmelee, H.L.B.; Parminter, J.; Parr, H.; Parry, F.; Parsons, E.M.R.; Parsons, G.H.; Patterson, M.W.; Patterson, R.E.; Payne, C.; Peat, A.; Peckham, P.A.; Pemberthy, E.; (Pembroke, M.S.H.); Pendleton, C.; Perkins, E.J.; Perry, N.; Petre, Lady C.H.; Pfeiffer, E.J.D.; Phelps, A.C.; Phillips, C.; Phillips, C.H.; Phillips, S.K.; Phillipson, C.G.L.; Piatt, S.M.B.; Pickard, K.E.R.; Pierson, B.A.; Piggott; Pimm, F.; Pindar; Plake, K.; Pleasants, Mrs. J.; Pleasants, J.; Pollard, R.S.; Ponsonby, Lady E.C.M.; Pope, M.E.F.; Potts, A.H.; Potts, E.; Poulter, L.F.; Power, M.A.; Power, S.A.; Powley; Poyas; Prentiss, E.P.; Preston, M.J.; Prichard, M.; Prideaux, F.A.B.; Procter, A.A.; Procter, A.A.; Proctor, E.D.; Pumpelly; Purdy; Pyper, M.

Raine, R.; Ramsey, V.G.M.; Rankin, S.B.L.; Ranyard, E.H.W.; Rathbone, H.M.R.; Raymond, E.L.; Reader, S.; Reddin; Reed, H.A.; Reeve, M.A.; Reno, L.M.; Rhoads, R.rachel.; Richards, E.B.; Richardson, M.; Richardson, M.E.; Richmond, C.L.V.S.H.T.;; Riddell, C.; Rigden; Ripley, M.A.; Ritchie, Mrs. C.; Ritchie, M.K.; Ritter, M.L.; Roberts, A.S.R.; Roberts, E.; Roberts, H.A.; Roberts, M.; Roberts, M.A.; Robinson, E.; Robinson, L.C.B.; Roby; Rogers, E.; Rogers, Mrs. J.; Rogers, M.E.; Rolleston; Roseboom; Rosling; Rossa; Rossetti; Rossiter; Rowbotham,; Rowland, C.A.; Rowley, F.A.; Rudland, M.; Runnells, E.B.D.; Rutland, J.

Salway, C.M.B.; Samuda; Sanders, M.R.; Sangster, M.E.; Satchell, A.F.; Saunders, E.S.; Saxby, J.E.B.; Saxby,

J.M.E.; Sayer, F.A.; Schenck; Scoones; Scott, J.M.; (Scott, J.H.K.); *Scott, M.L.D.; Scott, R.; Searle, A.A.; Sedgwick, C.M.; Sergeant, E.F.A.; (Seward, A.); Sewell, M.W.; Shannon, M.E.F.; Shaw, F.; *Shelley, M.W.G.; Shellock; Shepard, D.E.R.; Sherwin, E.; Sherwood, A.; Shipton, A.; Shore, A.; Shrimpton, A.; Shute; Sigourney, L.; Silsbee, M.C.D.; Simpson, J.C.B.; Sinclair, C.B.; Skelton, E.; Skelton, S.; Skiddy; Slaughter, L.W.; Smedley, M.B.; Smith, A.R.S.; Smith, B.; Smith, C.; Smith, C.B.; Smith, E.R.S.; Smith, E.S.; Smith, L.; Smith, M.; Smith, S.S.; Smythies, H.; Souder, E.B.T.; Southall, E.A.; Southey, C.; Spalding, L.H.B.; Spencer, Mrs. C.; Spire; Sprague, A.W.; Spurgeon, E.G.; Squirrell, M.E.; Staniforth, A.S.; Stapleton; Starr, E.A.; Steel, M.; Steele, A.C.W.; Steele, A.; Steele, E.A.; Stephens, H.M.W.; Stevenson, E.; Stone, E.; Stowe, H.E.B.; Streatfeild, S.C.; Strickland, A.; Strutt; Stuart, Lady L.; Stuart-Wortley; Sturt; Swain, M.P.; Swanwick, C.; Swift, F.E.C.; Swift, J.M.

Tanner, C.C.; Tatham, E.; (Taylor, C.); Taylor, J.M.; (Taylor, J.); Temple, R.E.H.; Templer, C.B.; Teulon, H.M.; Thackeray, R.E.; Thatcher, M.; Thaxter; Thaxter, C.; Thomas, E.; Thomas, J.H.; Thomas, J.P.; Thomas, L.; Thompson, A.S.; *Thomson, K.B.; Threlfall; Thurtell; Tilt, J.; Tincker, M.A.; Todd, S.H.; Toke; Tonkin; Toogood; Tovani; Townsend, E.; Townsend, E.F.; Townsend, M.A.V.V.; (Trench, M.C.); Trevanion; Trevelyan, F.A.; *Trevelyan, P.J.; Trevor, A.; Trinder; Trubshaw, S.; Truesdell; Tucker, C.M.; Tucker Lambert, M.; Tupper, E.I.; Tupper, M.F.; Turner, E.S.; Turner, F.; Tuthill; Tuttle, E.R.; Tweddell; Twentyman; Tylecoate; Tyler, J.

Underhill, C.

Varian, E.; Very, L.L.A.; Victor, F.A.F.; Vorse

W., E.A.; Wade, C.J.; Wadsworth, C.L.; Waisbrooker; Walbey; Walker, M.; Wallace; *Wakefield; Ward, E.S.P.; Ward, M.A.; Warfel; Waring, A.L.; Waring, C.W.; Warren, M.A.; Washburn, J.B.; Wassell, M.A.; Waterhouse, L.G.; Waterston, A.C.L.Q.; Watson, A.H.; Watson, A.A.; Watson, E.; Watt, Mrs. F.; Watts, A.M.H.; Watts, M.; Webb, L.S.; Webster, J.A.D.; Weeks, D.J.; Weiss, S.A.T.; Welby, A.B.C.; Wellman, M.W.B.; Wells, E.C.R.; West, T.C.J.W.; Westbrook, Mrs. J.C.; White, H.; White, I.; Whiteford, I.; Whitehead, E.; Whiteman, E.H.; Whiteside, L.T.; Whitman, S.H.P.; Whitney, A.; Whitney, Anne; Whittier, E.H.; Whittlesey, S.J.C.; Wight, L.M.; Wiglesworth; Wilbraham; Wilbur, J.A.; Wilcox, E.W.; Wilde, J.F.E.; Wilkinson, M.A.; Willard, F.J.; Williams, J.; Williams, M.L.; Williams, M.S.C.; Williams, S.; Williamson, J.; Williamson, J.M.; Willis, E.H.; Willoughby, E.; Willoughby, J.; Wills, R.; Willson; Willson, E.; Wilson, A.; Wilson, E.; Wilson, L.; Winter, M.; Wolferstan; Wood, A.; Wood, M.E.; Woodard, H.A.; (Woodrooffe, A.C.); Woodrooffe, S.; Woodward, H.; Woodward, M.A.; Worth, S.; Wright; Wright, E.C.; Wright, H.M.

Yates, J.; Young, A.M.N.

<u>1876-1899</u>

Ackroyd, L.G.; Adams, A.O.; Adams, Mrs. C.; Adams, E.C.; Adams, M.J.M.; Adams, N.E.; Adams, V.; Akerstrom, U.R.; Aldrich, A.R.; Aldrich, J.C.; Alexander, C.F.H.; Allen, A.L.; Allen, E.A.C.A.; Allen, G.F.; Allen, L.E.; Allerdice, E.W.; Allerton, E.P.; Alleyne; Allyn; Alma-Tadema; Alt; Ames, M.E.C.; Anagnos, J.R.H.; Anderson, J.W.; Anderson, M.J.; Angel, R.E.; Angier, A.L.; Arbuthnot; Archer, R.; Archibald, E.L.G.; Arey, H.E.G.; Argall, A.E.; Armour, M.; Armstrong, C.J.; Arnold, H.; Arthur, C.M.S.; Ashby, A.E.; Ashby, C.W.; Aston, M.; Attenborough, F.G.; Austin, M.C.; Austin, M.E.; Avery-Stuttle; Ayars

B.; Bachman, S.E.; Backus, E.W.; Bacon, F.E.; Bailey, A.W.; Bailey, F.H.; Bailey, S.L.; Bailey, U.L.S.; Baily, F.; Baines, W.; Baker, E.; Baker, E.M.; Baker, F.H.T.; Baker, Mrs. I.; Baker, L.S.; Baldwin, A.E.C.; Baldwin, E.F.; Baldwin, N.; Baldy; Ball, A.M.; Ballantyne, J.B.; Ballard, J.P.P.; Balmer, C.G.; Banks, E.; Banks, I.V.L.; Bannerman, F.; Banta; Barker, A.J.; Barlow, J.;

(Barnard, C.A.); Barnes, Mrs. G.; Barnes, M.L.F.; Barnes, N.L.D.; Barnes, S.L.; Barrett, R.M.; Barrows, E.A.C.; Barter, L.A.; Barton, A.; Barton, A.M.C.; Bass, C.C.; Bass, M.; Bateman, L.M.B.; Bateman, M.G.F.; Bates, A.P.; Bates, C.D.; Bates, T.; Battersby, C.M.; Battersby, H.S.; Baughan; Beach, E.J.; Beadle, J.E.; Beale, M.; Beardsley, J.M.M.; Beattie, E.; Beauchamp, E.; Beavan, M.; Beck, L.; Bednall, J.; Beers, E.E.; Begg, M.M.; Behenna; Bel, S.F.; Bell, C.L.; Bell, L.; Bell, M.T.B.; Bell, M.; Bell, M.A.P.; Bell, M.E.S.; Bell, O.K.; Beller, L.I.; Benedict, S.W.; Benn, R.; Bennett, E.M.; Bennett, L.A.; Bennett, M.A.; Bennett, N.P.K.; Bent, N.; Berry, L.; Bertoni; Besemeres; Bevan, E.F.A.; Bevington, L.S.; Bevis, S.C.H.; Bianchi; Bianciardi; Bicknell, E.L.; Bigg, L.; Bingham, A.; Bishop, K.; Bishop, M.J.; Black, A.C.; Blackwell, A.; Blackwell, E.; Blair, C.P.; Blair, O.E.; Blake, L.; Blake, M.J.; Blake, M.E.M.; Blanchard, M.E.; Bland, E.N.; Blankenship, M.A.; Blind, M.; Blodgett, L.; Bloede, G.; Bloomfield-Moore; Blount, Lady C.; Bolton, S.E.K.; Bolton, S.T.B.; Booth, E.S.; Bostwick, H.L.B.; Bosworth, E.A.; Botta; Boulger, M.C.; Boyd, N.; Boyden, E.M.B.; Boyden, H.F.; Boylan, G.D.; Boyle, M.; Boyle, S.R.; Boyle, V.F.; Boynton, J.P.; Brackenbury, C.A.; Bradbury, M.R.; Bradfield, M.B.; Bradford, N.K.; Bradley, K.A.; Bradley, K.H.; Bradley, M.E.N.; Bradt; Brainard, M.; Braithwaite; Bramhall; Bramston, M.; Branham, A.P.; Breese, C.A.; Bremont, A.D.; Brewster, C.E.S.; Briggs, E.; Brine, E.; Brine, M.D.N.; Brinton, B.; Bristol, A.C.; Brittingham, F.V.S.; Broadus; Brodie, E.R.; Brooks, L.W.; Brooks, M.S.; Brotherson, F.B.M.; Brotherton, A.W.; Brotherton, M.I.I.; Brown, A.; Brown, A.J.; Brown, E.A.B.; Brown, E.E.; Brown, H.E.; Brown, L.H.; Brown, M.; Brown, M.C.B.; Brown, M.F.; Brown, N.L.; Browne, L.L.; Brownell, A.G.H.; Bryan, H.M.; Bryan, J.M.; Bryan, M.E.; Bryant, M.; Buckingham, E.M.; Buckingham, E.M.; Budge; Budine; Bullens; Bullock, C.; Bumstead; Burge, J.P.; Burgess, A.M.; Burgess, E.; Burleigh, C.H.; Burnside, H.M.; Burt, E.F.; Bush, B.; Bush, C.; Bush, O.W.; Bushby, A.S.; Bussing, A.C.; Butcher, E.L.F.; Butler, A.; Butler, E.H.; Butler, M.R.; Butts, M.F.; Byron, M.C.G.

Caillard; Cake, L.B.; Cake, S.M.; Caldwell, M.; Callanan, H.; Callicotte; Calvert, E.H.M.; Camp, F.G.; Campbell, J.; Campbell, J.M.; Campbell, M.J.; Carpenter, A.D.; Carr, L.G.; Carroll, O.C.; Carson, S.; Carter, A.L.; (Cary, A.); Cary, P.; Case, V.R.; Chadwick, E.R.; Chamberlin, M.J.W.; Chambers, A.; Chandler, J.K.; Chandler, M.; Chant, L.O.D.; Chaplin, M.A.; Chapman, E.R.; Charles, B.E.; Charles, E.R.; Charles, E.T.; Chatelain; Cheever, E.H.W. ; Chesson, N.H.; Childe-Pemberton, H.L.; Chiltern; Choate; Churchill, R.; Claiborne, M.J.H.; Clapp, E.T.; Clapp, M.P.; Clark, A.M.L.; Clark, A.R.; Clark, E.D.; Clark, J.R.; Clark, J.; Clark, K.M.; Clarke, K.; Clarke, K.A.; Clarke, M.B.; Clarke, M.V.N.C.; Cleaveland, E.H.J.; Clement, A.; Clerke; Cleveland, L.; Clive; Cloud, V.W.; Clymer, E.M.D.; Coates, F.E.; Coats, J.B.; Cobbett, M.; Cobby, E.F.; Cocheron, A.J.; Cocke, Z.; Cockle, R.F.M.; Coghill, A.L.W.; Colborne-Veel; Colburn, M.S.; Colcord, M.; Cole, J.A.; Coleridge, M.E.A.; Collings, L.B.M.; Collins, E.G.; Collins, L.G.C.; Colvin, L.M.; Combermere; Commelin; Cone, H.G.; Conklin, J.E.D.; Conners, M.W.; Converse, H.M.; Conway, K.E.; Cook, A.G.; Cook, C.F.; Cook, E.; Cook, M.L.R.; Cooke, H.M.; Cooke, Mrs. M.A.; Cooke, R.T.; Coolbrith, I.D.; Cooley, H.A.; Coolidge, K.S.P.; Cooper, E.E.; Cooper, E.L.A.; Cork and Orrery; Corlett, T.; Cornaby, H.L.; Cornelius; Cornwall, C.; Cornwall, S.J.; Corpier; Corrie; Cortissoz; Cory, C.E.; Costley, R.F.; Cotes R.A.; Cotton, Mrs. F.P.; Courey, H.M.; Coursen; Cousin, A.R.C.; Coventry, M.; Cowell, E.S.; Cowen, H.E.A.G.; Cox, M.M.; Craig, C.P.; Craigmyle; Craik, D.M.M.; Craik, E.S.; Cranch, J.B.; Crawford, A.A.; Crawford, M.J.E.; Crewe, A.; Crist, M.B.; Crommelin, M.H.; Crosby, F.J.; Cross, A.C.; Cross, C.; Cross, M.; Crow, M.F.; Crowell, R.H.; Cruger, J.G.S.; Cummings, A.M.; Cummins, H.V.; Currie, M.M.L.S.; Currier, M.M.; Curtis, A.; Curtis, H.J.; Curzon, S.A.

Dabbs, M.A.; Dabney, J.P.; Dale, A.; Dale, C.; Dall, C.W.H.; Dalton, E.L.; Daly, M.A.; Daly, M.H.N.; Daman, J.; Dame, B.F.; Damon, F.A.; Dandridge, C.D.B.; Daniell, I.S.M.; Daniels, A.L.F.; Daniels, C.L.M.; Dannelly,

E.O.M.; Darling, I.F.; Darton, A.W.W.; Davis, C.M.A.B.; Davis, G.C.; Davis, H.E.B.; Davis, I.; Davis, K.B.; Davis, M.E.M.; Davis, Mary Evelyn (Moore); Davis, R.I.; Davis, S.W.; Davis, S.O.P.; Dawe, F.; Dawson, M.; Day, B.; Day, M.D.; Dean, C.A.; Deane, E.S.R.; DeBlaquiere; DeGeer, M.E.; DeGruchy; DeKantzow; Deland, M.W.C.; DeLaunay; Demarest, M.A.L.; Denison-Keeney; Dennis, A.E.; Dennis, E.A.; Denslow; Dent, A.J.; Denton, E.M.F.; Derby, C.R.; DeVere, C.; Dey, A.C.; Dickins, C.S.; Dickinson, E.E.; Dickinson, Emily; Dickinson, H.A.; Dickinson, M.L.; Dieudonne; Dignowity; Dimmick; Dixon, C.E.; Dixon, M.; Dodge, E.A.P.; Dodge, M.J.; Dodge, M.A.; Dodge, M.B.C.; Dolaro; Donne, A.; Donnelly, E.C.; Dorr, J.C.R.; Dorr, L.S.; Doudney, S.; Douglas, A.M.; Douglas, L.J.; Douglas, M.; Douglas, O.E.C.; Douglas, S.; Douglas, S.P.; Douglass, A.S.; Dow, M.R.; Dowd, A.M.; Dowden, E.D.W.; Dowling, H.T.; Down, E.; Downs, A.S.; Drane, A.T.; Dreyfus, L.G.S.; Duclaux, A.M.F.R.; Dudley, M.V.C.; Duer, C.K.; Duff, A.J.G.W.; Duff, H.A.; (Dufferin and Clandeboye); Duffy, A.V.; Dugan, A.A.S.; Duniway, A.J.S.; Dunlap, A.F.; Dunlop, A.H.; Dunning, F.A.B.; Dupuy, E.; Durant, H.; Duvall, L.M.

Easter, M.E.M.; Eastman, E.G.; Eastman, M.H..; Eaton, I.C.; Eaton, M.J.; Eddington, E.N.; Eddy, M.M.B.; Edelsten, J.; Edmonds, E.M.W.; Edson, H.R.; Edwards, M.B.B.; Edwards, M.C.S.; Edwards, V.P.; Eldred, E.E.; Eldred, O.P.; Elkins, L.M.; Ellard, V.G.; Eller; Ellerman, A.E.; Elliot, Lady C.; Elliott, E.E.S.; Elliott, L.L.; Ellis, L.A.S.; Elmore, B.; Elmore, L.A.M.; Embury, E.C.M.; Emerson, A.E.T.; Emma, Sister; Emmons, M.O.; Engle, A.C.S.; Enright, O.S.E.; Ensign, M.B.; Ericson, A.C.; Erskine, E.P.; Eta; (Evans, Anne); Evans, M.F.; Evans, M.A.B.; Ewer, M.H.; Eytinge

Fabbri; Fagan, F.; Fairbanks, A.L.; Fallon, S.A.; (Fanshawe, C.M.); Fanshawe, L.; Farley, H.H.M.; Farquhar; Farrer, G.; Farris, E.C.; Farrow, B.S.; Fawcett, M.H.; Fawkes; Fay, A.M.; Fay, J.D.; Fearing, L.B.; Feldsmith, M.D.; Felkin, E.T.F. ; Ferguson; Ferre, E.; Ferris, M.L.D.; Fessenden, L.C.S.D.; Fewkes, C.L.; Ffoulkes, L.F.W.; Ffrench, E.; Field, C.L.W.; Fields, A.A.; Fillmore, M.H.; Fillmore, S.F.; Finch, C.; Finch, M.B.; Fish, A.; Fisher, F.E.; Fisher, H.; Fisher, L.R.; Fisher, L.H.; Fisher, M.J.A.; Fitch, A.M.B.; Fitch, A.M.; Fitzgerald; Fitzgerald, M.A.; Fletcher, L.A.; Flowers, S.L.; Follett, M.A.; Folsom, F.B.; Foote, E.W.; Foote, L.Y.; Foott; Forbes, L.C.M.; Ford, A.M.; Ford, A.P.; Ford, E.E.F.; Ford, J.H.C.; Ford, L.M.; Forde, G.; Fordham, M.W.; Forman, E.S.; Forsayth, F.J.; Foster, E.; Foster, H.A.; (Foster, H.W.); Foster, H.T.; Foster, H.W.; Fouty; Fowle, M.L.W.; Fowles, M.A.; Foxworth, S.G.; Franklin, C.M.; Frantz, V.; Freeman, E.; Freeman, J.D.; Freeman, M.E.W.; French, A.L.; French, F.V.R.; French, L.V.S.; French, M.B.; Frere, H.M.; Frere, M.; Friend, S.E.; Frink, A.L.C.; Frink, Mrs. D.; Fronde; Fry, M.A.A.; Fry, M.C.; Fry, M.P.; Fuller, A.A.; Furlong, A.; Furlong, N.

G.; Gallagher, C.H.; Galloway, L.; Galway, V.G.M.A.; Gannett, A.M.; Gannon, A.; Garcia, P.V.; Gardner, A.; Gardner, C.E.; Gardner, M.R.; Gardyne; Garland, A.L.; Gary, A.C.; Gates, E.M.H.; Gates, J.E.; Gaylord, M.L.; Gazzam, A.R.; Gemmer, C.M.; Gerald, F.M.; Gibbons, S.A.; Gibbs, S.M.; Gielow, M.S.; Gifford, E.; Gilbert, F.C.; Gilbert, R.M.; Gilbert, S.V.; Gilchrist, A.S.; Gildea; Giles, S.R.H.; Gillen, A.; Gillett, E.E.; Gillette, F.L.; Gillette, L.F.W.; Gilligan, A.M.; Gilman, C.P.S.; Gilmore, M.L.; Gilstrap; Glazebrook, H.A.; Gleason, A.A.; Gleason, M.A.; Goddard, J.B.; Godwin, E.A.; Goodale, D.R.; Goodenough; Goodwin, M.M.B.; Gordon, D.H.; Gordon, E.; Gordon, M.E.; Gordon, R.; Gore-Booth; Gorton, M.J.; Gott, A.A.; Gould, A.W.; Gould, A.I.; Gould, E.P.; Gould, H.F.; Gower, J.M.; Gowing, C.; Gowing, E.A.B.; Graham, J.C.; Graham, M.; Grahame, A.V.; Granger, J.M.C.; Granger, L.N.; Granger, M.E.; Granniss, A.J.; (Grant, A.M.); Grant, E.; Grant, G.F.; Graves, A.C.S.; Gray, B.; Green, K.H.; Green, M.; Greene, A.; Greene, C.M.F.; Greene, M.B.; Greenough, S.D.L.; Greenwell, D.D.; Greenwood, A.D.O.; Greer, L.M.S.; Greer, M.; Gregg, L.B.; Gregory, K.; Gregory, P.; Grey, F.E.; Grey, G.; Griffiths, R.; Griggs, N.M.; Grose, C.E.; Gross, A.E.; Gue; Guild, M.L.P.; Guiney, L.I.; Gunther, A.B.; Gurdon, Lady E.C.N.; Gurney, E.P.K.; Gustafson; Guthrie, E.E.

Hagan, M.B.; Haggard, E.; Haigh, M.J.; Haight, S.J.; Haines, L.B.; Haines, P.; Haley, A.; Hall, E.M.; Hall, E.A.S.; Hall, H.M.M.; Hall, H.W.; Hall, L.J.P.; Hall, M.L.; Hall, S.A.M.A.; Ham, M.F.; Hamilton, A.S.; Hamilton, A.E.H.L.; Hamilton, S.J.; Hamlett, L.M.; Hamlin, F.E.; Hammond, L.; Hammond, M.C.W.; Hampton, Lady L.E.; Hanaford, P.A.C.; Hankin, M.L.; Hanna, H.L.; Hansbrough, M.B.C.; Hanscom, A.E.; Hardenbergh; Hardin, M.B.J.; Hardwicke, E.; Hardy, I.; Hardy, M.E.; Hardy, R.F.; Hargreaves, M.; Harlow, L.A.; Harper, F.E.W.; Harraden; Harrington, J.M.E.; Harris, A.; Harris, E.; Harris, E.M.; Harrison, M.; Hart, F.W.; Harter, E.M.; Harter, J.H.; Harvey, A.M.; Harvey, H.L.; Harvey, M.B.; Haslewood, F.C.; Hastings, L.W.; Hatheway, M.E.N.; Hattersley; Havergal, C.; Havergal, F.R.; Haviland, M.M.; Hawkey, C.; Hawkins, I.C.; Hawtrey; Haycraft, M.S.M.; Hayden, M.; Hayden, S.M.; Hayes, C.E.S.; Hayford, A.; Hayley, H.; Hayward, J.M.; Hayward, O.B.H.; Haywood, A.W.; Hazard, C.; Heard, J.D.H.; Hearn M.A.; Heath, C.B.S.; Heath, G.L.; Heath, M.I.; Heaton, E.O.P.; Hebron, E.E.; (Hemans, F.D.B.); Hempstead, F.; Henderson; Henderson, E.; Henderson, M.; Hendrix, L.E.G.; Hennah, A.; Henry, E.; Henry, S.M.I.; Henshaw, S.E.T.; Hensley, S.M.A.; Herbert, M.A.; Hernaman; Herrick, S.M.; Herritt, S.D.H.; Hibbard, A.M.; Hibbard, G.P.; Hickey, E.H.; Hickok, E.M.; Hicks, E.E.; Hicks, M.R.; Higginson, E.R.; Higginson, M.P.T.; Hildebrand, A.L.; Hill, E.L.C.; Hill, E.; Hill, E.S.; Hill, S.E.; Hills, C.P.; Hills, E.M.; Hime, R.H.; Hine, M.E.; Hines, N.W.; Hinkson; Hinkson, K.; Hinsdale, L.F.; Hippisley, E.F.; Hirst, E.H.; Hoard, M.A.; Hobart-Hampden; Hobbs, M.E.E.; Hoffman, M.L.; Hoffman, M.B.; Holahan, M.E.; Holbrook, J.E.; Holcombe, H.J.; Holden, F.G.; Holder, P.A.; Holland, M.C.; Holley, M.; Hollins, D.; Holloway, E.H.; Holmes, A.A.; Holmes, G.K.; Holmes, I.S.; Holmes, K.R.; Holyoke, M.B.; Honeywood, P.; Hoobler; Hopkins, J.E.; Hopkins, L.P.S.; Hopkins, S.A., M.D.; Hopkins, V.M.D.; Horn, L.M.; Horner, H.; Hosford, M.; Hottinger, E.; Housh, E.T.S.; Howard, A.G.; Howard, H.; Howe, C.D.; Howe, J.W.; Howe, L.T.; Howell, A.R.; Howell, A.; (Howland, S.H.); Hoxter, M.E.; Hubbard, J.P.; Huger; Hull, A.M.; Hull, M.E.B.; Hume, E.; Hunt, S.K.; Hunter, M.; Huntington, C.; Huntington, M.H.; Huntley, A.M.; Hurd, A.; Hurd, H.M.; Hussey, M.B.; Huston, A.H.; Hutter, N.L.; Hutton, R.L.S.; Huxley, H.A.H.; Hyde, E.R.; Hyde, M.C.; Hyde, M.E.; Hygema

Ingelow, J.; Ingham, J.S.C.; Inglis, C.H.; Ingram, W.; Iris; Irwin, A.; Isard; Iverson, W.A.; Ivory, B.M.

Jackson, C.N.; Jackson, H.M.F.H.; Jackson, H.M.; Jackson, L.E.; Jackson, L.M.; Jackson, T.F.B.; Jacques, M.J.; James, A.A.S.; Jay, K.; Jeffrey, R.V.J.; Jenkins, H.N.G.; Jennison, L.W.; (Jevons, M.A.R.); Johnson, E.M.; Johnson, E.S.; Johnson, E.P.; Johnson, K.H.; Johnson, M.K.; Johnston, J.H.; Jones, A.; Jones, A.T.; Jones, G.M.; Jones, H.W.; Jones, I.M.; Jones, J.C.; Jones, J.P.; Jones, M.W.; Jones, M.A.; Jordan, C.J.M.; Jordan, M.E.; Joseph, R.; Josephine, K.; Joynes, B.; Judson, E.C.C.

Kahn, R.W.; Kail; Katzenberger; Kautz; Keary, E.; Keene, K.; Kelley, S.A.U.; Kellogg, S.P.; Kelly, E.J.; Kelly, M.; Kelly, M.A.B.; Kemble, F.A.; Kendall, H.; Kendall, M.; Kendrew, M.E.; Ketcham, M.W.; Ketchum, A.C.B.; Kettle, M.R.S.; Kilburn-Brown; Kimball, E.A.; Kimball, H.P.; Kimball, H.M.; King, H.T.; King, H.E.B.H..; King, M.E.H.; King, S.A.; King, S.C.; Kirchhoffer; Knight, L.A.; Knowles, L.J.; Knowles, M.M.; Knowlton, A.I.; Knox, E.I.; Knox, Hon. L.S.R.; Kohaus; Kopta; Kossiter

Ladd, E.M.; Laffan, B.J.G.; Lahee, M.R.; Lamb, M.J.R.N.; Lambert, M.; Lambert, M.H.P.; Langston, C.B.; Larcom, L.; Larned, A.; Larned, J.; Lathbury, M.A.; Lathrap, M.T.; Lathrop, R.H.; Latimer, E.; Laurie, C.A.; Lawford, F.G.V.; Lawless; Lawrence, B.; Lawrence, M.O.W.; Lawson, M.J.K.; Layard, N.F.; Lazarus, E.; Leathley, M.E.S.D.; Leavitt, M.C.; Leck, J.; Lee, E.C.; Lefevre; Leicester, M.; Leighton, H.W.; Leith, E.; Leith, M.C.J.G.; Leland, H.M.P.; Lent, E.A.; Leonard, E.C.; Leonard, M.H.; Levy, A.; Lewis, H.J.W.; Lightfoot, C.A.; Lillie; Lincoln, M.D.; Lindsay, C.B.E.F.; Linn, E.L.W.; Lippincott; Litchfield, G.D.; Litchfield, H.E.; Littell, M.V.; Little, L.M.; Litzsinger;

Lloyd, J.G.; Lloyd, S.W.; Lodge, H.N.; Loftus; Logan, F.A.; Logan, M.A.; Logue, E.R.; Loiseau; Longstaff; Lonsdale, F.; Loomis, C.J.; Loomis, S.C.; Lord, A.E.S.; Lord, H.A.; Lothrop, H.M.S.; Loughery, F.L.; Lowe, M.A.P.; Lucas, A.; Lucas, W.M.; Luce, H.G.; Luders, C.; Luke, J.T.; Luke, M.; Lunt; Lunt, A.; Luquer; (Lushington, H.P.); Lushington, L.M.; Lyon, A.E.W.; Lytton, R.A.D.W.B.L.

Mabon, A.S.; McAboy, M.R.T.; Macalpine, M.; MacAndrew, B.M.; McCarthy, K.; MacCarthy, M.S., Sister; Mcclurg, M.V.D.; McConnell, M.D.D.; McConnell, S.J.; McCoy, K.C.; McCue, R.L.; McCullough, N.N.; Macdonald, A.E.; Macdonald, J.E.G.W.; McDowell, K.G.; McDowell, K.S.B.; Mace, F.P.L.; McFall, A.E.M.; McGill, A.; Machar; McIlvain, C.L.; Mackay, J.; McKean, M.F.; Mackellar, M.C.; Mackenzie, L.A.; McKinney, I.S.T.; McKinney, K.S.; McLanathan, M.L.; Maclean, J.; Maclean, K.S.; McLean, M.I.; Maclennan, A.; Maclintock, A.C.; McMillan, E.I.; McNinch, M.; McPherson, L.S.; McQueen, A.C.; Madison, R.W.; Magee, A.H.; Magie; Mair, E.H.S.; Maitland, E.F.; Maitland, F.S.F.; Makeever, I.; Malloy, M.L.; Maloney, M.T.; Manners, M.E.R.; Manning, C.C.; Manning, E.F.; Manning, J.W.; Mansell; Mansfield, C.; Marchbank, A.; Marean; Mark, A.; Marks, M.A.M.H.; Marr, F.H.; Marriott, I.L.; Marsden, E.A.R.R.; Marshall, A.P.; Martin, M.M.; Martin, M.; Marvin, L.H.; Mary Edith, Sister; Mason, C.A.B.; Mason, F.L.; Mason, M.; Mason, M.A.; Massey, L.F.; Massey, S.; Mather, D.M.; Matheson, A.; Mathews, J.A.; Mathis, J.E.; Matson, A.; Matson, C.A.; Matthew, M.H.; Maxim, R.; May, C.; May, C.B.; May, J.H.; Mears, A.G.; Medini; Meigs, M.N.B.M.; Melvin, F.B.; Mercedes, Sister; Mercur, A.H.; Meredith, H.R.; Meriwether, L.S.; Merritt, M.I.L.; Messenger, L.R.; Meynell; Meynell, A.; Meyrick, G.; Michener, A.P.; Michener, F.L.; Miller, A.R.; Miller, E.S.; Miller, E.C.H.; Miller, F.D.C.; Miller, L.; Miller, M.M.; Miller, Mary Morgan; Miller, M.W.B.; Mills, J.E.D.; Milne, F.M.T.; Mitchell, E.A.N.; Mitchell, E.H.R.; Moir, E.B.P.; Moise, P.; Monroe, H.; Montefiore; Montgomery, C.F.J.; Montgomery, E.E.; Moore, A.; Moore, C.S.J.B.; Moore, clara sophia (jessup) bloomfield.; Moore, E.M.S.; Moore, J.; Moore, J.E.; Moore, J.A.D.; Morehead, L.M.E.; Morehouse, C.W.; Morgan, H.P.; Morgan, L.S.; Morgan, M.; Morgan, S.R.D.; Morris, F.A.; Morris, M.H.; Morrison, S.P.; Morton, E.H.; Morton, H.C.; Mosher, A.A.; Mote, E.; Moulton, E.L.C.; Muchmore, J.; Muenster, M.C.F.M.; Muir, J.K.; Mulvany, A.A.; Munger; Murden; Murphy, E.S.; Murray, C.; Murray, J.G.

Naden, C.C.W.; (Nairne, C.O.); Nason, E.C.H.; Nason, E.C.H.; Neale, S.; Needham, E.A. ; Negreponte; Nelson, F.B.; Newall; Newcomb, F.W.D.; Newell, B.E.; Newton, E.; Nicholl, M.A.; Nichols, A.S.; Nichols, K.S.; Nichols, L.A.; Nicholson, E.C.; Nicholson, I.; Nicholson, K.M.; Norton, C.E.S.S.; Norton, M.; Nugent

Oakey, E.S.; Oates, C.M.B.; Oberholtzer; O'Brien, C.G.; O'Connor, R.A.; Odell, M.; O'Doherty, M.A.K.; Odom, M.H.M.; O'Donnell, J.F.; O'Donoghue, M.A.L.; O'Donoghue, N.P.L.; Oesterreicher; Ogden, E.L.; O'Hare, T.B.; O'Leary, E.; Ormond; Orne; Orred, M.; Orton, M.; Osgood, A.A.; Osgood, F.S.L.; O'Sheridan, M.G.; Overington, L.; Owen, F.B.; Owen, F.M.S.; Owen, G.M.; Owen, N.H.

Packman, A.; Page, E.A.S.; Page, J.H.; Paine, L.M.A.; Painter, L.E.F.; Palfrey; Palfrey, S.; Palmer, E.; Panton; Pardon, E.L.; Parham, H.B.R.; Parker, E.J.; Parker, H.B.; Parker, M.H.; Parker, M.H.; Parker, M.S.; Parkinson, A.; Parr, C.; Parr, O.K.; Parsons, K.L.; Pasmore; Paton, I.; Patterson; Patton, A.H.; Patton, E.Y.; Paull, M.E.K.; Payson, H.W.; Peacock, M.G.W.; Peacock, M.W.; Peacocke, G.; Pearson, E.C.M.; Peckham, L.G.C.; Peckham, M.C.P.; Peckham, P.A.; Pemberton, H.L.C.; Pendleton, C.; Pennefather; Pennell, A.I.; Perkin, A.; Perkins, A.S.; Perry, A.M.; Perry, C.A.; Perry, E.; Perry, E.R.; Perry, L.C.; Perry, M.A.; Perry, N.; Perry, S.T.; Peter, M.L.; Peterson, M.J.; Petre, Lady C.H.; Petrie, E.; Pfeiffer, E.J.D.; Phelps, J.A.C.; Phillips, E.S.; Phillips, S.A.; Phillips, S.K.; Piatt, S.M.B.; Pickens, A.E.; Pigott, J.S.; Pillsbury, L.B.; Pim, S.S.H.; Pimm, F.; Pinkney, J.V.; Pirtle, J.A.; Pitcairn, J.W.; Pitman, A.A.; Pittman, J.L.; Plumley, L.L.F.; Pocklington; Poe, A.H.; Pollard, J.; Pollard, R.S.; Pomeroy, M.S.; Poole,

E.L.T.E.; Poole, F.H.R.; Poole, H.M.H.; Pope, M.M.; Porter, E.E.; Porter, M.S.A.; Porter, M.J.; Porter, R.; Postgate, I.J.; Potter, E.C.; Potter, E.C.; Potts, E.D.; Poucher, E.E.; Powel, E.; Powers, O.A.; Pratt, R.B.; Prentiss, C.E.; Preston, M.J.; Price, C.A.; Prideaux, F.A.B.; Prime, L.H.; Probyn, M.; (Procter, A.A.); Proctor, E.D.; Proctor, E.D.; Purvis, T.T.; Putnam, E.D.; Putnam, I.

Quinn, M.

Radford, D.M.; Raeburn; Ralston, H.N.J.; Ramsey, V.G.M.; Rand, M.A.; Rankin, S.B.L.; Ranyard, E.H.W.; Ray, H.C.; Read, J.M.; Reader, E.E.; Reavis, R.M.; Reddin; Reed, A.; Reed, A.M.M.; Reese, L.W.; Reeve, A.; Reeves, H.B.M.; Renshaw, F.M.; Requa; Reskelly; Reynolds, C.M.; Rich, C.W.D.S.; Rich, H.H.; Rich, M.W.; Richards, A.M.; Richards, L.E.H.; Richards, L.P.; Richards, S.; Richardson, A.C.; Richardson, H.P.; Richey, I.G.; Richmond, C.L.V.; Richmond, E.Y.; Richmond, M.E.; Ricker, C.E.; Rickoff; Rigg, C.; Rittenhouse, L.J.; Ritter, F.M.R.; Robarts, L.W.; Robbins, C.A.; Roberts, B.A.S.; Roberts, M.; Roberts, S.; Roberts, S.B.; Robertson, A.H.; Robertson, J.L.; Robinson, E.W.; Robinson, M.D.; Rogers, A.M.; Rogers, E.; Rohlfs; Rollins; Rollins, A.; Rose, H.D.; Rosher; Ross, D.; Ross, N.; Rossetti; Rowe, E.S.; Rowe, M.F.; Rowley, M.S.; Ruddy, E.A.G.; Rude, E.S.; Ruffin, M.E.H.; Runcie, C.O.; Russell, C.E.; Russell, K.P.; Rutson, C.F.; Ryan, M.; Ryan, M.C.

Sanderson, A.C.; Sanford, K.I.; Sanford, M.F.; Sangster, M.E.M.; Santley, M.M.; Sargant, A.; Sargent, M.; Sartoris; Saunders, E.S.G.; Sawtelle; Sawyer, E.E.T.; Sawyer, H.A.; Saxby, J.M.; Sayers, F.H.; Scheyer; Schrack; Schuellermann; Schulte, M.J.M.; Scott, C.A.D.; Scott, C.; (Scott, M.L.D.); Scott, R.; Scramm, E.I.; Scudder; Seaton, R.; Serrano; Sewall, H.W.; Sewell, M.W.; Sharp, K.D.; Sharpe, M.; Shaw, G.E.; Shearer, F.M.; Shelby, H.; (Shelley, E.); (Shelley, M.W.G.); Shelton, A.S.; Shelton, J.F.; Sherman, A.F.M.; Sherrick, F.I.; Sherwood, K.M.B.; Sherwood, M.E.W.; Shipley, M.E.; Shipton, A.; Shore, A.; Shore, L.C.; Shorey; Shorter; Shorter, D.M.; Shortt; Shuey; Shultz, M.G.; Sidney, V.E.; Simmons, A.W.; Simpson, J.C.B.; Simpson, M.E.; Sinclair, A.M.; Sinclair, M.A.; Sinclair, M.; Skelton, E.; Skidmore, H.M.; Slaughter, E.S.M.; Slocum, G.L.; Smith, A.C.; Smith, C.F.; Smith, Mrs. E.J.; Smith, E.B.; Smith, E.L.; Smith, E.P.; Smith, H.; Smith, H.H.; Smith, Harriette; Smith, J.L.D.; Smith, J.O.D.; Smith, J.M.; Smith, L.H.; Smith, M.A.; Smith, M.; Smith, Mary A.; Smith, M.E.; Smith, M.L.R.; Smith, M.C.; Smith, S.H.; Smyth, F.W.; Snell, M.S.; Snow, F.L.; Solomons, R.J.; Somerset, I.C.S.C.; Southern, I.J.; Spalding, S.M.; Sparks, M.C.S.; Spaulding, E.A.; Spearing, A.B.; Spencer, A.H.; Spencer, E.B.; Spicer, I.; Spofford, H.E.P.; Spooner, M.A.; Springer, R.R.; Stanwood, E.H.; Stapleton; Starkey, E.A.H.; Starr, E.A.; Stebbins, S.B.; Stephens, A.S.W.; Stephens, E.J.; Stetson, G.E.C.; Stevens, B.R.; Stevens, F.E.; Stewart, B.; Stewart, E.M.; Stewart, J.F.; Stewart, M.L.; Stickney, J.N.; Stock, S.G.; Stockall, H.; Stockdale, J.; Stockdale, M.; Stoddard, E.D.B.; Stone, C.E.H.W.; Stone, K.M.; Stone, M.K.A.; Stonehewer; Strachan; Streatfeild, S.C.; Strong, M.E.; Strykor, C.; Stuart, E.G.; Stuart, H.M.; Stuart, J.I.; (Stuart, Lady L.); Sturm, O.L.; Sunter, J.; Sutfin; Sutherland, J.G.; Swain, S.; Swaine, C.J.; Swayne, M.; Swayne, M.S.; Sweat, M.J.M.; Sweetman, E.; Swift, F.E.C.; Swift, J.M.; Swingle, E.F.; Swinton; Swisher, B.F.

Tadlock, C.M.; Talcott, H.E.B.G.; Taney, M.F.; Tanner, M.J.; (Tatham, E.); Taylor, Mrs. E.; Taylor, J.L.P.; Taylor, M.S.; Taylor, M.; Teesdale; Teetzel; Temple, A.; Temple, R.; Teske, T.A.; Thackeray, R.E.; Thaxter, C.; Thomas, E.M.; Thomas, L.; Thomas, M.P.; Thomas, R.H.; Thompson, A.; Thompson, L.; Thompson, M.F.; Thompson, M.L.; Thompson, R.; (Thomson, K.B.); Thorndyke, E.P.; Thornton, C.A.E.; Thornton, F.; Thorpe; Thorpe, R.; Threlfall; Throop; Thurston, J.G.; Thwaites, C.; Tickner, C.; Tierney, C.A.; Tiffany, E.B.; Tiffany, O.E.F.; Tilbury, C.; Tilley, L.E.; Tillotson; Timlow; Tincker, M.A.; Tindal, H.; Titterington, S.B.; Todrig; Toland, M.B.M.; Tollemache ; Tomkins, Mrs. D.; Tomkins, Z.E.; Tomlinson, A.W.; Toms; Toogood, H.; Towle, M.L.W.; Townsend, M.A.; Townsend, M.E.;

Trask, K.N.; Tregelles; (Trevelyan, P.J.); Tritton, E.H.; Trollope, F.E.T.; Truesdell, A.W.; Tucker, C.M.; Tucker, F.; Tucker, M.A.; Tucker Lambert; Tupper, M.E.; Turnbull, F.H.L.; Turner, E.S.; Turner, M.E.W.; Turner, M.E.K.; Tuttiett; Tuttle, A.B.; Tuttle, E.R.; Tyler, J.

Ullman, D.; Underdown, E.

Vail, J.V.S.; Vale, V.; Valentine, C.S.; Van Allen, J.A.; Van Aulen; Van Loon; Van Nada; Van Norman; Vannah; Varian; Vaughan, V.; Veeder; Veley, M.; Verney; Very ; Vialls; Victor, F.A.F.B.; Visher; Vox; Vyse

Wagner, M.M.; Waite, B.; Waithman; (Wakefield); Walcott, J.; Waldo, F.; Waldron, A.C.; Walker, B.; Walker, M.W.; Wall, A.C.; Walter, C.S.; Walters; Walters, S.; Ward, E.S.P.; Ward, F.M.; Ward, L.A.C.; Ward, M.A.; Wardwell, M.E.; Waring, C.I.; Warne, E.; Warne, E.A.; Washburn, H.B.; Washburn, J.B.; Washington, L.H.W.; Wason; Waterhouse, E.; Waterman, M.B.; Waters, G.; Watres, H.G.H.; Watson, E.R.; Watson, Mrs. H.; Watson, R.B.M.; Watson-Taylor; Weatherhead, E.; Weaver, B.G.R.D.; Webb, L.S.; Webster, E.H.; Webster, J.A.D.; Weed, E.S.; Weeden, H.; Weeden, J.E.; Weeks, R.J.K.; Weitzel; Welby, A.B.C.; Welch, L.S.E.; Wellington, C.L.F.; Wells, A.M.F.; Wells, E.M.W.; Wells, E.H.; Wells, E.B.W.; Werner, A.; West, F.D.; West, M.; Westbrook, M.A.; Weston, E.G.; Wetherald; Wetherbee; Wharton, E.N.J.; Wheeler, E.G.L.; Wheeler, E.; Wheeler, K.L.; Whitaker, L.C.; White, I.L.; White, S.A.; Whitelock, L.C.; Whiteman; Whiting, L.; Whitman, S.H.P.; Whitney, A.; Whitney, H.H.; Whitten, M.E.H.; Whittier, I.C.; Whittlesey, S.J.C.; Whitworth, L.A.; Wightman, M.T.; Wiglesworth; Wigmore; Wilbraham; Wilcox, E.W.; Wilkins, A.; Williams, A.M.; Williams, G.M.; Williams, J.P.; Williamson, E.; Williamson, J.M.; Willing; Willoughby.; Wilson, A.; Wilson, C.C.H.; Wilson, I.M.; Wilson, L.; Wilson, M.L.G.P.C. ; Wilson, M.H.T.; Wing, A.K.; Winn, E.L.; Winser; Winston, C.P.; Winston, R.S.B.; Winthrop, A.C.; Wister, S.; Withers, E.; Witman, F.K.; Wolcott, J.A.; Wolf, M.I.; Wolverton, S.S.; Wood, H.J.; Wood, M.C.F.H.; Wood, M.W.; Woodbridge, S.A.; Woodbury, J.C.B.; Woodruff, B.C.; Woodruff, J.L.M.C.; Woods, C.E.; Woods, K.T.; Woods, M.L.B.; Woodward, C.A.; Woodward, M.C.S.; Woolford, B.E.; Woolsey, S.C.; Woolson, C.F.; Wordsworth, B.; Wordsworth, D.E.; Workman; Wray, A.W.; Wright, J.; Wylie, L.B.; Wynne, F.

Young, A.C.; Young, J.; Young, J.E.D.; Young, M.H.G.; Youngs, E.S.; Youngs, J.M.

SUBJECT INDEX

www.ingramcontent.com/pod-product-compliance
Lightning Source LLC
LaVergne TN
LVHW082005060826
844660LV00028B/1244
9781442639737